THE PRINCIPLES OF LEARNING AND BEHAVIOR

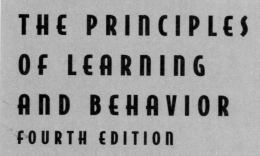

THE PRINCIPLES OF LEARNING AND BEHAVIOR
FOURTH EDITION

MICHAEL DOMJAN
University of Texas

Brooks/Cole Publishing Company

I(T)P® An International Thomson Publishing Company

Pacific Grove • Albany • Belmont • Bonn • Boston • Cincinnati • Detroit
Johannesburg • London • Madrid • Melbourne • Mexico City • New York
Paris • Singapore • Tokyo • Toronto • Washington

Sponsoring Editor: *Marianne Taflinger*
Marketing Team: *Marcy Perman/Christine Davis/ Alicia Barelli*
Editorial Assistant: *Scott Brearton*
Production Editor: *Tessa A. McGlasson*
Manuscript Editor: *Mary O'Briant*
Permissions Editor: *Mary Kay Hancharick*
Interior and Cover Design: *Donna Davis*

Cover Photo Composition: *Robert J. Western*
Art Editor: *Jennifer Mackres*
Interior Illustration: *Kathy Joneson*
Photo Editor: *Robert J. Western*
Indexer: James Minkin
Typesetting: *TBH/Typecast, Inc.*
Printing and Binding: *Courier/Westford*

I(T)P The ITP logo is a registered trademark under license.

For more information, contact:

BROOKS/COLE PUBLISHING COMPANY
511 Forest Lodge Road
Pacific Grove, CA 93950
USA

International Thomson Editores
Seneca 53
Col. Polanco
11560 México D.F., México

International Thomson Publishing Europe
Berkshire House 168–173
High Holborn
London WC1V 7AA
England

International Thomson Publishing GmbH
Königswinterer Strasse 418
53227 Bonn
Germany

Thomas Nelson Australia
102 Dodds Street
South Melbourne, 3205
Victoria, Australia

International Thomson Publishing Asia
221 Henderson Road
#05–10 Henderson Building
Singapore 0315

Nelson Canada
1120 Birchmount Road
Scarborough, Ontario
Canada M1K 5G4

International Thomson Publishing Japan
Hirakawacho Kyowa Building, 3F
2-2-1 Hirakawacho
Chiyoda-ku, Tokyo 102
Japan

Printed in the United States of America.

10 9 8 7 6 5 4

Library of Congress Cataloging-in-Publication Data

Domjan, Michael, [date]
    The principles of learning and behavior / Michael Domjan. — 4th ed.
        p.   cm.
    Includes bibliographical references and indexes.
    ISBN 0-534-34670-7
    1. Conditioned response.   2. Learning, Psychology of.
3. Behaviorism (Psychology)   I. Title.
BF319.D65   1998
150.19'43—dc21
                                                    97-21562
                                                       CIP

Cover images (clockwise from top): David Edmonson/SuperStock, Inc.; Corel Corporation–Apes CD-ROM; West Rim Enterprises; © David Young-Wolff/PhotoEdit; Corel Corporation–Apes CD-ROM; © David Young-Wolff/PhotoEdit.

TO MICHAEL R. BEST (1947–1996),
FRIEND AND COLLEAGUE

ABOUT THE AUTHOR

Michael Domjan is Professor of Psychology at the University of Texas at Austin, where he has been teaching undergraduate and graduate courses in learning since 1973. He has served as Editor of the *Journal of Experimental Psychology: Animal Behavior Processes* and Associate Editor of *Learning and Motivation.* He is noted for his research on food-aversion learning and learning mechanisms in sexual behavior. He is a recipient of the G. Stanley Hall Award of the American Psychological Association, and his research on sexual conditioning was selected for a MERIT Award by the National Institutes of Mental Health. In addition to *The Principles of Learning and Behavior,* 4th edition, he is also the author of *The Essentials of Conditioning and Learning,* with Brooks/Cole Publishing Company.

PREFACE

T HE investigation of learning and behavior has been an integral part of the study of psychology throughout much of the twentieth century. Studies of learning provide important insights into the ways in which experience can lead to long lasting changes in behavior. Basic associative learning phenomena also provide the building blocks for some prominent theories of cognitive function. In addition, studies of learning provide behavioral techniques that are useful in many allied fields, including behavioral neuroscience, psychopharmacology, behavioral medicine, and behavioral toxicology. These factors put the study of learning at the crossroads of many different approaches to the investigation of behavior.

Balance between contemporary and historical approaches in learning

The fourth edition, like earlier editions, introduces contemporary phenomena and theories about learning and behavior. For example, this edition discusses memory and complex cognition in detail, including a new discussion of directed forgetting, serial pattern learning in simultaneous arrays, and language learning in animals. Rather than advocate a particular point of view, the book strives to present a balanced perspective of the field in which strengths and weaknesses of each approach are discussed evenhandedly. Further, to help students see how ideas develop, contemporary findings are introduced within a historical context. Although some contemporary ideas cannot fully be integrated with previous findings, you'll find as integrated an account as possible.

Organized and streamlined for today's student

As with earlier editions, information is presented in increasing order of complexity, both within and across chapters. The basic ideas presented at the beginning of each chapter serve as a foundation for subsequent chapters with critical concepts repeated as needed. To make it even more accessible for today's student, this edition has been streamlined such that it is now 15% shorter, and I hope more readable. To make concepts more accessible, all of the art has been redone so that many of the figures, like the endpapers you see at the front of the book, read at a glance for the student. You'll also find a more user-friendly one-column design, researcher photos, and more frequent illustrations and subheadings, all in an attempt to make this edition work better for students.

What's remained the same?

This book covers both animal and human examples of learning phenomena so that students can see the relevance of animal models and can remember the concepts better. To make the human examples more apparent, you'll find an index of them directly following the table of contents. Throughout the book, boxes highlight human applications and extensions of the basic research findings. In addition, everyday examples and analogies are used to clarify concepts and make them more memorable for the student. For example, pay scales at a restaurant are used to illustrate the effects of schedules of reinforcement, the sounds of a symphony orchestra are used to illustrate configural cues, a shopping trip is used to illustrate the difference between retrospective and prospective memory, and miniature golf courses are used to illustrate the mechanisms of serial pattern learning.

Biological constraints on learning are integrated throughout the book instead of being segregated in one chapter, because they cannot easily be understood separately. Chapter 2 covers the ethological foundations of behavior, which are further described later on, as appropriate in other chapters. Adaptive specializations in learning are described in chapters on classical conditioning, instrumental conditioning, stimulus control, aversive control, and memory.

What's changed in the content?

- Of the 1,400 references more than a quarter have been published since l990
- Chapter 7 now covers behavioral regulation and the determinants of the elasticity of demand.
- Chapter 8 has been reorganized to clarify and simplify the material.
- Chapter 10 has been reorganized to better integrate historical and contemporary approaches to the interaction between classical and instrumental conditioning.
- Chapter 12 has a reorganized section on teaching language to chimps.
- Modern theoretical approaches such as Pearce's configural cue theory have been added—in the context of historical findings as much as possible.
- Memory interference accounts of the Conditioned Stimulus and the Unconditioned Stimulus pre-exposure effects have been added.
- Discussion of the conditioning model of drug tolerance has been updated.
- The directed forgetting section has been redone in light of recent methodological concerns about this area of research.

What's changed in the pedagogy?

- New chapter previews and outlines are provided at the beginning of each chapter.
- Boxes are highlighted to be more prominent, many focused on human examples.
- Technical terms are boldfaced when they first appear, and a list of key terms and their definitions appears at the end of each chapter.
- Thought questions for student review appear at the end of each chapter.
- "At-a-glance" endpapers enable students to easily compare habituation and classical, second-order, and instrumental conditioning.
- The art program has been revised for greater comprehension and appeal.

More instructor support

The improved and much-expanded instructor's manual with test bank includes for each chapter: chapter summaries, a list of key words and key concepts in their order of appearance, suggested readings, short-answer questions, essay questions, multiple-choice questions, suggested class exercises, transparency masters, and (where appropriate) specific suggestions for incorporating *Sniffy: The Virtual Rat, Version 4.5* for Macintosh and Windows into your learning class. Brooks/Cole offers special discounts for instructors who use *Sniffy the Virtual Rat, Version 4.5* together with the fourth edition of *The Principles of Learning and Behavior*. Contact Brooks/Cole at 1-800-354-0092 or marianne_taflinger@brookscole.com for more information on discounts available.

Acknowledgments

I am indebted to all those who provided thoughtful reviews of an earlier draft of the fourth edition and made numerous helpful suggestions: Robert W. Allan, Lafayette College; Robert H. Dale, Butler University; Nelson Freedman, Queen's University; John M. Hinson, Washington State University; Justin Hollands, University of Idaho; Jim Matthews, New York University; Michael Scavio, California State University, Fullerton; and Sherry Serdikoff, James Madison University. I am also grateful to Marianne Taflinger, for her editorial guidance; Tessa McGlasson, for skillfully coordinating the production process; Donald Dewsbury of the University of Florida for providing many of the photographs of major investigators; Kevin Holloway of Lewis and Clark College for preparing the accompanying Instructor's Manual (including test bank); and my wife, Karen, for her love, patience, and support.

Michael Domjan

BRIEF CONTENTS

1 Introduction 1

2 Elicited Behavior, Habituation, and Sensitization 27

3 Classical Conditioning: Foundations 57

4 Classical Conditioning: Mechanisms 87

5 Instrumental Conditioning: Foundations 122

6 Schedules of Reinforcement and Choice Behavior 159

7 Reinforcement: Theories and Experimental Analysis 189

8 Stimulus Control of Behavior 216

9 Aversive Control: Avoidance and Punishment 251

10 Classical-Instrumental Interactions and the Associative Structure of Instrumental Conditioning 284

11 Animal Cognition: Memory Mechanisms 307

12 Complex Animal Cognition 343

CONTENTS

1 INTRODUCTION 1

Historical Antecedents 3

    Historical Developments in the Study of the Mind 4

    Historical Developments in the Study of Reflexes 7

The Dawn of the Modern Era 9

    Comparative Cognition and the Evolution of Intelligence 9

    Functional Neurology 10

    Animal Models of Human Behavior 11

The Definition of Learning 13

    The Learning-Performance Distinction 13

    Distinction between Learning and Other Sources of Behavior Change 14

Methodological Aspects of the Study of Learning 16

    Learning as an Experimental Science 16

    The General-Process Approach to the Study of Learning 17

Use of Animals in Research on Learning 20

    Rationale for the Use of Animals in Research on Learning 20

    Laboratory Animals and Normal Behavior 21

    Public Debate about Animal Research 22

Sample Questions 25

Key Terms 25

2 ELICITED BEHAVIOR, HABITUATION, AND SENSITIZATION   27

The Nature of Elicited Behavior   28

The Concept of the Reflex   28

Modal Action Patterns   30

Eliciting Stimuli for Modal Action Patterns   31

Role of Response Feedback in Elicited Behavior   32

Effects of Repeated Stimulation: Two Examples   36

Visual Attention in Human Infants   36

Startle Response in Rats   37

The Concepts of Habituation and Sensitization   38

Adaptiveness and Pervasiveness of Habituation and Sensitization   39

Habituation versus Sensory Adaptation and Response Fatigue   40

The Dual-Process Theory of Habituation and Sensitization   41

Characteristics of Habituation and Sensitization   44

Time Course   45

Stimulus Specificity   46

Effects of Strong Extraneous Stimuli   47

The Standard Pattern of Affective Dynamics   48

Mechanisms of the Opponent-Process Theory   50

Examples of Opponent Processes   52

Concluding Comments   54

Sample Questions   54

Key Terms   55

3 CLASSICAL CONDITIONING: FOUNDATIONS   57

The Early Years of Classical Conditioning   58

The Discoveries of Wolfsohn and Snarsky   59

The Classical Conditioning Paradigm   60

Experimental Situations   61

Sign Tracking   61

Fear Conditioning   63

Eyeblink Conditioning   65

Taste Aversion Learning   66

Excitatory Pavlovian Conditioning 67

Common Pavlovian Conditioning Procedures 67

Measurement of Conditioned Responses 69

Control Procedures for Classical Conditioning 70

Effectiveness of Common Conditioning Procedures 71

Inhibitory Pavlovian Conditioning 73

Procedures for Inhibitory Conditioning 74

Measuring Conditioned Inhibition 77

Extinction 79

Extinction and Habituation 80

The Learning Involved in Extinction 81

Prevalence of Classical Conditioning 82

Acquired Food Preferences and Aversions in People 82

Infant and Maternal Responses during Nursing 83

The Conditioning of Sexual Behavior 84

Concluding Comments 84

Sample Questions 85

Key Terms 85

4 CLASSICAL CONDITIONING: MECHANISMS 87

What Makes Effective Conditioned and Unconditioned Stimuli? 88

Initial Response to the Stimuli 88

The Novelty of Conditioned and Unconditioned Stimuli 88

CS and US Intensity 89

CS-US Relevance, or Belongingness 90

The Concept of Biological Strength 92

What Determines the Nature of the Conditioned Response? 96

The Stimulus-Substitution Model 96

The Compensatory-Response Model 100

The CS as a Determinant of the Form of the CR 103

Behavior Systems Theory 104

How Do Conditioned and Unconditioned Stimuli Become Associated? 106

The Blocking Effect 107

The Rescorla-Wagner Model 109

Other Models of Classical Conditioning 113

Concluding Comments   120

Sample Questions   120

Key Terms   120

5 INSTRUMENTAL CONDITIONING: FOUNDATIONS   122

Early Investigations of Instrumental Conditioning   124

Modern Approaches to the Study of Instrumental Conditioning   125

    Discrete-Trial Procedures   125

    Free-Operant Procedures   127

Instrumental Conditioning Procedures   131

Fundamental Elements of Instrumental Conditioning   136

    The Instrumental Response   136

    The Instrumental Reinforcer   142

    The Response-Reinforcer Relation   145

Sample Questions   156

Key Terms   157

6 SCHEDULES OF REINFORCEMENT AND CHOICE BEHAVIOR   159

Simple Schedules of Intermittent Reinforcement   160

    Ratio Schedules   161

    Interval Schedules   163

    Comparison of Ratio and Interval Schedules   165

    Response-Rate Schedules of Reinforcement   167

Extinction   168

    Effects of Extinction Procedures   169

    Determinants of Extinction Effects   170

    Mechanisms of the Partial Reinforcement Extinction Effect   171

Choice Behavior: Concurrent Schedules   172

    Measures of Choice Behavior   173

    The Matching Law   174

    Mechanisms of the Matching Law   178

Complex Choice: Concurrent-Chain Schedules   181

Studies of "Self-Control"   183

Explanations of Self-Control   183

Concluding Comments   185

Sample Questions   186

Key Terms   187

7   REINFORCEMENT: THEORIES AND EXPERIMENTAL ANALYSIS   189

Reinforcers as Special Stimuli   190

Physiological Homeostasis and Drive Reduction   191

Primary Motivation and Incentive Motivation   191

Sensory Reinforcement   192

Brain-Stimulation Reinforcement and Motivation   193

Reinforcers as Special Responses   194

Consummatory Response Theory   194

Premack's Theory of Reinforcement   194

The Response Deprivation Hypothesis   200

Behavioral Regulation   201

The Behavioral Bliss Point Approach   201

Economic Concepts and Response Allocation   206

Optimal Foraging Theory and Behavioral Regulation   209

Concluding Comments   214

Sample Questions   215

Key Terms   215

8   STIMULUS CONTROL OF BEHAVIOR   216

Identification and Measurement of Stimulus Control   217

Differential Responding and Stimulus Discrimination   218

Stimulus Generalization   219

Stimulus Generalization Gradients as a Measure of Stimulus Control   220

Stimulus and Response Factors in Stimulus Control 222

Sensory Capacity and Orientation 223

Relative Ease of Conditioning Various Stimuli 224

Type of Reinforcement 225

Type of Instrumental Response 226

Stimulus Elements versus Configural Cues in Compound Stimuli 228

Learning Factors in Stimulus Control 229

Stimulus Discrimination Training 230

Effects of Discrimination Training on Stimulus Control 232

Range of Possible Discriminative Stimuli 233

What Is Learned in Discrimination Training? 235

Stimulus Equivalence Training 241

Contextual Cues and Conditional Relations 242

Control by Contextual Cues 242

Control by Conditional Relations 244

Concluding Comments 248

Sample Questions 249

Key Terms 249

9 AVERSIVE CONTROL: AVOIDANCE AND PUNISHMENT 251

Avoidance Behavior 252

Origins of the Study of Avoidance Behavior 252

The Discriminated Avoidance Procedure 253

Two-Process Theory of Avoidance 255

Experimental Analysis of Avoidance Behavior 256

Alternative Theoretical Accounts of Avoidance Behavior 265

The Avoidance Puzzle: Concluding Comments 271

Punishment 271

Experimental Analysis of Punishment 272

Theories of Punishment 277

Punishment Outside the Laboratory 281

Sample Questions 282

Key Terms 282

10 CLASSICAL-INSTRUMENTAL INTERACTIONS AND THE ASSOCIATIVE STRUCTURE OF INSTRUMENTAL CONDITIONING 284

The Role of Instrumental Reinforcement in Classical Conditioning Procedures 285

The Omission Control Procedure 286

Conditioned Response Modifications of the US 287

The Associative Structure of Instrumental Conditioning 289

S-R and S-O Associations and the r_g-s_g Mechanism 291

S-O Associations and Modern Two-Process Theory 293

R-O and S-(R-O) Associations 299

Concluding Comments 304

Sample Questions 305

Key Terms 306

11 ANIMAL COGNITION: MEMORY MECHANISMS 307

What Is Animal Cognition? 308

Animal Memory Paradigms 309

Delayed Matching to Sample 312

Spatial Memory in a Radial Maze 317

Spatial Memory in Food-Storing Birds 322

Memory Mechanisms 324

Acquisition and the Problem of Stimulus Coding 324

Retention and the Problem of Rehearsal 328

Retrieval 331

Forgetting 334

Proactive and Retroactive Interference 335

Retrograde Amnesia 337

Concluding Comments 341

Sample Questions 341

Key Terms 341

12 COMPLEX ANIMAL COGNITION 343

Timing 344

Techniques for the Measurement of Timing Behavior 344

The Concept of an Internal Clock 345

Characteristics of the Internal Clock 346

Models of Timing 347

Serial Pattern Learning 349

Possible Bases of Serial Pattern Behavior 349

Tests of Serial Pattern Learning with Simultaneous Stimulus Arrays 351

Effects of the Structure of Serial Patterns: Evidence of Chunking 353

Perceptual Concept Learning 355

Generalization to Novel Exemplars 357

Concept Training and Pseudoconcept Training Compared 357

Discrimination between Perceptual Categories 358

Development of Conceptual Errors 359

Mechanisms of Perceptual Concept Learning 361

Language Learning in Nonhuman Animals 363

Approaches to Language Training 364

Documenting Language Skills 366

Language Training Procedures 367

Components of Linguistic Competence 370

Sample Questions 375

Key Terms 375

References 377

Name Index 419

Subject Index 427

HUMAN EXAMPLES

1 INTRODUCTION 1

Historical antecedents   3–6

Animal models of human behavior   11–13

Definition of learning   13–16

2 ELICITED BEHAVIOR, HABITUATION, AND SENSITIZATION 27

Elicited behavior   28

Reflex   28–30

Feedback stimulus   32

Proprioceptive stimulus   32

Visual attention in human infants   36–37, 43

Adaptiveness and pervasiveness of habituation and sensitization   39–40

Sensory adaptation versus response fatigue   41

Box 2.2: Talking to a Fetus or a Pre-Verbal Infant   44

Stimulus specificity of habituation   46–47

Dishabituation   47

Opponent-process theory of motivation   48–49

Opponent-process theory: Drug addiction and love and attachment   52–54

3 CLASSICAL CONDITIONING: FOUNDATIONS 57

Stimulus-stimulus associations   58

Eyeblink conditioning   65

Conditioned inhibition   74

Box 3.2: Safety Signals and the Melioration of Stress   80

Acquired food preferences and aversions   82–83

Conditioning effects: Infant-mother nursing   83–84

4   CLASSICAL CONDITIONING: MECHANISMS   87

Stimulus relevance: human fears and phobias   92

Box 4.1: Behavior Approaches to the Control of Smoking   92

Box 4.2: Higher-Order Conditioning of Fear   94

Higher-order conditioning: Money   93–94

Conditioning in drug abuse patients   101–102

The blocking effect   107

Box 4.3: The Picture-Word Problem in Teaching Reading:
A Form of Blocking   109

The Rescorla-Wagner model   109

5   INSTRUMENTAL CONDITIONING: FOUNDATIONS   122

Instrumental human behavior   123

Shaping by reinforcing successive approximations   129

Box 5.2: Omission Training as a Therapeutic Procedure   135

Box 5.3: Detrimental Effects of Reward: More Myth than Reality   39

Response-reinforcer contiguity v. response-reinforcer contingency 145–146

Secondary reinforcement   147

Box 5.4: Human Extensions of Animal Research on the Controllability
of Reinforcers   153

**6   SCHEDULES OF REINFORCEMENT
AND CHOICE BEHAVIOR   159**

Intermittent reinforcement   160

Schedules of reinforcement: Management and education   160

Fixed ratio schedules   161

Variable ratio schedules   163

Box 6.1: The Postreinforcement Pause and Procrastination   163

Fixed interval schedules   164

Variable interval schedules   165

A limited hold in interval schedules 165

Human Examples

Response rate schedules   167

Box 6.2: Wage Scales and Schedules of Reinforcement   168

Extinction: frustrative aggression   169

Partial reinforcement extinction effect   170

Box 6.3: The Matching Law, Human Behavior, and Behavior Therapy   177

Concurrent-chain schedules   181

Self-control   183

Box 6.4: Can Self-Control Be Trained?   186

Developmental changes in human self-control   185

7 REINFORCEMENT: THEORIES AND EXPERIMENTAL ANALYSIS   189

Sensory reinforcement in human behavior   192

The Premack principle   195

Measuring the probability of a response   196–198

Box 7.1: Applications of the Premack Principle   198–199

Economic concepts and response allocation   207–209

Box 7.2: The Bliss Point Approach and Behavior Therapy   204–205

8 STIMULUS CONTROL OF BEHAVIOR   216

Stimulus control   217

Stimulus generalization   219

Sensory capacity   223

Sensory orientation   223–224

Box 8.1: Generalization of Treatment Outcomes   222

Overshadowing   224

Configural cues   228

Stimulus discrimination training   231–232

Box 8.2: Stimulus Control of Sleeping in Children   232

Control of behavior by contextual cues   243

9 AVERSIVE CONTROL: AVOIDANCE AND PUNISHMENT   251

Avoidance behavior   252

The first avoidance experiment: Bechterev, 1913   252

Extinction of avoidance   260

Observational learning of fear   266

Punishment outside the laboratory   281–282

Box 9.2: When Punishment Doesn't Work   278

Punishment   271

Timeout procedures   272

Overcorrection   272

Punishment and alternative sources of reinforcement   276

Discriminative punishment   276–277

Negative law of effect   280–281

11 ANIMAL COGNITION: MEMORY MECHANISMS   307

Animal cognition versus human thinking   308–309

Stages of memory   310

Working memory   311

Reference memory   312

Box 11.1: Matching to Sample in Elderly People   318–319

Stimulus coding   325

Retrospection and prospection   326

Changes in coding strategies with task demands   326–328

Rehearsal   329

Directed forgetting   329

Retrieval and retrieval failure   331–333

Memory interference   335

Amnesia and retrograde amnesia   337–338

12 COMPLEX ANIMAL COGNITION   343

Serial pattern learning   349–351

Chunking   353

Comparison of language comprehension in a bonobo chimpanzee
and a 2-year-old child   373–374

Human Examples

INTRODUCTION

Historical Antecedents

Historical Developments in the Study of the Mind

Historical Developments in the Study of Reflexes

The Dawn of the Modern Era

Comparative Cognition and the Evolution of Intelligence

Functional Neurology

Animal Models of Human Behavior

The Definition of Learning

The Learning-Performance Distinction

Distinction Between Learning and Other Sources of Behavior Change

Methodological Aspects of the Study of Learning

Learning as an Experimental Science

The General-Process Approach to the Study of Learning

Use of Animals in Research on Learning

Rationale for the Use of Animals in Research on Learning

Laboratory Animals and Normal Behavior

Public Debate about Animal Research

T HE goal of Chapter 1 is to introduce the reader to the study of learning and behavior. I will begin by discussing key concepts in the study of learning from a historical viewpoint and will describe the origins of experimental research in the area. These origins lie in studies of the evolution of intelligence, of functional neurology, and of animal models of human behavior. The defining characteristics of learning will be described next, followed by a discussion of methodological approaches to the study of learning. Because numerous experiments on learning have been performed with nonhuman animals, I will conclude the chapter by discussing the rationale for the use of animals in research.

You are probably already interested in understanding behavior, be it your own or the behavior of others. This interest is more than idle curiosity. Your quality of life is governed by your actions and the actions of others. Whether you receive a job offer depends on your prior education and record of employment, as well as the decisions of your prospective employer. Whether you get along well with your roommate depends on how he reacts to the things you do and how you react to the things he does. Whether you get to school on time depends on whether you get up early enough and on how crowded the roads are.

Any systematic effort to understand behavior must include consideration of what we learn and how we learn it. Numerous aspects of both human and animal behavior are the results of learning. We learn to read, to write, and to count. We learn how to walk down stairs without falling, how to open doors, how to ride a bicycle, and how to swim. We also learn when to relax and when to become anxious. We learn what foods are good for us and what will make us sick. We learn who is fun to visit and whose company is to be avoided. We learn how to tell when someone is unhappy and how to know when that person feels fine. We learn when to carry an umbrella and when to take an extra scarf. Life is filled with activities and experiences that are shaped by what we have learned.

Learning is one of the biological processes that promotes survival. The integrity of life depends on a variety of biological functions, including respiration, digestion, and the excretion of metabolic waste. Physiological systems have evolved to accomplish these tasks. However, finely tuned physiological processes are not enough to maintain the integrity of life. People and nonhuman animals are faced with climatic changes, changes in food resources, the coming and going of predators, and other environmental disruptions. Adverse effects of environmental change often have to be minimized by behavioral adjustments.

Animals have to learn to find new food sources as old ones become used up; they have to learn to avoid predators as new ones enter their territory; and they have to find new shelter when storms destroy their old one. Accomplishing these tasks obviously requires motor behavior such as walking and manipulating objects. These tasks also require the ability to predict important facts about the environment such as the availability of food in a particular location and at a particular time. Acquisition of new motor behavior and new anticipatory reactions involves learning. Animals learn to go to a new water hole when their old one dries up and learn to anticipate new sources of danger. These learned adjustments to the environment are as important as physiological processes such as respiration and digestion.

Most people tend to think about learning as involving the acquisition of new behavior. Indeed, learning is required before a child can read, ride a bicycle, or play a musical instrument. However, learning can just as well consist of the decrease or loss of some behavior in the organism's repertoire. A child, for example, may learn not to cross the street when the traffic light is red, not to grab food from someone else's plate, and not to yell and scream when her mother is trying to take a nap. Learning to withhold responses is just as important as learning to make responses, if not more so.

When considering learning, people commonly focus on the kinds of learning that require special training—the kinds of learning that take place in public schools and colleges, for example. Solving problems in calculus or making a triple somersault when diving does require special instruction. However, we learn all kinds of things without an expert teacher or coach during the course of routine interactions with our social and physical environment. Children, for example, learn how to open doors and windows, how to respond to a ringing telephone, when to avoid a hot stove, and when to duck so as not to get hit by a thrown ball. College students learn how to find their way around campus, how to avoid heartburn from cafeteria food, and how to predict when a roommate will stay out late at night—all without special instruction.

In the coming chapters, I will survey the research on basic principles of learning and behavior. I will discuss the types of learning and behavior that are fundamental to life but that, like breathing, are often ignored. The focus will be on pervasive and basic forms of learning that are a normal—though usually unnoticed—part of living. I will discuss the learning of simple relationships among events in the environment, the learning of simple motor movements, and the learning of emotional reactions to stimuli. These forms of learning are investigated in experiments that involve "training" procedures of various sorts. However, these forms of learning occur in the lives of people and animals without explicit or organized instruction or schooling.

HISTORICAL ANTECEDENTS

Theoretical approaches to the study of learning have their roots in the philosophy of René Descartes (see Figure 1.1). Before Descartes, most people thought of human behavior as entirely determined by conscious intent and free will. People's actions were not considered to be controlled by external stimuli or mechanistic natural laws. What a person did was presumed to be the result of his or her will or deliberate intent. Descartes took exception to this view of human nature because he recognized that many things people do are automatic reactions to external stimuli. However, he was not prepared to abandon entirely the idea of free will and the conscious control of actions. He therefore formulated a dualistic view of human behavior known as Cartesian **dualism.**

According to Cartesian dualism, there are two classes of human behavior: involuntary and voluntary. Some actions are involuntary and occur in response to external stimuli. These actions are called **reflexes.** Other aspects of human behavior involve voluntary actions that do not have to be triggered by external stimuli; rather, they occur because of the person's conscious choice to act in that manner.

The details of Descartes' dualistic view of human behavior are diagrammed in Figure 1.2. Let us first consider the mechanisms of involuntary, or reflexive, behavior. Stimuli in the environment are detected by the person's sense organs. The sensory information is then relayed to the brain through nerves. From the brain, the impetus for action is sent through nerves to the muscles that create the involuntary response. Thus, sensory input is *reflected* in response output. Hence, involuntary behavior is called *reflexive.*

Several aspects of this system are noteworthy. Stimuli in the external environment are seen as the cause of all involuntary behavior. These stimuli produce involuntary responses by way of a neural circuit that includes the brain. However, Descartes assumed that only one set of nerves was involved—that the same nerves transmitted information from the sense organs to the brain and from the brain down to the muscles. This circuit, he believed, permitted rapid reactions to external stimuli—for example, a person's quick withdrawal of his finger from a hot stove.

Descartes assumed that the involuntary mechanism of behavior was the only one available to animals other than humans. According to this view, all of nonhuman animal behavior occurs as reflex responses to external stimuli. Thus, Descartes believed that nonhuman animals lacked free will and were incapable of voluntary, conscious

Figure 1.1
René Descartes
(1596–1650).

behavior. He considered free will and voluntary behavior to be uniquely human attributes. This superiority of humans over other animals existed because only human beings were thought to have a mind, or soul.

The mind was assumed to be a nonphysical entity. Descartes believed that the mind is connected to the physical body by way of the pineal gland, which is near the brain. Because of this connection, the mind could be aware of and keep track of involuntary behavior. Through this mechanism, the mind could also initiate voluntary actions. Because he thought voluntary behavior is initiated in the mind, Descartes assumed that it could occur independently of external stimulation.

The mind-body dualism introduced by Descartes stimulated two intellectual traditions. One, *mentalism,* was concerned with the contents and workings of the mind; the other, *reflexology,* with the mechanisms of reflexive behavior. Let us turn to these next.

Historical Developments in the Study of the Mind

Philosophers concerned with the mind were interested in what is in the mind and how the mind works. Descartes had something to say about both these issues. Because Descartes thought the mind is connected to the brain by way of the pineal gland, he believed that some of the contents of the mind come from sense experiences. However, he also believed that the mind contains ideas that are innate and that exist in all human beings independent of personal experience. For example, he be-

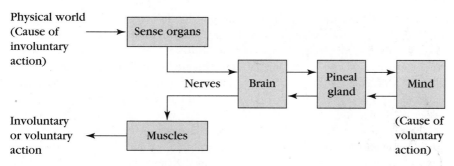

Figure 1.2 Diagram of Cartesian dualism. Events in the physical world are detected by sense organs. From here the information is passed along to the brain. The brain is connected to the mind by way of the pineal gland. Involuntary action is produced by a reflex arc that involves messages sent first from the sense organs to the brain and then from the brain to the muscles. Voluntary action is initiated by the mind, with messages sent to the brain and then the muscles.

lieved that all humans are born having a concept of God, a concept of self, and certain fundamental axioms of geometry (such as the fact that the shortest distance between two points is a straight line). The philosophical approach that assumes humans are born with innate ideas about certain things is called **nativism.**

Some philosophers after Descartes took issue with the nativist position. In particular, the British philosopher John Locke (1632–1704) believed that all the ideas people have are acquired directly or indirectly through experiences after birth. He believed that human beings are born without any preconceptions about the world. According to Locke, the mind starts out as a clean slate (*tabula rasa,* in Latin), to be gradually filled with ideas and information as the person has various sense experiences. This philosophical approach to the contents of the mind is called **empiricism.** Empiricism was accepted by a group of British philosophers who lived during the seventeenth, eighteenth, and nineteenth centuries and who came to be known as the *British empiricists.*

The nativist and empiricist philosophies differed not only on what the mind was assumed to contain but also on how the mind was assumed to operate. Descartes believed that the mind does not function in a predictable and orderly manner, according to discoverable rules or laws. One of the first to propose an alternative to this position was the British philosopher Thomas Hobbes (1588–1679). Hobbes accepted the distinction between voluntary and involuntary behavior stated by Descartes and also accepted the notion that voluntary behavior is controlled by the mind. However, unlike Descartes, he believed that the mind operates just as predictably and lawfully as reflex mechanisms. More specifically, he proposed that voluntary behavior is governed by the principle of **hedonism.** According to this principle, people do things in the pursuit of pleasure and the avoidance of pain. Hobbes was not concerned with whether the pursuit of pleasure and the avoidance of pain are laudable or desirable. For Hobbes, hedonism was simply a fact of life. As we will see, this conception of behavior has remained with us in one form or another to the present day.

According to the British empiricists, another important aspect of how the mind works involved the concept of **association.** Recall that empiricism assumes that all ideas originate from sense experiences. But how do the experiences of various colors, shapes, odors, and sounds allow the formation of more complex ideas? Consider, for example, the concept of a car. If you hear the word "car," you have an idea of what the thing looks like, what it is used for, and how you might feel if you sat in it. Where do all these ideas come from, given just the sound of the letters *c, a,* and *r*? The British empiricists proposed that simple sensations are combined into more complex ideas by associations. Because you had heard the word "car" when you saw a car, had considered using one to get to work, or had sat in one, associations may have become established between the word "car" and various aspects of cars. The British empiricists considered such associations very important in their explanation of how the mind works; hence, they devoted considerable effort to detailing the rules of associations.

Rules of Associations.   The British empiricists accepted two sets of rules for the establishment of associations, one primary and the other secondary. The primary rules were originally set forth by the ancient Greek philosopher Aristotle. He proposed three principles for the establishment of associations: (1) contiguity, (2) similarity, and (3) contrast. Of these, the contiguity principle has been the most prominent in studies of associations. It states that, if two events repeatedly occur together in space or time, they will become associated. Once an association has been established, the occurrence of one of the events will activate the memory of the other event. For example, if you encounter the smell of tomato sauce with spaghetti often enough, the smell of tomato sauce will become sufficient to get you to think about spaghetti. The similarity and contrast principles state that two things will become associated if they are similar in some respect (both are red, for example) or have some contrasting characteristics (one might be strikingly tall and the other strikingly short, for example).

Various secondary laws of associations were set forth by a number of empiricist philosophers—among them the Scotsman Thomas Brown (1778–1820). Brown proposed that a number of factors influence the formation of associations between two sensations. These include the intensity of the sensations and how frequently or recently the sensations occurred together. In addition, the formation of an association between two events was considered to depend on the number of other associations in which each event was already involved and the similarity of these past associations to the current one being formed.

The British empiricists discussed rules of association as a part of their philosophical discourse. They did not perform experiments to determine whether or not the rules were valid. Nor did they attempt to determine the circumstances in which one rule was more important than another. Empirical investigation of the mechanisms of associations did not begin until the pioneering work of the nineteenth-century German psychologist Hermann Ebbinghaus (1850–1909).

To study how associations are formed, Ebbinghaus invented **nonsense syllables.** These were three-letter combinations ("bap," for example), devoid of any meaning that might influence how a person might react to them. Ebbinghaus used himself as the experimental participant. He studied lists of nonsense syllables and measured his ability to remember the syllables under various experimental conditions. This general method enabled him to answer such questions as how the strength of an association improved with increased training, whether nonsense syllables that appeared close together in a list were associated more strongly than syllables that were farther apart, and whether a syllable became more strongly associated with the next one on the list than with the preceding one.

The concept of reflex action, that was introduced by Descartes greatly advanced the understanding of behavior. However, Descartes was mistaken in many of his beliefs about reflexes. He believed that sensory messages going from sense organs to the brain and motor messages going from the brain to the muscles travel along the same nerves. He thought that nerves are hollow tubes and that neural transmission involves gases called *animal spirits*. The animal spirits, released by the pineal gland, were assumed to flow through the neural tubes and enter the muscles, causing them to swell and create movement. Finally, Descartes considered all reflexive movements to be innate and to be fixed by the anatomy of the nervous system.

Later experimental work on animals by Charles Bell (1774–1842) in England and François Magendie (1783–1855) in France showed that separate nerves transmit sensory information from sense organs to the central nervous system and motor information from the central nervous system to muscles. If a sensory nerve is cut, an animal remains capable of muscle movements; if a motor nerve is cut, the animal remains capable of registering sensory information.

The idea that animal spirits are involved in neural transmission was also disproved after the death of Descartes. In 1669 John Swammerdam (1637–1680) showed that mechanical irritation of a nerve was sufficient to produce a muscle contraction. Thus, infusion of animal spirits from the pineal gland was not necessary. In other studies, Francis Glisson (1597–1677) demonstrated that muscle contractions are not produced by swelling due to the infusion of a gas, as Descartes had postulated. Glisson measured the swelling of the muscles of the arm by having people submerge their arm in water and then contract their arm muscle. If muscle contraction were resulting from the infusion of a gas, the muscle should have displaced more water when contracted than when relaxed. Contrary to this prediction, the amount of water displaced by the muscle did not change when the muscle was contracted. Such experiments indicate that neural conduction does not occur by the mechanisms Descartes had proposed.

Descartes and most philosophers after him assumed that reflexes are responsible only for simple reactions to stimuli. The energy in a stimulus was thought to be translated directly into the energy of the elicited response by the neural connections. The more intense the stimulus was, the more vigorous the resulting response would be. This view of reflexes is consistent with many casual observations. If you touch a stove, for example, the hotter the stove, the more quickly you withdraw your finger. However, reflexes can also be more complicated.

The physiological processes responsible for reflex behavior became better understood in the nineteenth century, and reflexes came to be used as an explanation for a greater range of behaviors. Two Russian physiologists, I. M. Sechenov (1829–1905) (see Figure 1.3) and Ivan Pavlov (1849–1936), were primarily responsible for these developments. Sechenov proposed that stimuli do not elicit reflex responses directly in all cases. Rather, in some cases a stimulus can release a response from inhibition. Where a stimulus released a response from inhibition, the vigor of the response would not depend on the intensity of the stimulus. This simple idea opened up all sorts of new possibilities.

Since the vigor of an elicited response does not invariably depend on the intensity of its triggering stimulus, it is possible for a very faint stimulus to produce a large response. Small pieces of dust in the nose, for example, can cause a vigorous sneeze. Sechenov took advantage of this type of mechanism to provide a reflex analysis of vol-

Figure 1.3
I. M. Sechenov
(1829–1905)

untary behavior. He suggested that complex forms of behavior (actions or thoughts) that occur in the absence of an obvious eliciting stimulus are in fact reflexive responses. In these cases, the eliciting stimuli are so faint as to be unnoticeable. Thus, according to Sechenov, voluntary behavior and thoughts are actually elicited by inconspicuous, faint stimuli.

Sechenov's ideas about voluntary behavior greatly extended the use of reflex mechanisms to explain a variety of aspects of behavior. However, his ideas were philosophical extrapolations from the research results he obtained. In addition, Sechenov did not address the question of how reflex mechanisms can account for the fact that the behavior of organisms is not fixed and invariant throughout an organism's lifetime but can be altered by experience. From the time of Descartes, reflex responses were considered to be innate and fixed by the anatomy of the nervous system. Reflexes were thought to depend on a pre-wired neural circuit connecting the sense organs to the relevant muscles. According to this view, a given stimulus could be expected to elicit the same response throughout an organism's life. Although this is true in some cases, there are also many examples in which responses to stimuli change as a result of experience. Explanation of such cases by reflex processes had to await the experimental and theoretical work of Ivan Pavlov.

Pavlov showed experimentally that not all reflexes are innate. New reflexes to stimuli can be established through mechanisms of association. Thus, Pavlov's role in the history of the study of reflexes is comparable to the role of Ebbinghaus in the study of the mind. Both were concerned with establishing the laws of associations through empirical research.

Experimental studies of basic principles of learning often are conducted with nonhuman animals and in the tradition of reflexology. Research in animal learning came to be pursued with great vigor starting a little more than 100 years ago. Impetus for the research came from three primary sources (see Domjan, 1987). The first of these was interest in comparative cognition and the evolution of the mind. The second was interest in how the nervous system works (functional neurology), and the third was interest in developing animal models to study certain aspects of human behavior. As we will see in ensuing chapters, comparative cognition, functional neurology, and animal models of human behavior continue to dominate contemporary research in learning processes.

Comparative Cognition and the Evolution of Intelligence

Interest in comparative cognition and the evolution of the mind was sparked by the writings of Charles Darwin (see Figure 1.4), who took Descartes' ideas about human nature one step further. Descartes had started chipping away at the age-old notion that human beings have a unique and privileged position in the animal kingdom by proposing that at least some aspects of human behavior (their reflexes) are animal-like. However, Descartes had preserved some privilege for human beings by assuming that humans (and only humans) have a mind.

Darwin attacked this last vestige of privilege. In his second major work, *The Descent of Man, and Selection in Relation to Sex,* Darwin argued that "man is descended from some lower form, notwithstanding that connecting-links have not hitherto been discovered" (Darwin, 1897, p. 146). In claiming a continuity from animals to humans, Darwin attempted to characterize not only the evolution of physical traits but also the evolution of psychological or mental abilities. Thus, he suggested that the human mind is a product of evolution. In making this claim, Darwin did not deny that human beings have such special mental abilities as the capacity for wonder, curiosity, imitation, attention, memory, reasoning, and aesthetic sensibility. Rather, he suggested that nonhuman animals also have these abilities. Moreover, he maintained that nonhuman animals are capable even of belief in spiritual agencies (Darwin, 1897, p. 95).

Darwin collected anecdotal evidence of various forms of intelligent behavior in animals in an effort to support his claims. Although the evidence was not compelling by modern standards, the research question was. Investigators ever since have been captivated by the possibility of tracing the evolution of intelligence by studying the abilities of various species of animals.

Before investigating the evolution of intelligence in a systematic fashion, a researcher must have a criterion for identifying intelligent behavior in animals. A highly influential proposal for a criterion was offered by George Romanes in his book *Animal Intelligence* (Romanes, 1884). Romanes suggested that intelligence can be identified by determining whether an animal learns "to make new adjustments, or to modify old ones, in accordance with the results of its own individual experience" (p. 4). Thus, Romanes defined intelligence in terms of the ability to learn. This definition was widely accepted by comparative psychologists at the end of the nineteenth and the start of the twentieth century and served to make the study of animal learning the key to obtaining information about the evolution of intelligence.

Figure 1.4
Charles Darwin
(1809–1882).

As we will see in the upcoming chapters, much research on the mechanisms of animal learning has not been concerned with trying to obtain evidence of the evolution of intelligence. Nevertheless, this issue remains of considerable contemporary interest (for example, Wasserman, 1993). I will describe some of the fruits of this contemporary research on animal cognition in Chapters 11 and 12.

Functional Neurology

As I previously mentioned, the modern era in the study of learning processes was also greatly stimulated by efforts to use studies of animal learning to gain insights into how the nervous system works. This line of research was led by the Russian physiologist Ivan Pavlov, quite independently of the work of Darwin, Romanes, and others interested in comparative cognition.

While still a medical student, Pavlov became committed to the principle of **nervism.** According to nervism, all key physiological functions are governed by the nervous system. Armed with this principle, Pavlov devoted his life to documenting how the nervous system controls various aspects of physiology. Much of his work was devoted to identifying the neural mechanisms of digestion.

For many years, Pavlov's research progressed according to plan. But in 1902, two British investigators (Bayliss and Starling) published results showing that the pancreas, an important digestive organ, was partially under hormonal rather than neural control. Writing some time later, Pavlov's friend and biographer noted that these novel findings produced a crisis in the laboratory because they "shook the very foundation of the teachings of the exclusive nervous regulation of the secretory activity of the digestive glands" (Babkin, 1949, p. 228).

The evidence of hormonal control of the pancreas presented Pavlov with a dilemma. If he continued his investigations of digestion, he would have to abandon his interest in the nervous system. On the other hand, if he maintained his commitment to nervism, he would have to stop studying digestive physiology. Nervism won out. In an effort to continue studying the nervous system, Pavlov changed from studying digestive physiology to studying the conditioning of reflexes. Thus, Pavlov regarded his studies of conditioning (which is a form of learning) as a way to obtain information about the functions of the nervous system—how the nervous system works. Pavlov's claim that studies of learning reveal how the nervous system functions is well accepted by contemporary neuroscientists. Kandel, for example, has commented that "the central tenet of modern neural science is that all behavior is a reflection of brain function" (Kandel, Schwartz, & Jessell, 1991, p. 3).

The behavioral psychologist is like a driver who tries to find out about an experimental car by immediately taking it out for a test drive instead of first looking at how the car was put together. By driving the car, a person can learn a great deal about how it functions. He can discover its acceleration, its top speed, the quality of its ride, its turning radius, and how quickly it comes to a stop. Driving the car will not tell us how these various functions are accomplished, but it will reveal the major functional characteristics of the internal machinery of the car.

Knowledge of the functional characteristics of a car can, in turn, provide clues about its internal machinery. For example, if the car accelerates sluggishly and never reaches high speeds, chances are it is not powered by a rocket engine. If the car only goes forward when facing downhill, it may be propelled by gravity rather than by an engine. On the other hand, if the car cannot be made to come to a stop quickly, it may not have brakes.

In a similar manner, behavioral studies of learning can provide clues about the machinery of the nervous system. Such studies show the kinds of plasticity the nervous system can exhibit, the conditions under which learning can take place, how long learned responses persist, and the circumstances under which learned information is accessible or inaccessible. By detailing the functions of the nervous system, behavioral studies of learning define the features or functions that have to be explained by neurophysiological investigations.

Animal Models of Human Behavior

The third major impetus for the modern era in the study of animal learning was the suggestion that animal research can provide information that may advance the understanding of human behavior. Animal models of human behavior are of more recent origin than comparative cognition or functional neurology. The approach was systematized by Dollard and Miller and their collaborators (Dollard, Miller, Doob, Mowrer, & Sears, 1939; Miller & Dollard, 1941) and developed further by B. F. Skinner (1953).

Drawing inferences about human behavior on the basis of research with animal participants can be hazardous and controversial. The inferences are hazardous if they are unwarranted; they are controversial if the rationale for the model system approach is poorly understood. Although animal models of human behavior have been developed based on research with a variety of species, most of the models were developed with rats and pigeons.

In generalizing from research with rats and pigeons to human behavior, scientists do not make the assumption that rats and pigeons are like people. Animal models are like other types of models. Architects, pharmacologists, medical scientists, and designers of automobiles all rely on models, and the models are often strikingly different from the real thing. Architects, for example, make small-scale models of buildings they are designing. Obviously, such models are not the same as the real building. They are much smaller, made of cardboard and small pieces of wood instead of bricks and mortar, and support little weight.

Models are commonly used because they permit the investigation of certain aspects of what they represent under conditions that are *simpler, more easily controlled,* and *less expensive* than the real thing. For example, with the use of a model, an architect can study the design of the exterior of a planned building without the expense of actual construction. The model can be used to determine what the building will look like from various vantage points and how it will appear relative to nearby buildings. Studying a model in a design studio is much simpler than studying a building on a busy street corner. Factors that may get in the way of getting a good view (other buildings, traffic, and power lines, for example) can be controlled and minimized in a model.

In a comparable fashion, a car designer can study the wind resistance of various design features of a new automobile with the use of a model in the form of a computer program. The program can be used to show how the addition of spoilers or changes in the shape of the car can cause changes in wind resistance. The computer model bears little resemblance to a real car. It has no tires or engine and cannot be driven. However, the model permits testing the wind resistance of a car design under conditions that are much simpler, better controlled, and less expensive than if the car were built and driven down the highway under various conditions in order to measure wind resistance.

What makes models valid for studying something, given all the differences between the model and the real thing? For a model to be valid, it must be comparable to the real thing in terms of the feature under study—the *relevant feature.* If the model of a building is used to study the building's exterior appearance, then all the exterior dimensions of the model must be proportional to the corresponding dimensions of the planned building. Other features of the model, such as its structural elements, are irrelevant. In contrast, if the model were used to study how well the building would withstand an earthquake, then its structural elements (beams and how they are connected) would be critical.

In a similar manner, the only thing relevant in a computer model of car wind resistance is that the computer program provide calculations for wind resistance that match the results obtained with real cars driven through real air. No other feature is relevant; therefore, the fact that the computer program lacks an engine or rubber tires is of no consequence.

The rationale and strategies associated with animal models of human behavior are similar to those pertaining to models in other areas of inquiry. Animal models permit the investigation of problems that are difficult, if not impossible, to investigate directly with people. A model permits the investigation to be carried out under circumstances that are simpler, better controlled, and less expensive. Furthermore, the validity of animal models is based on the same criterion as the validity of other types of models. The important thing is similarity between the animal model and human behavior in *relevant features* for the problem at hand. For example, similarities between rats and humans in the way they learn to avoid dangerous foods makes a rat model valid for the investigation of human food aversion learning. The fact that rats have long tails and walk on four legs rather than two is entirely irrelevant to food selection.

The critical task in constructing a successful animal model is to identify a relevant similarity between the animal model and the human behavior of interest. Because animal models are often used to push back the frontiers of knowledge, the correspondence between the animal findings and human behavior always must be carefully verified by empirical data.

The rationale and strategy for the development of animal models of human behavior were stated succinctly by Dollard and Miller (1950):

> In using the results from [research with rats] we are working on the hypothesis that people have all the learning capacities of rats. . . . Even though the facts must be verified at the human level, it is often easier to notice the operation of principles after they have been studied and isolated in simpler situations so that one knows exactly what to look for. Furthermore, in those cases in which it is impossible to use as rigorous experimental controls at the human level, our faith in what evidence can be gathered at that level will be increased if it is in line with the results of more carefully controlled experiments on other mammals. (p. 63)

Dollard and Miller advocated an interplay between animal and human research in which laboratory studies with animals are used to isolate and identify phenomena that can then be investigated in people more successfully. The animal research is also used to increase confidence in human data that are obtained with weaker research methods.

Animal models have been developed for a wide range of human problems and behaviors (see Overmier & Burke, 1992, for a bibliography). In the upcoming chapters I will discuss animal models of love and attachment, drug tolerance and addiction, food aversion learning, learning of fears and phobias, and stress and coping, among others. Animal models have also led to the development of numerous procedures now commonly employed with people, such as biofeedback, programmed instruction, systematic desensitization, token economies, and other techniques of behavior modification. I will provide examples of such applications throughout the text at relevant points.

THE DEFINITION OF LEARNING

Learning is such a common human experience that few people reflect on exactly what it means to say that something has been learned. A universally accepted definition of learning does not exist. However, many critical aspects of the concept are captured in the following statement:

> *Learning is an enduring change in the mechanisms of behavior involving specific stimuli and/or responses that results from prior experience with similar stimuli and responses.*

The Learning-Performance Distinction

Whenever we see evidence of learning, we see the emergence of a change in behavior—the performance of a new response or the suppression of a response that occurred previously. A child becomes skilled in snapping the buckles of her sandals or becomes more patient in waiting to eat dinner until everyone has been seated at the table. Such changes in behavior are the only way to tell whether or not learning has occurred. However, the preceding definition attributes learning to a change in the mechanisms of behavior, not to a change in behavior directly.

By *mechanisms of behavior,* I mean the underlying machinery that makes behavior happen. As Pavlov assumed, the physical machinery of learning resides in the nervous system. However, it is not necessary to observe the neural mechanisms of behavior directly to identify learning. Most investigators are satisfied with studying learning in terms of behavioral mechanisms or theoretical constructs. These theoretical constructs constitute a conceptual or hypothetical machinery that is assumed to be responsible for behavior. I have already mentioned one such theoretical concept— the concept of an association—which is used to explain certain changes in behavior that result from experience. In later chapters, I will discuss numerous other theoretical concepts or components of the hypothetical machinery that are used to explain learned changes in behavior.

Why should learning be defined in terms of a change in the mechanisms of behavior (be these conceptual or physical mechanisms) rather than a change in behavior itself? The main reason is that behavior is determined by many factors in addition to learning. Consider, for example, eating. Whether you eat something depends on how hungry you are, how much effort is required to obtain the food, how much you like the food, and whether you know where the food is. Of all these factors, only the last one necessarily involves learning.

Performance refers to an organism's actions at a particular time. Whether you do something or not (your performance) depends on many things. Even the occurrence of a simple response such as jumping into a swimming pool is multiply determined. Whether you jump depends on the availability, depth, and temperature of the water, your motivation to jump, your physical ability to spring away from the side of the pool, and so forth. Performance is determined by opportunity, motivation, and sensory and motor capabilities, in addition to learning. Therefore, a change in performance cannot be automatically considered to reflect learning.

The definition stated earlier identifies learning as a change in the mechanisms of behavior to emphasize the distinction between learning and performance. The behavior of an organism (its performance) is used to provide evidence of learning. However, because performance is determined by many factors in addition to learning, an observer must be very careful in deciding whether a particular aspect of performance does or does not reflect learning. Sometimes evidence of learning cannot be obtained until special test procedures are set up. Children, for example, learn a great deal about driving a car just by watching others drive, but this learning is not apparent until they are permitted behind the steering wheel. In other cases (next to be discussed), a change in behavior is readily observed but cannot be attributed to learning either because it is not sufficiently long lasting or because it does not result from experience with specific environmental events.

Distinction between Learning and Other Sources of Behavior Change

Evaluating various situations in terms of the abstract definition of learning I have stated may be difficult because some aspects of the definition are vague. For example, the definition does not specify exactly how long behavioral changes must last to be considered instances of learning. In other cases, it may be difficult to decide what constitutes sufficient experience with environmental events to classify something as an instance of learning. Therefore, it is useful to distinguish learning from other known mechanisms that can produce changes in behavior.

Several mechanisms produce changes in behavior that are too short-lasting to be considered instances of learning. One such process is **fatigue**. Physical exertion may result in a gradual weakening in the vigor of a response because the individual becomes tired or fatigued. This type of change is produced by experience. However, it is not considered an instance of learning because the decline in responding disappears if the individual is allowed to rest.

Behavior also may be temporarily altered by a *change in stimulus conditions*. If the house lights in a movie theater are suddenly turned on in the middle of the show, the behavior of the audience is likely to change dramatically. However, this is not an instance of learning because the audience is likely to return to watching the movie when the house lights are turned off again.

Another source of temporary change in behavior that is not considered learning is *alteration in the physiological or motivational state* of the organism. Hunger and thirst induce responses that are not observed at other times. Changes in the level of sex hormones cause changes in responsiveness to sexual stimuli. Short-lasting behavioral effects may also accompany the administration of psychoactive drugs.

Other mechanisms produce persistent changes in behavior, but without the type of experience with environmental events that satisfies the definition of learning. The most obvious process of this type is **maturation**. A child cannot get something from a high shelf until he grows tall enough. However, the change in behavior in this case is not an instance of learning because it occurs with the mere passage of time. A child does not have to be trained to reach high places as he becomes taller. Maturation can also result in the disappearance of certain responses. For example, touching an infant's feet shortly after birth results in foot movements that resemble walking, and stroking the bottom of the foot causes the toes to fan out. Both of these reflex reactions disappear as the infant gets older.

Generally, the distinction between learning and maturation is based on the importance of special experiences in producing the change in behavior. However, the distinction is blurred in instances where environmental stimulation has been found to be necessary for the occurrence of developmental changes that originally were thought to involve experience-independent maturation. Experiments with cats have shown that their visual system will not develop sufficiently for them to be able to see horizontal lines unless they are exposed to such stimuli early in life (for example, Blakemore & Cooper, 1970). The appearance of sexual behavior at puberty was originally thought to depend on experience-independent maturation. However, experiments suggest that successful sexual behavior requires interactions with playmates early in life (for example, Harlow, 1969).

So far I have discussed mechanisms that create changes in behavior during the lifetime of the organism. Changes in behavior may also occur across generations through evolutionary adaptation. Individuals possessing genetic characteristics that promote their reproduction are more likely to pass those characteristics on to future generations. Adaptation and evolutionary change produced by differential reproductive success can lead to changes in behavior, just as they lead to changes in the physical characteristics of species. Evolutionary changes are similar to learning in that they are also related to environmental influences. The characteristics of individuals that promote their reproductive success depend on the environment in which they live. However, evolutionary changes occur only across generations and are therefore distinguished from learning.

Although learning can be distinguished from maturation and evolution, it is not independent of these other sources of behavioral change. Whether a particular learning process occurs and how it operates depends on the organism's maturational level and evolutionary history. The dependence of learning on maturation is obvious in certain aspects of childrearing. For example, no amount of toilet training will be effective until a child's nerves and muscles have developed sufficiently to make bladder control possible. The dependence of learning on evolutionary history can be seen by comparing learning processes in various types of animals. For example, fish and turtles appear to learn differently than rats and monkeys in instrumental conditioning situations (Bitterman, 1975). I will have more to say about the interaction of evolutionary history and learning processes in later chapters (see also Plotkin & Odling-Smee, 1979; Rozin & Schull, 1988; Sherry & Schachter, 1987; Zeiler, 1992).

METHODOLOGICAL ASPECTS OF THE STUDY OF LEARNING

There are two prominent methodological features of investigations of learning processes. One of these is the exclusive use of experimental, as contrasted with observational, research methods. The second is reliance on a general-process approach. The exclusive use of experimental research methods is an inevitable consequence of the nature of learning. The phenomena of learning simply cannot be studied any other way. By contrast, reliance on a general-process approach is more a matter of preference than of necessity.

Learning as an Experimental Science

To review for a moment, I have argued that learning is identified by changes in behavior that result from prior experience with specific stimuli and/or responses, provided those changes are sufficiently long lasting to rule out other possible factors such as fatigue, temporary shifts in motivation, and the like. The fact that my definition restricts learning to the effects of prior experience has some important implications. To say that a change in behavior results from prior experience is to attribute the behavior to something the organism encountered previously—in other words, to make a claim about the causes of the behavior change. Therefore, *the study of learning is a study of certain types of causes of behavior*—causes that alter behavior through prior experience. Prior experience may be thought of as a "training procedure" that causes a long lasting change in behavior.

The fact that learning involves certain types of causes of behavior sets tight limits on the kinds of evidence that can be used to make claims about learning. The study of learning is limited to the investigative methods that are required to identify causes. The basic problem with studying causes is that they cannot be observed directly; causes can only be inferred from the results of experimental manipulations.

Consider the following example. Mary opens the door to a dark room. She quickly turns on a switch near the door, and the lights in the room go on. Can you conclude that turning on the wall switch "caused" the lights to go on? Not from the information provided. Perhaps the lights were on an automatic timer and would have gone on anyway just when Mary entered the room. Alternatively, the door may have had a built-in switch that turned on the lights after a slight delay. Or, there may have been a motion detector in the room that activated the lights.

How could you determine that manipulation of the wall switch caused the lights to go on? You would have to see what would happen under other circumstances. More specifically, you would have to instruct Mary to enter the room again but ask her not to turn on the wall switch. If the lights did not go on under these circumstances, you could conclude that the lights were not turned on by a motion detector or by a switch built into the door. To identify a cause, an experiment must be conducted in which the presumed cause is removed. The results obtained with and without the presumed cause can then be compared. The conclusion that one thing causes another is based on such comparisons.

In studying learning, the behavior of living organisms is of interest, not lights. But the investigator must proceed in a similar fashion to identify causes. Experiments must be conducted in which behavior is observed with and without the presumed cause. In studies of learning, the cause that is of interest has to do with prior experience (the training experience). Studies of learning require comparisons between individuals who previously received the training experience in question and individuals who did not have that experience. The only conclusive way to prove that the training experience is causing the behavior change of interest is to experimentally vary the presence and absence of that experience. For this reason, *learning can be investigated only with experimental techniques.* Also for this reason, the study of learning is primarily a laboratory science.

The need to use experimental techniques to investigate learning is not always appreciated. Many aspects of behavior can be studied with observational procedures that do not involve experimental manipulations of behavioral causes. For example, observational studies can provide a great deal of information about whether and how certain animals set up territories, the manner in which they defend those territories, the activities involved in the animals' courtship and sexual behavior, the ways in which they raise their offspring, and the change in activities of the offspring as they mature. Many aspects of animal behavior are open to observational study, and much fascinating information has been obtained with observational techniques that involve minimal, if any, disruption of the ongoing activities of the animals.

Unfortunately, learning cannot be observed directly in the same manner as activities such as grooming, aggression, or parental behavior. Researchers can form hypotheses about what animals may be learning by observing their behavior unobtrusively in nature. However, to be sure that the changes in behavior are not due to changes in motivation, sensory development, hormonal fluctuations, or other possible nonlearning mechanisms, it is necessary to conduct experiments in which the presumed training experiences are systematically manipulated.

The General-Process Approach to the Study of Learning

The second prominent methodological feature of studies of learning is the use of a general-process approach. This is more a matter of preference than of necessity. However, in adopting a general-process approach, investigators of animal learning are following a longstanding tradition in science.

Elements of the General-Process Approach. The most obvious feature of nature is its diversity. Consider, for example, the splendid variety of minerals that exist in the world. Some are soft, some are hard, some are brilliant, others are dull in appearance, and so on. Plants and animals also are many different shapes and sizes. And the dynamic properties of objects are diverse; some things float up, whereas others rapidly drop to the ground. Some remain still; others remain in motion.

In studying nature, an investigator can either focus on differences or ignore the differences and search for commonalities. Scientists ranging from physicists to chemists to biologists to psychologists have all elected to follow the latter strategy. Rather than being overwhelmed by the tremendous diversity in nature, scientists have chosen to focus on the commonalities. They have attempted to formulate *general laws* with which to organize and explain the diversity of events in the universe. Investigators of animal learning also have taken this approach.

Whether or not general laws are discovered often depends on the level of analysis that is pursued. The diversity of the phenomena scientists try to understand and organize makes it difficult to formulate general laws at the level of the observed phenomena. It is difficult, for example, to discover the general laws that govern chemical reactions by focusing on the nature of the chemicals involved in various reactions. Similarly, it is difficult to explain the diversity of species on Earth by cataloging the features of various animals. Major progress in science has often come from analyzing phenomena at a more elemental or molecular level. For example, by the nineteenth century, chemists knew many specific facts about what would happen when various chemicals were combined. However, a general account of chemical reactions had to await the development of the periodic table of the elements, which describes and organizes chemical elements in terms of their constituent atomic components.

A fundamental assumption of the general-process approach is that the phenomena of interest are the products of more elemental processes. Furthermore, those elemental processes are assumed to operate in pretty much the same manner no matter where they are found. Thus, generality is assumed to exist at the level of basic or elemental processes.

Investigators of conditioning and learning have been committed to the general-process approach from the inception of this field of psychology. They have focused on the commonalities of various instances of learning and have assumed that learning phenomena are products of elemental processes that operate in much the same way in different learning situations.

The commitment to a general-process approach guided Pavlov's work on functional neurology and conditioning. Commitment to a general-process approach to the study of learning is also evident in the writings of early comparative psychologists. For example, Darwin (1897) emphasized commonalities among species in cognitive functions. "My object . . . is to show that there is no fundamental difference between man and the higher mammals in their mental faculties" (p. 66). Jacques Loeb (1900) pointed out that commonalities occur at the level of elemental processes. "Psychic phenomena . . . appear, invariably, as a function of an elemental process, namely the activity of associative memory" (p. 213). Another prominent comparative psychologist of the time, C. Lloyd Morgan, stated in 1903 that elementary laws of association "are, we believe, universal laws" (p. 219).

The assumption that universal, elemental laws of association are responsible for learning phenomena does not deny the diversity of stimuli that different animals may learn about, the diversity of responses they may learn to perform, or species differences in rates of learning. The generality is assumed to exist in the rules or processes of learning—not in the content or speed of learning. This idea was clearly expressed nearly a century ago by Edward Thorndike:

Formally, the crab, fish, turtle, dog, cat, monkey, and baby have very similar intellects and characters. All are systems of connections subject to change by the laws of exercise and effect. The differences are: first, in the concrete particular connections, in what stimulates the animal to response, what responses it makes, which stimulus connects with what response, and second, in the degree of ability to learn. (Thorndike, 1911, p. 280)

What an animal can learn about (the stimuli, responses, and stimulus-response connections it learns about) varies from one species to another. Animals also differ in how fast they learn ("in the degree of ability to learn"). However, Thorndike assumed that the rules of learning are universal. We no longer share Thorndike's view that these universal rules of learning are the "laws of exercise and effect." Contemporary scientists, however, continue to adhere to the idea that universal rules of learning exist. The job of the learning psychologist is to discover those universal laws. (More about the work of Thorndike will follow in Chapter 5.)

Evidence of the Generality of Learning Phenomena. The available evidence suggests that elementary principles of learning of the sort that will be described in this text have considerable generality. Most research on animal learning has been performed with pigeons, rats, and (to a lesser extent) rabbits. Similar forms of learning have been found with fish, hamsters, cats, dogs, human beings, dolphins, and sea lions. In addition, some of the principles of learning observed with these vertebrate species also have been demonstrated in newts (Ellins, Cramer, & Martin, 1982), fruit flies (Holliday & Hirsch, 1986; Platt, Holliday, & Drudge, 1980), honeybees (Bitterman, 1988, 1996), terrestrial mollusks (Sahley, Rudy, & Gelperin, 1981), and various marine mollusks (Carew, Hawkins, & Kandel, 1983; Farley & Alkon, 1980; Rogers, Schiller, & Matzel, 1996; Susswein & Schwarz, 1983).

Examples of learning in diverse species provide support for the general-process approach. However, the evidence should be interpreted cautiously. With the exception of the extensive program of research on learning in honeybees conducted by Bitterman and his colleagues, the various invertebrate species in the studies I have cited have been tested on a limited range of learning phenomena. Thus it is unclear whether their learning was mediated by the same type of processes responsible for analogous instances of learning observed in vertebrate species.

Methodological Implications of the General-Process Approach. If we assume that universal rules of learning exist, then we should be able to discover those rules in any situation in which learning occurs. Thus, an important methodological implication of the general-process approach is that general rules of learning may be discovered by studying any species or response system that exhibits learning. Another consequence of the general-process approach is that it justifies studying learning in a small number of experimental situations. If the processes of learning are in fact universal, then there is no need to study learning in a great number of situations.

Although the total list of species and situations in which learning has been investigated is rather long, the general-process approach has encouraged investigators to develop a few "standard" or conventional experimental paradigms. Most studies of learning are conducted in one of these paradigms. I will give examples of standard experimental paradigms in discussions of various learning phenomena in later chapters.

Conventional experimental paradigms have been fine-tuned over the years to fit well with the behavioral predispositions of the research animals. Because of these improvements, conventional experimental preparations permit laboratory study of reasonably naturalistic responses (Timberlake, 1990).

Proof of the Generality of Learning Phenomena.   The general-process approach has dominated studies of animal learning throughout the twentieth century. As I will show in the chapters that follow, the approach has provided an extensive and sophisticated body of knowledge. Given the successes of the general-process approach, it is tempting to conclude that learning processes are indeed universal. However, it is important to keep in mind that the generality of learning processes is not proven by adopting a general-process approach. Assuming the existence of common elemental learning processes is not the same as empirically demonstrating those commonalities.

Direct empirical verification of the existence of common learning processes in a variety of situations remains necessary in efforts to build a truly general account of how learning occurs. A general theory of learning cannot be empirically verified by investigating learning in a few standard experimental paradigms. The generality of learning processes has to be proven by studying learning in many different species and situations.

USE OF ANIMALS IN RESEARCH ON LEARNING

Many of the experiments I will be describing in subsequent chapters have been conducted with animal participants. Numerous types of animals have been used, including rats, mice, rabbits, fish, pigeons, and monkeys. Animals are used in the research for both theoretical and methodological reasons.

Rationale for the Use of Animals in Research on Learning

As I have argued, experimental methods are needed to investigate learning. Experimental methods make it possible to attribute the acquisition of new behaviors to particular previous experiences. Such experimental control of past experience cannot be achieved to the same degree of precision in studies with human participants as in studies with laboratory animals. With animals, the learning involved in acquiring food, in avoiding pain or distress, and in finding potential sexual partners can be studied, as well as how strong emotional responses are learned. With people, investigators are limited to trying to modify maladaptive emotional responses after such responses have been already acquired. However, even the development of successful therapeutic procedures for the treatment of maladaptive emotional responses has required knowledge of how strong emotional responses are acquired in the first place—knowledge that required studies with laboratory animals.

Knowledge of the evolution and physiology of learning also cannot be obtained without the use of animals in research. The question of how cognition and intelligence evolved, first formulated by Darwin, is one of the fundamental questions about human nature. The answer to this question will shape our view of human nature, just as knowledge of the solar system has changed our view of the role of the Earth in the universe. As we have seen, investigation of the evolution of cognition and intelligence rests heavily on studies of learning in animals.

Knowledge of the physiology of learning may not change anyone's view of human nature, but it is apt to yield important dividends in the treatment of learning and memory disorders. Such knowledge also rests heavily on research with animals. The kind of detailed physiological investigations that are necessary to unravel the mysteries of the physiology of learning simply cannot be conducted with people. As I have argued, a search for the physiology of learning first requires documenting the nature of learning processes at the behavioral level. Therefore, behavioral studies of learning in animals are an inescapable prerequisite to any animal research on the physiology of learning.

Laboratory animals also provide important conceptual advantages over people in studies of learning processes; the processes of learning may be simpler in animals reared in controlled laboratory situations than in people, whose backgrounds are much more varied. Animal behavior is not complicated by the linguistic processes that have a prominent role in certain kinds of human behavior. Another important advantage of using animals is that demand characteristics of an experiment do not come into play. In research with people, the investigator has to make sure that the actions of the participants are not governed by their efforts to please (or displease) the experimenter. Such factors are not likely to determine what rats and pigeons do in an experiment.

Laboratory Animals and Normal Behavior

Some theorists have suggested that domesticated laboratory strains of animals may not provide useful information because such animals have degenerated as a result of many generations of inbreeding and long periods of captivity (for example, Lockard, 1968). However, this notion is probably mistaken. In an interesting test, Boice (1977) took five male and five female albino rats of a highly inbred laboratory stock and housed them in an outdoor pen in Missouri without artificial shelter. All ten rats survived the first winter with temperatures as low as −22°F. The animals reproduced normally and reached a stable population of about 50 members. Only three of the rats died before showing signs of old age during the two-year period. Given the extreme climatic conditions, this level of success is remarkable. Furthermore, the behavior of these domesticated rats in the outdoors was very similar to the behavior of wild rats observed in similar circumstances.

The vigor of inbred laboratory rats in outdoor living conditions indicates that they are not inferior to their wild counterparts. Domesticated rats act similarly to wild rats in other tests as well, and there is some indication that they perform better than wild rats in learning experiments (see, for example, Boice, 1973, 1981; Kaufman & Collier, 1983). Therefore, the results I will be describing in this text should not be discounted simply because many of the experiments were conducted with domesticated animals. In fact, laboratory animals may be preferable in research to their wild counterparts. Human beings in civilized society are raised and live in somewhat contrived environments. Therefore, research with animals may prove most relevant to human behavior if the animals are domesticated and live in artificial laboratory situations. As Boice (1973) commented, "The domesticated rat may be a good model for domestic man" (p. 227).

Public Debate about Animal Research

There has been much public debate about the pros and cons of animal research. Part of the debate has centered on the humane treatment of animals. Other aspects of the debate have centered on what constitutes ethical treatment of animals, whether human beings have the right to benefit at the expense of animals, and possible alternatives to research with animals.

The Humane Treatment of Animals.   Concern for the welfare of laboratory animals has resulted in the adoption of strict federal standards for animal housing and for the supervision of animal research. Many of these changes were necessary and desirable. D. E. Koshland, editor of the prestigious journal *Science,* commented in 1989 that "ten years ago, before the current wave of legislation, it could fairly be said that some animal experiments were done improperly, in inadequate facilities, or with inappropriate supervision. These days are largely past. The current protocols for care and treatment of animals are so stringent that most modern animal facilities are models for responsible and considerate treatment" (Koshland, 1989, p. 1253).

Sometimes scientists involved in animal research are portrayed as being so intent on completing their experiments that they disregard the welfare of their research animals in the process. Scientists, especially those studying behavior, must be concerned about the welfare of their research subjects. Information about normal learning and behavior cannot be obtained from diseased and terrorized animals. Investigators of animal learning must ensure the welfare of their animals if they are to obtain useful scientific data.

Laboratory rats cower in a corner if they are sick and anxious. No useful information about their learning and behavior can be obtained under such circumstances. Investigators have to take great pains to make sure their animals are not upset by serving in an experiment. The animals must be healthy and adapted to handling; the experimental chambers must be suitable for the species; and the animals must be comfortable being in the chamber.

Learning experiments sometimes do involve discomfort. However, every effort is made to minimize the degree of discomfort. In studies of food reinforcement, for example, animals are food-deprived before each experimental session to ensure their interest in food. However, the hunger imposed is no more severe than the hunger animals are likely to encounter in the wild, and often it is less severe (Poling, Nickel, & Alling, 1990).

The investigation of certain forms of learning and behavior requires the administration of aversive stimulation. Important topics such as punishment or the learning of fear and anxiety cannot be studied without some discomfort to the participants. However, even in such cases, efforts are made to keep the discomfort to a minimum.

Electric shock is often used in studies of fear and avoidance learning. The term "electric shock" may conjure up images of an electric chair used to impose the death penalty or the pain a child suffers when he accidentally puts his finger in an electrical outlet. However, shock is not used in studies of learning because it can be made horrendously painful but because it can produce mild, yet effective, levels of discomfort. Unlike other sources of aversive stimulation, electric shock can be precisely regulated, enabling an experimenter to administer shock at controlled low levels. The shock levels employed in studies of animal learning are far lower than the levels experienced from a wall outlet or an electric chair. In addition, in many procedures the animals are permitted to control their exposure by making escape or avoidance responses.

| TABLE 1.1 | NUMBERS OF ANIMALS USED ANNUALLY IN THE UNITED STATES |

TYPE OF USE[a]	NUMBER USED	% OF TOTAL
Food	6,086,000,000	96.5
Hunting	165,000,000	2.6
Killed in animal shelters	27,000,000	.4
Fur garments	11,000,000	.2
All teaching and research	20,000,000	.3
Grand Total	6,309,000,000	100.0
Graduate Departments of Psychology[b]	198,019	.003

[a]From "Analysis of Animal Rights Literature Reveals the Underlying Motives of the Movement: Ammunition for Counter Offensive by Scientists," by C. S. Nicoll and S. M. Russell, 1990, *Endocrinology, 127,* pp. 985–989. Copyright © 1990 by Williams & Wilkins. Reprinted by permission.

[b]From *Animal Research Survey,* 1985, by the American Psychological Association.

What Constitutes the Ethical Treatment of Animals?   Although treating laboratory animals as humanely as possible is in the best interest of the animals as well as the research, formulating general ethical principles is difficult. Animal "rights" cannot be identified in the way human rights can be, (Lansdell, 1988), and animals seem to have different "rights" under different circumstances.

Currently, substantial efforts are made to house laboratory animals in conditions that promote their health and comfort. However, a laboratory mouse or rat loses the protection afforded by federal standards when it escapes from the laboratory and takes up residence in the walls of the building (Herzog, 1988). The trapping and extermination of rodents in buildings is a common practice that has not been the subject of either public debate or restrictive federal regulation. Mites, fleas, and ticks are also animals, but we do not tolerate them in our hair or on our pets. Which species have the right to life, and under what circumstances do they have that right? Such questions defy simple answers.

Should Human Beings Benefit from the Use of Animals?   Part of the public debate about animal rights has been fueled by the argument that human beings have no right to benefit at the expense of animals; humans have no right to "exploit" animals. This argument goes far beyond issues concerning the use of animals in research, so I will not discuss the argument in detail here except to try to put its implications for animal research in perspective.

The number of animals used in research is a small fraction of the number of animals used in other realms of human activity. Table 1.1 summarizes estimates of the number of animals used each year in all forms of teaching and research as compared to the numbers of unwanted animals killed in animal shelters or sacrificed for food, for clothing, and in hunting.

By far the greatest numbers of animals are used for food and in hunting. The number of animals used in all forms of teaching and research is substantial (about 20 million), but this is just .3% of the total usage. Moreover, only about 200,000 animals are used each year in psychological research. This is but .003% of the total number of animals used for various purposes in the United States each year. Studies of animal learning account for less than one-half of all animals used in psychological research. Thus, the number of animals that serve in learning experiments is minuscule compared with other human uses of animals.

In addition to the explicit human uses of animals for such things as food, clothing, and recreation, a comprehensive account of the human "exploitation" of animals has to include disruptions of habitats that occur whenever roads, housing developments, and factories are built. The millions of animals that are killed by insecticides and other pest-control efforts in agriculture and elsewhere should also be considered. In this context, the contributions of animal research to the so-called exploitation of animal life takes on even more trivial dimensions.

In a survey of animal rights advocates, 85% agreed with the statement, "If it were up to me, I would eliminate all research using animals" (Plous, 1991). When asked what should be the top priority of the animal rights movement, only 4% said that they should work to eliminate the use of animals in sports or entertainment, 12% said that they should work to eliminate the use of animals in clothing or fashion, and 24% considered it most important to try to discourage the use of animals for food (see also Nicoll & Russell, 1990).

The focus of animal rights advocates on curbing animal research efforts is puzzling, given the far greater numbers of animals used in other ways. This anti-research focus is also puzzling in light of the fact that alternatives to the use of animals are much more readily available when it comes to foods, clothing or fashion, and sports and entertainment.

Alternatives to Research with Animals. As Gallup and Suarez (1985) pointed out, good research on learning processes cannot be conducted without experiments on live organisms, be they animal or human. Nevertheless, public debate on the pros and cons of animal research has focused interest on possible alternatives to testing animals. Some of these alternatives are considered in the following list:

1. *Observational techniques.* As I said earlier, learning processes cannot be investigated with unobtrusive observational techniques. Experimental manipulations of past experience are necessary in studies of learning. Field observations of undisturbed animals cannot yield information about the mechanisms of learning.

2. *Plants.* Learning cannot be investigated in plants because plants lack a nervous system, which is required for learning.

3. *Tissue cultures.* Although tissue cultures may reveal the operation of cellular processes, how these cellular processes operate in an intact organism can be discovered only by studying the intact organism. Furthermore, as I pointed out earlier, a search for cellular mechanisms of learning first requires characterizing learning at the behavioral level.

4. *Computer simulations.* Writing a computer program to simulate a natural phenomenon requires a great deal of knowledge about the phenomenon. In the case of learning, precise and detailed information about the nature of learning phenomena and the mechanisms and factors that determine learning would be needed before a

computer simulation of learning could be constructed. The absence of such knowledge necessitates experimental research with live organisms. Thus, experimental research with live organisms is a prerequisite for effective computer simulations. For that reason, computer simulations cannot be used in place of experimental research.

Computer simulations can serve many useful functions in science. Simulations are effective in showing the implications of the experimental observations that have been already obtained. Computer simulations are often used in studies of behavior to show the implications of various theoretical assumptions; they can be used to identify gaps in knowledge; and they can be used to suggest important future lines of research. However, they cannot be used to generate new, previously unknown facts about behavior. That can only be done by studying live organisms.

Earlier in this chapter, I used the example of a computer simulation to measure the wind resistance of various automobile designs. Why is it possible to construct a computer program to study wind resistance, but it is not possible to construct one to study learning processes? The critical difference is that a lot more is known about wind resistance than about learning. Wind resistance is determined by the laws of mechanics—laws that have been thoroughly explored since the days of Sir Isaac Newton. Application of those laws to wind resistance has received special attention in recent years, as the wind resistance of automobiles has become an important factor in increasing gas mileage.

Designing automobiles with low wind resistance is an engineering task. It involves the application of existing knowledge rather than the discovery of new knowledge and new principles. Research on animal learning involves the discovery of new facts and new principles. It is science, not engineering.

SAMPLE QUESTIONS

1. Describe how historical developments in the study of the mind contributed to the contemporary study of learning.

2. Describe Descartes' conception of the reflex and how the concept of the reflex has changed since his time.

3. Describe three major themes in contemporary studies of animal learning.

4. Describe the definition of learning, and describe its methodological implications.

5. Describe several alternatives to the use of animals in research, and describe their advantages and disadvantages.

KEY TERMS

association A connection between the representations of two events (two stimuli or a stimulus and a response) such that the occurrence of one of the events activates the representation of the other.

dualism The view of behavior according to which actions can be separated into two categories: voluntary behavior controlled by the mind and involuntary behavior controlled by reflex mechanisms.

empiricism A philosophy according to which all ideas in the mind arise from experience.

fatigue A temporary decrease in behavior caused by repeated or excessive use of the muscles involved in the behavior.

hedonism The philosophy proposed by Hobbes according to which the actions of organisms are determined entirely by the pursuit of pleasure and the avoidance of pain.

learning An enduring change in the mechanisms of behavior involving specific stimuli and/or responses that results from prior experience with similar stimuli and responses.

maturation A change in behavior caused by physical or physiological development of the organism in the absence of experience with particular environmental events.

nativism A philosophy according to which human beings are born with innate ideas.

nervism The philosophical position adopted by Pavlov that all behavioral and physiological processes are regulated by the nervous system.

nonsense syllable A three-letter combination (two consonants separated by a vowel) that has no meaning.

performance An organism's activities at a particular time.

reflex A mechanism that enables a specific environmental event to elicit a specific response.

CHAPTER 2

ELICITED BEHAVIOR, HABITUATION, AND SENSITIZATION

The Nature of Elicited Behavior

The Concept of the Reflex

Modal Action Patterns

Eliciting Stimuli for Modal Action Patterns

Role of Response Feedback in Elicited Behavior

Effects of Repeated Stimulation: Two Examples

Visual Attention in Human Infants

Startle Response in Rats

The Concepts of Habituation and Sensitization

Adaptiveness and Pervasiveness of Habituation and Sensitization

Habituation versus Sensory Adaptation and Response Fatigue

The Dual-Process Theory of Habituation and Sensitization

Characteristics of Habituation and Sensitization

Time Course

Stimulus Specificity

Effects of Strong Extraneous Stimuli

Changes in Complex Emotional Responses

The Standard Pattern of Affective Dynamics

Mechanisms of the Opponent-Process Theory

Examples of Opponent Processes

Concluding Comments

I will begin discussing contemporary principles of learning and behavior in Chapter 2 by describing elicited behavior—behavior that occurs in reaction to specific environmental stimuli. Numerous aspects of behavior are elicited by discrete stimuli, and some of the most extensively investigated response systems involve elicited behavior. The discussion will progress from a description of the simplest form of elicited behavior, reflexive behavior, to a discussion of complex emotional responses elicited by stimuli. Along the way I will describe two of the simplest and most common forms of behavioral change: habituation and sensitization. Habituation and sensitization occur in a wide variety of response systems and are therefore fundamental properties of behavior.

THE NATURE OF ELICITED BEHAVIOR

All animals, whether they be single-celled organisms such as paramecia or complex human beings, react to events in their environment. The calls of an intruder elicit territorial defensive responses in white-crowned sparrows. The odor of a sexually receptive female dog or cat elicits approach and sexual behavior in male dogs and cats. If something moves in the periphery of a woman's vision, she is likely to turn her head in that direction. A particle of food in the mouth elicits salivation. Exposure to a bright light causes the pupils of the eyes to constrict. Touching a hot surface elicits a quick withdrawal response. Irritation of the respiratory passages causes sneezing and coughing. These and numerous similar examples illustrate that much of behavior occurs in response to stimuli—that is, it is elicited.

Elicited behavior has been the subject of extensive investigation. Many of the chapters of this text deal, in one way or another, with elicited behavior. I begin the discussion of elicited behavior by describing its simplest form—reflexive behavior.

The Concept of the Reflex

A light puff of air directed at the cornea makes the eye blink. A tap just below the knee causes the leg to kick. A loud noise causes a startle reaction. These are all examples of reflexes. A reflex involves two closely related events—an *eliciting stimulus* and a *corresponding response*. The stimulus and response are linked. Presentation of the stimulus is followed by the occurrence of the response; moreover, the response rarely occurs in the absence of the stimulus. For example, dust in the nasal passages elicits sneezing, which does not occur in the absence of nasal irritation.

The specificity of the relation between a stimulus and its associated reflex response is a consequence of the organization of the nervous system. In vertebrates (including humans), simple reflexes are typically mediated by three neurons, as illustrated in Figure 2.1. The environmental stimulus for a reflex activates a **sensory neuron** (also called **afferent neuron**) that transmits the sensory message to the spinal cord. Here the neural impulses are relayed to the **motor neuron** (also called **efferent**

Figure 2.1 Neural organization of simple reflexes. The environmental stimulus for a reflex activates a sensory neuron, which transmits the sensory message to the spinal cord. Here, the neural impulses are relayed to an interneuron, which in turn relays the impulses to the motor neuron. The motor neuron activates muscles involved in movement.

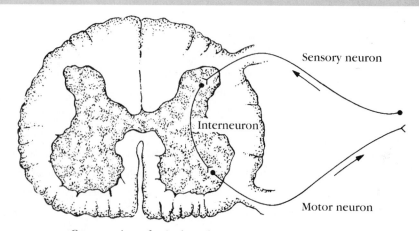

Sensory neuron

Interneuron

Motor neuron

Cross-section of spinal cord

Figure 2.2 Painful stimulation of one limb of a dog causes withdrawal (flexion) of that limb and extension of the opposite limb. (From "Reflexive Behavior," by B. L. Hart in G. Bermant (Ed.), *Perspectives in animal behavior.* Copyright © 1973 by Scott, Foresman. Reprinted by permission.)

neuron), which activates the muscles involved in the reflex response. However, sensory and motor neurons rarely communicate directly; rather, the impulses from one to the other are relayed through at least one **interneuron.** The neural circuitry ensures that particular sensory neurons are connected to a corresponding set of motor neurons. Because of this restricted system of connections, a particular reflex response is elicited only by a restricted set of stimuli. The afferent neuron, interneuron, and efferent neuron together constitute the **reflex arc.**

The reflex arc in vertebrates represents the fewest neural connections necessary for reflex action. However, additional neural structures also may be involved in the elicitation of reflexes. For example, the sensory messages may be relayed to the brain, and through that circuitry the reflex reaction may be modified in various ways. I will discuss such effects later in the chapter. For now, it is sufficient to say that the occurrence of even simple reflexes can be influenced by higher nervous system functions.

Most reflexes promote the well-being of the organism in obvious ways. For example, in many animals painful stimulation of one limb causes withdrawal, or flexion, of that limb and extension of the opposite limb (Hart, 1973). If a dog, for example, stubs a toe while walking, it will automatically withdraw that leg and simultaneously extend the opposite leg. This combination of responses removes the first leg from the source of pain and at the same time allows the animal to maintain balance.

Reflexes constitute much of the behavioral repertoire of newborn infants. If you touch an infant's cheek with your finger, the baby will reflexively turn her head in that direction, with the result that your finger will fall into the baby's mouth. This head-turning reflex probably evolved to facilitate finding the nipple. The sensation of an object in the mouth causes reflexive sucking. The more closely the object resembles a nipple, the more vigorously the baby will suck.

Another important reflex, the *respiratory occlusion reflex,* is stimulated by a reduction of air flow to the baby, which can be caused by a cloth covering the baby's face or by the accumulation of mucus in the nasal passages. In response to the reduced air flow, the baby's first reaction is to pull her head back. If this does not remove the eliciting stimulus, the baby will move her hands in a face-wiping motion. If this also fails to remove the eliciting stimulus, the baby will begin to cry. Crying involves a vigorous expulsion of air, which is often sufficient to remove whatever was obstructing the air passages.

The respiratory occlusion reflex is obviously essential for survival. If the baby does not get enough air, she may suffocate. A problem arises, however, when the

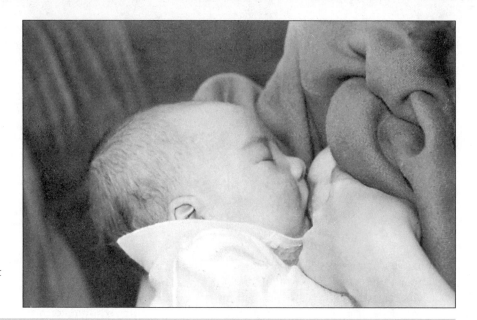

Figure 2.3 Sucking is one of the most prominent reflexes in infants. (Photo courtesy of Allen Zak.)

respiratory occlusion reflex is triggered during nursing. While nursing, the baby can get air only through her nose. If the mother presses the baby too close to the breast during feeding so that the baby's nostrils are covered by the breast, the respiratory occlusion reflex will be triggered. The baby will attempt to pull her head back from the nipple, may paw at her face to get released from the nipple, and may begin to cry. Successful nursing requires a bit of experience. The mother and child have to adjust their positions so that nursing can progress without stimulation of the respiratory occlusion reflex (Gunther, 1961). (See Figure 2.3.)

Modal Action Patterns

Simple reflex responses such as pupillary constriction to a bright light and startle reactions to a brief loud noise are evident in many species. By contrast, other forms of elicited behavior occur in just one species or in a small group of related species. For example, sucking in response to objects placed in the mouth is a characteristic of mammalian infants. Herring-gull chicks are just as dependent on parental feeding as are human infants. However, their feeding behavior is very different. When a herring-gull parent returns to the nest from a foraging trip, the baby chicks peck at the tip of the parent's bill (see Figure 2.4). This causes the parent to regurgitate. As the chicks continue to peck, they manage to get some of the parent's regurgitated food, and this provides their nourishment.

Response sequences, such as those involved in infant feeding, that are typical of a particular species are referred to as **modal action patterns** or **MAPs.** Species-characteristic response patterns have been identified in many aspects of animal behavior, including sexual behavior, territorial defense, aggression, and prey capture. Ring doves, for example, begin their sexual behavior with a courtship interaction that culminates in the selection of a nest site and the cooperative construction of the nest by the male and female. By contrast, in the three-spined stickleback—a species of small fish—the male first establishes a territory and constructs a nest. Females that enter the

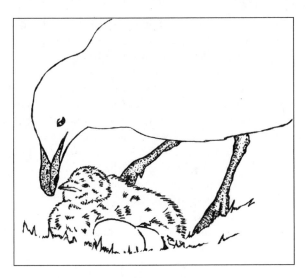

Figure 2.4   Feeding of herring-gull chicks. The chicks peck a red patch near the tip of the parent's bill, causing the parent to regurgitate food for the chicks.

territory after the nest has been built are courted and induced to lay their eggs in the nest. Once a female has deposited her eggs, she is chased away, leaving the male to care for and defend the eggs until the offspring hatch.

An important feature of MAPs is that the threshold for eliciting such activities varies a great deal as a function of circumstances (Baerends, 1988; Camhi, 1984). The same stimulus can have widely different effects, depending on the physiological state of the animal and its recent actions. A male stickleback, for example, will not court a female ready to lay eggs until he has completed building his nest. And after the female has deposited her eggs, the male will chase her away rather than court her as he did earlier. In many species, including the stickleback, stimuli that elicit male territorial and sexual behavior do so only during the breeding season.

MAPs were initially identified by *ethologists*—scientists interested in the study of the evolution of behavior. Early ethologists such as Lorenz and Tinbergen referred to species-specific action patterns as "fixed action patterns" to emphasize that the activities involved occurred pretty much the same way in all members of a species. However, subsequent detailed observations have indicated that action patterns are not performed in exactly the same fashion each time. Because of this variability, the term *modal action pattern* is preferred now (Baerends, 1988).

Eliciting Stimuli for Modal Action Patterns

The eliciting stimulus is fairly easy to identify in examples of simple reflexes such as the startle response to a brief loud noise. The stimulus responsible for a modal action pattern can be more difficult to identify, especially if the response occurs in the course of social interaction among several animals. For example, let us consider again the feeding of a herring-gull chick. To get fed, the chick has to peck the parent's beak to stimulate the parent to regurgitate. Something about the parent elicits the chick's pecking response. However, from casual observation, the critical eliciting stimuli cannot be identified.

G. P. Baerends

Adult herring gulls have a long, yellow bill with a striking red patch near the tip. Pecking in the chicks may be elicited by the color, shape, or length of the parent's bill, the noises the parent makes, the head movements of the parent, or some other stimulus. To isolate which of these stimuli elicits pecking, Tinbergen and Perdeck (1950) tested chicks with various artificial models instead of live adult gulls. From this research they concluded that a model had to have several characteristics to elicit strong pecking. It had to be a long, thin, moving object that was pointed downward and that had a contrasting red patch near the tip. These experiments suggest that neither the yellow color of the adult's bill, nor the shape and coloration of its head, nor the noises it makes is required for eliciting pecking in the gull chicks. The specific features that were found to be required to elicit the pecking behavior are called, collectively, the **sign stimulus** or **releasing stimulus** for this behavior.

A sign or releasing stimulus is sufficient for eliciting an MAP. However, a given action pattern may be controlled by several stimulus features in an additive fashion. In addition, the most effective stimulus for eliciting an MAP may not be one that is likely to occur under natural conditions. These principles are nicely illustrated by a study of the egg retrieval behavior of herring gulls (Baerends & Drent, 1982). Brooding herring gulls will pull into their nest eggs that are placed on the rim of the nest. To determine which features of eggs best stimulate this egg retrieval behavior, Baerends and Drent tested gulls with wooden eggs of various sizes, colors, and speckling.

Results of this study indicate that the gulls preferred to retrieve green speckled eggs more than yellow ones, yellow eggs more than brown, and brown eggs more than blue. The preference for green and yellow eggs over brown eggs is remarkable because the brown wooden eggs were most similar to a real gull egg. Increases in the number of speckles and their contrast with the background also increased egg retrieval behavior, as did increases in the size of the wooden eggs (see Figure 2.5).

Color, speckling, and size appeared to control the egg retrieval behavior in an additive fashion. Thus, the attractiveness of an egg could be increased by making it more green, more speckled, or larger. Optimizing all three of these stimulus dimensions resulted in a green, highly speckled, and abnormally large egg. Interestingly, such an egg was more effective in stimulating egg retrieval behavior than was a real gull egg. Thus, once the stimulus features that controlled egg retrieval were identified, they could be combined to form an object that was more effective than a naturally occurring egg in eliciting the action pattern. Such an unusually effective stimulus is called a **supernormal stimulus.**

Role of Response Feedback in Elicited Behavior

Responses usually produce specific stimulus consequences. This is true for all behavior, including responses elicited by environmental events. When the pupils constrict in bright light, for example, less light reaches the retina as a result. The salivation elicited by food in the mouth makes the food softer and more diluted. Coughing in response to irritation of the respiratory passages produces a loud noise and rapid expulsion of air. A stimulus that results from a particular response is called a **feedback stimulus** for that response.

Feedback stimuli may arise from sources internal or external to the organism. Internal feedback cues are provided by sensory neurons that allow the animal to feel the muscle and joint movements involved in making the response. For example, if a man's knee is tapped in the appropriate place and the knee-jerk reflex is elicited, he would feel his leg kick because of sensory neurons located in the leg muscles and the knee joint. Such internal feedback cues are called **proprioceptive stimuli.**

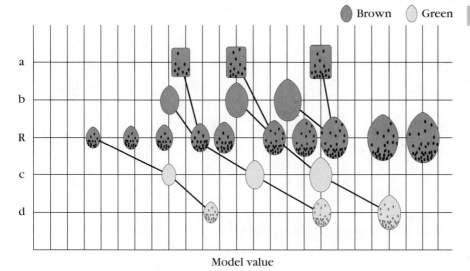

Figure 2.5 Relative effectiveness of various artificial eggs in stimulating egg retrieval behavior in gulls. Going from left to right, the models increase in effectiveness. Row "R" (for reference series) shows eggs of normal color and speckling. Row "a" shows block-shaped eggs; "b" shows plain brown eggs; "c" shows plain green eggs; and "d" shows speckled green eggs. The oblique lines connect models of the same size. Notice that eggs of a given size can be made more effective by making them green and adding speckling. Eggs of a particular color can be made more effective by an increase in size. (From "The Herring Gull and Its Egg. Part II: The Responsiveness to Egg Features," by G. P. Baerends and R. H. Drent [Eds.], *Behaviour*, 1982, *82*, 1–417. Reprinted by permission.)

The movement of most skeletal muscles provides proprioceptive sensations. However, not all reflex responses are accompanied by proprioceptive cues. For example, constriction of the pupils creates few internal sensations. Rather, the feedback that results from pupillary constriction occurs because less light reaches the retina. This feedback changes the external stimuli to which the organism is exposed. Let us now turn to the role of such external feedback cues in elicited behavior. Some action patterns are largely independent of external feedback cues. In other cases, the behavior is almost exclusively controlled by feedback.

Elicited Behavior Independent of Feedback Stimuli. Once started, some responses go to completion largely independent of the consequences of the behavior. This is the case with many modal action patterns. Familiar examples occur in common pets. When cats are eating, for example, they shake their heads to the right and left a bit after taking a bite and then proceed to chew and swallow. The shaking response is very useful when the cat is about to eat a live mouse because it helps to kill the mouse. This part of the MAP continues to occur, even when the food does not have to be killed. Another common MAP in domestic cats is seen when they use the litter box. Elimination in cats ends with their scratching the litter to cover up their waste. However, this scratching response is independent of its stimulus consequences; cats scratch for awhile after eliminating whether or not the litter they scratch covers up

BOX **2.1**

THE LEARNING OF "INSTINCT"

Because modal action patterns occur in a similar fashion among members of a given species, they include activities that are informally characterized as "instinctive." Instinctive behavior is considered primarily to reflect an individual's genetic history, leading to the impression that modal action patterns are not the product of learning and experience. However, the fact that all members of a species exhibit similar forms of responding does not necessarily mean that the behavior was not learned through experience. As Tinbergen (1951) recognized many years ago, similar behavior on the part of all members of a species may reflect similar learning experiences. In a more recent expression of this sentiment, Baerends (1988) wrote that "learning processes in many variations are tools, so to speak, that can be used in the building of some segments in the species-specific behavior organization" (p. 801). Thus, learning may be involved in what is commonly referred to as "instinctive" behavior (Hailman, 1967).

their waste. In fact, sometimes they scratch on the side of the litter box without moving any litter at all.

Another dramatic example of a modal action pattern is the cocoon spinning behavior of the spider *Ciprennium salei* (see Eibl-Eibesfeldt, 1970). The spider begins by spinning the bottom of the cocoon; then it spins the sides. It lays its eggs inside the cocoon and then spins the top of the cocoon, thereby closing it. This response sequence is remarkable because it occurs in the same order, even if the usual outcome of the response is altered by an experimenter. For example, the spider will continue to spin the sides of the cocoon and lay the eggs, even if the bottom of the cocoon is destroyed and the eggs fall through the cocoon. If the spider is placed on a partly completed cocoon, it will nevertheless begin the spinning response sequence as if it had to start an entirely new cocoon. Another remarkable aspect is that the spinning response occurs in much the same way, even if the spider is unable to produce the material with which to construct the cocoon. Thus, although the spider seems to go through the spinning movements to create a place to lay its eggs, the consequences of the behavior do not control its occurrence.

Presence or Absence of the Eliciting Stimulus as Feedback. An elicited response may either maintain the animal in contact with the eliciting stimulus or remove the animal from the stimulus. Which of these feedback events takes place strongly determines the future occurrence of the response. If the response maintains the animal in contact with the eliciting stimulus, the response will persist. By contrast, if the behavior removes the animal from the eliciting stimulus, the response will cease.

I have already described responses in which feedback is provided by the presence or absence of the eliciting stimulus. Consider, for example, the sucking response of newborn babies. When presented with a nipple, the baby begins to suck. This response serves to maintain contact between the baby and the nipple. The continued contact, in turn, elicits further sucking behavior. In other cases, the outcome of the response removes the eliciting stimulus. Reflexive sneezing and coughing, for example, usually result in removal of the irritant that originally elicited the behavior. When the irritant is removed, the sneezing and coughing cease.

Feedback involving the presence or absence of the eliciting stimulus is very important in controlling reflexive locomotor movements. In one type of reflexive locomotion, the eliciting stimulus produces a change in the speed of movement (or the speed of turning), irrespective of direction. Such locomotion is called a **kinesis.** The behavior of woodlice provides a good example. The woodlouse (*Porcellio scaber*) is a small isopod usually found under rocks, boards, and leaves. From a casual observation of the places in which woodlice are found, it is tempting to conclude that they go to damp places because they prefer high humidity. However, their tendency to congregate in damp places is a result of a kinesis. Low levels of humidity elicit locomotor movement in the lice. As long as the air is dry, the lice continue to move. When they reach a sufficiently humid spot, they become inactive. Thus, they tend to congregate in areas of high humidity not because they prefer such areas and "voluntarily" seek them out but because in damp places, the stimulus that causes their movement is absent (Fraenkel & Gunn, 1961).

In contrast to woodlice, both adult and larval grasshoppers are active in moist areas and quiescent in dry places (Riegert, 1959). This response increases the likelihood that they will remain in dry areas. In flatworms kinesis is controlled by illumination rather than humidity. Several types of flatworms are more likely to stop in dark than in well-lit places (Walter, 1907; Welsh, 1933).

Kinesis produces movements toward (or away from) a stimulus as an indirect result of changes in the rate of random movement triggered by that stimulus. In another type of reflexive locomotion process, the stimulus directly creates movements toward or away from it. This type of locomotion is called a **taxis** (plural, *taxes*). A taxis is identified by the nature of the eliciting stimulus and whether the movement is toward or away from the stimulus. Earthworms tend to turn away from bright light (Adams, 1903). This is an example of a *negative phototaxis.* The South American bloodsucker orients and goes toward warm bodies (Wigglesworth & Gillett, 1934). In the laboratory, for example, the bloodsucker will go toward a test tube of warm water. This is an example of a *positive thermotaxis.* The tree snail exhibits a *negative geotaxis* (Crozier & Navez, 1930). Pulling of the shell in one direction causes the snail to move in the opposite direction. In nature the result is that the snail climbs trees because gravity pulls its shell toward the ground.

Taxes and kineses are remarkable because they appear to be goal-directed and voluntary but in fact are produced by simple and mechanistic reflex processes. To explain the behavior of woodlice, for example, it is not necessary to postulate that they enjoy and seek out damp places. Similarly, tree snails are not trying to move up tree branches. Rather, these apparently goal-directed movements are a result of reflex responses controlled by feedback cues involving the presence or absence of the eliciting stimulus. The locomotor/orientation movement persists as long as the response feedback involves continued contact with the eliciting stimulus; the movement ceases when the response removes the organism from the eliciting stimulus.

Responses Elicited and Guided by Different Stimuli. There is yet a third category of elicited behavior. In these cases the elicited behavior is guided by feedback cues that are different from the eliciting stimulus. A good example is provided by the mouth-breeding cichlid (*Tilapia mossambica*), a bass-like fish that incubates its eggs in its mouth. After hatching, the young remain close to the mother for a number of days. The approach of a large object or turbulence in the water causes the young to swim toward the mother. More specifically, they approach her lower parts and dark areas. When they reach the mother, they push on the surface and penetrate into holes, and hence many of them end up in the mother's mouth. If the mother is replaced by a model, the young also approach its lower parts and dark patches and push against these areas (Baerends, 1957). The stimulus that elicits the response sequence is the approach of a large object or water turbulence. However, the behavior is guided by other cues—the lower side of the mother (or model) and dark patches.

In summary, we have seen three different ways in which elicited behavior can be related to feedback cues. Some elicited responses occur largely independently of feedback cues. Other elicited responses are controlled by feedback involving the presence or absence of the eliciting stimulus. Yet other responses are elicited by one stimulus and controlled by feedback involving other types of stimuli.

EFFECTS OF REPEATED STIMULATION: TWO EXAMPLES

Because elicited behavior involves a close relationship between the eliciting stimulus and the resulting response, people tend to think that elicited behavior is invariant or fixed. The common assumption is that an elicited response—particularly a simple reflex response—will occur the same way automatically every time the eliciting stimulus is presented. Most people assume, for example, that a baby will suck with the same vigor every time a nipple is presented. However, if elicited behavior occurred the same way every time, it would be of limited interest, particularly for investigators of learning.

Contrary to common assumptions, elicited behavior is not invariant. One of the most impressive features of behavior is its plasticity. Even simple elicited responses do not occur the same way each time. My description of the role of feedback cues indicated that in some cases the nature of elicited behavior is altered by the feedback cues that result from responding. Alterations in the nature of elicited behavior often also occur simply as a result of repeated presentations of the eliciting stimulus. The following examples illustrate such results.

Visual Attention in Human Infants

Human infants have a lot to learn about the world. One way they obtain information is by looking at things in their environment. Visual cues elicit a looking response, which can be measured by how long the infant keeps his eyes on one object before shifting his gaze elsewhere.

In one study of visual attention (Bashinski, Werner, & Rudy, 1985; see also Kaplan, Werner, & Rudy, 1990), 4-month-old infants were assigned to one of two groups, and each group was tested with a different visual stimulus. The stimuli are shown in the right panel of Figure 2.6. Both were checkerboard patterns, but one had 4 squares on each side (the 4×4 stimulus), and the other had 12 squares on each side (the 12×12 stimulus). Each stimulus presentation lasted 10 seconds, and the stimuli were presented eight times at 10-second intervals.

Both stimuli elicited visual attention initially, with the babies spending an average of about 5.5 seconds looking at the stimuli. With repeated presentations of the 4×4 stimulus, visual attention progressively decreased. By contrast, the babies

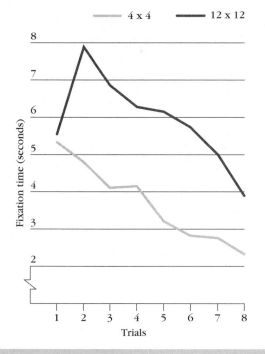

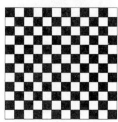

The 4 x 4 stimulus

The 12 x 12 stimulus

Figure 2.6 Time infants spent looking at a visual stimulus during successive trials. For one group, the stimulus consisted of a 4 × 4 checkerboard pattern. For a second group, the stimulus consisted of a 12 × 12 checkerboard pattern. The stimuli are illustrated to the right of the results. (From "Determinants of Infant Visual Attention: Evidence For a Two-Process Theory," by H. Bashinski, J. Werner, and J. Rudy, *Journal of Experimental Child Psychology,* 1985, *39,* pp. 580–598. Copyright © 1985 by Academic Press. Reprinted by permission.)

increased their gaze at the 12 × 12 stimulus during the second trial as compared to the first. But, after that, visual attention to the 12 × 12 stimulus also decreased.

This relatively simple experiment reveals a great deal about visual attention. The results show that visual attention elicited by a novel stimulus changes as babies gain familiarity with the stimulus. The nature of the change is determined by the nature of the stimulus. With a relatively simple 4 × 4 pattern, visual attention progressively declines. With a more complex 12 × 12 pattern, attention initially increases and then declines. Thus, far from being invariant, the elicited behavior of looking at checkerboard patterns changes in different ways as a result of experience with the stimuli.

Startle Response in Rats

Variations in elicited behavior of the type that occur when a stimulus is repeatedly presented to elicit visual attention also occur in other response systems. One system that has been extensively investigated involves the startle response. The startle is a defensive response evident in many species, including humans. For example, unexpectedly blowing a clown's horn behind a child's back is likely to make him jump. This is the startle response. It consists of a sudden jump and tensing of the muscles of the upper part of the body, usually involving raising of the shoulders. In rats, the reaction can be measured by placing the animal in a *stabilimeter chamber* (see Figure 2.7). The chamber rests on pressure sensors. When startled, the animal jumps, producing a bouncing movement of the chamber. Sudden movements are precisely measured by the pressure sensors under the chamber to indicate the vigor of the startle reaction.

The startle reaction can be elicited in rats by all sorts of stimuli, including brief tones and lights. In one experiment, Davis (1974) investigated the startle reaction of

Figure 2.7 Stabilimeter apparatus to measure the startle response of rats. A small chamber rests on pressure sensors. Sudden movements of the rat are detected by the pressure sensors and recorded on a computer. (Adapted from Hoffman and Fleshler, 1964.)

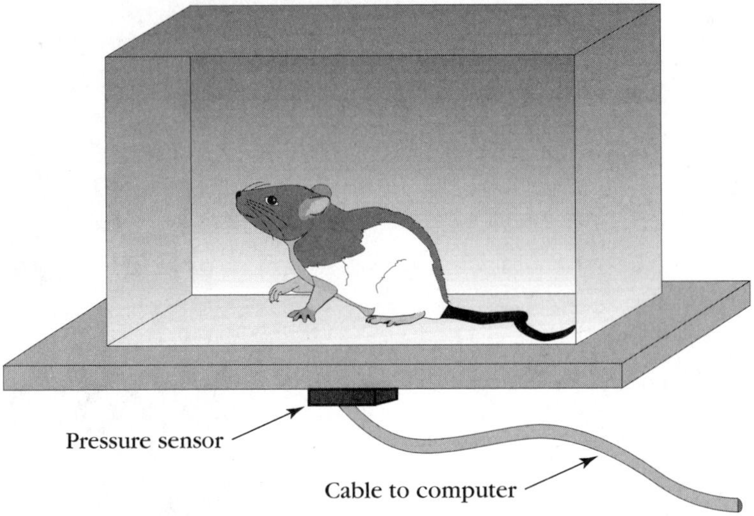

Pressure sensor

Cable to computer

rats to presentations of a brief (90-millisecond) loud tone (110 dB, 4000 cps). Two groups of rats were tested. Each group received 100 successive tone presentations separated by 30 seconds. In addition, a noise generator provided background noise that sounded something like water running from a faucet. For one group, the background noise was relatively quiet (60 dB); for the other, the background noise was rather loud (80 dB) but of lower intensity than the brief startle-eliciting tones.

The results of the experiment are shown in Figure 2.8. As was true of the visual-attention response, repeated presentations of the eliciting stimulus (the 4000-cps tone) did not always produce the same startle response. For rats tested in the presence of the soft background noise (60 dB), repetitions of the tone resulted in weaker and weaker startle reactions. This outcome is similar to what was observed when the 4×4 checkerboard pattern was repeatedly presented to elicit visual attention in babies. By contrast, when the background noise was loud (80 dB), repetitions of the tone elicited more vigorous startle reactions. This outcome is comparable to what was observed at first with the 12×12 checkerboard pattern. Thus, as with visual attention, repeated elicitations of the startle reflex produced a decrease in the magnitude of the startle reaction in one situation and an increase under other circumstances.

THE CONCEPTS OF HABITUATION AND SENSITIZATION

The two studies described in the previous section show that both decreases and increases in responding can occur with repeated presentation of an eliciting stimulus. My next task is to characterize and analyze these effects more systematically.

Decreases in responsiveness produced by repeated stimulation are technically referred to as **habituation effects.** Increases in responsiveness are called **sensitization**

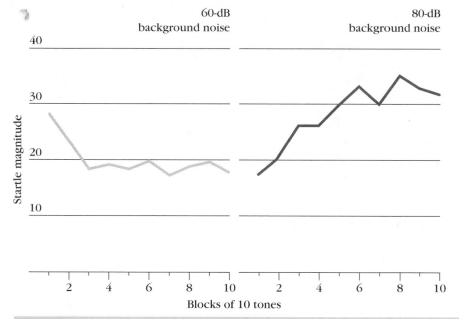

Figure 2.8 Magnitude of the startle response of rats to successive presentations of a tone with background noise of 60 and 80 dB. (From "Sensitization of the Rat Startle Response by Noise," by M. Davis, *Journal of Comparative and Physiological Psychology,* 1974, *87,* pp. 571–581. Copyright © 1974 by the American Psychological Association. Reprinted by permission.)

effects. Habituation and sensitization effects are two basic types of behavior change that result from prior experience. They are such fundamental features of how organisms adjust to their environment that they occur in nearly all species and response systems (for example, Peeke & Petrinovich, 1984).

Adaptiveness and Pervasiveness of Habituation and Sensitization

Organisms are constantly being bombarded by a host of stimuli. Consider sitting at your desk, for example. Even such a simple situation involves a myriad of sensations. You are exposed to the color, texture, and brightness of the paint on the walls, the sounds of the air conditioning system, noises from other rooms, odors in the air, the color and texture of the desk, the tactile sensations of the chair against your legs, seat, and back, and so on. If you were to respond to all of these stimuli, your behavior would be disorganized and chaotic. Habituation and sensitization effects reflect how you end up sorting out what to ignore and what to respond to. Habituation and sensitization effects are the end products of processes that help you organize and focus your behavior in the sea of ongoing stimulation.

There are numerous instances of habituation and sensitization in common human experience (Simons, 1996). Consider a grandfather clock, for example. Most people who own such a clock do not notice each time it chimes. They have completely habituated to the clock's sounds. In fact, they are more likely to notice when the clock misses a scheduled chime. In a sense, this is unfortunate, because they may have purchased the clock because they liked its chime. Similarly, people who live on a busy street, near a railroad track, or close to an airport may become entirely habituated to the noises that frequently intrude into their homes. Visitors who have not become familiarized with such sounds are much more likely to react and be bothered by them.

Driving a car involves exposure to a large array of complex visual and auditory stimuli. In becoming an experienced driver, a person habituates to the numerous stimuli that are irrelevant to driving, such as details of the color and texture of the road, the kind of telephone poles that line the sides of the highway, tactile sensations of the steering wheel, and sounds from the engine. Habituation to irrelevant cues is particularly prominent during long driving trips. If you drive continuously for several hours, you are likely to become oblivious to all kinds of stimuli that are irrelevant to keeping the car on the road. If you then come across an accident or arrive in a new town, you are likely to "wake up" and again pay attention to various things that you had been ignoring. Passing a bad accident or coming to a new town is arousing and sensitizes various orientation responses that were previously habituated.

If you visit a new place or meet a new person, you are likely to pay attention to all sorts of stimuli that you ordinarily ignore. In a strange home, for example, you are likely to take notice of the quality of the furniture, the drapes, and some of the knickknacks on the shelves. You are likely to ignore such details in familiar places— so much so that you may not be able to describe the color of the walls in a hallway you pass through every day or to recall the type of knob attached to a door you use regularly.

Habituation versus Sensory Adaptation and Response Fatigue

The key characteristic of habituation effects is a decline in the response that was initially elicited by a stimulus. However, not all instances in which repetitions of a stimulus result in a decline in responding represent habituation. To understand alternative sources of response decrement, I must return to the concept of a reflex. A reflex consists of three components. First, a stimulus activates one of the sense organs such as the eyes or ears. This generates sensory neural impulses that are relayed to the central nervous system (spinal cord and brain). The second component involves relay of the sensory messages through interneurons to motor nerves. Finally, the neural impulses in motor nerves in turn activate the muscles that create the observed response.

Given the three components of a reflex, there are several reasons why an elicited response may decline with repeated stimulation (see Figure 2.9). The elicited response will not be observed if for some reason the sense organs become temporarily insensitive to stimulation. A person may be temporarily blinded by a bright light, for example, or suffer a temporary hearing loss because of repeated exposures to a loud noise. Such decreases in sensitivity are called **sensory adaptation**. The reflex response

Figure 2.9 Sensory adaptation occurs in the sense organs, and response fatigue occurs in effector muscles. In contrast, habituation and sensitization occur in the nervous system.

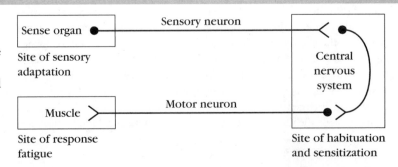

will also fail to occur if the muscles involved become incapacitated by **fatigue**. Sensory adaptation and response fatigue are impediments to the elicited response that are produced outside the nervous system, in sense organs and muscles.

The likelihood of a response will also change if the neural processes involved in the elicited behavior are altered. Various types of changes in the nervous system can hinder or facilitate the transmission of neural impulses from sensory to motor neurons. Habituation and sensitization are assumed to involve such neurophysiological changes. Thus, habituation is different from sensory adaptation and response fatigue. In habituation, the organism ceases to respond to a stimulus, even though it remains fully capable of sensing the stimulus and of making the muscle movements required for the response. The response fails to occur because changes in the nervous system block the relay of sensory neural impulses to the motor neurons.

In studies of habituation, sensory adaptation is ruled out by evidence that *habituation is response-specific*. An organism may stop responding to a stimulus in one aspect of its behavior while continuing to respond to the stimulus in other ways. When a teacher makes an announcement while you are concentrating on taking a test, you may look up from your test at first, but only briefly. However, you will continue to listen to the announcement until it is over. Thus, your orienting response habituates quickly, but other attentional responses to the stimulus persist.

Response fatigue as a cause of habituation is ruled out by evidence that *habituation is stimulus-specific*. A habituated response will quickly recover when a new stimulus is introduced. After your orienting response to the teacher's announcement has habituated, if the teacher mentions your name you are likely to look up again. Thus, a new stimulus will elicit the previously habituated orienting response, indicating that failure of the response was not due to fatigue.

The Dual-Process Theory of Habituation and Sensitization

Habituation and sensitization effects are changes in behavior or performance—a habituation effect being a decrease in responding and a sensitization effect being an increase in responding. What factors are responsible for such changes? To answer this question I must shift the level of analysis from behavior to the presumed underlying processes causing the behavior. In other words, I must discuss theory. The dominant theory of habituation and sensitization remains the dual-process theory proposed by Groves and Thompson (1970).

The dual-process theory assumes that different types of underlying neural processes are responsible for increases and decreases in responsiveness to stimulation. One neural process produces decreases in responsiveness. This is called the **habituation process.** Another process produces increases in responsiveness. This is called the **sensitization process.** The habituation and sensitization processes are not mutually exclusive. Rather, both may be activated at the same time. The behavioral outcome of these underlying processes depends on which process is stronger. Thus habituation and sensitization processes compete for control of behavior. This is illustrated in Figure 2.10.

The left-hand graph in Figure 2.10 illustrates a hypothetical situation in which repetitions of a stimulus intensify the habituation process more than the sensitization process. The net effect of these changes is a decline in the elicited response across trials (a habituation effect). The right-hand graph illustrates the opposite outcome. Here, repetitions of a stimulus strengthen the sensitization process more than the habituation process, and the net result is an increase in the magnitude of the elicited

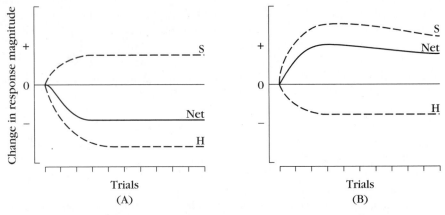

Figure 2.10 Hypothetical data illustrating the dual-process theory of habituation and sensitization. The strength of the habituation process (H) is indicated by the dashed lines that extend below the horizontal 0 line. The strength of the sensitization processes (S) is indicated by the dashed lines that extend above the horizontal 0 line. The solid lines indicate the net effects of the habituation and sensitization processes. In panel A (left), the habituation process becomes stronger than the sensitization process across trials, which leads to a progressive decrement in responding. In panel B (right), the sensitization process becomes stronger than the habituation process across trials, which leads to a progressive increase in responding.

response across trials (a sensitization effect). As these cases illustrate, the change in the elicited response that actually occurs in a particular situation represents the net effect of the habituation and sensitization processes.

It is unfortunate that the underlying processes that suppress and facilitate responding are called habituation and sensitization. That makes it tempting to think that decreased responding or a habituation effect is a direct reflection of the habituation process and that increased responding or a sensitization effect is a direct reflection of the sensitization process. In fact, as is illustrated in Figure 2.10, both habituation and sensitization effects are the sum or net result of both habituation and sensitization processes. Whether the net result is an increase or a decrease in behavior depends on which underlying process is stronger in a particular situation. The distinction between *effects* and *processes* in habituation and sensitization is analogous to the distinction between *performance* and *learning* discussed in Chapter 1. Effects refer to observable behavior, and processes refer to underlying mechanisms.

On the basis of neurophysiological research, Groves and Thompson (1970) suggested that habituation and sensitization processes occur in different parts of the nervous system (see also Thompson, Groves, Teyler, & Roemer, 1973). Habituation processes are assumed to occur in what is called the **S-R system.** This system consists of the shortest neural path that connects the sense organs activated by the eliciting stimulus and the muscles involved in making the elicited response. The S-R system may be viewed as the reflex arc. Each presentation of an eliciting stimulus activates the S-R system and causes some build-up of habituation.

Sensitization processes are assumed to occur in what is called the **state system.** This system consists of other parts of the nervous system that determine the organism's general level of responsiveness or readiness to respond. In contrast to the S-R system, which is activated every time an eliciting stimulus is presented, only arousing events activate the state system. The state system is relatively quiescent during sleep, for example. Drugs such as stimulants or depressants may alter the functioning of the state system and thereby change responsiveness. The state system is also altered by emotional experiences. For example, the jumpiness that accompanies fear is caused by activation of the state system.

In summary, the state system determines the animal's readiness to respond, whereas the S-R system enables the animal to make the specific response that is elicited by the stimulus of interest. Changes in behavior that occur with repetitions of a stimulus reflect the combined actions of the S-R and state systems.

Applications of the Dual-Process Theory. The examples of habituation and sensitization illustrated in Figures 2.6 and 2.8 can be easily interpreted in terms of the dual-process theory. Repeated exposure to the 4×4 checkerboard pattern produced a decrement in responding. This presumably occurred because the 4×4 stimulus did not create much arousal. Rather, the 4×4 stimulus activated primarily the S-R system and hence activated primarily the habituation process. The more complex 12×12 checkerboard pattern produced a greater level of arousal. It presumably activated not only the S-R system but also the state system. The activation of the state system resulted in the increment in visual attention that occurred after the first presentation of the 12×12 pattern. However, the arousal or sensitization process was not strong enough to entirely counteract the effects of habituation. As a result, after a few trials visual attention also declined in response to the 12×12 stimulus.

The dual-process theory is also consistent with the habituation and sensitization effects I noted in the startle reaction of rats (Figure 2.8). When the rats were tested with a relatively quiet background noise (60 dB), there was little to arouse them; the experimental procedures probably did not produce changes in the state system. Repeated presentations of the startle-eliciting tone merely activated the S-R system, which resulted in habituation of the startle response.

The opposite outcome occurred when the animals were tested in the presence of a loud background noise (80 dB). In this case, stronger startle reactions occurred to successive presentations of the tone. Because the identical tone was used for both groups, the difference in the results cannot be attributed to the tone. Rather, the loud background noise probably increased arousal or readiness to respond in the second group. This sensitization of the state system was presumably responsible for increasing the startle reaction to the tone in the second group.

Implications of the Dual-Process Theory. The preceding interpretations of changes in visual attention and startle responding illustrate several important features of the dual-process theory. As we have seen, the state and S-R systems are activated differently by repeated presentations of a stimulus. *The S-R system is activated every time a stimulus elicits a response* because it is the neural circuit that conducts impulses from sensory input to response output. By contrast, *the state system becomes involved only in special circumstances.* Some extraneous event (such as an intense background noise) may increase the individual's alertness and sensitize the state system. Alternatively, the state system may be sensitized by the repeated presentations of the test stimulus itself if that stimulus is sufficiently intense or excitatory (a 12×12 checkerboard pattern, as compared with a 4×4 pattern). If the arousing stimulus is repeated soon enough so that the second presentation occurs while the organism remains sensitized from the preceding trial, an increase in responding will be observed.

The dual-process theory of habituation and sensitization has been very influential in the study of the plasticity of elicited behavior, although it has not been successful in explaining all habituation and sensitization effects. One of the important contributions of the theory has been the assumption that elicited behavior can be strongly influenced by neurophysiological events taking place outside the reflex arc that are directly involved in a particular elicited response. In the dual-process theory, the state system is assumed to modulate the activity of reflex arcs. The basic idea that certain parts of the nervous system serve to modulate S-R systems that are more directly involved in elicited behavior has been developed in more recent studies of habituation and sensitization (for example, Borszcz, Cranney, & Leaton, 1989; Davis & File, 1984; Davis, Hitchcock, & Rosen, 1987). (For a detailed discussion of other theories of habituation, see Stephenson & Siddle, 1983.)

CHARACTERISTICS OF HABITUATION
AND SENSITIZATION

Much research has been performed to determine how various factors influence habituation and sensitization processes. Although the characteristics of habituation and sensitization are not perfectly uniform across all species and response systems, there are many commonalties. I will describe some of the most important of these.

Most of the forms of behavior change I will describe in later chapters are retained for long periods (weeks or months). In fact, this is one of the defining characteristics of learning phenomena (see Chapter 1). Instances of habituation and sensitization do not always have this characteristic, and therefore not all instances of habituation and sensitization are properly considered examples of learning.

Time Course of Sensitization. Sensitization processes generally have temporary effects. Although in some instances sensitization persists for more than a week (for example, Heiligenberg, 1974), in most situations the increased responsiveness is short-lived. Davis (1974), for example, investigated the sensitizing effect of a 25-minute exposure to a loud noise (80 dB) in rats. As expected, the loud noise sensitized the startle response to a tone. However, this increased reactivity lasted only 10–15 minutes after the loud noise was turned off. In other response systems, sensitization dissipates more rapidly. For example, sensitization of the spinal hindlimb-flexion reflex in cats persists for only about 3 seconds (Groves & Thompson, 1970).

In all response systems the duration of sensitization effects is determined by the intensity of the sensitizing stimulus. More intense stimuli produce greater increases in responsiveness, and with more intense stimuli the sensitization effects persist longer.

Time Course of Habituation. Habituation also persists for varying amounts of time. With sensitization, differences in the time course of the effect usually reflect only quantitative differences in the same underlying mechanism. By contrast, there are two qualitatively different types of habituation effects. One is similar to most cases of sensitization in that it dissipates relatively quickly—within seconds or minutes. This is called *short-term habituation*. The other type is much longer lasting and may persist for many days. This type is called *long-term habituation.*

Short-term and long-term habituation effects are clearly illustrated in an experiment on the startle response of rats by Leaton (1976). The test stimulus was a high-pitched, loud tone presented for 2 seconds. The animals were first allowed to get used to the experimental chamber without any tone presentations. Each rat then received a single test trial with the tone stimulus once a day for 11 days. Because of the long (24-hour) interval between trials, any decrements in responding produced by the stimulus presentations were assumed to exemplify long-term habituation. The short-term habituation process was illustrated in the next phase of the experiment by giving the rats 300 closely spaced tone presentations (every 3 seconds). Finally, the animals were given a single tone presentation 1, 2, and 3 days later to measure recovery from the short-term habituation effect.

Figure 2.11 shows the results. The most intense startle reaction was observed the first time the tone was presented. Progressively less intense reactions occurred during the next 10 days. Because the animals were tested only once every 24 hours in this phase, the progressive decrements in responding indicate that the habituating effects of the stimulus presentations persisted throughout the 11-day period. However, this long-term habituation did not result in complete loss of the startle reflex. Even on the 11th day, the animals still reacted a little.

By contrast, startle reactions quickly ceased when the tone presentations occurred every 3 seconds in the next phase of the experiment. However, this dramatic loss of responsiveness was only temporary. In the third phase of the experiment, when

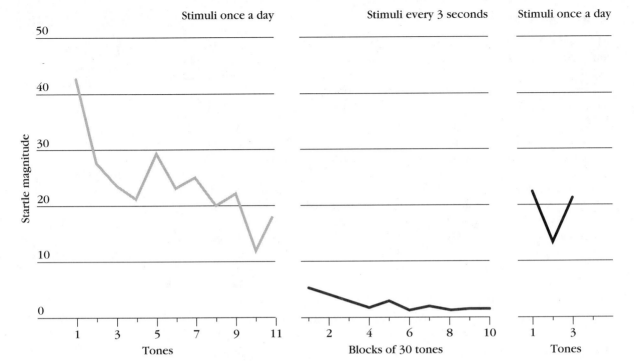

Stimuli once a day   Stimuli every 3 seconds   Stimuli once a day

Startle magnitude

Tones   Blocks of 30 tones   Tones

Figure 2.11 Startle response of rats to a tone presented once a day in Phase 1, every 3 seconds in Phase 2, and once a day in Phase 3. (From "Long-Term Retention of the Habituation of Lick Suppression and Startle Response Produced by a Single Auditory Stimulus," by R. N. Leaton, *Journal of Experimental Psychology: Animal Behavior Processes,* 1976, *2,* 248–259. Copyright © 1976 by the American Psychological Association. Reprinted by permission.)

the animals were tested again just once a day, the startle response recovered to the level of the 11th day of the experiment. This recovery, known as **spontaneous recovery,** occurred simply because the tone had not been presented for a long time (24 hours). Spontaneous recovery is the identifying characteristic of the short-term habituation effect.

Repeated presentations of a stimulus do not always result in both long-term and short-term habituation effects. With the spinal leg-flexion reflex in cats, for example, only the short-term habituation effect is observed (Thompson & Spencer, 1966). In such cases, spontaneous recovery completely restores the animal's reaction to the eliciting stimulus if a long enough period of rest is permitted after habituation. By contrast, spontaneous recovery is never complete in situations that also involve long-term habituation effects, as in Leaton's experiment. As Figure 2.11 indicates, the startle response was restored to some extent in the last phase of the experiment, but the animals did not react as vigorously to the tone as they had the first time it was presented.

Few theories can explain satisfactorily the qualitative differences between short- and long-term habituation. The dual-process theory was formulated to explain only short-term habituation and sensitization. Differences between short-term and long-term habituation effects were addressed by Wagner's priming theory (for example, Whitlow & Wagner, 1984). However, critical predictions of that theory have not been confirmed (see, for example, Honey, Pye, Lightbown, Rey, & Hall, 1992; Marlin & Miller, 1981).

Stimulus Specificity

Stimulus Specificity of Habituation. Habituation processes are typically highly specific to the stimulus that is repeatedly presented. A response that has been habituated to one stimulus can be evoked in full strength by a new eliciting stimulus. After a woman has become completely habituated to the chimes of her grandfather clock, for example, if the clock malfunctions and makes a new sound, her attention to the clock is likely to become entirely restored. After complete habituation of the orienting response to one stimulus, the response will occur in its normal strength if a sufficiently novel stimulus is presented. Stimulus specificity characterizes all examples of habituation and therefore has been considered one of the defining characteristics of habituation (Thompson & Spencer, 1966).

Although habituation effects are always stimulus-specific, some generalization of the effects may occur. The woman who has become habituated to a particular clock chime may also fail to respond to another clock chime that is similar to the original one. This phenomenon is called *stimulus generalization of habituation*. However, even in cases of stimulus generalization, as test stimuli are made increasingly different from the habituated stimulus, the organism will show progressively less habituation or suppression of responding to the test stimuli.

Stimulus Specificity of Sensitization.   Unlike habituation, sensitization is not highly stimulus-specific. If an animal becomes aroused or sensitized for some reason, its reactivity will increase to a range of cues. For example, pain induced by footshock increases the reactivity of laboratory rats to both auditory and visual cues. Similarly, feelings of sickness or internal malaise increase the reactivity of rats to a wide range of novel tastes. However, shock-induced sensitization appears to be limited to exteroceptive cues, and illness-induced sensitization is limited to gustatory stimuli (Miller & Domjan, 1981). Cutaneous pain and internal malaise seem to activate separate sensitization systems.

Effects of Strong Extraneous Stimuli

As I have noted, changing the nature of the eliciting stimulus can produce recovery of a habituated response. However, this is not the only way to quickly restore responding after habituation. The habituated response can also be restored by sensitizing the organism with exposure to an extraneous stimulus. This phenomenon is called **dishabituation.**

Figure 2.12 illustrates the results of a study involving dishabituation of the visual-attention response of human infants (Kaplan, Werner, & Rudy, 1990). The infants were shown a 4×4 checkerboard pattern during each of the first eight trials of the experiment and displayed a familiar habituation effect. During Trial 9, a 75-dB, 1000-cps tone was sounded along with the visual stimulus for one group of infants, while the other group continued to receive the visual stimulus without the tone as before. The presence of the tone greatly elevated responding. Furthermore, responding continued to be elevated on Trials 10, 11, and 12, during which the tone was again omitted, and only the 4×4 visual stimulus was available.

It is important to keep in mind that dishabituation refers to recovery in the response to the previously habituated stimulus—the 4×4 pattern in the example. Responding directly to the sensitizing or dishabituating tone is not of interest. In fact, the increased visual fixation that was observed when the tone was presented on Trial 9 could not be explained as a response to the tone because the tone was presented through a speaker located above and behind the infant. Thus, if the infant had oriented toward the source of the tone, he or she would have ended up looking away from the visual stimulus.

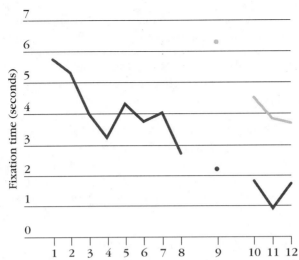

Figure 2.12   Fixation time of human infants plotted as a function of presentations of a 4 × 4 checkerboard pattern. On the ninth trial, some of the infants were exposed to a 10-second, 1000-Hz, 75 dB tone. This caused an increase in responding to the checkerboard pattern. (From "Habituation, Sensitization, and Infant Visual Attention," by P. S. Kaplan, J. S. Werner, and J. W. Rudy, *Advances in Infancy Research,* 1990, Vol. 6, pp. 61–109 by C. Rovee-Collier and L. P. Lipsitt (Eds.). Copyright © 1990 by Ablex Publishing Company. Reprinted by permission.)

CHANGES IN COMPLEX EMOTIONAL RESPONSES

R. L. Solomon

To this point, my discussion of changes produced by repetitions of an eliciting stimulus has been limited to relatively simple responses. However, a stimulus may also evoke complex emotional responses such as love, fear, euphoria, terror, satisfaction, or uneasiness. In this section I will describe the standard pattern of emotions evoked by complex emotion-arousing stimuli and show how this pattern is altered by repetitions of the stimulus. These issues have been most systematically addressed by the opponent-process theory of motivation proposed by Solomon and his collaborators (Hoffman & Solomon, 1974; Solomon, 1977; Solomon & Corbit, 1973, 1974). Therefore, my discussion will focus on that theory.

The Standard Pattern of Affective Dynamics

The standard pattern of affective dynamics describes what happens when an emotion-arousing stimulus is presented and then removed. Consider the reactions of a 16-year-old student who is given a car to drive for the first time. Initially, the teenager will be extremely excited and happy. This excitement will subside a bit as time passes.

Nevertheless, the car will continue to give pleasure. If after a day or two the car becomes no longer available, the teenager's emotions will not simply return to neutrality. Rather, for a while after surrendering the car, a longing for it will persist. This longing will then gradually dissipate.

Obviously, different emotion-arousing stimuli elicit different types of emotional responses. However, the pattern of the emotional changes that are elicited has certain common characteristics. Solomon and his associates have called these characteristics the **standard pattern of affective dynamics** (Solomon & Corbit, 1974). The key elements of the pattern are shown in Figure 2.13.

The onset of the emotion-arousing stimulus, such as receipt of a car, elicits a strong emotional response (happiness) that quickly reaches a peak. This *peak reaction* is followed by an *adaptation phase* during which the emotional response subsides a bit until it reaches a *steady state*. The stimulus (the car) continues to elicit the emotion (happiness) during the steady state but at a lower level than at the peak.

When the stimulus ceases (the teenager has to surrender the car), the emotional state quickly changes to feelings opposite to those that occurred in the presence of the stimulus. Now the teenager feels unhappy and has a longing for the car. This reversal of the emotional state, called the *affective after-reaction,* gradually decays and the organism returns to its baseline state.

How will a teenager react to getting a car once such an experience has become routine? If the student has had access to a car many times before, receipt of the car will not elicit the same intense happiness that occurred the first time. Getting the car is likely to produce only a mild reaction. However, this time, if the car becomes unavailable, the unhappiness and longing for it that result will be much more intense than the first time. Once a person has become accustomed to having a car, losing access to it creates intense unhappiness. Thus, the pattern of emotional changes to a habituated emotion-arousing stimulus is different from the standard pattern of affective dynamics. This habituated pattern is shown in Figure 2.14. The habituated stimulus elicits only a slight emotional response. However, the affective after-reaction is much more intense than in the standard pattern.

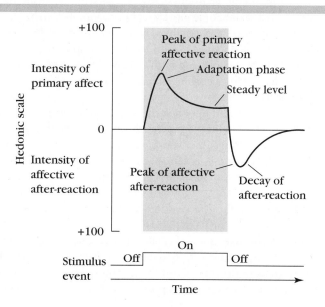

Figure 2.13 Standard pattern of affective dynamics. (From "An Opponent-Process Theory of Motivation: I. The Temporal Dynamics of Affect," by R. L. Solomon and J. D. Corbit, *Psychological Review,* 1974, *81,* 119–145. Copyright © 1974 by the American Psychological Association. Reprinted by permission.)

Figure 2.14 Pattern of affective changes to a habituated stimulus. (From "An Opponent-Process Theory of Motivation: I. The Temporal Dynamics of Affect," by R. L. Solomon and J. D. Corbit, *Psychological Review,* 1974, *81,* 119–145. Copyright © 1974 by the American Psychological Association. Reprinted by permission.)

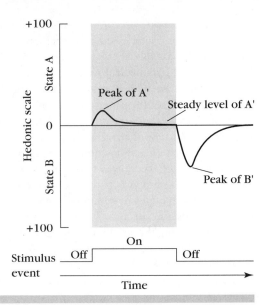

Mechanisms of the Opponent-Process Theory

What underlying mechanisms produce the standard pattern of affective dynamics and modifications of this pattern with habituation to the emotion-arousing stimulus? The opponent-process theory of motivation assumes that neurophysiological mechanisms involved in emotional behavior serve to maintain emotional stability. Thus, the opponent-process theory is a *homeostatic* theory. It assumes that an important function of mechanisms that control emotional behavior is to minimize deviations from emotional neutrality or stability. (The concept of homeostasis has been very important in the analysis of behavior. I will discuss other types of homeostatic theories in later chapters.)

How might neurophysiological mechanisms maintain emotional stability or neutrality? Maintaining any system in a neutral or stable state requires that a disturbance that moves the system in one direction be met by an opposing force that counteracts the disturbance. Consider, for example, trying to keep a seesaw level. If something pushes one end of the seesaw down, the other end will go up. To keep the seesaw level, a force pushing one end down has to be met by an opposing force on the other side.

The concept of opponent forces or processes serving to maintain a stable state is central to the opponent-process theory of motivation. The theory assumes that an emotion-arousing stimulus pushes a person's emotional state away from neutrality. This shift away from emotional neutrality is assumed to trigger an opponent process that counteracts the shift. The patterns of emotional behavior observed initially and after extensive experience with a stimulus are the net results of the opponent process and changes in the opponent process with experience.

The opponent-process theory assumes that the presentation of an emotion-arousing stimulus initially elicits what is called the **primary process**, or *a* **process**, which is responsible for the quality of the emotional state (happiness, for example) that occurs in the presence of the stimulus. The primary, or *a*, process is assumed to elicit, in turn, an **opponent process**, or *b* **process**, that generates the opposite emotional reaction (unhappiness, for example). The emotional changes observed when a stimulus is presented and then removed are assumed to reflect the net result of the primary and opponent processes. The strength of the opponent process subtracts from the strength of the primary process to provide the emotions that actually occur. Thus, the primary and opponent processes are internal mechanisms whose net effects are the emotional changes that are observed, in much the same way that habituation and sensitization processes are internal mechanisms whose net effects are observed in the magnitude of the startle reflex (see Figure 2.9).

An additional assumption that is basic to the opponent process theory is that the opponent process is assumed to be a bit inefficient. It lags behind the primary emotional disturbance at first and is not strong enough to entirely counteract the primary emotion initially. However, the opponent process becomes quicker and more powerful with practice or repeated experience with the emotion-arousing stimulus. Thus, in a sense the opponent process becomes sensitized as a result of repeated activation.

Explanation of the Standard Pattern of Affective Dynamics. Figure 2.15 shows how the primary and opponent processes determine the standard pattern of affective dynamics. When the stimulus is first presented, the *a* process occurs unopposed by the *b* process. The primary emotional reaction can therefore reach its peak quickly. The *b* process then becomes activated and begins to oppose the *a* process. The *b* process reduces the strength of the primary emotional response and is therefore responsible for the adaptation phase of the standard pattern.

The primary emotional response reaches a steady state when the *a* and *b* processes have each reached their maximum strength during the stimulus presentation. When the stimulus is withdrawn, the *a* process quickly stops, but the *b* process lingers for awhile. At this point the *b* process has nothing to oppose. Therefore, emotional responses characteristic of the opponent process become evident for the first time.

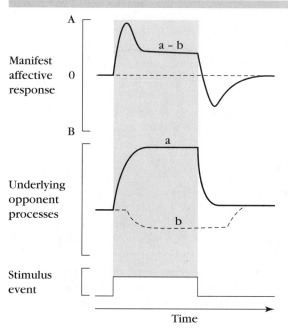

Figure 2.15 Opponent-process mechanism that produces the standard pattern of affective dynamics. (From "An Opponent-Process Theory of Motivation: I. The Temporal Dynamics of Affect," by R. L. Solomon and J. D. Corbit, *Psychological Review,* 1974, *81,* 119–145. Copyright © 1974 by the American Psychological Association. Reprinted by permission.)

Figure 2.16 Opponent-process mechanism that produces the affective changes to a habituated stimulus. (From "An Opponent-Process Theory of Motivation: I. The Temporal Dynamics of Affect," by R. L. Solomon and J. D. Corbit, *Psychological Review,* 1974, *81,* 119–145. Copyright © 1974 by the American Psychological Association. Reprinted by permission.)

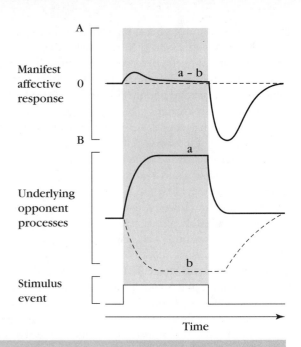

These emotions are typically opposite to those observed during the presence of the stimulus.

Explanation of the Habituated Pattern   As shown in Figure 2.14, after extensive exposure, a stimulus ceases to elicit strong emotional reactions, and the affective after-reaction becomes much stronger when the stimulus is terminated. The opponent-process theory explains this outcome by assuming that the *b* process becomes strengthened by repeated exposures to the stimulus. The strengthening of the *b* process is reflected in several of its characteristics. The *b* process becomes activated sooner after the onset of the stimulus, its maximum intensity becomes greater, and it becomes slower to decay when the stimulus ceases. In contrast, the *a* process is assumed to remain unchanged. Thus, after repeated presentations of a stimulus, the primary emotional responses are more strongly opposed by the opponent process. This growth in the opponent process reduces the intensity of the observed primary emotional responses during presentation of the emotion-arousing stimulus. It also leads to the excessive affective after-reaction when the stimulus is withdrawn (see Figure 2.16).

Examples of Opponent Processes

Drug Addiction.   Psychoactive drugs are taken mainly for their emotional effects. The emotional changes that result from initial and habitual drug use are accurately described by the opponent-process theory of motivation in many cases (Solomon, 1977). The opponent-process theory predicts that psychoactive drugs produce a biphasic emotional effect initially. One set of emotional responses is experienced when the drug is active (the primary affective response), and the opposite emotions occur when the drug has worn off (the affective after-reaction). Such biphasic changes are evident with a variety of psychoactive drugs, including alcohol, opiates (such as heroin), amphetamine, and nicotine.

Consider what happens with alcohol, for example. Shortly after taking a drink, the drinker becomes mellow and relaxed because the drug is a sedative. The opponent after-reaction to alcohol is evident in headaches, nausea, and other symptoms of a hangover. With amphetamine, the presence of the drug creates feelings of euphoria, a sense of well-being, self-confidence, wakefulness, and control. After the drug has worn off, the drug-taker is likely to be fatigued, depressed, and drowsy.

The opponent-process theory predicts that with repeated and frequent use, the primary emotional response to a drug will become less evident and the opponent after-reaction will become more prominent. Habituation of the primary drug reactions is an example of **drug tolerance,** which refers to a decline in the effectiveness of a drug with repeated exposures. Habitual users of alcohol, nicotine, heroin, caffeine, and other drugs are not as greatly affected by the presence of the drug as first-time users. An amount of alcohol that would make a casual drinker a bit tipsy is not likely to have any effect on a frequent drinker. (I will revisit the role of opponent processes in drug tolerance in Chapter 4.)

Because of the development of tolerance, habitual drug users sometimes do not enjoy taking the drug as much as naive users. People who smoke frequently, for example, do not always derive much enjoyment from doing so. Accompanying this decline in the primary drug reaction is a growth in the opponent after-reaction. Accordingly, habitual drug users experience much more severe hangovers on termination of the drug than naive users. A person who stops smoking cigarettes, for example, will experience headaches, irritability, anxiety, tension, and general dissatisfaction. A heavy drinker who stops taking alcohol is likely to experience hallucinations, memory loss, psychomotor agitation, delirium tremens, and other physiological disturbances. For a habitual user of amphetamine, the fatigue and depression that characterize the opponent after-effect may be so severe as to cause suicide.

If the primary pleasurable effects of a psychoactive drug are gone for habitual users, why do they continue taking the drug? Why are they addicted? The opponent-process theory suggests that drug addiction is mainly an attempt to reduce the aversiveness of the affective after-reaction to the drugs—the bad hangovers, the amphetamine "crashes," and the irritability that comes from not having the usual cigarette. There are two ways to reduce the aversive opponent after-reactions of drugs. One is to simply wait long enough for them to dissipate. This is what is known as "going cold turkey." For heavy drug users, going cold turkey may take a long time and may be very painful. The opponent after-reaction can be much more quickly eliminated by taking the drug again. This will reactivate the primary process and stave off the agonies of withdrawal. According to the theory, addicts are not "trapped" by the pleasure they derive from the drug directly. Rather, they take the drug to reduce withdrawal pains.

Love and Attachment.   The opponent-process theory also has been used in the analysis of love and attachment. Newlyweds are usually very excited about each other and are very affectionate whenever they are together. This primary emotional reaction habituates as years go by. Gradually, the couple settles into a comfortable mode of interaction that lacks the excitement of the honeymoon. However, this habituation of the primary emotional reaction is accompanied by a strengthening of the affective after-reaction. The more time a couple spends together, the more unhappy the partners become when separated for some reason, and this unhappiness lasts longer. ("Absence makes the heart grow fonder.") After the partners have been together for several decades, the death of one is likely to cause an intense grief reaction in the survivor. This strong affective after-reaction is remarkable, considering that by this stage in their relationship the couple may have entirely ceased to show any overt signs of affection.

The predictions of the opponent-process theory for human love and attachment have not been tested experimentally. However, animal research provides some support for the theory (see Hoffman & Solomon, 1974; Mineka, Suomi, & DeLizio, 1981; Starr, 1978; Suomi, Mineka, & Harlow, 1983).

CONCLUDING COMMENTS

The quality of life and survival itself depend on an intricate coordination of behavior with the complexities of an animal's environment. Elicited behavior represents one of the fundamental ways in which the behavior of all animals—from single-celled organisms to people—is adjusted to environmental events.

As we have seen, elicited behavior takes many forms, ranging from simple reflexes mediated by just three neurons to complex emotional reactions. Although elicited behavior occurs as a reaction to a stimulus, it is not rigid and invariant. In fact, one of the remarkable features of elicited behavior is that it is altered by experience. If an eliciting stimulus does not arouse the organism, repeated presentations of the stimulus will evoke progressively weaker responses (a habituation effect). If the eliciting stimulus is particularly intense or of significance to the individual, repeated presentations will create arousal and lead to progressively stronger reactions (a sensitization effect).

Environmental events activate habituation and sensitization processes to varying degrees. The resultant responses reflect the net effect of the habituation and sensitization processes. Therefore, without knowing the past experiences of the organism, it is impossible to predict how strong a reaction will be elicited by a particular stimulus presentation.

Repeated presentations of an eliciting stimulus produce changes in simple responses as well as in more complex emotional reactions. Organisms tend to minimize changes in emotional state caused by external stimuli. According to the opponent-process theory of motivation, emotional responses stimulated by an outside event are counteracted by an opposing process in the organism. This compensatory, or opponent, process is assumed to become stronger each time it is elicited, leading to a reduction of the primary emotional responses. The strengthened opponent emotional state is evident when the stimulus is removed.

Habituation, sensitization, and changes in the strength of opponent processes are the simplest mechanisms whereby organisms adjust their reactions to environmental events on the basis of past experience.

SAMPLE QUESTIONS

1. What are modal action patterns, and how are they controlled by response feedback?

2. Describe the distinction between habituation, sensory adaptation, and fatigue.

3. What is the difference between habituation and sensitization effects and habituation and sensitization processes?

4. Describe the two processes of the dual-process theory of habituation and sensitization and the differences between these processes.

5. What aspects of the opponent-process theory of motivation lead to habituation effects? What aspects lead to sensitization effects?

KEY TERMS

afferent neuron A neuron that transmits messages from sense organs to the central nervous system. Also called *sensory neuron.*

a **process** Same as *primary process* in the opponent-process theory of motivation.

b **process** Same as *opponent process* in the opponent-process theory of motivation.

dishabituation Recovery of a habituated response as a result of a strong extraneous stimulus.

drug tolerance Reduction in the effectiveness of a drug as a result of repeated use of the drug.

efferent neuron A neuron that transmits impulses to muscles. Also called a *motor neuron.*

fatigue A temporary decrease in behavior caused by repeated or excessive use of the muscles involved in the behavior.

feedback stimulus A stimulus that results from the performance of a response.

habituation effect A progressive decrease in the vigor of elicited behavior that may occur with repeated presentations of the eliciting stimulus.

habituation process A neural mechanism activated by repetitions of a stimulus that reduces the magnitude of responses elicited by that stimulus.

interneuron A neuron in the spinal cord that transmits impulses from afferent (or sensory) to efferent (or motor) neurons.

kinesis An instance in which a stimulus produces a change in the speed of movement, irrespective of the direction of the movement.

MAP Abbreviation for *modal action pattern.*

modal action pattern A response pattern exhibited by most, if not all, members of a species in much the same way. Modal action patterns are used as basic units of behavior in ethological investigations of behavior.

motor neuron Same as *efferent neuron.*

opponent process A compensatory mechanism that occurs in response to the primary process elicited by biologically significant events. The opponent process causes physiological and behavioral changes that are the opposite of those caused by the primary process. Sometimes referred to as the *b process.*

primary process The first process that is elicited by a biologically significant stimulus. Sometimes referred to as the *a process.*

proprioceptive stimulus An internal response feedback stimulus that arises from the movement of muscles and/or joints. (Compare with exteroceptive stimulus.)

reflex arc Neural structures, consisting of the afferent (sensory) neuron, interneuron, and efferent (motor) neuron that enable a stimulus to elicit a reflex response.

releasing stimulus Same as *sign stimulus.*

sensitization effect An increase in the vigor of elicited behavior that may result from repeated presentations of the eliciting stimulus or from exposure to a strong extraneous stimulus.

sensitization process A neural mechanism that increases the magnitude of responses elicited by a stimulus.

sensory adaptation A temporary reduction in the sensitivity of sense organs caused by repeated or excessive stimulation.

sensory neuron Same as *afferent neuron.*

sign stimulus A specific feature of an object or animal that elicits a modal action pattern in another organism. Also called *releasing stimulus.*

spontaneous recovery Recovery of a response produced by a period of rest after habituation or extinction. (Extinction is discussed in Chapters 3 and 6.)

S-R system The shortest neural pathway that connects the sense organs stimulated by an eliciting stimulus and the muscles involved in making the elicited response.

standard pattern of affective dynamics As specified by the opponent-process theory of motivation, a pattern of emotional changes that is frequently observed when a novel, biologically significant event is presented.

state system Neural structures that determine the general level of responsiveness, or readiness to respond, of the organism.

supernormal stimulus An artificially enlarged or exaggerated sign stimulus that elicits an unusually vigorous response.

taxis An orientation movement toward or away from an eliciting stimulus.

CLASSICAL CONDITIONING: FOUNDATIONS

The Early Years of Classical Conditioning

The Discoveries of Wolfsohn and Snarsky

The Classical Conditioning Paradigm

Experimental Situations

Sign Tracking

Fear Conditioning

Eyeblink Conditioning

Taste Aversion Learning

Excitatory Pavlovian Conditioning

Common Pavlovian Conditioning Procedures

Measurement of Conditioned Responses

Control Procedures for Classical Conditioning

Effectiveness of Common Conditioning Procedures

Inhibitory Pavlovian Conditioning

Procedures for Inhibitory Conditioning

Measuring Conditioned Inhibition

Extinction

Extinction and Habituation

The Learning Involved in Extinction

Prevalence of Classical Conditioning

Acquired Food Preferences and Aversions in People

Infant and Maternal Responses during Nursing

Conditioning of Sexual Behavior

Concluding Comments

 HAPTER 3 provides an introduction to another basic form of learning—classical conditioning. Investigations of classical conditioning began with the work of Pavlov, who studied how dogs learn to anticipate feeding episodes. Since then, the research has been extended to a variety of other organisms and response systems. Some classical conditioning procedures establish an excitatory association between two stimuli. Others serve to inhibit the operation of excitatory associations. I will describe excitatory and inhibitory conditioning procedures, as well as how conditioned responding can be extinguished. I will conclude the chapter by considering how classical conditioning is involved in food preferences, breast feeding, and sexual behavior.

In the preceding chapter, I described how elicited behavior is modified by sensitization and habituation processes. These relatively simple processes permit organisms to adjust their behavior to some environmental challenges. However, if animals only had the behavioral mechanisms described in Chapter 2, they would remain rather limited in the kinds of things they could do. Habituation, for example, involves learning about just one stimulus. However, events in the world do not occur in isolation, independent of other things. Rather, they occur in predictable and consistent combinations. Habituation processes are not sufficient to allow an organism to take advantage of predictable relationships between stimuli in the environment and adjust their behavior accordingly.

Cause and effect relationships in the world ensure that certain things occur in combination with others. Your car's engine does not run unless the ignition has been turned on; you cannot walk through a doorway unless the door is open; it does not rain unless there are clouds in the sky. Social institutions and customs also ensure that events occur in a predictable order. Classes are scheduled at predictable times; people are better dressed at church than at a public park; you can predict whether someone will engage you in conversation by the way the person greets you. Learning to predict events in the environment and learning what stimuli tend to occur together are important ways in which behavior becomes better coordinated with the environment. Imagine how much trouble you would have if you could never predict how long something would take to cook, when stores would be open, or whether your door key would work to unlock your apartment.

The simplest mechanism whereby organisms learn about relations between stimuli and come to alter their behavior accordingly is classical conditioning. Classical conditioning enables animals to take advantage of the orderly sequence of events in the environment and learn which stimuli tend to go with which events. On the basis of this learning, animals come to make new responses to stimuli. For example, classical conditioning is the process whereby animals learn to approach signals for food and to salivate when they are about to be fed. It is also integrally involved in the learning of emotional reactions such as fear and pleasure to stimuli that initially do not elicit these emotions.

THE EARLY YEARS OF CLASSICAL CONDITIONING

Systematic studies of classical conditioning began with the work of the great Russian physiologist Ivan P. Pavlov (see Box 3.1). Classical conditioning was independently discovered by Edwin B. Twitmyer. In a Ph.D. dissertation submitted to the University of Pennsylvania in 1902 (see Twitmyer, 1974), Twitmyer repeatedly tested the knee-jerk reflex of college students by sounding a bell .5 seconds before hitting their patellar tendon. After several trials of this sort, the bell was sufficient to elicit the reflex in some of the students. However, Twitmyer did not develop the implications of his discoveries, and his findings were ignored for many years.

Pavlov's studies of classical conditioning were an extension of his research on the processes of digestion. Pavlov made major advances in the study of digestion by developing surgical techniques that enabled dogs to survive for many years with artificial tubes or fistulae that permitted the collection of digestive juices. With the use of a stomach fistula, for example, Pavlov was able to collect stomach secretions in dogs

Figure 3.1 Diagram of the Pavlovian salivary conditioning preparation. A cannula attached to the animal's salivary duct conducts drops of saliva to a data-recording device. (From "The Method of Pavlov in Animal Psychology," by R. M. Yerkes and S. Morgulis, *Psychological Bulletin*, 1909, *6, 257–273*.)

that otherwise lived normally. Technicians in the laboratory soon discovered that the dogs would secrete stomach juices in response to the sight of food, or even just upon seeing the person who usually fed them. The laboratory produced considerable quantities of stomach juice in this manner and sold the excess to the general public. The popularity of this juice as a remedy for various stomach ailments supplemented the income of the laboratory for several years.

Assistants in the laboratory referred to stomach secretions elicited by food-related stimuli as "psychic secretions" because they seemed to be a response to the expectation or thought of food. However, for many years the phenomenon of psychic secretions generated little scientific interest.

The Discoveries of Wolfsohn and Snarsky

The first systematic studies of classical conditioning were performed by Stefan Wolfsohn and Anton Snarsky in Pavlov's laboratory (Boakes, 1984). Both of these students focused on the salivary glands, which are the first digestive glands involved in the breakdown of food. Some of the salivary glands are rather large and have ducts that are accessible and can be easily externalized with a fistula (see Figure 3.1). Wolfsohn studied salivary responses to various substances placed in the mouth: dry food, wet food, sour water, and sand, for example. After the dogs had experienced these substances placed in the mouth, the mere sight of the substances was enough to make them salivate.

Whereas Wolfsohn used naturally occurring substances in his studies, Snarsky extended these observations to artificial substances. In one experiment, for example, Snarsky first gave his dogs sour water (such as strong lemon juice) that was artificially colored black. After eliciting salivation with black sour water, Snarsky found that the dogs would also salivate to plain black water or to the sight of a bottle containing a black liquid.

The substances tested by Wolfsohn and Snarsky had both visual and orosensory stimulus features. *Orosensory stimuli* are the sensations of taste and texture that are

IVAN P. PAVLOV: BIOGRAPHICAL SKETCH

Born in 1849 into the family of a priest in Russia, Pavlov dedicated his life to scholarship and discovery. He received his early education in a local theological seminary and planned a career of religious service. However, his interests soon changed, and when he was 21 he entered the university in St. Petersburg, where his studies focused on chemistry and animal physiology. After obtaining the equivalent of a bachelor's degree, he went to the Imperial Medico-Surgical Academy in 1875 to further his education in physiology. Eight years later, he received his doctoral degree for his research on the efferent nerves of the heart and then began investigating various aspects of digestive physiology. In 1888 he discovered the nerves that stimulate the digestive secretions of the pancreas—

a finding that initiated a series of experiments for which Pavlov was awarded the Nobel Prize in Physiology in 1904.

Pavlov did a great deal of original research while a graduate student, as well as after obtaining his doctoral degree. However, he did not have a faculty position or his own laboratory until 1890, when he was appointed professor of pharmacology at the St. Petersburg Military Medical Academy. In 1895 he became professor of physiology at the same institution. Pavlov remained active in the laboratory until close to his death in 1936. In fact, much of the research for which he is famous today was performed after he received the Nobel Prize.

produced when something is placed in the mouth. The first time sand was placed in a dog's mouth, only the sensations it produced in the mouth elicited salivation. However, after sand had been placed in the mouth several times, the sight of sand (its visual features) also came to elicit salivation. Presumably the dog learned to associate the visual features of the sand with its orosensory features. Such learning is referred to as **object learning** because it involves associating different features of the same object.

To study the mechanisms of associative learning, the stimuli to be associated have to be manipulated independently of one another. This is difficult to do when the two stimuli are properties of the same object. Therefore, in later studies of conditioning, Pavlov used procedures in which the stimuli to be associated came from different sources.

The Classical Conditioning Paradigm

Pavlov's basic procedure for the study of conditioned salivation is familiar. The procedure involved two stimuli. One of these was a tone or a light. On its first presentation, this stimulus might have elicited an orienting response, but it did not elicit salivation. The other stimulus was food or the taste of a sour solution placed in the mouth. In contrast to the first stimulus, this second one elicited vigorous salivation, even the first time it was presented.

Pavlov referred to the tone or light as the **conditional stimulus** because the effectiveness of this stimulus in eliciting salivation depended on (was conditional on) pairing it several times with the presentation of food. By contrast, the food or sour-taste stimulus was called the **unconditional stimulus** because its effectiveness in eliciting salivation was not dependent on any prior training. The salivation that eventually came to be elicited by the tone or light was called the **conditional response,** and the salivation that was always elicited by the food or sour taste was called the **unconditional response.** Thus, stimuli and responses whose properties and occurrence did not depend on prior training were called "unconditional," and stimuli and responses whose properties and occurrence depended on special training were called "conditional."

In the first English translation of Pavlov's writings, the term uncondition*al* was erroneously translated as uncondition*ed,* and the term condition*al* was translated as condition*ed.* The "ed" suffix was used exclusively in English writings for many years. However, the term condition*ed* does not capture Pavlov's original meaning of "dependent on" as well as the term condition*al* (Gantt, 1966). The words conditional and unconditional are more common in modern writings on classical conditioning and are now used interchangeably with conditioned and unconditioned.

Because the terms conditioned (and unconditioned) stimulus and conditioned (and unconditioned) response are used frequently in discussions of classical conditioning, they are often abbreviated. Conditioned stimulus and conditioned response are abbreviated **CS** and **CR,** respectively. Unconditioned stimulus and unconditioned response are abbreviated **US** and **UR,** respectively.

EXPERIMENTAL SITUATIONS

Classical conditioning has been investigated in a variety of situations involving many different species (see Turkkan, 1989). Pavlov did most of his experiments with dogs using the salivary fistula technique. Most contemporary experiments on Pavlovian conditioning are carried out with domesticated rats, rabbits, and pigeons using procedures developed by North American scientists during the second half of the twentieth century.

Sign Tracking

Pavlov's research concentrated on salivation and other highly reflexive responses and encouraged the belief that classical conditioning occurs only in reflex response systems. In recent years, however, such a restrictive view of Pavlovian conditioning has been abandoned (for example, Rescorla, 1988b). One experimental paradigm that has contributed significantly to modern conceptions of Pavlovian conditioning is called **sign tracking** or **autoshaping** (Hearst, 1975; Hearst & Jenkins, 1974; Locurto, Terrace, & Gibbon, 1981).

Animals tend to approach and contact stimuli that signal the availability of food. In the natural environment, the availability of food is usually indicated by a feature of the food (its odor, perhaps) that is apparent at a distance. By approaching and contacting these stimuli, animals end up in contact with the food. For a predator, for example, the sight, movements, odor, and perhaps noises of the prey are cues indicating the possibility of a meal. By tracking these stimuli, the predator is likely to catch its prey.

Sign tracking is investigated in the laboratory by presenting a discrete, localized visual stimulus just before each delivery of a small amount of food. The first experiment of this sort was performed by Brown and Jenkins (1968) with pigeons. The animals were placed in an experimental chamber that had a small circular key that could be illuminated and that the pigeons could peck. Periodically, the birds were given access to food for a few seconds. The key light was illuminated for 8 seconds immediately before each food delivery.

The pigeons did not have to do anything for the food to be presented. The food was automatically delivered after each illumination of the response key no matter what the animals did. Since the birds were hungry, it would seem that when they saw the key light, they would go to the food dish and wait for the forthcoming food presentation. Interestingly, however, that is not what happened. Instead of using the key light as a guide to when they would go to the food dish, the pigeons started pecking the key itself. This behavior was remarkable because it was not required in order for the pigeon to gain access to the food.

Many experiments have been done on the sign tracking phenomenon using a variety of species, including chicks, quail, goldfish, lizards, rats, rhesus monkeys, squirrel monkeys, and human adults and children. (For a recent review, see Tomie, Brooks, & Zito, 1989.) These experiments have shown that sign tracking is a useful technique for the investigation of how associations between one stimulus and another are learned. In pigeon sign tracking experiments, the *conditioned stimulus* is an illuminated response key, and the *unconditioned stimulus* is a presentation of food. Learning proceeds most rapidly when the CS is presented just before the US. Pigeons do not come to approach and peck the CS if the CS and US are presented at random times in relation to each other (Gamzu & Williams, 1971, 1973).

The tracking of signals for food is dramatically illustrated by instances in which the signal is located far away from the food cup. In one such experiment (see Hearst & Jenkins, 1974), pigeons were placed in a 6-foot (182-cm) alley that had a food dish in the middle (see Figure 3.2). Each end of the alley had a circular disk or response key. Presentation of food was always preceded by illumination of the key at one end of the alley. The key light at the opposite end was uncorrelated with food. One other aspect of the experiment is important to point out. The food was available for only 4 seconds each time. Therefore, if the animal did not reach the food cup within 4 seconds, it did not get any food on that trial.

As conditioning progressed, the pigeons started behaving in a most remarkable manner. As soon as the light came on signaling food, they would run to that end of the alley, peck the key, and then run to the center of the alley to get the food. Because the alley was very long, the pigeons did not always get to the food dish before the food was removed. The sign tracking behavior was amazing because it was entirely unnecessary. The animals did not have to peck the key light to get the food US. They could have just stayed in the middle of the alley and waited for the food. The fact that they approached the key light is evidence of the compelling attraction of classically conditioned signals for food. By contrast, the pigeons did not consistently approach the light at the other end of the box, which was uncorrelated with food presentations (for a similar study in sexual conditioning, see Burns & Domjan, 1996).

Sign tracking is possible only when the conditioned stimulus is localized and therefore can be approached and "tracked." In one study, diffuse spatial and contextual cues of the chamber in which pigeons were given food periodically served as the conditioned stimulus. This time the learning of an association was evident in an

Key light signaling food

Food dish

Key light uncorrelated with food

Figure 3.2 The "long box" used in the sign tracking experiment with pigeons by Jenkins. The conditioned stimulus was illumination of the key light at one end of the experimental chamber. Food was delivered in the middle of the chamber. (Based on Jenkins, personal communication, 1980.)

increase in activity, rather than in a specific approach response (Rescorla, Durlach, & Grau, 1985). In another experiment (conducted with laboratory rats), a localized light and a sound were compared as conditioned stimuli for food (Cleland & Davey, 1983). Only the light stimulated conditioned approach or sign tracking behavior. The conditioned sound stimulus elicited approach to the food cup rather than approach to the sound source. These experiments illustrate that for sign tracking to occur, the conditioned stimulus has to be of the proper modality and configuration.

Fear Conditioning

Classical conditioning is also involved in the learning of emotional responses. One area of special interest is the acquisition of fear. Laboratory studies of fear conditioning typically are conducted with rats. The aversive unconditioned stimulus is a brief electrical current delivered to the rats' feet through a metal grid floor. The brief shock is probably aversive primarily because it is startling—unlike anything the animal has encountered before. The CS may be a tone or a light. Unlike sign tracking, which is recorded by measuring directly the approach and contact with the CS, conditioned fear is measured indirectly by measuring how the CS disrupts the animal's ongoing activity.

A popular technique for indirect measurement of conditioned fear is called the **conditioned emotional response,** or **conditioned suppression,** procedure (abbreviated CER). The CER procedure was devised by Estes and Skinner (1941) and has since been used extensively in the study of Pavlovian conditioning (Kamin, 1965). Rats are first trained to press a response lever for food reward in a small experimental chamber (see Figure 3.3A). Food is provided for every few lever presses. After sufficient training, the rats press the lever at a steady rate. The classical conditioning phase of the experiment is then introduced. During each conditioning trial, the CS is presented for 1 or 2 minutes, followed immediately by brief exposure to the shock US. Trials are scheduled 15–30 minutes apart.

The acquisition of fear to the CS results in disruption of the food-rewarded lever press response. After several pairings of the CS with shock, the animals suppress their lever pressing when the CS appears. Within 3–5 conditioning trials, the conditioned

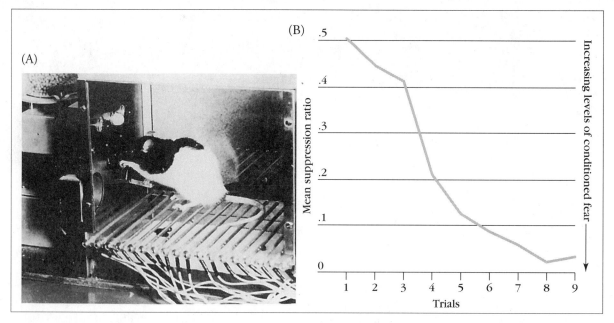

(B)

Mean suppression ratio

Increasing levels of conditioned fear →

Trials

Figure 3.3 (A) A rat pressing a response lever for food reward in a conditioned suppression experiment. (B) Sample results of a conditioned suppression experiment with rats (from Domjan, unpublished). Three conditioning trials were conducted on each of 3 days of training. The CS was an audiovisual stimulus, and the US was a brief shock through the grid floor. A suppression ratio of .5 indicates that the participants did not suppress their lever pressing during the CS. A suppression ratio of 0 indicates total suppression of responding during the CS.

suppression may be complete (Kamin & Brimer, 1963), with the rats not pressing the lever at all during the CS. However, the suppression is specific to the CS. Soon after the CS is turned off, the animals resume their food-rewarded behavior.

The suppression of lever pressing in the CER procedure occurs in part because becoming motionless (or freezing) is one of the innate reactions of rats to fearful and aversive stimuli (Bolles, 1970). Rats cannot press the lever when they freeze due to fear. This makes the CER procedure useful for measuring response suppression induced by fear (Bouton & Bolles, 1980; Mast, Blanchard, & Blanchard, 1982; for additional factors involved in conditioned suppression, see Bevins & Ayres, 1994).

Conditioned suppression is measured quantitatively with the use of a ratio. The ratio compares the number of lever presses that occur during the CS with the number that occur during a comparable baseline period before the CS is presented (the pre-CS period). The specific formula is as follows:

Suppression Ratio = CS responding ÷ (CS responding + pre-CS responding)

The *suppression ratio* has a value of 0 if the rat suppresses lever pressing completely during the CS, because in this case the numerator of the formula is 0. At the other extreme, if the rat does not alter its rate of lever pressing at all when the CS is presented, the ratio has a value of .5. For example, let us assume that the CS is presented for 3 minutes and that in a typical 3-minute period the rat makes 45 responses. If the CS does not disrupt lever pressing, the animal will make 45 responses during the CS so that the numerator of the ratio will be 45. The denominator will be 45 (CS responses) + 45 (pre-CS responses), or 90. Therefore, the ratio will be 45 ÷ 90 or .5. Decreasing values of the ratio from .5 to 0 indicate greater response suppression, or conditioned fear.

Figure 3.3B shows sample results of a conditioned suppression experiment with rats. Three conditioning trials were conducted on each of 3 days of training. Very little suppression occurred the first time the CS was presented, and not much acquisition of suppression was evident during the first day of training. However, a substantial increase in suppression occurred from the last trial on Day 1 (Trial 3) to the first trial on Day 2 (Trial 4). With continued training, responding gradually became more and more suppressed, until the animals hardly ever pressed the response lever when the CS was presented.

Interpreting conditioned suppression data can be confusing because the scale is inverse. Greater levels of conditioned fear are evident in lower values of the suppression ratio. It is important to keep this in mind. The smaller the suppression ratio, the more motionless is the animal, presumably because the CS elicits more conditioned fear.

Eyeblink Conditioning

The eyeblink reflex is a discrete reflex, much like the patellar knee-jerk response. It is an early component of the startle response and occurs in a variety of species. Getting a person to blink, for example, only requires clapping your hands near his eyes or blowing a puff of air through a straw directed toward his eyes. If the air puff is preceded by a brief tone, the person is likely to learn to blink when the tone comes on, in anticipation of the puff.

Eyeblink conditioning has been the subject of extensive investigation in people, and it is useful in studying learning in both infants and the elderly (Durkin, Prescott, Furchtgott, Cantor, & Powell, 1993; Little, Lipsitt, & Rovee-Collier, 1984). However, in contemporary research eyeblink conditioning is frequently conducted with albino laboratory rabbits that provide a convenient preparation for the study of the neurophysiology of learning.

The rabbit eyeblink preparation was developed by I. Gormezano (see Gormezano, 1966; Gormezano, Kehoe, & Marshall, 1983). Domesticated albino rabbits are typically used. Gormezano focused on the eyeblink response because in the absence of special training, rabbits rarely blink. Therefore, if a rabbit blinks after the presentation of a stimulus, it is pretty certain that the response was elicited by that stimulus.

Domesticated rabbits are sedentary and tend to sit in one place, even if they are not restrained. In an eyeblink conditioning experiment, the rabbit is placed in a small enclosure and attached to equipment that enables measurement of the blink response. The US to elicit blinking is provided by a small puff of air or mild irritation of the skin below the eye with a brief (.1-second) pulse of electrical current. The CS may be a light, a tone, or mild vibration of the animal's abdomen.

I. Gormezano

In the typical conditioning experiment, the CS is presented for half a second and is followed immediately by delivery of the US, which elicits a rapid and vigorous eyelid closure. As the CS is repeatedly paired with the US, the eyeblink response also comes to be made to the CS. Investigators record the percentage of trials in which a conditioned blink response is observed.

Eyeblink conditioning is a relatively slow process, and even after extensive training conditioned responding does not occur on every trial. Figure 3.4 shows a typical learning curve for eyeblink conditioning for a group of 12 rabbits. The animals received 82 conditioning trials each day. By the eighth day of training (656 trials), conditioned responses occurred on about 70% of the trials. Control groups in such experiments, which do not receive the CS paired with the US, typically blink on fewer than 5% of the trials.

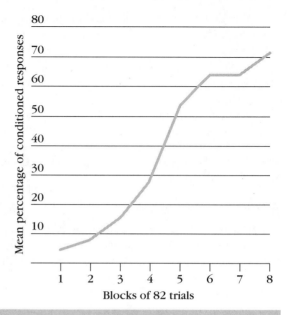

Figure 3.4 A typical learning curve for eyeblink conditioning. (From "Acquisition and Extinction of the Classically Conditioned Eyelid Response in the Albino Rabbit," by N. Schneiderman, I. Fuentes, and I. Gormezano, *Science,* 1962, *136,* 650–652. Copyright © 1962 by the American Association for the Advancement of Science. Reprinted by permission.)

Taste Aversion Learning

Another popular procedure for investigating classical conditioning involves taste aversion learning (see Barker, Best, & Domjan, 1977; Braveman & Bronstein, 1985). The taste aversion conditioning technique takes advantage of an important form of learning that is involved in how animals (and people) select what to eat. Most things in the environment are inedible; eating them results in illness, if not death. One of the ways in which animals manage to select safe foods is to learn to avoid poisonous ones. Given the importance of poison avoidance learning for survival, it is not surprising that such learning can occur in a single trial.

In learning to avoid a poisonous food, the animal learns to associate the taste and/or smell of the food with its ill effects. Then it can avoid the food just by smelling or tasting it. Thus, poison avoidance learning is an instance of object learning in that the source of the conditioned and unconditioned stimuli is the same object. I previously discussed object learning in connection with Wolfsohn's pioneering study of conditioned salivation in which dogs became conditioned to the sight of sand. For increased analytical power, subsequent studies in Pavlov's laboratory employed conditioned and unconditioned stimuli that originated from different sources. For the same reason, investigators of poison avoidance learning have developed procedures that permit presenting taste or odor stimuli independent of the source of the illness that serves as the US.

In taste aversion conditioning, animals are given a flavored solution to drink and are then made to feel sick by the injection of a drug or exposure to radiation. As a result of the illness after the taste exposure, the animals acquire an aversion to the taste. Their ingestion of the taste solution is suppressed by the conditioning procedure.

Taste aversion learning is a result of the pairing of a CS (in this case a taste) and a US (drug injection or radiation exposure) in much the same manner as in other examples of classical conditioning; it follows standard rules of learning in many respects (for example, Domjan, 1980, 1983). However, it also has some special features. First, strong taste aversions can be learned with just one pairing of the flavor and illness. Although one-trial learning also occurs in fear conditioning, such rapid learning is rarely, if ever, observed in eyeblink conditioning, salivary conditioning, or sign tracking.

The second unique feature of taste aversion learning is that it occurs even if the animals do not get sick until several hours after exposure to the novel taste (Garcia, Ervin, & Koelling, 1966; Revusky & Garcia, 1970). Toxic materials in food often do not have their bad effects until the food has been digested, absorbed in the bloodstream, and distributed to various body tissues. This process takes time. *Long-delay learning* of taste aversions probably evolved to enable animals to avoid poisonous foods that have delayed ill effects.

A dramatic example of long-delay, taste aversion learning was provided by an experiment by Smith and Roll (1967). Laboratory rats were first adapted to a water deprivation schedule so that they would readily drink when a water bottle was placed on their cage. On the conditioning day, the rats were given a novel (.1% saccharin) solution to drink for 20 minutes. At various times after the saccharin presentation, ranging from 0 to 24 hours, different groups of rats were exposed to radiation from an X-ray machine. Control groups of rats were also taken to the X-ray machine but were not irradiated. They were called the "sham-irradiated" groups. Starting a day after the radiation or sham treatment, each rat was given a choice of saccharin solution or plain water to drink for 2 days.

J. Garcia

The preference of each group of animals for the saccharin solution is shown in Figure 3.5. Animals exposed to radiation within 6 hours after tasting the saccharin solution showed a profound aversion to the saccharin flavor in the postconditioning test. They drank less than 20% of their total fluid intake from the saccharin drinking tube. Much less of an aversion was evident in animals irradiated 12 hours after the saccharin exposure, and hardly any aversion was observed in rats irradiated 24 hours after the taste exposure. In contrast to this gradient of saccharin avoidance observed in the irradiated rats, all the sham-irradiated groups strongly preferred the saccharin solution. They drank more than 70% of their total fluid intake from the saccharin drinking tube.

EXCITATORY PAVLOVIAN CONDITIONING

During excitatory conditioning, organisms learn an association between the conditioned and unconditioned stimuli. As a result of this association, presentation of the CS activates processes related to the US—in the absence of the actual presentation of the US. These US-related processes are responsible for the conditioned responses that are observed. Thus, dogs come to salivate in response to the sight of sand or black water, pigeons learn to approach and peck a key light that was followed by food, rats learn to freeze to a sound that preceded footshock, rabbits learn to blink in response to a tone that preceded a puff of air, and rats learn to avoid drinking saccharin that was followed by illness. In all these cases, the CS comes to activate behavior related to the associated US.

Common Pavlovian Conditioning Procedures

One of the critical factors that determines the course of classical conditioning in each of the situations I have described is the relative timing of the CS and the US.

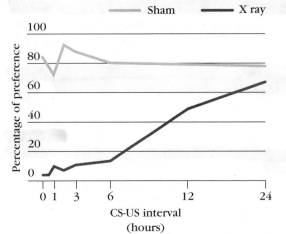

Figure 3.5 Mean percent preference for the CS flavor during a test session conducted after the CS flavor was paired with X irradiation (the US) or sham exposure. Percent preference is the percentage of a participant's total fluid intake (saccharin solution plus water) that consisted of the saccharin solution. During conditioning, the interval between exposure to the CS and the US ranged from 0 to 24 hours for different groups of rats. (From "Trace Conditioning with X-rays as an Aversive Stimulus," by J. C. Smith and D. L. Roll, *Psychonomic Science,* 1967, *9,* 11–12. Copyright © 1967 by Psychonomic Society. Reprinted by permission.)

Seemingly small and trivial variations in how a CS is paired with a US can have profound effects on the rate and extent of classical conditioning.

Five common classical conditioning procedures are illustrated by the diagrams in Figure 3.6. The horizontal distance in each diagram represents the passage of time; vertical displacements represent when a stimulus begins and ends. Each configuration of CS and US represents a single **conditioning trial.**

In a typical classical conditioning experiment, CS-US episodes are repeated in one or more *training sessions.* The time from the end of one conditioning trial to the start of the next trial is called the **intertrial interval.** By contrast, the time from the start of the CS to the start of the US during a conditioning trial is called the **interstimulus interval** or **CS-US interval.** The interstimulus interval is always much shorter than the intertrial interval. In many experiments the interstimulus interval is less than 1 minute, whereas the intertrial interval may be 5 minutes or more. (A more detailed discussion of these parameters is provided in Chapter 4.)

1. *Short-delayed conditioning.* The most frequently used procedure for Pavlovian conditioning involves delaying the start of the US slightly after the start of the CS on each trial. This procedure is called **short-delayed conditioning.** The critical feature of short-delayed conditioning is that the CS starts each trial, and the US is presented after a brief (less than 1-minute) delay. The CS may continue during the US or end as soon as the US starts.

2. *Trace conditioning.* The **trace conditioning** procedure is similar to the short-delayed procedure in that the US occurs after the CS. However, in trace conditioning

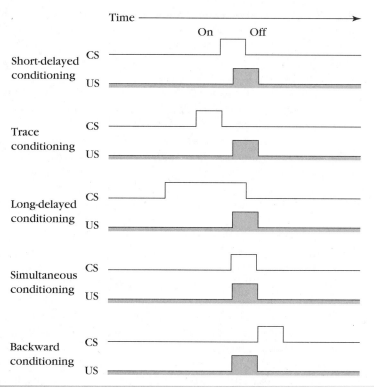

Figure 3.6 Five common classical conditioning procedures.

the US is not presented until some time after the CS has ended. This leaves a gap between the CS and US. The gap is called the **trace interval.**

3. *Long-delayed conditioning.* The long-delayed conditioning procedure is also similar to the short-delayed conditioning in that the US is delayed until after the start of the CS. However, in this case the US is delayed much longer (5–10 minutes) than in the short-delay procedure. There is no trace interval. The CS remains until the US occurs.

4. *Simultaneous conditioning.* Perhaps the most obvious way to expose subjects to a CS in conjunction with a US is to present the two stimuli at the same time. This procedure is called **simultaneous conditioning.** The critical feature of simultaneous conditioning is that the conditioned and unconditioned stimuli are presented concurrently.

5. *Backward conditioning.* The last procedure depicted in Figure 3.6 differs from the others in that the US occurs shortly before, rather than after, the CS. This technique is called **backward conditioning** because the CS and US are presented in a "backward" order compared to the other procedures.

Measurement of Conditioned Responses

Pavlov and others after him have conducted systematic investigations of procedures like those depicted in Figure 3.6 to find out how the conditioning of a CS depends on the temporal relation between CS and US presentations. To make comparisons among the various procedures, the investigator must use a method for measuring conditioning that is equally applicable to all the procedures. This is typically done with the use of a **test trial.** A test trial consists of presenting the CS by itself (without the US). Responses elicited by the CS can then be observed without contamination from responses elicited by the US. Such CS-alone test trials can be introduced periodically during the course of training to track the progress of learning.

Behavior during presentation of the CS can be quantified in several ways. One aspect of conditioned behavior is how much of it occurs. This is called the **magnitude of the conditioned response.** Pavlov, for example, measured the number of drops of saliva that were elicited by a CS. Other examples of the magnitude of CRs are the degree of response suppression that occurs in the CER procedure (see Figure 3.3) and the degree of preference for a flavored solution that is observed in taste aversion learning (see Figure 3.5).

The vigor of responding can be also measured by how often the CS elicits a CR. For example, the percentage of trials on which a CR is elicited by the CS can be measured. This measure is frequently used in studies of eyeblink conditioning (see Figure 3.4) and reflects the likelihood or **probability of responding.**

A third aspect of conditioned responding is how soon the CR occurs after presentation of the CS. This measure of the vigor of conditioned behavior is called the **latency** of the CR, that is, the amount of time that elapses between the start of the CS and the occurrence of the CR.

In the delayed and trace conditioning procedures, the CS occurs by itself at the start of each trial (see Figure 3.6). Any conditioned behavior that occurs during these initial CS-alone periods is uncontaminated by behavior elicited by the US and therefore can be used as a measure of learning. In contrast, responding on simultaneous and backward conditioning trials is bound to reflect the presence or recent presentation of the US. Therefore, test trials are critical for assessing learning in simultaneous and backward conditioning.

Control Procedures for Classical Conditioning

Devising an effective test trial is not enough to obtain conclusive evidence of classical conditioning. As I noted in Chapter 1, learning is an inference about the causes of behavior based on a comparison of at least two conditions. To be certain that a conditioning procedure is responsible for certain changes in behavior, those changes must be compared to the effects of a control procedure. What should the control procedure be? In studies of habituation and sensitization, only the effects of prior exposure to a stimulus were of interest. Therefore, the comparison or control procedure was rather simple: it consisted of no prior stimulus exposure. In studies of classical conditioning, interest is in how conditioned and unconditioned stimuli become associated. This is a more complicated issue. Hence, more complicated control procedures are required.

An association between a CS and a US implies that the two events have become connected in some way. After an association has been established, the CS can activate processes related to the US. An association requires more than just familiarity with the CS and US. It presumably depends on having the two stimuli experienced in connection with each other. Therefore, to conclude that an association has been established, the investigator must make sure that any observed change in behavior could not have been produced by prior separate presentations of the CS or the US.

As we saw in the discussion of sensitization in Chapter 2, presentations of an arousing stimulus such as food to a hungry animal can increase the behavior elicited by a more innocuous stimulus such as a tone without an association having been established between the two stimuli. (Recall, for example, the phenomenon of dis-habituation, discussed under "Characteristics of Habituation and Sensitization" in Chapter 2.) Therefore, increases in responding observed with repeated CS-US pairings can sometimes result from exposure just to the US. Instances in which exposure to the US alone produces responses like the CR are called **pseudo-conditioning.** Control procedures are required to determine whether responses that develop to the CS represent an association between the CS and US rather than pseudo-conditioning or sensitization effects of exposure to the conditioned and unconditioned stimuli.

Investigators have debated at great length about the proper control procedure for classical conditioning. Ideally, a control procedure for the learning of an association would involve the same number and distribution of CS and US presentations as the experimental procedure but with the CSs and USs arranged so that they would not become associated. One possibility involves presenting the conditioned and the unconditioned stimuli in a random order with respect to each other (Rescorla, 1967b). This is called the **random control** procedure. Unfortunately, evidence from a variety of sources indicates that the random control procedure can produce associative learning (see Papini & Bitterman, 1990.)

A more successful control procedure involves presenting the conditioned and unconditioned stimuli on separate trials. Such a procedure is called the **explicitly unpaired control.** In the explicitly unpaired control, the CS and US are presented far enough apart to prevent their association. How much time has to elapse between them depends on the response system. In taste aversion learning, much longer separation is necessary between the CS and US than in other forms of conditioning. In one variation of the explicitly unpaired control, only CSs are presented during one session, and only USs are presented during a second session. (For a further discussion of control methodology, see Gormezano et al., 1983.)

Effectiveness of Common Conditioning Procedures

Using test trials and measures of response latency, magnitude, or probability, the effectiveness of the various procedures depicted in Figure 3.6 can be compared. Rarely have all five procedures been compared in the same experiment. Furthermore, the results of the comparisons that have been performed sometimes differ depending on the type of behavior that is conditioned. However, some generalizations can be made on the basis of the available evidence.

Short-Delayed Conditioning.   In many situations, the short-delayed conditioning procedure is most effective in producing behavioral evidence of learning. As I noted earlier, the interval between the start of the CS and the start of the US is called the interstimulus or CS-US interval. Generally, an increase in the CS-US interval facilitates conditioned responding up to a point. Beyond this optimal point, further increases in the CS-US interval produce a decline in conditioned responding (for example, Ost & Lauer, 1965; Schneiderman & Gormezano, 1964).

Trace Conditioning.   In each trial of the short-delayed procedure, the CS starts just before the US and persists until the US occurs. The trace conditioning procedure is similar in that here the CS also starts shortly before the US (see Figure 3.6). However, in the trace procedure the CS is terminated for a short time before the US occurs. As with delayed conditioning, less conditioned responding is evident with the trace procedure if the interval between the CS and US is increased (Kehoe, Cool, & Gormezano, 1991). In addition, whether there is a trace interval between the CS and the US has a significant effect on learning. The trace procedure is often less effective than the delayed procedure in producing excitatory conditioning (for example, Ellison, 1964; Kamin, 1965). Furthermore, under certain circumstances the trace procedure results in inhibition rather than excitation of the conditioned response (Hinson & Siegel,1980; Kaplan, 1984).

Because the CS ends before the start of the US in a trace conditioning procedure, the best predictor of the US is the gap between the CS and the US. During this gap, just the background contextual cues of the experimental chamber are present. Perhaps not surprisingly, organisms come to associate those background cues with the US (Marlin, 1981). Interestingly, trace conditioning of the CS is facilitated when the gap between the CS and US is filled with another stimulus—a gap filler (Kaplan & Hearst, 1982; Rescorla, 1982a). A gap filler may facilitate conditioning by making the CS more memorable (Thomas, Robertson, & Lieberman, 1990).

Long-Delayed Conditioning. Conditioning with a long CS-US interval is generally not effective. However, there are some exceptions. One of these is taste aversion learning. As we have seen, taste aversion learning is possible with delays of several hours between exposure to a flavor and subsequent illness (see Figure 3.5).

Pavlov also investigated learning in a long-delayed conditioning procedure, but he used much more extensive training than is common in taste aversion learning. With continued training he discovered an unusual effect that he called **inhibition of delay**. Pavlov observed that during early stages of learning, his dogs started salivating shortly after the CS was presented. However, with continued CS-US pairings, the dogs appeared to learn that the US does not occur for some time after the beginning of the CS. As they learned the delayed timing of the US, they began to delay their conditioned responding to better coincide with the delivery of the US (see Figure 3.7). Inhibition of delay refers to this delay of conditioned responding to the end of the CS-US interval. The phenomenon has been observed in salivary conditioning and fear conditioning (for example, Pavlov, 1927; Rescorla, 1967a; Williams, 1965) and also appears to occur in sign tracking with a sexual US (Burns & Domjan, 1996).

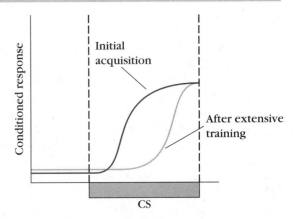

Figure 3.7 Comparison of conditioned responding during initial acquisition and after extensive training in a delayed conditioning procedure. With extensive training, there is an increase in the latency of the conditioned response. This phenomenon is called *inhibition of delay.* (Hypothetical data.)

Simultaneous Conditioning. Simultaneous conditioning procedures have produced puzzling results. Since Aristotle, philosophers have assumed that associations are formed largely based on the closeness or *contiguity* between stimuli. This assumption suggests that simultaneous presentations of a CS and a US should be especially effective in producing conditioned responding. Contrary to this prediction, some investigators have found that simultaneous conditioning is not as effective in generating conditioned responding as a short-delayed conditioning procedure (Heth & Rescorla, 1973; Schafe, Sollars, & Bernstein, 1995), and in many experiments no conditioned responding at all has been observed following simultaneous conditioning (for example, Bitterman, 1964; Smith, Coleman, & Gormezano, 1969). However, these results appear to reflect a failure of performance rather than a failure of learning.

As I will describe in Chapter 4, conditioned responding reflects an organism's anticipation of the US. Since the CS and US are presented at the same time in a simultaneous procedure, conditioned anticipatory behavior does not occur. However, tests that do not depend on anticipatory behavior (such as second-order conditioning, see Chapter 4) reveal good evidence of learning after simultaneous conditioning (Barnet, Arnold, & Miller, 1991; Matzel, Held, & Miller, 1988; Rescorla, 1980b).

Backward Conditioning. Like simultaneous conditioning, backward conditioning has produced mixed results. Some investigators have reported excitatory associations produced by backward pairings of a CS and US (for example, Ayres, Haddad, & Albert, 1987; Hearst, 1989; Shurtleff & Ayres, 1981; Spetch, Wilkie, & Pinel, 1981). Others have reported primarily inhibition of conditioned responding as a result of backward conditioning (for example, Maier, Rapaport, & Wheatley, 1976; Siegel & Domjan, 1971). To make matters even more confusing, in a rather remarkable experiment Tait and Saladin (1986) reported both excitatory and inhibitory conditioning effects resulting from the same backward conditioning procedure.

The factors that determine the outcome of backward conditioning remain poorly understood. The results appear to be influenced by the number of conditioning trials that are conducted (Heth, 1976); the nature of the presentations of the US—signaled or unsignaled (Dolan, Shishimi, & Wagner, 1985; Williams & Overmier, 1988a); the interval between trials (Williams & Overmier, 1988); and the assessment procedure used to evaluate learning (Tait & Saladin, 1986). These various outcomes illustrate the complexities of conditioning processes and may be best understood by assuming that unconditioned stimuli have multiple effects. Different aspects of the US may be captured by different conditioning parameters and test procedures. (I will have more to say about this idea in Chapter 4 when I discuss the SOP and AESOP models of conditioning.)

INHIBITORY PAVLOVIAN CONDITIONING

When people mention Pavlovian conditioning, they are usually thinking about excitatory conditioning. However, an equally important aspect of Pavlovian conditioning is **inhibitory conditioning.** Much of learning may be viewed as involving regulatory processes—processes that regulate or control how an organism interacts with its environment (for example, Hollis, 1982). As we saw in Chapter 2, regulatory processes require two opposing mechanisms. We will encounter numerous examples of opposing mechanisms during the course of our study. In Chapter 2, I discussed habituation and sensitization, along with the opponent processes related to the regulation of emotional reactions. In Pavlovian conditioning, two opposing mechanisms are *conditioned excitation* and *conditioned inhibition.*

Opposing mechanisms are not necessarily symmetrical opposites of one another. Sensitization, for example, is not the symmetrical opposite of habituation. Sensitization is activated by different types of stimuli and involves different neural processes. Even so, the sensitization process can counteract the effects of the habituation process. In an analogous fashion, the *b* process in the opponent-process theory of motivation is not the symmetrical opposite of the *a* process. The *a* and *b* processes differ in their latency and duration, for example. Nevertheless, the *b* process can counteract the *a* process.

Like other opposing processes, Pavlovian conditioned inhibition is not the symmetrical opposite of conditioned excitation, but it serves to counteract conditioned excitation. Whereas an excitatory CS comes to activate behavior related to the US, an inhibitory CS comes to suppress or inhibit such behavior. This suppression is evident in decreased levels of excitatory conditioned responding. In fact, conditioned inhibition is typically measured indirectly by measuring the suppression of excitatory responding.

Although Pavlov discovered inhibitory conditioning early in the twentieth century, this type of learning did not command the serious attention of psychologists until the mid-1960s (Boakes & Halliday, 1972; Rescorla, 1969b). The concept of conditioned inhibition was ignored because investigators thought evidence for inhibitory processes could be explained in other ways (for a historical discussion, see Williams, Overmier, & LoLordo, 1992). In contrast to excitatory conditioning, conditioned inhibition remains a controversial topic (for example, Miller & Matzel, 1988; Papini & Bitterman, 1993). Nevertheless, a considerable body of research has addressed problems related to conditioned inhibition (for reviews, see Fowler, Lysle, & DeVito, 1991; Miller & Spear, 1985). Therefore, I will describe the major procedures used to produce conditioned inhibition and special tests that are necessary to detect and measure conditioned inhibition.

Procedures for Inhibitory Conditioning

Excitatory conditioning results from procedures in which the CS is paired with or presented just before the US. In contrast, in inhibitory conditioning procedures, the CS is presented in the absence of the US or signals that the US will not occur.

For the absence of the US to be a significant event, the US has to occur periodically in the situation. There are many signals for the absence of events in our daily lives. Signs such as "Closed," "Out of Order," and "No Entry" are all of this type. However, these signs provide meaningful information and influence behavior only if they indicate the absence of something that is otherwise expected. For example, upon encountering the sign "Out of Gas" at a service station people may become frustrated and disappointed; the sign provides important information here because service stations are expected to have gas. However, the same sign does not reveal anything of interest if it is in the window of a lumberyard, and it is not likely to discourage anyone from going to buy lumber.

The example I just described illustrates the general rule that inhibitory conditioning and inhibitory control of behavior occur only if there is an excitatory context for the US in question (for example, Baker & Baker, 1985; Fowler, Kleiman, & Lysle, 1985; LoLordo & Fairless, 1985). This principle makes inhibitory conditioning very

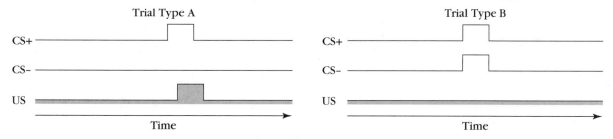

different from excitatory conditioning. Excitatory conditioning is not dependent on a special context in the same fashion.

Standard Procedure for Conditioned Inhibition.   Pavlov recognized the importance of an excitatory context for the conditioning of inhibition and was careful to provide such a context in his standard inhibitory training procedure (Pavlov, 1927). The procedure he used, diagrammed in Figure 3.8, involves two conditioned stimuli and two kinds of conditioning trials, one for excitatory conditioning and the other for inhibitory conditioning. The US is presented on excitatory conditioning trials (trial Type A in Figure 3.8), and whenever the US occurs, it is announced by the conditioned stimulus labeled CS+ (a tone, for example). Because of its pairings with the US, the CS+ becomes a signal for the US and can then provide the excitatory context for the development of conditioned inhibition.

During inhibitory conditioning trials (trial Type B in Figure 3.8), the CS+ is presented together with the second conditioned stimulus, the CS– (a light, for example), and the US does not occur. Thus, the CS– is presented in the excitatory context provided by the CS+, but the CS– is not paired with the US. This makes the CS– a conditioned inhibitor. During the course of training, trials with and without the US are alternated randomly. As the animal receives repeated trials of CS+ followed by the US and CS+/CS– followed by no US, the CS– gradually acquires inhibitory properties (Marchant, Mis, & Moore, 1972).

The standard conditioned inhibition procedure is analogous to a situation in which something is introduced that prevents an outcome that would occur otherwise. A red traffic light at a busy intersection is a signal (CS+) of potential danger (the US). However, if a police officer indicates that you should cross the intersection despite the red light (perhaps because the traffic lights are malfunctioning), you probably will not have an accident. The red light (CS+) together with the gestures of the officer (CS–) are not likely to be followed by danger. The gestures act like a CS– to inhibit, or block, your hesitation to cross the intersection because of the red light.

Differential Inhibition.   Another frequently used procedure for conditioning inhibition is called **differential inhibition**. This procedure is very similar to the standard procedure just described. As in the standard procedure, the US is presented on some trials, and its occurrence is always announced by the presentation of the CS+. On other trials the US does not occur, and the organism receives only the CS–. Thus, the differential inhibition procedure involves two types of trials: CS+ followed by the US and CS– followed by no US (see Figure 3.9). As in the standard procedure, the CS– becomes a conditioned inhibitory stimulus (for example, Rescorla & LoLordo, 1965).

The differential inhibition procedure is analogous to having two traffic lights at an intersection, one red and one green. The red light (CS+) signals danger (US) to

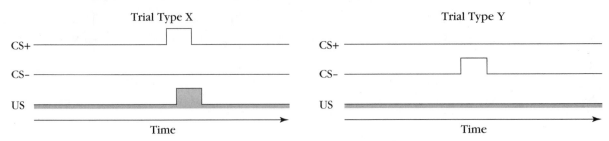

| Trial Type X | Trial Type Y |

Figure 3.9 Procedure for differential inhibition. On some trials (trial Type X), the CS+ is paired with the US. On other trials (trial Type Y), the CS– is presented alone. The procedure is effective in conditioning inhibitory properties to the CS–.

those crossing the intersection, whereas the green light (CS–) signals the absence of danger (no US). People crossing the intersection during the green light (CS–) can be reasonably confident that they will not be involved in an accident.

It is not obvious what provides the excitatory context for the conditioning of inhibition in the differential procedure. In contrast to the standard procedure, the CS+ is not presented on the CS– trials of the differential procedure. In fact, this is the main difference between the two procedures. As it turns out, contextual cues of the experimental situation provide the excitatory context (for example, Miller, Hallam, Hong, & Dufore, 1991). Because the US is presented periodically in the differential procedure, the stimuli of the experimental situation become associated with the US. As a consequence, the animal has some expectation of the US whenever it is in the experimental situation, and the contextual cues of the experimental situation provide the excitatory context for the learning of inhibition. If the contextual cues of the experimental situation do not become associated with the US for some reason, inhibitory properties will not become conditioned to the CS–. Therefore the differential procedure is not always as effective in producing conditioned inhibition as the standard procedure. (See LoLordo & Fairless, 1985, for an extensive discussion of this issue.)

R. A. Rescorla

Negative CS-US Contingency or Correlation. Conditioned inhibition can also result from procedures in which there is only one explicit conditioned stimulus, provided that this CS is negatively correlated with the US. A negative correlation or contingency means that the US is less likely to occur after the CS than at other times. Thus, the CS signals a reduction in the probability that the US will occur. A sample arrangement that meets this requirement is diagrammed in Figure 3.10. The US is periodically presented by itself. However, each occurrence of the CS is followed by the predictable absence of the US for awhile.

Consider a child who periodically gets picked on by his classmates when the teacher is out of the room. This is like periodically getting an aversive stimulus or US. When the teacher returns, the child can be sure he will not be bothered. Thus, the teacher serves as a CS– that signals a period free from harassment, or the absence of the US.

Conditioned inhibition is reliably observed in procedures in which the only explicit conditioned stimulus is negatively correlated with the US (Rescorla, 1969a). What provides the excitatory context for this inhibition? As with differential inhibition, the environmental cues of the experimental chamber provide the excitatory context (Dweck & Wagner, 1970). Because the US occurs periodically in the experimental situation, the contextual cues of the experimental chamber acquire excitatory properties. This in turn permits the acquisition of inhibitory properties to the CS.

Time

Measuring Conditioned Inhibition

How are conditioned inhibitory processes manifest in behavior? For conditioned excitation, the answer to the corresponding question is straightforward. Conditioned excitatory stimuli come to elicit responses related to the US that were not evident before. Conditioned excitatory stimuli come to elicit new responses such as salivation, approach, or eye blinking, depending on what the unconditioned stimulus is. Conditioned inhibitory stimuli might be expected to elicit the opposites of these reactions—namely, suppression of salivation, approach, or eye blinking. But how can these response opposites be measured?

Bidirectional Response Systems.   Identification of opposing response tendencies is easy with response systems that can change in opposite directions from baseline (normal) performance. This is characteristic of many physiological responses. Heart rate, respiration, and temperature, for example, can either increase or decrease from a baseline level. Certain behavioral responses are also bidirectional. For example, animals can either approach or withdraw from a stimulus, and their rate of lever pressing for a food reward can either increase or decrease. In these cases, conditioned excitation results in a change in behavior in one direction, and conditioned inhibition results in a change in behavior in the opposite direction.

The sign tracking procedure, for example, has been used to provide evidence of inhibitory conditioning through bidirectional responses. As I noted earlier, pigeons approach visual stimuli associated with the forthcoming presentation of food. By contrast, if an inhibitory conditioning procedure is used, the pigeons withdraw from the CS (Hearst & Franklin, 1977; Wasserman, Franklin, & Hearst, 1974; Janssen, Farley, & Hearst, 1995; see also Palya, 1993).

Evidence of inhibitory conditioning through bidirectional responses has also been obtained with the conditioned suppression technique with rats. As we saw, stimuli that have been associated with impending shock suppress the rate of food-rewarded lever pressing in rats. By contrast, stimuli that have become associated with the absence of shock increase the rate of food-rewarded lever pressing (Hammond, 1966; see also Wesierska & Zielinski, 1980). Another good example of bidirectionality involves taste preference. The association of a flavor with illness reduces preference for that flavor. On the other hand, the association of a flavor with the absence of illness increases preference for the flavor (for example, Best, Dunn, Batson, Meachum, & Nash, 1985).

It is important to note that the simple observation of a response opposite to the reaction to a conditioned excitatory stimulus is not sufficient to conclude that inhibitory conditioning was involved. The researcher must also make certain that the opposing response was due to the inhibitory conditioning procedure rather than some other process. Consider, for example, changes in taste preference. Mere exposure to a flavor CS by itself often increases preference for that flavor (Domjan, 1976).

Figure 3.10   A negative CS-US contingency procedure for conditioning inhibitory properties to the CS. Notice that the CS is always followed by a period without the US.

The association of a flavor with the absence of illness (inhibitory conditioning) also increases taste preference (Best et al., 1985). To conclude that an increase in taste preference is due to conditioned inhibition, the inhibitory conditioning procedure has to produce a higher taste preference than what is observed with mere CS exposure. (For a more detailed discussion of control problems in studies of conditioned inhibition, see Papini & Bitterman, 1993.)

The Compound-Stimulus, or Summation, Test. Inhibitory conditioning can be investigated directly in bidirectional response systems. However, many responses cannot change in both directions. Eye blinking in rabbits is a good example. In the absence of an eliciting stimulus, rabbits rarely blink. If a stimulus had been conditioned to inhibit the eyeblink response, eyeblinks would not be observed when this stimulus was presented. But, then again, the animal also would not blink when the stimulus was absent. Therefore, it is not clear whether the lack of responding reflects an active suppression of blinking or merely the low baseline level of this behavior. To conclude that a stimulus actively inhibits blinking, more sophisticated test procedures must be used.

The most versatile procedure for assessing inhibition is the **compound-stimulus test,** or **summation test.** This procedure was particularly popular with Pavlov (for example, Pavlov, 1927) and is generally regarded as the most acceptable procedure for the measurement of conditioned inhibition in contemporary research (see Miller & Spear, 1985). Difficulties created by low baseline levels of responding are overcome in the compound stimulus test by presenting an excitatory conditioned stimulus that elicits the conditioned response. Conditioned inhibition is then measured in terms of the reduction or inhibition of this conditioned responding. Thus, the test involves observing the effects of an inhibitory CS in compound with an excitatory CS+. The procedure may also be conceptualized as one that involves observing the summation of the effects of an inhibitory stimulus (CS−) and an excitatory stimulus (CS+).

An experiment by Reberg and Black (1969) illustrates the use of the compound-stimulus test to evaluate inhibition in a conditioned suppression experiment. Laboratory rats in the conditioned inhibition group received differential conditioning in which a CS+ was periodically presented ending in a brief shock. A CS− was also periodically presented, but in the absence of shock. (Visual and auditory stimuli were used as the CS+ and CS−.) The control group received only the CS+ paired with shock during this part of the experiment so that, for them, the CS− did not become associated with the absence of shock. Then, both groups received two types of test trials. During one test trial, only the CS+ was presented to determine the degree of response suppression the animals learned to this stimulus. During the other test trial, the CS+ was presented simultaneously with the CS−.

The results are summarized in Figure 3.11. For the conditioned inhibition group (shown by the two bars on the left), less response suppression occurred when the CS− was presented simultaneously with the CS+ than when the CS+ was presented alone. Thus, the CS− attenuated conditioned responding to the CS+. Such an outcome did not occur in the control group (shown by the two bars on the right). In the control group, the CS− had not been conditioned to signal the absence of shock. In fact, the CS− was presented for the first time during the test trials. The presence of the CS− did not inhibit the response suppression produced by the CS+ in the comparison group. In fact, it slightly increased suppression.

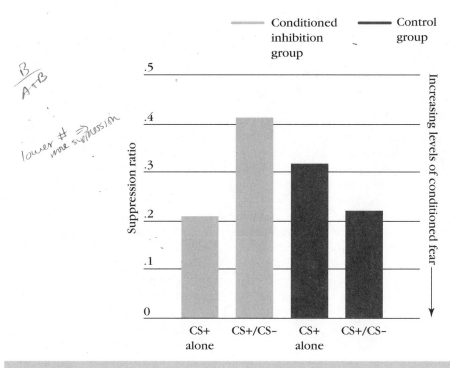

B/A+B

lower # more suppression

Figure 3.11 Compound-stimulus test of inhibition in a conditioned suppression experiment. For the conditioned inhibition group, the CS– was a predictor of the absence of shock. For the control group, the CS– was a novel stimulus. The CS– reduced the degree of response suppression produced by a shock-conditioned CS+ in the conditioned inhibition group (two bars on the left) but not in the control group (two bars on the right). (Adapted from Reberg and Black, 1969.)

The Retardation-of-Acquisition Test. Another frequently used indirect test of conditioned inhibition is the **retardation-of-acquisition test** (for example, Hammond, 1968; Rescorla, 1969a). The rationale for this test is also rather straightforward. If a stimulus actively inhibits a particular response, then it should be especially difficult to condition that stimulus to elicit the behavior. In other words, the rate of acquisition of an excitatory CR should be retarded if the CS is a conditioned inhibitor.

Conditioned inhibition can be difficult to distinguish from other behavioral processes. Therefore, the best strategy is to use more than one test and be sure that the different tests all point to the same conclusion. Rescorla (1969b) advocated using both the compound stimulus test and the retardation-of-acquisition test. This dual test strategy has remained popular in the ensuing quarter century (Williams et al., 1992).

EXTINCTION

So far, my presentation of classical conditioning has centered on various aspects of the acquisition of new associations between conditioned and unconditioned stimuli and the resultant new responses or behavioral tendencies that the conditioned stimuli come to elicit. The question arises, Are the results of such conditioning permanent, or are there ways to reverse the effects of conditioning? Many investigators, including Pavlov, have puzzled over this question. The focus of the research effort has been on reversing the effects of excitatory conditioning. (For relevant studies on conditioned inhibition, see DeVito & Fowler, 1986; Fiori, Barnet, & Miller, 1994; Williams, 1986; Witcher & Ayres, 1984.)

One highly effective procedure for reducing conditioned responses that result from excitatory conditioning procedures is **extinction**. In an extinction procedure, the CS is repeatedly presented by itself, without the US. If the organism had been conditioned to approach a CS for food, for example, repeated presentations of the CS without food would result in loss of the conditioned approach response.

The loss of the conditioned response (CR) that occurs as a result of extinction is not the same as the loss of behavior that may occur because of **forgetting**. Extinction is produced by repeated presentations of the CS by itself. Forgetting, by contrast, is a decline in the strength of the CR that may occur simply because of the passage of time. Extinction involves a particular experience with the CS. Forgetting occurs with prolonged absence of exposure to the CS.

Extinction and Habituation

The procedure for extinction following Pavlovian conditioning is very similar to the procedures discussed in Chapter 2 for producing habituation. Both extinction and habituation involve repeated presentation of a stimulus. The critical difference between them is that, in extinction, the stimulus involved was previously conditioned. In contrast, a history of conditioning is not required for habituation.

Because of the similarity in the procedures for extinction and habituation, similarities in the results observed might be expected. Such similarities are indeed being uncovered. For example, it has been shown that the effects of the interval between successive presentations of a stimulus are similar in habituation and extinction paradigms (Westbrook, Smith, & Charnock, 1985). Another important characteristic of habituation is that the habituated stimulus recovers its effectiveness in eliciting the response with the passage of time. As noted in Chapter 2, this phenomenon is called the *spontaneous recovery* of habituation. A similar effect is observed with extinguished stimuli or responses. If, after a series of extinction trials, the animal is given a period of rest away from the experimental environment, spontaneous recovery of the extinguished response may occur (Brooks & Bouton, 1993; Pavlov, 1927; Robbins, 1990).

Habituation and extinction are also similar in the effects of novel stimuli on the loss of responsiveness. In Chapter 2 I described how the presentation of a novel stimulus can result in recovery of the response elicited by the habituated stimulus (*dishabituation*). A comparable effect occurs in extinction. If, after a series of extinction trials, a novel stimulus is presented, recovery may occur in the response to the extinguished CS (Pavlov, 1927). This recovery in the CR produced by novelty is called *disinhibition.*

It is important to differentiate disinhibition from spontaneous recovery. Even though both processes are forms of recovery of the CR, in spontaneous recovery the response is reestablished simply because of the passage of time. In disinhibition the response is reestablished because of the presentation of a novel stimulus.

The Learning Involved in Extinction

The phenomenon of extinction fits the definition of learning used in this book in that it involves a change in behavior (loss of responsiveness to a stimulus) as a result of experience (repeated presentations of the CS). However, it is not clear what is actually learned in extinction. A common but erroneous belief is that extinction involves the unlearning of the previously conditioned response. According to this view, the gradual decline in the conditioned response in extinction simply reflects the loss of what was learned earlier.

In contrast to the unlearning interpretation of extinction, Pavlov (1927) suggested that during extinction animals somehow learn to inhibit making the CR to the CS. According to this view, extinction does not involve the unlearning of the original CS-US association but rather the acquisition of a new inhibitory process that prevents the appearance of the CR.

The primary evidence for Pavlov's inhibition interpretation of extinction was provided by the phenomenon of disinhibition. Pavlov reasoned that if extinction involved inhibition of the CR, then the response should recover if this inhibition was disrupted somehow. Presentation of a novel stimulus presumably disrupts the inhibition and thereby produces recovery of the CR in the disinhibition phenomenon.

Despite the phenomenon of disinhibition, extinction does not appear to involve the same type of active inhibition that occurs when a CS becomes associated with the absence of a US (Rescorla, 1969b). An extinguished CS does not have any of the three identifying properties of a conditioned inhibitory stimulus that I discussed earlier (see "Measuring Conditioned Inhibition"). Extinguished conditioned stimuli have not been observed to elicit responses opposite to those elicited by excitatory conditioned stimuli in bidirectional response systems. An extinguished conditioned stimulus is also no more difficult to condition than a novel stimulus. Indeed, the opposite result is sometimes observed; that is, conditioning may proceed more rapidly with previously extinguished conditioned stimuli than with novel stimuli (Konorski & Szwejkowska, 1950, 1952; Napier, Macrae, & Kehoe, 1992). Finally, an extinguished stimulus does not inhibit the conditioned responses elicited by an effective conditioned stimulus in a compound test. Rather, it is not unusual to observe some facilitation of responding when the extinguished CS is presented together with an excitatory test CS (Reberg, 1972).

Extinction procedures produce suppression of behavior through some mechanism other than conditioned inhibition. Although the precise nature of that mechanism is not well understood, investigators are becoming increasingly convinced that Pavlov was correct in suggesting that extinction involves new learning rather than the unlearning of a CS-US association. This conclusion is supported by growing evidence that extinction does not eliminate previously conditioned associations and responses. The phenomena of disinhibition and spontaneous recovery show that a CS-US association is not lost during the course of extinction. For additional evidence that extinction does not involve unlearning of a CS-US association, see Bouton (1991, 1993, 1994).

M. E. Bouton

PREVALENCE OF CLASSICAL CONDITIONING

Classical conditioning is typically investigated in laboratory situations. However, we do not have to know much about classical conditioning to realize that it may also occur in a wide range of situations outside the laboratory. Classical conditioning is most likely to develop when one event reliably precedes another in a short-delayed CS-US pairing. This occurs in many aspects of life. As I mentioned at the beginning of the chapter, stimuli in the environment occur in an orderly temporal sequence, largely because of the physical constraints of causation. Some events simply cannot happen before other things have occurred. Social institutions and customs also ensure that things happen in a predictable order. Whenever certain stimuli reliably precede others, classical conditioning may take place (see Turkkan, 1989, for a wide range of examples). In the next section, I will describe examples of Pavlovian conditioning in food preferences, mother-infant interactions, and sexual behavior.

Acquired Food Preferences and Aversions in People

The normal course of eating provides numerous opportunities for the learning of associations. Rozin and Zellner (1985) concluded a review of the role of Pavlovian conditioning in people's food likes and dislikes with the note that "Pavlovian conditioning is alive and well, in the flavor-flavor associations of the billions of meals eaten each day, . . . in the associations of foods and offensive objects, and in the associations of foods with some of their consequences" (p. 199).

Taste aversion and taste preference learning, as examples of Pavlovian conditioning, have been extensively investigated in various animal species (see Riley & Tuck, 1985). A growing body of evidence indicates that many human taste aversions are also the result of Pavlovian conditioning. Much of this evidence has been provided by questionnaire studies (Garb & Stunkard, 1974; Logue, Ophir, & Strauss, 1981; Logue, 1985, 1988a). People report having acquired at least one food aversion during their lives. Furthermore, the reported circumstances of food aversion learning in people are often comparable to circumstances that have been shown to facilitate aversion learning in animals. For example, the aversions are more likely to have resulted from a forward pairing of the food with subsequent illness than from simultaneous or backward pairings. As in the animal experiments, the aversions are often learned in one trial, and learning can occur even if illness is delayed several hours after ingestion of the food.

Another interesting finding is that in about 20% of the cases, the individuals were certain that their illness was not caused by the food they ate. Nevertheless, they learned an aversion to the food. This indicates that food aversion learning can be independent of rational thought processes and can go against a person's conclusions about the causes of their illness.

Serious problems can arise because food aversions develop to novel foods eaten prior to illness. For example, food aversions can develop as a result of cancer chemotherapy. Chemotherapy for cancer often causes nausea as a side effect. Both child and adult cancer patients have been shown to acquire aversions to foods eaten before a chemotherapy session (Bernstein, 1978, 1991; Bernstein & Webster, 1980; Carrell, Cannon, Best, & Stone, 1986). Such conditioned aversions may contribute to the lack of appetite commonly found among chemotherapy patients.

Conditioned food aversions also may contribute to the suppression of food intake or anorexia observed in other clinical situations (see Bernstein & Borson, 1986, for a review.) The anorexia that accompanies the growth of some tumors may result from food aversion learning. Animal research indicates that the growth of tumors can result in the conditioning of aversions to food ingested during the disease. Food aversion learning may also contribute to anorexia nervosa, a disorder characterized by severe and chronic weight loss. Suggestive evidence indicates that people suffering from anorexia nervosa experience digestive disorders that may increase their likelihood of learning food aversions. Increased susceptibility to food aversion learning may also contribute to the loss of appetite that is evident in people suffering from severe depression. Finally, animal research suggests that food aversion learning may be involved in the suppression of food intake that results from two surgical procedures—intestinal bypass surgery and vagotomy—sometimes used to treat excessively obese individuals.

Infant and Maternal Responses during Nursing

Infants begin to suckle soon after birth. Suckling involves mutual stimulation between the infant and the mother. Placement of a nipple in the baby's mouth, for example, stimulates the baby to suck. The sucking response of the infant in turn stimulates the milk let-down reflex in the mother. Both of these reflexes can come to be conditioned to additional stimuli the infant and mother provide each other, and such conditioning facilitates the nursing interaction.

To successfully nurse an infant, the mother has to hold the baby in a particular position, which provides special tactile stimuli for the infant. These tactile stimuli may become conditioned to elicit both orientation and pucker-suck responses on the part of the baby. In a study of newborn human infants, Blass, Ganchrow, and Steiner (1984) employed a small squirt of sucrose solution to the infants' lips as a US. The sucrose elicited orientation and sucking as URs. A tactile CS was used, consisting of stroking the infants' forehead at a rate of about once per second for 10 seconds. For babies in the experimental group, the sucrose US was delivered at the end of the 10-second CS. For babies in the control group, the US was presented unpaired with the CS. After just 18 trials of conditioning, infants in the experimental group showed strong conditioned orientation and pucker-suck responses to the tactile CS. Such results were not obtained with the infants in the control group.

Tactile stimuli provided by the baby to the mother may also become conditioned, in this case to elicit the milk let-down response of the mother in anticipation of having the infant suckle. Mothers who nurse their babies frequently may experience the milk let-down reflex when the baby cries or when the usual time for breast-feeding arrives. All these stimuli (special tactile cues, the baby's crying, and the time of normal feedings) reliably precede suckling by the infant. Therefore, they may become conditioned by the suckling stimulation and come to elicit milk secretion as a conditioned response.

Conditioning of Sexual Behavior

Pavlovian conditioning is also important in learning about sexual situations. Although clinical observations indicate that human sexual behavior is shaped by learning experiences, the best experimental evidence of sexual conditioning has been obtained in studies with animals (see review by Domjan & Holloway, 1997). In these studies, males typically serve as participants, and the US is provided either by the sight of a sexually receptive female or by physical access to a female.

Sexual Pavlovian conditioning has been investigated using a variation of the sign tracking procedure in which a localized stimulus such as a light is used as a signal for visual or physical access to a female. As I noted earlier, organisms come to approach a localized CS that has become associated with the presentation of food. Similar results are obtained when a localized visual stimulus becomes associated with access to a potential sexual partner. In one study (Burns & Domjan, 1996), a wood block was presented briefly to male Japanese quail immediately before they were allowed access to a female quail. Within a few trials, the male birds came to approach and remain near the CS object. Similar conditioned approach behavior has been observed in studies of sexual conditioning with the blue gourami, a fish species (Hollis, Cadieux, & Colbert, 1989).

The presentation of sexually conditioned stimuli also has been observed to facilitate a variety of aspects of reproductive behavior. After exposure to a sexual CS, males are quicker to perform copulatory responses (Domjan, Lyons, North, & Bruell, 1986; Zamble, Hadad, Mitchell, & Cutmore, 1985), compete more successfully with other males for access to a female (Gutiérrez & Domjan, 1996), show more courtship behavior (Hollis et al., 1989), and produce more offspring (Hollis et al., 1997). Some of these results may be mediated by sexually conditioned hormonal changes. Sexually conditioned stimuli have been observed to stimulate the release of testosterone and leuteinizing hormone in male rats (Graham & Desjardins, 1980).

K. L. Hollis

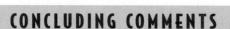

CONCLUDING COMMENTS

In Chapter 3 I continued the discussion of elicited behavior by turning from habituation and sensitization to classical conditioning. Classical conditioning is a bit more complex than habituation and sensitization in that it involves associatively mediated elicited behavior. In fact, classical conditioning is one of the major techniques for investigating how associations are learned. As we have seen, classical conditioning may be involved in many important aspects of behavior. Depending on the procedure used, the learning may occur quickly or slowly. With some procedures, excitatory response tendencies are learned; with other procedures, the organism learns to inhibit a particular response in the presence of the conditioned stimulus. Finally, if the CS is repeatedly presented without the US after conditioning, it will become extinguished and lose its response-evoking properties.

SAMPLE QUESTIONS

1. Describe similarities and differences between habituation, sensitization, and classical conditioning.

2. What is object learning, and how is it similar to or different from conventional classical conditioning?

3. What is the most effective procedure for excitatory conditioning, and how is it different from other possibilities?

4. What is a control procedure for excitatory conditioning, and what processes is the control procedure intended to rule out?

5. Are conditioned excitation and conditioned inhibition related, and if so how?

KEY TERMS

autoshaping Same as *sign tracking.*

backward conditioning A procedure in which the conditioned stimulus is presented after the unconditioned stimulus on each trial.

compound-stimulus test A test procedure that identifies a stimulus as a conditioned inhibitor if that stimulus reduces the responding elicited by a conditioned excitatory stimulus. Also called *summation test.*

conditional or conditioned response The response that comes to be made to the conditioned stimulus as a result of classical conditioning. Abbreviated *CR.*

conditional or conditioned stimulus A stimulus that does not elicit a particular response initially but comes to do so as a result of becoming associated with an unconditioned stimulus. Abbreviated *CS.*

conditioned emotional response Suppression of positively reinforced instrumental behavior caused by the presentation of a stimulus that has become associated with an aversive stimulus. Abbreviated *CER.* Also called *conditioned suppression.*

conditioned suppression Same as *conditioned emotional response.*

conditioning trial A training episode involving presentation of a conditioned stimulus with (or without) an unconditioned stimulus.

CR Abbreviation for *conditioned response.*

CS Abbreviation for *conditioned stimulus.*

CS-US interval Same as *interstimulus interval.*

differential inhibition A classical conditioning procedure in which one stimulus (the CS+) is paired with the unconditioned stimulus on some trials and another stimulus (the CS–) is presented without the unconditioned stimulus on other trials. As a result of this procedure the CS+ comes to elicit a conditioned response, and the CS– comes to inhibit this response. Also called the *stimulus-discrimination procedure* (in classical conditioning).

explicitly unpaired control A procedure in which both conditioned and unconditioned stimuli are presented, but with sufficient time between them so that they do not become associated with each other.

extinction Reduction of a learned response that occurs because the conditioned stimulus is no longer paired with the unconditioned stimulus (in classical conditioning). Also, the procedure of repeatedly presenting a conditioned stimulus without the unconditioned stimulus.

forgetting A reduction of a learned response that occurs because of the passage of time, not because of particular experiences.

inhibition of delay Progressive increase in the latency of the conditioned response that occurs with extended training with a long-delay conditioning procedure.

inhibitory conditioning A type of classical conditioning in which the conditioned stimulus becomes a signal for the absence of the unconditioned stimulus.

interstimulus interval The amount of time that elapses between presentations of the conditioned stimulus (CS) and the unconditioned stimulus (US) during a classical conditioning trial. Also called the *CS-US interval.*

intertrial interval   The amount of time that elapses between two successive trials.

latency   The time elapsed between a stimulus (or the start of a trial) and the response that is made to the stimulus.

magnitude of a response   A measure of the size, vigor, or extent of a response.

object learning   Learning associations between different stimulus elements of an object.

probability of a response   The likelihood of making the response, usually represented in terms of the percentage of trials on which the response occurs.

pseudoconditioning   Increased responding that may occur to a stimulus whose presentations are intermixed with presentations of an unconditioned stimulus (US) in the absence of the establishment of an association between the stimulus and the US.

random control   A procedure in which the conditioned and unconditioned stimuli are presented at random times with respect to each other.

retardation-of-acquisition test   A test procedure that identifies a stimulus as a conditioned inhibitor if that stimulus is slower to acquire excitatory properties than a comparison stimulus.

short-delayed conditioning   A classical conditioning procedure in which the conditioned stimulus is initiated shortly before the unconditioned stimulus on each conditioning trial.

sign tracking   Movement toward and possibly contact with a stimulus that signals the availability of a positive reinforcer such as food. (Also called *autoshaping.*)

simultaneous conditioning   A classical conditioning procedure in which the conditioned stimulus and the unconditioned stimulus are presented simultaneously on each conditioning trial.

summation test   Same as *compound-stimulus test.*

test trial   A trial in which the conditioned stimulus is presented without the unconditioned stimulus. This allows measurement of the conditioned response in the absence of the unconditioned response.

trace conditioning   A classical conditioning procedure in which the unconditioned stimulus is presented after the conditioned stimulus has been terminated for a short period.

trace interval   The interval between the end of the conditioned stimulus and the start of the unconditioned stimulus in trace-conditioning trials.

unconditional or **unconditioned response**   A response that occurs to a stimulus without the necessity of prior training.

unconditional or **unconditioned stimulus**   A stimulus that elicits a particular response without the necessity of prior training.

UR   Abbreviation for *unconditioned response.*

US   Abbreviation for *unconditioned stimulus.*

CLASSICAL CONDITIONING: MECHANISMS

What Makes Effective Conditioned and Unconditioned Stimuli?

Initial Response to the Stimuli

The Novelty of Conditioned and Unconditioned Stimuli

CS and US Intensity

CS-US Relevance, or Belongingness

The Concept of Biological Strength

What Determines the Nature of the Conditioned Response?

The Stimulus-Substitution Model

The Compensatory-Response Model

The CS as a Determinant of the Form of the CR

Behavior Systems Theory

How Do Conditioned and Unconditioned Stimuli Become Associated?

The Blocking Effect

The Rescorla-Wagner Model

Other Models of Classical Conditioning

Concluding Comments

I N Chapter 4 I will continue discussing classical conditioning by focusing on the mechanisms and outcomes of this type of learning. The discussion is organized around three key issues. First, I will describe features of conditioned and unconditioned stimuli that influence their effectiveness in classical conditioning procedures. Then I will discuss factors that determine the types of responses that come to be made to conditioned stimuli. In the third and final section of the chapter, I will focus on the mechanisms involved in the formation of associations between conditioned and unconditioned stimuli.

WHAT MAKES EFFECTIVE CONDITIONED AND UNCONDITIONED STIMULI?

The question of what makes some stimuli effective as conditioned stimuli and others effective as unconditioned stimuli is perhaps the most basic question about classical conditioning. Traditionally, Western investigators have been concerned with how classical conditioning is influenced by various temporal arrangements and signal relations between conditioned and unconditioned stimuli. The issue of what makes stimuli effective as CSs and USs was originally addressed by Pavlov and is increasingly attracting the attention of contemporary researchers.

Initial Response to the Stimuli

Pavlov addressed the effectiveness criteria for conditioned and unconditioned stimuli in his definitions of the terms *conditioned* and *unconditioned.* According to these definitions, the CS does not elicit the CR initially but comes to do so as a result of becoming associated with the US. By contrast, the US is effective in eliciting the target response without any special training.

Pavlov's definitions are stated in terms of the elicitation of a particular response—the one to be conditioned. Because of this, identifying potential CSs and USs requires comparing the responses elicited by each stimulus before conditioning. Such a comparison makes the identification of CSs and USs *relative.* A particular event may serve as a CS relative to one stimulus and as a US relative to another.

Consider, for example, a palatable saccharin solution for thirsty rats. This stimulus may serve as a CS in a taste aversion experiment, with illness serving as the US. In this case, conditioning trials would consist of exposure to the saccharin flavor followed by injection of a drug that induces malaise, and animals would learn to stop drinking the saccharin solution.

A palatable saccharin solution may also serve as an unconditioned stimulus—in a sign tracking experiment, for example. The conditioning trials in this case might involve the illumination of a light just before each presentation of a small amount of saccharin. After a number of trials of this sort, the animals would begin to approach the light CS. Thus, whether the saccharin solution is considered a US or a CS depends on its relation to other stimuli in the situation. In the sign tracking experiment, the saccharin solution serves as the US because it elicits the response in question (approach) without conditioning. In the taste aversion experiment, the saccharin solution serves as the CS because it elicits the CR (withdrawal or aversion) only after pairings with sickness.

The Novelty of Conditioned and Unconditioned Stimuli

As we saw in studies of habituation, the behavioral impact of a stimulus depends on its novelty. Highly familiar stimuli do not elicit as vigorous reactions as do novel stimuli. Novelty is also very important in classical conditioning. If either the CS or the US is highly familiar, learning proceeds more slowly than if both the CS and US are novel.

Investigations of the role of novelty in classical conditioning are usually conducted in two phases. For example, animals may be first given repeated exposure to the stimulus that is later to be used as the CS. During this initial phase of the experiment, the CS-to-be is always presented by itself. After this stimulus familiarization, the CS may be paired with a US using conventional classical conditioning procedures. Initial familiarization with a stimulus presented by itself usually retards the subsequent conditioning of that stimulus. This phenomenon is called the **CS-preexposure effect** or **latent-inhibition effect** (Hall, 1991; Lubow, 1989; Lubow & Gewirtz, 1995).

The function of the CS preexposure effect is similar to the function of habituation. Both phenomena serve to limit processing and attention to stimuli that have proven to be inconsequential. Habituation serves to bias elicited behavior in favor of novel stimuli; latent inhibition serves to bias learning in favor of novel stimuli. As Lubow and Gewirtz (1995) noted, latent inhibition "promotes the stimulus selectivity required for rapid learning" (p. 87).

Experiments that address the issue of US novelty are conducted in a manner similar to the CS-preexposure experiments. In the first phase of the study, animals are given repeated exposures to the US presented alone. The US is then paired with a CS, and the progress of learning is monitored. Animals familiarized with a US before its pairings with a CS are slower to develop conditioned responding to the CS than animals for which the US is novel during the CS-US pairings. This result is called the **US-preexposure effect** (Randich, 1981; Randich & LoLordo, 1979; Saladin, ten Have, Saper, Labinsky, & Tait, 1989).

The mechanisms of the CS- and US-preexposure effects have been the subject of extensive research and debate. No one theory has been successful in explaining all of the data. A reasonable conclusion at the present time is that several mechanisms are involved (see Hall, 1991, for a discussion of this in relation to the CS-preexposure effect). One mechanism involves *associative interference* (Lubow, Weiner, & Schnur, 1981). According to the associative interference mechanism, preconditioning exposures to the CS or US make these stimuli less able to enter into new associations.

The second factor responsible for the CS- and US-preexposure effects is *memory interference*. According to the memory interference mechanism, conditioned responding is disrupted because animals remember what happened in both phases of the experiment. They remember having received the CS (or US) by itself repeatedly during the preexposure phase and having received the CS paired with the US in the conditioning phase. The memory of CS (or US) preexposure disrupts responding because the preexposure procedures do not stimulate the CR. Consistent with this mechanism, procedures that reduce the memory of preexposure at the time of testing result in enhanced conditioned responding (Aguado, Symonds, & Hall, 1994; Kraemer, Randall, & Carbary, 1991; Miller, Jagielo, & Spear, 1993).

CS and US Intensity

Another important stimulus variable for classical conditioning is the intensity of the conditioned and unconditioned stimuli. Most biological and physiological effects of stimulation are related to the intensity of the stimulus input. This is also true for learning. The association of a CS with a US occurs more rapidly, and the final level of conditioned responding is greater, when more intense stimuli are used (for example, Kamin & Brimer, 1963; Kamin & Schaub, 1963; Scavio & Gormezano, 1974). This relation is observed over a broad range of stimulus intensities.

The fact that conditioning is facilitated by increasing the intensity of the CS and US may be related to the novelty of the conditioned and unconditioned stimuli. Organisms rarely encounter stimuli of high intensity. Therefore, high-intensity

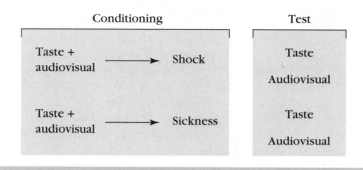

Figure 4.1 Diagram of Garcia and Koelling's (1966) experiment. A compound taste-audiovisual stimulus was first paired with either shock or sickness. The subjects were then tested with the taste and audiovisual stimuli separately.

conditioned and unconditioned stimuli may be more novel than lower-intensity stimulation. Thus, novelty may be at least partly responsible for stimulus-intensity effects in classical conditioning (see Kalat, 1974).

CS-US Relevance, or Belongingness

Another variable that governs the rate of classical conditioning is the extent to which the CS is relevant to, or belongs with, the US. The importance of stimulus relevance was first clearly demonstrated in a classic experiment by Garcia and Koelling (1966). The investigators compared learning about peripheral pain (induced by footshock) and learning about illness (induced by irradiation or a drug injection) in a study conducted with laboratory rats.

In their natural environment, rats are likely to get sick after eating a poisonous food. In contrast, they are likely to encounter peripheral pain after being chased and bitten by a predator that they can hear and see. To represent food-related cues, Garcia and Koelling tested learning about a taste CS; to represent predator-related cues they tested learning about an audiovisual CS.

The experiment, diagrammed in Figure 4.1, involved having the rats drink from a drinking tube before administration of one of the unconditioned stimuli. The drinking tube was filled with flavored water, either salty or sweet. In addition, each lick on the tube activated a brief audiovisual stimulus (the click of a relay and a flash of light). Thus, the rats encountered the taste and audiovisual stimuli at the same time. After exposure to these conditioned stimuli, the animals either received shock through the grid floor or were made sick.

Because the unconditioned stimuli used were aversive, the rats were expected to learn some kind of aversion. The investigators measured the response of the animals to the taste and audiovisual stimuli separately after conditioning. During tests of response to the taste CS, the water was flavored as before, but now licks did not activate the audiovisual stimulus. During tests of response to the audiovisual CS, the water was unflavored, and the audiovisual stimulus was briefly turned on whenever the animal drank. The degree of conditioned aversion to the taste or audiovisual CS was inferred from the suppression of drinking.

The results of the experiment are summarized in Figure 4.2. Animals conditioned with shock subsequently suppressed their drinking much more when tested with the audiovisual stimulus than when tested with the taste CS. The opposite result occurred when animals were conditioned with sickness. These rats suppressed their

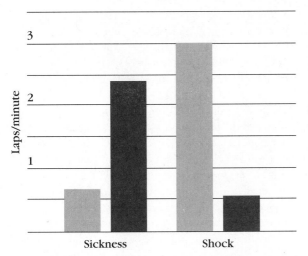

Figure 4.2 Results of Garcia and Koelling's (1966) experiment. Rats conditioned with sickness learned a stronger aversion to taste than to audiovisual cues. By contrast, rats conditioned with shock learned a stronger aversion to audiovisual than to taste cues. (Adapted from Garcia and Koelling, 1966.)

drinking much more when the taste CS was present than when drinking produced the audiovisual stimulus.

Garcia and Koelling's experiment demonstrates the principle of CS-US relevance, or belongingness. Learning depended on the relevance or appropriateness of the CS to the US that was administered. Taste became readily associated with illness, and audiovisual cues became readily associated with peripheral pain. Rapid learning occurred only if the CS was combined with the appropriate US. The audiovisual CS, for example, was not generally more effective than the taste CS. Rather, the audiovisual CS was more effective only when shock served as the US. Correspondingly, the shock US was not generally more effective than the sickness US. Rather, shock conditioned stronger aversions than sickness only when the audiovisual cue served as the CS.

The CS-US relevance effect obtained by Garcia and Koelling was not readily accepted at first. However, numerous subsequent studies have confirmed the original findings (for a review, see Domjan, 1983). Gemberling and Domjan (1982), for example, demonstrated that the effect occurs in rats 1 day after birth. This observation indicates that extensive experience with tastes and sickness (or audiovisual cues and peripheral pain) is not necessary for the stimulus-relevance effect. Rather, the phenomenon appears to reflect a genetic predisposition for the selective association of certain combinations of conditioned and unconditioned stimuli. (For evidence of stimulus relevance in human food aversion learning, see Garb & Stunkard, 1974; Logue et al., 1981; Pelchat & Rozin, 1982).

Stimulus relevance effects have been documented in other situations as well. For example, LoLordo and his associates investigated how pigeons learn about food as compared with peripheral pain. They found that pigeons associate visual cues with food much more easily than they associate auditory cues with food. By contrast, if the conditioning situation involves shock, auditory cues are more effective as the CS than visual cues. These results suggest that, for pigeons, visual cues are relevant to feeding and auditory cues are relevant to defensive behavior (see LoLordo, Jacobs, & Foree, 1982; Kelley, 1986; Shapiro, Jacobs, & LoLordo, 1980; Shapiro & LoLordo, 1982).

BOX 4.1

BEHAVIOR APPROACHES TO THE CONTROL OF SMOKING

A variety of aversion conditioning procedures have been developed to discourage cigarette smoking (Hall, Hall, & Ginsberg, 1990). Early efforts involved aversion therapy in which smoking was paired with pain induced by electric shock. More recently, techniques have been developed based on findings indicating that aversion conditioning is more effective if the aversive stimulus is "relevant" to the situation. In these procedures, cigarette smoking itself is used to provide the aversive stimulus. A frequently employed procedure is called "rapid smoking." This procedure requires the person to inhale every 6 seconds for either a fixed period or until nausea or dizziness develops. Such rapid smoking is aversive and serves to condition an aversion to smoking.

Aversion conditioning procedures are most effective in discouraging smoking when they are combined with other behavior modification techniques. Rapid smoking, for example, may be effectively combined with training in self-monitoring and self-management procedures. Individuals are first required to maintain an accurate record of the number of cigarettes they smoke and the time, place, and circumstances of the smoking. Once information has been obtained on the frequency and circumstances of a person's usual smoking behavior, goals can be introduced with the intent of gradually reducing smoking. Two types of goals are adopted. One goal is to reduce the total number of cigarettes smoked each day; the other is to reduce the number of situations in which the person is allowed to smoke. These goals serve in combination to restrict smoking behavior. Compliance with the goals can be encouraged by setting up a contract system. For example, the person may deposit a sizable sum of money at the start of treatment and receive portions of this deposit back each time a specified goal is met.

Stimulus relevance effects are also evident in the acquisition of fear. Rhesus monkeys can become fearful of a live snake or a toy snake as a result of observing another monkey react with fear to the snakes. Cook and Mineka (1990) found that observational learning of fear was more likely if the demonstrator showed fear of a toy snake than if the demonstrator appeared to be afraid in the presence of artificial flowers. However, the artificial flower CS was just as effective as the toy snake in a learning task involving food. Thus, monkeys seem to be predisposed to learn a fear of snakes.

People also exhibit stimulus selectivity in their learning of fear. People are more likely to report being afraid of snakes and spiders than of electric outlets or hammers, which can also inflict severe pain (Seligman, 1971). Laboratory studies have shown that human participants associate pictures of snakes and spiders with shock more readily than pictures of flowers and houses (Öhman, Dimberg, & Öst, 1985). The mechanisms of these selective learning effects remain the subject of lively investigation (Davey, 1995).

The Concept of Biological Strength

In all the examples of classical conditioning discussed so far, the CS did not elicit as strong responses as the US prior to conditioning. The familiar example of salivary conditioning is a good case in point. In this situation, the CS (a tone) initially elicits only weak orientation movements. By contrast, the US (food) elicits vigorous approach, ingestion, salivation, chewing, swallowing, and so on. Pavlov was aware of this large difference in the "biological strength" of the stimuli and considered the difference necessary for their effectiveness as conditioned and unconditioned stimuli (Pavlov, 1927). Pavlov suggested that for a stimulus to become conditioned, it had to be of weaker biological strength than the unconditioned stimulus with which it is paired. By "weaker biological strength," he meant that the CS initially elicited fewer and weaker responses than the US.

Higher-Order Conditioning.   One implication of Pavlov's biological strength criterion is that a stimulus may serve as a US after it has become strongly conditioned. Consider, for example, a tone that is repeatedly paired with food. After sufficient pairings, the tone will come to elicit salivation, as well as strong orientation and approach (sign tracking) responses. According to the concept of biological strength, at this point the tone should be effective in conditioning salivation to a novel light stimulus that does not initially elicit strong responses. Pairings of the previously conditioned tone with the novel light should gradually result in the conditioning of salivation to the light. Indeed, this effect is often observed and is called **higher-order conditioning.** Figure 4.3 summarizes the sequence of events that brings about higher-order conditioning.

As the term "higher order" implies, conditioning may be considered to operate at different levels. In the preceding example, conditioning of the tone with food is considered *first-order conditioning*. Conditioning of the light with the previously conditioned tone is considered *second-order conditioning*. If after becoming conditioned, the light were used to condition yet another stimulus—say, an odor—that would be *third-order conditioning*.

The procedure for second-order conditioning shown in Figure 4.3 is similar to the standard procedure for inhibitory conditioning discussed in Chapter 3 (see Figure 3.8). In both cases, one CS (CS1 or the CS+) is paired with the US, and a second CS (CS2 or CS–) is paired with the first one. Why does such a procedure produce conditioned inhibition in some cases and excitatory second-order conditioning under other circumstances? The critical factor appears to be amount of training. With a few conditioning trials, second-order excitatory conditioning occurs. With extensive training, conditioned inhibition develops (Yin, Barnet, & Miller, 1994).

Although there is no doubt that second-order conditioning is a robust phenomenon (Rescorla, 1980a), little research has been done to evaluate the mechanisms of third-order and higher orders of conditioning. However, even the existence of second-order conditioning is of considerable significance because it greatly increases the range of situations in which classical conditioning can take place. With higher-order conditioning, classical conditioning can occur without a primary unconditioned stimulus. The only requirement is that a previously conditioned stimulus be available.

Many instances of conditioning in human experience involve higher-order conditioning. For example, money is a powerful conditioned stimulus for human behavior

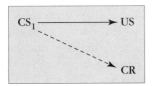 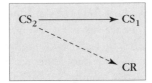

Figure 4.3   Procedure for higher-order conditioning. CS1 is first paired with the US and comes to elicit the conditioned response. A new stimulus (CS2) is then paired with CS1 and also comes to elicit the conditioned response.

BOX **4.2**

HIGHER-ORDER CONDITIONING OF FEAR

Irrational fears sometimes develop through higher-order conditioning. For example, Wolpe (1990) described the case of a woman who initially developed a fear of crowds. How this fear was originally conditioned is unknown, but somehow crowds became fear-eliciting stimuli. To avoid arousing her fear, the woman would go to the movies only in the daytime when few people were present. On one such visit,

the theater suddenly became crowded with students. The woman became extremely upset by this and came to associate movie houses with crowds. Thus, one fear-conditioned stimulus (crowds) had conditioned fear to other stimuli (movie houses) that previously were innocuous, as in higher-order conditioning.

After her frightening experience in the movie house, the woman avoided going to the movies, even when she was unlikely to encounter many other people there. Furthermore, her newly acquired fear of movie houses generalized to other public places such as restaurants, churches, and public buildings. She also avoided these, even if they were empty.

because of its association with candy, toys, movies, and other things money can buy. A child may learn to like a particular uncle if the uncle gives him money on each visit. The positive conditioned emotional response to the uncle develops because the child comes to associate the uncle with money—a case of second-order conditioning.

Second-order conditioning is also of interest as a technique for confirming the occurrence of first-order conditioning. For example, as noted in Chapter 3, second-order conditioning has been used successfully to reveal first-order conditioning produced by simultaneous pairings of a CS with a US (Barnet, Arnold, & Miller, 1991).

Counterconditioning. Many instances of association learning, including higher-order conditioning, satisfy the criterion of differential biological strength. However, this criterion is not met in all situations that permit the learning of associations between stimuli. Two stimuli can become associated with one another, even though both elicit strong responses initially. This occurs in **counterconditioning**. In counterconditioning the response an animal makes to a stimulus is reversed, or "countered," by associating this stimulus with a US that promotes the opposite type of reaction.

In one study of counterconditioning (Pearce & Dickinson, 1975), the aversive properties of brief shock were reduced or reversed by pairing the shock with food. In the first phase of the experiment, rats in the counterconditioned group received shock periodically, but each shock delivery ended with delivery of a food pellet. Animals in control groups received the shocks and food pellets either unpaired or they received only one or the other of the USs. How these treatments changed the aversiveness of shock was then measured by using the shock in a conditioned-suppression procedure. As expected, the animals that previously had shock paired with food showed less conditioned suppression than the control groups. This result indicates that the counterconditioning procedure reduced the aversive properties of the shock. (For other examples of counterconditioning, see Dickinson & Dearing, 1979.)

Sensory Preconditioning. Counterconditioning involves the learning of an association between two stimuli, each of which elicits a vigorous response before conditioning. Associations between two stimuli can also be learned when each elicits only a mild orienting response before conditioning. One situation in which this type of learning is often investigated is called **sensory preconditioning,** the procedure for which is shown in Figure 4.4.

In a sensory preconditioning experiment, animals first receive repeated pairings of two biologically weak stimuli or CSs. The stimuli may be two visual cues—a triangle presented close to a square, for example. No response conditioning is evident in this phase of training. Neither the triangle nor the square comes to elicit a CR. Conditioned behavior is acquired in the second phase of the experiment, in which the triangle is now paired with an unconditioned stimulus such as food. A conditioned approach response, or sign tracking, comes to be elicited by the triangle as a result of its pairings with food.

Once the triangle has come to elicit sign tracking, an interesting thing happens: the square now also elicits this response because of its prior association with the triangle. Thus, the association of the two innocuous visual cues with each other becomes evident when one of the stimuli is later conditioned to elicit a vigorous response. (For additional examples, see Berridge & Schulkin, 1989; Lavin, 1976; Rescorla & Durlach, 1981.)

Differential Biological Strength as a Performance Variable Rather than a Learning Variable. The phenomenon of sensory preconditioning suggests that differential biological strength is important in instances of association learning because it permits observing the effects of learning more easily—not because it facilitates the learning process. In sensory preconditioning, organisms learn to associate two innocuous stimuli, CS1 and CS2, with each other. However, this learning is not observable at first because the stimuli are of little behavioral significance. The association between CS1 and CS2 becomes evident when one of the stimuli (CS1) is made to elicit a strong response—when CS1 is made biologically strong, in Pavlov's terminology. The association can then be seen when a corresponding response is elicited by CS2.

The somewhat roundabout method used to give behavioral expression to a learned association in the sensory preconditioning procedure is not necessary in other procedures I have described. In these other procedures, cues are associated with stimuli that already elicit strong responses. In standard first-order conditioning, an innocuous stimulus (CS) is associated with a biologically strong event (US). By virtue of this association, the CS comes to elicit a response corresponding to the US. Higher-order conditioning is similar in that an initially "neutral" stimulus (CS2) becomes associated with one that already elicits stronger responses (CS1). In counterconditioning, the associated stimulus is likewise biologically strong, so that associations with it result in an observable change in elicited behavior.

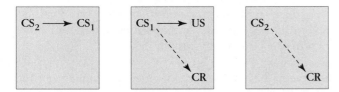

Figure 4.4 Procedure for sensory preconditioning. First CS2 is paired with CS1 without an unconditioned stimulus. Then CS1 is paired with a US and comes to elicit a CR. In a later session, CS2 is also found to elicit a CR, even though CS2 was never paired with the US.

WHAT DETERMINES THE NATURE OF THE CONDITIONED RESPONSE?

In the present and preceding chapters, I described numerous examples of classical conditioning. Throughout the discussion, conditioning was identified by the development of new responses to the conditioned stimulus. I described a variety of responses that can become conditioned, including salivation, eye blinking, fear, locomotor approach and withdrawal, and aversion responses. However, I have not yet discussed why one set of responses becomes conditioned in one situation and other responses are learned in other circumstances.

The Stimulus-Substitution Model

The oldest idea about what animals learn in classical conditioning is based on a model of conditioning proposed by Pavlov. As I noted earlier, Pavlov was primarily a physiologist. Not unexpectedly, therefore, his model of conditioning has a decidedly physiological orientation. For purposes of theorizing, Pavlov viewed the brain as consisting of discrete neural centers, as illustrated in Figure 4.5. He suggested that one brain center is primarily responsible for processing the US and that a different center is primarily responsible for processing the CS. A third brain center was assumed to be responsible for generating the UR. Because the UR occurred whenever the US was presented, Pavlov assumed there is a neural connection between the center for the US and the center for the UR. Furthermore, because the reaction to the US did not have to be learned, the functional pathway between the US and UR centers was assumed to be innate (see Figure 4.5).

Pavlov suggested that conditioning results in the establishment of new functional neural pathways. During the course of repeated pairings of the conditioned and unconditioned stimuli, a new connection develops between the brain center for the CS and the brain center for the US. Once this new connection has been established, presentation of the CS results in excitation of the US neural center. Excitation of the US center in turn generates the UR because of the preexisting connection between the US and UR centers. Therefore, according to Pavlov's model, conditioning enables the CS to elicit the UR.

The response to the CS may not always be identical to the response to the US. Differences between the two may occur if, for example, the CS is not as intense as the US and therefore produces less excitation of the UR center. However, the Pavlovian model predicts that the general form of the CR will be similar to the form of the UR. Because of the new functional pathway established between the CS center and the US center, the CS comes to have effects on the nervous system similar to those of the US. That is why the model is called **stimulus substitution.** In Pavlov's model, the CS becomes a surrogate US—a substitute for the US.

The US as a Determining Factor for the CR.   According to the stimulus-substitution model, each US is assumed to have its own unique brain center, which is connected to a unique UR center. If conditioning turns a CS into a surrogate US, the model predicts that CSs conditioned with different USs will elicit different types of CRs. This is obviously true. Animals learn to salivate when conditioned with food and to blink when conditioned with a puff of air to the eye. Salivation is not condi-

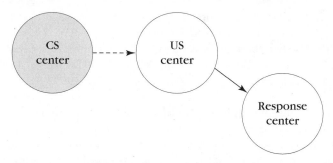

Figure 4.5 Diagram of Pavlov's stimulus substitution model. The solid arrow indicates an innate neural connection. The dashed arrow indicates a learned neural connection. The CS comes to elicit a response by activating the US center, which automatically elicits the response.

tioned in eyeblink conditioning experiments, and eyeblink responses are not conditioned in salivary conditioning experiments.

The unconditioned stimuli involved in salivary and eyeblink conditioning differ in numerous respects. For example, food is a desirable or appetitive stimulus, whereas a puff of air to the eyes is a mildly aversive stimulus. What would happen if the two unconditioned stimuli were more similar? For example, would two different appetitive unconditioned stimuli also support different conditioned responses? The available evidence indicates that the answer is yes. However, some of the changes in behavior produced by conditioning will be common to the two USs.

Consider, for example, food and water as USs. Food and water are both desirable, appetitive stimuli. However, they elicit different URs. A pigeon eating grain makes rapid, hard pecking movements directed at the grain with its beak slightly open at the moment of contact. By contrast, it drinks by lowering its beak into the water, sucking up some water, and then raising its head gradually to allow the water to flow down its throat. Thus, the URs of eating and drinking differ in both speed and form.

Jenkins and Moore (1973) compared sign tracking in pigeons with food and with water as the US. In both experimental situations, the CS was illumination of a small disk or response key for 8 seconds before the US. With repeated pairings of the key light with the presentation of grain, the pigeons gradually became conditioned to peck the illuminated key. Pecking also developed with repeated pairings of the key light with water. However, the form of the CR was different with water. In the food experiment, the pigeons pecked the response key as if eating: the pecks were rapid, with the beak slightly open at the moment of contact. In the water experiment the pecking movements were slower, made with the beak closed, and often accompanied by swallowing. Thus, the form of the CR was determined by, and resembled, the form of the UR. Eating-like pecks occurred in conditioning with food, and drinking-like pecks occurred in conditioning with water (see also Allan & Zeigler, 1994; Ploog & Zeigler, 1996; Spetch, Wilkie, & Skelton, 1981; Stanhope, 1992).

Similar findings have been obtained with food pellets and milk as unconditioned stimuli with laboratory rats. In one study, the insertion of a response lever into the experimental chamber 10 seconds before the delivery of a food pellet or milk served as the CS. With both food and milk, the rats learned to approach and touch the response lever. However, they were much more likely to lick the lever when it was associated with milk as compared to food pellets (Davey & Cleland, 1982; Davey, Phillips, & Cleland, 1981). (For additional examples of CRs determined by the nature of the US, see Meachum & Bernstein, 1990; Parker, 1988; Pelchat et al., 1983; Peterson, Ackil, Frommer, & Hearst, 1972; Zalaquett & Parker, 1989.)

Difficulties with the Stimulus-Substitution Model. Doubts arose about the stimulus-substitution model very early in North American investigations of classical conditioning. The problem was that in many situations the conditioned and unconditioned responses were significantly different. Hilgard reviewed several examples many years ago (Hilgard, 1936). He noted, for example, that whereas the UR to shock is an increase in respiration rate, the CR to a CS paired with shock is a decrease in respiration. Detailed study of the form of conditioned eyeblink responses also showed that humans blink differently in response to conditioned and unconditioned stimuli.

In other research of this type, Zener (1937) carefully observed both salivation and motor responses to a bell that had been paired with food in dogs. The UR to food always involved lowering the head to the food tray and chewing one or more pieces of food. After conditioning, the bell rarely elicited chewing movements, and if chewing occurred, it was not sustained; the CR to the bell only sometimes included orientation to the food tray. On some trials the dog looked toward the bell instead. On other trials the dog's orientation vacillated between the food tray and the bell, and on still other occasions the dog held its head between the food tray and the bell when the bell sounded. Thus, the CRs elicited by the bell were often different from the URs elicited by the food.

Modern Approaches to Stimulus Substitution. Contemporary investigators do not believe that the CS becomes a substitute for the US. However, they have retained the idea that the CR is elicited by way of a US "center" of some sort, because the US is clearly one factor that determines the nature of the CR. The contemporary view is stated in more abstract language than Pavlov used in his model. The new model states that animals learn two things from repeated pairings of a CS with a US: (1) they learn a CS-US association, and (2) they form an image, or representation, of the US. According to the model, the CR depends on both these factors. The CS elicits the CR because of its association with the US representation. If either the CS-US association or the US representation is weak, the CR will be correspondingly weak.

Evidence for the importance of the US representation in classical conditioning is provided by experiments in which the US representation is altered without changing the CS-US association. For example, the value of the US may be reduced after conditioning. Reducing the value of the US is called **US devaluation.** The basic strategy of a US devaluation experiment is illustrated in Figure 4.6. Holland and Rescorla (1975a), for example, first conditioned two groups of mildly food-deprived rats by repeatedly pairing a tone with pellets of food. This initial phase of the experiment was assumed to establish an association between the tone CS and the food US, as well as to get the rats to form a representation of the food US. Conditioned responding was evident in the increased activity elicited by the tone.

In the next phase of the experiment, the experimental group received a treatment designed to devalue the US representation. The animals were given sufficient free food to completely satisfy their hunger. Food satiation presumably reduces the value

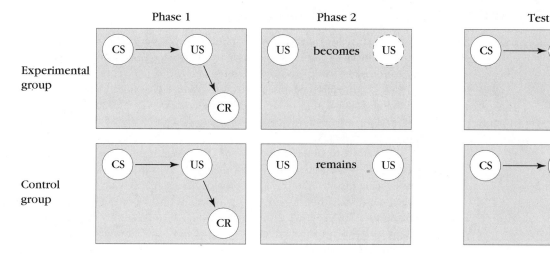

Figure 4.6 Basic strategy and rationale involved in US-devaluation experiments. In Phase 1 the experimental and control groups receive conventional conditioning to establish an association between the CS and the US and to lead the participants to form a representation of the US. In Phase 2 the US representation is devalued for the experimental group but remains unchanged for the control group. If the CR is elicited by way of the US representation, devaluation of the US representation should reduce responding to the CS.

of food and thus devalues the US representation. The deprivation state of the control group was not changed in Phase 2. Thus, the US representation was assumed to remain intact for the control group (see Figure 4.6). Both groups then received a series of test trials with the tone-conditioned stimulus. During these tests, the experimental group showed significantly less conditioned responding than the control group. These results indicate that devaluation of the US representation reduced the power of the tone CS to elicit the activity conditioned response. The experiment demonstrates in an ingenious way that the CR was elicited by way of a US representation.

S-S versus S-R Learning. In the Holland-Rescorla US devaluation experiment, whether or not the CS elicited the CR critically depended on the status of the US representation. If conditioning had established a new reflex connection between the CS and CR, the CR would have been elicited whenever the CS occurred. That did not happen. Rather, conditioning resulted in an association between the CS and a representation of the US. Presentation of the CS activated the US representation, and the CR was a reflection of that US representation. This type of outcome is called **stimulus-stimulus learning,** or **S-S learning.**

In S-S learning, organisms learn an association between two stimuli, and the CR is an indirect reflection of this association. Whether the CR occurs depends on the behavioral impact of the associated stimulus (the US) at the time of testing. If the associated stimulus is reduced in behavioral impact (by food satiation, for example), the elicited CR will also be reduced.

Evidence of S-S learning is available from a variety of classical conditioning situations (for example, Cleland & Davey, 1982; Colwill & Motzkin, 1994; Holland & Straub, 1979; Holloway & Domjan, 1993; Kraemer, Hoffmann, Randall, & Spear, 1992; Rescorla, 1973). However, not all instances of classical conditioning involve S-S learning. In some cases, the participants appear to learn a direct association between the CS and the CR. This type of learning is called **stimulus-response learning,** or **S-R learning.** Evidence for S-R learning comes from studies of second-order conditioning (for example, Holland & Rescorla, 1975a, 1975b). However, some instances of second-order conditioning involve S-S learning (Rashotte, Griffin, & Sisk, 1977; Rescorla, 1982b).

The Compensatory-Response Model

As we have seen, Pavlov's idea that conditioning involves stimulus substitution has met critical challenges over the years. Perhaps the most serious challenge has come from the **conditioned compensatory-response** model, to which we turn next. The conditioned compensatory-response model was stimulated by research in which drugs served as unconditioned stimuli, and it assumes (contrary to stimulus-substitution) that conditioned responses are opposite in form to the responses elicited by the unconditioned stimulus.

We previously encountered the idea of compensatory, or opposing, reactions in connection with the opponent-process theory of motivation in Chapter 2. The opponent-process theory of motivation provides a mechanism for minimizing the disruptive effects of an emotion-arousing stimulus. According to the theory, an emotion-arousing stimulus produces a primary reaction, which is soon counteracted by an opponent process that activates responses opposite those initially elicited by the stimulus (see Figures 2.15 and 2.16).

The conditioned compensatory-response model takes advantage of some of the same ideas. Like the opponent-process theory, it is a homeostatic model in that it provides a mechanism for minimizing the disruptive effects of stimuli. It focuses on disruptions produced by drug stimuli. Also like the opponent-process theory, the basic mechanism for reducing the disruptive effects of stimuli involves the activation of a compensatory or opponent response. The primary difference between the two models concerns the source of the opponent response. In the opponent-process theory of motivation, the opponent response is a delayed effect of the US. Thus, in a sense it is a *delayed unconditioned response.* By contrast, in the compensatory-response model, the opponent is a reaction to a CS that has become associated with the US. Thus, the opponent response is a *drug anticipatory conditioned response.*

The compensatory-response model was encouraged by observations showing that when a drug serves as the US, the form of the CR is often opposite the direct effects of the drug. For example, epinephrine causes a decrease in gastric secretion, but the response to a CS that has been paired with epinephrine is increased gastric secretion (Guha, Dutta, & Pradhan, 1974). Dinitrophenol causes increased oxygen consumption and increased temperature; the response to a CS for dinitrophenol involves decreased oxygen consumption and decreased temperature (Obal, 1966). Compensatory CRs have been also observed with morphine, lithium, ethanol, chlorpromazine, amphetamine, and other drugs (see Siegel, 1977, 1989).

A Conditioning Model of Drug Tolerance. The compensatory-response model has been used as the basis for an innovative explanation of the development of **drug tolerance.** Tolerance to a drug is said to develop when repeated administrations of the drug have progressively less effect. Because of this, increasing doses are required to produce the same drug response. Traditionally, drug tolerance has been considered to result from pharmacological processes. In contrast to this traditional approach, Shepard Siegel has proposed a model of drug tolerance based on classical conditioning (see Siegel, 1983, 1989).

The conditioning model assumes that each drug administration constitutes a classical conditioning trial in which the stimuli that accompany the drug administration are paired with the effects of the drug. These conditioned stimuli might be the time of day, the sensations involved in preparing a syringe, or the distinctiveness of

S. Siegel

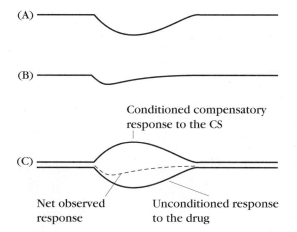

(A)

(B)

Conditioned compensatory
response to the CS

(C)

Net observed
response

Unconditioned response
to the drug

Figure 4.7 Diagram of the Pavlovian conditioning model of drug tolerance. The strength of the drug reaction is represented by deviations from the horizontal line. (A) Reaction to the CS plus the drug before conditioning, illustrating the UR to the drug. (B) Attenuated reaction to the CS plus the drug after extensive experience with the drug, illustrating drug tolerance. (C) Components of the reaction after conditioning, showing that the net attenuated drug response is due to a compensatory conditioned response to the CS that counteracts the UR to the drug.

the place where the drug is usually taken. As a result of association with the drug effects, the drug administration cues are assumed to elicit CRs that are opposite the direct effects of the drug. Because the CRs compensate for the drug effects, the reaction otherwise elicited by the drug is reduced. Therefore, the response to the drug is attenuated when the drug is taken in the presence of these conditioned stimuli (see Figure 4.7).

The conditioning model of drug tolerance attributes tolerance to compensatory responses conditioned to environmental stimuli paired with drug administration. If the model is valid, then manipulations of the external environment should influence the effectiveness of drugs. Various aspects of this prediction have been confirmed by Siegel and his colleagues, as well as by numerous other investigative teams in laboratory studies with opiates (morphine and heroin), alcohol, scopolamine, benzodiazepines, and amphetamine. (See reviews by Siegel, 1989; Stewart & Eikelboom, 1987.)

Evidence of Conditioning in Drug-Abuse Patients. Conditioning also occurs during the course of drug use outside the laboratory. In a study of naturally acquired drug-conditioned responses, Ehrman, Robbins, Childress, and O'Brien (1992) tested men with a history of free-basing and smoking cocaine (but no history of heroin use). A control group that had never used cocaine or heroin also provided data. The participants were observed under three test conditions. In one test, cues related to cocaine use were presented. The participants listened to an audiotape of people talking about their experiences free-basing and smoking cocaine, watched a videotape of people buying and using cocaine, and were asked to go through the motions of free-basing and smoking. In another test, cues related to heroin use were presented in the same manner as the cocaine stimuli. Finally, in the third test, control stimuli unrelated to drug use were presented. During each test, both physiological responses and self-reports of feelings were recorded.

Both the physiological measures and self-reports of mood provided evidence that cocaine-related stimuli elicited conditioned responses. Figure 4.8 shows the results of measures of heart rate. Cocaine users exposed to cocaine-related stimuli experienced a significant increase in heart rate during the test. Furthermore, this increased heart rate

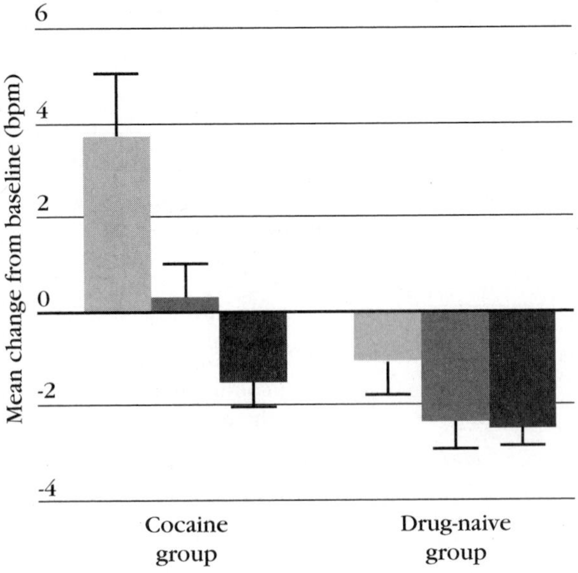

Figure 4.8 Mean change in heart rate from baseline levels for men with a history of cocaine use and a drug-naive control group during tests involving exposure to cocaine-related stimuli (light bars), heroin-related stimuli (medium bars), or nondrug stimuli (dark bars). (From "Conditioned Responses to Cocaine-Related Stimuli in Cocaine Abuse Patients," by R. N. Ehrman, S. J. Robbins, A. R. Childress, and C. P. O'Brien, *Psychopharmacology,* 1992, *107,* 523–529. Copyright © 1992 by Springer-Verlag. Reprinted by permission.)

response was specific to the cocaine-related stimuli. The heart rate of cocaine users did not change in response to heroin-related stimuli or nondrug stimuli. The increased heart rate response was also specific to the cocaine users. Participants in the control group did not show elevations in heart rate in any of the tests.

Participants with a history of cocaine use also reported feelings of cocaine craving and withdrawal elicited by the cocaine-related stimuli. They did not report these emotions in response to the heroin-related or nondrug stimuli. Feelings of cocaine craving and withdrawal were also not reported by participants in the control group.

The results of this study suggest that cocaine users acquire conditioned physiological and emotional responses to cocaine-related stimuli during the course of their drug use. The self-reports of conditioned cocaine craving and withdrawal are consistent with the compensatory-response model, because these feelings are opposite the feelings of being high that are experienced during cocaine use. However, the physiological conditioned response (increased heart rate) is similar to, rather than opposite, the physiological activating effects of cocaine. Thus, overall, the results of this study were not entirely consistent with the compensatory-response model.

Evaluation of the Compensatory-Response Model. Numerous studies of the conditioned compensatory-response model of drug tolerance have confirmed that variables that influence other forms of classical conditioning also influence reactivity to many psychoactive drugs. A truly remarkable body of evidence has been developed in this area. However, a recurrent problem has been that contrary to the model, not all learned modifications of drug effects are accompanied by the conditioned drug-compensatory responses called for by the model (for recent reviews, see Cunningham, 1993, 1997). As in the study of drug-abuse patients discussed above, some conditioned responses are similar to reactions to the drug, whereas others are opposite.

Inconsistencies in the form of drug-conditioned responses have encouraged alternative formulations. Some theorists have advocated explaining learning influences on drug tolerance using a behavioral model of habituation that makes no assumptions about the form of drug-conditioned responses (Baker & Tiffany, 1985). However, this approach is limited in its ability to explain evidence of conditioned drug-withdrawal effects (for example, Falls & Kelsey, 1989). Another approach is to assume that drug-compensatory responses exist but may be difficult to observe (Siegel, 1989). For example, some drug-conditioned responses may involve physiological changes that are not expressed in behavior (King, Bouton, & Musty, 1987) or that may require special test procedures for their expression (Hinson, Poulos, & Cappell, 1982; Krank, 1987). Although no entirely satisfactory account of drug-conditioning effects is available, such an account will no doubt emerge from more detailed investigations of the physiological regulatory processes that determine how drugs produce various physiological and emotional changes in organisms (Dworkin, 1993; Stewart & Eikelboom, 1987).

The CS as a Determinant of the Form of the CR

In the discussion thus far I have shown how the form of the CR is determined by the US—that is, whether the CR mimics or compensates for the UR. However, the US is not the only important factor. The form of the CR is also influenced by the nature of the CS. This was first illustrated by a rather unusual experiment by Timberlake and Grant (1975).

Timberlake and Grant investigated classical conditioning in rats, with food as the US. However, instead of a conventional light or tone, the CS was the presentation of another rat just before food delivery. One side of the experimental chamber was equipped with a sliding platform that could be moved in and out of the chamber through a flap door (see Figure 4.9). A live rat was gently restrained on the stimulus platform. Ten seconds before each delivery of food, the platform was moved into the experimental chamber, thereby transporting the stimulus rat through the flap door.

The stimulus-substitution model predicts that CS-US pairings will generate responses to the CS that are similar to responses elicited by the food US. Since the US elicits gnawing and biting, gnawing and biting should also come to be elicited by the CS, even if the CS is the presentation of a live rat. Contrary to this prediction, the CS did not elicit gnawing and biting. Rather, as the CS rat was repeatedly paired with food, it came to elicit orientation, approach, and sniffing movements, as well as social contacts. Such responses did not develop if the CS rat was not paired with food or was presented at times unrelated to food.

The outcome of this experiment does not support any model that explains the form of the CR solely in terms of the US that is used. The pattern of CRs, particularly the social behavior elicited by the CS rat, was no doubt determined by the nature of the CS (see also Timberlake, 1983a). Other kinds of food-conditioned stimuli elicit different CRs. For example, Peterson et al. (1972) inserted an illuminated response lever into the experimental chamber immediately before presenting food to rats. With the protruding metal lever as the CS, the CRs were "almost exclusively oral and consisted mainly of licking . . . and gnawing" (p. 1010). (For other investigations of how the CS determines the nature of the conditioned response, see Holland, 1977, 1980, 1984; Kim, Rivers, Bevins, & Ayres, 1996; Sigmundi & Bolles, 1983).

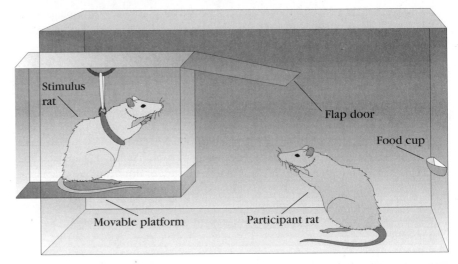

Figure 4.9 Diagram of the experiment by Timberlake and Grant (1975). The CS for food is presentation of a stimulus rat on a movable platform through a flap door on one side of the experimental chamber.

Behavior Systems Theory

The approaches to the form of the conditioned response I have been describing have their intellectual roots in Pavlov's physiological model systems method for the study of learning. In this method, one or two responses are isolated for investigation. Pavlov's approach focuses on how changes in an isolated response can be used to gain information about underlying learning mechanisms. This approach is continuing to provide rich dividends in new knowledge. However, it is also becoming evident that answers to questions about the nature of the CR will require considering the animal's behavior from a broader perspective. Holland (1984), for example, has commented that a comprehensive account of the nature of conditioned behavior will require "knowledge of the normal functions of behavior systems engaged by the various CSs, the natural, unlearned organization within those systems, and the ontogeny of those systems" (p. 164).

It is convenient to conceptualize the full range of things animals do as being organized into various systems of behavior. There are behavior systems for procuring and eating food, for territorial defense, for sexual behavior, for maintaining warmth (thermoregulation), and so on. Each behavior system consists of a series of response modules, each with its own controlling stimuli and responses, arranged spatially and/or temporally. For example, in territorial defense, the distant approach of an intruder initially provides only weak stimuli that elicit correspondingly mild responses of vigilance and orientation. As the intruder moves closer, the stimuli it provides become more intense and distinctive, and the elicited responses also change, perhaps to vigorous patrolling. Finally, as the intruder enters the defended territory, the elicited responses change again, to threat gestures and aggression.

Behavior systems theory assumes that Pavlovian conditioning procedures activate the behavior system relevant to the US that is employed. Food unconditioned stimuli activate the foraging and feeding system. By contrast, aversive unconditioned stimuli activate the predatory-defensive behavior system. Classical conditioning procedures involve superimposing a CS-US relationship on the behavioral system activated by the US. As a CS becomes associated with the US, it becomes integrated into the behavioral system and comes to elicit component responses of that system. Thus, food-conditioned stimuli come to elicit components of the feeding system, and shock-conditioned stimuli come to elicit components of the defense system.

An experiment on the conditioning of baby chicks with heat as the US nicely illustrates some of the concepts of the behavior systems approach. To predict what might happen in such a situation, the researcher must first consider the thermoregulatory behavior of chicks. When baby chicks are cold and seek warmth, they approach the mother hen, peck at the feathers on the underpart of her body, and snuggle up to her (rubbing and pushing their heads up into her feathers). Once they have nestled in under the mother hen's feathers, the chicks stop moving, twitter, and close their eyes. Thus, the behavior system involves first approach-and-pecking responses, then snuggling responses, and finally quiescence and closing of the eyes upon attainment of warmth.

Wasserman (1973) used a small lighted disk as the CS and paired this with brief exposure to heat in young chicks. As the light became conditioned, the chicks started to approach and peck it. Later the pecking responses became less forceful as the chicks pushed the lighted disk and shook their heads in a snuggling type of movement. These CRs were very different from the reactions to the heat US itself, which included napping. However, the CRs resembled what chicks do when they seek warmth from a mother hen in the barnyard. Thus, the CS became integrated into early portions of the thermoregulatory behavior system of the chicks (see also Hogan, 1974; Jenkins, Barrera, Ireland, & Woodside, 1978; Wasserman, 1974, 1981).

Behavior systems theory has been most extensively developed by William Timberlake (Timberlake, 1983a, 1983b; Timberlake & Lucas, 1989) and is consistent with much of what is known about the nature of classically conditioned behavioral responses. The theory is clearly consistent with the fact that the form of CRs is determined by the nature of the US. Since different unconditioned stimuli activate different behavior systems, CSs integrated into these systems will also elicit different CRs. However, as we saw in the thermal conditioning of chicks, behavior systems theory does not require that the form of the CR be the same (or opposite) the form of the UR.

The behavior systems view is also consistent with the fact that the form of the CR is determined by the nature of the CS. Certain types of stimuli may be more effective in eliciting particular component responses of a behavior system than other types of stimuli. Therefore, the nature of the CS is expected to determine how the CS becomes incorporated into the behavior system.

An especially provocative prediction of behavior systems theory is that the form of the CR will depend on the CS-US interval that is used. The CS-US interval is assumed to determine where the CS becomes incorporated into the sequence of responses that makes up the behavior system. Consider, for example, the sexual behavior of a male bird. When sexually motivated, the male will engage in a general search response to bring it into the proximity of a female. Once he is in the vicinity of the female, the male will engage in a more focal search response to actually locate her. Finally, once he finds her, the male will engage in courtship and copulatory responses. This sequence is illustrated in Figure 4.10.

Consider now what might happen if a Pavlovian conditioning procedure were superimposed on the sexual behavior system. In a sexual conditioning procedure, access to a female is the US. Access to the female activates the courtship and copulatory responses that characterize the end of the behavior sequence. With a short CS-US interval, the CS occurs shortly before access to the female. If the CS becomes incorporated into the behavior system at this point, the CS should elicit focal search

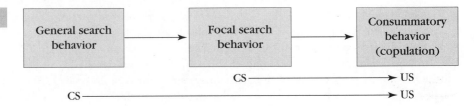

Figure 4.10 Sequence of responses, starting with general search and ending with copulatory behavior, that characterize the sexual behavior system. A conditioning procedure is superimposed on this behavior system. The CS-US interval determines where the CS becomes incorporated into the behavioral sequence.

behavior: the male should approach and remain near the CS. The CR should be different if a long CS-US interval is used. In this case (see Figure 4.10), the CS should become incorporated into an earlier portion of the behavior system and elicit general search rather than focal search behavior. General search behavior should be manifest in nondirected locomotion.

The predictions I described were recently tested in an experiment conducted with domesticated quail (Akins, Domjan, and Gutiérrez, 1994). Akins et al. used a large rectangular experimental chamber. During each conditioning trial, a small visual CS was presented at one end either 1 minute before the male birds received access to a female or 20 minutes before the release of the female. Control groups were exposed to the CS and US in an unpaired fashion. To detect focal search behavior, Akins et al. measured how much time the males spent close to the CS. To detect general search behavior, they measured pacing between one half of the experimental chamber and the other.

The results of the focal search and general search CR measures are presented in Figure 4.11. With a 1-minute CS-US interval, the conditioning procedure produced significant focal search but not general search behavior. In contrast, with the 20-minute CS-US interval, conditioning produced significant general search but not focal search responding. These results are precisely what was predicted by behavior systems theory. According to behavior systems theory, the CS does not come to either substitute for or compensate for the US. Rather, it comes to substitute for a stimulus in the behavior system at a point that is determined by the CS-US interval.

HOW DO CONDITIONED AND UNCONDITIONED STIMULI BECOME ASSOCIATED?

I have described numerous situations in which classical conditioning occurs and have discussed various factors that determine what responses result from this learning. However, I have yet to address in detail the critical issue of how conditioned and unconditioned stimuli become associated. What are the mechanisms of association learning—the underlying processes that are activated by conditioning procedures to produce learning? This question has been the subject of intense scholarly work. The evolution of theories of classical conditioning continues today, as investigators strive

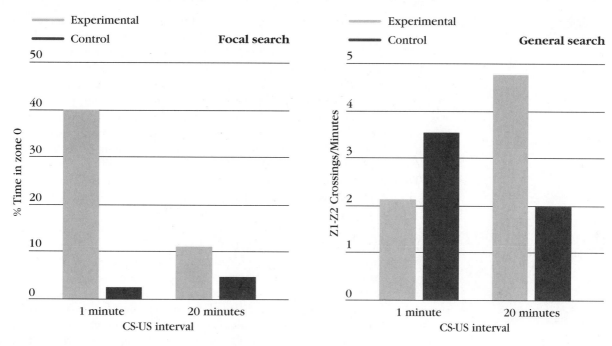

Figure 4.11 Effects of the CS-US interval on the conditioning of focal search and general search responses in male domesticated quail. When the CS-US interval was 1 minute, conditioning resulted in increased focal search behavior. When the CS-US interval was 20 minutes, conditioning resulted in increased general search behavior. (Adapted from Akins, Domjan, & Gutiérrez, 1994.)

to formulate comprehensive accounts of the mechanisms of association learning that can embrace all the diverse research results. (For recent reviews, see Hall, 1994; Wasserman & Miller, 1997).

The Blocking Effect

The modern era in theories of classical conditioning got under way about 30 years ago with the discovery of several provocative phenomena that stimulated the application of information processing ideas to the analysis of classical conditioning (for example, Rescorla, 1967b, 1968b; Wagner, Logan, Haberlandt, & Price, 1968). One of the most prominent of these phenomena was the **blocking effect.**

To get an intuitive sense of the blocking effect, consider the following scenario. Each Sunday afternoon you visit your grandmother, who always serves a rice pudding that slightly disagrees with you. Not wanting to upset her, you politely eat the pudding during each visit, and consequently acquire an aversion to rice pudding. One of the visits falls on a holiday, and to make the occasion a bit more festive, your grandmother serves tea cookies with the rice pudding this time. As usual, you eat some of everything that is offered, and as usual you get a bit sick to your stomach. Will you now learn an aversion to the tea cookies? Probably not. Knowing that rice pudding disagrees with you, you probably will attribute your illness to the proven culprit and not learn to dislike the tea cookies.

The blocking effect involves a similar sequence of events. First, an association is established between one conditioned stimulus (stimulus A) and the US. Once CSA is well conditioned, a second stimulus (stimulus B) is added to stimulus A during the conditioning trials. The basic finding is that prior conditioning of stimulus A interferes with or blocks the acquisition of conditioned responding to the added stimulus B.

L. J. Kamin

The blocking effect was initially investigated using the conditioned suppression technique with rats (Kamin, 1968, 1969). The basic procedure involved three phases (see Figure 4.12). Two conditioned stimuli were employed, a tone and a light. In Phase 1, the experimental group received repeated pairings of one of the CSs (stimulus A) with the US. This phase of training was continued until the rats totally suppressed lever pressing whenever stimulus A was presented. In the next phase of the experiment, stimulus B was presented together with stimulus A and paired with the US. After several such conditioning trials, stimulus B was presented alone in a test trial to see if it would also elicit conditioned suppression. Interestingly, very little suppression to stimulus B was observed on this test trial.

The control group in the blocking design received the same kind of conditioning trials with stimulus B as the experimental group, as indicated in Phase 2 (shown in Figure 4.12). That is, for the control group, stimulus B was also presented simultaneously with stimulus A during its conditioning trials. However, for the control group, stimulus A was not conditioned to elicit fear prior to these compound-stimulus trials. In many replications of the experiment, stimulus B invariably produced less conditioned suppression in the experimental group than in the control group.

Since the time of Aristotle, temporal contiguity has been considered the primary means by which stimuli become associated. The blocking effect has become a landmark phenomenon in classical conditioning because it called into question the assumption that temporal contiguity is sufficient for learning. The blocking effect clearly shows that pairings of a CS with a US are not enough for conditioned responding to develop. During Phase 2 of the blocking experiment, CSB is paired with the US in an identical fashion for the experimental and the control groups. Nevertheless, CSB comes to elicit vigorous conditioned responding only in the control group.

Why does the presence of the previously conditioned stimulus A block the acquisition of responding to the added cue B? Kamin explained the blocking effect by proposing that a US has to be surprising to be effective in producing learning. If the US is signaled by a previously conditioned stimulus (A), it will not be surprising and therefore it will not function well in conditioning the added stimulus (B). Kamin reasoned that if the US is not surprising, it will not startle the animal and stimulate the "mental effort" needed for the formation of an association. Unexpected events are

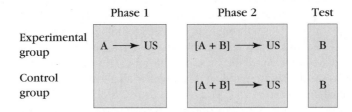

	Phase 1	Phase 2	Test
Experimental group	A ⟶ US	[A + B] ⟶ US	B
Control group		[A + B] ⟶ US	B

Figure 4.12 Diagram of the blocking procedure. During Phase 1, stimulus A is conditioned with the US in the experimental group, while the control group does not receive conditioning trials. During Phase 2, both the experimental and control groups receive conditioning trials in which stimulus A is presented simultaneously with stimulus B and paired with the US. A later test of stimulus B alone shows that less conditioned responding occurs to stimulus B in the experimental group than in the control group.

THE PICTURE-WORD PROBLEM IN TEACHING READING: A FORM OF BLOCKING

Early instruction in reading often involves showing children a written word, along with a picture of what that word represents. Thus, two stimuli are presented (picture and word). The children have already learned what the picture is called (a "horse," for example). Therefore, the two stimuli in the picture-word compound include one that is already known (the picture) and one that is not (the word). This makes the picture-word compound much like the compound stimulus in a blocking experiment: a previously conditioned stimulus is presented along with a new stimulus, not yet conditioned. Animal research on the blocking effect indicates that the presence of the previously conditioned stimulus disrupts conditioning of the new one. Singh and Solman (1990) found that a similar effect occurs with picture-word compounds in teaching reading to mentally retarded students.

The children were taught to read words such as knife, lemon, radio, stamp, and chalk. Some of the words were taught using a variation of the blocking design in which the picture of the object was presented first, and the student was asked to name it. The picture was then presented, together with its written word, and the student was asked, "What is that word?" In other conditions, the words were presented without their corresponding pictures. All eight students in the experiment showed the slowest learning of the words that were taught in the blocking procedure. By contrast, six of the eight students showed the fastest learning of the words that were taught without their corresponding pictures. (The remaining two students learned most rapidly with a modified procedure.) These results suggest that processes akin to blocking may occur in learning to read. The results also suggest that pictorial prompts should be used with caution in reading instruction because they may disrupt rather than facilitate learning.

events to which the organism has not adjusted yet. Therefore, unexpected events activate processes leading to new learning. To be effective, the US has to be unexpected or surprising.

The Rescorla-Wagner Model

The idea that the surprisingness of an unconditioned stimulus determines its effectiveness in producing new learning was developed into a formal mathematical model of conditioning by Robert Rescorla and Allan Wagner (Rescorla & Wagner, 1972; Wagner & Rescorla, 1972). With the use of this model, the implications of the concept of US surprisingness were extended to a wide variety of conditioning phenomena. The Rescorla-Wagner model dominated research on classical conditioning for about 10 years after its formulation and continues to be used in a variety of areas of psychology (Siegel & Allan, 1996).

How might the surprisingness of an unconditioned stimulus be measured? What does it mean to say that something is surprising? By definition, *an event is surprising if it is different from what is expected.* If you expect a small gift for your birthday, and you get a car, you will be very surprised. This is analogous to an unexpectedly large US. Correspondingly, if you expect a car and receive a box of candy, you will also be surprised. This is analogous to an unexpectedly small US. According to the Rescorla-Wagner model, an unexpectedly large US is the basis for excitatory conditioning or increases in associative value, and an unexpectedly small US is the basis for inhibitory conditioning or decreases in associative value.

109

Rescorla and Wagner assumed that the surprisingness, and hence the effectiveness, of a US depends on how different the US is from what the individual expects. Furthermore, they assumed that expectation of the US is related to the conditioned or associative properties of the stimuli that precede the US. Strong conditioned responding indicates strong expectation that the US will occur; weak conditioned responding indicates a low expectation of the US.

These ideas can be expressed mathematically by using λ to represent the magnitude of the US and V to represent the associative value of the stimuli that precede the US. The surprisingness of the US will then be $(\lambda - V)$. Learning on a given conditioning trial is a change in the associative value of a stimulus. That change can be represented as ΔV. Using these symbols, the idea that learning depends on the surprisingness of the US can be expressed as follows:

$$\Delta V = k(\lambda - V),$$

where "k" is a constant. This is the fundamental equation of the Rescorla-Wagner model.

Application to the Blocking Effect. The basic ideas of the Rescorla-Wagner model clearly predict the blocking effect. In applying the model, it is important to keep in mind that expectations of the US are based on all of the cues available to the organism during the conditioning trial. As shown in Figure 4.12, the experimental group in the blocking design first receives extensive conditioning of stimulus A so that it acquires a perfect expectation that the US will occur whenever it encounters stimulus A. In Phase 2, stimulus B is presented together with stimulus A, and the two CSs are followed by the US. According to the Rescorla-Wagner model, no conditioning of stimulus B will occur in Phase 2 because the US is now perfectly predicted by the presence of stimulus A.

The control group receives the identical training in Phase 2, but for them the presence of stimulus A does not lead to an expectation of the US. Therefore, the US is surprising for the control group and produces new learning.

Loss of Associative Value Despite Pairings with the US. Although the Rescorla-Wagner model is consistent with fundamental facts of classical conditioning such as acquisition and the blocking effect, much of the importance of the model has come from its unusual predictions. One unusual prediction is that under certain circumstances the conditioned properties of stimuli will decline despite continued pairings with the US. How might this happen? Stimuli are predicted to lose associative value if they are presented together on a conditioning trial after having been trained separately. Such an experiment is outlined in Figure 4.13.

Figure 4.13 shows a two-phase experiment. In Phase 1, stimuli A and B are paired with the same US (one pellet of food, for example) on separate trials. This continues until both A and B have been conditioned completely—until both stimuli predict perfectly the one-food-pellet US. Phase 2 is then initiated. In Phase 2, stimuli A and B are presented simultaneously for the first time, and the CSs are followed by the same US—one food pellet. The question is, What happens to the conditioned properties of stimuli A and B as a result of the Phase 2 training?

Note that the same US that was used in Phase 1 continues to be presented in Phase 2. Given that there is no change in the US, informal reflection suggests that the conditioned properties of stimuli A and B should also remain unchanged during Phase 2. In contrast to this commonsense prediction, the Rescorla-Wagner model

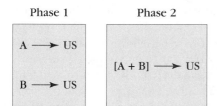

Phase 1   Phase 2

A ⟶ US   [A + B] ⟶ US

B ⟶ US

Figure 4.13   Loss of associative value despite continued presentations of the US. Stimuli A and B are conditioned separately to asymptote in Phase 1 so that each CS perfectly predicts the US. In Phase 2, stimuli A and B are presented simultaneously and paired with the same US that was used in Phase 1. This produces an over-expectation of the US. Because the delivered US is surprisingly small at the start of Phase 2, the conditioned properties of stimuli A and B decrease until the simultaneous presentation of the two CSs no longer produces the over-expectation.

predicts that the conditioned properties of the individual stimuli A and B will decrease in Phase 2.

As a result of training in Phase 1, stimuli A and B both come to predict the one-food-pellet US. When stimuli A and B are presented simultaneously for the first time in Phase 2, the expectations based on the individual stimuli are assumed to add together, with the result that two food pellets are predicted as the US. This is an over-expectation because the US remains only one food pellet. Thus, there is a discrepancy between what is expected (two pellets) and what occurs (one pellet). At the start of Phase 2, the participants find the US surprisingly small. To bring their expectations of the US in line with what actually occurs in Phase 2, the participants have to decrease their expectancy of the US based on stimuli A and B. Thus, stimuli A and B are predicted to lose associative value despite continued presentations of the same US. The loss in associative value is predicted to continue until the sum of the expectancies based on A and B equals one food pellet. The predicted loss of conditioned responding to the individual stimuli A and B in this type of procedure is highly counterintuitive but has been verified experimentally (see Kremer, 1978; Khallad & Moore, 1996).

Conditioned Inhibition.   How does the Rescorla-Wagner model explain the development of conditioned inhibition? Consider, for example, the standard inhibitory conditioning procedure (see Figure 3.8). This procedure involves two kinds of trials—trials on which the US is presented (reinforced trials) and trials on which the US is omitted (nonreinforced trials). On reinforced trials, a conditioned excitatory stimulus (CS+) is presented. On nonreinforced trials, the CS+ is presented together with the conditioned inhibitory stimulus, CS–.

Application of the Rescorla-Wagner model to such a procedure requires considering reinforced and nonreinforced trials separately. To accurately anticipate the US on reinforced trials, the CS+ has to gain excitatory properties. The development of such conditioned excitation is illustrated in the left-hand panel of Figure 4.14. Excitatory conditioning involves the acquisition of positive associative value and ceases once the organism predicts the US perfectly on each reinforced trial.

What happens on nonreinforced trials? On these trials, both the CS+ and CS– occur. Once the CS+ has acquired some degree of conditioned excitation (because of its presentation on reinforced trials), the organism will expect the US whenever the CS+ occurs, including on nonreinforced trials. However, the US does not happen on nonreinforced trials. Therefore, this is a case of over-expectation, similar to the example illustrated in Figure 4.13. To accurately predict the absence of the US on nonreinforced trials, the associative value of the CS+ and the value of the CS– have to sum to zero. How can this be achieved? Given the positive associative value of the CS+, the only way to achieve a net zero expectation of the US on nonreinforced trials is to make the associative value of the CS– negative. Hence, the Rescorla-Wagner model explains conditioned inhibition by assuming that the CS– acquires negative associative value (see the left-hand panel of Figure 4.14).

Extinction of Excitation and Inhibition. Predictions of the Rescorla-Wagner model for extinction are illustrated in the right-hand panel of Figure 4.14. The standard procedure for extinction involves omitting the unconditioned stimulus on each trial. If a CS has acquired excitatory properties (see CS+ in Figure 4.14), there will be an over-expectation of the US at the start of extinction. The expectation elicited by the CS gradually will be brought in line with the absence of the US during extinction by reduction of the associative value of the CS+ to zero.

The Rescorla-Wagner model predicts an analogous scenario for extinction of conditioned inhibition. At the start of extinction, the CS– has negative associative value. This may be thought of as creating an underprediction of the US; the organism predicts less than the zero US that occurs on extinction trials. To bring expectations

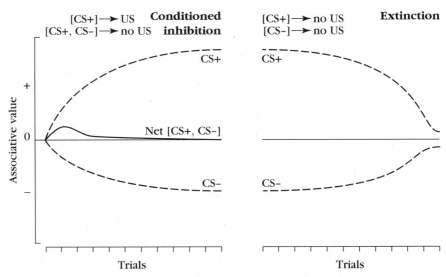

Figure 4.14 Predicted associative values of CS+ and CS– during the course of conditioned inhibition training (left) and extinction (right). During conditioned inhibition training, when the CS+ is presented alone, it is followed by the US; by contrast, when the CS+ is presented with the CS–, the US is omitted. The net associative value of CS+ and CS– is the sum of the associative values of the individual stimuli. During extinction the conditioned stimuli are presented alone, and the US never occurs.

in line with the absence of the US, the negative associative value of the CS– is gradually lost, and the CS– ends up with zero associative strength.

Evaluation of the Rescorla-Wagner Model.   The Rescorla-Wagner model stimulated a great deal of research and led to the discovery of many new and important phenomena in classical conditioning. Not unexpectedly, however, the model has also encountered some difficulties since it was proposed nearly 30 years ago. (For a recent review of these difficulties, see Miller, Barnet, & Grahame, 1995).

One of the difficulties that became evident early on is that the model's analysis of the extinction of conditioned inhibition is incorrect. As I said earlier (see Figure 4.14), the model predicts that repeated presentations of a conditioned inhibitor (CS–) by itself will lead to loss of conditioned inhibition. However, this does not seem to be the case (Zimmer-Hart & Rescorla, 1974; Witcher & Ayres, 1984). In fact, some investigators have found that repeated nonreinforcement of a CS– can enhance its conditioned inhibitory properties (for example, DeVito & Fowler, 1987; Hallam, Grahame, Harris, & Miller, 1992). Curiously, an effective procedure for reducing the conditioned inhibitory properties of a CS– does not involve presenting the CS– at all. Rather, it involves extinguishing the excitatory properties of the CS+ with which the CS– was presented during inhibitory training (Best et al., 1985; Lysle & Fowler, 1985). (For a more complete discussion of procedures for extinguishing conditioned inhibition, see Fowler et al., 1991.)

Another difficulty is that the Rescorla-Wagner model views extinction as the reverse of acquisition, or the return of the associative value of a CS to zero. However, as I mentioned in Chapter 3, a growing body of evidence indicates that extinction should not be viewed as simply the reverse of acquisition. Rather, extinction appears to involve the learning of a new relationship between the CS and the US (namely that the US no longer follows the CS).

Another puzzling finding that has been difficult to incorporate into the Rescorla-Wagner model is that under certain conditions, the same CS may have both excitatory and inhibitory properties (Matzel, Gladstein, & Miller, 1988; Robbins, 1990; Tait & Saladin, 1986; Williams & Overmier, 1988). The Rescorla-Wagner model allows for conditioned stimuli to have only one associative value. That value can be excitatory or inhibitory, but not both.

Other Models of Classical Conditioning

The formulation of a comprehensive theory of classical conditioning is a formidable challenge. Given the nearly 100 years of research on classical conditioning, a comprehensive theory must account for many diverse findings. No theory available today has been entirely successful in accomplishing that goal. Nevertheless, interesting new ideas about classical conditioning have been proposed. Some of these new models supplement the Rescorla-Wagner model. In contrast, others are incompatible with the Rescorla-Wagner model and serve to replace it.

US-Modification versus CS-Modification Models.   In the Rescorla-Wagner model, how much is learned on a conditioning trial depends on the effectiveness of the US, which in turn is determined by how surprising the US is. Much more learning occurs if the US is surprising than if it is expected. The outcome of various procedures is explained by how those procedures alter the surprisingness of the US on a trial. Therefore, the Rescorla-Wagner model is a *US-modification model* of classical conditioning.

N. J. Mackintosh

North American psychologists have favored US-modification models. By contrast, British psychologists have approached phenomena such as the blocking effect by assuming that the effectiveness or ability of the CS to enter into an association is altered under various circumstances (Mackintosh, 1975; Pearce & Hall, 1980). Thus, they have attempted to explain differences in learning in terms of changes in the effectiveness of the CS. Such models are called *CS-modification models*.

CS-modification models emphasize that for conditioning to take place, the CS has to be noticeable, or salient; it has to attract attention. The salience of a CS on a conditioning trial is assumed to determine how much learning occurs on that trial. If a stimulus has lost its salience and no longer commands attention, the organism will not learn much about it.

CS-modification models differ in their assumptions about what determines the salience, or noticeability, of the CS on a given trial. Pearce and Hall (1980), for example, assumed that how much attention an animal devotes to the CS on a given trial is determined by how surprising the US was on the preceding trial (see also Hall, Kaye, & Pearce, 1985). Animals have a lot to learn in situations where the US is surprising. Therefore, if a CS is followed by a surprising US, the organism will pay closer attention to that CS on the next trial. In contrast, if a CS is followed by an expected US, the animal will pay less attention to that CS on the next trial. An expected US is assumed to decrease the salience of the CS.

An important feature of CS-modification models is that they assume that the surprisingness of the US on a given trial alters the degree of attention commanded by the CS on future trials. If Trial 10, for example, ends in the presentation of a surprising US, that outcome increases the salience of the CS on Trial 11. The surprisingness of the US on Trial 10 does not determine what is learned on Trial 10. How much attention the CS attracts on Trial 10 is assumed to have been determined by Trials 1–9. Thus, US surprisingness is assumed to have only a *prospective* or *proactive* influence on conditioning. This is an important contrast to US-reduction models, in which the surprisingness of the US determines what is learned on the same trial the US is presented.

The assumption that the US on a given trial influences only what is learned on the next trial has permitted CS reduction models to explain certain findings (for example, Mackintosh, Bygrave, & Picton, 1977). However, that assumption has made it difficult for the models to explain other results. In particular, the models cannot explain blocking that occurs on the first trial of Phase 2 of the blocking experiment (for example, Azorlosa & Cicala, 1986; Balaz, Kasprow, & Miller, 1982; Dickinson, Nicholas, & Mackintosh, 1983; Gillan & Domjan, 1977). According to CS-reduction models, blocking occurs because in Phase 2 of the blocking experiment the lack of surprisingness of the US reduces the salience of the added CS. However, that reduction in salience can occur only after the first Phase 2 trial. Therefore, CS-reduction models cannot explain blocking that occurs on the first trial of Phase 2 of the blocking experiment.

The Relative Waiting Time Hypothesis.   Neither the Rescorla-Wagner model nor CS modification models were designed to explain the effects of time in conditioning. By contrast, temporal factors are the focus of the **relative waiting time hypothesis** (Gibbon & Balsam, 1981; Jenkins, Barnes, & Barrera, 1981). This hypothesis, also referred to as the *scalar expectancy hypothesis,* was developed to explain the results of studies of sign tracking in which the duration of the CS and the interval between tri-

J. Gibbon

als or successive food presentations were systematically varied. The findings indicate that the strength of conditioned responding is determined by a comparison of two time intervals: how long the organism has to wait for food in the presence of the CS (*CS waiting time*) and how long the organism has to wait for food in the experimental situation irrespective of the conditioned stimulus (*context waiting time*) (see Cooper, 1991, for a review).

A CS is informative about the occurrence of the US only if the participant has to spend less time waiting for the US during the CS than in the experimental situation irrespective of the CS. The relative waiting time hypothesis states that conditioned responding to the CS will develop only if the CS waiting time is much less than the context waiting time. If the CS waiting time is similar to the context waiting time, conditioned responding will not be observed.

The relative waiting time hypothesis has been tested in studies of the effects of introducing extra unconditioned stimuli between trials involving pairings of a target CS and a US. These extra USs during the intertrial interval should decrease the context waiting time and thereby reduce the ratio between the context and CS waiting times. A smaller ratio of context-to-CS waiting times should result in less conditioned responding to the CS. This prediction of the relative waiting time hypothesis has been confirmed. Extra intertrial USs invariably result in less responding to the CS. However, an important corollary of the hypothesis has yielded more controversial results.

The corollary is that context waiting time is to be measured independent of any signals that might permit prediction of the extra USs. Some studies have reported that extra USs disrupt conditioned responding whether or not these USs are signaled (for example, Jenkins et al., 1981), whereas others have observed that signaling the extra USs makes them less effective in disrupting conditioned responding (for example, Durlach, 1983). These and other data have encouraged revisions of the relative waiting time hypothesis (see Cooper, 1991; Cooper, Aronson, Balsam, & Gibbon, 1990).

The Comparator Hypothesis. The relative waiting time hypothesis was developed to explain certain temporal features of excitatory conditioning and manipulations of CS-US contingency. One of its important contributions was to emphasize that conditioned responding depends not only on what happens during the CS but also on what happens in the experimental situation in general. The idea that both of these factors influence many learning phenomena has been developed in greater detail by R. Miller and his collaborators in the **comparator hypothesis** (Miller & Matzel, 1988, 1989).

The comparator hypothesis is similar to the relative waiting time hypothesis in its assumption that conditioned responding depends not only on associations between a target CS and the US but also on possible associations that may be learned between contextual cues and the US. The associative strength of other cues present during training with the target CS is especially important. Another restriction of the comparator hypothesis is that it only allows for the formation of excitatory associations with the US. Whether conditioned responding reflects excitation or inhibition is assumed to be determined by the relative strengths of excitation conditioned to the target CS as compared to the excitatory value of the contextual cues that were present with the target CS during training.

The comparator process is represented by the balance shown in Figure 4.15. As Figure 4.15 illustrates, a comparison is made between the excitatory value of the

P. D. Balsam

R. R. Miller

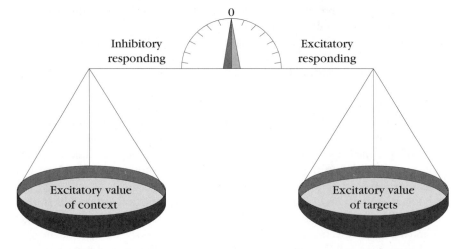

Figure 4.15 Illustration of the comparator hypothesis. Responding to the target CS is represented by the reading on the balance. If the excitatory value of the target CS exceeds the excitatory value of the other cues present during training of the target CS, the balance tips in favor of excitatory responding to the CS. As the associative value of the contextual cues increases, the comparison becomes less favorable for excitatory responding and may tip in favor of inhibitory responding.

target CS and the excitatory value of the other cues that are present during the training of the CS. If CS excitation exceeds the excitatory value of the contextual cues, the balance of the comparison will be tipped in favor of excitatory responding to the target CS. As the excitatory value of the other cues becomes stronger, the balance of the comparison will become less favorable for excitatory responding. In fact, if the excitatory value of the contextual cues becomes sufficiently strong, the balance may become tipped in favor of inhibitory responding to the target CS.

Unlike the relative waiting time hypothesis, the comparator hypothesis emphasizes associations rather than time. It assumes that organisms learn three associations during the course of conditioning: an association between the target CS and the US, an association between other contextual stimuli and the US, and an association between the target CS and those other contextual cues. When the target CS is presented, all three of these associations are activated, permitting the organism to compare the CS-US association to the context-US association. That comparison determines conditioned responding.

It is important to note that the comparator hypothesis makes no assumptions about how associations become established. Rather, it describes how CS-US and context-US associations determine responding to the target CS. Thus, unlike US-modification and CS-modification models, the comparator hypothesis is a theory of *performance,* not a theory of learning.

An important corollary to the comparator hypothesis is that the comparison of CS-US and context-US associations is made at the time of testing for conditioned responding. Because of this assumption, the comparator hypothesis makes the unusual prediction that extinction of context-US associations following training of

a target CS will enhance responding to that target CS. This prediction has been confirmed in several studies (Hallam, Matzel, Sloat, & Miller, 1990; Matzel, Brown, & Miller, 1987; Miller, Barnet, & Grahame, 1992). US-modification and CS-modification theories of learning do not predict such an outcome.

The comparator hypothesis has been most extensively tested in studies of conditioned inhibition (see Kasprow, Schachtman, & Miller, 1987; Schachtman, Brown, Gordon, Catterson, & Miller, 1987). The hypothesis attributes inhibitory responding to situations in which the association of the target CS with the US is weaker than the association of contextual cues with the US. The contextual cues in this case are the stimuli that provide the excitatory context for inhibitory conditioning. Interestingly, the hypothesis predicts that extinction of these conditioned excitatory stimuli following inhibitory conditioning will reduce inhibitory responding. Thus, the comparator hypothesis is unique in predicting that extinction of conditioned inhibition is best accomplished not by presenting the CS– alone but by extinguishing the CS+ cues that provided the excitatory context for inhibitory conditioning. As I noted earlier in my discussion of the extinction of conditioned inhibition, this unusual prediction has been confirmed (Best et al., 1985; Lysle & Fowler, 1985).

Although the comparator hypothesis has accurately predicted the results of studies involving extinction of contextual cues after training, efforts to obtain the opposite effect have been less successful. The model predicts that increasing the excitatory value of contextual cues after training will reduce conditioned responding to the target CS (see Figure 4.15). However, a number of experiments have failed to find this outcome (Miller, Hallam, & Grahame, 1990; Robbins, 1988).

On balance the comparator hypothesis has identified some important contextual constraints on conditioned responding, especially following inhibitory training. It is the only major theory that can explain why postconditioning extinction of the training context increases excitatory conditioned responding. However, as with other models, the hypothesis has not been totally successful.

SOP and AESOP. Each of the new models I have described emphasizes a different aspect of classical conditioning. The relative waiting time hypothesis addresses a fairly small range of phenomena involving the temporal distribution of conditioned and unconditioned stimuli. The comparator hypothesis is more ambitious, but it is a theory of performance rather than learning, and therefore it does not provide an explanation of how associations are acquired. CS-modification models attempt to address the same wide range of phenomena as does the Rescorla-Wagner model, but they have some of the same difficulties as the Rescorla-Wagner model. All of these models have been important in directing attention to previously ignored aspects of classical conditioning. However, none of them has come to dominate the study of classical conditioning as the Rescorla-Wagner model did in the 1970s.

The last two models I will discuss—SOP and AESOP—are the most ambitious in attempting to provide a new, comprehensive approach to classical conditioning (Wagner, 1981; Wagner & Brandon, 1989; Wagner & Larew, 1985). These models provide not only an account of the acquisition of conditioned excitation and inhibition but also an explanation of the form of conditioned responses (Paletta & Wagner, 1986). Thus, unlike the other models that characterize only learning *or* performance, these models provide an account of both aspects of classical conditioning. Furthermore, SOP and AESOP are "real time" models, and hence can explain time-dependent conditioning effects.

A. R. Wagner

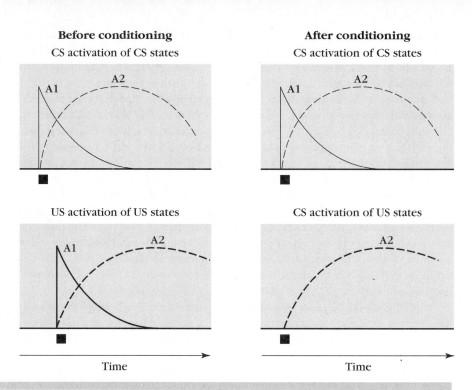

Before conditioning

CS activation of CS states

A1   A2

US activation of US states

A1   A2

After conditioning

CS activation of CS states

A1   A2

CS activation of US states

A2

Time   Time

Figure 4.16 Mechanisms of the SOP model. Before the CS has been conditioned (left), the CS and the US elicit their own respective A1 and A2 states. After the CS has been conditioned (right), it continues to elicit its own A1 and A2 states. In addition, the CS elicits the A2 state of the US.

1-SOP. SOP is an acronym for both "standard operating procedures" of memory and "sometimes opponent process." The SOP model provides a general characterization of how stimuli are processed by the nervous system. Its starting assumptions bear striking resemblance to the opponent-process ideas already presented in discussions of the opponent-process theory of motivation in Chapter 2 and compensatory conditioned responses discussed earlier in this chapter. As illustrated in Figure 4.16, each stimulus is presumed to have a primary (A1) and a secondary (A2) effect. The A1 and A2 states are analogous to the primary (*a*) and opponent (*b*) states of the opponent-process theory of motivation. When the stimulus starts, the A1 state predominates; the A2 state then gradually takes over, followed by its own decay.

An excitatory association between a CS and a US is presumed to develop if the A1 state of the CS overlaps with the A1 state of the US, as is the case for the CS and US diagrammed in Figure 4.16. Once a CS-US association has been learned, the CS continues to elicit its own A1 and A2 states, as shown in the upper right-hand graph of Figure 4.16. Moreover, the CS comes to activate neural processes related to the US as well. After excitatory conditioning, however, the CS is not assumed to act as a substitute for the US. Rather, it activates only the A2 state of the US.

Because excitatory conditioning is presumed to occur only if the A1 states of the CS and the US overlap, the model predicts systematic changes in the degree of excitatory conditioning as a function of variations in the CS-US interval. None of the other models of conditioning considered so far explain the effects of variations in the CS-US interval on associative strength.

SOP also provides rules for predicting the form of the conditioned response. Before conditioning, the CS is not a biologically significant stimulus. Hence, the A1 and A2 states of the CS are not manifest in strong behavioral reactions. By contrast, the A1 and A2 states of the US create easily observed behavior. The initial reaction to an injection of morphine, for example, is a decrease in activity, which is followed by hyperactivity as a delayed or secondary response. Because an excitatory CS is presumed to elicit the A2 state of the US, the CR to morphine is expected to be the hyperactivity response. Thus, in cases where the secondary effects of the US are opposite the initial reactions to the US, the CR is expected to be this opposing response.

As I have noted, however, not all USs produce biphasic URs. For example, an aversive stimulus elicits a reduction in pain sensitivity, which is not followed by enhanced pain sensitivity. Therefore, in such a case the CR, which mimics the delayed effects of the US, will not be opposite in form to the initial effects of the US. SOP predicts that the form of the CR will be opposite the form of the UR only with USs that have biphasic behavioral effects. Hence, SOP is a "sometimes opponent process" model. These predictions have been confirmed in studies of conditioned morphine effects and conditioned hypoalgesia (see Wagner & Brandon, 1989). However, the generality of these ideas remains to be tested.

2-AESOP. SOP was subsequently extended in recognition of the fact that unconditioned stimuli are complex events that have multiple aspects of potential significance for learning. In particular, unconditioned stimuli may be viewed as having motivational-emotional aspects as well as simple sensory features. AESOP is an extension of SOP designed specifically to incorporate the motivational emotional aspects of unconditioned stimuli. Thus, AESOP is the "affective extension" of SOP. The basic assumption of AESOP is that unconditioned stimuli activate two sets of A1 and A2 processes—one set related to sensory features of the US and the other set related to the emotional features of the US. Emotional reactivity is generally slower than the simple sensation of a stimulus. (If someone tells you that your best friend is sick and will not be able to visit you, your disappointment may not be immediate and will last longer than your awareness of the spoken message.) Therefore, the A1 and A2 processes related to emotional effects of a US are also presumed to be longer lasting.

The added assumption that unconditioned stimuli have multiple features with different time courses enables AESOP to explain a greater range of findings concerning the nature of conditioned responses (see Wagner & Brandon, 1989). In addition, it provides an account for the puzzling finding that a given CS can have both conditioned excitatory and conditioned inhibitory properties (for example, Tait & Saladin, 1986). The CS can have excitatory associations with one aspect of the US and inhibitory associations with other US features at the same time.

SOP and AESOP have been remarkably successful in explaining a wide range of phenomena and offer an approach to integrating issues relevant to both learning and performance. However, even these models leave many important phenomena unaccounted for. For example, it is not clear how SOP and AESOP would explain comparator effects in inhibitory conditioning. The models also may have difficulty with findings concerning extinction. For example, they assume that extinction of excitation occurs by the same process responsible for conditioned inhibition, even though empirical evidence fails to support a conditioned inhibition view of extinction. The models also cannot explain how the nature of the conditioned stimulus determines the form of the conditioned response or why, in some situations, the conditioned response appears to bear little resemblance to the unconditioned responses. Thus, the task of integrating all knowledge about classical conditioning remains a challenge as investigators approach the second century of research in this area.

CONCLUDING COMMENTS

Traditionally, classical conditioning has been regarded as a relatively simple and primitive type of learning that is involved in the regulation only of glandular and visceral responses such as salivation. The establishment of CS-US associations was assumed to occur fairly automatically with the pairing of a CS and a US. Given the simple and automatic nature of the conditioning and its limitation to glandular and visceral responses, it was not viewed as important in explaining the complexity and richness of human experience. This view of classical conditioning is no longer tenable.

The research reviewed in Chapters 3 and 4 has shown that classical conditioning involves numerous complex processes and is involved in the control of a wide variety of responses, including emotional behavior and locomotor movements. The learning does not occur automatically with the pairing of a CS with a US. Rather, it depends on the organism's prior experience with each of these stimuli, the presence of other stimuli during the conditioning trial, and the extent to which the CS and US are relevant to each other. Furthermore, the processes of classical conditioning are not limited to CS-US pairings. Learned associations can occur between two biologically weak stimuli (sensory preconditioning), in the absence of an unconditioned stimulus (higher-order conditioning), or in the absence of conventional conditioned stimuli (counterconditioning).

Given these and other complexities of classical conditioning processes, it is a mistake to disregard classical conditioning in attempts to explain complex forms of behavior. The richness of classical conditioning mechanisms makes them potentially quite relevant to the richness and complexity of human experience.

SAMPLE QUESTIONS

1. What, if any, limits are there on the kinds of stimuli that can serve as conditioned and unconditioned stimuli in Pavlovian conditioning?

2. How can Pavlovian conditioning mechanisms explain drug tolerance, and what are some of the implications of these mechanisms?

3. How can S-R and S-S learning be distinguished experimentally?

4. Describe the basic idea of the Rescorla-Wagner model. What aspect of the model allows it to explain the blocking effect and make some unusual predictions?

5. In what respects are attentional theories of learning different from other theories?

KEY TERMS

blocking effect Interference with the conditioning of a novel stimulus because of the presence of a previously conditioned stimulus.

comparator hypothesis The idea that conditioned responding depends on a comparison between the associative strength of the conditioned stimulus (CS) and the associative strength of other cues present during training of the target CS.

conditioned compensatory-response A conditioned response opposite in form to the reaction elicited by the unconditioned stimulus and which therefore compensates for this reaction.

counterconditioning A conditioning procedure that reverses the organism's previous response to a stimulus. For example, an animal may be conditioned to approach a stimulus that initially elicited withdrawal reactions.

CS-preexposure effect Interference with conditioning produced by repeated exposures to the conditioned stimulus before the conditioning trials. Also called *latent-inhibition effect*.

drug tolerance Reduction in the effectiveness of a drug as a result of repeated use of the drug.

higher-order conditioning A procedure in which a previously conditioned stimulus (CS1) is used to condition a new stimulus (CS2).

latent-inhibition effect Same as *CS-preexposure effect*.

relative waiting time hypothesis The idea that conditioned responding depends on how long the organism has to wait for the unconditioned stimulus (US) in the presence of the conditioned stimulus (CS), as compared to how long the organism has to wait for the US in the experimental situation irrespective of the CS.

S-R learning The learning of an association between a stimulus (S) and a response (R), with the result that the stimulus comes to elicit the response.

S-S learning The learning of an association between two stimuli, with the result that exposure to one of the stimuli comes to activate a representation, or mental image, of the other stimulus.

sensory preconditioning A procedure in which one biologically weak stimulus (CS2) is repeatedly paired with another biologically weak stimulus (CS1). Then, CS1 is conditioned with an unconditioned stimulus. In a later test trial, CS2 also will elicit the conditioned response, even though CS2 was never directly paired with the unconditioned stimulus.

stimulus-response learning Same as *S-R learning*.

stimulus-stimulus learning Same as *S-S learning*.

stimulus substitution The idea that the outcome of classical conditioning is that organisms come to respond to the conditioned stimulus in much the same way that they respond to the unconditioned stimulus.

US-preexposure effect Interference with conditioning produced by repeated exposures to the unconditioned stimulus before the conditioning trials.

US devaluation Reduction in the attractiveness of an unconditioned stimulus, usually achieved by aversion conditioning or satiation.

INSTRUMENTAL CONDITIONING: FOUNDATIONS

Early Investigations of Instrumental Conditioning

Modern Approaches to the Study of Instrumental Conditioning

Discrete-Trial Procedures

Free-Operant Procedures

Instrumental Conditioning Procedures

Fundamental Elements of Instrumental Conditioning

The Instrumental Response

The Instrumental Reinforcer

The Response-Reinforcer Relation

C HAPTER 5 begins a discussion of instrumental conditioning and goal-directed behavior. In this type of conditioning, presentations of stimuli depend on the prior occurrence of designated responses. I will first discuss the origins of research on instrumental conditioning and the investigative methods used in contemporary research. This discussion lays the groundwork for the section following, in which the four basic types of instrumental conditioning procedures are described. I will conclude the chapter with a discussion of three fundamental elements of the instrumental conditioning paradigm: the instrumental response, the goal event, and the relation between the instrumental response and the goal event.

In the preceding chapters I described various aspects of how responses are elicited by discrete stimuli. Studies of habituation, sensitization, and classical conditioning are all concerned with analyses of the mechanisms of elicited behavior. Because of this emphasis, experiments on habituation, sensitization, and classical conditioning use procedures in which the organism has no control over the stimuli to which it is exposed. In the present chapter, I will turn to the analysis of learning situations in which the stimuli an organism encounters are a direct result of its behavior. Such behavior is commonly referred to as "goal-directed."

By studying hard, a student can earn a better grade in a class; by turning the car key in the ignition, a driver can start the engine; by putting a coin in a vending machine, a child can obtain a piece of candy. In all these instances, some aspect of the person's behavior is instrumental in producing a significant stimulus or outcome. Furthermore, the behavior occurs because similar actions produced the same type of outcome in the past. Students would not study if studying did not yield interesting information or good grades at least occasionally, drivers would not turn the ignition key if this did not start the engine, and children would not put coins in a candy machine if they did not get candy in return. Behavior that occurs because it was previously instrumental in producing certain consequences is called instrumental behavior.

The fact that the consequences of an action can determine future occurrences of that action is obvious to everyone. If you happen to find a dollar bill when you glance down, you will keep looking at the ground as you walk. How such consequences influence future behavior is not so readily apparent. Much of the remainder of this text is devoted to a discussion of the mechanisms responsible for the control of behavior by its consequences. In the present chapter, I will describe some of the history, basic techniques, procedures, and issues in the experimental analysis of instrumental, or goal-directed, behavior.

How might instrumental behavior be investigated? One way would be to go to the natural environment and look for examples of goal-directed behavior. However, this approach is not likely to lead to definitive results because factors responsible for goal-directed behavior are difficult to isolate without experimental manipulation.

Consider, for example, a dog sitting comfortably in its yard. When an intruder approaches, the dog starts to bark vigorously, with the result that the intruder goes away. Because the dog's barking has a clear consequence (departure of the intruder), it is tempting to conclude that the dog barked in order to produce this consequence— that barking was goal-directed. However, an equally likely possibility is that barking was elicited by the novelty of the intruder and persisted as long as the eliciting stimulus was present. The response consequence—departure of the intruder—may have been incidental to the dog's barking. Deciding between such alternatives is difficult without experimental manipulations of the relation between barking and its consequences. (For an experimental analysis of a similar situation in a fish species, see Losey & Sevenster, 1995).

The type of research I will discuss brings instrumental behavior into the laboratory. The idea, as with elicited behaviors, is to study representative instrumental responses in the hope of discovering general principles.

EARLY INVESTIGATIONS OF INSTRUMENTAL CONDITIONING

Laboratory and theoretical analyses of instrumental conditioning began in earnest with the work of E. L. Thorndike. Thorndike's original intent was to study animal intelligence (Thorndike, 1898, 1911). As I noted in Chapter 1, the publication of Darwin's theory of evolution stimulated people to speculate about the extent to which human intellectual capacities such as reasoning were present in animals. Thorndike pursued this question through empirical research. He devised a series of puzzle boxes for his experiments. His training procedure consisted of placing a hungry cat (or dog or chicken) in the puzzle box with some food left outside in plain view of the animal. The task for the cat was to learn how to get out of the box and obtain the food.

Different puzzle boxes required different responses to get out. Some were easier than others. In the simplest boxes, the cat's random movements initially led to escape and access to the food. With repeated trials, the cat escaped more and more quickly. In more complicated boxes, such as box "K" shown in Figure 5.1, escape also improved with practice, but more slowly. In box "K," the cat had to pull a string, depress a pedal, and open one of two latches to get out. Figure 5.1 shows the median times for escape for five cats. None of the cats escaped on the first trial in the 10-minute maximum time that was allowed. Their performance improved on later trials; toward the end of the experiment they escaped in 2–3 minutes.

Thorndike interpreted the results of his studies as reflecting the learning of an association. When a cat was initially placed in a box, it displayed a variety of responses typical of a confined animal. Eventually, some of these responses resulted in opening the door. Thorndike believed that such successful escapes led to the learning of an association between the stimuli inside the puzzle box and the escape response. As the association, or connection, between the box cues and the successful response became stronger, the cat came to make that response more quickly. The consequence of the successful response—escaping the box—strengthened the association between the box stimuli and that response.

Figure 5.1 Thorndike's puzzle box "K" and the median escape times of five cats tested in the box on 40 successive trials. The cats took less and less time to get out of the box with practice. (Left: From "Animal Intelligence: An Experimental Study of the Association Processes in Animals," by E. L. Thorndike, 1898, *Psychological Review Monograph, 2* (*Whole no. 8*). Right: Adapted from "Thorndike's (1898) Puzzle-Box Experiments Revisited," by H. Imada and S. Imada, 1983, Kwansie Gakuin University Annual Studies, *32,* pp. 167–184. Reprinted by permission.)

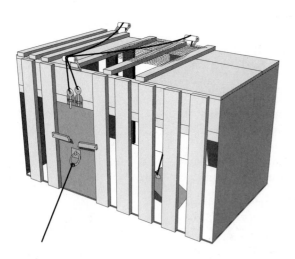

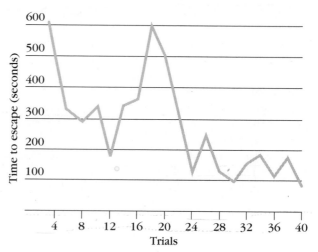

E. L. THORNDIKE: BIOGRAPHICAL SKETCH

Edward Lee Thorndike was born in 1874 and died in 1949. As an undergraduate at Wesleyan University, he became interested in the work of William James, then at Harvard. Thorndike himself entered Harvard as a graduate student in 1895. During his stay he began his research on instrumental behavior, at first using chicks. Since there was no laboratory space at Harvard, he set up his project in William James's cellar. Soon after that, he was offered a fellowship at Columbia University. This time his laboratory was located in the attic of psychologist James Cattell.

Thorndike received his Ph.D. from Columbia in 1898 for his work entitled "Animal Intelligence: An Experimental Analysis of Associative Processes in Animals." This included the famous puzzle-box experiments. Thorndike stayed on in New York at Columbia University Teachers College, where for many years he served as professor of educational psychology. Among other things, he attempted to apply to children the principles of trial-and-error learning he had uncovered with animals. He also became interested in psychological testing and became a leader in this newly formed field. Several years before his death, Thorndike returned to Harvard as the William James Lecturer—a fitting honor considering the origins of his interests in psychology.

On the basis of his research, Thorndike formulated the law of effect. The law of effect states that if a response in the presence of a stimulus is followed by a *satisfying event,* the association between the stimulus (S) and the response (R) is strengthened. If the response is followed by an *annoying event,* the S-R association is weakened. It is important to stress here that, according to the law of effect, animals learn an association between the response and the stimuli present at the time of the response. The consequence of the response is not one of the elements in the association. The satisfying or annoying consequence simply serves to strengthen or weaken the association, or bond, between the response and the stimulus situation. Thus, Thorndike's law of effect involves *S-R learning.*

MODERN APPROACHES TO THE STUDY OF INSTRUMENTAL CONDITIONING

Thorndike used 15 different puzzle boxes in his investigations. Each box required different manipulations for the cat to get out. As more scientists became involved in studying instrumental learning, the range of tasks they used became much smaller. A few of these became "standard" and have been used repeatedly to facilitate comparison of results obtained in different laboratories.

Discrete-Trial Procedures

Discrete-trial procedures are similar to the method Thorndike used in that each training trial ends with removal of the animal from the apparatus, and the instrumental response is performed only once during each trial. Discrete-trial investigations of instrumental behavior are often conducted in some type of maze. The use of mazes

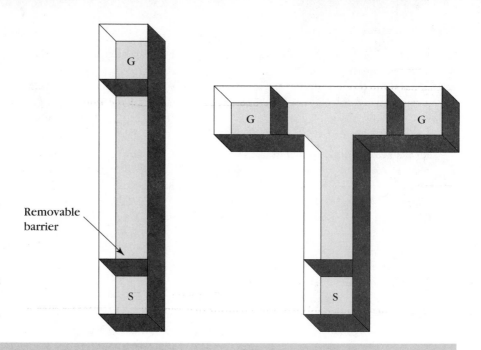

Figure 5.2 Top view of a runway and a T-maze. S is the start box; G is the goal box.

Removable barrier

in investigations of learning was introduced at the turn of the twentieth century by W. S. Small (1899, 1900), an American psychologist. Small was interested in studying rats and was encouraged to use a maze by an article he had read in *Scientific American* describing the complex system of underground burrows that kangaroo rats build in their natural habitat. Small reasoned that a maze would take advantage of the rats' "propensity for small winding passages."

Figure 5.2 shows two mazes frequently used in contemporary research. (For other mazes, see Figures 5.12 and 11.4.) The runway or straight-alley maze contains a start box at one end and a goal box at the other. The rat is placed in the start box at the beginning of each trial. The movable barrier separating the start box from the main section of the runway is then lifted. The rat is allowed to make its way down the runway until it reaches the goal box, which usually contains a reinforcer such as food or water.

Another frequently used maze is the T-maze, shown on the right in Figure 5.2. The T-maze consists of a start box and alleys arranged in the shape of a T. A goal box is located at the end of each arm of the T. Because it has two goal boxes, the T-maze is well suited to studying choice behavior. For example, the one goal box may be baited with plain food and the other with food flavored with NutraSweet®. By seeing which arm the rat chooses over a series of trials, the experimenter can measure preference for one food over the other.

Behavior in a maze can be quantified by measuring how fast the animal gets from the start box to the goal box. This is called the **running speed.** The running speed typically increases with repeated training trials. Another common measure of behavior in runways is the **latency.** The latency of the running response is the time it takes the animal to leave the start box and begin moving down the alley. Typically, latencies become shorter as training progresses.

In a runway or a T-maze, after reaching the goal box, the animal is removed from the apparatus for awhile before being returned to the start box for its next trial. Thus, the animal has limited opportunities to respond, and those opportunities are scheduled by the experimenter. By contrast, free-operant procedures allow the animal to repeat the instrumental response "freely" over and over again. The free-operant method was devised by B. F. Skinner (1938) to study behavior in a more continuous manner than is possible with mazes.

Skinner (Figure 5.3) was interested in analyzing in the laboratory a form of behavior that would be representative of all naturally occurring ongoing activity. However, he recognized that before behavior can be experimentally analyzed, a measurable unit of behavior must be defined. Casual observation suggests that ongoing behavior is continuous; one activity leads to another. Behavior does not fall neatly into units as do molecules of a chemical solution. Skinner proposed the concept of the operant as a way of dividing behavior into meaningful measurable units.

Figure 5.4 shows a typical Skinner box used to study free-operant behavior in rats. The box is a small chamber that contains a lever that the rat can push down repeatedly. The chamber also has a mechanism that can deliver a reinforcer such as

Figure 5.3   B. F. Skinner (1904–1990) (Bettman Archive).

Figure 5.4 A Skinner box equipped with a response lever and a food delivery device. Electronic equipment is used to program procedures and record responses automatically. (Omikron/Photo Researchers, Inc.)

food or water. In the simplest experiment, a hungry rat is placed in the chamber. The lever is electronically connected to the food delivery system. When the rat depresses the lever, a pellet of food falls into the food cup.

An **operant response,** such as the lever press, is defined in terms of the effect that it has on the environment. Activities that have the same environmental effect are considered to be instances of the same operant. The critical thing is not the muscles involved in the behavior but the way in which the behavior "operates" on the environment. For example, the lever-press operant in rats is typically defined as sufficient depression of the lever to cause the closure of a microswitch. The rat may press the lever with its right paw, its left paw, or its tail. These different muscle responses constitute the same operant if they all depress the lever the required amount. Various ways of pressing the lever are assumed to be functionally equivalent because they all have the same effect on the environment—namely, closing the microswitch.

Magazine Training and Shaping. Most rats, when placed in a Skinner box, do not press the lever frequently. There are some preliminary steps for establishing the lever-press behavior. First, the animals have to learn when food is available in the food cup. This involves classical conditioning: the sound of the food delivery device is repeatedly paired with the delivery of a food pellet into the cup. The food delivery device is called the *food magazine.* After enough pairings of the sound of the food magazine with food delivery, the sound comes to elicit a sign tracking response: the animal goes to the food cup and picks up the food pellet. This preliminary phase of conditioning is called magazine training.

After magazine training, the organism is ready to learn the required instrumental response. If the response is not something the animal already does occasionally, it may never "discover" on its own what it has to do to obtain food. To facilitate the acquisition of a new operant response, experimenters employ a strategy that has been used

128

by animal trainers for centuries. At first food is given if the animal does anything remotely related to the desired response. For example, at first a rat may be given a food pellet each time it gets up on its hind legs anywhere in the experimental chamber. Once the rearing response has been established, the food pellet may be given only if the rat rears over the response lever. Rearing in other parts of the chamber would no longer be reinforced. Once rearing over the lever has been established, the food pellet may be given only after the rat actually depresses the lever. Such a sequence of training steps is called shaping. Shaping involves two complementary tactics: *reinforcement of successive approximations* to the required response and *nonreinforcement of earlier response forms.*

As is illustrated in the preceding example, the shaping of a new operant requires training response components or approximations to the final behavior. Once an operant response such as lever pressing has become established, the manner in which the organism accomplishes the required operation on the environment does not matter. Nevertheless, the steps used in shaping the behavior continue to influence how the response is made. For example, if rearing was one of the reinforced approximations during shaping, the rat is likely to continue to rear as it presses the lever (Stokes & Balsam, 1991). With extensive training, responding becomes more efficient and comes to involve less energy expenditure (Brener & Mitchell, 1989; Mitchell & Brener, 1991)

Shaping of Response Form.   Shaping procedures can be used not only to train new operants but also to train new features or parameters of an operant response. For example, after a child has been taught how to hit a baseball with a bat properly, the teacher may want to shape increases in the force of the batting response to enable the child to hit the ball farther. Many aspects of sports involve such training of response parameters: learning to throw or kick a football farther, to jump off a higher diving board, to swim faster, to hold a bow and arrow more steadily, and so forth.

In a laboratory study, Deich, Allan, and Zeigler (1988) shaped the gape response of pigeons pecking for food reinforcement. Pigeons peck for food with their beaks opened a bit. Deich and his associates used a special transducer to measure how far the birds kept their beaks open as they pecked a response key. In a baseline phase, the pigeons were reinforced for pecking irrespective of their gape. In another phase of the experiment, food was provided only if the pigeons' beaks were opened wider than a criterion value. The criterion was chosen based on the previous day's performance so that at least 20% of the birds' pecks would be reinforced. As the birds met each new criterion, the criterion was made more stringent, thereby shaping the birds to peck with increasingly wider gapes. In a comparable manner, decreases in the gape response were shaped in another phase of the experiment.

Figure 5.5 shows the results for one pigeon. During the baseline phase, when reinforcement was independent of the bird's gape, the pigeon made intermediate gape responses. After the shaping procedure in which the criterion for reinforcement required progressively wider gapes, the pigeon learned to peck with its beak opened wider. By contrast, after shaping in which the criterion for reinforcement involved progressively smaller gapes, the pigeon learned to peck with its beak more tightly closed. These changes occurred fairly rapidly. The data in the middle panel of Figure 5.5 were obtained during the fifth training session, and the data in the bottom panel came from the seventh session of that condition. (Each session had 32 trials.)

The results presented in Figure 5.5 illustrate several important aspects of the process of shaping. Most responses are like the gape response in that they occur with

Figure 5.5 llustration of the shaping of gape size in pigeons. Each panel shows the relative frequency of gapes of various sizes observed in the pecking behavior of a pigeon. During the baseline phase (top panel), pecking was reinforced with food irrespective of the size of the gape. In the other phases, pecking was reinforced only if it occurred with gapes that either exceeded a progressively increasing criterion (middle panel) or were less than a progressively decreasing criterion (bottom panel). (From "Conjunctive Differentiation of Gape During Food-Reinforced Keypecking in the Pigeon," by J. D. Deich, R. W. Allan, and H. P. Zeigler, *Animal Learning & Behavior,* 1988, *16,* 268–276. Copyright © 1988 by the Psychonomic Society. Reprinted by permission.)

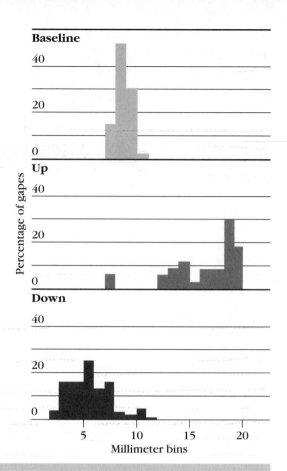

some variability. The gape response was most uniform during the baseline phase. However, even then, the pigeon pecked with a range of gapes—its gape ranged from 7 to 10 mm during different pecks. This variability in responding helps to ensure that at least a few responses occur that are in the direction the investigator wants to shape. Thus, *shaping takes advantage of the inherent variability of behavior.* Without such variability, shaping procedures could not succeed.

When a gape-size criterion was introduced, the distribution of gape sizes shifted in the direction of the reinforcement criterion. Presenting food only if the gape exceeded a certain size, for example, served to shift the distribution of gape sizes to higher values. However, it was important to set each criterion so that at least some of the pigeon's existing responses could be reinforced. For example, the first shaping criterion could not have been set at 15 mm because during the baseline phase the pigeon never made a peck with its beak more than 10 mm apart.

As the criterion for reinforcement was gradually shifted during shaping, the pigeon's responses shifted correspondingly. As this process continued, the pigeon started making responses that it had never displayed prior to training. For example, after the pigeon was trained to peck with progressively larger gapes, it pecked with its beak opened 20 mm some of the time. By contrast, during the baseline phase, gapes had never exceeded 10 mm. In an analogous fashion, shaping of small gapes produced pecks with gapes as small as 4 mm, which never had been observed during the baseline phase. These aspects of the results illustrate that *shaping can produce new response forms*—forms never before performed by the organism. (For additional discussions of shaping, see Galbicka, 1988; Midgley, Lea, & Kirby, 1989; Pear & Legris, 1987; Platt, 1973.)

Response Rate as a Measure of Operant Behavior.   The major advantage of free-operant methods over discrete-trial techniques for studying instrumental behavior is that free-operant methods permit continuous observation of behavior over long periods. With continuous opportunity to respond, the organism rather than the experimenter determines the frequency of its instrumental response. Hence, free-operant techniques provide a special opportunity to observe changes in the likelihood of behavior over time.

How might a researcher take advantage of this opportunity and measure the probability of an operant response? Measures of response latency and speed that are commonly used in discrete-trial procedures do not characterize the likelihood of repetitions of a response. Skinner proposed that the *rate of occurrence* of operant behavior (frequency of the response per minute, for example) be used as a measure of response probability. Highly likely responses occur frequently and have a high rate. In contrast, unlikely responses occur seldom and have a low rate.

The Cumulative Recorder.   Free-operant investigations are typically concerned with measuring the rate of behavior over time. Skinner devised a data-recording instrument—the **cumulative recorder**—that is ideally suited to display such information. As shown in Figure 5.6, the cumulative recorder consists of a rotating drum that pulls paper out of the recorder at a constant speed. A pen rests on the surface of the paper. If no responses occur, the pen remains stationary and makes a horizontal line as the paper comes out of the machine. If the animal performs a lever-press response, the pen moves one step vertically on the paper. Since each lever-press response causes

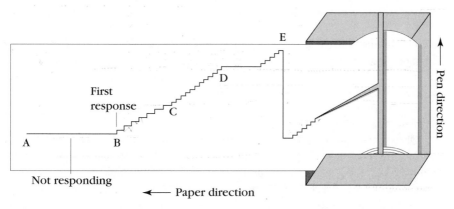

Figure 5.6   Cumulative recorder used for the continuous recording of behavior. The paper moves out of the machine toward the left at a constant speed. Each response causes the pen to move up the paper one step. No responses occurred between points A and B. A moderate rate of responding occurred between points B and C, and a rapid rate occurred between points C and D. At point E, the pen reset to the bottom of the page.

the pen to move one step up the paper, the total vertical distance traveled by the pen represents the cumulative (or total) number of responses the animal has made. Because the paper comes out of the recorder at a constant speed, the horizontal distance on the cumulative record is a measure of how much time has elapsed in the session. The slope of the line made by the cumulative recorder represents the rate of responding.

The cumulative record provides a complete visual representation of when and how frequently the animal responds during a session. In the record of Figure 5.6, for example, the animal did not perform the response between points A and B, and a slow rate of responding occurred between points B and C. Responses occurred more frequently between points C and D, but the animal paused at D. After responding resumed, the pen reached the top of the page (at point E) and reset to the bottom for additional responses.

INSTRUMENTAL CONDITIONING PROCEDURES

In all instrumental conditioning situations, a response is related to an environmental event. The event may be *pleasant* or *unpleasant*. A pleasant event is technically called an **appetitive stimulus.** An unpleasant event is technically called an **aversive stimulus.** The instrumental response may turn on the stimulus. In this case a positive contingency is said to be in effect between the response and its stimulus outcome. Alternatively, the instrumental response may turn off or eliminate a stimulus, in which case a negative contingency is said to be in effect between the response and its outcome. Whether the result of a conditioning procedure is an increase in the rate of responding or a decrease in the response rate depends both on response-outcome contingency and on the nature of the outcome.

Table 5.1 describes four common instrumental conditioning procedures. The procedures differ in what type of stimulus (appetitive or aversive) is controlled by the instrumental response and whether the response produces or eliminates the stimulus.

Positive Reinforcement. The term **positive reinforcement** refers to procedures in which the instrumental response turns on or produces an appetitive stimulus. If the response occurs, the appetitive stimulus is presented; if the response does not occur, the appetitive stimulus is not presented. There is a positive contingency between the instrumental response and an appetitive stimulus, and the procedure produces an increase in the rate of responding.

Giving a hungry rat a food pellet whenever it presses a response lever but not when it does not press the lever is a laboratory example of positive reinforcement. There are also many examples of positive reinforcement outside the laboratory. A father may give his daughter a cookie only when she puts away her toys; a teacher may praise a student only when the student hands in a good report; or an employee may receive a bonus check only when he performs well on the job.

Punishment. The term **punishment** refers to procedures in which the instrumental response produces or turns on an unpleasant, or aversive, stimulus. If the individual performs the instrumental response, it receives the aversive stimulus; if it does not perform the instrumental response, the aversive stimulus is not presented. A mother may reprimand her child for running into the street; a boss may criticize her assistant

**TABLE
5.1** **TYPES OF INSTRUMENTAL
CONDITIONING PROCEDURES**

NAME	RESPONSE-OUTCOME CONTINGENCY	RESULT
Positive reinforcement	*Positive:* Response produces an appetitive stimulus	*Reinforcement,* or increase in response rate
Punishment (positive punishment)	*Positive:* Response produces an aversive stimulus	*Punishment,* or decrease in response rate
Negative reinforcement (escape or avoidance)	*Negative:* Response eliminates or prevents the occurrence of an aversive stimulus	*Reinforcement,* or increase in response rate
Omission training (DRO)	*Negative:* Response eliminates or prevents the occurrence of an appetitive stimulus	*Punishment,* or decrease in response rate

for being late to a meeting; a teacher may give a failing grade to a student who answers too many test questions incorrectly. Such procedures decrease the future likelihood of the instrumental response and hence are called *punishment* procedures. Because there is a positive contingency between the instrumental response and the aversive stimulus, the procedures are also sometimes called *positive punishment*.

Negative Reinforcement.   The first two types of procedures I described involved a positive contingency between the instrumental response and a stimulus outcome. If the response occurred, the consequent stimulus was delivered; if the response did not occur, the consequent stimulus was not delivered. I now turn to procedures that involve a *negative contingency* between the instrumental response and an environmental event. In a negative contingency the response turns off or prevents the presentation of the environmental event. If the response occurs, the stimulus is eliminated or withheld; if the response does not occur, the stimulus remains. Such a procedure increases the likelihood of the instrumental response if the stimulus is an aversive event. Procedures in which the instrumental response terminates or prevents the delivery of an aversive stimulus are called **negative reinforcement**.

There are two types of negative reinforcement procedures. In one case the aversive stimulus is present but can be terminated by the instrumental response. This type of procedure is called escape. The unpleasant static of a radio may be escaped by turning it off. People may leave a movie theater to escape the experience of a bad movie. In the laboratory, a rat may be exposed to a continuous loud noise at the beginning of a trial. By jumping over a barrier or pressing a lever, the rat can escape the noise. In all these cases, the presence of the aversive stimulus sets the occasion for the instrumental response. The instrumental response is then reinforced by termination of the aversive stimulus.

The second type of negative reinforcement procedure involves an aversive stimulus that is scheduled to be presented some time in the future. In this case the instrumental response prevents delivery of the aversive stimulus. This type of procedure is called *avoidance.* People do many things to prevent the occurrence of something bad. Students study before an examination to avoid receiving a bad grade; responding to a fire alarm may permit a person to avoid injury; people get their cars tuned up regularly to avoid unexpected breakdowns. In the laboratory, a rat may be scheduled to receive shock at the end of a warning stimulus. However, if it makes the instrumental response during the warning stimulus, the shock will not be delivered. I will have much more to say about avoidance behavior in Chapter 9.

Omission Training. Another type of procedure that involves a negative contingency between the instrumental response and an environmental event is called **omission training.** In this case, the instrumental response prevents the delivery of a pleasant or appetitive stimulus. If the organism makes the instrumental response, the appetitive stimulus is omitted; if the organism does not respond, the appetitive stimulus occurs. Thus, the appetitive stimulus is delivered only if the individual withholds the instrumental response. Because of that, omission training discourages responding or produces a punishment effect.

Omission training is often a preferred method of discouraging human behavior because, unlike punishment, it does not involve delivering an aversive stimulus. Omission training is being used when a child is told to go to his room after doing something bad. The child does not receive an aversive stimulus when he is told to go to his room. There is nothing aversive about the child's room. Rather, by sending the child to the room, the parent is withdrawing sources of positive reinforcement such as playing with friends or watching television. Suspending a person's driver's license for drunken driving also constitutes omission training (withdrawal of the pleasure and privilege of driving).

Omission training procedures are also sometimes called **differential reinforcement of other behavior,** abbreviated **DRO.** This term highlights the fact that in omission training the individual periodically receives the appetitive stimulus, provided he or she is engaged in behavior other than the response specified by the procedure. Making the target response results in omission of the reward that would have been delivered had the individual performed some "other" behavior. Thus, omission training involves the reinforcement of "other" behavior.

A Final Note on Terminology. The terms used to describe instrumental conditioning procedures are a bit confusing. Several comments may help clarify matters. First, in the terms positive and negative reinforcement, "positive" and "negative" do not refer to pleasant and unpleasant outcomes. Rather, they refer to positive and negative contingencies between the instrumental response and its environmental consequence. Positive reinforcement involves a positive contingency between behavior and the reinforcer (presentation of an appetitive stimulus); negative reinforcement involves a negative contingency between behavior and the reinforcer (removal of an aversive stimulus). The term "reinforcement" is used in both cases because both positive and negative reinforcement procedures produce increases in the rate of the instrumental response. "Reinforcement" refers to strengthening or increased rate of responding.

There also may be confusion regarding negative reinforcement and punishment. An aversive stimulus is used in both procedures. However, the relation of the instrumental response to the aversive stimulus is drastically different in the two cases. In what is commonly called "punishment," there is a positive contingency between the instrumental response and the aversive stimulus. (The response results in delivery of the aversive stimulus.) By contrast, in negative reinforcement, there is a negative

BOX 5.2

OMISSION TRAINING AS A THERAPEUTIC PROCEDURE

Omission training or differential reinforcement of other behavior (DRO) involves the delivery of an appetitive stimulus when the individual fails to perform the target response. Therefore, such procedures can be used to discourage undesired responses. In one study (Barton, Brulle, & Repp, 1986), omission training was used with mentally retarded students of elementary school age. The reinforcers were things like apples, raisins, grapes, and juice. One student engaged in recurrent handflapping (moving the hand up and down or back and forth). The rate of this behavior was first observed under baseline conditions (in the absence of special intervention) for 12 days. Then, an omission training procedure (DRO) was introduced

for the next 29 days. Omission training consisted of providing a reinforcer whenever a 1-minute period elapsed without any handflapping. The omission training phase was then followed by return to the baseline condition, followed by reintroduction of omission training.

The results of the study are summarized in Figure 5.7. During the first baseline phase, the student engaged in handflapping about once a minute. This rate of responding declined to near zero during the first omission training (DRO) phase. Removal of the omission procedure resulted in recovery of the handflapping response. Reintroduction of omission training at the end of the study produced another decline in responding. Interestingly, responding dropped to close to zero faster the second time the omission contingency (DRO) was introduced. These results indicate that omission training is an effective procedure for suppressing responding and illustrate that the suppression of responding is easily reversed by removing the omission procedure.

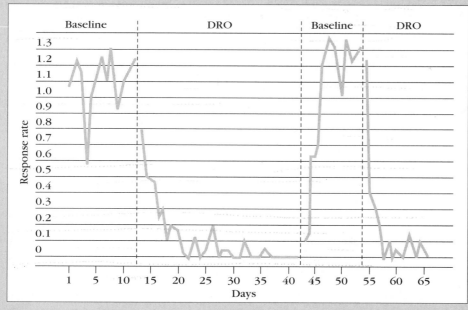

Figure 5.7 Rate of handflapping (responses per minute) by a mentally retarded student during baseline conditions, when reinforcement was not provided, and during omission training phases (DRO), when reinforcement was provided for 1-minute periods without handflapping. (From "Maintenance of Therapeutic Change by Momentary DRO," by L. E. Barton, A. R. Brulle, and A. C. Repp, *Journal of Applied Behavior Analysis*, 1986, *19*, 277–282. Copyright © 1986 by the Journal of Applied Behavior Analysis. Reprinted by permission.)

response-outcome contingency. (The response either terminates or prevents the delivery of the aversive stimulus.) This difference in the contingencies produces very different outcomes. The instrumental response is decreased by the punishment procedure and increased by negative reinforcement.

FUNDAMENTAL ELEMENTS OF INSTRUMENTAL CONDITIONING

As I will show in the coming chapters, the analysis of instrumental conditioning involves numerous factors and variables. However, the essence of instrumental behavior is that it is controlled by its consequences. Thus, instrumental conditioning fundamentally involves three elements: a response, an outcome (the reinforcer), and a relation, or contingency, between the response and the outcome. In the remainder of this chapter, I will discuss how each of these elements influences the course of instrumental conditioning.

The Instrumental Response

The outcome of instrumental conditioning procedures depends in part on the nature of the response being conditioned. Some responses are more easily modified than others. In Chapter 9 I will describe how the nature of the response influences the outcome of negative reinforcement (avoidance) and punishment procedures. The present section describes how the nature of the response determines the results of positive reinforcement procedures.

Reinforcement of an Existing Response. I have already described several contemporary techniques for the study of instrumental conditioning that involve different types of responses. In a runway (or T-maze), animals have to go from the start box to the goal box to obtain the reinforcer. Participants in these experiments do not have to learn the response involved in the task. A rat already knows how to run when it is first put into a runway. But, the rat does not know where the food is or that it will receive a bit of food when it gets to the goal box. Thus, the runway (and the T-maze) require learning where to run and what to run for.

The Creation of New Response Units. In contrast to a runway or T-maze, free-operant lever-press training does require learning a new response. Most of the rats that serve in Skinner box experiments have never had the opportunity to press a lever before. Therefore, the lever-press behavior has to be shaped by the reinforcement of successive approximations. Exactly how is this shaping done, and what does it accomplish?

Although rats may come into a lever-press experiment never having pressed a lever before, they are not entirely inexperienced in the various behavioral components of pressing a lever. Lever pressing requires that the rat get up on its hind legs, that it reach out a paw, and that it press down. All these are responses the rat is likely to have made before. What, then, does a rat learn that is new? It learns to put the various components of the lever-press behavior together into a coordinated and effective lever-press response. Unless rearing, reaching out a paw, and pressing down occur in the correct sequence and in the correct place in the experimental chamber, these actions do not constitute pressing the lever. Thus, instrumental conditioning of lever pressing involves the rearrangement of familiar components of the rat's behavior. Reinforcement leads to the creation of a *new response unit made up of familiar response components* (for example, Schwartz, 1981, 1982, 1986; Midgley et al., 1989).

Behavioral Variability versus Stereotypy. Thorndike described instrumental behavior as involving the "stamping in" of an S-R association. Skinner wrote about behavior being "reinforced" or strengthened. Both pioneers emphasized that reinforcement increases the likelihood that the instrumental response will be repeated in the future. This emphasis encouraged the belief that instrumental conditioning produces repetitions of the same response—that it produces uniformity or stereotypy in behavior. Increasingly stereotyped responding does develop if that is allowed or required by the instrumental conditioning procedure (for example, Pisacreta, 1982; Schwartz, 1980, 1985, 1988.) However, that does not mean that instrumental conditioning cannot be also involved in producing creative or variable responses.

Researchers are accustomed to thinking about the requirement for obtaining reinforcement as being an observable action such as a leg, body, or hand movement. Interestingly, however, the criteria for obtaining reinforcement can also be defined in terms of more abstract dimensions of behavior, such as its variability. For example, organisms can learn to obtain reinforcement in a situation where they are required to do something new, something unlike what they did on the preceding four or five trials. Thus, *response variability* can be the basis for instrumental reinforcement.

In one study of the instrumental conditioning of response variability (Page & Neuringer, 1985), pigeons had to peck two response keys eight times to obtain food. The eight pecks could be distributed between the two keys in any manner. All the pecks could be on the left or the right key, or the pigeons could alternate between the keys in various ways (two pecks on the left, followed by one on the right, one on the left, three on the right, and one on the left, for example). However, to obtain food on a given trial, the sequence of left-right pecks had to be different from the pattern of left-right pecks the bird made on the preceding 50 trials. Thus, to obtain reinforcement, the pigeons had to generate novel patterns of left-right pecks and not repeat any pattern for 50 trials. In a control condition, food reinforcement was provided at the same frequency for eight pecks distributed between the two keys, but now the sequence of right and left pecks did not matter. The pigeons did not have to generate novel response sequences in the control condition.

Sample results of the experiment are presented in Figure 5.8 in terms of the percentage of response sequences performed during each session that were different from each other. Results for the first and last 5 days on each procedure are presented separately. About 50% of the response sequences performed were different from each other during the first five sessions of each procedure. When the instrumental conditioning procedure required response variability, variability in responding increased to about 75%. By contrast, in the control condition, when the pigeons were reinforced regardless of the sequence of left-right pecks they made, variability in performed sequences dropped to less than 20%.

This study illustrates two interesting facts about instrumental conditioning. First, it shows that variability in responding can be maintained and increased by reinforcement. Thus, response variability can be established as an operant (see also Machado, 1989, 1992; Morgan & Neuringer, 1990; C. J. Morris, 1987; Neuringer, 1991, 1992, 1993). The results also show that in the absence of explicit reinforcement of response variability, responding becomes more stereotyped with continued

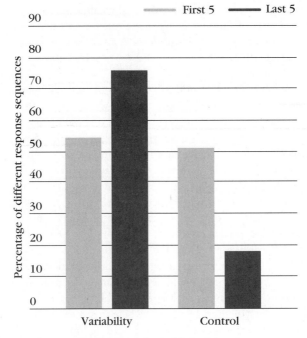

Figure 5.8 Percentage of novel left-right response sequences pigeons performed when variability in response sequences was required for food reinforcement (left) and when food reinforcement was provided regardless of the response sequence performed (right). Data are presented separately for the first five and last five sessions of each procedure. (From "Variability as an Operant," by S. Page and A. Neuringer, *Journal of Experimental Psychology: Animal Behavior Process,* 1985, *11,* 429–452. Copyright © 1985 by the American Psychological Association. Reprinted by permission.)

instrumental conditioning. Pigeons in the control condition decreased the range of different response sequences they performed as training progressed. Thus, the typical consequence of instrumental reinforcement is a decrease in response variability.

Relevance or Belongingness in Instrumental Conditioning. As we saw in the preceding discussion, instrumental conditioning can act on overt response components or on abstract dimensions of behavior. How far do these processes extend? Are there any limits on the types of new behavioral units or response dimensions that may be modified by instrumental conditioning? A growing body of evidence indicates that there are important limitations.

In Chapter 4 I described how classical conditioning occurs at different rates depending on the combination of CS and US that is used. Rats readily learn to associate tastes with sickness, for example, whereas associations between tastes and shock are not so easily learned. Such examples suggest that, for conditioning to occur rapidly, the CS has to "belong" with the US, or be "relevant" to the US. Analogous belongingness—relevance—relations occur in instrumental conditioning.

Thorndike was the first to observe differences in the conditionability of various responses with reinforcement. In many of the puzzle-box experiments, the cat had to manipulate a latch or string to escape from the box. However, Thorndike also tried to condition such responses as yawning and scratching. The cats could learn to make these responses. However, interestingly, the form of the responses changed as training proceeded. At first, the cat would scratch itself vigorously to be let out of the box. On later trials, it would only make aborted scratching movements. It might put its leg to its body but would not make a true scratch response. Similar results were obtained in attempts to condition yawning. As training progressed, the animal would open its mouth to be let out of the box, but it would not give a bona fide yawn.

Thorndike proposed the concept of **belongingness** to explain the failures to train scratching and yawning. According to this concept, certain responses naturally "belong with" the reinforcer because of the animal's evolutionary history. Operating a latch and pulling a string are manipulatory responses that naturally belong with release from confinement. By contrast, scratching and yawning characteristically do not help animals escape from confinement and therefore do not belong with release from a puzzle box. Presumably this is why scratching and yawning do not persist as vigorous bona fide instrumental responses when reinforced by release from the box.

The concept of belongingness in instrumental conditioning is nicely illustrated by a more recent study involving the three-spined stickleback fish (*Gasterosteus aculeatus*). During the mating season each spring, male sticklebacks establish territories from which they court females but chase away and fight other males. Sevenster (1973) used the presentation of another male or a female as a reinforcer in instrumental conditioning of male sticklebacks. One group of fish was required to bite a rod to obtain access to the reinforcer. Biting is a component of the aggressive behavior that occurs when a resident male encounters an intruder male. When the reinforcer was another male, biting behavior increased; access to another male was an effective reinforcer for the biting response. By contrast, biting did not increase when it was reinforced with courtship opportunity. However, courtship opportunity was an effective reinforcer for other responses such as swimming through a ring. Evidently, a belongingness relation exists between biting and the consequent presentation of

139

another male. By contrast, biting does not "belong with" presentation of a female, which typically elicits courtship rather than aggression.

Various limitations on instrumental conditioning were also observed by Breland and Breland (1961) in attempts to condition instrumental responses with food reinforcement in several species. Their goal was to train animals to perform entertaining response chains for displays to be used in amusement parks and zoos. During the course of this work, they observed dramatic behavior changes that were not consistent with the reinforcement procedures they were using. For example, they describe a raccoon that was reinforced for picking up a coin and depositing it in a coin bank.

> We started out by reinforcing him for picking up a single coin. Then the metal container was introduced, with the requirement that he drop the coin into the container. Here we ran into the first bit of difficulty: he seemed to have a great deal of trouble letting go of the coin. He would rub it up against the inside of the container, pull it back out, and clutch it firmly for several seconds. However, he would finally turn it loose and receive his food reinforcement. Then the final contingency: we [required] that he pick up [two] coins and put them in the container.
>
> Now the raccoon really had problems (and so did we). Not only could he not let go of the coins, but he spent seconds, even minutes, rubbing them together (in a most miserly fashion), and dipping them into the container. He carried on this behavior to such an extent that the practical application we had in mind—a display featuring a raccoon putting money in a piggy bank—simply was not feasible. The rubbing behavior became worse and worse as time went on, in spite of nonreinforcement. (p. 682).

M. Breland-Bailey

The Brelands had similar difficulties with other species. Pigs, for example, also could not learn to put coins in a piggy bank. After initial training, they began rooting the coins along the ground. The Brelands called the development of such responses as rooting in the pigs and rubbing coins together in the raccoons **instinctive drift.** As the term implies, the extra responses that developed in these food reinforcement situations were activities the animals instinctively perform when obtaining food. Pigs root along the ground in connection with feeding, and raccoons rub and dunk food-related objects. These natural food-related responses were apparently very strong and competed with the responses required by the experimenter. The Brelands emphasized that such instinctive response tendencies have to be taken into account in the analysis of behavior.

Behavior Systems and Constraints on Instrumental Conditioning   The limitations on instrumental conditioning I have described are consistent with behavior systems theory. I previously mentioned this theory in Chapter 4, in discussions of the nature of the conditioned response (see Timberlake, 1983a; Timberlake & Lucas, 1989). According to behavior systems theory, when an animal is food-deprived and is in a situation where it might encounter food, its feeding system becomes activated, and it begins to engage in foraging and other food-related responses. An instrumental conditioning procedure is superimposed on this behavior system. The effectiveness of the procedure in increasing an instrumental response will depend on the compatibility of that response with the preexisting organization of the feeding system. Furthermore, the nature of other responses that emerge during the course of training (or instinctive drift) will depend on the behavioral components of the feeding system that become activated by the instrumental conditioning procedure.

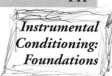

Instrumental Conditioning: Foundations

Racoons are adept at doing some things, like tearing up a package, but it is difficult to condition them to drop coins into a container for food reinforcement.

According to the behavior systems approach, it should be predictable which responses will increase with food reinforcement by studying what animals do when their feeding system is activated in the absence of instrumental conditioning. This prediction has been confirmed. In a study of hamsters, Shettleworth (1975) found that food deprivation decreases the probability of self-care responses such as face washing and scratching but increases the probability of environment-directed activities such as digging, scratching at a wall (scrabbling), and rearing on the hind legs. These results suggest that self-care responses (face washing and scratching) are not part of the feeding system activated by hunger, whereas environment-directed activities (digging, scrabbling, and rearing) do belong to the feeding system. Given these findings, behavior systems theory predicts that food reinforcement should produce increases in digging, scrabbling, and rearing but not increases in face washing and scratching. This pattern of results is precisely what has been observed in studies of instrumental conditioning (Shettleworth, 1975). Thus, the susceptibility of various responses to food reinforcement can be predicted from how those responses are altered by food deprivation, which presumably reflects their compatibility with the feeding system.

S. J. Shettleworth

As we saw in Chapter 4, another way to diagnose whether a response is a part of a behavior system is to perform a classical conditioning experiment. Through classical conditioning, a CS comes to elicit components of the behavior system activated by the US. If "instinctive drift" reflects responses of the behavior system, responses akin to instinctive drift should be evident in a classical conditioning experiment. Timberlake and his associates (see Timberlake, 1983b; Timberlake, Wahl, & King, 1982) tested this prediction with rats in a modification of the coin-handling studies conducted by Breland and Breland.

Instead of a coin, the apparatus used by Timberlake et al. (1982) delivered a ball bearing into the experimental chamber at the start of each trial. The floor of the chamber was tilted so that the ball bearing would roll from one end of the chamber to the other and exit through a hole. In one experimental condition, the rats were required to make contact with the ball bearing to obtain food reinforcement. Other conditions employed a classical conditioning procedure: food was provided after the ball bearing rolled across the chamber whether or not the rat touched the ball bearing. Consistent with the behavior systems view, in both procedures the rats came to touch and extensively handle the ball bearings instead of letting them roll into the hole. (Some animals picked up the bearing, put it in their mouth, carried it to the other end of the chamber, and sat and chewed it.) Such "instinctive drift" developed with both instrumental and classical conditioning procedures. These results indicate that touching and handling the ball bearing are manifestations of the feeding behavior system in rats. Thus, instinctive drift represents the intrusion of responses appropriate to the behavior system that is activated during the course of instrumental conditioning.

According to the behavior systems approach, differences in the preexisting responses of the behavior system activated by a conditioning procedure will lead to differences in the type of responses that are easily conditioned by that procedure. The preexisting responses of a behavior system may vary across species and reinforcers. The behavior systems approach predicts that such differences should lead to corresponding differences in the ease of conditioning those responses. This prediction has been confirmed in comparisons of the conditioning of carnivorous versus herbivorous species of rodents, and in a comparison of conditioning with food versus water in rats (Timberlake, 1983b; Timberlake & Washburne, 1989).

The Instrumental Reinforcer

Having discussed the nature of the instrumental response, I now turn to the nature of the reinforcer in instrumental conditioning. Several aspects of a reinforcer determine its effects on the learning and performance of instrumental behavior. I will first discuss the direct effects of the quantity and quality of a reinforcer on instrumental behavior and then show how responding to a particular reward amount and type depends on the organism's past experience with other reinforcers.

Quantity and Quality of the Reinforcer. Although the quantity and quality of the reinforcer are logically different characteristics, sometimes it is difficult to separate them experimentally. A change in the quantity of the reinforcer may also make the reinforcer qualitatively different. In a systematic study, Hutt (1954) tried to isolate the effects of the quantity and quality of a liquid food reinforcer by varying both of these features at the same time. Independent groups of rats were trained to press a response lever for either a small, medium, or large amount of the fluid. The fluid was a mixture of water, milk, and flour. For each reward quantity, some of the rats were tested with the basic mixture. For others, the quality of the mixture was improved by adding saccharin. For yet other rats, the quality of the fluid was reduced by adding a small amount of citric acid. Figure 5.9 shows the average rate of bar pressing for each group. Increases in either the quality or the quantity of the reinforcer produced higher rates of responding.

Results similar to the findings of Hutt are typically obtained in runway experiments (see Mackintosh, 1974, for a review). Rats, for example, run faster for larger and more palatable reinforcers. In free-operant situations, however, the effects of reinforcer magnitude are more complex and depend on the schedule of reinforcement used and other factors (for example, Collier, Johnson, & Morgan, 1992; Reed, 1991; Reed & Wright, 1989). (I will discuss schedules of reinforcement in Chapter 6.)

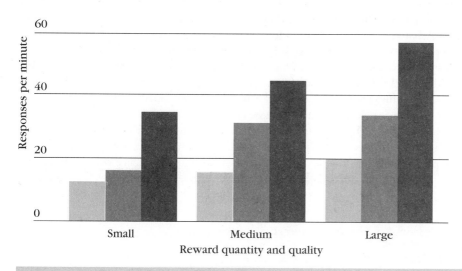

Figure 5.9 Average rates of responding in groups of rats for which responding was reinforced with reinforcers varying in quantity and quality. (From "Rate of Bar Pressing as a Function of Quality and Quantity of Food Reward," by P. J. Hutt, *Journal of Comparative and Physiological Psychology,* 1954, *47,* 235–239.)

C. F. Flaherty

Shifts in Reinforcer Quality or Quantity. In the study by Hutt (1954), a given group of rats received only one particular quantity and quality of liquid food throughout the experiment. What would happen if the quantity or quality of the reinforcer were shifted from one value to another for the same individuals? This is an interesting question because it raises the possibility that the effectiveness of a reinforcer depends not only on its own properties but also on how that reinforcer compares with others the individual has experienced.

I noted in Chapter 4 that the effectiveness of an unconditioned stimulus in classical conditioning depends on how the US compares with the individual's expectations based on prior experience. If the US is larger (or more intense) than expected, it will support excitatory conditioning. By contrast, if it is smaller (or weaker) than expected, the US will support inhibitory conditioning. Are there analogous effects in instrumental conditioning? Evidently so. Numerous studies have shown that the effects of a particular amount and type of reinforcer depend on the quantity and quality of the reinforcers the individual experienced previously. (For reviews, see Flaherty, 1982, 1991.) Speaking loosely, the research has shown that a good reward is treated as especially good after reinforcement with a poor reward, and a poor reward is treated as especially poor after reinforcement with a good reward.

Effects of a shift in the quantity of reward were first described by Crespi (1942). The basic results are also nicely illustrated by a more recent study by Mellgren (1972). Four groups of rats served in a runway experiment. During Phase 1, two of the groups received a small reward (2 food pellets) each time they reached the end of the runway. The other two groups received a large reward (22 pellets) for each trip down the runway. (Delivery of the food was always delayed for 20 seconds after the rats reached the end of the runway so that they would not run at their maximum speed.) After 11 trials of training in Phase 1, one group of rats receiving each reward quantity was shifted to the alternate quantity. Thus, some rats were shifted from small to large reward (S-L), and others were shifted from large to small reward (L-S). The remaining

143

two groups continued to receive the same amount of reward in Phase 2 as they had received in Phase 1. (These groups were designated as L-L and S-S.)

Figure 5.10 summarizes the results. At the end of Phase 1, the animals that received the large reward ran slightly, but not significantly, faster than the rats that received the small reward. For groups that continued to receive the same amount of reward in Phase 2 as in Phase 1 (groups L-L and S-S), instrumental performance did not change much during Phase 2. By contrast, significant deviations from these baselines of running were observed in groups that received shifts in reward magnitude with the start of Phase 2. Rats shifted from large to small reward (group L-S) rapidly decreased their running speeds, and rats shifted from small to large reward (group S-L) soon increased their running speeds.

The most significant finding was that, following a shift in reward magnitude, running speed was not entirely determined by the new reward magnitude. Rather, response to the new reward was enhanced by previous experience with a contrasting reward magnitude. Rats shifted from a small to a large reward (group S-L) ran faster

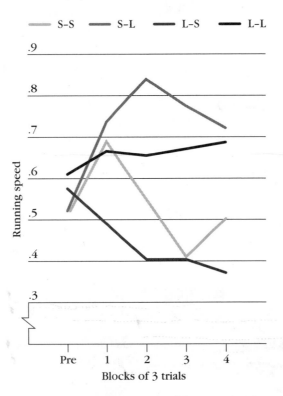

Figure 5.10 Running speeds of four groups of rats in blocks of three trials. Block "Pre" represents running speeds at the end of Phase 1. Blocks 1–4 represent running speeds in Phase 2. At the start of Phase 2, groups S-L and L-S experienced a shift in amount of reward from small to large and large to small, respectively. Groups S-S and L-L received small and large rewards, respectively, throughout the experiment. (From "Positive and Negative Contrast Effects Using Delayed Reinforcement," by R. L. Mellgren, *Learning and Motivation,* 1972, *3,* 185–193. Copyright © 1972 by Academic Press. Reprinted by permission.)

for the large reward than rats that always received the large reward (group L-L). Correspondingly, animals shifted from a large to a small reward (group L-S) ran more slowly for the small reward than animals that always received the small reward (group S-S).

The results Mellgren obtained illustrate the phenomena of successive positive and negative behavioral contrast. **Positive behavioral contrast** refers to elevated responding for a favorable reward resulting from prior experience with a less attractive outcome. More informally, the favorable reward looks especially good to individuals who experienced a worse outcome previously. **Negative behavioral contrast** refers to depressed responding for an unfavorable reward because of prior experience with a better outcome. In this case, the unfavorable reward looks especially bad to individuals who experienced a better reward previously.

Mellgren's results illustrate successive behavioral contrast effects because the two reward conditions were presented in different phases of the experiment, and only one shift in reward magnitude occurred for the shifted groups. Positive and negative behavioral contrast are also obtained if reward conditions are shifted back and forth frequently, with a different cue signaling each reward condition (for example, McSweeney & Melville, 1993; Williams, 1983, 1990, 1992). These effects are examples of **simultaneous behavioral contrast**. Different contrast effects are mediated by different mechanisms (for example, Flaherty & Rowan, 1986). However, all contrast effects illustrate that the effectiveness of a reinforcer in one situation is determined in part by the organism's experiences with reinforcers in other situations.

R. L. Mellgren

The Response-Reinforcer Relation

As I have said, instrumental behavior produces and is controlled by its consequences. In some cases, there is a strong relation between what a person does and the consequence that follows. If you put 65¢ into a soda machine, you will get a can of soda. As long as the machine is working, you will get a can of soda every time you put in the required 65¢. In other cases, there is no relation between behavior and an outcome. You may wear a red shirt to an examination and receive a good grade. However, the grade would not be related to your having worn the red shirt. In yet other situations, the relation between behavior and its consequences may be imperfect. You might have to make several phone calls before finding someone who is willing to help you with a problem.

Animals and people perform a continual stream of responses and experience all kinds of environmental events. You are always doing something, even if it is just sitting still, and things are continually happening in your environment. An organism must organize its behavior to meet various challenges, and it must do so in a way that makes the best use of its time and energy. To be efficient, an animal has to be responsive to the ways in which it can and cannot control its environment. There is no point in working hard to make the sun rise each morning, because that will happen anyway. It makes more sense to devote energy to building a shelter or hunting for food—things that do not become available without effort. Efficient instrumental behavior requires sensitivity to the response-reinforcer relation.

The response-reinforcer relation actually consists of two independent factors. One of these involves *timing*: the time between the response and the reinforcer. If the reinforcer is presented immediately after the response, this is called **temporal contiguity**. The **second** component of the response-reinforcer relation involves *causation*: the extent to which the instrumental response is necessary and sufficient for the occurrence of the reinforcer. This is called the **response-reinforcer contingency.** Temporal and causal factors are independent of each other. For example, there is strong causation between submitting an application for admission to a college and getting accepted, but the temporal relation is weak. You may not hear about the acceptance for several weeks after submitting the application.

Effects of Temporal Contiguity.   Since the early work of Grice (1948), the conventional wisdom has been that instrumental conditioning requires providing the reinforcer immediately after occurrence of the instrumental response. Grice reported that instrumental learning can be disrupted by delays as short as 0.5 seconds. More recent research has indicated that instrumental learning is possible with delays as long as 30 seconds (Critchfield & Lattal, 1993; Lattal & Gleeson, 1990; Lattal & Metzger, 1994; Wilkenfield, Nickel, Blakely, & Poling, 1992). However, the fact remains that instrumental learning is disrupted by delaying the delivery of the reinforcer after the occurrence of the instrumental response.

Figure 5.11 shows a recent example of the effects of delayed reinforcement on learning to press a response lever (Dickinson, Watt, & Griffiths, 1992). Each time a rat pressed the lever, a food pellet was set up to be delivered after a fixed delay. For some rats the delay was short (2–4 seconds). For others the delay was considerable (64 seconds). If a rat pressed the lever again during the delay interval, the new response resulted in another food pellet after the specified delay. In Figure 5.11, response rates are shown as a function of the mean delay of reinforcement experienced by each group. The results indicate that responding dropped off fairly rapidly with increases in the delay of reinforcement. With this procedure, no learning occurred with a 64-second delay of reinforcement.

Why is instrumental conditioning sensitive to a delay of reinforcement? A potential answer to this question is provided by reconsidering the fact that behavior consists of an ongoing, continual stream of activities. When reinforcement is delayed after performance of a specified response (R1) the organism does not stop doing things. After performing R1, the organism may perform R2, R3, R4, and so on. If the reinforcer is set up by R1 but not delivered until some time later, the reinforcer may occur

Figure 5.11   Effects of delay of reinforcement on acquisition of lever pressing in rats. (From "Free-Operant Acquisition with Delayed Reinforcement," by A. Dickinson, A. Watt, and W. J. H. Griffiths, *The Quarterly Journal of Experimental Psychology,* 1992, *45B,* 241–258. Copyright © 1992 by The Experimental Psychology Society. Reprinted by permission.)

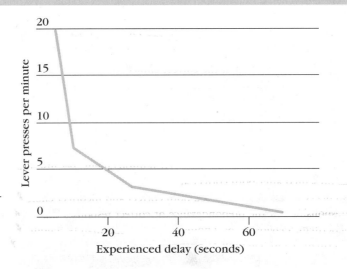

immediately after some other response, let's say R6. To associate R1 with the reinforcer, the organism has to have some way to distinguish R1 from the other responses it performs during the delay interval.

Research has identified two ways to facilitate learning with delayed reinforcement. The first procedure, used by animal trainers and coaches for centuries, is to provide a secondary or conditioned reinforcer immediately after the instrumental response, even if the primary reinforcer cannot occur until some time later. A secondary or **conditioned reinforcer** is a conditioned stimulus that was previously associated with the reinforcer. Verbal prompts in coaching, such as "good" and "that's the way," are conditioned reinforcers that can provide immediate reinforcement for appropriate behavior. Conditioned reinforcers can serve to "bridge" a delay between the instrumental response and delivery of the primary reinforcer (Cronin, 1980; Winter & Perkins, 1982; Williams, 1991, 1993).

Another technique that facilitates learning with delayed reinforcement is to *mark* the target instrumental response in some way to make it distinguishable from the other activities of the organism. The effectiveness of a marking procedure was first demonstrated by Lieberman, McIntosh, and Thomas (1979). Rats served in the experiment, and the apparatus was a special maze, shown at the top in Figure 5.12. After release from the start box, the rats had a choice between entering a white or a black side arm. Entering the white arm was designated as the correct instrumental response and was reinforced with access to food in the goal box after a delay of 60 seconds.

Two groups of animals were tested, and they were differentiated by what happened to them immediately after making the correct choice. Rats in the "marked" group were picked up by the experimenter and placed in the delay box. By contrast, the animals in the "unmarked" group were undisturbed. After they made the correct response, the door at the end of the choice alley was opened for them, and they were allowed to walk into the delay box without being handled. Sixty seconds after the instrumental response, both groups were placed in the goal box to obtain the reinforcer. The same sequence of events occurred when the rats made an incorrect response except that in this case they were not reinforced at the end of the delay interval. Because the same marking stimulus (handling) occurred on reinforced and nonreinforced trials, the marking stimulus was not specifically correlated with reinforcement.

Results of the experiment are shown in the graph in Figure 5.12. Rats in the marked group learned the instrumental response with the 60-second delay of reinforcement much better than animals in the unmarked group. At the end of 50 training trials, the marking procedure resulted in the correct choice 90% of the time. By contrast, without the marking procedure, the correct choice occurred about 50% of the time, which is chance performance.

In another experiment, Lieberman and his colleagues demonstrated successful learning with delayed reinforcement when the instrumental response was marked by a brief, intense light or noise (Lieberman et al., 1979). These effects of marking cannot be explained in terms of secondary or conditioned reinforcement, because the marking stimulus was presented after both correct and incorrect choices. Any conditioned reinforcement effects would have increased both correct and incorrect choices and thus cannot be responsible for the preponderance of correct responses that was observed (see also Lieberman, Davidson, & Thomas, 1985; Lieberman & Thomas, 1986; Thomas & Lieberman, 1990; Urcuioli & Kasprow, 1988).

D. A. Lieberman

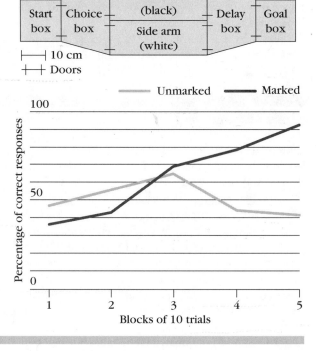

Figure 5.12 Top view of apparatus and results of an experiment to test the effects of marking an instrumental response on instrumental conditioning with reinforcement delayed 60 seconds. Choosing the white side arm was designated as the correct response. Rats spent the delay interval in the delay box. Those in the "Marked" group were placed in the delay box after each choice response. Those in the "Unmarked" group were allowed to walk into the delay box undisturbed. (From "Learning When Reward Is Delayed: A Marking Hypothesis," by D. A. Lieberman, D. C. McIntosh, and G. V. Thomas, *Journal of Experimental Psychology: Animal Behavior Processes,* 1979, 5, 224–242. Copyright © 1979 by the American Psychological Association. Reprinted by permission.)

The Response-Reinforcer Contingency. As I noted earlier, the response-reinforcer contingency refers to the extent to which the delivery of the reinforcer is dependent on the prior occurrence of the instrumental response. In studies of delay of reinforcement, there is a perfect causal relation between the response and the reinforcer. Although the reinforcer is delayed, it is only provided if the organism makes the instrumental response. Studies of delay of reinforcement show that a perfect causal relation between the response and the reinforcer is not sufficient to produce vigorous instrumental responding. Even with a perfect causal relation, conditioning does not occur if reinforcement is delayed too long. Such data encouraged early investigators to conclude that response-reinforcer contiguity rather than contingency was the critical factor producing instrmental learning. However, this view has turned out to be unjustified by subsequent research.

Skinner's Superstition Experiment. A landmark experiment in the debate about the role of contiguity versus contingency in instrumental learning was Skinner's superstition experiment (Skinner, 1948). Skinner placed pigeons in separate experimental chambers and set the equipment to deliver a bit of food every 15 seconds irrespective of what the pigeons were doing. The birds were not required to peck a key or perform any other response to get the food. After some time, Skinner returned to see what the birds were doing. He described some of what he saw as follows:

> In six out of eight cases the resulting responses were so clearly defined that two observers could agree perfectly in counting instances. One bird was conditioned to turn counterclockwise about the cage, making two or three turns between reinforcements. Another repeatedly thrust its head into one of the upper corners of the cage. A third developed a "tossing" response, as if placing its head beneath an invisible bar and lifting it repeatedly. (p. 168)

The pigeons appeared to Skinner to be responding as if their behavior controlled the delivery of the reinforcer when, in fact, food was provided independently of behavior. Accordingly, Skinner called this **superstitious behavior.**

Skinner's explanation of superstitious behavior rests on the idea of **accidental,** or **adventitious, reinforcement.** Adventitious reinforcement refers to the accidental pairing of a response with delivery of the reinforcer. Animals are always doing something, even if no particular responses are required to obtain food. Skinner suggested that whatever response a pigeon happened to make just before it got free food became strengthened and subsequently increased in frequency because of adventitious reinforcement. One accidental pairing of a response with food increases the chance that the same response will just before the next delivery of the food. A second accidental response-reinforcer pairing further increases the probability of the response. In this way, each accidental pairing helps to "stamp in" a particular response. After awhile, the response will occur frequently enough to be identified as superstitious behavior.

Skinner's interpretation of his experiment was appealing and consistent with views of reinforcement that were widely held at the time. Impressed by studies of delay of reinforcement, theorists thought that temporal contiguity was the main factor responsible for learning. Skinner's experiment appeared to support this view and suggested that a positive response-reinforcer contingency is not necessary for instrumental conditioning.

1. *Reinterpretation of the superstition experiment.* Skinner's bold claim that response-reinforcer contiguity rather than contingency is most important for instrumental conditioning has been challenged by subsequent empirical evidence. In a landmark study, Staddon and Simmelhag (1971) reported their attempt to replicate Skinner's experiment with pigeons. Staddon and Simmelhag made much more extensive and systematic observations than Skinner. They defined and measured the occurrence of many responses such as orienting to the food hopper, pecking the response key, wing flapping, turning in quarter circles, and preening. They recorded the frequency of each response according to when it occurred during the interval between successive free deliveries of food.

J. E. R. Staddon

Figure 5.13 shows the data obtained by Staddon and Simmelhag for several responses for one pigeon. Clearly, some of the responses occurred predominantly toward the end of the interval between successive reinforcers. For example, R1 and R7 (orienting to the food magazine and pecking at something on the magazine wall) were much more likely to occur at the end of the interval between food deliveries than at other times. Staddon and Simmelhag called these **terminal responses.** Other activities increased in frequency after the delivery of food and then decreased as the time for the next food delivery drew closer. The pigeons were most likely to engage in R8 and R4 (moving along the magazine wall and making a quarter turn) somewhere near the middle of the interval between food deliveries. These activities were called **interim responses.**

Which actions were terminal responses and which were interim responses did not vary much from one pigeon to another. Furthermore, Staddon and Simmelhag failed to find evidence of accidental reinforcement effects. Responses did not always increase in frequency merely because they occurred coincidentally with food delivery. Food delivery appeared to influence only the strength of terminal responses, even in the initial phases of training.

Subsequent research has provided much additional evidence that periodic presentations of a reinforcer produce behavioral regularities, with certain responses

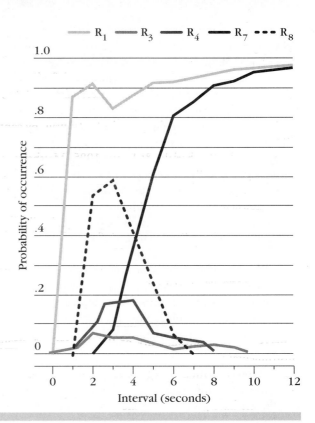

Figure 5.13 Probability of several responses as a function of time between successive deliveries of a food reinforcer. R1 (orienting toward the food magazine wall) and R7 (pecking at something on the magazine wall) are terminal responses, having their highest probabilities at the end of the interval between food deliveries. R3 (pecking at something on the floor), R4 (a quarter turn), and R8 (moving along the magazine wall) are interim responses, having their highest probabilities somewhere near the middle of the interval between food deliveries. (From "The 'Superstition' Experiment: A Reexamination of Its Implications for the Principles of Adaptive Behavior," by J. E. R. Staddon and V. L. Simmelhag, *Psychological Review, 78*, 3–43. Copyright © 1971 by the American Psychological Association. Reprinted by permission.)

predominating late in the interval between successive food presentations and other responses predominating earlier in the interfood interval (Anderson & Shettleworth, 1977; Innis, Simmelhag-Grant, & Staddon, 1983). It is not clear why Skinner failed to observe such regularities in his pigeons. One possibility is that he focused on different aspects of the behavior of different birds in an effort to document that each bird responded in a unique fashion. For example, he may have focused on the terminal response of one bird and interim responses in other birds. Subsequent investigators have also noted some variations in behavior between individuals but have emphasized what are even more striking similarities among animals that are given food periodically, independent of their behavior.

2. *Explanation of the periodicity of interim and terminal responses.* What is responsible for the development of similar terminal and interim responses in animals exposed to the same schedule of response-independent food presentations? Staddon and Simmelhag (1971) suggested that terminal responses are species-typical responses that reflect the anticipation of food as time draws closer to the next food presentation. By contrast, they viewed interim responses as reflecting other sources of motivation that become prominent early in the interfood interval, when food presentation is unlikely. In contrast, subsequent investigators have favored approaches in which terminal and interim responses are considered to be different manifestations of the same motivational system (for example, Innis, Reberg, Mann, Jacobson, & Turton, 1983; Matthews, Bordi, & Depollo, 1990; but see Lawler & Cohen, 1992). The best developed of these alternative formulations is behavior systems theory (Lucas, Timberlake, & Gawley, 1988; Timberlake & Lucas, 1985, 1991).

Instrumental Conditioning: Foundations

According to behavior systems theory, the feeding system (and its accompanying foraging responses) is activated in food-deprived animals that are given small portions of food periodically. Behavior under these circumstances is assumed to be a reflection of preorganized species-typical foraging and feeding behavior. Just before the predictable delivery of food, behavior is directed toward the place where food is about to appear. Notice that in Figure 5.13 the terminal responses (R1 and R7) involved orienting and pecking something on the feeder wall. By contrast, just after food delivery (R4 in Figure 5.13), turning and moving away from the feeder area were likely to occur (see also Timberlake & Lucas, 1985; Matthews et al., 1990). These turning-away responses reflect earlier components of foraging behavior—responses pigeons make when food has become depleted in one place and the birds move on to look for food elsewhere.

Consistent with behavior systems theory, the distribution of activities that develops with periodic deliveries of a reinforcer depend on the nature of that reinforcer. For example, different patterns of behavior develop with food versus water presentations (Innis et al., 1983; Papadouka & Matthews, 1995; Reberg, Innis, Mann, & Eizenga, 1978; Timberlake & Lucas, 1991), presumably because food and water activate different foraging patterns.

Effects of the Controllability of Reinforcers. A strong contingency between an instrumental response and a reinforcer essentially means that the response controls the reinforcer. With a strong contingency, whether the reinforcer occurs depends on whether the instrumental response has occurred. Studies of the effects of control over reinforcers have provided the most extensive body of evidence on the sensitivity of behavior to response-reinforcer contingencies. Although some of these studies have involved positive reinforcement (for example, Caspy & Lubow, 1981; Job, 1987, 1989), most of the research has focused on the effects of control over aversive stimulation (see Maier & Jackson, 1979; Maier & Seligman, 1976; Minor, Dess, & Overmier, 1991; Seligman & Weiss, 1980; Peterson, Maier, & Seligman, 1993).

S. F. Maier

Contemporary research on the effects of the controllability of aversive stimulation on learning originated with the pioneering studies of Seligman, Overmier, and Maier (for example, Overmier & Seligman, 1967; Seligman & Maier, 1967), who investigated the effects of exposure to uncontrollable shock on subsequent escape-avoidance learning in dogs. The typical finding was that exposure to uncontrollable shock disrupted subsequent learning. This phenomenon has come to be called the **learned helplessness effect.**

1. *The triadic design.* Learned helplessness experiments are usually conducted using the *triadic design* presented in Table 5.2. The design involves two phases, an exposure phase and a conditioning phase. During the exposure phase, one group (E, for *escape*) is exposed to periodic shocks that can be terminated by performing an escape response (rotating a small wheel or tumbler, for example). Each individual in the second group (Y, for *yoked*) is yoked to an animal in Group E and receives the same shocks as its Group E partner. However, animals in Group Y cannot do anything to turn off the shocks. The third group (R, for *restricted*) receives no shocks during the exposure phase but is restricted to the apparatus for as long as the other groups. During the conditioning phase, all three groups receive escape-avoidance training. This is usually conducted in a shuttle apparatus that has two adjacent compartments (see Figure 9.4). The animals have to go back and forth between the two compartments to avoid shock (or escape any shocks that they did not avoid).

M. E. P. Seligman

| TABLE 5.2 | THE TRIADIC DESIGN USED IN STUDIES OF THE LEARNED HELPLESSNESS EFFECT | | |

GROUP	EXPOSURE PHASE	CONDITIONING PHASE	RESULT
Group E	Escapable shock	Escape-avoidance	Rapid avoidance learning
Group Y	Yoked inescapable shock	Escape-avoidance	Slow avoidance learning
Group R	Restricted to apparatus	Escape-avoidance	Rapid avoidance learning

The remarkable finding in experiments on the learned helplessness effect is that the effects of aversive stimulation during the exposure phase depend on whether or not shock is escapable. Exposure to uncontrollable shock in Group Y during the exposure phase produces a severe disruption in subsequent escape-avoidance learning. By contrast, often little or no deleterious effects are observed after exposure to escapable shock. In the conditioning phase of the experiment, Group Y typically shows much poorer escape-avoidance performance than Group E and Group R. Similar detrimental effects of exposure to yoked inescapable shock have been reported on subsequent responding for food reinforcement (for example, Rosellini & DeCola, 1981; Rosellini, DeCola, & Shapiro, 1982; see also DeCola & Rosellini, 1990).

The fact that Group Y shows a deficit in subsequent learning in comparison to Group E indicates that the animals are sensitive to the procedural differences between escapable and yoked inescapable shock. The primary procedural difference between groups E and Y is the presence of a response-reinforcer contingency for Group E but not for Group Y. Therefore, the difference in the rate of learning between these two groups shows that the animals are sensitive to the response-reinforcer contingency.

2. *The learned helplessness hypothesis.* The first major explanation of studies employing the triadic design—the **learned helplessness hypothesis**—was based on the conclusion that animals can perceive the contingency between their behavior and the delivery of a reinforcer (Maier & Seligman, 1976; Maier, Seligman, & Solomon, 1969). The learned helplessness hypothesis assumes that during exposure to uncontrollable shocks, animals learn that the shocks are independent of their behavior—that there is nothing they can do to control the shocks. Furthermore, they come to expect that their behavior will continue to be independent of reinforcers in the future. This expectation of future lack of control undermines their ability to learn new instrumental responses. The learning deficit occurs for two reasons. First, expectation of future lack of control makes it more difficult to learn a subsequent response-reinforcer contingency. Second, expectation of future lack of control reduces the motivation for instrumental responding.

It is important to distinguish the learned helplessness *hypothesis* from the learned helplessness *effect*. The learned helplessness effect is the pattern of results obtained with the triadic design (poorer learning in Group Y than in Groups E and R). The

HUMAN EXTENSIONS OF ANIMAL RESEARCH ON THE CONTROLLABILITY OF REINFORCERS

The fact that a history of lack of control over reinforcers can severely disrupt subsequent instrumental performance has important implications for human behavior. The concept of helplessness has been extended and elaborated to a variety of areas of human concern, including aging, athletic performance, chronic pain, academic achievement, susceptibility to heart attacks, and victimization and bereavement (see Garber & Seligman, 1980; Peterson, Maier, & Seligman, 1993). Perhaps the most prominent area to which the concept of helplessness has been applied is depression (Seligman, 1975; see also Abramson, Metalsky, & Alloy, 1989; Peterson & Seligman, 1984).

Animal research on uncontrollability and unpredictability has also been used to gain insights into human posttraumatic stress disorder (Foa, Zinbarg, & Rothbaum, 1992). Victims of rape, assault, or combat stress have symptoms that correspond to the effects of chronic uncontrollable and unpredictable shock in animals. Recognition of these similarities promises to provide new insights into the origin and treatment of posttraumatic stress disorder.

learned helplessness effect has been replicated in numerous studies and is a well-established finding. By contrast, the learned helplessness hypothesis, which assumes that the learning deficit in Group Y is produced by the perception of lack of control, has been a provocative and controversial explanation of the learned helplessness effect since its introduction (see Black, 1977; Levis, 1976).

3. *Activity deficits.* Early in the history of research on the learned helplessness effect, investigators became concerned that the learning deficit observed in Group Y was a result of these animals learning to be inactive in response to shock during the exposure phase. Consistent with this hypothesis, in some situations, inescapable shock produces a decrease in motor movement, or response perseveration, and this is responsible for subsequent performance deficits (Anderson, Crowell, Cunningham, & Lupo, 1979; Anisman, de Catanzaro, & Remington, 1978; Anisman, Hamilton, & Zacharko, 1984; Irwin, Suissa, & Anisman, 1980). However, there are also situations in which effects on learning are not likely to be due to the suppression of movement caused by inescapable shock (for example, Jackson, Alexander, & Maier, 1980; Rosellini, DeCola, Plonsky, Warren, & Stilman, 1984). Therefore, a learned inactivity hypothesis cannot explain all instances of learned helplessness effects (Maier & Jackson, 1979).

4. *Attentional deficits.* Why might lack of control over reinforcers produce a deficit in learning if the effect is not due to a deficit in activity? One interesting possibility is that inescapable shock causes animals to pay less attention to their actions. If an animal fails to pay attention to its behavior, it will have difficulty associating its actions with reinforcers in escape-avoidance or other forms of instrumental conditioning.

In a fascinating experiment, Maier, Jackson, and Tomie (1987) tested this attention-deficit hypothesis with rats. They reasoned that an animal that fails to pay attention to its behavior because of exposure to inescapable shock is faced with the same problem as an animal that receives delayed reinforcement. In both cases, the animals have difficulty figuring out which of their actions causes the delivery of the reinforcer. This analogy suggested to Maier and his colleagues that manipulations that facilitate learning with delayed reinforcement might also help animals exposed to inescapable shock.

As I noted earlier in this chapter, the problem of identifying which response is responsible for delayed reinforcement can be solved by marking the target response with an immediate external feedback stimulus of some sort. Maier and his colleagues reasoned that reduced attention to instrumental behavior also may be alleviated by introducing an external response feedback cue or marking stimulus. Thus, their prediction was that rats given inescapable shock will not be disrupted in their subsequent escape learning if each instrumental response was marked by an external stimulus.

The relevant results of their experiment are presented in Figure 5.14. The figure shows the latency of escape responses performed by various groups during the second phase—the conditioning phase—of the experiment. Higher values indicate slower escape responses, and hence poorer escape learning. Groups E, Y, and R were the standard groups of the triadic design and yielded the usual learned helplessness effect. Group E, which received escapable shocks during the exposure phase, performed with as short latencies as Group R, which was not given shock during the exposure phase. By contrast, Group Y, which received inescapable shocks at first, had significantly longer escape latencies.

The fourth group, Group Y-M (yoked-marker) received the same type of shocks as Group Y during the exposure phase. During the conditioning phase, Group Y-M received a marking stimulus after each escape response. The marker consisted of turning off the house lights for 0.75 second and having the floor tilt slightly as the rat crossed from one side of the shuttle box to the other. The presence of this marker completely eliminated the deficit in learning that was otherwise produced by prior exposure to inescapable shock. Group Y-M performed much better than Group Y

Figure 5.14 Mean escape latency during the conditioning phase for four groups of rats in a learned helplessness experiment. During the exposure phase, Group E received escapable shocks, Groups Y and Y-M received yoked inescapable shocks, and Group R received no shock. During the conditioning phase, a brief marking stimulus was presented after each escape response for subjects in Group Y-M. (From "Potentiation, Overshadowing, and Prior Exposure to Inescapable Shock," by S. F. Maier, R. L. Jackson, and A. Tomie, *Journal of Experimental Psychology: Animal Behavior Processes*, 1987, *13*, 260–270. Copyright © 1987 by the American Psychological Association. Reprinted by permission.)

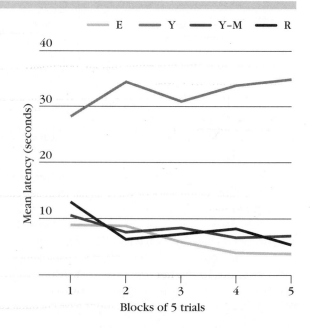

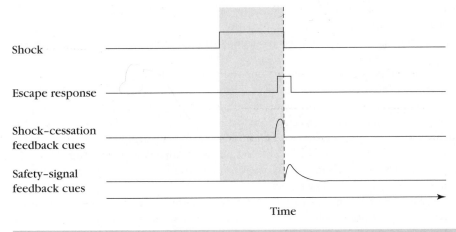

Figure 5.15 Stimulus relations in an escape conditioning trial. Shock-cessation feedback cues are experienced at the start of the escape response, just before the termination of shock. Safety-signal feedback cues are experienced just after the termination of shock, at the start of the intertrial interval.

and as well as Groups R and E. (Other aspects of the experiment ruled out nonspecific effects of the marking stimulus.) Thus, as predicted, marking the instrumental response overcame the learned helplessness deficit. This outcome suggests that one of the sources of the learning deficit is a reduction in attention to the responses the animal performs (see also Lee & Maier, 1988).

5. *Stimulus relations in escape conditioning.* The interpretations of the learned helplessness effect I have discussed so far have focused on the deleterious effects of exposure to inescapable shock. However, an equally important question is why exposure to shock is not as harmful if the animal can perform a response to escape the shock (Minor et al., 1991). This question has stimulated a closer look at what happens when animals are permitted to escape shock in the exposure phase of the triadic design. It is apparent that escape training is far more complex than was previously thought.

The defining feature of escape behavior is that the instrumental response results in the termination of an aversive stimulus. However, there are also special stimulus relations in an escape procedure that are potentially very important. These are illustrated in Figure 5.15. Making the escape response results in internal response feedback cues. Some of these response-produced stimuli are experienced at the start of the escape response, just before the shock is turned off, and are called *shock-cessation feedback cues.* Other response-produced stimuli are experienced as the animal completes the response, just after the shock has been turned off at the start of the intertrial interval. These are called *safety-signal feedback cues.*

At first, investigations of stimulus factors involved with escapable shock centered on the possible significance of safety-signal feedback cues. Safety-signal feedback cues are reliably followed by the intertrial interval, and hence by the absence of shock. Therefore, such feedback cues can become conditioned inhibitors of fear and limit or inhibit fear elicited by contextual cues of the experimental chamber. No such safety signals exist for animals given yoked inescapable shock because, for them, shocks and shock-free periods are not predictable. Therefore, contextual cues of the chamber in which shocks are delivered are more likely to become conditioned to elicit fear with inescapable shock. These considerations have encouraged analyzing the triadic design in terms of group differences in signals for safety rather than in terms of differences in response-reinforcer contingencies.

Although some studies have indicated that group differences in signals for safety can account for the learned helplessness effect (Jackson & Minor, 1988), findings from other experiments have not supported this conclusion (DeCola, Rosellini, & Warren, 1988; Maier, 1990; Maier & Warren, 1988; Rosellini, Warren, & DeCola, 1987). These considerations have encouraged focusing on other aspects of escape responding that may protect animals from the deleterious effects of exposure to shock. One study suggests, for example, that the critical aspect of an escape response may be that it indicates that the shock is being terminated (Minor, Trauner, Lee, & Dess, 1990). Thus, cessation signals may mimic critical features of an escape response more effectively than safety signals.

Focusing on stimulus factors in escape conditioning rather than on response-reinforcer contingencies has not yet yielded a comprehensive account of the results of all experiments with the triadic design. However, the available evidence indicates that significant differences in how animals cope with aversive stimulation can result from differences in signal relations. The more restricted focus of the learned helplessness hypothesis cannot explain such findings. On balance, the triadic design has been invaluable in focusing attention on the possible importance of response-reinforcer contingencies. However, research has uncovered important factors other than the response-reinforcer contingency that also determine the effects of exposure to uncontrollable aversive stimulation.

Contiguity and Contingency: Concluding Comments. As we have seen, organisms are sensitive to the contiguity as well as the contingency between an instrumental response and a reinforcer. Typically, these two aspects of the relation between response and reinforcer act jointly to produce learning (Davis & Platt, 1983). Both factors serve to focus the effects of reinforcement on the instrumental response. The causal relation, or contingency, ensures that the reinforcer is delivered only after occurrence of the specified instrumental response. The contiguity relation ensures that other activities do not intrude between the specified response and the reinforcer to interfere with conditioning of the target response.

SAMPLE QUESTIONS

1. Compare and contrast free-operant and discrete-trial methods for the study of instrumental behavior.

2. What are the similarities and differences between positive and negative reinforcement?

3. What are the effects of a delay of reinforcement on instrumental learning, and how can those effects be reduced?

4. What was the purpose of Skinner's superstition experiment? What were the results and how have those results been reinterpreted?

5. Describe alternative explanations of the learned helplessness effect.

accidental reinforcement An instance in which the delivery of a reinforcer happens to coincide with a particular response, even though that response was not responsible for the reinforcer presentation. Also called *adventitious reinforcement*.

adventitious reinforcement Same as *accidental reinforcement*.

appetitive stimulus A pleasant or satisfying stimulus that can be used to positively reinforce an instrumental response.

aversive stimulus An unpleasant or annoying stimulus than can be used to punish an instrumental response.

avoidance An instrumental conditioning procedure in which the instrumental response prevents the delivery of an aversive stimulus.

belongingness The theoretical idea, originally proposed by Thorndike, that an organism's evolutionary history makes certain responses fit, or belong with, certain reinforcers. Belongingness facilitates learning.

conditioned reinforcer A stimulus that becomes an effective reinforcer because of its association with a primary or unconditioned reinforcer. Also called *secondary reinforcer*.

contiguity The simultaneous (or almost simultaneous) occurrence of two events, such as a response and a reinforcer. Also called *temporal contiguity*.

cumulative recorder An automatic event recorder that records occurrences of a particular response cumulatively as a function of the passage of time.

differential reinforcement of other behavior An instrumental conditioning procedure in which a positive reinforcer is periodically delivered only if the participant fails to perform a particular response. Abbreviated *DRO*.

discrete-trial method A method of instrumental conditioning in which the participant can perform the instrumental response only during specified periods usually determined either by placement of the participant in an experimental chamber or by the presentation of a stimulus.

DRO Abbreviation for *differential reinforcement of other behavior*.

escape An instrumental conditioning procedure in which the instrumental response terminates an aversive stimulus. (See also *negative reinforcement*.)

free-operant method A method of instrumental conditioning that permits repeated performance of the instrumental response without the participant being removed from the experimental chamber. (Compare with *discrete-trial method*.)

instinctive drift A gradual drift of instrumental behavior away from the responses required for reinforcement to species-typical or "instinctive" responses related to the reinforcer and to other stimuli in the experimental situation.

instrumental behavior An activity that occurs because it is effective in producing a particular consequence or reinforcer.

interim response A response that increases in frequency after the delivery of a periodic reinforcer and then declines as time for the the next reinforcer approaches.

latency The time between the start of a trial (or the start of a stimulus) and the instrumental response.

law of effect A rule for instrumental behavior, proposed by Thorndike, which states that if a response in the presence of a stimulus is followed by a satisfying event, the association between the stimulus and the response will be strengthened; if the response is followed by an annoying event, the association will be weakened.

learned helplessness effect Interference with the learning of new instrumental responses as a result of exposure to inescapable and unavoidable aversive stimulation.

learned helplessness hypothesis A theoretical idea that assumes that during exposure to inescapable and unavoidable aversive stimulation, participants learn that their behavior does not control environmental events.

magazine training A preliminary stage of instrumental conditioning in which a stimulus is repeatedly paired with the reinforcer to enable the participant to learn to go and get the reinforcer when it is presented. The sound of the food delivery device, for example, may be repeatedly paired with food so that the animal will learn to go to the food cup when food is delivered.

marking procedure A procedure in which the instrumental response is immediately followed by a distinctive event (the participant is picked up or a flash of light is presented) that makes the instrumental response more memorable and helps overcome the deleterious effects of delayed reinforcement.

negative behavioral contrast Less responding for an unfavorable reinforcer following previous experience with a more desired reinforcer than in the absence of such prior experience.

negative reinforcement An instrumental conditioning procedure in which there is a negative contingency between the instrumental response and an aversive stimulus. If the instrumental response is performed, the aversive stimulus is terminated or prevented from occurring; if the instrumental response is not performed, the aversive stimulus is presented.

omission training An instrumental conditioning procedure in which the instrumental response prevents the delivery of a reinforcing stimulus. (See also *differential reinforcement of other behavior.*)

operant response A response that is defined by the effect it produces on the environment. Examples include pressing a lever and opening a door. Any sequence of movements that depresses the lever or opens the door constitutes an instance of that particular operant.

positive behavioral contrast Greater responding for a favorable reinforcer following previous experience with a less desired reinforcer than in the absence of such prior experience.

positive reinforcement An instrumental conditioning procedure in which there is a positive contingency between the instrumental response and a reinforcing stimulus. If the participant performs the response, it receives the reinforcing stimulus; if the participant does not perform the response, it does not receive the reinforcing stimulus.

punishment An instrumental conditioning procedure in which there is a positive contingency between the instrumental response and an aversive stimulus. If the participant performs the instrumental response, it receives the aversive stimulus; if the participant does not perform the instrumental response, it does not receive the aversive stimulus.

response-reinforcer contingency The relation of a response to a reinforcer defined in terms of the probability of getting reinforced for making the response as compared to the probability of getting reinforced in the absence of the response.

running speed How fast (in feet per second, for example) an animal moves in a runway.

secondary reinforcer Same as *conditioned reinforcer.*

shaping Reinforcement of successive approximations to a desired instrumental response.

simultaneous behavioral contrast Behavioral contrast effects (positive and negative contrast) that are produced by frequent shifts between a favorable and an unfavorable reward condition, with each reward condition associated with its own distinctive stimulus.

superstitious behavior Behavior that increases in frequency because of accidental pairings of the delivery of a reinforcer with occurrences of the behavior.

temporal contiguity Same as *contiguity.*

terminal response A response that is most likely at the end of the interval between successive presentations of a reinforcer at fixed intervals.

SCHEDULES OF REINFORCEMENT AND CHOICE BEHAVIOR

Simple Schedules of Intermittent Reinforcement
    Ratio Schedules
    Interval Schedules
    Comparison of Ratio and Interval Schedules
    Response-Rate Schedules of Reinforcements

Extinction
    Effects of Extinction Procedures
    Determinants of Extinction Effects
    Mechanisms of the Partial Reinforcement Extinction Effect

Choice Behavior: Concurrent Schedules
    Measures of Choice Behavior
    The Matching Law
    Mechanisms of the Matching Law

Complex Choice: Concurrent-Chain Schedules
    Studies of Self-Control
    Explanations of Self-Control

Concluding Comments

I N Chapter 6 I will continue discussing the importance of the response-reinforcer relation in instrumental behavior by describing the effects of various schedules of reinforcement. A schedule of reinforcement is a program, or rule, that determines how presentations of the reinforcer are related to occurrences of the instrumental response. To begin, I will describe simple fixed and variable ratio and fixed and variable interval schedules, as well as the patterns of instrumental responding that are produced by these schedules. I will also describe how the schedule of reinforcement in effect during the conditioning and maintenance of a response determines the persistence of the response during extinction, when reinforcement is no longer provided. In the last sections of the chapter, I will describe how concurrent and concurrent-chain schedules of reinforcement are used in the empirical and theoretical analyses of choice behavior.

In describing various instrumental conditioning procedures in Chapter 5, I may have given the impression that every occurrence of the instrumental response invariably results in delivery of the reinforcer in these procedures. Casual reflection suggests that such a perfect contingency between response and reinforcement is rare outside the laboratory. You do not get a high grade on a test every time you spend many hours studying. You cannot get on a bus every time you go to the bus stop. Inviting a friend over for dinner does not always result in a pleasant evening. In fact, in most cases the relation between instrumental responses and consequent reinforcement is rather complex. Attempts to study how these complex relations control the occurrence of instrumental responses have led to laboratory investigations of schedules of reinforcement.

A **schedule of reinforcement** is a program, or rule, that determines how and when the occurrence of a response will be followed by a reinforcer. There are an infinite number of ways that such a program could be set up. The delivery of a reinforcer may depend on the occurrence of a certain number of responses, the passage of time, the presence of certain stimuli, the occurrence of other responses, or any number of other things. Cataloging the behavioral effects produced by the various possible schedules of reinforcement might seem to be a difficult task. However, research has shown that the job is quite manageable. Reinforcement schedules that involve similar relations among stimuli, responses, and reinforcers usually produce similar patterns of behavior. The exact rate of responding may differ from one situation to another, but the pattern of results is highly predictable. This regularity has made the study of the effects of reinforcement schedules both interesting and fruitful.

Schedules of reinforcement influence both how an instrumental response is learned and how it is then maintained by reinforcement. Traditionally, however, investigators of schedule effects have been concerned primarily with the maintenance of behavior. Reinforcement schedules are typically investigated in Skinner boxes that permit continuous observation of behavior so that changes in the rate of responding can be readily observed and analyzed (Ferster & Skinner, 1957). The manner in which the operant response is initially shaped and conditioned is rarely of interest. Thus, investigations of reinforcement schedules have provided a great deal of information about the factors that control the maintenance and repetitive performance of instrumental behavior rather than its original acquisition.

Schedules of reinforcement are important for managers who have to make sure their employees continue to perform a job after having learned it. Even teachers are often concerned with encouraging the occurrence of already learned responses rather than with teaching new responses. Many students who do poorly in school know how to do their homework and how to study, but simply choose not to. Schedules of reinforcement can be used to motivate more frequent studying behavior.

SIMPLE SCHEDULES OF INTERMITTENT REINFORCEMENT

Processes that organize and direct instrumental performance are activated in different ways by different schedules of reinforcement. I will begin with a discussion of "simple" schedules of reinforcement. In simple schedules, a single factor determines which occurrence of the instrumental response is reinforced.

Ratio Schedules

The defining characteristic of a **ratio schedule** is that reinforcement depends only on the number of responses the organism has performed. A ratio schedule requires merely counting the number of responses that have occurred and delivering the reinforcer each time the required number is reached. If the required number is 1, every occurrence of the instrumental response results in delivery of the reinforcer. Such a schedule is technically called **continuous reinforcement** (abbreviated CRF).

Continuous reinforcement rarely occurs outside the laboratory because the world is not perfect. Pushing an elevator button usually brings the elevator. But all elevators occasionally malfunction, so on occasion nothing may happen when you push the button. Other forms of instrumental behavior also may result in reinforcement only some of the time. Situations in which responding is reinforced only some of the time are said to involve **partial** or **intermittent reinforcement**.

Fixed Ratio.   Consider, for example, delivering the reinforcer after every tenth lever-press response in a study with laboratory rats. In such a schedule, there would be a fixed ratio between the number of responses the rat made and the number of reinforcers it got. (There would always be 10 responses per reinforcer.) This makes such a procedure a **fixed ratio schedule.** More specifically, the procedure would be called a fixed ratio 10 schedule of reinforcement (abbreviated FR 10).

Fixed ratio schedules are found in daily life whenever a fixed number of responses are always required for reinforcement. The delivery person who always has to visit the same number of houses to complete his route is working on a fixed ratio schedule. Piecework in factories is usually set up on a fixed ratio schedule: workers get paid for every so many "widgets" they put together. Flights of stairs provide another example. In a given staircase, you always have to go up the same number of steps to reach the next landing.

A continuous reinforcement schedule is also a fixed ratio schedule. Continuous reinforcement involves a fixed ratio of one response per reinforcer. On a continuous reinforcement schedule, organisms typically respond at a steady but moderate rate. Only brief and unpredictable pauses occur. On a CRF schedule, a pigeon, for example, will peck a key for food steadily at first and will then slow down as it satisfies its hunger.

A very different pattern of responding occurs when an intermittent fixed ratio schedule of reinforcement is in effect. Figure 6.1 shows the cumulative record of a pigeon that had stabilized its responding on an FR 120 schedule. Access to the food reinforcer required 120 pecks at the response key. Each food delivery is indicated by the small downward deflections of the recorder pen. The bird stopped responding after each food delivery. However, when it resumed pecking, it responded at a high and steady rate. The zero rate of responding that occurs just after reinforcement is called the **postreinforcement pause.** The high and steady rate of responding that completes each ratio requirement is called the **ratio run.**

If the ratio requirement is increased a little (from FR 120 to 150, for example), the rate of responding during the ratio run may remain the same. However, with higher ratio requirements, the postreinforcement pause becomes longer (for example, Felton & Lyon, 1966). If the ratio requirement is suddenly increased a great deal (from FR 120 to FR 500, for example), the animal is likely to pause periodically before the completion of the ratio requirement. This effect is called **ratio strain.** In extreme cases, ratio strain may be so great that the animal stops responding altogether.

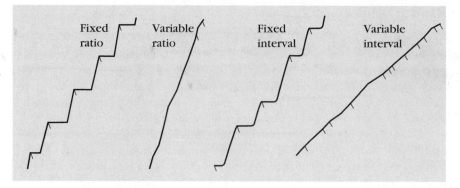

Figure 6.1   Sample cumulative records of different pigeons pecking a response key on four simple schedules of food reinforcement: fixed ratio 120, variable ratio 360, fixed interval 4 minute, and variable interval 2 minute. (From *Schedules of Reinforcement* by C. B. Ferster and B. F. Skinner, 1957, Appleton-Century-Crofts.)

In using ratio schedules, an investigator must be careful not to raise the ratio requirement (or, more generally, the difficulty of a task) too quickly, or ratio strain may occur and the organism may give up altogether.

Variable Ratio.   In a fixed ratio schedule, a predictable number of responses is required for each reinforcer. This predictability can be disrupted by varying the number of responses required for reinforcement from one occasion to the next. Such a procedure is still a ratio schedule because reinforcement still depends on how many responses the organism makes. However, a different number of responses is required for the delivery of each reward. Such a procedure is called a **variable ratio schedule.** An investigator may, for example, require a pigeon to make 10 responses to earn the first reward, 13 to earn the second reward, 7 for the next one, and so on. The numerical value of a variable ratio schedule indicates the average number of responses required per reinforcer. Thus, the procedure in the above example would be a variable ratio 10 schedule (abbreviated VR 10).

Because the number of responses required for reinforcement is not predictable, predictable pauses in the rate of responding are less likely with variable ratio schedules than with fixed ratio schedules. Rather, organisms respond at a fairly steady rate on VR schedules. Figure 6.1 shows a cumulative record for a pigeon whose pecking behavior was maintained on a VR 360 schedule of reinforcement. Notice that even though on average the VR 360 schedule required many more pecks for each reinforcer than the FR 120 schedule shown in Figure 6.1, the VR 360 schedule maintained a much more steady pattern of responding.

Although postreinforcement pauses can occur on variable ratio schedules (see Blakely & Schlinger, 1988; Schlinger, Blakely, & Kaczor, 1990), such pauses are longer and more prominent with fixed ratio schedules. The overall response rate on fixed and variable ratio schedules is similar provided that, on average, similar numbers of responses are required. However, the overall response rate tends to be distributed in a pause-run pattern with fixed ratio schedules, whereas a more steady pattern of responding develops with variable ratio schedules (for example, Crossman, Bonem, & Phelps, 1987).

THE POSTREINFORCEMENT PAUSE AND PROCRASTINATION

The postreinforcement pause that occurs in fixed ratio schedules in the laboratory is also evident in common human experience. In fixed ratio schedules, the pause occurs because a predictably large number of responses are always required to produce the next reward. In a sense, the animal is "procrastinating" before embarking on the large effort necessary for reinforcement. Similar procrastination is legendary in human behavior. Consider, for example, a semester in which you have several term papers to write. You are likely to work on one term paper at a time. However, when you have completed one paper, you probably will not start working on the next one right away. Rather, there will be a postreinforcement pause. After completing a large project, people tend to take some time off before starting the next task. In fact, procras-tination between tasks or before the start of a new job is the rule rather than the exception.

Laboratory results provide a suggestion for overcoming procrastination. Fixed ratio schedule performance in the laboratory indicates that once animals begin to respond on a ratio run, they respond at a high and steady rate until they complete the ratio requirement. This suggests that if somehow you got yourself to start on a job, chances are you would not find it difficult to keep working to finish it. Only the beginning is hard. One technique that works pretty well in getting started is to tell yourself that you will begin with only a small part of the new job. If you are trying to write a paper, tell yourself that you will write only one paragraph to start with. You may find that once you have completed the first paragraph, it will be easier to write the second one, then the one after that, and so on. If you are procrastinating about spring cleaning, instead of thinking about doing the entire job, start with a small part of it, such as washing the kitchen floor. The rest will then come more easily.

Variable ratio schedules are found in daily life whenever an unpredictable amount of effort is required to obtain a reinforcer. For example, each time a custodian goes into a room on his rounds, he knows that some amount of cleaning will be necessary, but he does not know exactly how dirty the room will be. Gamblers playing a slot machine are also responding on a variable ratio schedule. They have to play the machine to win. However, they never know how many plays will produce the winning combination. Variable ratio schedules are also common in sports. A certain number of strokes are always required to finish a hole in golf, for example. However, players can never be sure how many strokes they will need to make when they start.

Interval Schedules

In ratio schedules, reinforcement depends only on the number of responses the organism has performed. In other situations, a response is reinforced only if it occurs after a certain amount of time has passed. **Interval schedules** illustrate this type of situation.

Fixed Interval. In a simple interval schedule, a response is reinforced only if it occurs more than a set amount of time after the last delivery of the reinforcer. In a **fixed interval schedule,** the set time is constant from one occasion to the next. Consider, for example, a fixed interval 4-minute schedule (FI 4 min) for pecking in pigeons. A bird on this schedule would get reinforced for the first peck it made after 4 minutes have passed since the last food delivery (or the beginning of the session).

Because pecks made less than 4 minutes after each food delivery are never reinforced on an FI 4 min schedule, animals learn to wait to respond until the end of the FI interval (see Figure 6.1). As the time for the availability of the next reinforcer draws closer, the response rate increases. This increase in response rate is evident as an acceleration in the cumulative record toward the end of the interval. The pattern of responding that develops with fixed interval reinforcement schedules is accordingly called the **fixed interval scallop**.

It is important to realize that a fixed interval schedule does not guarantee that the animal will be reinforced at fixed intervals of time. Pigeons on an FI 4-min schedule do not automatically receive the reinforcer every 4 minutes. Instrumental responses are required for the reinforcer in interval schedules, just as in ratio schedules. The interval determines only when the reinforcer becomes available. In order to receive the reinforcer after it has become available, the organism still has to make the instrumental response. (For recent analyses of fixed interval schedule performance, see Baron & Leinenweber, 1994; Hoyert, 1992; Lejeune & Wearden, 1991).

Fixed interval schedules are found in situations in which a fixed amount of time is required to prepare or set up the reinforcer. Consider, for example, washing clothes in an automatic washer. A certain amount of time is required to complete the wash cycle. No matter how many times you open the washing machine before the required amount of time has passed, you will not be reinforced with clean clothes. Once the cycle is finished, the reinforcer becomes available, and you can pick up your clean clothes any time after that.

The scheduling of tests in college courses has important similarities to the basic fixed interval schedule. In many courses there are few tests, and the tests are evenly distributed during the term. There may be only a midterm and a final exam. The pattern of studying that such a schedule of tests produces is very similar to what is observed with an FI schedule in the laboratory. Students spend little effort studying at the beginning of the semester or just after the midterm exam. Rather, they begin to study a week or so before each exam, and the rate of studying rapidly increases as the day of the exam approaches. Studying at the beginning of the term or after the midterm exam is not reinforced by the receipt of good grades at that time. Therefore, students do not study at these times in the semester.

Variable Interval. In fixed interval schedules, responses are reinforced if they occur after a fixed amount of time has passed since the delivery of the previous reinforcer (or the beginning of the session). Interval schedules also can be unpredictable. With a **variable interval schedule,** responses are reinforced if they occur after a variable interval since the delivery of the previous reinforcer (or the beginning of the session). An investigator may set up a schedule, for example, in which the first reinforcer becomes available when at least 1 minute has passed since the beginning of the session; the second reinforcer becomes available when at least 3 minutes have passed since the first reward; and the third reinforcer becomes available when at least 2 minutes have passed since the second reward. In this procedure, the average interval that has to pass before successive rewards become available is 2 minutes. Therefore, the procedure is a variable interval 2-minute schedule, abbreviated VI 2 min.

As in fixed interval schedules, the organism has to perform the instrumental response to obtain the reinforcer. Reinforcers are not given "free." Rather, they are given if the organism responds after the variable interval. Like variable ratio schedules, variable interval schedules maintain steady and stable rates of responding without regular pauses (see Figure 6.1).

Variable interval schedules are found in situations in which an unpredictable amount of time is required to prepare or set up the reinforcer. A mechanic who cannot tell you how long it will take to fix your car has imposed a variable interval schedule on you. The car will not be ready for some time, during which attempts to get it will not be reinforced. However, the amount of time that has to pass before the car will be ready is unpredictable. A sales clerk at a bakery is also on a VI schedule of reinforcement. Some time has to pass after waiting on a customer before another will enter the store to buy something. However, the interval between customers is unpredictable.

The Concept of a Limited Hold. In simple interval schedules, once the reinforcer becomes available, it remains available until the required response is made, no matter how long that may take. On an FI 2-minute schedule, for example, the reinforcer becomes available 2 minutes after the previous reward. If the animal responds at exactly this time, it will be reinforced. If it waits and responds 90 minutes later, it will still get the reward. Once the reinforcer has been set up, it remains available until the response occurs.

With interval schedules outside the laboratory, it is more common for reinforcers to become available for only limited periods. Consider, for example, a dormitory cafeteria. Meals are served only at fixed intervals. Therefore, going to the cafeteria is reinforced only after a certain amount of time has passed since the last meal. However, once a meal becomes available, you have a limited amount of time in which to get it. This kind of restriction on how long reward remains available is called a **limited hold**. Limited hold restrictions can be added to both fixed interval and variable interval schedules.

Comparison of Ratio and Interval Schedules

There are striking similarities between the patterns of responding maintained by simple ratio and interval schedules. As we have seen, with both fixed ratio and fixed interval schedules, there is a marked pause after each delivery of the reinforcer (the postreinforcement pause). In addition, both FR and FI schedules produce high rates of responding just before the delivery of the next reinforcer. By contrast, variable ratio and variable interval schedules both maintain steady rates of responding, without predictable pauses. Does this mean that interval and ratio schedules activate similar processes? Hardly! The surface similarities hide fundamental differences in underlying mechanisms between time-based and ratio schedules.

Ratio and interval schedules activate different neurochemical changes in the brain (Barrett & Hoffmann, 1991). As might be expected, behavior maintained by interval schedules is mediated by the organism's sense of time, whereas timing mechanisms are not involved with ratio performance (Staddon, Wynne, & Higa, 1991). (I will discuss mechanisms of timing in greater detail in Chapter 12.)

Early evidence of fundamental differences between ratio and interval schedules was provided by an important experiment by Reynolds (1975). Reynolds compared the rate of key pecking in pigeons reinforced on variable ratio and variable interval schedules. Two pigeons were trained to peck the response key for food reinforcement. One of the birds was reinforced on a VR schedule. Therefore, for this bird the frequency of reinforcement was entirely determined by its rate of responding. The other bird was reinforced on a VI schedule. To make sure that the opportunities for

Figure 6.2 Cumulative records for two pigeons, one reinforced on a variable ratio (VR) schedule and the other yoked to it on a variable interval (VI) schedule. Although the two pigeons received the same rate of reinforcement, the VR bird responded five times as fast as the VI bird. (From *A Primer of Operant Conditioning,* 2nd ed. by G. S. Reynolds. Copyright © 1975 by Scott, Foresman. Reprinted by permission of the author.)

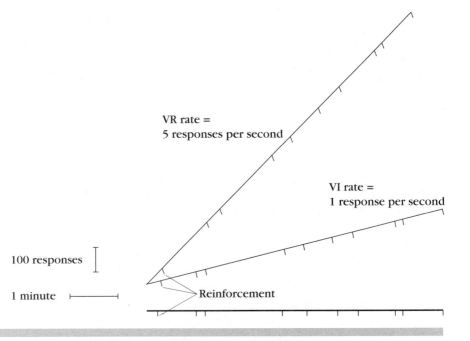

VR rate = 5 responses per second

VI rate = 1 response per second

100 responses

1 minute

Reinforcement

reinforcement would be identical for the two birds, the VI schedule was controlled by the behavior of the bird reinforced on the VR schedule. Each time the VR pigeon was just one response short of the requirement for reinforcement on that trial, the experimenter set up the reinforcer for the VI bird. With this arrangement, the next response made by each bird was reinforced. Thus, the VR bird controlled the VI schedule for its partner. This yoking procedure ensured that the frequency of reinforcement was virtually identical for the two animals.

Figure 6.2 shows the cumulative record of pecking exhibited by each bird. Even though the two pigeons received the same frequency of reinforcers, they behaved very differently. The pigeon reinforced on the VR schedule responded at a much higher rate than the pigeon reinforced on the VI schedule. The VR schedule motivated much more vigorous instrumental behavior. (For more recent demonstrations of this effect, see Baum, 1993; Cole, 1994.)

Why might ratio schedules produce higher rates of responding than interval schedules? The answer requires considering how the rate of responding is related to the frequency of reinforcement in the two types of schedules. In a sense, reinforcement constitutes feedback for the instrumental response. Because of this, the relationship between rate of responding and rate of reinforcement is technically called the **feedback function.** Each schedule of reinforcement has its own feedback function.

In ratio schedules, the feedback loop between responses and reinforcers is very strong. On a VR 10 schedule, for example, the only thing that determines whether the organism will be reinforced is the number of responses it makes. Therefore, the rate of responding totally determines the frequency of reinforcement. By responding at a higher rate, the organism can always obtain reinforcers at a higher rate.

In interval schedules, the relationship between rate of responding and frequency of reinforcement is not as close. Consider, for example, an FI 2-min schedule of food reinforcement. Each food pellet becomes available 2 minutes after the last one was delivered. If the animal responds right away when the food pellet is set up, the pellet is delivered and the next cycle begins. However, no matter how frequently the animal responds, it will never be reinforced more than once every 2 minutes. Therefore, the interval schedule sets a maximum limit on the frequency of reinforcers the organism can obtain. With an FI 2-min schedule, the limit is 30 reinforcers per hour. If the animal does not respond as soon as each pellet becomes available, it will not earn the maximum 30 pellets per hour possible. Therefore, the rate of responding determines the frequency of reinforcement to some extent. However, the delivery of the reinforcer depends more on exactly *when* the animal responds than on *how often* it responds.

The available evidence indicates that ratio schedules produce higher rates of responding than interval schedules because of the difference in the feedback functions of the two types of schedules. The strong link between response rate and reinforcement rate in ratio schedules encourages higher rates of responding. (For further discussion of these issues, see Baum, 1993; Cole, 1994; Dawson & Dickinson, 1990; McDowell & Wixted, 1988; Wearden & Clark, 1988).

Response-Rate Schedules of Reinforcement

Although ratio schedules produce higher rates of responding than comparable interval schedules, neither type of schedule requires a specific rate of responding for reinforcement. By contrast, other types of procedures specifically require that the organism respond at a particular rate to get reinforced. Such procedures are called **response-rate schedules.**

In response-rate schedules, whether a response is reinforced depends on how soon it occurs after the preceding response. A reinforcement schedule can be set up, for example, in which a response is reinforced only if it occurs within 5 seconds following the preceding response. If the animal makes a response every 5 seconds, its rate of response will be 12 per minute. Thus, the schedule provides reinforcement if the rate of response is 12 per minute or greater. The organism will not be reinforced if its rate of response falls below 12 per minute. As you might suspect, this procedure encourages responding at high rates. Therefore, it is called **differential reinforcement of high rates,** or DRH.

In DRH schedules, a response is reinforced only if it occurs *before* a certain amount of time has elapsed following the preceding response. The opposite result is achieved if a response is reinforced only if it occurs *after* a certain amount of time has elapsed following the previous response. This type of procedure is called **differential reinforcement of low rates,** abbreviated DRL. As you might suspect, DRL schedules encourage subjects to respond slowly.

Response-rate schedules are found outside the laboratory in situations that require particular rates of responding. DRH schedules are in effect in sports where speed is of the essence. For example, running from home plate to first base in a baseball game is reinforced only if it occurs faster than the time it takes to throw the ball to first base. In other circumstances, responding is reinforced only if it occurs at a specified rate. This is typically the case in dancing and music. Response-rate schedules are also in effect on an assembly line, where the speed of movement of the line dictates the rate of response for the workers. If an employee responds more slowly than the specified rate, he or she will not be reinforced and may, in fact, get fired. However, workers have to be careful not to work too fast. Those who work faster than the accepted norm are likely to be disliked by their peers.

EXTINCTION

So far I have shown how organisms behave when their responses are reinforced according to various schedules of reinforcement. A related and very important issue concerns what happens when reinforcement is no longer available. Reinforcement schedules do not necessarily remain in effect throughout an organism's lifetime. Responses that are successful in producing reinforcement at one time may cease to be effective as circumstances change. Children, for example, are praised for drawing crude representations of people and objects in nursery school, but the same type of drawing is not considered good if made in sixth grade. Dating someone may be extremely pleasant and rewarding at first, but stops being reinforcing when that person falls in love with someone else.

The nonreinforcement of a response that was previously reinforced is called **extinction.** I previously described extinction in Chapter 3 in connection with classical conditioning. The extinction procedure for classical conditioning involves presenting the conditioned stimulus (CS) by itself, no longer paired with the unconditioned stimulus (US). The typical outcome is a decline in conditioned responding. The instrumental analogue of presenting the CS by itself is permitting the instrumental response to occur by itself. The extinction procedure for instrumental conditioning involves allowing the instrumental response to occur without reinforcement.

Effects of Extinction Procedures

Instrumental extinction procedures have both behavioral and emotional effects. The behavioral effects are illustrated in Figure 6.3. When extinction is first introduced after a period of reinforcement, there is a burst of responding. This is called the *extinction burst.* Following the extinction burst, the rate of responding gradually declines, as is shown by the leveling off of the cumulative record. If the organism is placed back in the experimental situation the next day, there may be a small and temporary recovery in the rate of responding. This is called *spontaneous recovery.* Spontaneous recovery in instrumental conditioning is similar to spontaneous recovery after extinction in classical conditioning (see Chapter 3).

In addition to the behavioral effects illustrated in Figure 6.3, extinction procedures may also produce strong emotional effects. If an organism has become accustomed to receiving reinforcement for a particular response, it may become upset when reinforcers are no longer delivered. The emotional reaction induced by withdrawal of an expected reinforcer is called **frustration.** Under certain conditions, frustration may be sufficiently severe to include aggressive reactions. When a vending machine breaks down and no longer delivers a soft drink or candy after you put in your money, you may become abusive and pound and kick the machine. If a secretary has a cup of coffee ready for the boss every morning, the first time the secretary fails to prepare the coffee, the boss is likely to become angry. If a man takes his partner on a date every Saturday evening, she will surely be very disturbed if he unexpectedly calls to cancel the date.

Frustrative aggression induced by extinction is dramatically demonstrated by experiments in which two animals (pigeons, for example) are placed in the same Skinner box (Azrin, Hutchinson, & Hake, 1966). One of them is initially reinforced for pecking a response key, while the other animal is restrained in a corner of the experimental chamber. The key-pecking bird largely ignores the other one as long as reinforcers are provided. However, when extinction is introduced and reinforcement ceases, the previously rewarded animal is likely to attack its innocent partner. Similar

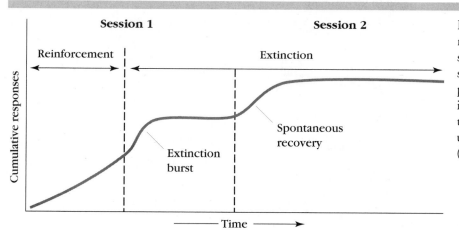

Figure 6.3 Cumulative record of responding during successive sessions of an instrumental conditioning experiment. Extinction was introduced midway during the first session and continued in the second session. (Hypothetical data.)

aggression occurs if a stuffed model instead of a real animal is placed in the Skinner box. Extinction-induced aggression has also been investigated with rats and with people (Nation & Cooney, 1982; Tomie, Carelli, & Wagner, 1993).

Determinants of Extinction Effects

The most important variable that determines the magnitude of both the behavioral and emotional effects of an extinction procedure is the schedule of reinforcement in effect before the extinction procedure is introduced. Various subtle features of reinforcement schedules can influence the subsequent extinction of instrumental responses. However, the dominant schedule characteristic that determines extinction effects is whether the instrumental response was reinforced every time it occurred (*continuous reinforcement*) or only some of the times it occurred (*intermittent, or partial, reinforcement*). The general finding is that extinction is much slower and involves fewer frustration reactions if partial reinforcement rather than continuous reinforcement was in effect before introduction of the extinction procedure (see Figure 6.4). This phenomenon is called the **partial reinforcement extinction effect,** or PREE.

The persistence in responding that is created by intermittent reinforcement can be remarkable. Habitual gamblers are at the mercy of intermittent reinforcement. Occasional winnings encourage them to continue gambling during long strings of losses. Intermittent reinforcement can also have undesirable consequences in parenting. Consider, for example, a child riding in a grocery cart while the parent is shopping. The child asks the parent to buy a piece of candy. The parent says no. The child asks again and again and then begins to throw a temper tantrum because the parent continues to say no. At this point, the parent is likely to give in to avoid public

Figure 6.4 Cumulative records of extinction of instrumental behavior following various simple schedules of reinforcement. (Hypothetical data.)

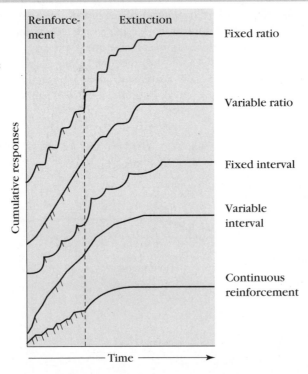

embarrassment. By finally buying the candy, the parent will have provided intermittent reinforcement for the repeated demands for candy. The parent will also have reinforced the tantrum behavior. The intermittent reinforcement the parent used will make the child very persistent in asking for candy during shopping trips in the future.

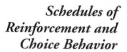
Mechanisms of the Partial Reinforcement Extinction Effect

Perhaps the most obvious explanation of the PREE is that the introduction of extinction is easier to detect after continuous reinforcement than after partial reinforcement. If an organism does not receive the reinforcer after each response during training, it may not immediately notice when reinforcers are omitted altogether. The absence of reinforcement is presumably much more noticeable after continuous reinforcement. This explanation of the partial reinforcement extinction effect is called the **discrimination hypothesis.**

Although intuitively attractive, the discrimination hypothesis was disproved some years ago (Jenkins, 1962; Theios, 1962). Current thinking is that the advantage of partial reinforcement does not come from greater difficulty in detecting the introduction of an extinction procedure. Rather, organisms learn something important during partial reinforcement training that enables them to continue responding in extinction. What is learned that produces persistence has been the subject of numerous experiments. These studies indicate that partial reinforcement training promotes persistence during extinction in two ways.

One of the mechanisms of the partial reinforcement extinction effect—**frustration theory**—was developed by Amsel (for example, 1958, 1962, 1967, 1992). According to frustration theory, persistence in extinction results from learning something paradoxical, namely, to continue responding when nonreinforcement or frustration is expected. Frustration theory assumes that intermittent reinforcement results in learning to respond in the face of expected nonreinforcement. However, this paradoxical outcome requires a considerable amount of experience with intermittent reinforcement.

Frustration theory assumes that learning during the course of intermittent reinforcement occurs in stages. Intermittent reinforcement involves both rewarded and nonrewarded trials. Rewarded trials lead organisms to expect reinforcement, and nonrewarded trials lead them to expect the absence of reward. Consequently, animals develop expectations of both reward and nonreward. At first, the anticipation of reward encourages the animals to respond, and the anticipation of nonreinforcement discourages responding. Thus, early in training the animals are in a conflict about what to do. However, as training continues, this conflict is resolved in favor of responding.

A. Amsel

The resolution of the conflict occurs because with a partial reinforcement schedule, on some occasions when animals expect nonreward, performance of the instrumental response may in fact be followed by the reinforcer. Because of such experiences, the instrumental response becomes conditioned to the expectation of nonreward. According to frustration theory, this is the key to persistent responding in extinction. With sufficient training, *intermittent reinforcement results in learning to make the instrumental response as a reaction to the expectation of nonreward.* Once the response has become conditioned to the expectation of nonreward, responding persists when extinction is introduced. By contrast, there is nothing about the experience of continuous reinforcement that teaches organisms to respond when they expect nonreward. Therefore, continuous reinforcement does not produce persistence in extinction.

E. J. Capaldi

The second prominent explanation of the partial reinforcement extinction effect was proposed by Capaldi (for example, 1967, 1971) and is known as **sequential theory**. Sequential theory is stated in terms of memory concepts. It assumes that animals can remember whether or not they were reinforced for performing the instrumental response in the recent past. They remember both recent rewarded and nonrewarded trials. The theory assumes further that during intermittent reinforcement training, the memory of nonreward becomes a cue for performing the instrumental response. According to sequential theory, this produces persistence in extinction. Precisely how this happens depends a great deal on the sequence in which rewarded (R) and nonrewarded (N) trials are administered in the intermittent reinforcement schedule. That is why the theory is labeled "sequential."

Consider the following sequence of trials: RNN<u>R</u>RN<u>R</u>. In this sequence the animal is rewarded on the first trial, not rewarded on the next two trials, then rewarded twice, then not rewarded, and then rewarded again. The fourth and last trials are critical in this schedule and are therefore underlined. On the fourth trial, the animal is reinforced after receiving nonreward on the preceding two trials. It is assumed that the animal remembers the two nonrewarded trials when it is reinforced on the fourth trial. Because of this, the memory of two nonrewarded trials becomes a cue for responding. Responding in the face of the memory of nonreward is again reinforced on the last trial, when the animal is reinforced for responding during the memory of one nonreinforced trial. With enough experiences of this type, the animal learns to respond whenever it remembers not having been reinforced on the preceding trials. This learning creates persistence of the instrumental response in extinction. (For recent studies of this mechanism, see Capaldi, Alptekin, & Birmingham, 1996; Capaldi, Alptekin, Miller, & Barry, 1992; Haggbloom, Lovelace, Brewer, Levins, & Owens, 1990).

Some theorists have regarded frustration theory and sequential theory as competing explanations of the partial reinforcement extinction effect. However, since the two mechanisms were originally proposed, a large and impressive body of evidence has been obtained in support of each theory. Therefore, neither of the theories can be regarded as correct and the other as incorrect. Rather, the two theories point out two different ways in which partial reinforcement can promote responding during extinction. In some situations one or the other mechanism may predominate; in other cases, both processes may contribute to persistent responding in extinction.

CHOICE BEHAVIOR: CONCURRENT SCHEDULES

The reinforcement schedules I have discussed thus far have involved an analysis of the relation between occurrences of a particular response and reinforcement of that response. However, experiments in which only one response is being measured are not likely to provide a complete account of behavior. Behavior involves more than the repetition of individual responses. Even in a simple situation such as a Skinner box, organisms engage in a variety of activities and are continually choosing between possible alternatives. People are also constantly having to make choices about what to do. Should you go to the movies or stay at home and study? Should you go shopping tonight or watch television and go shopping tomorrow? Understanding the mechanisms of response choice is fundamental to the understanding of behavior because the choices organisms make determine the occurrence of individual responses.

Choice situations can be rather complicated. For example, a person may have a choice of 12 different activities (reading the newspaper, watching television, going for a walk, playing with the dog, and the like), each of which produces a different type of reinforcer according to a different reinforcement schedule. Analyzing all the factors that control the individual's behavior in such a situation is a formidable task, if not an impossible one. Therefore, psychologists have begun experimental investigations of the mechanisms of choice by studying simpler situations. The simplest choice situation is one in which the organism has two response alternatives, and each response is followed by a reinforcer according to its own schedule of reinforcement.

Historically, research on choice behavior was conducted using mazes, particularly the T-maze (see Woodworth & Schlosberg, 1954). More recent approaches to the study of choice use Skinner boxes equipped with two manipulanda, such as two pecking keys. In the typical experiment, responding on each key is reinforced on some schedule of reinforcement. The two schedules are in effect at the same time (or concurrently), and the animal is free to switch from one response key to the other. This type of procedure is called a **concurrent schedule**. Concurrent schedules of reinforcement allow for continuous measurement of choice because the organism is free to change back and forth between the response alternatives.

Figure 6.5 shows an example of a concurrent schedule. If the pigeon pecks the key on the left, it receives food according to a VI 60-sec schedule. Pecks on the right key produce food according to an FR 10 schedule. The animal is free to peck on either side at any time. The point of the experiment is to see how the animal distributes its pecks on the two keys and how the schedule of reinforcement on each key influences its choices.

Measures of Choice Behavior

The animal's choice in a concurrent schedule is reflected in the distribution of its behavior between the two response alternatives. This can be measured in several ways.

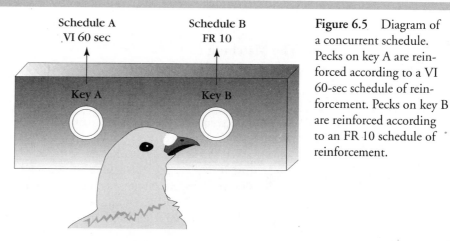

Schedule A
VI 60 sec

Schedule B
FR 10

Key A

Key B

Figure 6.5 Diagram of a concurrent schedule. Pecks on key A are reinforced according to a VI 60-sec schedule of reinforcement. Pecks on key B are reinforced according to an FR 10 schedule of reinforcement.

One common technique is to calculate the *relative rate of responding* on each alternative. The relative rate of responding on key A, for example, is calculated by dividing the response rate on key A by the total rate of responding (rate on key A plus rate on key B):

$$R_A/(R_A + R_B) \qquad\qquad (6.1)$$

where R_A is the rate of responding on key A, and R_B is the rate on key B. If the pigeon pecks equally often on the two response keys, this ratio will be 0.5. If the rate of responding on key A is greater than the rate of responding on key B, the ratio will be greater than 0.5. On the other hand, if the rate of responding on key A is less than the rate of responding on key B, the ratio will be less than 0.5. The relative rate of responding on key B can be calculated in a comparable manner.

As you might suspect, how an organism distributes its behavior between the two response alternatives is greatly influenced by the reinforcement schedule in effect for each response. For example, if the same variable interval reinforcement schedule is available for each response alternative, as in a concurrent VI 60-sec VI 60-sec procedure, the pigeon will peck the two keys equally often. The relative rate of responding for pecks on each side will be 0.5. This result is intuitively reasonable. If the pigeon spent all its time pecking on one side, it would receive only the reinforcers programmed for that side. The bird can get more reinforcers by pecking on both sides. Since the VI schedule available on each side is the same, there is no advantage in responding more on one side than on the other.

By responding equally often on each side of a concurrent VI 60-sec VI 60-sec schedule, the pigeon will also earn reinforcers equally often on each side. The relative rate of reinforcement earned for each response alternative can be calculated in a manner comparable to the relative rate of response. For example, the relative rate of reinforcement for alternative A is the rate of reinforcement of response A divided by the total rate of reinforcement (the sum of the rate of reward earned on side A plus the rate of reward earned on side B). This is expressed in the formula

$$r_A/(r_A + r_B) \qquad\qquad (6.2)$$

where r_A and r_B represent the rates of reinforcement earned on each response alternative. On a concurrent VI 60-sec VI 60-sec schedule, the relative rate of reinforcement for each response alternative will be 0.5 because the subject earns rewards equally often on each side.

The Matching Law

As we have seen, with a concurrent VI 60-sec VI 60-sec schedule, both the relative rate of responding and the relative rate of reinforcement for each response alternative are 0.5. Thus, the relative rate of responding is equal to the relative rate of reinforcement. Will this equality also occur if the two response alternatives are not reinforced according to the same schedule in the concurrent procedure? This important question was asked by Herrnstein (1961).

Herrnstein studied the distribution of responses on various concurrent VI-VI schedules in which the maximum total rate of reinforcement the pigeons could earn was 40 per hour. However, depending on the exact value of each VI schedule, different proportions of the 40 reinforcers could be obtained by each response alternative.

Consider, for example, a concurrent VI 6-min VI 2-min schedule. With such a schedule, a maximum of 10 reinforcers per hour could be obtained by responding on the VI 6-min alternative, and a maximum of 30 reinforcers per hour could be obtained by responding on the VI 2-min alternative.

Herrnstein studied the effects of a variety of concurrent VI-VI schedules. There was no constraint on which side the pigeons could peck. They could respond exclusively on one side or the other, or they could distribute their pecks between the two sides in some manner. As it turns out, the pigeons distributed their responses in a highly predictable fashion. The results, summarized in Figure 6.6, indicate that the relative rate of responding on a given alternative was always very nearly equal to the relative rate of reinforcement earned on that alternative. If the pigeons earned a greater proportion of their reinforcers on alternative A, they made a correspondingly greater proportion of their responses on alternative A. Thus, the relative rate of responding on an alternative *matched* the relative rate of reinforcement on that alternative. Similar findings have been obtained in a variety of situations, which encouraged Herrnstein to state the relation as a law of behavior—the **matching law.**

There are two common mathematical expressions of the matching law. In one formulation, rates of responding and reinforcement on one alternative are expressed as a proportion of total response and reinforcement rates, as follows:

$$R_A/(R_A + R_B) = r_A/(r_A + r_B) \qquad (6.3)$$

As before, R_A and R_B in this equation represent the rates of responding on keys A and B, and r_A and r_B represent the rates of reinforcement earned on each response alternative.

R. J. Herrnstein

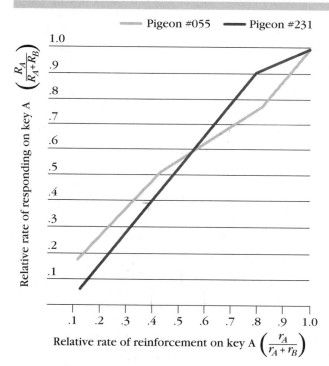

Figure 6.6 Various combinations of VI schedules were tested whose combined reinforcement rate was 40 reinforcements per hour. Note that throughout the range of schedules, the relative rate of responding nearly equals (matches) the relative rate of reinforcement. (From "Relative and Absolute Strength of Response as a Function of Frequency of Reinforcement" by R. J. Herrnstein, *Journal of the Experimental Analysis of Behavior,* 1961, *4,* pp. 267–272. Copyright © 1961 by the Society for the Experimental Analysis of Behavior, Inc. Reprinted by permission.)

The second formulation of the matching law is simpler but mathematically equivalent to equation 6.3. In the second version, the rates of responding and reinforcement on one alternative are expressed as a proportion of the rates of responding and reinforcement on the other alternative, as follows:

$$R_A/R_B = r_A/r_B \qquad (6.4)$$

Both mathematical expressions of the matching law express the same basic principle, namely that *relative rates of responding match relative rates of reinforcement.*

Undermatching, Overmatching, and Response Bias. The matching law clearly indicates that choices are not made capriciously; they are, rather, an orderly function of rates of reinforcement. However, the precise characterization of the function is the subject of continuing research (see reviews by Baum, 1979; Davison & McCarthy, 1988; Wearden & Burgess, 1982; Williams, 1988, 1994.) Although the matching law has enjoyed considerable success and has guided much research over the past 25 years, relative rates of responding do not always match relative rates of reinforcement perfectly.

Most instances in which choice behavior does not correspond perfectly to the matching relation can be accommodated by adding two parameters, *b* and *s,* to equation 6.4. This generalized form of the matching law (Baum, 1974) is as follows:

$$R_A/R_B = b(r_A/r_B)^s \qquad (6.5)$$

The parameter "s" represents *sensitivity* of the choice behavior to the relative rates of reinforcement for the response alternatives. Perfect matching occurs if "s" is equal to 1.0. In that case, relative response rates are a direct function of relative rates of reinforcement.

One type of deviation from perfect matching involves reduced sensitivity of the choice behavior to the relative rate of reinforcement. Such results are referred to as **undermatching** and can be accommodated by equation 6.5 by making the exponent "s" less than 1.0. Notice that if the exponent "s" is less than 1.0, the value of the term representing relative reinforcer rates—$(r_A/r_B)^s$—becomes smaller, indicating the reduced sensitivity to the relative rate of reinforcement.

In other instances, the relative rate of responding is more sensitive to the relative rate of reinforcement than what is predicted by perfect matching. Such outcomes are called **overmatching** and can be accommodated by equation 6.5 by making the exponent greater than 1.0. In this case, the value of the term representing the relative rate of reinforcement—$(r_A/r_B)^s$—is increased, indicating the increased sensitivity to this factor.

Choices are more likely to exhibit reduced sensitivity to relative reinforcement rates than they are to exhibit enhanced sensitivity to reinforcement rates. Therefore, undermatching is found more often than overmatching. Numerous variables have been found to influence the sensitivity parameter, including the species tested, effort or difficulty involved in switching from one alternative to the other, and the details of how the schedule alternatives are constructed (for some recent studies, see Davison, 1991a; Davison & Jones, 1995; Dreyfus, DePorto-Callan, & Pesillo, 1993; Elliffe & Alsup, 1996; Foster, Temple, Robertson, Nair, & Poling, 1996). In general, making it more difficult to switch from one response alternative to the other increases the sensitivity parameter; when switching is more difficult, organisms are more sensitive to the relative rates of reinforcement for the response alternatives.

W. M. Baum

The matching law and its implications have been found to apply to a wide range of human behavior (see, for example, Baum, 1975; Conger & Killeen, 1974; Martens, Lochner, & Kelly, 1992; McDowell, 1982). In addition, the matching law has important implications for behavior therapy (McDowell, 1982). According to the matching law, the tendency to make a particular response depends not only on the rate of reinforcement for that response but also on the rates of reinforcement available for alternative activities. This implies that analysis of a problematic behavior (truancy from school, for example) has to include not only consideration of the rewards available for that particular behavior but also the rewards the person can obtain in other ways. Thus, the matching law suggests that accurate assessment of a behavior problem requires consideration of the individual's full range of activities and sources of reinforcement.

The matching law also suggests novel techniques for decreasing undesired responses and increasing desired responses. According to the matching law, an undesired response can be decreased by providing more reinforcement for other activities or by simply providing more "free" reinforcers. Conversely, a desired response can be increased by withdrawing reinforcement for other activities.

Implications of the matching law for behavior therapy are illustrated by the treatment of a mildly retarded 22-year-old man to decrease his oppositional behavior (McDowell, 1981). The man periodically became very uncooperative, and his oppositional behavior sometimes escalated to the point of assault. Given the potential for aggression in the situation, punishment was judged to be an unsuitable therapeutic procedure. The undesired behavior was successfully treated by introducing a system that permitted the man to earn positive reinforcement by engaging in a variety of other activities. He could earn points for performing various personal hygiene, job, and educational tasks and then exchange the points for money. Increasing the rate of reinforcement for other activities significantly decreased the rate of oppositional behavior.

The parameter "b" in equation 6.5 represents response *bias*. In Herrnstein's original experiment (and in most others that have followed), animals choose between two responses of the same type (pecking a response key), and each response is reinforced by the same type of reinforcer (a short period of access to food). Response bias influences choice when the response alternatives are different (one may be pecking a key and the other stepping on a treadle). Parameter "b" is also important when the reinforcer provided for the two responses is different. In the case of pigeons, one reinforcer may be buckwheat and the other hemp (seed). A preference (or bias) for one response or one reinforcer over the other influences the bias parameter "b" (see Hanson & Green, 1986; Miller, 1976). In the absence of bias, "b" is equal to 1.0. Depending on the nature of the bias or preference, "b" will be greater or less than 1.0.

The Matching Law and Reinforcer Value. The matching relation has been extended to aspects of reinforcers other than their rate of occurrence. For example, the relative rate of responding has been found to be a function of the relative amount of each reinforcer, as well as the relative delay of reinforcement (for example, Gibbon & Fairhurst, 1994; Grace, 1995). Relative rates of responding have also been found to be determined by the palatability of the reinforcers (Shah, Bradshaw, & Szabadi, 1991). Features of a reinforcer such as its amount, palatability, and delay can be considered to be aspects of the general value of the reinforcer. Larger, more palatable, and more immediate reinforcers presumably are of greater value. However, it is not yet clear exactly how various features of a reinforcer combine to determine reinforcer value. (For a detailed recent discussion of this issue, see Williams, 1994.)

The Matching Law and Simple Reinforcement Schedules. If the matching law represents a fundamental fact about behavior, then it should also characterize responding on simple schedules of reinforcement. But, in a simple schedule, only one response manipulandum is provided. How can a law that describes the distribution of responses among several alternatives be applied to single-response situations?

As Herrnstein (1970) pointed out, even single-response situations can be considered to involve a choice. The choice is between making the specified response (bar pressing or pecking a key, for example) and engaging in other possible activities (grooming, walking around, pecking the floor, sniffing holes in the experimental chamber). On a simple schedule, the animal receives explicit reinforcement for making a specific operant response. In addition, it no doubt receives intrinsic rewards for the other activities in which it may engage. Hence, the total reinforcement in a simple schedule experiment includes the programmed extrinsic rewards as well as other unprogrammed sources of reinforcement. This type of analysis permits application of the matching law to single-response reinforcement schedules.

Let us assume that R_A represents the rate of the specified operant response in the schedule, R_O represents the rate of the animal's other activities, r_A is the rate of the explicit programmed reinforcement, and r_O is the rate of the intrinsic reinforcement for the other activities. With these values substituted into equation 6.4, the matching law for single-response situations can be stated as follows:

$$R_A/R_O = r_A/r_O \qquad\qquad (6.6)$$

Extensions of the matching law to single-response situations have enjoyed considerable success in recent years (for example, Beardsley & McDowell, 1992; Belke & Heyman, 1994a, 1994b; Heyman & Monaghan, 1994; Petry & Heyman, 1994).

Mechanisms of the Matching Law

The matching law describes how organisms distribute their responses in a choice situation but does not explain what mechanisms are responsible for this response distribution. Factors that may be responsible for matching in choice situations have been the subject of continuing experimentation and theoretical debate (see Commons, Herrnstein, & Rachlin, 1982; Davison & McCarthy, 1988; Williams, 1988, 1994).

The matching law is stated in terms of rates of responding and reinforcement averaged over the entire duration of experimental sessions. It ignores when and how individual responses are made. Some theories are similar in that they ignore what might occur at the level of individual responses. Such explanations are called *molar theories*. Molar theories operate at the level of aggregates of responses. They deal with the overall distribution of responses and reinforcers in choice situations.

In contrast to molar theories, other explanations of the matching relation attempt to explain what happens at the level of individual responses and view the matching relation as the net result of these individual choices. Such explanations are called *molecular theories*. Finally, yet other theories provide characterizations of behavior that are neither molar nor molecular but somewhere in between. One such theory is melioration. I now will turn to a discussion of molecular, molar, and melioration theories of choice.

B. A. Williams

Matching and Maximizing Rates of Reinforcement. The most extensively investigated explanations of choice behavior are based on the intuitively reasonable idea that organisms distribute their actions among response alternatives so as to receive the maximum amount of reinforcement possible in the situation. According to this idea, animals switch back and forth between response alternatives so as to receive as many reinforcers as they possibly can. The idea that organisms maximize reinforcement has been used to explain choice behavior at both molecular and molar levels of analysis.

1. *Molecular maximizing.* According to molecular theories of maximizing, organisms always choose whichever response alternative is most likely to be reinforced at the time (Hinson & Staddon, 1983a, 1983b). Shimp (1966, 1969) proposed an early version of molecular matching. He suggested that when two schedules (A and B) are in effect simultaneously, the animal switches from schedule A to schedule B as the probability of reinforcement for schedule B increases. Consider, for example, a pigeon working on a concurrent VI-VI schedule. As the pigeon pecks key A, the timer controlling reinforcement for key B is still operating. The longer the pigeon stays on key A, the greater the probability that the requisite interval for key B will elapse and reinforcement will become available for pecking key B. By switching, the pigeon can pick up the reinforcer on key B. Now, the longer it continues to peck key B, the more likely key A will become set for reinforcement. Shimp proposed that the matching relation is a by-product of prudent switching, when the probability of reinforcement on the alternative response key becomes greater than the probability of reinforcement on the current response key.

Detailed studies of the patterns of switching from one to another response alternative have not always supported the molecular maximizing theory proposed by Shimp. In fact, some studies have shown that matching is possible in the absence of momentary maximizing (for example, Nevin, 1969, 1979). (For more recent evidence contrary to molecular maximizing, see Machado, 1994; Williams, 1991, 1992a)

2. *Molar maximizing.* Molar theories of maximizing assume that organisms distribute their responses among various alternatives so as to maximize the amount of reinforcement they earn over the long run (for example, Rachlin, Battalio, Kagel, & Green, 1981; Rachlin, Green, Kagel, & Battalio, 1976). What is long enough to be considered a "long run" is not clearly specified. However, in contrast to molecular theories, molar theories focus on aggregates of behavior over some period of time rather than on individual choice responses.

Molar maximizing theory was originally formulated to explain choice on concurrent schedules made up of ratio components. In concurrent ratio schedules, animals rarely switch back and forth between response alternatives. Rather, they respond exclusively on the ratio component that requires the fewest responses. On a concurrent FR 20-FR 10 schedule, for example, the organism is likely to respond only on the FR 10 alternative. In this way it maximizes its rate of reinforcement with the least effort.

In many situations, molar maximizing accurately predicts the results of choice procedures. However, certain findings present difficulties for molar maximizing theories. One difficulty arises from the results of concurrent VI-VI schedules of reinforcement. On a concurrent VI-VI schedule, organisms can earn close to all of the available rewards on both schedules, provided they occasionally sample each alternative. Therefore, the total amount of reinforcement obtained on a concurrent VI-VI schedule can be close to the same, despite wide variations in how responding is distributed between the two alternatives. The matching relation is only one of many

E. Fantino

different possibilities that yield close to maximal rates of reinforcement. Because other response distributions can yield similar amounts of total reward, molar maximizing cannot explain why choice behavior is distributed so close to the matching relation on concurrent VI-VI schedules and not in other, equally effective ways (Heyman, 1983).

Another challenge for molar matching is provided by the results of studies in which there is a choice between a variable ratio and a variable interval schedule. On a variable ratio schedule, the organism can obtain reinforcement at any time by making the required number of responses. By contrast, on a variable interval schedule, the animal only has to respond occasionally to obtain close to the maximum number of rewards possible. Given these differences, for maximum return on a concurrent VR-VI schedule, animals should concentrate their responses on the variable ratio alternative and respond only occasionally on the variable interval component. Evidence shows that animals do favor the VR component but not as strongly as molar maximizing predicts (Baum, 1981; DeCarlo, 1985; Herrnstein & Heyman, 1979; Heyman & Herrnstein, 1986; see also Vyse & Belke, 1992). Human participants also respond much more on the VI alternative than is prudent if they are trying to maximize their rate of reinforcement (Savastano & Fantino, 1994).

Melioration. The third major mechanism of choice that I will discuss—**melioration**—is neither a molecular nor a molar mechanism. Molecular mechanisms operate at the level of individual responses, whereas molar mechanisms deal with response rates that are calculated over an entire experimental session. In contrast, melioration operates at the level of local rates of responding. The *local rate* of a response is calculated over just the time the organism devotes to that particular response.

The local rate of a response is always higher than its overall rate. Consider, for example, a situation with two response alternatives, A and B. If the animal responds 75 times in an hour on response A, the overall rate for response A will be 75/hour. However, those 75 responses might be made during just 20 minutes of the session, with the animal working on response B the rest of the time. Therefore, the local rate of response A will be 75/20 minutes, or 225/hour.

Melioration theory assumes that animals change from one response alternative to another to improve on the local rate of reinforcement they are receiving (Herrnstein & Vaughan, 1980; Vaughan, 1981, 1985). Adjustments in the distribution of behavior between alternatives are assumed to continue until the organism is obtaining the same local rate of reward on all alternatives. It can be shown mathematically that when animals distribute their responses so as to obtain the same local rate of reinforcement on each response alternative, they are behaving in accordance with the matching law. Therefore, the mechanism of melioration results in matching.

To see how melioration works, consider a concurrent VI 1-min VI 3-min schedule. During the first hour of exposure to this schedule, a pigeon will switch back and forth between the two alternatives and may end up accumulating a total of 30 minutes responding on each component, earning all of the available reinforcers. On a VI 1-min schedule, at most 60 reinforcers are available in 1 hour. The pigeon could get all of these during the course of spending just 30 minutes on the VI 1-min schedule, provided it spaced out its responses appropriately. If the pigeon received all 60 reinforcers during the course of accumulating 30 minutes on the VI 1 min schedule, its local rate of reinforcement would be 60 reinforcers in 30 minutes, or *120 per hour*. On a VI 3-min schedule, at most 20 reinforcers are available in 1 hour. If the pigeon got all of these during the course of accumulating a total of 30 minutes on the VI

3-min schedule, its local rate of reinforcement on the VI 3-min component would be 20 reinforcers in 30 minutes, or *40 per hour.*

According to melioration theory, the pigeon will shift its preference in favor of the response alternative that yields the higher local rate of reinforcement. Since the local rate of reinforcement on the VI 1-min schedule (120 hr) is much higher than on the VI 3-min schedule (40/hr), the pigeon will shift its behavior in favor of the VI 1-min alternative. However, if it begins to spend too much time on the VI 1-min schedule and samples the VI 3-min schedule only rarely, it may be reinforced every time it pecks the VI 3-min key. This will make the local rate of reinforcement on the VI 3-min key higher than the local rate of reinforcement on the VI 1-min alternative. That in turn would produce a shift in favor of the VI 3-min schedule. According to melioration theory, such shifts back and forth will continue until the local rates of reinforcement earned on the two alternatives are equal.

Although tests of the melioration hypothesis have yielded confirmatory evidence (for example, McSweeney, Melville, Buck, & Whipple, 1983), the hypothesis has also encountered some difficulties (for example, Belke, 1992; Williams, 1993). Therefore, investigators are continuing their exploration of alternative approaches to explaining how organisms choose between different sources of reinforcement (for example, Davis, Staddon, Machado, & Palmer, 1993; McDowell & Wood, 1985; Myerson & Hale, 1988; Staddon, 1988).

COMPLEX CHOICE: CONCURRENT-CHAIN SCHEDULES

In a standard concurrent schedule of reinforcement, two (or more) response alternatives are available at the same time, and switching from one to the other can occur at any time. Many choice situations outside the laboratory are of this type. If you have a plate of roast beef, vegetables, and mashed potatoes, you can switch from one food to another at any time during the meal. You can similarly switch back and forth among television channels or parts of the newspaper you are reading. However, in other situations choosing one alternative may make other alternatives unavailable, and the choice may involve assessing complex, long-range goals.

Should you go to college and get a degree in engineering or start in a full-time job without a college degree? You cannot switch back and forth between such alternatives frequently. Furthermore, to make the decision, you need to consider long-range goals. A degree in engineering may enable you to get a higher-paying job eventually, but it may require significant economic sacrifices initially. Getting a job without a college degree would enable you to make money sooner, but in the long run you would not be able to earn as much money.

Obviously, we cannot conduct experiments that directly involve such complex choices as choosing between college and employment. However, simplified analogous questions may be posed in laboratory experiments. For example, does a pigeon prefer to work on an FR 10 schedule of reinforcement for 15 minutes, or does it prefer to work on a VI 60-sec schedule for the same amount of time? Answers to such questions can be obtained with the use of **concurrent-chain schedules.**

A concurrent-chain schedule of reinforcement involves at least two stages, or links (see Figure 6.7). The first stage is called the *choice link.* In this link, the participant is

Figure 6.7 Diagram of a concurrent-chain schedule. Pecking the left key in the choice link puts into effect reinforcement schedule A in the terminal link. Pecking the right key in the choice link puts into effect reinforcement schedule B in the terminal link.

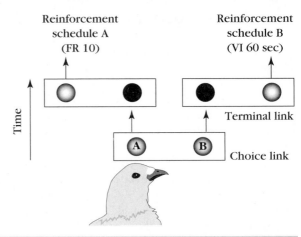

allowed to choose between two schedule alternatives by making one of two responses. In the example diagrammed in Figure 6.7, the pigeon makes its choice by pecking either the left or the right response key. Pecking the left key produces alternative A, the opportunity to peck the left key for 15 minutes on an FR 10 schedule of reinforcement. If the pigeon pecks the right key in the choice link, it produces alternative B, which is the opportunity to peck the right key for 15 minutes on a VI 60-sec schedule. Responding on either key during the choice link does not produce reinforcement. The opportunity for reinforcement occurs only after the initial choice has been made, and the pigeon has entered the *terminal link*. Another important feature of the concurrent-chain schedule is that once the participant has made a choice, it is stuck with that choice until the end of the terminal link of the schedule (in the hypothetical example, for 15 minutes). Thus, concurrent-chain schedules involve *choice with commitment*.

The pattern of responding that occurs in the terminal component of a concurrent-chain schedule is characteristic of whatever schedule of reinforcement is in effect during that component. In the example, if the pigeon selected alternative A, its pattern of pecking during the terminal component would be similar to the usual response pattern for an FR 10 schedule. If the pigeon selected alternative B, its pattern of pecking during the terminal component would be characteristic of a VI 60-sec schedule.

Concurrent-chain schedules are useful for studying preference between different schedules of reinforcement. An organism's preference for one or the other terminal link schedule is measured by how often it chooses alternative A over B during the choice link. Studies of concurrent-chain schedules focus on how behavior during the choice link is determined by the schedules of reinforcement that are in effect in the terminal links.

Concurrent-chain schedules can be used to investigate many interesting questions about how various aspects of reinforcers and their contingent relation to behavior combine to influence choice. Some experiments, for example, have explored the conditions under which animals prefer a schedule in which reinforcers are unpredictable over a schedule that provides reinforcement in a predictable fashion (for example, Belke & Spetch, 1994; Bruner, Gibbon, & Fairhurst, 1994; Mazur, 1991; Mazur & Romano, 1992; Spetch, Mondloch, Belke, & Dunn, 1994). Other experiments have explored how amount and delay of reinforcement determine choice.

These latter investigations have led to the development of an experimental model of "self-control."

Studies of "Self-Control"

Self-control is often a matter of choosing a large delayed reward over an immediate small reward. For example, self-control in eating involves selecting the large delayed reward of being thin over the immediate small reward of eating a piece of cake. When a piece of cake is in plain view, it is very difficult to choose the delayed reward; it is difficult to pass up the piece of cake in favor of being thin. Self-control is easier if the tempting alternative is not as readily available. It is easier to pass up a piece of cake if you are deciding on what to eat at the next meal. Rachlin and Green (1972) set up a laboratory analog of self-control with pigeons based on these ideas.

The basic concurrent-chain schedule used by Rachlin and Green is shown in Figure 6.8. In the terminal components of the schedule, responding was rewarded by either immediate access to a small amount of grain (alternative A) or access to a large amount of grain that was delayed by 4 seconds (alternative B). The pigeons could choose between these two alternatives by pecking either key A or key B during the initial component of the schedule.

Rachlin and Green tested the choice behavior of the pigeons under two different conditions. In one case (labeled "direct-choice procedure" in Figure 6.8), the small immediate reward and the delayed large reward were available as soon as the pigeons pecked the corresponding choice key once. Under these conditions, the pigeons lacked self-control. They predominantly selected the small immediate reward. In the second case (labeled "concurrent-chain procedure" in Figure 6.8), the terminal components of the concurrent-chain schedule were delayed after the pigeons made their initial choice. If a sufficient delay was imposed before the terminal components, the pigeons showed self-control; they primarily selected the large delayed reward.

The phenomenon of self-control as illustrated by the Rachlin and Green experiment has stimulated much research and theorizing. Numerous investigators have found, in agreement with Rachlin and Green, that preferences shift in favor of the delayed large reward as participants are required to wait longer to receive either reward after making their choice. If rewards are delivered shortly after a choice response, organisms generally favor an immediate small reward over a delayed large reward. However, if a constant delay is added to the delivery of both rewards, individuals are more likely to show self-control and favor the delayed large reward. This crossover in preference has been obtained in experiments with both people and non-human organisms and thus represents a general property of choice behavior. (For a review, see Logue, 1988b.)

Explanations of Self-Control

The results of animal studies of self-control have been generally consistent with concepts related to the matching law. The matching approach assumes that the value of a reinforcer is directly related to its size or amount and inversely related to how long the individual has to wait to obtain it (delay). The longer a reinforcer is delayed, the less valuable it becomes. These relationships are illustrated in Figure 6.9 for a small and a large reward. The value of the reinforcer is represented by the height of the vertical bars. The bar for the large reward is taller than the bar for the small reward. Time is represented by distance along the horizontal axis. Notice that the figure is set up so

L. Green

A. W. Logue

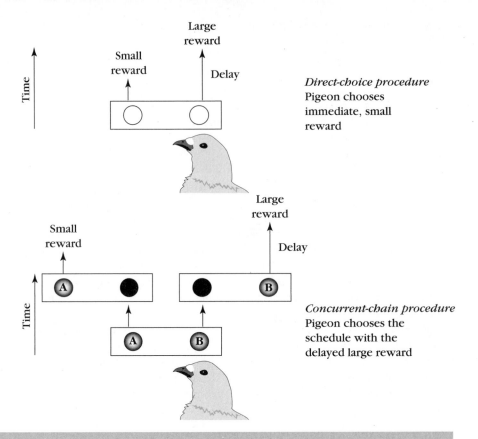

Figure 6.8 Diagram of the experiment by Rachlin and Green (1972) on self-control. The direct-choice procedure is shown at the top; the concurrent-chain procedure at the bottom.

that the large reinforcer is delivered later than the small one. Decreases in the value of the reinforcer with time are illustrated by the curves that decrease toward the left from each reinforcer.

Figure 6.9 identifies two points in time—T1 and T2—before delivery of the small and large rewards. The waiting time to reward delivery is much less at T1 than at T2. The reward-value curves shown in Figure 6.9 predict the choice behavior that is typically observed in self-control experiments. When the waiting time for reward delivery is short (at T1), the value of the small reward is greater than the value of the large reward. Hence, at this point, participants will choose the small reward. By contrast, when the waiting time to reward delivery is long (at T2), the value of the large reward is greater than the value of the small reward. At T2, participants will choose the large reward. Thus, the model depicted in Figure 6.9 predicts the crossover from preference for the small reward to preference for the more remote large reward as the waiting time for both rewards is increased.

The approach based on the matching law illustrated in Figure 6.9 accurately characterizes the results of many animal experiments (see Logue, 1988b). Various outcomes can be accommodated by changing how fast the reinforcer value is assumed to decline with delay. For example, in some situations organisms seem to be more sensitive to reinforcer amounts than to reinforcer delays. This increases the likelihood of their choosing the large delayed reward (see Box 6.4). Such cases can be accommodated by assuming that the reinforcer value decreases more slowly with delay than the functions shown in Figure 6.9.

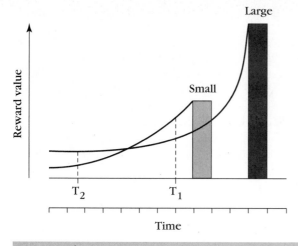

Figure 6.9 Hypothetical relations between reward value and waiting time to reward delivery for a small reward and a large reward presented some time later.

In comparison to pigeons and rats, the choice behavior of macaque monkeys and human beings is less sensitive to reinforcer delays. As a consequence, macaques and people are more likely than pigeons and rats to select the large delayed reward in a self-control procedure (for example, King & Logue, 1987; Logue, King, Chavarro, & Volpe, 1990; Logue, Peña-Correal, Rodriguez, & Kabela, 1986; Tobin, Logue, Chelonis, Ackerman, & May, 1996). These results suggest that in macaques and people, choice of the large delayed reward reflects maximizing obtained reinforcers rather than the matching of choices to relative reinforcer value (see also Sonuga-Barke, Lea, & Webley, 1989a).

Interestingly, preference for the large delayed reward in humans emerges with age. Four-year-old children are more likely to respond like pigeons, selecting the small immediate reward, than are 6- or 9-year-old children, who exclusively select the large delayed reward (Sonuga-Barke, Lea, & Webley, 1989b). The reasons for these species and developmental differences are the subject of continuing investigation (Forzano & Logue, 1994; Logue, Forzano, & Tobin, 1992). Learning is probably a contributing factor. Box 6.4, on the next page, illustrates that the development of self-control can be facilitated by training that involves exposure to large delayed rewards. However, other variables are also no doubt responsible for species and developmental differences in self-control.

CONCLUDING COMMENTS

The basic principle of instrumental conditioning is very simple: reinforcement increases (and punishment decreases) the future probability of an instrumental response. However, as we have seen, the experimental analysis of instrumental behavior can be rather intricate. Many important aspects of instrumental behavior are determined by the schedule of reinforcement. There are numerous schedules by which responses can be reinforced. Reinforcement can depend on how many responses have occurred, when a response occurs, or the rate of responding. Furthermore, more than one reinforcement schedule may be available to the organism at the same time. The pattern of instrumental behavior, as well as choices between various response alternatives, are

A person who cannot tolerate the delay involved in obtaining large rewards has to forgo obtaining those reinforcers. Self-control, or the preference for a large delayed reward over a small immediate reward, is often a sensible strategy. In fact, some have suggested that self-control is a critical component of socialization and emotional adjustment. This raises an interesting question: Can self-control be trained? The answer seems to be yes.

Training people with delayed reward appears to have generalized effects in increasing their tolerance for delayed reward. In one study (Eisenberger & Ardonetto, 1986), second- and third-grade students in a public elementary school were first tested for self-control by being asked whether they wanted to get 2¢ immediately or 3¢ at the end of the day. Children

who elected the immediate reward were given 2¢. For those who elected the delayed reward, 3¢ was placed in a cup to be given to the child later. The procedure was repeated eight times to complete the pretest. The children then received three sessions of training with either immediate or delayed reward.

During each training session, various problems were presented: one involved counting objects on a card, another was a picture-memory task, and the third was a shape-matching task. For half the students, correct responding was reinforced immediately with 2¢. For the remaining students, correct responses resulted in 3¢ being placed in a cup that was given to the child at the end of the day. After the third training session, preference for small immediate reward versus larger delayed reward was measured as in the pretest. Provided that the training tasks involved low effort, training with delayed reward increased preference for the larger delayed reward during the posttest. Thus, training with delayed reinforcement produced generalized self-control (see also Schweitzer & Sulzer-Azaroff, 1988).

strongly determined by the schedule of reinforcement that is in effect. Reinforcement schedules also determine the extent to which individuals persist in responding when reinforcement becomes unavailable. These various findings have told us a great deal about how reinforcement controls behavior in a variety of circumstances and have encouraged numerous powerful applications of reinforcement principles to human behavior.

SAMPLE QUESTIONS

1. Compare and contrast ratio and interval schedules in terms of how the contingencies of reinforcement are set up and the effects they have on the instrumental response.

2. Describe the partial reinforcement extinction effect and major explanations of the phenomenon.

3. Describe the generalized matching law equation and explain each of its parameters.

4. How are concurrent-chain schedules different from concurrent schedules, and what kinds of research questions require the use of concurrent-chain schedules?

5. Describe how self-control might be studied in the laboratory and factors that have been proven to facilitate the occurrence of self-control.

concurrent-chain schedules A complex reinforcement procedure in which the participant is permitted to choose which of several simple reinforcement schedules will be in effect. Once a choice has been made, the rejected alternatives become unavailable for some time.

concurrent schedule A complex reinforcement procedure in which the participant can choose any one of two or more simple reinforcement schedules that are available simultaneously. Concurrent schedules allow for the measurement of choice between simple schedule alternatives.

continuous reinforcement A schedule of reinforcement in which every occurrence of the instrumental response produces the reinforcer. Abbreviated *CRF.*

differential reinforcement of high rate A reinforcement schedule in which a response is reinforced only if it occurs before a specified amount of time has elapsed following the preceding response. Abbreviated *DRH.*

differential reinforcement of low rate A reinforcement schedule in which a response is reinforced only if it occurs after a specified amount of time has elapsed following the preceding response. Abbreviated *DRL.*

discrimination hypothesis An explanation of the partial reinforcement extinction effect according to which extinction is slower after partial reinforcement than after continuous reinforcement because the onset of extinction is more difficult to detect following partial reinforcement.

extinction (in instrumental conditioning) Reduction of the instrumental response that occurs because the response is no longer followed by the reinforcer. Also, the procedure of no longer reinforcing the instrumental response.

feedback function The relation between rates of responding and rates of reinforcement allowed by a particular reinforcement schedule.

fixed interval scallop The gradually increasing rate of responding that occurs between successive reinforcements on a fixed interval schedule.

fixed interval schedule A reinforcement schedule in which the reinforcer is delivered for the first response that occurs after a fixed amount of time following the last reinforcer. Abbreviated *FI.*

fixed ratio schedule A reinforcement schedule in which a fixed number of responses must occur in order for the next response to be reinforced. Abbreviated *FR.*

frustration An aversive emotional reaction that results from the unexpected absence of reinforcement.

frustration theory A theory of the partial reinforcement extinction effect, according to which extinction is retarded after partial reinforcement because the instrumental response becomes conditioned to the anticipation of frustrative nonreward.

intermittent reinforcement A schedule of reinforcement in which only some of the occurrences of the instrumental response are reinforced. The instrumental response is reinforced occasionally, or intermittently. Also called *partial reinforcement.*

interval schedule A reinforcement schedule in which a response is reinforced only if it occurs after a set amount of time following the last reinforcement.

limited hold A restriction on how long reinforcement remains available. In order for a response to be reinforced, it must occur during the limited hold period.

matching law A rule for instrumental behavior proposed by R. J. Herrnstein that states that the relative rate of responding on a particular response alternative equals the relative rate of reinforcement for that response alternative.

melioration A mechanism for achieving matching that involves increased responding on the choice alternative that produces the highest local rate of reinforcement.

overmatching Greater sensitivity to the relative rate of reinforcement than predicted by the matching law.

partial reinforcement Same as *intermittent reinforcement.*

partial reinforcement extinction effect The term used to describe greater persistence in instrumental responding in extinction after partial (intermittent) reinforcement training than after continuous reinforcement training. Abbreviated *PREE.*

postreinforcement pause A pause in responding that typically occurs after the delivery of the reinforcer on fixed ratio and fixed interval schedules of reinforcement.

ratio run The high and invariant rate of responding observed after the postreinforcement pause on fixed ratio reinforcement schedules. The ratio run ends when the necessary number of responses have been performed, and the participant is reinforced.

ratio schedule A reinforcement schedule in which reinforcement depends only on the number of responses the participant performs, irrespective of when those responses occur.

ratio strain Disruption of responding that occurs when a fixed ratio response requirement is increased too rapidly.

response-rate schedule A reinforcement schedule in which a response is reinforced depending on how soon that response is made after the previous occurrence of the behavior.

schedule of reinforcement A program, or rule, that determines how and when the occurrence of a response will be followed by the delivery of the reinforcer.

sequential theory A theory of the partial reinforcement extinction effect, according to which extinction is retarded after partial reinforcement because the instrumental response becomes conditioned to the memory of nonreward.

undermatching Less sensitivity to the relative rate of reinforcement than predicted by the matching law.

variable interval schedule A reinforcement schedule in which reinforcement is provided for the first response that occurs after a variable amount of time from the last reinforcement. Abbreviated *VI*.

variable ratio schedule A reinforcement schedule in which the number of responses necessary to produce reinforcement varies from trial to trial. The value of the schedule refers to the average number of responses needed for reinforcement. Abbreviated *VR*.

Reinforcers as Special Stimuli
  Physiological Homeostasis and Drive Reduction
  Primary Motivation and Incentive Motivation
  Sensory Reinforcement
  Brain-Stimulation Reinforcement and Motivation

Reinforcers as Special Responses
  Consummatory Response Theory
  Premack's Theory of Reinforcement

The Response Deprivation Hypothesis

Behavioral Regulation
  The Behavioral Bliss Point Approach
  Economic Concepts and Response Allocation
  Optimal Foraging Theory and Behavioral Regulation

Concluding Comments

 HAPTER 7 is devoted to a detailed discussion of the development of theories of reinforcement. The discussion illustrates dramatic changes in thinking as investigators sought to develop theories that provide satisfactory explanations for a growing diversity of experimental findings. Early theories of reinforcement assumed that reinforcers were special types of stimuli. However, investigators soon realized that reinforcers could also involve special types of responses. Problems with early response theories of reinforcement encouraged looking for the roots of reinforcement in the instrumental conditioning procedure itself. This approach led to behavioral regulation theories that describe how an organism's repertoire is constrained by instrumental contingencies and how instrumental contingencies produce a redistribution of the actions of the organism. Behavior regulation theories describe reinforcement effects within the broader context of an organism's behavioral repertoire, using concepts from several areas of inquiry, including behavioral economics and behavioral ecology.

In Chapters 5 and 6, I described instrumental behavior and showed how such behavior is influenced by various experimental manipulations, including schedules of reinforcement. This research has provided much information about the characteristics of instrumental behavior in a variety of circumstances. In the present chapter, I will analyze the mechanisms of instrumental reinforcement further and will consider why certain events are effective reinforcers and why reinforcers increase instrumental behavior. The answers to these questions involve some of the most exciting and important aspects of behavior theory today.

During the past 20 years, there has been a major reorientation in how psychologists view the mechanisms of reinforcement (see Timberlake, 1993). Early investigators followed Thorndike and Skinner in assuming that reinforcement involved the "stamping in" or "strengthening" of the instrumental response by the presentation of a special kind of stimulus (a reinforcer). More recent conceptualizations of the reinforcement process take a broader view of an organism's behavior. According to contemporary perspectives, reinforcement involves much more than the presentation of a special stimulus. Reinforcing events usually also involve an activity of some sort, such as eating a food pellet. In addition, modern views are concerned not only with changes in the reinforced response but also with changes in other activities related to the instrumental conditioning procedure. In contemporary theorizing, instrumental conditioning is viewed as creating a new distribution or balance of activities, not just as strengthening a particular response. This shift in perspective has involved a change from thinking about reinforcement as a form of physiological regulation to thinking about reinforcement as a form of behavioral regulation.

REINFORCERS AS SPECIAL STIMULI

Reinforcers were initially considered to be special kinds of stimuli. Thorndike, for example, characterized a reinforcer as a stimulus that produces a "satisfying state of affairs." Various proposals have been made about the special characteristics a stimulus must have for it to serve as a reinforcer. However, all theories that consider the reinforcer as a special kind of stimulus share the view that reinforcement "strengthens" the instrumental response in some way.

If I were to name all the stimuli that have been used as reinforcers for instrumental behavior, the list would be very long. Included would be familiar reinforcers such as food, water, and access to a social partner. The list would also include oxygen and a comfortable temperature, as well as less obvious things such as diet drinks, watching a moving electric train, playing a video game, running, and even exposure to electrical shock. Also included might be reinforcers that are difficult to define, such as the approval of others, self-satisfaction, and the like. What do all these things have in common that makes them effective reinforcers?

An intuitively attractive answer is that reinforcers are pleasurable stimuli. But, what is a pleasurable stimulus? How can we tell if something is pleasurable? We may conclude that something is pleasurable if the organism is willing to work for it. However, defined in this way, a pleasurable stimulus is whatever will reinforce instrumental behavior. This makes the definition of a reinforcer circular (Meehl, 1950). We cannot define a reinforcer as something that provides pleasure if we define something that provides pleasure as a reinforcer. What is needed is a definition of pleasure that is not stated in terms of a reinforcement effect.

Theories of reinforcement endeavor to explain why some things are reinforcing without resorting to the kind of circularity that is inherent in the idea that reinforcers are pleasurable events. An early and highly influential proposition was that reinforcers were effective because they reduce a drive state.

Physiological Homeostasis and Drive Reduction

In much of the research on instrumental learning, biologically important stimuli such as food and water are used as reinforcers. Participants are first deprived of food or water; food and water then serve as reinforcers. Because these reinforcers are necessary for the physiological functioning of the body, early theories of reinforcement have employed physiological concepts.

The procedures of deprivation and reinforcement are two opposing processes that regulate the organism's physiological state. The concept of **physiological homeostasis** is useful to describe the operation of these two processes. According to this concept, organisms have a preferred or optimal physiological state that they strive to maintain. A deprivation procedure causes a shift away from the preferred state. By contrast, reinforcement returns the organism to its optimal or homeostatic state. A shift away from the homeostatic level motivates the organism to perform the instrumental response and return to its preferred state. According to this view, reinforcement works because organisms seek to return to their homeostatic level.

One of the first theorists to make extensive use of a physiological homeostatic mechanism was Clark Hull. (For a review of Hullian theory, see Amsel & Rashotte, 1984.) Hull believed that deprivation procedures used in experiments that employ food and water as reinforcers create a biological *drive state.* Reinforcers were assumed to have the common characteristic of reducing this drive state. Hence, this mechanism was called **drive reduction theory.** According to drive reduction theory, each time an organism obtains a reinforcer, it moves a step closer to its homeostatic level. The tendency of organisms to return to their homeostatic level motivates the instrumental response. Therefore, according to Hull, the degree of drive determines (in part) the degree of responding.

Physiological needs or drives are assumed to be related to elements of the environment that are necessary for survival. Therefore, need or drive states presumably can be identified with physiology experiments. Consistent with this view, food, water, and a return to a more comfortable temperature have all been used successfully as instrumental reinforcers.

Primary Motivation and Incentive Motivation

Drive reduction theory illustrates that the analysis of reinforcement is part of the broader field of motivation. Reinforcement is one way of inducing behavior to change. Where, though, does the force for change—the motivation—originate? Sometimes the force seems to lie within the organism as a biological drive state. Motivation induced by a biological drive state is called **primary motivation.** Thirst and hunger are sources of primary motivation. Motivation for behavior may also come from the reinforcer itself. Sometimes just the presence of food, water, or a sexual partner can trigger behavior. Motivation created by the reinforcer itself is called **incentive motivation.**

Consider, for example, a T-maze experiment in which laboratory rats received 300 mg of food as the reinforcer. Capaldi, Miller, and Alptekin (1989) found that this amount of food was a more effective reinforcer if it was given as four 75-mg pellets than if it was given as one 300-mg pellet, even though the level of food deprivation of the rats was identical. These results cannot be explained in terms of differences in drive level or primary motivation because the amount of food was identical. Rather, these results illustrate the importance of incentive motivation. Evidently, four food pellets are more attractive to hungry rats than a single large pellet that contains the same amount of food.

We thus have two possible sources of motivation: (1) the drive state and (2) the incentive properties of the reinforcer. The role of each of these sources of motivation has been discussed at length in the psychology literature (see Bolles, 1975). At present it appears that reinforcement is neither solely drive reduction nor solely incentive motivation. Both aspects play a role. Miller and Kessen (1952), for example, compared the reinforcing effects of food delivered directly into the stomach of rats through a fistula and food consumed in the normal fashion. They found that fistula feeding was an effective reinforcer. Drive reduction from fistula feeding was sufficient to produce a reinforcement effect. However, the reinforcing effect was not as powerful as that produced by normal eating. Normal eating may have been more effective in increasing the instrumental response because it involved both primary and incentive motivation.

Sensory Reinforcement

The evidence for both primary and incentive motivation indicates that drive reduction mechanisms do not explain all reinforcement effects. External stimuli also have an important role in the motivation of instrumental behavior. Other lines of evidence suggest that drive reduction may not even be necessary for reinforcement. Sheffield, Wulff, and Backer (1951), for example, demonstrated that a male rat will run down a runway to gain access to a female, even though it is not allowed to complete the sexual act with the female. In this case, the instrumental behavior was acquired without drive reduction. In fact, the drive level or excitement of the male was probably increased when it was exposed to the female but not allowed to copulate. Thus, a reinforcement effect was obtained in the face of an increase rather than a decrease in drive.

The fact that reinforcement can occur without drive reduction is also illustrated by numerous examples of the reinforcing effects of stimuli that are not biologically or physiologically significant in any obvious sense. One prominent reinforcement theorist has commented that "virtually anything can act as a reward in suitable circumstances" (Berlyne, 1969, p. 182). Activities such as watching a moving toy train can be used to reinforce the behavior of monkeys. Turning on a light, having an opportunity to explore, and drinking a saccharin solution (which has no nutritive value), can all be effective reinforcers. (For a recent study of sensory reinforcement in laboratory rats, see Reed, Mitchell, & Nokes, 1996.) Motivation of behavior by the sensory properties of stimuli is also common in human experience. Fine works of art and music, for example, provide primarily sensory reinforcement.

To explain the effectiveness of sensory reinforcers, the existence of a drive state corresponding to each sensory reinforcer might be hypothesized. For example, a hypothesized curiosity drive might explain why the sight of a moving toy train can act as a reinforcer for monkeys. However, this approach reintroduces the circularity problem I discussed earlier. The only evidence for the existence of a curiosity drive is that moving toy trains can reinforce instrumental behavior. Drive reduction theory compels the addition of an item to the list of drives each time a reinforcer is found that

Listening to music provides primarily sensory reinforcement.

does not satisfy a biological drive previously identified by other means. However, this does not provide a way to identify reinforcers independent of the outcome of instrumental conditioning. Therefore, the drive reduction hypothesis has not been successful in specifying a common feature of all reinforcers independent of their reinforcement effects.

Brain-Stimulation Reinforcement and Motivation

I will describe one final approach to reinforcers as special kinds of stimuli. This approach focuses on the physiological effects of reinforcers. It attempts to identify reinforcers on the basis of the areas of the brain or neural pathways that are activated by reinforcing stimuli. The approach is based on the pioneering work of James Olds and Peter Milner, who implanted electrodes in the septal area of rats' brains. The rats were then observed while they were given brief, mild electrical pulses through the electrodes. The rats tended to move toward the area of the chamber·where they last received the brain stimulation. Olds and Milner then connected a response lever to the electrical stimulator and discovered that the rats would press the lever at high rates hour after hour to receive the brain stimulation. The phenomenon sparked a great deal of interest and was called **intracranial self-stimulation** (Olds & Milner, 1954). Intracranial self-stimulation raised the hope that a mechanism common to all reinforcers could be discovered at the physiological level (see Liebman & Cooper, 1989).

Following the seminal studies of Olds and Olds (1963), many experiments have been performed to map out the various areas of the brain that, when stimulated, yield a reinforcement effect (for example, Phillips & Fibiger, 1989; Shizgal & Murray, 1989; Yeomans, 1990). In addition, studies have documented the neurochemical pathways that are involved in brain stimulation reward (for example, Stellar & Rice, 1989; Vaccarino, Schiff, & Glickman, 1989.) However, the hope that studies of intracranial self-stimulation would reveal neurophysiological substrates common to

193

natural reinforcers remains to be fulfilled. As Phillips and Fibiger (1989) noted, "An animal may choose to stimulate its brain for a variety of reasons, including the induction of a mood or a state of incentive motivation, and perhaps simply [to activate] circuits that facilitate memory processes" (p. 95).

REINFORCERS AS SPECIAL RESPONSES

As we have seen, the assumption that reinforcers are special kinds of stimuli has encountered various problems over the years. A radically different approach to the analysis of reinforcement involves thinking about reinforcers as responses rather than as stimuli.

Consummatory Response Theory

The possibility that certain responses may serve as reinforcers was first recognized by Sheffield and his co-workers, who formulated the **consummatory response theory**. The consummatory response theory was proposed in an effort to explain why particular incentive stimuli, such as food, are effective reinforcers. Many reinforcers, like food and water, elicit species-typical unconditioned responses such as chewing, licking, and swallowing. The consummatory response theory attributes reinforcement to these species-typical behaviors. It asserts that species-typical consummatory responses—eating, drinking, and the like—are themselves the critical feature of reinforcers.

According to consummatory response theory, drive reduction might follow a consummatory response, but drive reduction is not essential for producing an increase in the instrumental response. Research on the consummatory response theory focused on demonstrations that consummatory responses could reinforce instrumental behavior in the absence of drive reduction. Famous experiments were performed showing that saccharin is an effective reinforcer for rats (for example, Sheffield, Roby, & Campbell, 1954). A mild solution of saccharin has a pleasant taste and stimulates consummatory behavior but is not nutritive and therefore presumably does not reduce the hunger drive.

Premack's Theory of Reinforcement

The consummatory response theory was a radical innovation in reinforcement theory because it moved the search for reinforcers from special kinds of stimuli to special types of responses. Reinforcer responses were assumed to be special because they involved the consummation of an instinctive behavior sequence. (See the discussion of consummatory behavior in Chapter 2.) The theory assumed that consummatory responses (chewing and swallowing, for example) are fundamentally different from various potential instrumental responses such as running, jumping, or pressing a lever. David Premack took issue with this and suggested that reinforcer responses are special only because they are more likely to occur than the responses they reinforce.

Premack pointed out that responses involved with commonly used reinforcers are activities that animals are highly likely to perform. For example, animals in a food reinforcement experiment are typically food-deprived and therefore are highly likely to engage in eating behavior. By contrast, instrumental responses are typically low-probability activities. An experimentally naive rat, for example, is much less likely to press a response lever than it is to eat. Premack (1965) proposed that this difference in response probabilities is critical for reinforcement. Formally, his reinforcement principle can be stated as follows:

> Given two responses H and L, the opportunity to perform the higher-probability response H after the lower-probability response L will result in reinforcement of response L. (L→H reinforces L.) The opportunity to perform the lower-probability response L after the higher-probability response H will not result in reinforcement of response H. (H→L does not reinforce H.)

The Premack principle focuses on the difference in the likelihood of the instrumental and reinforcer responses. Therefore, it is also called the **differential probability principle.**

Eating will reinforce bar pressing because eating is typically more probable than bar pressing. Under ordinary circumstances, bar pressing cannot reinforce eating. However, Premack's theory suggests that if for some reason bar pressing became more probable than eating, it would reinforce eating. Thus, Premack's theory denies that there is a fundamental distinction between reinforcers and instrumental responses. According to Premack, the particular characteristic that makes a reinforcer act as such is not something intrinsic to the reinforcing response. Rather, the reinforcing response is simply a response that is more likely to occur than the instrumental response. Consequently, it is possible to use a wide variety of responses as reinforcers.

Experimental Evidence.   Premack and his colleagues conducted many experiments to test his theory (see Premack, 1965, 1971a). One of the early studies was conducted with young children. Premack first gave the children two response alternatives (eating candy and playing a pinball machine) and measured which response was more probable for each child. Some of the children preferred eating candy over playing pinball; others preferred the pinball machine. In the second phase of the experiment (see Figure 7.1), the children were tested with one of two procedures. In one procedure, eating was specified as the reinforcing response, and playing pinball was the instrumental response. That is, the children had to play the pinball machine in order to gain the opportunity to eat the candy. The question was whether all the children would increase their pinball playing. Consistent with Premack's theory, only those children who preferred eating to playing pinball showed a reinforcement effect under these circumstances.

In another test, the roles of the two responses were reversed. Eating was the instrumental response, and playing pinball was the reinforcing response. The children had to eat candy to gain the opportunity to play the pinball machine. In this situation, only those children who preferred playing pinball to eating showed a reinforcement effect.

Premack (1962) also tested his theory in studies of drinking and wheel running in laboratory rats. The study is illustrated in Figure 7.2. Premack altered the probabilities of the drinking and wheel-running responses by changing deprivation conditions. In Experiment 1, the rats were water-deprived but not deprived of the opportunity to run in the wheel. Under these circumstances drinking was more probable than running, and the opportunity to drink could be effectively used to reinforce running. In Experiment 2, the rats were not deprived of water. Under these circumstances, they were more likely to run in the wheel than to drink. Now the

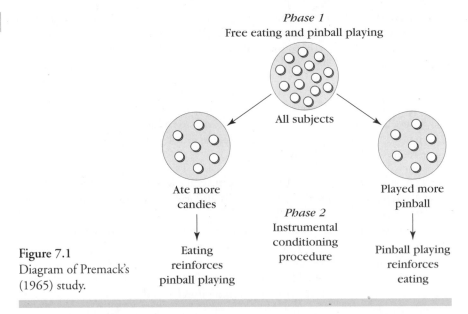

Figure 7.1
Diagram of Premack's (1965) study.

opportunity to run in the wheel could be effectively used to reinforce drinking. However, drinking could no longer be used to reinforce running. This study shows that running and drinking could be used interchangeably as instrumental and reinforcing responses, depending on the animal's state of water deprivation.

Measuring Response Probability. Both of the preceding experiments had two parts. In the first part, behavior was measured in a situation in which the participants had unlimited opportunity to engage in either of the responses to be used later as the instrumental and the reinforcing responses. This is called the *baseline phase.* In the second part of the experiments, the opportunity to engage in one of the responses was provided only after the organism performed the other response. This is called the *response contingency phase.* As we saw, what happened in the response contingency phase depended on the relative probabilities of the two responses during the baseline phase. Therefore, before precise predictions can be made about whether one response will (or will not) reinforce another, there must be some way to measure and compare the baseline probabilities of the two responses.

One possible measure of response probability is the frequency with which each response occurs in a set amount of time. This measure serves well as long as responses that require similar amounts of time are being compared—responses such as pressing two alternative but otherwise identical response levers. What would happen, however, if a researcher wanted to compare the probability of two very different responses, such as doing a crossword puzzle and eating? Comparing frequencies of response here would be very cumbersome. The researcher would have to specify what constituted an instance, or unit, of puzzle-solving behavior and an instance, or unit, of eating. Would completing one word in a crossword puzzle constitute a unit of puzzle-solving behavior, or would completing all the items in a certain direction (horizontal or vertical) constitute one unit of this behavior? Correspondingly, would a unit of eating be taking one bite, completing one course, or eating an entire meal?

Experiment 1: Limited access to water

Experiment 2: Unlimited access to water

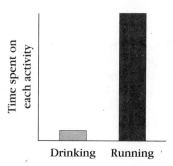

Figure 7.2 When a rat is water-deprived (Experiment 1), it drinks more than it runs. Therefore, drinking reinforces running, but running does not reinforce drinking. When a rat is not water-deprived (Experiment 2), it runs more than it drinks. This time running reinforces drinking, but drinking does not reinforce running.

As suggested by the preceding discussion, it is difficult to formulate comparable units of behavior for diverse activities. However, a common dimension to all responses is time. Premack proposed that response probability should be measured in terms of the amount of time an organism spends engaged in the response during a specified period. This idea can be expressed in the following equation:

$$\text{Probability of response} = \frac{\text{Time spent on that response}}{\text{Total time}}$$

By this definition, responses taking up a greater proportion of the available time are considered more probable than responses on which the organism spends less time. If in an hour you spend 45 minutes reading a novel and 15 minutes studying, we would say that reading was more probable than studying during this hour. Therefore, reading should reinforce studying.

Although time is a dimension for measuring the likelihood of diverse activities, it has its own difficulties. The first problem is empirical. Several studies have shown that the duration of an activity is not as basic to behavior (or as important to the organism) as other aspects of behavior such as response frequency (for example, Allison, Moore, Gawley, Mondloch, & Mondloch, 1986; Davison, 1991b). Other difficulties with time as a measure of response probability are conceptual. With certain activities, it is difficult to decide how to identify the duration of the behavior. For example, eating involves a series of brief bites. It may be obvious that the first bite

197

BOX **7.1**

APPLICATIONS OF
THE PREMACK PRINCIPLE

Using reinforcement procedures to encourage appropriate behavior in children requires identifying an effective reinforcer. Food is an effective reinforcer. However, practical and ethical considerations have encouraged investigators to identify other forms of reinforcement. The Premack principle has been a great help in this regard because it suggests that any activity that is more likely than the response to be reinforced can serve as an effective reinforcer.

Like other people, children differ in their preferred activities. Some may prefer playing ball after school; others may prefer talking to friends on the phone. By measuring the relative probability of different activities for each individual, reinforcement procedures can be personalized to take advantage of each individual's unique response preferences. This may result in some rather unusual responses serving as reinforcers.

Children with autism often engage in repetitive aberrant behaviors. One such behavior, called *delayed echolalia,* involves repeating words. For example, one autistic child was heard to say over and over again, "Ding! ding! ding! You win again," and "Match Game

83." Another form of aberrant behavior, *perseverative behavior,* involves persistent manipulation of an object. For example, the child may repeatedly manipulate only certain plastic toys.

The high probability of echolalia and perseverative behavior in children with autism suggests that these responses may be effectively used as reinforcers in treatment procedures. This possibility has been explored by several investigators. In a study by Charlop, Kurtz, and Casey (1990), the effectiveness of different forms of reinforcement was compared in training various academic-related skills in autistic children. The tasks included identifying which of several objects was the same or different from the one held up by the teacher, adding up coins, and correctly responding to sentences designed to teach receptive pronouns or prepositions. In one experimental condition, a preferred food (such as a small piece of chocolate, cereal, or a cookie) served as the reinforcer, in the absence of programmed food deprivation. In another condition, the opportunity to perform an aberrant response for 3 to 5 seconds served as the reinforcer.

Some of the results of the study are illustrated in Figure 7.3. Each panel represents the data for a different student. Notice that in each case, the opportunity to engage in a prevalent aberrant response resulted in better performance on the training tasks than food reinforcement. Delayed echolalia and perseverative

marks the start of a bout of eating, but the end of the bout is more difficult to identify. How long does the organism have to pause between bites before it is clear that the bout is finished? There is no easy answer to this question.

Another decision to be made concerns the observation period during which the duration of an activity is measured. A long observation period can yield results very different from a short observation period. Consider, for example, a comparison between sexual behavior and studying. A student may spend a good deal more time studying than engaging in sexual behavior. Nevertheless, most students would find sexual behavior more reinforcing. This paradox may be resolved by taking into account the duration of the baseline observations. Given a choice between sex and studying in a 2-hour period, sexual behavior will most likely predominate. However, over a 2-year period, students will probably accumulate more time studying than engaging in sexual behavior.

The duration of the total observation period is critical for assessing the probability of responses that occur only periodically. For example, although you spend a good deal of time eating during a 24-hour period, eating is not uniformly distributed over the course of a day. Rather, it is highly likely only at certain times. In addition, the

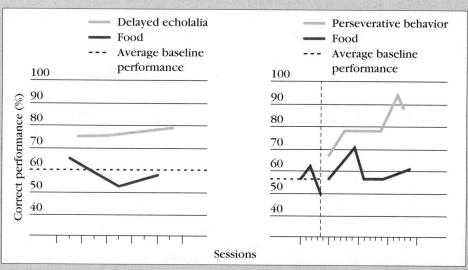

Figure 7.3 Task performance data for three children with autism. One student's behavior was reinforced with food or the opportunity to engage in delayed echolalia. Another student's behavior was reinforced with food or the opportunity to engage in perseverative responding. (Responding during baseline periods was also reinforced with food.) (From "Using Aberrant Behaviors as Reinforcers for Autistic Children" by M. H. Charlop, P. F. Kurtz, & F. G. Casey, *Journal of Applied Behavior Analysis*, 1990, *23*, pp. 163–181. Copyright © 1990 by the Society for the Experimental Analysis of Behavior, Inc. Reprinted by permission.)

behavior both served to increase task performance above what was observed with food reinforcement. These results indicate that high-probability responses can serve to reinforce lower-probability responses, even if the reinforcer responses are not characteristic of normal behavior.

more time you devote to eating, the less likely the response becomes. After an hour of eating, you are unlikely to eat again for some time.

Because response probabilities vary with time, Premack went on to suggest that momentary probability is the best measure for making predictions about reinforcement. Opportunity to perform response A will serve to reinforce response B only if at that moment the probability of A is higher than the probability of B.

Contributions of the Premack Principle. The Premack principle advanced our thinking about reinforcement in significant ways. It encouraged thinking about reinforcers as responses rather than as stimuli, and it greatly expanded the range of things investigators started to use as reinforcers. With the Premack principle, any activity could serve as a reinforcer, provided that it was more likely than the instrumental response. Differential probability as the key to reinforcement paved the way for applications of reinforcement procedures to all sorts of human problems. However, problems with the measurement of response probability and a closer look at instrumental conditioning procedures encouraged further theoretical developments in the analysis of reinforcement.

In most instrumental conditioning procedures, the momentary probability of the reinforcer response is kept at a high level by restricting access to the reinforcing response. A rat lever pressing for food, for example, typically comes into the experimental situation not having eaten much and does not receive a whole meal for each lever-press response. These limitations on the reinforcing response are very important. If an investigator were to give a rat a full meal for pressing the lever once, chances are its rate of responding would not increase very much. Restrictions on the opportunity to engage in the reinforcing response serve to increase its effectiveness as a reinforcer.

Premack (1965) recognized the importance of restricting access to the reinforcer response for instrumental conditioning. He regarded response deprivation as a necessary condition for reinforcement. However, he regarded it as an adjunct to the differential probability principle. In his view, the reinforcer response still had to be a more likely behavior than the instrumental response. By contrast, Timberlake and Allison (1974; see also Allison, 1993) abandoned the differential probability principle altogether and argued that restriction of the reinforcer response was the critical factor for instrumental reinforcement. This proposal is called the **response deprivation hypothesis.**

In several studies, investigators found that depriving participants of a low-probability response can make access to that response an effective reinforcer, even if the initial probability of the instrumental response is higher (Allison & Timberlake, 1974; Eisenberger, Karpman, & Trattner, 1967). Such evidence indicates that with response deprivation, a low-probability response can be used to reinforce a higher-probability response. Thus, response deprivation can lead to reinforcement effects, even if Premack's differential probability principle is violated. This shows that response deprivation is more basic to reinforcement than the differential probability principle.

W. Timberlake

The response deprivation hypothesis provides a new principle for predicting what will serve as an effective reinforcer. It also provides a new procedure for creating reinforcers—restricting access to the reinforcer response. It is interesting to note that restricting access to the reinforcer response is inherent in all instrumental conditioning procedures. By definition, instrumental conditioning involves imposing a response-reinforcer contingency. Setting up a response-reinforcer contingency requires that the reinforcer be withheld until the specified instrumental response has been performed. The response deprivation hypothesis points out that this fundamental feature of instrumental conditioning is critical for producing a reinforcer.

Traditional views of reinforcement assume that a reinforcer is something that exists independent of an instrumental conditioning procedure. Stimulus views of reinforcement and the consummatory response theory all assume that reinforcers exist whether or not they are used in an instrumental conditioning procedure. The response deprivation hypothesis makes explicit the radically different idea that a reinforcer is produced by the instrumental contingency itself. The Premack principle was the first theory to suggest that reinforcers do not exist in an absolute sense. In the Premack principle, whether a response was a reinforcer depended on how its likelihood of occurrence compared with that of the instrumental response. However, the Premack principle did not imply that the instrumental conditioning procedure itself was responsible for the creation of a reinforcer. How instrumental contingencies create reinforcers and reinforcement effects has been developed further in behavioral regulation theories, which I will discuss next.

BEHAVIORAL REGULATION

I mentioned regulatory processes earlier in this chapter in connection with the concept of physiological homeostasis. As I noted at that point, organisms have a preferred, or optimal, physiological state that they strive to maintain. A shift away from the optimal, or homeostatic, level motivates efforts to return to that state. Behavioral regulation theories assume that analogous homeostatic mechanisms exist with respect to behavior. That is, the behaving organism may be considered to have a preferred or optimal distribution of activities that it tries to maintain in the face of disruptions. Behavioral regulation theories do not focus on the relative probabilities of the instrumental and reinforcing responses but on the extent to which an instrumental response-reinforcer contingency disrupts behavioral stability and forces the individual away from its preferred or optimal distribution of activities (see Allison, 1983, 1989; Hanson & Timberlake, 1983; Timberlake, 1980, 1984).

An individual has to eat, breathe, drink, keep warm, exercise, entertain itself, and so on. All these activities have to occur in particular proportions—an individual shouldn't eat too much or too little, or exercise too much or too little. If the preferred, or optimal, balance of activities is upset, behavior is assumed to change so as to correct the deviation from the homeostatic level. This basic assumption of behavioral regulation is fairly simple. However, as we will see, numerous factors (some of which are a bit complicated) can influence how organisms meet challenges to their preferred or optimal distribution of responses.

J. Allison

The Behavioral Bliss Point Approach

Every situation provides various response opportunities. In an experimental situation, for example, an animal can run in a wheel, drink, eat, scratch itself, sniff holes, or manipulate a response lever. Behavioral regulation theory assumes that if organisms are free to distribute their responses among the available alternatives, they will do so in a way that is most comfortable or in some sense "optimal" for them. This response distribution defines the **behavioral bliss point.**

The particular distribution of activities that constitutes the bliss point will vary from one situation to another. For example, if the running wheel is made very difficult to turn or if the participant is severely deprived of water, the relative likelihood of running and drinking will change. However, for a given circumstance, the behavioral bliss point, as revealed in unconstrained choices among response alternatives, is assumed to be stable across time.

Behavioral regulation theory assumes that the behavioral bliss point will be defended against disruptions caused by limitations on the opportunity to engage in particular responses. Such limitations often result from instrumental conditioning procedures because an instrumental contingency does not permit access to the reinforcer response unless the individual has previously performed the instrumental response in the required fashion.

The behavioral bliss point can be identified by the relative frequency of occurrence of all the responses of an organism in an unconstrained situation. To simplify analysis, let us focus on two responses that might be performed by laboratory rats—running in a running wheel and pressing a response lever (see, for example, Iversen, 1993b). If no restrictions are placed on running and lever pressing, these activities may occur in any relation to each other. The animal may spend a lot of time on both activities, spend more time on one than the other, or spend little time on both. Figure 7.4 represents time spent running on the horizontal axis and time spent lever pressing on the vertical axis. Let us assume that in a free-baseline situation the animal spends equal amounts of time running and lever pressing, as represented by the open circle. The rat spends 15 minutes lever pressing and runs for 15 minutes in the observation period. This defines its behavioral bliss point in this situation.

Imposing an Instrumental Contingency. How would the introduction of an instrumental contingency between running and lever pressing disrupt the behavioral bliss? That depends on the nature of the contingency. Figure 7.4 shows three possible contingent relations between running and lever pressing. These are represented by the solid lines emanating from the origin in the figure. These lines specify how long the animal has to run to obtain a particular amount of time lever pressing. Thus, these lines are feedback functions (see Chapter 6).

Line B represents a contingency in which 1 minute of running is required for each minute of lever-pressing opportunity. Line B passes through the bliss point obtained in the free-baseline condition. This makes the contingency represented by line B rather special because it permits participants to reach the behavioral bliss point and satisfy the response-reinforcer contingency at the same time. The contingencies represented by lines A and C do not allow that.

Line A specifies a contingency in which the animal receives access to the lever for half the time it spends running. If the animal runs for 15 minutes, it gets to press the lever for only 7.5 minutes. The contingency specified by line A involves a restriction of lever pressing because at the behavioral bliss point, 15 minutes of running is associated with 15 minutes of lever pressing. Line C represents a different kind of restriction; here the animal gets to run for half the time it spends lever pressing. If the animal presses the lever for 15 minutes, it only gets to run for 7.5 minutes. In this case, the response-reinforcer contingency involves a restriction of running relative to the behavioral bliss point. Lines A and C represent instrumental conditioning procedures that challenge maintenance of the behavioral bliss point in different ways.

Effects of Contingency Constraints. Behavioral regulation theory states that organisms will defend against challenges to the behavioral bliss point, just as physiological regulation involves defense against challenges to a physiological set point. However, the interesting thing is that the free-baseline behavioral bliss point cannot always be reestablished after an instrumental contingency has been introduced. In the example, the behavioral bliss point was 15 minutes of lever pressing and 15 minutes of running during a standard observation period. Consider the possible adjustments an animal could make when the schedule of reinforcement represented by line C in Figure 7.4 is imposed on the free-response situation. Now the bliss point cannot be reached with respect to running without strongly deviating from the optimal level for lever pressing, and vice versa.

The line C contingency requires twice as much lever pressing as running. To achieve the optimal level of 15 minutes of running, the organism would have to press

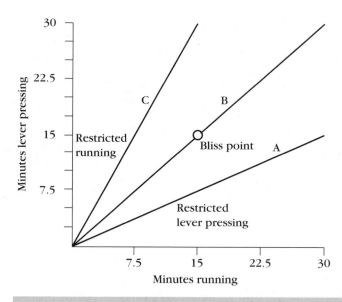

Figure 7.4 Allocation of behavior between running and lever pressing. The open circle shows the optimal allocation, or behavioral bliss point, obtained in a free-baseline session. Lines A, B, and C represent different contingent relations imposed between running and lever pressing. The contingency represented by line A restricts lever pressing, whereas the contingency represented by line C restricts running. Line B, which passes through the bliss point, exerts no restriction.

the lever for 30 minutes—twice its optimal level. Alternatively, if the animal achieved its optimal 15 minutes of lever pressing, its running would be at 7.5 minutes—half the optimal level. Line A represents similar problems. Schedule lines A and C make it impossible for the organism to achieve "bliss" with respect to one response without strongly deviating from the optimal level for the other behavior.

Although schedules of reinforcement such as those represented by lines A and C in Figure 7.4 make it impossible to return to the behavioral bliss point, this does not mean that return to the behavioral set point is irrelevant in such cases. To the contrary. The bliss point still provides the motivation for instrumental behavior. Behavioral regulation theory assumes that returning to the behavioral set point remains a goal of response allocation. When this goal cannot be reached, the redistribution of responses between the instrumental and contingent behaviors becomes a matter of compromise. The rate of one response is brought as close as possible to its preferred level without moving the other response too far away from its preferred level.

Staddon, for example, has proposed a **minimum deviation model** of behavioral regulation (Staddon, 1979; see also Staddon, 1983). According to this model, introduction of a response-reinforcer contingency causes organisms to redistribute their behavior between the instrumental and contingent responses in a way that minimizes the total deviation of the two responses from the optimal point. For situations in which the free-baseline behavioral bliss point cannot be achieved, the minimum deviation model provides one view of how organisms settle for the next best thing.

Explanation of Reinforcement Effects. How are reinforcement effects produced by behavioral regulation? Behavioral regulation involves the defense of a behavioral bliss point in the face of restrictions on responding imposed by a response-reinforcer contingency. Often this defense involves settling not for the free-baseline bliss point but for the next best thing possible in the situation. How do these mechanisms lead to increases in instrumental behavior in typical instrumental conditioning procedures?

BOX **7.2**

Behavior regulation theories of reinforcement not only provide new insights into age-old theoretical issues concerning reinforcement but also suggest new approaches to behavior therapy (Timberlake & Farmer-Dougan, 1991). The bliss point approach, for example, forces us to consider the behavioral context in which an instrumental contingency is introduced. Depending on that behavioral context, a reinforcement procedure may increase or decrease the target response. Thus, the bliss point approach can provide insights into situations in which a reinforcement procedure produces an unexpected decrease in the instrumental response.

One area of behavior therapy in which reinforcement procedures are surprisingly ineffective is the use of parental social reinforcement to increase a child's prosocial behavior. A parent whose child frequently misbehaves is encouraged to provide more social reinforcement for positive behavior on the assumption that low rates of parental reinforcement are responsible for the child's misbehavior. Viken and McFall (1994) have pointed out that the common failure of such reinforcement procedures is predictable if we consider the behavioral bliss point of the child.

Figure 7.5 shows the behavioral space for parental social reinforcement and positive child behavior. The open circle represents the child's presumed bliss point. Left to his own devices, the child prefers a lot of social reinforcement while emitting few positive behaviors. The dashed line represents the low rate of parental reinforcement in effect before a therapeutic intervention. According to this schedule line, the child has to perform two positive responses to receive each social reinforcer from the parent. The filled point on the line indicates the equilibrium point, where positive responses by the child and social reinforcers earned are equally far from their respective bliss point values.

The therapeutic procedure involves increasing the rate of social reinforcement, let's say to a ratio of 1:1. This is illustrated by the solid line in Figure 7.5. Now the child receives one social reinforcer for each positive behavior. The equilibrium point is again illustrated by the filled data point. Notice that with the increased social reinforcement, the child can get more

A reinforcement effect is identified by an increase in the occurrence of an instrumental response above the level of that behavior in the absence of the response-reinforcer contingency. As Figure 7.4 illustrates, instrumental contingencies that do not go through the behavioral bliss point invariably restrict access to a response below the level specified by the bliss point. In line A of Figure 7.4, for example, the organism's lever pressing is restricted relative to running. To move toward the behavioral bliss point, the animal has to increase its running so as to gain more opportunity to press the lever. This is precisely what occurs in typical instrumental conditioning procedures. Access to the reinforcer is restricted; to gain more opportunity to engage in the reinforcer response, the individual has to perform more of the instrumental response. Increased performance of the instrumental response (a reinforcement effect) results from behavioral regulatory mechanisms that function to minimize deviations from the behavioral bliss point.

Problems with the Bliss Point Approach. The bliss point approach has done much to change the way we think about reinforcement and instrumental conditioning. However, recent experimental evidence suggests that the approach has two major shortcomings.

First, as we have seen, the behavioral bliss point is determined by giving individuals access to two response alternatives without restriction. The bliss point is based on a measure of each response totaled over the entire free-baseline session. Thus, the

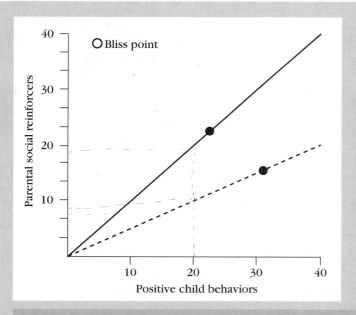

Figure 7.5 Hypothetical data on parental social reinforcement and positive child behavior. The behavioral bliss point for the child is indicated by the open circle. The dashed line represents the rate of social reinforcement for positive behavior in effect prior to introduction of a treatment procedure. The solid line represents the rate of social reinforcement for positive behavior set up by the behavior therapy procedure. The solid point on each line represents the equilibrium point for each schedule.

of the social reinforcers he wants without having to make more positive responses. In fact, the child can increase his rate of social reinforcement while performing fewer positive responses. No wonder, then, that the therapeutic reinforcement procedure does not increase the rate of positive responses. The unexpected results of increased social reinforcement illustrated in Figure 7.5 suggest that solutions to behavior problems require considering the complex context in which reinforcement procedures are introduced.

behavioral bliss point is a molar feature of behavior. A given molar bliss point can be achieved in a variety of ways. In the hypothetical example in Figure 7.4, the animal was allowed to choose between lever pressing and running in a wheel, and it ended up spending 15 minutes on each activity during the free-baseline session. This could have been achieved by doing all the lever pressing before any running (or vice versa). An accumulation of 15 minutes on each response could also occur if the animal frequently switched back and forth between the two responses. According to the behavioral bliss point approach, such differences should not matter. But experimental evidence indicates that how the molar bliss point is achieved is important (for example, Gawley, Timberlake, & Lucas, 1987; Tierney, Smith, & Gannon, 1987). Therefore, an adequate characterization of "behavioral bliss" requires information about molecular response patterns.

Another, and perhaps more serious, difficulty for the behavioral bliss point approach is that responses occurring in a situation that is unconstrained by the experimenter do not appear to have the same "value" as responses occurring as a part of an arranged instrumental contingency. In behavioral regulation theory, the outcome of instrumental contingencies is predicted from the free-baseline distribution of responses. For such predictions to work, it must be assumed that responses performed in the absence of experimenter-imposed contingency constraints are basically the same as the responses that occur when an instrumental contingency is imposed. For example, running in a wheel in the absence of experimenter-imposed response constraints (free running) has to be considered to be the same as running in order to gain access to a response lever (contingent running). This assumption has been found to be incorrect in several experiments (Allison, Buxton, & Moore, 1987; Gawley et al., 1987; Tierney et al., 1987). Doing something when there are no externally imposed requirements (jogging for pleasure, for example) appears to be different from doing the same thing when it is required by an imposed instrumental contingency (jogging in a physical education class, for example).

Contributions of the Bliss Point Approach.   The bliss point approach followed up on theoretical developments that were started by Premack's differential probability principle. Although this line of theorizing has encountered some serious difficulties, it has also made major contributions to how we think about instrumental reinforcement. It is instructive to review some of these contributions.

1.   The bliss point approach and the Premack principle have moved us away from thinking about reinforcers as special kinds of stimuli or as special kinds of responses. We are now encouraged to look for the causes of reinforcement in how instrumental contingencies constrain the organism's free flow of behavior. Reinforcement effects are seen as produced by schedule constraints on an organism's ongoing activities.

2.   Instrumental conditioning procedures are no longer considered to "stamp in" or to "strengthen" instrumental behavior. Rather, instrumental conditioning is seen as creating a new distribution, or allocation, of responses. Typically, the reallocation of behavior involves an increase in the instrumental response and a decrease in the reinforcer response. These two changes are viewed as equally important features of the redistribution of behavior.

3.   There is no fundamental distinction between instrumental and reinforcer responses. Reinforcer responses are not assumed to be more likely than instrumental responses. They are not assumed to provide any special physiological benefits or to have any inherent characteristics that make them different from instrumental responses. Rather, instrumental and reinforcer responses are distinguished only by the roles assigned to them by an instrumental conditioning procedure.

4.   The bliss point approach embraces the assumption that organisms respond so as to maximize their benefits. The idea of optimization is not original with the bliss point approach. In drive reduction theories of reinforcement, optimization referred to a return to physiological homeostasis and a drive-free state. We also encountered the idea of optimization (maximizing rates of reinforcement) in discussions of concurrent schedules and choice. The bliss point approach suggests that the optimal distribution of activities is determined not only by physiological needs but also by the organism's ecological niche and natural or phylogenetically determined response tendencies. These additional aspects of optimization are developed further in optimal foraging theory, to be discussed shortly.

Economic Concepts and Response Allocation

The bliss point approach redefined the fundamental question that a theory of reinforcement needs to answer. Given the bliss point approach, we are no longer interested in what makes something act as a reinforcer. Rather, the fundamental question has become, How do the constraints of an instrumental conditioning procedure produce changes in behavior?

Psychologists have become interested in discovering principles that describe how behavior changes as a result of schedule constraints. Students who have studied economics may recognize a similarity here to problems addressed by economists. Economists, like psychologists, strive to understand changes in behavior in terms of preexisting preferences and restrictions on fulfilling those preferences. Thus, as Bickel, Green, and Vuchinich (1995) noted, "Economics is the study of the allocation of behavior within a system of constraint" (p. 258). In the economic arena, the restrictions on behavior are imposed by a person's income and the price of the goods that person wants to purchase. In instrumental conditioning situations, the restrictions are provided by the number of responses an organism is able to make and the number of responses required to obtain each reinforcer.

Psychologists have become interested in the similarities between economic restrictions in the marketplace and schedule constraints in instrumental conditioning. Let us now consider how economic ideas have influenced behavior regulation theories of reinforcement. For the sake of simplicity, I will focus on the basic ideas that have had the most impact on understanding reinforcement. (For further details, see Allison, 1983, 1993; Hursh, 1980, 1984; Lea, 1978; Rachlin, 1989; Rachlin et al., 1976; Staddon, 1980.)

Consumer Demand.   Fundamental to the application of economic concepts to the problem of reinforcement is the relation between the price of a commodity and how much of it is purchased. This relation is called the **demand curve.** Figure 7.6 shows three examples of demand curves. Curve A illustrates a situation in which the consumption of a commodity is very easily influenced by its price. This is the case with candy. If the price of candy increases substantially, the amount purchased quickly drops. Other commodities are less responsive to price changes (curve C in Figure 7.6). The purchase of gasoline, for example, is not as easily discouraged by increases in price. People continue to purchase gas for their cars, even if the price increases substantially.

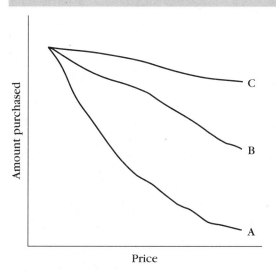

Figure 7.6   Hypothetical consumer demand curves illustrating high sensitivity to price (curve A), intermediate sensitivity (curve B), and low sensitivity (curve C).

The degree to which price influences consumption is called **elasticity of demand.** Demand for candy is highly elastic. The more candy costs, the less people will buy. In contrast, demand for gasoline is much less elastic. People continue to purchase gas, even if the price increases a great deal.

The concept of consumer demand can be used to analyze instrumental reinforcement by considering the number of responses performed (or time spent responding) to be analogous to money. The total number of responses the organism can make is analogous to a person's income—the total amount of money a person has available to spend. The "price" of a reinforcer is the time or number of responses required to obtain the reinforcer, as specified by the schedule of reinforcement. The goal is to understand how instrumental behavior ("spending") is controlled by instrumental contingencies ("prices").

In a study of cigarette smokers, for example, the instrumental response was pushing a plunger, and the reinforcer was the opportunity to take puffs on a cigarette (Bickel, DeGrandpre, Hughes, & Higgins, 1991). Price was increased by requiring more responses for each reinforcer (using fixed ratio schedules) or by decreasing the number of puffs the participants could take with each access to the reinforcer. Increases in the price of smoking decreased the amount participants smoked, regardless of how the price was determined. Thus, cigarette smoking was highly sensitive to price in the laboratory situation. It showed high elasticity.

Determinants of the Elasticity of Demand. The application of economic concepts to the analysis of instrumental conditioning would be of little value if the application did not provide new insights into the mechanisms of reinforcement effects. As it turns out, economic concepts have helped to identify three major factors that influence how schedule constraints shape the reallocation of behavior. Each of these factors determines the degree of elasticity of demand—the extent to which increases in price cause a decrease in consumption.

1. *Availability of substitutes.* A major determinant of the elasticity of demand is the availability of substitutes. Whether increases in the price of one item cause a decline in consumption depends on the availability (and price) of other goods that can be used in place of the original item. The availability of substitutes increases the sensitivity of the original item to higher prices.

A common example involves coffee and tea, both of which are common sources of caffeine. Many people find tea a good substitute for coffee. Therefore, if the price of coffee increases substantially, they will switch to tea. The elasticity of the demand for coffee is influenced by the availability of tea as a substitute for coffee. In contrast to coffee, how much gasoline people buy is not highly influenced by price because there are no readily available substitutes for gasoline.

Two experiments nicely illustrate the effects of substitutability (Kagel et al., 1975; see also Rachlin et al., 1976). Laboratory rats lived in Skinner boxes with two levers. Each rat was allowed a fixed number of lever presses it could perform each day (its daily income). In the first experiment, pressing one lever produced dry food pellets, whereas pressing the other lever produced water. In the second study, lever presses could be "spent" on two sweet drinks (root beer and Tom Collins mix). Food pellets and water are poor substitutes for each other. In fact, these commodities are *complementary.* The more dry food pellets a rat eats, the more it needs to drink. By contrast, the two sweet drinks used in the second study were presumed to be good substitutes.

In each experiment, the "price" of one of the reinforcers was increased by increasing the schedule requirement. Changes in price were not accompanied by changes in how much food the rats worked to obtain. Demand for food was inelastic. Furthermore, the rats did not substitute the "cheaper" water for the more "expensive" food. By contrast, substitution occurred in the second experiment. As the price of one sweet drink increased, the rats spent more of their responses obtaining the other drink. Demand for the sweet drinks was elastic. (For a comprehensive review of substitutability and instrumental behavior, see Green & Freed, 1993.)

2. *Price range.* Another important determinant of the elasticity of demand is the price range of the commodity. Generally, an increase in price has less of an effect at low prices than at high prices. Consider, for example, the cost of candy. A 10% increase in the price from 50¢ to 55¢ is not likely to discourage consumption. But if the candy costs $5.00, a 10% increase to $5.50 might well discourage purchases.

Such effects of price on the elasticity of demand for food have been documented in studies with both laboratory rats and baboons (Hursh, Raslear, Shurtleff, Bauman, & Simmons, 1988; Foltin, 1991, 1994). The price of food was increased by increasing the number of responses required for reinforcement, using fixed ratio schedules. As the price of food increased, the animals at first increased their responding correspondingly to obtain the same amount of food as before. Thus, over a range of low prices, demand for food was inelastic. However, responding failed to keep up with further increases in price, and at the high FR schedules, food consumption declined. This outcome is remarkable because it shows that there is some elasticity in demand, even for a commodity as important as food, provided that prices are raised sufficiently.

3. *Income level.* A third factor that determines elasticity of demand is the level of income. In general, the higher your income, the less deterred you will be by increases in price. This is also true for reinforcers obtained on schedules of reinforcement. In studies of instrumental conditioning, the number of responses or amount of time available for responding corresponds to income. These are resources an organism can use to respond to a schedule constraint. The more responses or time animals have available, the less their behavior is influenced by increases in the cost of the reinforcer (Hastjarjo, Silberberg, & Hursh, 1990a; Silberberg, Warren-Boulton, & Asano, 1987; see also Hastjarjo & Silberberg, 1992; DeGrandpre, Bickel, Rizvi, & Hughes, 1993).

The Contribution of Economic Concepts.   Economic concepts have provided psychologists with new ways of analyzing behavioral regulation—the reallocation of behavior in response to schedule constraints. Like the bliss point approach, economic models assume that changes in behavior serve to maximize something. It is not always clear what is being maximized. In fact, studies of behavior can be used to identify what organisms value and work to conserve (Rachlin, 1995).

Economic concepts have provided new and precise ways of describing constraints that various instrumental conditioning procedures impose on an organism's repertoire of behavior. More importantly, they have emphasized that instrumental behavior cannot be described in a vacuum. Rather, the entire repertoire of the organism at a given time must be considered as a system. Changes in one part of the system influence changes in other parts. Constraints imposed by instrumental procedures are more or less effective depending on the nature of the constraint, the availability of substitutes, and the organism's level of "income."

Optimal Foraging Theory and Behavioral Regulation

Behavioral economics is just one of several interdisciplinary approaches that have contributed significantly to our understanding of reinforcement. Another interdisciplinary

The use of illicit drugs such as heroin and cocaine is instrumental behavior. Going to obtain an illicit drug and paying for it provides the opportunity to use it. Government efforts to reduce the use of illicit drugs have involved manipulating various aspects of its cost, or "price." Confiscating shipments limits the availability of a drug and increases its monetary cost, as shortages drive up the price. Severe penalties for drug possession also impose a "cost," but only after the drug has been obtained.

Laboratory studies of rats, monkeys, and people self-administering drugs under various schedules of reinforcement have shown that the concepts of consumer demand are useful in the analysis of instrumen-

tal drug-seeking behavior (for example, Bickel et al., 1991; Carroll, Carmona, & May, 1991; English, Rowlett, & Woolverton, 1995; Petry & Heyman, 1995). The results of experimental studies of consumer demand have also been extended to analyses of drug abuse policy (Hirsh, 1991).

The effectiveness of policies intended to curb drug use depend on the drug's elasticity of demand. As we have seen, increasing the cost of a commodity fails to reduce its consumption if the price remains relatively low, if there are no substitutes for the item, or if the individual has a high income level. These considerations suggest that to discourage drug use, more than the cost of the drug needs to be considered. A highly effective technique for increasing the elasticity of demand for an item involves making an effective substitute available. Interestingly, under certain circumstances, nondrug reinforcers can serve as effective substitutes for a drug reinforcer (for example, Carroll, Carmona, & May, 1991).

effort relevant to reinforcement is the study of foraging behavior. Here psychologists have joined with zoologists in trying to understand how animals distribute their efforts to obtain food in an optimally efficient fashion.

Foraging is a rather complex system of behaviors that may involve specialized perceptual mechanisms for recognizing foods, motor responses for getting to the food and handling it, memory mechanisms for remembering which food sources have already been depleted or locations where food might have been stored, and social behavior such as avoidance of competitors and predators or defense of a feeding area (see Commons, Kacelnik, & Shettleworth, 1987; Kamil, Krebs, & Pulliam, 1987; Kamil & Sargent, 1981). In Chapter 11 I will discuss some special memory mechanisms involved in the foraging behavior of food-storing birds. The aspect of foraging that is relevant to analyses of instrumental behavior is the relation between effort expended and food obtained (Shettleworth, 1988).

Research on foraging behavior has been dominated by theories of optimal foraging (see Krebs & McCleery, 1984; Stephens & Krebs, 1986). The basic assumption of optimal foraging theories is that animals search for and obtain food in a manner that maximizes their energy intake (E) per unit time (T) spent foraging. Thus, animals are assumed to maximize E/T.

A. C. Kamil

Comparisons with Other Optimality Approaches. Optimal foraging theories are similar to other optimality theories that I have already discussed, such as molar maximizing models of choice (see Chapter 6), behavioral bliss point models, and behavioral economics. However, unlike the other optimality theories, which are applicable to a variety of responses and reinforcers, theories of foraging are restricted to analyses of activities involved in obtaining and consuming food and water. Another important difference is that investigators of foraging are concerned with ecological validity. Foraging was first studied by zoologists and field biologists interested in understanding foraging behavior in the wild. Investigators of foraging continue to be concerned with the extent to which experimental studies of optimal foraging accurately represent the behavior of animals in their natural environment (Mellgren, 1982; Shettleworth, 1989).

The roots of research on optimal foraging in zoology and field biology have also stimulated greater interest in species differences and adaptive specializations in response reallocation. Foraging behavior occurs in diverse forms in the animal kingdom. Animals that eat only plants (herbivores) have to eat a great deal to obtain enough nutrition from their relatively poor-quality food. The response cost of procuring plants to eat is usually low, but herbivores have to eat frequent meals. By contrast, animals that hunt and eat mostly meat (carnivores) can get by with far less food because the nutritional quality of their food is so much better. However, their procurement costs (effort required to capture a prey) are much greater. Foraging theory, with its biological perspective, highlights that a complete theory of response allocation must address such species differences.

Key Elements of the Foraging Problem. For most animals, food is distributed in patches. For example, a hummingbird forages among patches of flowers for nectar, and a squirrel forages among tree branches for nuts. Foraging involves two essential decisions: (1) whether to enter a patch in search of food—to visit a clump of flowers or a tree branch—and (2) whether to continue looking for food in that location or to go elsewhere in hopes of finding a patch that has more food. Both of these aspects of foraging have been investigated in great detail.

Whether to enter a patch. Other things being equal, animals will, of course, elect to enter a patch that has lots of food in favor of one that has little food. However, they rarely have the luxury of choosing between two food sources that are available at the same time. Rather, patches of food are encountered in succession, one after another, and an animal may have to wait a long time (or travel a long distance) between leaving one patch and finding the next one. This makes foraging choices more difficult. Upon encountering a lean patch, should the animal continue on its way in the hope of finding a richer source of food, or should it stop and harvest the food from the lean patch that it found? Optimal foraging theory predicts that choice of the leaner patch depends on when the organism is likely to encounter a richer patch (see Ito & Fantino, 1986; Fantino & Preston, 1988). If it is likely to find a richer source of food soon, there is no need to accept the poor alternative now. (For other studies of patch choice, see Bateson & Kacelnik, 1995; Case, Nichols, & Fantino, 1995; Plowright & Shettleworth, 1991.)

Whether to leave a patch. The second major decision involved in foraging is whether or not to remain in the selected patch or go to another one. Interestingly, the considerations involved in this decision are similar in some respects to those involved in entering a patch. In the natural environment, patches of food have a fixed amount of food in them, so that the longer an animal harvests food from a chosen patch, the less food there is to be had. As the patch becomes depleted, the animal has to decide whether to stay there or try to find a richer source of food. The decision is a difficult one. Optimality requires leaving at just the right time. If the animal leaves too early, it will give up food that is readily at hand. By contrast, if it stays too long, it will be wasting its time on a depleting patch, when it could be harvesting a richer one. As in the decision to enter a patch, optimality in leaving a patch requires comparing the current situation to possible future gains.

Various laboratory procedures have been devised to investigate the foraging problem posed by a depleting patch (see Shettleworth, 1988). In one approach, animals are given a choice between two patches of food. One patch always provides food at a moderate rate and is therefore a nondepleting patch. The second patch starts out much richer in food but becomes depleted (see for example, Bhatt & Wasserman, 1987; Redhead & Tyler, 1988; Wanchisen, Tatham, & Hineline, 1988). Optimal choice in this situation requires selecting the depleting patch at first (since it is richer in food initially). However, as food becomes harder to get in the depleting patch, the animal should switch to the nondepleting patch (see also Davison, 1992; Davison & McCarthy, 1994; Jacobs & Hackenberg, 1996; McCarthy, Voss, & Davison, 1994).

Kamil, Yoerg, and Clements (1988) tested this prediction in a study of the foraging behavior of blue jays using a variation on a concurrent-chain schedule (see also Kamil & Clements, 1990). Blue jays eat insects such as moths. In this experiment, encounter with an insect was simulated by presenting a picture of a moth. The birds faced a wall with two small rectangular panels on which pictures could be projected from the back (see Figure 7.7). The pictures either showed a conspicuous black and white moth on a pink background or just showed the background. If a picture of a moth appeared, the birds got a bit of food. The right panel represented a nondepleting patch, and the left panel represented a depleting patch. Both patches were available throughout the experiment.

The birds selected the depleting or the nondepleting patch by pecking a small circular pecking key below the rectangular picture panels. If they selected the nondepleting patch, a picture of a moth appeared 25% of the time, each appearance being followed by access to food reinforcement. Thus, selection of the nondepleting patch was reinforced intermittently. No matter how often the birds encountered a moth on the nondepleting side, the probability of finding another one in that patch (and hence the probability of reinforcement) remained 25%.

If the birds selected the depleting patch, finding a prey item was more likely at first. The birds encountered a picture of a moth (and food reinforcement) 50% of the time at the start of a session. However, the depleting side had a limited number of moths available during each session. After the birds had obtained the available number, no more were to be had there for the remainder of the session. In different parts of the experiment, each session started with 9, 6, or 3 moths in the depleting patch. Thus, initially the probability of reinforcement on the depleting side was greater than on the nondepleting side (50% as compared to 25%). However, as the session progressed and all the moths on the depleting side were found, the relative probabilities reversed, with the depleting side now having a lower probability of reinforcement (0%) than the nondepleting side (25%).

As expected, the choice behavior of the blue jays tracked the probabilities of reinforcement in the two patches. At the start of a session, the blue jays were more likely to select the depleting patch. However, as each session progressed, they switched to the nondepleting patch. The birds learned to respond quite efficiently, obtaining more than 90% of all possible moths in each session.

Optimality: Description Rather than Mechanism.   Deciding when to enter a patch and when to depart from it in a way that optimizes the rate of obtaining food involves complex judgments. The food density of the current and possible future patches has to be accurately assessed, impending changes in the current patch (depletion) have to be correctly judged, the likelihood of encountering another patch soon has to be determined, and the effort and risk involved in traveling to the next patch have to be

Figure 7.7 A blue jay in an experiment on the effects of patch depletion on foraging behavior. Patches were represented by slides projected from the rear on the rectangular displays on either side of the food dish above the pecking keys. The slides sometimes showed a black and white *Cotocala relicta* moth. (Drawing based on a photograph provided by A. Kamil.)

considered in comparison to the likely benefits. Optimal foraging theories say nothing about the mechanisms animals use to accomplish all of this successfully. They just describe what constitutes optimal performance.

To assume that optimality is a mechanism of foraging would require assuming that animals have fabulous abilities to calculate probabilities and weigh costs and benefits over a large span of time. That is unlikely. But if animals do not make complex optimality calculations, how do they manage to approximate optimal choice performance? Answers to this question are beginning to emerge from the interactive efforts of biologists and psychologists. Psychologists are beginning to explore the behavioral processes involved in foraging situations and the ways in which those behavioral processes contribute to near-optimal performance (for example, Fantino & Abarca, 1985; Gibbon, Church, Fairhurst, & Kacelnik, 1988; Timberlake, Gawley, & Lucas, 1987, 1988).

One interesting conclusion that has emerged is that animals do not have to make complicated optimality calculations in order to perform optimally. Following some simple rules of thumb often can lead to nearly the same outcome as precise calculations of optimality. Consider, for example, the study of foraging in blue jays described earlier. In this experiment, the animals had to decide when to switch from a depleting patch to a nondepleting patch. Kamil and his associates (1988) discovered that the probability of leaving the depleting patch was determined by two factors. One of these was the number of times in a row the birds failed to find a moth in the depleting patch. This factor is called the *run of bad luck*. According to the rule of thumb, the longer the run of bad luck in the depleting patch, the more likely the birds were to switch to the nondepleting patch.

213

The other rule of thumb was related to *the number of moths the birds had already found* in the depleting patch. The depleting patch had a limited number of moths at the start of each session. When all of those had been found, there were no more for the rest of the session. The blue jays evidently detected this aspect of the situation and were more likely to switch to the nondepleting patch once they had obtained close to the total number of moths available on the depleting patch that day. The two rules of thumb (run of bad luck and number of prey already found) were used in combination. The birds were more likely to switch in response to a particular run of bad luck if they had already obtained most of the available prey.

Contributions of the Foraging Approach. Studies of foraging behavior have enriched our knowledge of the mechanisms of response allocation in the same manner as behavioral economics; that is, such studies have focused attention on some previously ignored factors that are important determinants of choice. Studies of foraging behavior have also expanded the conceptual framework for the investigation of instrumental conditioning by emphasizing the ecological validity of laboratory studies and by raising questions about species differences in response allocation.

CONCLUDING COMMENTS

The research and theories about reinforcement discussed in this chapter represent several points of view. No one approach is comprehensive. Each starts from a particular set of assumptions about what a reinforcer is. The choice of whether to regard a reinforcer as a stimulus or as a response leads, as we have seen, in different directions. In fact, a reinforcer in most cases involves both stimuli and responses. Determining a common feature for all reinforcers is therefore an extremely complex task.

Explaining the mechanism of reinforcement likewise rests on a set of starting assumptions about instrumental behavior. The instrumental response was originally viewed as a single behavior that increases in frequency with reinforcement. Drive reduction theorists suggested a physiologically based mechanism to account for this "stamping in" effect. However, with more research it became clear that the motivating circumstances are not so simple. As we have seen, more comprehensive approaches to the problem of reinforcement take a broader view of the organism's behavior. An instrumental conditioning procedure is considered to be a constraint on the organism's free flow of activities, and increases in the instrumental response are by-products of a comprehensive reorganization or reallocation of behavior. The nature of the response reallocation depends on the availability of substitutes and the costs and benefits of alternative strategies.

So far, the most productive working assumption has been that the response reallocation results in optimality in some sense. However, what is being optimized and how the optimization is achieved are questions that remain to be answered.

The story of the development of theories of reinforcement is an exciting illustration of the course of scientific inquiry. It spans intellectual developments from simple stimulus-response, drive reduction formulations to comprehensive considerations of how the organism's repertoire is constrained by instrumental contingencies and how organisms solve complex ecological problems. In this aspect of the study of conditioning and learning, perhaps more so than in any other, investigators have moved boldly to explore radically new conceptions when older ideas did not meet the challenges posed by new empirical findings.

SAMPLE QUESTIONS

1. Describe the drive reduction theory of reinforcement and its successes and failures.
2. In what ways is the Premack principle different from drive reduction theory?
3. Describe similarities and differences between the Premack principle and subsequent behavioral regulation theory.
4. What are the shortcomings of behavioral regulation theory?
5. What economic concepts have been used in reinforcement theory, and how have these concepts been used?

KEY TERMS

behavioral bliss point The preferred distribution of an organism's activities before an instrumental conditioning procedure is introduced that sets constraints and limitations on response allocation.

consummatory response theory A theory that assumes that species-typical consummatory responses (eating, drinking, and the like) are critical features of reinforcers.

demand curve The relation between how much of a commodity is purchased and the price of the commodity.

differential probability principle A principle that assumes that reinforcement depends on how much more likely the organism is to perform the reinforcer response than the instrumental response before an instrumental conditioning procedure is introduced. The greater the differential probability of the reinforcer and instrumental responses during baseline conditions, the greater will be the reinforcement effect of providing opportunity to engage in the reinforcer response after performance of the instrumental response. Also known as the *Premack principle.*

drive reduction theory A theory of reinforcement according to which reinforcers are effective because they reduce the participant's drive state and enable a return to homeostasis.

elasticity of demand The degree to which price influences the consumption or purchase of a commodity. If price has a large effect on consumption, elasticity of demand is high. If price has a small effect on consumption, elasticity of demand is low.

incentive motivation Motivation for instrumental behavior created by the sensory properties of a reinforcer.

intracranial self-stimulation Performance of an instrumental response that is reinforced by brief pulses of current passed through an electrode implanted in certain areas of the brain.

minimum deviation model A model of instrumental behavior, according to which participants respond to a response-reinforcer contingency in a manner that gets them as close as possible to their behavioral bliss point.

physiological homeostasis The preferred or optimal state of a biological system. Deviations from this state stimulate adjustments to return the system to its preferred state.

primary motivation Motivation for instrumental behavior created by a drive state.

response deprivation hypothesis An explanation of reinforcement according to which restricting access to a response below its baseline rate of occurrence (response deprivation) is sufficient to make the opportunity to perform that response an effective positive reinforcer.

Identification and Measurement of Stimulus Control

    Differential Responding and Stimulus Discrimination

    Stimulus Generalization

    Stimulus Generalization Gradients as a Measure of
        Stimulus Control

Stimulus and Response Factors in Stimulus Control

    Sensory Capacity and Orientation

    Relative Ease of Conditioning Various Stimuli

    Type of Reinforcement

    Type of Instrumental Response

    Stimulus Elements versus Configural Cues in Compound
        Stimuli

Learning Factors in Stimulus Control

    Stimulus Discrimination Training

    Effects of Discrimination Training on Stimulus Control

    Range of Possible Discriminative Stimuli

    What Is Learned in Discrimination Training?

    Stimulus Equivalence Training

Contextual Cues and Conditional Relations

    Control by Contextual Cues

    Control by Conditional Relations

Concluding Comments

C HAPTER 8 is organized around the principles of stimulus control. Although most of the chapter deals with the ways in which instrumental behavior comes under the control of particular stimuli that are present when the response is reinforced, the concepts I will discuss are equally applicable to classical conditioning. I will begin with the definition of stimulus control and the basic concepts of stimulus discrimination and generalization and then discuss factors that determine the extent to which behavior comes to be restricted to particular stimulus values. Along the way, I will describe special forms of stimulus control (intradimensional discrimination) and control by special categories of stimuli (compound stimuli and contextual cues). I will conclude this chapter with a discussion of the learning of conditional relations in both instrumental and classical conditioning.

In the discussion of instrumental behavior so far, I have emphasized the relation between the instrumental response and the reinforcer. As we have seen in Chapters 5–7, the response-reinforcer relation is a very important aspect of instrumental conditioning. However, it is not the only factor that determines when and where an instrumental response will be performed. Responses and reinforcers do not occur in a vacuum; rather, they occur in the presence of particular stimuli. Such stimuli can come to determine whether or not the instrumental response is performed. In Chapter 8 I will describe the stimulus control of instrumental behavior and the processes that are responsible for such control.

Stimulus control of instrumental behavior is evident in many aspects of life. For most students, for example, studying is under the strong control of school-related stimuli. College students who have fallen behind in their work may make determined resolutions to study a lot when they return home during the holidays. However, such good intentions are rarely carried out. The stimulus context of the holidays is very different from the stimuli students experience when classes are in session. Therefore, the holiday stimuli do not evoke effective studying behavior.

Stimulus control of behavior is an important aspect of how organisms adjust to their environment. The survival of animals in the wild depends on their ability to perform responses that are appropriate to the stimulus circumstances. With seasonal changes in their food supply, for example, animals have to change how they forage for food. Within the same season, they have to respond one way in the presence of predators or intruders and in other ways in the absence of nearby danger. In cold weather, animals may seek comfort by going to areas warmed by the sun; on rainy days, they may seek comfort by going to sheltered areas. To effectively obtain comfort and avoid pain, animals have to behave in ways that are appropriate to their changing circumstances.

The proper fit between an instrumental response and the stimulus context in which the response is performed is so important that the failure of appropriate stimulus control is often considered abnormal. Getting undressed, for example, is acceptable instrumental behavior in the privacy of your bedroom. The same behavior on a public street is highly inappropriate. Staring at a television set is considered appropriate if the set is turned on. Staring at a blank television screen may be a symptom of behavior pathology. If you respond in a loving manner in the presence of your spouse or other family members, your behavior generally has positive consequences. The same behavior directed toward strangers is likely to be greeted with far less pleasant consequences.

IDENTIFICATION AND MEASUREMENT OF STIMULUS CONTROL

Before beginning an investigation of the stimulus control of behavior, ways to identify and measure instances of stimulus control must be established. How can a researcher tell that an instrumental response has come under the control of certain stimuli? Consider, for example, a pigeon pecking for food on a variable interval reinforcement schedule in a Skinner box. While in the Skinner box, the pigeon is exposed to a wide variety of stimuli, including the color and texture of the walls of the chamber, the sight of the nuts and bolts holding the chamber together, the odor of the chamber, and the noises of the ventilating fan. In addition, let us assume that the pigeon's pecking key is illuminated by a pattern consisting of a white triangle on a red background. How can the investigator determine which of these stimuli control the pigeon's key-pecking behavior?

Differential Responding and Stimulus Discrimination

Reynolds (1961) conducted an experiment using stimuli similar to those I just described. Two pigeons were reinforced on a variable interval schedule for pecking a circular response key. Reinforcement for pecking was available whenever the response key was illuminated by a visual pattern consisting of a white triangle on a red background (see Figure 8.1). The stimulus on the key thus had two components—the white triangle and the red color of the background. Reynolds was interested in finding out which of these stimulus components gained control over the pecking behavior.

After the pigeons learned to peck steadily at the triangle on the red background, Reynolds measured the amount of pecking that occurred when only one of the stimuli was presented. On some of the test trials, the white triangle was projected on the response key without the red color. On other test trials, the red background color was projected on the response key without the white triangle.

The results are summarized in Figure 8.1. One of the pigeons pecked a great deal more when the response key was illuminated with the red light than when it was illuminated with the white triangle. This outcome shows that its pecking behavior was much more strongly controlled by the red color than by the white triangle. By contrast, the other pigeon pecked a great deal more when the white triangle was projected on the response key than when the key was illuminated by the red light. Thus, for the second bird, the pecking behavior was more strongly controlled by the triangle than by the color stimulus. (For a recent variation of this experiment, see Cheng & Spetch, 1995.)

This experiment illustrates several important ideas. First, it shows how to experimentally determine whether instrumental behavior has come under the control of a particular stimulus. *The stimulus control of instrumental behavior is demonstrated by differential responding in the presence of different stimuli.* If an organism responds in one way in the presence of one stimulus and in a different way in the presence of another stimulus, it is possible to conclude that its behavior has come under the control of the stimuli involved. Such differential responding was evident in the behavior of both pigeons Reynolds tested. Both of the birds responded more frequently in the presence of one of the stimuli (red color or triangle) than in the presence of the other.

Differential responding to two stimuli also indicates that the animals are discriminating between them—that they are treating each stimulus as different from the other. This is called **stimulus discrimination.** *An animal is said to show stimulus discrimination if it responds differently to two or more stimuli.* Stimulus discrimination and stimulus control are two ways of considering the same phenomenon. There is no way to have one without the other. If an organism does not discriminate between two stimuli, its behavior is not under the control of those cues.

Another interesting aspect of the results of Reynolds' experiment is that the pecking behavior of each bird came under the control of a different stimulus. The behavior of one bird came under the control of the red color, whereas the behavior of the other bird came under the control of the triangle.

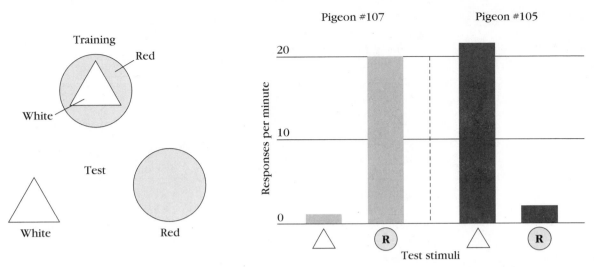

Figure 8.1 Summary of procedure and results of an experiment by Reynolds (1961). Two pigeons were first reinforced for pecking whenever a compound stimulus consisting of a white triangle on a red background was projected on the response key. The rate of pecking was then observed with each pigeon when the white triangle and the red background stimuli were presented separately.

The procedures used in the experiment did not direct attention to one of the stimuli at the expense of the other. Therefore, it is not surprising that each bird came to respond to a different aspect of the situation. The experiment was comparable to showing a group of children a picture of a cowboy grooming a horse. Some of the children may focus on the cowboy, whereas others may find the horse more interesting. In the absence of special procedures that I will describe later in the chapter, it is not always possible to predict which of the various stimuli an organism experiences will gain control over its instrumental behavior.

Stimulus Generalization

In the discussion so far, I have treated stimuli as if they were clearly identifiable and distinguishable entities in the world. However, identifying and differentiating various stimuli is not a simple matter (Fetterman, 1996). Stimuli may be defined in all kinds of ways. Sometimes widely different objects or events are considered instances of the same stimulus because they all share the same function. A wheel, for example, may be small or large, spoked or not spoked, and made of wood, rubber, or metal— but it is still a wheel. By contrast, in other cases stimuli are identified and distinguished in terms of precise physical features such as the wavelength of light or the frequency of radio waves. For example, to tune in a particular FM radio station, you have to tune your radio within a very small range of the FM band. Small variations in the frequency to which your radio is tuned will significantly distort the quality of the reception.

Psychologists and physiologists have long been concerned with how organisms identify and distinguish different stimuli. In fact, some have suggested that this is the single most important question in psychology (Stevens, 1951). The problem is central to the analysis of stimulus control. As I will show, numerous factors are involved in the identification and differentiation of stimuli. Experimental analyses of the problem have depended mainly on the phenomenon of **stimulus generalization.** In a sense, stimulus generalization is the opposite of differential responding, or stimulus discrimination. *An animal is said to show stimulus generalization if it responds in a*

219

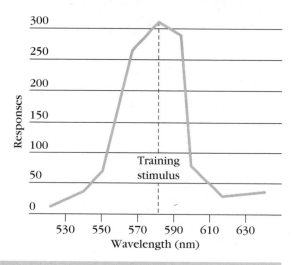

Figure 8.2 Stimulus generalization gradient for pigeons that were trained to peck in the presence of a colored light of 580-nm wavelength and were then tested in the presence of other colors. (From "Discriminability and Stimulus Generalization" by N. Guttman and H. I. Kalish, 1956, *Journal of Experimental Psychology, 51,* pp. 79–88.)

similar fashion to two or more stimuli—if the same level of behavior is observed in the presence of different stimuli.

The phenomenon of stimulus generalization was first observed by Pavlov. He found that after one stimulus was used as a CS, his dogs would also make the conditioned response to other, similar stimuli. That is, they failed to respond differentially to stimuli that were similar to the original CS.

Stimulus generalization has also been investigated in instrumental conditioning. In a landmark experiment, Guttman and Kalish (1956) first reinforced pigeons on a variable interval schedule for pecking a response key illuminated by a yellowish-orange light with a wavelength of 580 nm. After training, the animals were tested with a variety of other colors presented in a random order without reinforcement, and the rate of responding in the presence of each color was recorded.

The results of the experiment are summarized in Figure 8.2. The highest rate of pecking occurred in response to the original 580-nm light. But, the birds also made substantial numbers of pecks when lights of 570- and 590-nm wavelength were tested. This indicates that responding generalized to the 570-nm and 590-nm stimuli. However, as the color of the test stimuli became increasingly different from the color of the original training stimulus, progressively fewer responses occurred. The results showed a gradient of responding as a function of how similar each test stimulus was to the original training stimulus. This is an example of a **stimulus generalization gradient.**

Stimulus Generalization Gradients as a Measure of Stimulus Control

Stimulus generalization gradients are often used to measure stimulus control because they provide information about how sensitive the organism's behavior is to variations in a particular aspect of the environment (see Honig & Urcuioli, 1981). With the use of stimulus generalization gradients, an investigator can determine

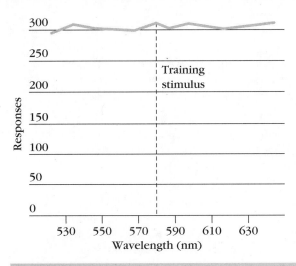

Figure 8.3 Hypothetical stimulus generalization gradient for color-blind pigeons trained to peck in the presence of a colored light of 580-nm wavelength and then tested in the presence of other colors.

exactly how much an environmental stimulus has to be altered to produce a change in behavior.

Consider, for example, the gradient in Figure 8.2. The pigeons responded much more when the original 580-nm training stimulus was presented than when the response key was illuminated by lights whose wavelengths were 520, 540, 620, and 640 nm. Thus, differences in color controlled different levels of responding. However, this control was not very precise. Responding to the 580-nm color generalized to the 570- and 590-nm stimuli. The wavelength of the 580-nm training stimulus had to be changed by more than 10 nm before a decrement in performance was observed. This aspect of the stimulus generalization gradient provides precise information about how much an environmental stimulus has to be changed for the organism to show a change in its behavior.

How do you suppose pigeons would have responded in this experiment if they had been color-blind? If the birds had been color-blind, they could not have distinguished lights on the basis of color or wavelength. Therefore, they would have responded in much the same way regardless of what color was projected on the response key. Figure 8.3 presents hypothetical results of an experiment of this sort. If the pigeons did not respond on the basis of the color of the key light, similar high rates of responding would have occurred as different colors were projected on the key. Thus, the stimulus generalization gradient would have been flat.

A comparison of the results obtained by Guttman and Kalish and our hypothetical experiment with color-blind pigeons indicates that *the steepness of a stimulus generalization gradient provides a precise measure of the degree of stimulus control.* A flat generalization gradient (Figure 8.3) is obtained if the organism responds in a similar fashion to all the test stimuli. Such lack of differential responding shows that the stimulus feature that is varied in the generalization test does not control the instrumental behavior. By contrast, a steep generalization gradient (Figure 8.2) is obtained if the organism responds more to some of the test stimuli than to others. Such differential responding is evidence that the instrumental behavior is under the control of the stimulus feature that is varied among the test stimuli.

BOX **8.1**

GENERALIZATION OF TREATMENT OUTCOMES

Stimulus generalization is critical to the success of behavior therapy. Behavior therapy, like other forms of therapy, is typically conducted under specific circumstances (in a therapist's office, for example). For the treatment to be maximally useful, what is learned during treatment should generalize outside the training situation. An autistic child, for example, who is taught certain communicative responses in interactions with a particular therapist should also exhibit those responses in interactions with other people. The following techniques have been proposed to facilitate generalization of treatment outcomes (for example, Schreibman, Koegel, Charlop, & Egel, 1990; Stokes & Baer, 1977):

1. The treatment situation should be made as similar as possible to the natural environment of the client. Thus, if the natural environment provides reinforcement only intermittently, it is a good idea to reduce the frequency of reinforcement during treatment sessions as well. Another way to increase the similarity of the treatment procedure to the natural environment is to use the same reinforcers the client is likely to encounter in the natural environment.

2. Generalization also may be increased by conducting the treatment procedure in new settings. This strategy is called *sequential modification.* After a behavior has been conditioned in one situation (a class-

room), training is conducted in a new situation (the playground). If that does not result in sufficient generalization, training can be extended to a third environment (the school cafeteria, for example).

3. Using numerous exemplars during training also facilitates generalization. In trying to extinguish fear of elevators, for example, training should be conducted with numerous different types of elevators.

4. Generalization may be also encouraged by conditioning the new responses to stimuli that are common to various situations. Language provides effective mediating stimuli. Responses conditioned to verbal or instructional cues are likely to generalize to new situations in which those instructional stimuli are encountered.

5. Another approach is to make the training procedure indiscriminable or incidental to other activities. In one study (McGee, Krantz, & McClannahan, 1986), for example, the investigators took advantage of the interest that autistic children showed in specific toys during a play session to teach the children how to read the names of the toys.

6. Finally, generalization outside a training situation is achieved if the training helps to bring the individual in contact with contingencies of reinforcement available in the natural environment (Baer & Wolf, 1970). Once a response is acquired through special training, the behavior often can be maintained by naturally available reinforcers. Reading, calculating simple arithmetic problems, and riding a bicycle are all responses that are maintained by natural reinforcers once the responses have been acquired through special training.

Generalization and differential responding may be considered opposites. If a great deal of generalization occurs, there is little differential responding. If responding is highly differential to stimuli, little generalization is obtained.

STIMULUS AND RESPONSE FACTORS IN STIMULUS CONTROL

In the experiment by Reynolds (1961) that I described at the outset of the chapter, pigeons pecked a response key that had a white triangle on a red background. Such a stimulus obviously has two features—the color of the background and the shape of the triangle. Perhaps less obvious is the fact that all stimulus situations involve multiple stimulus features. Even if the response key only had the red background, the situation could be analyzed as being composed of several stimulus elements. These elements include, for example, the wavelength of the red light, its brightness, the shape of the response key, and the location of the key in the experimental chamber.

Situations outside the laboratory are even more complex. During a football game, for example, cheering is reinforced by social approval if the people near you are all rooting for the same team as you are and if your team is doing well. The cues that accompany appropriate cheering include your team making a good play on the field, the announcer describing the play, cheerleaders dancing exuberantly, and the people around you cheering. As another example, consider placing your groceries on a checkout counter. Such behavior is appropriate in the presence of cues that include the customer before you being finished, the checkout counter being free of someone else's groceries, and the cashier indicating that it is your turn.

The central question in the analysis of stimulus control is, What determines which of the elements of a stimulus situation gain control over the instrumental behavior? Stimuli as complex as those found at a football game or a checkout counter are difficult to analyze experimentally. Therefore, laboratory studies are typically conducted with stimulus compounds that consist of more easily identified elements, or features. In the present section I will discuss stimulus and response factors that determine which cues come to control behavior. In the following section I will describe learning factors.

Sensory Capacity and Orientation

Consideration of the factors that determine whether, and to what extent, a particular stimulus feature comes to control responding has to begin with the organism's sensory capacity and orientation. The range of stimuli that can potentially influence behavior is determined by the organism's sensory world—the world of sensations a particular individual experiences. Sensory capacity and orientation determine which stimuli are included in an organism's sensory world. Presentation of stimuli with certain features of interest to one organism does not guarantee that another organism will respond to the same features. The individual's own (and possibly unique) point of view or sensory world must always be considered.

An individual's behavior can come under the control of a particular stimulus only if the individual is sensitive to that stimulus. Events outside the range of what an organism can detect with its sense organs simply do not exist for that individual unless the stimuli are amplified or transduced into something the individual can detect. People, for example, cannot detect sounds when the pitch is above about 20,000 cps. Such stimuli are called "ultrasounds" because they are outside the range of human hearing. Because ultrasounds are inaudible to people, such sounds cannot come to control human behavior. Other species, however, are able to hear ultrasounds. Dogs, for example, can hear whistles outside the range of human hearing and therefore can be trained to respond to such sounds.

Limitations on the stimuli that can come to control behavior are also set by whether the individual comes in contact with the stimulus. Consider, for example, a child's crib. Parents often place mobiles and other decorations on and around the crib to provide interesting stimuli for the child to look at. The crib shown in Figure 8.4 is decorated with such a mobile. The mobile consists of several thin needlework animal figures (including a giraffe, a seal, and a lion).

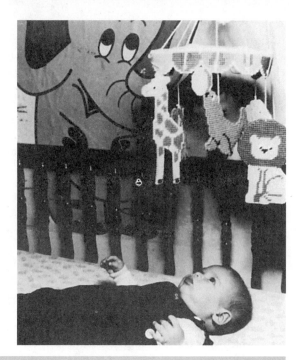

Figure 8.4 An infant looking up at a mobile.

Which aspects of the stimuli in the crib can potentially control the child's behavior? To answer this question, the first thing to consider is what the child sees about the mobile rather than what the mobile looks like to adults. From the child's vantage point under the mobile, only the bottom edges of the animal figures are visible. The shapes of the animals and their surface decorations are not easily visible from below. Therefore, these other features are not likely to gain control of the child's looking behavior. These considerations illustrate that an individual's orientation with respect to the various features of its environment greatly influences which stimuli can gain control over its behavior. (For research findings illustrating the importance of orientation for the acquisition of stimulus control, see, for example, Gillette, Martin, & Bellingham, 1980.)

Relative Ease of Conditioning Various Stimuli

Having the necessary sense organs and the appropriate sensory orientation does not guarantee that the organism's behavior will come under the control of a particular stimulus. Whether a stimulus comes to control behavior also depends on the presence of other cues in the situation. In particular, how strongly organisms learn about one stimulus depends on how easily other cues in the situation can become conditioned. This phenomenon is called **overshadowing.**

Consider, for example, getting sick after eating an unfamiliar dessert that is very sweet and also has a weak vanilla flavor. Because of the illness experience, you will learn an aversion to the food. However, you may not learn a strong aversion to both of its taste features. The conditioned aversion is likely to be controlled primarily by the strong, sweet taste of the dessert, with little of the aversion being elicited by the weak vanilla flavor.

I disagree

Pavlov (1927) was the first to observe that if two stimuli are presented simultaneously, the presence of the stimulus that is easier to condition may hinder learning about the other one. In many of Pavlov's experiments, the two stimuli differed in intensity. Generally, the more intense stimulus became conditioned more rapidly and overshadowed learning about the weaker stimulus. Pavlov found that the weak stimulus could become conditioned (somewhat slowly) if it was presented by itself and repeatedly paired with the US. However, much less conditioning occurred if the weak stimulus was presented simultaneously with a more intense stimulus. (For recent studies of overshadowing, see March, Chamizo, & Mackintosh, 1992; Schachtman, Kasprow, Meyer, Bourne, & Hart, 1992; Spetch, 1995.)

Type of Reinforcement

V. M. LoLordo

The development of stimulus control also depends on the type of reinforcement that is used. Certain types of stimuli are more likely to gain control over the instrumental behavior with positive than with negative reinforcement. This relation has been extensively investigated in experiments with pigeons (see LoLordo, 1979).

In one study (Foree & LoLordo, 1973), two groups of pigeons were trained to press a foot treadle in the presence of a compound stimulus consisting of a red light and a tone whose pitch was 440 cps. When the light/tone compound was absent, responses were not reinforced. For one group of pigeons, reinforcement for treadle pressing consisted of food. For the other group, treadle pressing was reinforced by the avoidance of shock. If the avoidance group pressed the treadle in the presence of the light/tone stimulus, no shock was delivered on that trial; if they failed to respond during the light/tone stimulus, a brief shock was periodically applied until a response occurred.

Both groups of pigeons learned to respond during the light/tone compound. Foree and LoLordo then sought to determine which of the two elements of the compound stimulus, the light or the tone, was primarily responsible for the treadle-press behavior. Test trials were conducted during which the light and tone stimuli were presented one at a time. Responding during these tests with the stimulus elements was then compared with the pigeons' behavior when the light and the tone were presented simultaneously, as during training.

The results are summarized in Figure 8.5. Pigeons that were trained with food reinforcement responded much more when tested with the light stimulus alone than when tested with the tone alone. In fact, their rate of treadle pressing in response to the isolated presentation of the red light was nearly as high as when the light was presented simultaneously with the tone. Therefore, it is clear that the behavior of these birds was nearly exclusively controlled by the red light stimulus.

A very different pattern of results occurred with the animals that were trained with shock-avoidance reinforcement. These animals responded much more when tested with the tone alone than when tested with the light alone. Thus, with shock-avoidance reinforcement the tone acquired more control over the treadle response than the red light.

Similar results have been obtained in a variety of other experiments (for example, Kelley, 1986; Kraemer & Roberts, 1985; Schindler & Weiss, 1982; Shapiro et al., 1980; Shapiro & LoLordo, 1982). These findings indicate that stimulus control of instrumental behavior is determined in part by the type of reinforcement used. Although the mechanisms responsible for this effect are still being worked out (Weiss, Panlilio, & Schindler, 1993a, 1993b), the results are clear. Visual stimuli are more

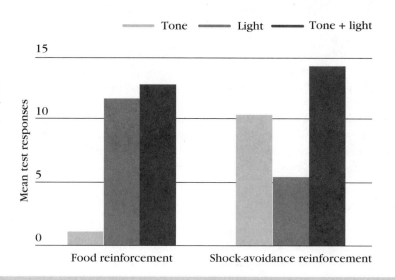

Figure 8.5 Effects of type of reinforcement on stimulus control. A treadle-press response in pigeons was reinforced in the presence of a compound stimulus consisting of a tone and a red light. With food reinforcement, the light gained much more control over the behavior than the tone. With shock-avoidance reinforcement, the tone gained more control over behavior than the light. (Adapted from Foree & LoLordo, 1973.)

likely to gain control over behavior than auditory cues in appetitive situations, whereas auditory cues are more likely to gain control in aversive situations.

The dominance of visual control in appetitive situations and auditory control in aversive situations is probably related to the behavior systems that are activated in the two cases. Food-reinforcement procedures activate the feeding system. Responding to visual cues may be particularly useful for pigeons in seeking food. Therefore, activation of the feeding system may involve increased sensitivity to visual stimuli. In contrast, shock-avoidance procedures activate the defensive behavior system. Responding to auditory cues may be particularly adaptive in avoiding danger.

Unfortunately, we do not know enough about the behavioral ecology of pigeons to be able to calculate the adaptive value of different types of stimulus control in feeding versus defensive behavior; nor do we know how stimulus control varies as a function of type of reinforcement in other species. Thus, this issue remains a fertile area for future research.

Type of Instrumental Response

Another factor that can determine which of several features of a compound stimulus gains control over behavior is the nature of the response required for reinforcement. The importance of the instrumental response for stimulus control is illustrated by an experiment by Dobrzecka, Szwejkowska, and Konorski (1966). These investigators studied the control of instrumental behavior by auditory stimuli in dogs. The dogs were gently restrained in a harness, with a metronome placed in front of them and a buzzer placed behind them. The metronome and buzzer provided qualitatively different types of sounds—a periodic beat versus a continuous rattle. The two stimuli also differed in spatial location. One was in front of the animal and the other behind it. The investigators were interested in which of these two stimulus characteristics (quality of the sound or its location) would come to control behavior.

Two groups of dogs served in the experiment (see Figure 8.6). The two groups differed in what responses were required for reinforcement in the presence of the buzzer and the metronome stimuli. Group 1 received training in a right/left task.

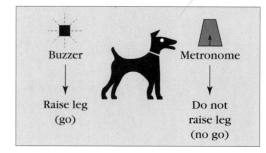

Figure 8.6 — Group 1 (right/left discrimination) and Group 2 (go/no-go discrimination)

Group 1
(right/left discrimination)

Training

Buzzer → Raise left leg
Metronome → Raise right leg

Testing

Metronome → Raised left leg
Buzzer → Raised right leg

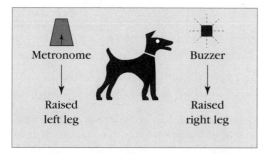

Group 2
(go/no-go discrimination)

Training

Buzzer → Raise leg (go)
Metronome → Do not raise leg (no go)

Testing

Metronome → Did not raise leg
Buzzer → Raised leg

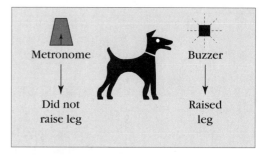

Figure 8.6 Diagram of the experiment by Dobrzecka, Szwejkowska, and Konorski (1966). Dogs were trained on a left/right or go/no-go task (Groups 1 and 2, respectively) with auditory stimuli that differed both in location (in front or in back of the animals) and in quality (the sound of a buzzer or a metronome). During testing, the location of the two sounds was reversed. The results showed that the left/right differential response was controlled mainly by the location of the sounds, whereas the go/no-go differential response was controlled mainly by the quality of the sounds.

When the metronome was sounded, dogs in this group were reinforced for raising the right leg; when the buzzer was sounded, they were reinforced for raising the left leg. Thus, the location of the response (right/left) was important for reinforcement in this group.

Group 2 received training on a go/no-go task. In this case, the dogs had to raise the right leg when the buzzer sounded and not raise the leg when the metronome sounded. Thus, the quality of the response (go/no-go) rather than its location was important for reinforcement for this group.

What aspect of the auditory cues—quality or location—gained control over the instrumental behavior in the two groups? To answer this question, the dogs were tested with the positions of the metronome and buzzer reversed. During these tests, the buzzer was placed in front of the animals and the metronome behind them (see Figure 8.6). This manipulation produced very different results in the two groups.

Dogs trained on the right/left task (in which the location of the response was critical for reinforcement) had learned to respond mainly on the basis of the location of the auditory cues rather than their quality. The participants in Group 1 raised their right leg in response to sound from the front, regardless of whether the sound was made by the metronome or the buzzer. When the sound came from the back, they raised the left leg, again regardless of whether the sound was made by the metronome or the buzzer. Thus, the location of the sounds controlled their behavior much more than sound quality.

A contrasting outcome was observed in the animals trained on the go/no-go task. These dogs responded mainly on the basis of the quality of the sound rather than its location. They raised a leg in response to the buzzer regardless of whether the sound came from the front or the back, and they did not raise a leg when the metronome was sounded, again irrespective of the location of the metronome.

These results indicate that responses that are differentiated by location (right/left) are more likely to come under the control of the spatial feature of auditory cues. By contrast, responses that are differentiated by quality (go/no-go) are more likely to come under the control of the quality of auditory cues (see also Bowe, Miller, & Green, 1987; Williams, Butler, & Overmier, 1990). Although some suggestions have been made for why such relations exist (see Neill & Harrison, 1987), a definitive explanation has yet to be found. However, the research to date clearly indicates that the activities required for reinforcement can determine which stimulus features come to control the instrumental behavior.

Stimulus Elements versus Configural Cues in Compound Stimuli

In the discussion so far of control of behavior by various stimulus elements, I have assumed that organisms treat stimulus elements as distinct and separate events. This is called the **stimulus-element approach.** The assumption of this approach is that stimulus elements retain their individuality in their control of behavior, even if they are presented simultaneously as a compound stimulus. An important alternative theoretical approach assumes that organisms treat a compound stimulus as an integral whole that is not divided into parts or elements. This is called the **configural-cue approach.**

According to the configural-cue approach, individuals respond to a compound stimulus in terms of the unique configuration of its elements. It is assumed that the elements are not treated as separate entities. In fact, they may not even be identifiable in the stimulus compound. Stimulus elements are important not because of their individuality but because of the way they contribute to the entire configuration of stimulation provided by the compound.

The concept of a configural cue may be illustrated by considering the sound made by a symphony orchestra. The orchestral sound originates from the sounds of the individual instruments. However, the sound of the entire orchestra is very different from the sound of any of the individual instruments, some of which are difficult to identify when the entire orchestra is playing. We primarily hear the configuration of the sounds made by the individual instruments.

J. M. Pearce

The configural-cue approach to the analysis of control by compound stimuli has enjoyed considerable success (Pearce, 1987, 1994b). Under certain conditions, animals clearly seem to respond to compound stimuli in terms of the configuration of the elements that make up the compound (Kehoe, 1986; Kehoe & Graham, 1988; Lachnit & Kimmel, 1993; Pearce & Redhead, 1993; Pearce & Wilson, 1990a, 1990b; Redhead & Pearce, 1995a, 1995b).

Let us consider, for example, how a configural approach might explain the phenomenon of overshadowing (see Table 8.1). An overshadowing experiment involves two groups of animals and two stimulus elements, one of low intensity (*a*) and the other of high intensity (*B*). For the overshadowing group, the two stimuli are pre-

TABLE 8.1	**CONFIGURAL EXPLANATION OF OVERSHADOWING**		
GROUP	TRAINING STIMULI	TEST STIMULUS	GENERALIZATION FROM TRAINING TO TEST
Overshadowing group	aB	a	Decrement
Control group	a	a	No decrement

sented together (aB) as a compound cue and paired with reinforcement during conditioning. For the control group, only the low-intensity stimulus (a) is presented during conditioning. Tests are then conducted with the weaker stimulus element (a) for each group, and less responding occurs to a in the overshadowing group than in the control group. This outcome indicates that the presence of B during conditioning disrupted control of behavior by the weaker stimulus a for the overshadowing group.

According to the configural-cue approach, overshadowing reflects different degrees of generalization decrement from training to testing for the overshadowing and the control groups (Pearce, 1987). There is no generalization decrement for the control group when it is tested with the weak stimulus a because that is the same as the stimulus it received during conditioning. In contrast, considerable generalization decrement occurs when the overshadowing group is tested with stimulus a after conditioning with the compound aB. For the overshadowing group, responding becomes conditioned to the aB compound, which is very different from a presented during testing. Therefore, responding conditioned to aB suffers considerable generalization decrement. This greater generalization decrement is assumed to be responsible for the overshadowing effect according to the configural-cue approach.

Despite its considerable successes, the configural-cue approach cannot explain all of the results of compound-stimulus experiments. For example, the configural-cue approach cannot explain findings, described earlier, indicating that stimulus control is a function of the type of reinforcement used and the response required. The most prudent conclusion at this point is that organisms respond to stimulus compounds both in terms of the stimulus elements that make up the compound and in terms of unique stimulus configurations created by the stimulus elements. Under certain circumstances elemental control may predominate; under other conditions control by configural features of stimulus compounds may predominate; or elemental and configural control may coexist.

LEARNING FACTORS IN STIMULUS CONTROL

In the preceding section, I described how the stimulus control of instrumental behavior is influenced by sensory capacity and orientation, the presence of more easily conditioned stimuli, the behavior system (feeding or defense) activated by the reinforcer, and the response required for reinforcement. These stimulus and response factors are not determined by the organism's previous experiences but set the preconditions for how animals learn about the environmental stimuli they encounter. I next will turn to a discussion of how the acquisition of stimulus control is influenced by experience. The fact that certain stimuli can be perceived does not ensure that those stimuli will come to control behavior. Whether or not certain stimuli come to control behavior often depends on what the organism has learned about those stimuli.

The suggestion that experience with stimuli may determine the extent to which those stimuli come to control behavior originated in efforts to explain the phenomenon of stimulus generalization. As I noted earlier, stimulus generalization refers to the fact that a response conditioned to one stimulus will also occur when other stimuli that are similar to the original cue are presented. Pavlov suggested that stimulus generalization occurs because learning about a CS becomes transferred to other stimuli on the basis of the physical similarity of the test stimuli to the CS.

In a spirited attack, Lashley and Wade (1946) took exception to Pavlov's proposal. They rejected the idea that stimulus generalization reflects the transfer of learning. Rather, they suggested that stimulus generalization reflects the *absence* of learning. In particular, they proposed that stimulus generalization occurs if animals have not learned to distinguish differences among the stimuli. Lashley and Wade proposed that animals have to learn to treat stimuli as different from one another. Thus, in contrast to Pavlov, Lashley and Wade considered the shape of a stimulus generalization gradient to be determined primarily by the organism's previous learning experiences rather than by the physical properties of the stimuli tested.

Stimulus Discrimination Training

As it has turned out, Lashley and Wade identified a powerful determinant of stimulus control. Numerous studies have shown that stimulus control can be dramatically altered by learning experiences. Perhaps the most powerful procedure for bringing behavior under the control of a stimulus is stimulus discrimination training. In a **stimulus discrimination procedure,** the participants are exposed to at least two different stimuli—let us say a red and a green light. However, reinforcement for performing the instrumental response is available only in the presence of one of the colors. For example, the participants could be reinforced for responding on trials when the red light is on but not when the green light is on. In this procedure, diagrammed in Figure 8.7, the red light signals the availability of reinforcement for responding. The green light signals that responding will not be reinforced. The stimulus that signals the availability of reinforcement is often called the S+ or S^D (pronounced "ess dee"). By contrast, the stimulus that signals the lack of reinforcement is often called the S− or S^Δ (pronounced "ess delta").

With sufficient exposure to a discrimination procedure, participants will come to respond whenever the S+ is presented and withhold responding whenever the S− is presented. The acquisition of this pattern of responding is illustrated in the cumulative record in Figure 8.7. Initially, organisms respond similarly in the presence of the S+ and the S−. However, as training progresses, responding in the presence of the S+ persists, and responding in the presence of the S− declines. The emergence of greater responding to the S+ than to the S− indicates differential responding to these stimuli. Thus, *stimulus discrimination procedures establish control by the stimuli that signal when reinforcement is and is not available.* Once the S+ and S− have gained control over the organism's behavior, they are called **discriminative stimuli.** The S+ is a discriminative stimulus for performing the instrumental response, and the S− is a discriminative stimulus for not performing the response.

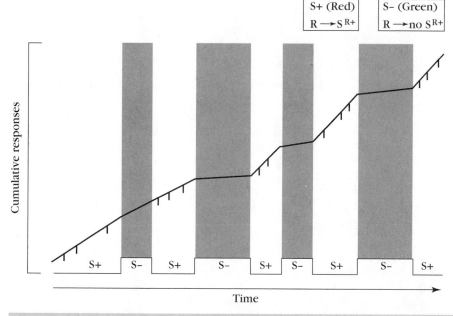

Figure 8.7 Procedure and hypothetical results (presented as a cumulative record) of stimulus discrimination training. Responding is reinforced on a variable interval schedule in the presence of the S+ (a red light) and is not reinforced in the presence of the S– (a green light). Differential responding gradually develops to the two stimuli. (Hatch marks on the cumulative record indicate reinforcements.)

The procedure diagrammed in Figure 8.7 is the standard procedure for stimulus discrimination training in instrumental conditioning. Stimulus discriminations can be also established with the use of classical conditioning procedures. In this case one stimulus (the CS+) is paired with the US and another (the CS–) is presented in the absence of the US. With repeated pairings of the CS+ with the US, and presentations of the CS– by itself, conditioned responding comes to be elicited by the CS+ but not by the CS–. (I discussed this procedure in Chapter 3; see Figure 3.9.)

Instrumental stimulus discrimination procedures are different from classical conditioning procedures only in that the reinforcer is presented contingent on responding during the S+. Responding is not required for pairings of the CS+ with the US in classical conditioning procedures. Unlike a CS+, an S+ does not signal that the reinforcer will inevitably occur. Rather, the S+ indicates that performance of the instrumental response will be reinforced.

The stimulus discrimination procedure shown in Figure 8.7 is a special case of a **multiple schedule of reinforcement.** In a multiple schedule, different schedules of reinforcement are in effect in the presence of different stimuli. For example, a VI schedule of reinforcement may be in effect when a light is turned on, and an FR schedule may be in effect when a tone is presented. With sufficient exposure to such a procedure, the pattern of responding during each stimulus will correspond to the schedule of reinforcement in effect during that stimulus. The participants will show a steady rate of responding during the VI stimulus and a stop-run pattern during the FR stimulus.

Stimulus discrimination and multiple schedules are common outside the laboratory. Nearly all reinforcement schedules that exist outside the laboratory are in effect only in the presence of particular stimuli. Playing a game yields reinforcement only in the presence of enjoyable or challenging partners. Driving rapidly is reinforced when you are on the highway but not when you are on a crowded city street. Loud and boisterous discussions with your friends are reinforced at a party. The same type of behavior is not reinforced during a sermon in church. Eating with your fingers is reinforced when you are on a picnic but not when you are in a fine restaurant. Daily activities typically consist of going from one situation to another (to the kitchen to get breakfast, to the bus stop, to your office, to the grocery store, and so on), and each situation involves a different schedule of reinforcement.

Effects of Discrimination Training on Stimulus Control

Discrimination training brings the instrumental response under the control of the S+ and S–. How precise is the control that S+ acquires over the instrumental behavior, and what factors determine the precision of the stimulus control that is achieved? To answer such questions, it is not enough to note differential responding to S+ versus S–. The researcher must also find out how steep the generalization gradient is when the participants are tested with stimuli that systematically vary from the S+ along some stimulus dimension. Furthermore, which aspect of the discrimination training procedure is responsible for the type of stimulus generalization gradient that is obtained must be determined. These issues were first addressed in classic experiments by Jenkins and Harrison (1960, 1962).

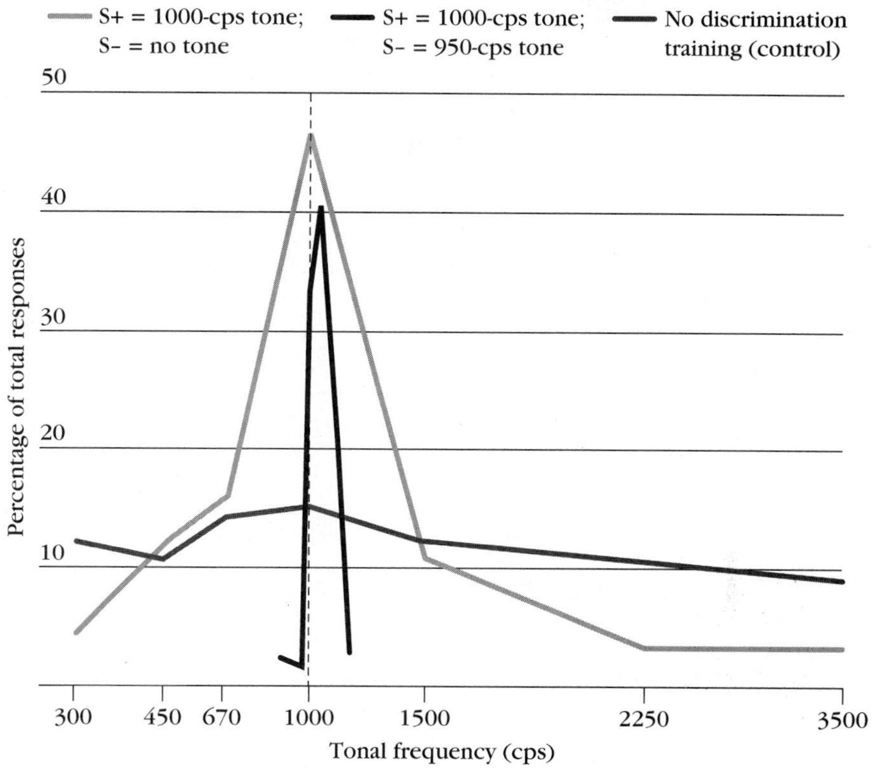

Figure 8.8 Generalization gradients of response to tones of different frequencies after various types of training. One group received discrimination training in which a 1000-cps tone served as the S+, and the absence of tones served as the S−. Another group received training in which a 1000-cps tone served as the S+, and a 950-cps tone served as the S−. The control group did not receive discrimination training before the generalization test. (From Jenkins & Harrison, 1960; Jenkins & Harrison, 1962.)

Jenkins and Harrison investigated how auditory stimuli that differed in pitch came to control the pecking behavior of pigeons reinforced with food. They measured how pigeons responded to tones of various frequencies after three types of training procedures. One group of birds was reinforced for pecking in the presence of a 1000-cps tone and received no reinforcement when the tone was off. Therefore, for these pigeons the 1000-cps tone served as the S+, and the absence of tones served as the S−.

A second group also received discrimination training. The 1000-cps tone again served as the S+. However, for the second group the S− was a 950-cps tone. Thus, these pigeons were reinforced for pecking whenever the 1000-cps tone was presented and were not reinforced whenever the 950-cps tone was presented. The third group of pigeons served as a control group and did not receive discrimination training. The 1000-cps tone was continuously turned on for these animals, and they could always receive reinforcement for pecking in the experimental chamber.

Upon completion of the preceding training procedures, each pigeon was tested for pecking in the presence of tones of various frequencies to see how precisely pecking was controlled by pitch. Figure 8.8 shows the generalization gradients that were obtained. The control group, which had not received discrimination training, responded nearly equally in the presence of all the test stimuli: the pitch of the tones did not control behavior. Each of the other two training procedures produced control over pecking by the frequency of the tones. The steepest generalization gradient, and hence the strongest stimulus control, was observed in animals that were trained with the 1000-cps tone as S+ and the 950-cps tone as S−. Pigeons that previously received

233

discrimination training between the 1000-cps tone (S+) and the absence of tones (S–) showed an intermediate degree of stimulus control by tonal frequency.

The results of the Jenkins and Harrison experiment suggest two important conclusions. First, they show that discrimination training increases the stimulus control of instrumental behavior. Second, a particular stimulus dimension (such as tonal frequency) is most likely to gain control over responding if the S+ and S– differ along that stimulus dimension. The most precise control by tonal frequency was observed after discrimination training in which the S+ was a tone of one frequency (1000 cps) and the S– was a tone of another frequency (950 cps). Discrimination training did not produce as strong control by pitch if the S+ was a 1000-cps tone and the S– was the absence of tones. In this case, the pigeons learned a discrimination between the presence and absence of the 1000-cps tone and could have been responding in part on the basis of the loudness or timbre of the tone in addition to its frequency. (For further discussion of discrimination training and stimulus control, see Balsam, 1988.)

Range of Possible Discriminative Stimuli

Discrimination procedures can be used to bring an organism's instrumental behavior under the control of a wide variety of stimuli. D'Amato and Salmon (1982), for example, used two different tunes as discriminative stimuli for rats and monkeys. Porter and Neuringer (1984) showed that pigeons are able to discriminate the music of Bach from music by Stravinsky and generalize this discrimination to music of other composers from the same periods in musical history. In another study, pigeons learned to distinguish color slides of paintings by Monet from paintings by Picasso (Watanabe, Sakamoto, & Wakita, 1995). Discrimination procedures also can be based on internal cues related to level of hunger (Davidson, Flynn, & Jarrard, 1992) or physiological states created by drugs such as caffeine, pentobarbital, and methamphetamine (Lamb & Henningfield, 1994; Silverman, Mumford, & Griffiths, 1994; Snodgrass & McMillan, 1996).

The fact that stimulus discrimination procedures can be used to bring behavior under the control of a wide variety of stimuli makes these procedures powerful tools for the investigation of how animals process information. We will see some impressive fruits of this research in the discussions of animal cognition in Chapters 11 and 12. Studies of discrimination learning have also yielded some unexpected information about animal social behavior.

In several bird and mammalian species, sexually inexperienced males fail to discriminate between males and females of their own species. Male ruffed grouse, for example, have been observed to respond similarly to male and female grouse (Allen, 1934), and young male, red-winged blackbirds have been observed to copulate with taxidermic models of various bird species, seemingly unaware of the sex of the models (Noble & Vogt, 1935). In more recent research, male Japanese quail have been observed to copulate with both male and female quail, also apparently unaware of the sex of the other birds (for example, Wilson & Bermant, 1972).

Laboratory research has shown that male quail can learn to distinguish the sex of other quail if they receive discrimination training in which exposure to females is paired with sexual reinforcement (in the form of copulatory opportunity) and exposure to males is provided without reinforcement (Domjan & Ravert, 1991; Nash, Domjan, & Askins, 1989). Thus, if female quail serve as the S+, and male quail serve as the S– for sexual reinforcement, males learn to discriminate stimulus females from stimulus males and come to prefer the company of females. Interestingly, learning to discriminate males from females occurs in much the same way as other, more conventional forms of discrimination learning. The critical factor is differential reinforcement of the female and male cues (see also Nash & Domjan, 1991).

What Is Learned in Discrimination Training?

As we have seen, if an instrumental response is reinforced in the presence of one stimulus (S+) and not in the presence of another (S–), these stimuli will come to control occurrences of the instrumental behavior. Because of the profound effect that discrimination training has on stimulus control, investigators have been interested in what is learned during discrimination training.

Consider the following relatively simple situation: Responses are reinforced whenever a red light is turned on (S+) and not reinforced whenever a loud tone is presented (S–). What strategies could be used to make sure that most responses were reinforced in this situation? One possibility is to learn to respond whenever the S+ is present and not learn anything about the S–. If an organism adopted this strategy ("Respond only when S+ is present"), it would end up responding much more to S+ than to S– and could obtain all the available reinforcers. Another possibility is to learn to suppress responding during S– but not learn anything about S+. This would constitute following the rule "Suppress responding only when S– is present." This strategy would also lead to more responding during S+ than S–. A third possibility is to learn the significance of both S+ and S–, to learn both to respond to S+ and to suppress responding to S–.

Spence's Theory of Discrimination Learning. One of the first and most influential theories of discrimination learning was proposed by Kenneth Spence in 1936. Spence advocated the last of the possibilities I have just described. According to his theory, reinforcement of a response in the presence of the S+ conditions excitatory properties to the S+ that encourage responding to S+. By contrast, nonreinforcement of responding during presentations of S– is assumed to condition inhibitory properties to S– that serve to suppress the instrumental behavior on future presentations of S–. Differential responding to S+ and S– is assumed to reflect both the excitation of responding to S+ and inhibition of responding to S–.

How can the excitation-inhibition theory of discrimination learning be experimentally evaluated? As I have noted, mere observation that organisms respond more to S+ than to S– is not sufficient to prove that they have learned something about both of these stimuli. More sophisticated experimental tests are required. One possibility is to use stimulus generalization gradients.

If an excitatory tendency has become conditioned to S+, then stimuli that increasingly differ from S+ should be progressively less effective in evoking the instrumental response. In other words, a steep generalization gradient should be observed, with the greatest amount of responding occurring to S+. Such an outcome is called an **excitatory stimulus generalization gradient.** Conversely, if an inhibitory tendency has become conditioned to S–, then stimuli that increasingly differ from S– should be progressively less effective in inhibiting the instrumental response. Such an outcome is called an **inhibitory stimulus generalization gradient.**

Behavioral techniques were not sufficiently sophisticated when Spence proposed his theory to allow direct observation of the excitatory and inhibitory generalization gradients his theory assumed. However, experimental tests conducted decades later proved that his ideas were substantially correct. In a landmark experiment, two groups of pigeons received discrimination training with visual stimuli before tests of stimulus generalization (Honig, Boneau, Burstein, & Pennypacker, 1963). One group was reinforced for pecking when the response key was illuminated by a white light that had a black vertical bar superimposed on it (S+) and was not reinforced when the white light was presented without the vertical bar (S–).(See Figure 8.9.) The second group of animals received the same type of discrimination training; however, for them the S+ and S– stimuli were reversed. The black vertical bar served as the S–, and the white key without the bar served as the S+. After both groups had learned to respond much more to S+ than to S–, tests of stimulus generalization were conducted to see how much control the vertical bar had gained over the instrumental behavior in the two groups. The test stimuli consisted of the black bar on a white background, with the bar tilted at various angles away from the vertical position during the test trials.

The results of the experiment are summarized in Figure 8.9. Let us first consider the outcome for Group 1. Recall that for this group the vertical bar had served as the S+ during discrimination training. Therefore, these birds came to respond in the presence of the vertical bar. During the generalization test, the highest rate of responding occurred when the bar was presented in the original vertical position, and progressively less responding was observed when the bar was tilted more and more away from the vertical. These results indicate that the position of the vertical bar had gained control over the pecking behavior when the vertical bar served as S+.

Let us consider next the results for Group 2. For these pigeons, the vertical bar had served as the S– during discrimination training. At the end of discrimination training, these birds did not peck when the vertical bar was projected on the response key. Results of the generalization test indicated that this failure to respond to the vertical bar was due to active inhibition of the pecking behavior in response to the position of the vertical bar. As the bar was tilted away from the original vertical position, progressively more pecking occurred. Stimuli that were increasingly different from the original S– produced progressively less inhibition of the pecking behavior.

This experiment shows that discrimination training can produce both excitatory conditioning to S+ and inhibitory conditioning to S–. An excitatory stimulus generalization gradient around the vertical bar was obtained when the bar served as the S+, and an inhibitory gradient of generalization around the vertical bar was obtained when the bar served as the S–. The excitatory gradient had an inverted-U shape, with greatest responding occurring to the original S+. The inhibitory gradient had the opposite shape, with the least responding occurring to the original S–. The fact that gradients of excitation and inhibition can occur around S+ and S– provides strong support for Spence's theory of discrimination learning.

The choice of the stimuli that served as S+ and S– was very important for the success of this experiment. Consider, for example, Group 2, which received the vertical bar on a white background as the S– and the white background without a bar as the S+. Responding in the inhibitory generalization gradient increased as the bar was tilted away from vertical. This outcome could not be explained by claiming that tilting the black bar made the test stimuli more similar to the S+. Changing the orientation of the black bar does not make the bar stimulus more or less similar to the white background alone (the S+). The bar stimuli are qualitatively different from the background alone. As I will discuss in the next section, different results occur if the S+ and S– stimuli differ quantitatively rather than qualitatively.

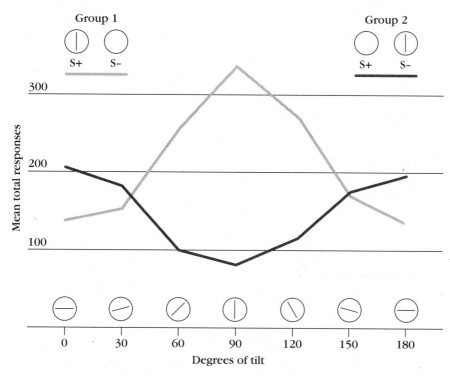

Figure 8.9 Stimulus generalization gradients for line-tilt stimuli in two groups of pigeons after discrimination training. For Group 1 a vertical black bar on a white background served as the S+, and the white light without the bar served as the S–. For Group 2 the functions of the stimuli were reversed. (From Honig et al., 1963.)

Intradimensional Discrimination Training and the Peak-Shift Effect. So far I have discussed the general characteristics of stimulus discrimination training that can be found with any combination of stimuli serving as the S+ and the S–. In addition to the effects already described, certain special problems and phenomena arise if the S+ and S– differ from each other in only one stimulus characteristic. Stimulus features such as color, brightness, and pitch are called *stimulus dimensions*. A training procedure in which the S+ and S– differ only in terms of one stimulus feature is called an **intradimensional discrimination.**

Consider, for example, discrimination training in which the S+ and S– are identical in every respect except color. What effect will the similarity in the colors of S+ and S– have on the stimulus control of the instrumental behavior? Will the rate of response to S+ be determined mainly by the availability of reinforcement in the presence of S+, or will the rate of response to S+ also be influenced by how similar the color of S+ is to the color of S–?

In an important experiment, Hanson (1959) investigated the effects of intradimensional discrimination training on the extent to which various colors controlled the pecking behavior of pigeons. All the participants in the experiment were reinforced for pecking in the presence of a light whose wavelength was 550 nm. Thus, the S+ was the same for all animals (see Figure 8.10). The groups differed in how similar the S– was to the S+. One group, for example, received discrimination training in which the S– was a color of 590-nm wavelength. For another group the S– was much more similar to the S+; the wavelength of the S– was 555 nm, only 5 nm away from the S+. The performance of these pigeons was compared with the behavior of a control group that did not receive discrimination training but was reinforced for pecking in the presence of the 550-nm stimulus.

237

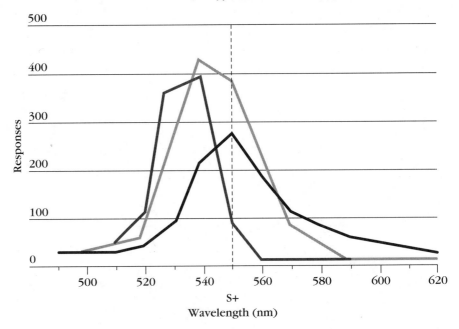

Figure 8.10 Effects of intradimensional discrimination training on stimulus control. All three groups of pigeons were reinforced for pecking in the presence of a 550-nm light (S+). One group received discrimination training in which the S– was a 590-nm light. Another group received discrimination training in which the S– was a 555-nm light. The third group served as a control and did not receive discrimination training before the test for stimulus generalization. (From "Effects of Discrimination Training on Stimulus Generalization" by H. M. Hanson, *Journal of Experimental Psychology,* 1959, *58,* pp. 321–333.)

After their different training experiences, all of the birds were tested for their rate of pecking in the presence of stimuli of various colors. The results are shown in Figure 8.10. Let us consider first the performance of the control group. These animals showed the highest rate of response to the S+ stimulus, and progressively lower rates of responding occurred as the pigeons were tested with stimuli increasingly different from the S+. Thus, the control group showed the usual excitatory stimulus generalization gradient around the S+.

Different results were obtained after discrimination training with the 590-nm color as S–. These pigeons also responded at high rates to the 550-nm color that had served as the S+. However, the birds showed much more generalization of the pecking response to the 540-nm color. In fact, their rate of response was slightly higher to the 540-nm color than to the original 550-nm S+. This shift of the peak responding away from the original S+ was even more dramatic after discrimination training with the 555-nm color as S–. These birds showed much lower rates of responding to the original S+ (550 nm) than either of the other two groups. Furthermore, their highest response rates occurred to colors of 540- and 530-nm wavelength. This shift of the peak of the generalization gradient away from the original S+ is remarkable because in the earlier phase of discrimination training, responding was never reinforced in the presence of the 540-nm or 530-nm stimuli. The highest rates of pecking occurred to stimuli that had never even been presented during the original training.

The shift of the peak of the generalization gradient away from the original S+ is called the **peak-shift** phenomenon. The results of Hanson's experiment indicate that the peak-shift effect occurs following intradimensional discrimination training. A shift in the peak of the generalization gradient did not occur in the control group, which had not received discrimination training. The peak of the generalization gradient was shifted away from S+ in a direction opposite the stimulus that was used as the S− in the discrimination procedure.

The peak-shift effect was a function of the similarity of the S− to the S+ used in discrimination training. The greatest shift in peak responding occurred after training in which the S− was very similar to the S+ (555 nm and 550 nm, respectively). Less of a peak shift occurred after discrimination training with more widely different colors (590 nm compared with 550 nm). It is interesting to note that a small peak-shift effect is also evident in Figure 8.8 for pigeons that received discrimination training with the 1000-cps tone as S+ and the 950-cps tone as S−.

The peak-shift effect can result from any intradimensional discrimination, not just pitch and color. The S+ and S− may be lines of different orientations, tones of different loudness, and squares of different size. (For examples of the peak-shift effect, see Dougherty & Lewis, 1991; Moye & Thomas, 1982; Weiss & Schindler, 1981; Weiss & Weissman, 1992.)

Spence's Explanation of Peak-Shift. The peak-shift effect is remarkable because it shows that the only stimulus in whose presence responding is reinforced (the S+) is not necessarily the stimulus that evokes the highest rate of responding. How can this be? In an experiment I described earlier, Honig et al. (1963) reported an excitatory stimulus generalization gradient that showed peak responding at S+ (see Figure 8.9). That seems inconsistent with the peak-shift phenomenon. How can peak shift be explained in terms of the excitatory and inhibitory gradients that result from discrimination training? In an ingenious analysis, Spence (1937) suggested that excitatory and inhibitory gradients may in fact produce the peak-shift phenomenon. His analysis is particularly remarkable because it was proposed more than 20 years before the peak-shift effect and gradients of excitation and inhibition were experimentally demonstrated.

Spence assumed that intradimensional discrimination training produces excitatory and inhibitory stimulus generalization gradients centered at S+ and S−, respectively, in much the same way as other types of discrimination training. However, because the S+ and S− are similar in intradimensional discrimination tasks (both being colors, for example), the generalization gradients of excitation and inhibition are assumed to overlap. Responding to a particular test stimulus reflects generalized excitation to that stimulus minus generalized inhibition to that stimulus. By subtracting the assumed gradient of inhibition centered at S− from the assumed gradient of excitation centered at S+, Spence was able to predict the phenomenon of peak shift under certain circumstances.

Spence's explanation of the peak-shift effect is illustrated in Figure 8.11. S+, S−, and S1, S2, S3, and S4 represent different colors of light, as in Figure 8.10. The dashed lines represent the excitatory and inhibitory generalization gradients that will presumably develop around the S+ and S− stimuli. Notice that because S+ and S− are close together on the stimulus dimension, the excitatory and inhibitory gradients overlap a great deal. To predict the level of response that will occur to

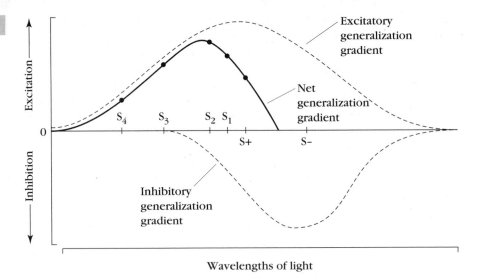

Figure 8.11 Spence's explanation of the peak-shift effect. Excitatory and inhibitory stimulus generalization gradients (dashed curves) are assumed to become established around S+ and S–, respectively. The organism's behavior is assumed to reflect the net generalization gradient. The net gradient is calculated by subtracting the level of inhibition that is assumed to be generalized to a particular stimulus from the level of excitation that is assumed to be generalized to that stimulus.

various wavelengths of light, the researcher simply has to subtract the level of generalized inhibition to a particular stimulus from the level of generalized excitation to that stimulus.

The inhibitory gradient in Figure 8.11 does not extend to stimuli S3 and S4. Therefore, no generalized inhibition is subtracted from the generalized excitation for these test stimuli. The greatest amount of inhibition is subtracted from the generalized excitatory strength of stimulus S–, with lesser amounts subtracted from the S+ and test stimuli S1 and S2. The dots connected with a solid line in Figure 8.11 represent the net excitatory strength of S–, S+, and test stimuli S1 through S4.

The net excitatory gradient in Figure 8.11 is a prediction of the organism's behavior. This prediction is consistent with the peak-shift effect. Note that the peak of the net generalization gradient in Figure 8.11 is not at the S+ but is displaced away from S+ in a direction opposite S–. This is precisely what is observed in peak-shift experiments (see Figure 8.10).

Predictions from Spence's model depend on the exact shape of the excitatory and inhibitory gradients around S+ and S–, respectively. The shift in the peak of the net excitatory gradient away from S+ depends on the inhibitory generalization gradient extending to S+. If the S+ and S– stimuli are too far apart for this to happen (or the inhibitory gradient is not broad enough to extend to S+), the excitatory potential of S+ will not be reduced by generalized inhibition, and the peak-shift effect will not be observed.

As mentioned previously, experimental techniques were unavailable to obtain direct evidence of excitatory and inhibitory gradients at the time Spence proposed his model. However, more recent research conducted with modern operant conditioning techniques has provided impressive evidence for the types of generalization gradients Spence assumed served as the basis for peak-shift (see Hearst, 1968, 1969; Klein & Rilling, 1974; Marsh, 1972).

Alternative Accounts of Peak-Shift. As I noted earlier, studies of stimulus control can tell us a great deal about how animals (and people) view the world. An important question that has been a source of debate for decades is whether we view stimuli in terms of their individual and absolute properties or in terms of their relation to other stimuli that we experience (for example, Köhler, 1939). Evidence consistent with each of these approaches to the analysis of stimulus control is available, suggesting that both types of mechanisms are involved in how organisms respond (for example, Hulse, Page, & Braaten, 1990).

Spence's model of discrimination learning is an absolute stimulus learning model. It predicts behavior based on the net excitatory properties of individual stimuli. An alternative approach assumes that organisms learn to respond to a stimulus based on the relation of that stimulus to other cues in the situation. An interesting prediction of this approach is that the shape of a generalization gradient will change as a function of the range of test stimuli that are presented during the generalization test session. These and other predictions of the relational approach have been confirmed in studies with human participants (see Thomas, 1993).

M. E. Rilling

Stimulus Equivalence Training

The peak-shift effect is a curious and counterintuitive outcome of intradimensional discrimination training. However, as the studies of Jenkins and Harrison showed (see Figure 8.8), even with this effect, discrimination training dramatically increases the stimulus control of behavior. It limits the generalization of behavior to other cues and increases the steepness of generalization gradients. This raises the question, Are there learning procedures that have the opposite effect? Are there learning procedures that increase the generalization of behavior? How might such procedures be constructed?

In a discrimination procedure, stimuli are treated differently; they have different consequences. One stimulus is associated with reinforcement, whereas another is associated with nonreinforcement. The differential treatment or significance of the stimuli leads organisms to respond to the stimuli as distinct from each other. What would happen if two different stimuli were treated in the same or equivalent fashion? Would such a procedure lead organisms to respond to the stimuli as being similar or equivalent? The answer seems to be yes. Just as discrimination training encourages differential responding, equivalence training appears to encourage generalized responding or **stimulus equivalence.**

Several approaches are available to promote generalization rather than discrimination among stimuli. In Chapter 12 I will describe research on perceptual concept learning that involves learning to treat various physically different instances of a concept in the same manner. For example, pigeons can be trained to respond in a similar fashion to different photographs, all of which include water in some form (ocean, lake, puddle, stream) (Herrnstein, Loveland, & Cable, 1976). The basic training strategy is to reinforce the same response (pecking a response key) in the presence of various pictures containing water, and not to reinforce that response when photographs without water appear. Herrnstein et al. trained such a discrimination using 500–700 photographs of various scenes in New England. Once the pigeons learned the water/no-water discrimination, their behavior generalized to novel photographs that had not been presented during training. (For additional discussion of perceptual concept learning, see Chapter 12.)

Investigators have also explored the possibility that functional equivalence between two different stimuli might be established by linking each of the distinct cues with a common third stimulus. In an experiment by Honey and Hall (1989), for example, rats first received presentations of two different auditory cues, a noise and a clicker. For one group of animals, both the noise and the clicker were paired with food. The common food outcome was expected to create an equivalence between the noise and clicker stimuli. The control group also received presentations of the noise and the clicker, but in this case only the clicker was paired with food. Both groups then had the noise paired with mild foot-shock, resulting in the conditioning of fear to the noise. The investigators were interested in the extent to which this conditioned fear of the noise would generalize to the clicker. Significantly more generalization occurred in the equivalence-trained animals than in the control group. The equivalence-trained animals were more apt to treat the clicker and noise similarly than the control group. (For additional research along these lines, see Bonardi, Rey, Richmond, & Hall, 1993; Hall, 1991; Hall, Ray, & Bonardi, 1993; Honey & Hall, 1991.)

Perhaps the most extensively used technique for the study of equivalence training involves complicated versions of the matching to sample procedure (see Sidman, 1990, 1994; Sidman & Tailby, 1982). I will describe the matching to sample procedure in Chapter 11.

CONTEXTUAL CUES AND CONDITIONAL RELATIONS

So far I have been discussing the control of behavior by discrete stimuli such as a tone or a light, presented individually or in combination. A stimulus is said to be discrete if it is presented for a brief period and has a clear beginning and end. The use of discrete stimuli in studies of stimulus control has its roots in reflexology. In studies of reflexes, a discrete stimulus (a puff of air, for example) is employed to elicit a specific response (an eyeblink). As we have seen, instrumental behavior can also come under the control of discrete stimuli, especially when a discrimination training procedure is employed. For example, if a pigeon is reinforced for pecking a key when a vertical line is presented and not reinforced when a horizontal line appears, the pecking behavior will come to be controlled by the line-angle stimuli. Presentation of the S+ will stimulate pecking, in a manner analogous (but not identical) to the elicitation of an eyeblink response by a puff of air.

Control by Contextual Cues

Although studies with discrete stimuli have provided much information about the stimulus control of instrumental behavior, such studies do not tell the whole story. A more comprehensive analysis of the stimuli organisms experience during the course of instrumental conditioning indicates that discrete discriminative stimuli occur in the presence of background contextual cues. The contextual cues may be provided by visual, auditory, or olfactory cues of the room or place where the discrete discriminative stimuli are presented. Recent research indicates that contextual cues can provide an important additional source of control of learned behavior.

Several of the examples of stimulus control described at the beginning of this chapter involve the control of behavior by contextual cues. It is easier to concentrate on your studies when you are in the school library than when you are at home during holidays because of the contextual control of studying behavior by stimuli experienced in the library. Cheering at a football game but not during a church sermon also illustrates the power of contextual cues.

Contextual cues can come to control behavior in a variety of ways (see Balsam, 1985; Balsam & Tomie, 1985). For example, contextual cues can be used in place of discrete discriminative stimuli in a discrimination procedure and thereby come to function in much the same manner as discrete stimuli. Consider a procedure in which pigeons are placed in a noisy chamber on some occasions where they receive food periodically (the S+ context). At other times, the birds are placed in a quiet experimental chamber where they never receive food (the S– context). The pigeons will soon show increased locomotor behavior in the S+ chamber, which is indicative of the expectation of food. Such increased locomotion will not occur in the S– chamber. The S+ and S– contexts will become signals for food and the absence of food in the same way as other types of discriminative stimuli.

Do contextual cues come to control behavior when they do not serve as a signal for reinforcement—when they are truly "background" stimuli that the organism is not specifically required to pay attention to? This is a major issue in the stimulus control of instrumental behavior. Much work has been devoted to it, and the answer appears to be yes.

In one experiment, for example, Thomas, McKelvie, and Mah (1985) first trained pigeons on a line-orientation discrimination in which a vertical line (90°) served as the S+ and a horizontal line (0°) served as the S–. The pigeons were periodically reinforced with food for pecking on S+ trials and were never reinforced on S– trials. The training took place in a standard Skinner box (Context 1), but the availability of reinforcement was signaled by the line-orientation S+ and S– stimuli rather than by contextual cues.

After the discrimination was well learned, the contextual cues of the experimental chamber were changed by altering both the lighting and the type of noise in the chamber. In the presence of these new contextual cues (Context 2), the discrimination training contingencies were reversed. Now, the horizontal line (0°) served as the S+, and the vertical line (90°) served as the S–. Notice that the pigeons were not specifically required to pay attention to the contextual cues. They were simply required to learn a new discrimination problem in which the original S+ and S– stimuli were reversed. (They could have learned this new problem had the contextual cues not been changed.)

After the reversal training, the birds received generalization tests in which lines of various orientations between 0° and 90° were presented. One such generalization test was conducted in Context 1, and another was conducted in Context 2. The results of these tests are presented in Figure 8.12. Remarkably, the shape of the generalization gradient in each context was appropriate to the discrimination problem that was experienced in that context. Thus, in Context 1, the birds responded most to the 90° stimulus, which had served as the S+ in that context, and least to the 0° stimulus, which had served as the S–. The opposite pattern of results occurred in Context 2. Here, the pigeons responded most to the 0° stimulus and least to the 90° stimulus, appropriate to the reverse discrimination contingencies that had been in effect in Context 2.

These results clearly illustrate that contextual cues can come to control instrumental behavior. The results also illustrate that contextual stimulus control can occur

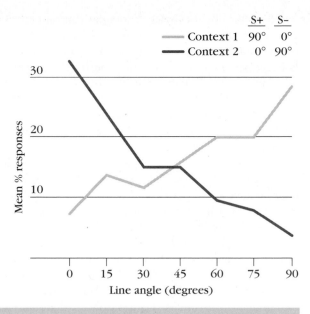

Figure 8.12 Generalization gradients obtained with various line-angle stimuli following training in two different contexts. In Context 1, the 90° stimulus served as the S+, and the 0° stimulus served as the S−. In Context 2, the 0° stimulus served as the S+, and the 90° stimulus served as the S−. (From "Context as a Conditional Cue in Operant Discrimination Reversal Learning" by D. R. Thomas, A. R. McKelvie, & W. L. Mah, *Journal of Experimental Psychology: Animal Behavior Processes,* 1985, *11,* pp. 317–330. Copyright © 1985 by the American Psychological Association. Reprinted by permission.)

without one context being more strongly associated with reinforcement than another. In both Context 1 and Context 2, the pigeons received discrimination training involving reinforced (S+) and nonreinforced (S−) trials. Therefore, one context was not a better signal for the availability of reinforcement than the other context. (See also Hall & Honey, 1989; Honey, Willis, & Hall, 1990; Swartzentruber, 1993.)

How did Context 1 and Context 2 come to produce different types of responding? Since one context was not a better signal for reinforcement than the other, direct associations of each context with food cannot explain the results. A different kind of mechanism must have been involved. One possibility is that each context activated a different memory. Context 1 activated the memory of reinforcement with 90° and nonreinforcement with 0°. In contrast, Context 2 activated the memory of reinforcement with 0° and nonreinforcement with 90°. Instead of being associated with a particular stimulus, each context appeared to be associated with a different S+/S− contingency. Such associations are called conditional relations.

Control by Conditional Relations

In much of the discussion so far, I have emphasized relations that involved just two events: a CS and US, or a response and a reinforcer. Relations between two events are called *binary relations.* Under certain circumstances, the nature of a binary relation is determined by a third event, called a **modulator.** In the experiment I described earlier by Thomas et al. (1985), each context was a modulator. Whether or not a particular line-angle stimulus was associated with reinforcement depended on which contextual cues were present. The relation of a modulator to the binary relation that it signals is called a **conditional relation.** Numerous recent experiments have indicated that animals can learn to use modulators to tell when a particular binary relation is in effect (see reviews by Holland, 1984, 1992; Swartzentruber, 1995).

We have already encountered some conditional relations without having identified them as such. One example is instrumental stimulus discrimination training. In an instrumental discrimination procedure, the organism is reinforced for responding in the presence of the S+ but is not reinforced in the presence of the S–. The discriminative stimuli S+ and S– are modulators that signal the relation between the response and the reinforcer. One response-reinforcer relation exists during S+ (positive reinforcement), and a different relation exists during S– (extinction). Thus, instrumental discrimination procedures in fact involve conditional control of the relation between the response and the reinforcer (Davidson, Aparicio, & Rescorla, 1988; Goodall & Mackintosh, 1987; Holman & Mackintosh, 1981; Jenkins, 1977; Skinner, 1938).

Conditional Control in Pavlovian Conditioning. The mechanisms involved in the control of behavior by conditional relations have been extensively investigated using Pavlovian conditioning procedures. The fundamental concept of conditional control is that one event signals the relation between two other events. Classical conditioning is typically conceived as involving a binary relation between a conditioned and an unconditioned stimulus. The CS may be brief illumination of a localized response key with an orange light, and the US may be food. A strong relation exists between the CS and US if the food is presented immediately after each occurrence of the CS but not at other times. How could conditional control over such a CS-US relation be established?

Establishing a conditional relation requires introducing a third event (the modulator) that indicates when presentation of the key light will end in food. For example, a noise stimulus could be used, in the presence of which the key light would be followed by food. In the absence of the noise stimulus, the key light would not end with food. This procedure is diagrammed in Figure 8.13. As in instrumental discrimination procedures, the participants receive both reinforced and nonreinforced trials. During reinforced trials, the noise stimulus is turned on for 15 seconds. Ten seconds later, the orange key-light CS is turned on for 5 seconds and is immediately followed by the food US. During nonreinforced trials, the noise stimulus is not presented. The key-light CS is simply turned on alone for 5 seconds without the food US.

The procedure I just described is similar to one that was investigated in a sign tracking experiment with pigeons by Rescorla, Durlach, and Grau (1985). A noise stimulus was used as the modulator on reinforced trials for half the pigeons. For the rest of the birds, a diffuse flashing light was used in place of the noise. The conditioned response that was measured was pecking the response key when it was illuminated with the orange key-light CS. Since pecking is not elicited by diffuse auditory or visual stimuli, the key-peck behavior could be interpreted as a response only to the orange key-light CS.

Reinforced trials	*Nonreinforced trials*
Noise	No noise
Key light → food	Key light → no food

Figure 8.13 Procedure for establishing conditional stimulus control in classical conditioning. On reinforced trials, a noise stimulus (the modulator) is presented, and a key-light CS is paired with food. On nonreinforced trials, the noise stimulus is absent, and the key-light CS is presented without food.

The results of the experiment are illustrated in Figure 8.14. The birds pecked the orange key much more when it was presented in compound with the modulator cue than when it was presented as an isolated element. Thus, the presence of the modulator facilitated responding to the key-light CS. It is important to keep in mind that the modulator itself did not elicit pecking because pigeons do not peck in response to diffuse auditory and visual stimuli. Rather, the modulator increased the ability of the orange key-light CS to elicit pecking. The diffuse modulator gained conditional control over the effectiveness of the key-light CS in eliciting the conditioned response. Just as a discriminative stimulus facilitates instrumental behavior, the modulator facilitated CS-elicited responding in the present study. (See also Parker, Serdikoff, Kaminski, & Critchfield, 1991.)

In instrumental discrimination procedures, modulators (S+ and S–) are called "discriminative stimuli." In Pavlovian conditioning, some investigators have called conditional control of responding **facilitation** because the modulator facilitates elicitation of the CR by the CS (Rescorla, 1985; Rescorla, Durlach, & Grau, 1985). In this terminology, the modulator is called a *facilitator*. Others have preferred to call conditional control in classical conditioning **occasion setting** because the modulator sets the occasion for pairings of the CS with the US (Holland, 1985; Ross, 1983; Ross & Holland, 1981). In this terminology, the modulator is called an *occasion setter*.

It is interesting to note that the procedure outlined in Figure 8.13 is the converse of the standard procedure for inhibitory conditioning (see Figure 3.8). To turn the procedure outlined in Figure 8.13 into one that will result in the conditioning of inhibitory properties to the noise, all the investigator has to do is to reverse the type of trial on which the noise is presented. Instead of being presented on reinforced trials, the noise would be presented on nonreinforced trials.

As I noted in Chapter 3, conditioned inhibition develops if a stimulus signals the absence of the US that is otherwise expected to occur. Presenting the noise stimulus

Figure 8.14 Acquisition of pecking to an orange key light in a study of conditional stimulus control of Pavlovian conditioned key pecking in pigeons. An orange key-light CS was paired with food in the presence of a modulator (compound trials) and was presented without food in the absence of the modulator (element trials). (From "Contextual Learning in Pavlovian Conditioning" by R. A. Rescorla, P. J. Durlach, & J. W. Grau. In P. Balsam & A. Tomie (Eds.), *Context and Learning*. Copyright © 1985, Lawrence Erlbaum and Associates. Reprinted by permission.)

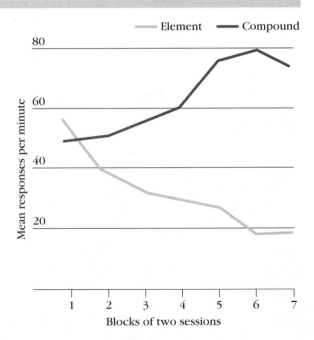

on nonreinforced trials would make the noise a signal for nonreinforcement of the key light and would make the noise a conditioned inhibitor. This illustrates that the procedure for inhibitory Pavlovian conditioning involves conditional relations, just as positive occasion-setting and facilitation procedures do. This argument also suggests that conditioned inhibition may be the conceptual opposite of facilitation rather than the opposite of conditioned excitation. In certain circumstances, this indeed appears to be the case (Rescorla, 1987, 1988a).

Distinction between Excitation and Modulation. Facilitation, or occasion setting, is an important aspect of classical conditioning not only because it illustrates that classical conditioning is subject to conditional control but also because it appears to involve different mechanisms of learning from those considered so far. As discussed in Chapter 4, during pairings of a CS with a US, organisms learn an association between the two events such that presentation of the CS comes to activate a representation of the US. I have referred to this kind of learning as the conditioning of excitation to the CS. A modulator, by contrast, has properties that are different from conditioned excitation.

Several lines of evidence indicate that modulators have unique properties that involve conditional relations rather than simple conditioned excitatory properties. In several studies, attempts to obtain evidence of conditioned excitatory properties of modulators failed to reveal such evidence (for example, Bouton & Swartzentruber, 1986; Puente, Cannon, Best, & Carrell, 1988). These experiments indicate that a stimulus can set the occasion for conditioned responding elicited by another cue without itself eliciting visible conditioned responding. Other studies have shown that conditioning simple excitatory properties to a stimulus does not make that stimulus function as a modulator (see Holland, 1985; Rescorla, 1985).

Additional evidence for a distinction between modulation and conditioned excitation is based on the effects of extinction procedures. As I noted in Chapter 3, a conditioned excitatory stimulus that is repeatedly presented by itself gradually loses the capacity to elicit the conditioned response; it undergoes extinction. The same procedure applied to a modulator has no effect. Once a stimulus has become established as a conditional cue signaling a CS-US relation, repeated presentations of the stimulus by itself do not reduce its ability to facilitate conditioned responding to the CS (for example, Holland, 1989a; Rescorla, 1985; Ross, 1983).

The difference in the effects of extinction on conditioned excitatory stimuli and modulators appear to be related to what is signaled. A conditioned excitatory stimulus signals the forthcoming presentation of the US. The absence of the US following presentation of the CS during extinction is a violation of the expectancy conditioned to the CS. Hence, the signal value of the CS has to be readjusted in extinction to bring it in line with the new reality. Such a readjustment is not required by an extinction procedure for a modulator stimulus.

A modulator signals a relation between a CS and a US. The absence of the US when the modulator is presented alone in extinction does not mean that the relation between the CS and the US has changed. The information signaled by a modulator is not proved incorrect by presenting the modulator by itself during extinction. Therefore, the ability of the modulator to promote responding elicited by another CS remains intact during extinction. However, a modulator's effectiveness is reduced if the CS-US relation signaled by the modulator is altered (Rescorla, 1986).

The last type of evidence to consider that supports the conclusion that modulation is distinct from conventional excitation has been obtained from transfer tests.

These tests were conducted to determine whether a stimulus that has been conditioned to set the occasion for responding to a particular target CS will also increase responding to other CSs. Evidence of successful transfer of the effects of a modulator to new target CSs has been obtained. Of particular interest is the type of properties transfer targets must have in order to be subject to the influence of a modulator. Transfer effects are most likely to be obtained if the new target stimuli had previously served as targets of other modulator stimuli (Holland, 1992; Swartzentruber, 1995). Little transfer is obtained if the new target previously served as a conditioned excitatory stimulus, or if it had a history of reinforcement and nonreinforcement but was not a part of a conditional relation. Such limitations on transfer effects would not occur if a modulator increased responding to a target stimulus because the excitatory properties of the modulator summated with the excitatory properties of the target. Therefore, limitations on transfer provide additional evidence that modulators operate by different mechanisms from conventional excitation.

Modulation versus Configural Conditioning.   Not all conditional discrimination procedures of the type illustrated in Figure 8.13 result in the learning of a conditional relation between the stimuli involved. On reinforced trials in this procedure, a compound stimulus consisting of the noise and the key light was presented. As I noted earlier, organisms can respond to a compound stimulus either in terms of the elements that make up the compound or in terms of the unique stimulus configuration produced by the elements. For the noise to signal that the key light will be paired with food, the noise and key light have to be treated as independent stimuli rather than as a combined configural cue. Thus, modulatory effects require responding to the stimulus compound as consisting of independent stimulus elements (Holland, 1992).

   To encourage organisms to treat stimulus compounds as consisting of independent elements, investigators have presented the elements one after the other, rather than simultaneously, in what is called a *serial compound*. On reinforced trials, the modulator is usually presented first, followed by the target CS and reinforcement. In many of his experiments on occasion setting, Holland, for example, has even inserted a 5-second gap between the modulator and the target CS. Such procedures discourage the perception of a stimulus configuration based on the modulator and the target CS. In numerous studies, Holland and his associates have found that organisms respond to conditional discriminations involving serial compounds in terms of conditional relations. By contrast, the use of simultaneous compounds in conditional discriminations often does not result in modulatory effects (for example, Holland, 1986, 1989a, 1989c, 1991; Ross & Holland, 1981; see also Holland, 1989b; Thomas, Cook, & Terrones, 1990; Thomas, Curran, & Russell, 1988).

CONCLUDING COMMENTS

Stimulus control refers to how precisely tuned an organism's behavior is to specific features of the environment. Therefore, issues concerning the stimulus control of behavior are critical for understanding how an organism interacts with its environment. Stimulus control is measured in terms of the steepness of generalization gradients. A steep generalization gradient indicates that small variations in a stimulus produce large differences in responding. Weaker stimulus control is evidenced by flatter generalization gradients.

The degree of stimulus control is determined by numerous factors, including the sensory capacity and sensory orientation of the organism, the relative salience of other cues in the situation, the type of reinforcement used, and the type of response required for reinforcement. Stimulus control is also a function of learning. Discrimination training increases the stimulus control of behavior whether that training involves stimuli that differ in several respects or stimuli that differ in only one respect. Discrimination training with stimuli that differ in only one dimension produces more precise stimulus control and may lead to the counterintuitive outcome that the peak level of responding is shifted away from the reinforced stimulus. The converse of discrimination training is equivalence training, which increases the generalization of behavior.

Not only discrete stimuli but also background contextual cues can come to control behavior. Stimulus control by contextual cues can develop, even if attention to contextual cues is not required to optimize reinforcement. Finally, behavior can come to be influenced by conditional relations among stimuli.

SAMPLE QUESTIONS

1. Describe the relationship between stimulus discrimination and stimulus generalization.

2. Describe the phenomenon of overshadowing, and describe how it may be explained by elemental and configural approaches to stimulus control.

3. Describe how the steepness of a generalization gradient may be altered by experience and learning.

4. Describe the peak-shift effect and how it can be explained in terms of conditioned excitatory and inhibitory generalization gradients.

5. Compare and contrast conditioned excitation and occasion setting, or facilitation.

KEY TERMS

conditional relation A relation in which the significance of one stimulus or event depends on the status of another stimulus.

configural-cue approach An approach to the analysis of control by compound stimuli that assumes that organisms respond to a compound stimulus as an integral whole rather than a collection of separate and independent stimulus elements. (Compare with *stimulus element approach*.)

discriminative stimulus A stimulus that controls the performance of instrumental behavior because it signals the availability (or nonavailability) of reinforcement.

excitatory stimulus generalization gradient A gradient of responding that is observed when organisms are tested with the S+ from a discrimination procedure and with stimuli that increasingly differ from the S+. The highest level of responding occurs to stimuli similar to the S+; progressively less responding occurs to stimuli that increasingly differ from the S+. Thus, the gradient has an inverted-U shape.

facilitation A procedure in which one cue designates when another cue will be reinforced. Also called *occasion setting*.

inhibitory stimulus generalization gradient A gradient of responding observed when organisms are tested with the S− from a discrimination procedure and with stimuli that increasingly differ from the S−.

The lowest level of responding occurs to stimuli similar to the S−; progressively more responding occurs to stimuli that increasingly differ from S−. Thus, the gradient has a U shape.

intradimensional discrimination A discrimination between stimuli that differ in only one stimulus characteristic, such as color, brightness, or pitch.

modulator A stimulus that signals the relation between two other events. The nature of the binary relation is determined by the modulator.

multiple schedule of reinforcement A procedure in which different reinforcement schedules are in effect in the presence of different stimuli presented in succession. Generally, each stimulus comes to evoke a pattern of responding that corresponds to whatever reinforcement schedule is in effect during that stimulus.

occasion setting Same as *facilitation*.

overshadowing Interference with the conditioning of a stimulus because of the simultaneous presence of another stimulus that is easier to condition.

peak-shift A displacement of the highest rate of responding in a stimulus generalization gradient away from the S+ in a direction opposite the S− after intradimensional discrimination training.

stimulus discrimination Differential responding in the presence of two or more stimuli.

stimulus discrimination procedure (in classical conditioning) A classical conditioning procedure in which one stimulus (the CS+) is paired with the uncondi-

tioned stimulus on some trials and another stimulus (the CS−) is presented without the unconditioned stimulus on other trials. As a result of this procedure the CS+ comes to elicit a conditioned response, and the CS− comes to inhibit this response. (Also called *differential inhibition*.)

stimulus discrimination procedure (in instrumental conditioning) A procedure in which reinforcement for responding is available whenever one stimulus (the S+, or S^D) is present and not available whenever another stimulus (the S−, or S^D) is present.

stimulus-element approach An approach to the analysis of control by compound stimuli that assumes that participants respond to a compound stimulus in terms of the stimulus elements that make up the compound. (Compare with configural-cue.)

stimulus equivalence Responding to physically distinct stimuli as if they were the same because of common prior experiences with the stimuli.

stimulus generalization The occurrence of behavior learned through habituation or conditioning in the presence of stimuli that are different from the stimuli used during training.

stimulus generalization gradient A gradient of responding that is observed if participants are tested with stimuli that increasingly differ from the stimulus that was present during training. (See also *excitatory stimulus generalization gradient* and *inhibitory stimulus generalization gradient*.)

AVERSIVE CONTROL: AVOIDANCE AND PUNISHMENT

Avoidance Behavior

Origins of the Study of Avoidance Behavior

The Discriminated Avoidance Procedure

Two-Process Theory of Avoidance

Experimental Analysis of Avoidance Behavior

Alternative Theoretical Accounts of Avoidance Behavior

The Avoidance Puzzle: Concluding Comments

Punishment

Experimental Analysis of Punishment

Theories of Punishment

Punishment Outside the Laboratory

I N Chapter 9 I will discuss how behavior can be controlled by aversive stimulation. My presentation will focus on two types of instrumental aversive
control—avoidance and punishment. Avoidance conditioning increases the performance of a target behavior, and punishment decreases the target behavior. However,
in both cases individuals learn to minimize their exposure to aversive stimulation.
Because of this similarity, theoretical analyses of avoidance and punishment share
some of the same concepts. Nevertheless, for the most part, experimental analyses
of avoidance and punishment have proceeded independently of each other. I will
describe the major theoretical puzzles and empirical findings in both areas of
research.

Aversive stimulation is a fact of life and influences much of what we do. It is natural, then, that we should be interested in how behavior is controlled by aversive stimuli. Two procedures have been extensively investigated in studies of aversive control—avoidance and punishment. In an **avoidance procedure,** the individual has to make a specific response to prevent an aversive stimulus from occurring—for example, grabbing a handrail to avoid slipping on the stairs. Thus, an avoidance procedure involves a negative contingency between an instrumental response and the aversive stimulus. If the response occurs, the aversive stimulus is not presented. By contrast, a punishment procedure involves a positive contingency between the response and the aversive stimulus. Here, if the individual performs the response, the aversive stimulus occurs. For example, if you cut in line at a ticket window, you are likely to be reprimanded by others waiting in the line.

Avoidance procedures increase the occurrence of instrumental behavior, whereas punishment procedures suppress instrumental responding. However, with both procedures, the behavior that develops serves to minimize contact with the aversive stimulus. The critical difference is that, in avoidance, taking specific action is required to prevent the aversive stimulus whereas, in punishment, refraining from action minimizes contact with the aversive stimulus. Because of this, avoidance behavior is sometimes referred to as *active avoidance,* and punishment is sometimes referred to as *passive avoidance.* The terms active and passive avoidance emphasize the fact that both avoidance and punishment involve minimizing contact with an aversive stimulus.

Despite similarities between them, avoidance and punishment have stimulated different investigative approaches. Research on avoidance behavior has focused primarily on theoretical issues. What mechanisms are responsible for behavior whose primary consequence is the absence of aversive stimulation? By contrast, research on punishment has focused on practical considerations. What procedures are effective in suppressing behavior, and what factors influence their effectiveness?

AVOIDANCE BEHAVIOR

Origins of the Study of Avoidance Behavior

The study of avoidance behavior was initially closely allied to investigations of classical conditioning. The first avoidance conditioning experiments were conducted by the Russian psychologist Vladimir Bechterev (1913), as an extension of Pavlov's research. Unlike Pavlov, however, Bechterev investigated conditioning mechanisms in people. In one situation, participants were asked to place a finger on a metal plate. A warning stimulus (the CS) was periodically presented, followed by a brief shock (the US) through the plate. As you might suspect, the participants quickly lifted their finger off the plate upon being shocked. After a few trials, they also learned to make this response to the warning stimulus.

Bechterev's experiment was viewed as a standard example of classical conditioning. However, in Bechterev's method the participants determined whether or not they were exposed to the US. If they lifted their finger off the plate in response to the CS, they did not experience the shock scheduled on that trial. This aspect of the procedure constitutes a significant departure from Pavlov's methods because in standard classical conditioning, the delivery of the US does not depend on performance of the CR.

Figure 9.1 Modern running wheel for rodents.

The fact that Bechterev did not use a standard classical conditioning procedure went unnoticed for many years. However, starting in the 1930s, several investigations focused attention on the difference between a standard classical conditioning procedure and a procedure that had an instrumental avoidance component added (for example, Schlosberg, 1934, 1936). One of the most influential of these studies was performed by Brogden, Lipman, and Culler (1938).

Brogden and his collaborators tested two groups of guinea pigs in a rotating wheel apparatus (see Figure 9.1). A tone served as the CS, and shock served as the US. The shock stimulated the guinea pigs to run and thereby rotate the wheel. For the classical conditioning group, the shock was always presented 2 seconds after the beginning of the tone. For the avoidance conditioning group, the same type of CS-US pairings were conducted when the animals did not make the CR (a small movement of the wheel). However, if the avoidance animals moved the wheel during the tone CS before the shock occurred, the scheduled shock was omitted. Figure 9.2 shows the percentage of trials on which each group made the conditioned response. The avoidance group quickly learned to make the conditioned response and was responding on 100% of the trials within 8 days of training. In contrast, the classical conditioning group never achieved this high level of performance.

The results obtained by Brogden and his collaborators proved that avoidance conditioning is different from standard classical conditioning and ushered in several decades of research on avoidance learning.

The Discriminated Avoidance Procedure

Although avoidance behavior is not just another case of classical conditioning, the classical conditioning heritage of the study of avoidance behavior has greatly influenced its experimental and theoretical analysis. Investigators have been concerned with the importance of signals for the aversive event in avoidance procedures and with how such warning signals are related to the aversive US and the instrumental response. Experimental issues of this type have been extensively investigated with procedures similar to those used by Brogden and his colleagues. This method is called **discriminated**, or **signaled**, **avoidance**. The standard features of the discriminated avoidance procedure are diagrammed in Figure 9.3.

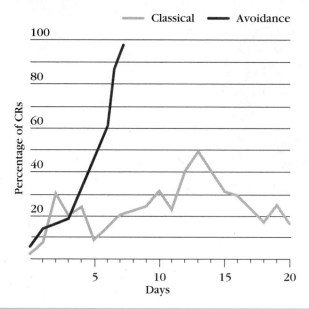

Figure 9.2 Percentage of trials with a conditioned response on successive days of training. The conditioned response prevented shock delivery for the avoidance group but not for the classical group. (From "The Role of Incentive in Conditioning and Extinction" by W. J. Brogden, E. A. Lipman, & E. Culler, *American Journal of Psychology*, 1938, *51*, pp. 109–117.)

The first thing to note about the discriminated avoidance procedure is that it involves discrete trials. Each trial is initiated by the CS. The events that occur after that depend on what the participant does. There are two possibilities. If the organism makes the response required for avoidance during the CS but before the shock is scheduled, the CS is turned off and the US is omitted on that trial. This is a successful **avoidance trial**. If the organism fails to make the required response during the CS-US interval, the scheduled shock is presented and remains on until the response occurs, whereupon both the CS and the US are terminated. In this case, the instrumental response results in escape from the shock; hence, this type of trial is called an **escape trial**. During early stages of training, most of the trials are escape trials. Once the avoidance response has been well established, avoidance trials predominate.

Discriminated avoidance procedures are often conducted in a shuttle box like that shown in Figure 9.4. The shuttle box consists of two compartments separated by an archway open at floor level. The animal is placed on one side of the apparatus. At the start of a trial, the CS is presented (a light or a tone, for example). If the animal crosses over to the other side before the shock occurs, no shock is delivered, and the CS is turned off. At the end of the intertrial interval, the next trial can be administered, starting with the animal in the second compartment. With this procedure, the animal shuttles back and forth between the two sides on successive trials. The response is therefore called **shuttle avoidance**.

There are two types of shuttle avoidance procedures. In the procedure just described, the animal moves from left to right on the first trial and back the other way on the second trial. This type of procedure is technically called *two-way shuttle avoidance* because the animal moves in different directions on successive trials. In the second type of shuttle avoidance, the animal is placed on the same side of the apparatus at the start of each trial and always moves in the same direction, to the other side. This type of procedure is called *one-way avoidance*. Generally, one-way avoidance is easier to learn than the two-way procedure.

| Avoidance trial | Escape trial |

CS ⎯⎯⎯⎯⎯⎯⎯⎯⎯⎯⎯⎯⎯⎯⎯

US ⎯⎯⎯⎯⎯⎯⎯⎯⎯⎯⎯⎯⎯⎯⎯

R ⎯⎯⎯⎯⎯⎯⎯⎯⎯⎯⎯⎯⎯⎯⎯

Two-Process Theory of Avoidance

Avoidance procedures involve a negative contingency between a response and an aversive stimulus. If you make the appropriate avoidance responses, you will not fall, bump into things, or drive off the road. No particular pleasure is derived from these experiences. You simply do not get hurt. The absence of the aversive stimulus is presumably the reason that avoidance responses are made. However, how can the absence of something provide reinforcement for instrumental behavior? This is the fundamental question in the study of avoidance.

Mowrer and Lamoreaux (1942) pointed out more than a half-century ago that "not getting something can hardly, in and of itself, qualify as rewarding" (p. 6). Since then, much intellectual effort has been devoted to figuring out what else is involved in avoidance conditioning procedures that might provide reinforcement for avoidance responding. In fact, the investigation of avoidance behavior has been dominated by this theoretical problem. The first and most influential solution to the puzzle, proposed by Mowrer (1947) and elaborated by Miller (for example, 1951) and others, is known as the **two-process theory of avoidance.**

In one form or another, two-process theory has been the dominant theoretical viewpoint on avoidance learning for many years and continues to enjoy success and support (Levis, 1989; McAllister & McAllister, 1991; Zhuikov, Couvillon, & Bitterman, 1994). Because other approaches deal more directly with certain findings, two-process theory is no longer viewed as a complete explanation of avoidance learning. Nevertheless, the theory remains the standard against which all other explanations of avoidance behavior are always measured.

As its name implies, two-process theory assumes that two mechanisms are involved in avoidance learning. The first is a classical conditioning process activated by pairings of the warning stimulus (CS) with the aversive event (US) on trials when the organism fails to make the avoidance response. Because the US is an aversive stimulus, through classical conditioning the CS also becomes aversive; Mowrer (1947) assumed that it thus comes to elicit fear. The first component of two-process theory is therefore the *classical conditioning of fear to the CS.*

Fear is an emotionally arousing unpleasant state. As I noted in Chapter 5, the termination of an unpleasant or aversive event provides negative reinforcement for instrumental behavior. Since fear is elicited by the CS, termination of the CS presumably results in a reduction in the level of fear, which can be a source of negative reinforcement. The second process in two-process theory is based on this negative reinforcement. Mowrer assumed that learning of the instrumental avoidance response occurs because the response terminates the CS and thereby reduces the conditioned fear elicited by the CS. Thus, the second component in two-process theory is *instrumental reinforcement of the avoidance response through fear reduction.*

Figure 9.3 Diagram of the discriminated, or signaled, avoidance procedure. *Avoidance trial:* If the participant makes the response required for avoidance during the CS (the signal) but before the US (for example, shock) is scheduled, the CS is turned off, and the US is omitted on that trial. *Escape trial:* If the participant fails to make the required response during the CS-US interval, the scheduled shock is presented and remains on until the response occurs, whereupon both the CS and the US are terminated.

N. E. Miller

255

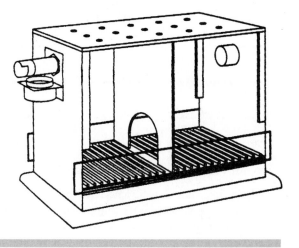

Figure 9.4 A shuttle box. The box has a metal grid floor and is separated into two compartments by an archway. The instrumental response consists of crossing from one side of the box to the other.

There are several noteworthy aspects of two-process theory. First, and perhaps most important, is that the classical and instrumental processes are not assumed to provide independent sources of support for avoidance behavior. Rather, the two processes are very much interdependent. Instrumental reinforcement through fear reduction is not possible until fear has become conditioned to the CS. Therefore, the classical conditioning process has to occur first. After that, the instrumental conditioning process may create extinction trials for the classical conditioning process. This occurs because each successful avoidance response prevents the occurrence of the US. Thus, two-process theory predicts a constant interplay between classical and instrumental processes.

Another important aspect of two-process theory is that it explains avoidance behavior in terms of escape from conditioned fear rather than in terms of the prevention of shock. The fact that the avoidance response prevents shock is seen as a byproduct in two-process theory, not as the critical event that motivates avoidance behavior. Escape from conditioned fear provides the critical reinforcement for avoidance behavior. Thus, according to two-process theory, the instrumental response is reinforced by a tangible event (fear reduction) rather than merely the absence of aversive stimulation.

Experimental Analysis of Avoidance Behavior

Avoidance learning has been extensively investigated. Much of the research has been stimulated in one way or another by two-process theory. I cannot review all the evidence here. However, I will discuss several important types of results that must be considered in any effort to fully understand the mechanisms of avoidance behavior.

Acquired Drive Experiments. In the typical avoidance procedure, classical conditioning of fear and instrumental reinforcement through fear reduction occur intermixed in a series of trials. However, if these two processes make separate contributions to avoidance learning, it should be possible to demonstrate their operation when the two types of conditioning are not intermixed. This is the goal of acquired drive experiments.

The basic strategy is to first condition fear to a CS with a "pure" classical conditioning procedure in which the organism's responses do not influence whether the US is presented. In the next phase of the experiment, the animals are periodically exposed to the fear-eliciting CS and allowed to perform an instrumental response that is effective in terminating the CS (and thereby reducing fear). No shocks are scheduled in this phase. Therefore, the instrumental response is not required to avoid shock presentations. If two-process theory is correct, and escape from the fear-eliciting CS can reinforce instrumental behavior, then the instrumental response should become conditioned in the second phase of the experiment. This type of experiment is called an **acquired drive** study because the drive to perform the instrumental response (fear) is learned through classical conditioning. (It is not an innate drive such as hunger or thirst.)

One of the first definitive acquired drive experiments was performed by Brown and Jacobs (1949), who tested rats in a shuttle box. During the first phase of the experiment, the door between the two shuttle compartments was closed. The rats were individually placed on one side of the apparatus, and a pulsating light/tone CS was presented, ending in shock through the grid floor. Twenty-two such Pavlovian conditioning trials were conducted, with the rats confined on the right and left sides of the apparatus on alternate trials. The control group received the same training except that no shocks were delivered.

Instrumental conditioning was conducted during the next phase of the experiment. Each animal was placed on one side of the shuttle box, and the center barrier was removed. The CS was then presented and remained on until the rat turned it off by crossing to the other side. The animal was then removed from the apparatus until the next trial. No shocks were delivered during the instrumental conditioning phase. The investigators wanted to determine whether the rats would learn to cross rapidly from one side to the other when the only reinforcement for crossing was termination of the previously conditioned light/tone CS.

How long the rats took to cross the shuttle box and turn off the CS was measured for each trial in the instrumental conditioning phase. Figure 9.5 summarizes these response latencies for both the shock-conditioned group and the control group. The two groups had similar response latencies at the beginning of instrumental training. However, as training progressed, the shock-conditioned animals learned to cross the shuttle box faster (and thus turn off the CS sooner) than the control group. This outcome shows that termination of a fear-conditioned stimulus is sufficient to provide reinforcement for an instrumental response. Such findings have been obtained in a variety of experimental situations (for example, Dinsmoor, 1962; McAllister & McAllister, 1971; see also Delprato, 1969; Israel, Devine, O'Dea, & Hamdi, 1974; Katzev, 1967, 1972). These results provide strong support for two-process theory.

Independent Measurement of Fear During Acquisition of Avoidance Behavior.
Another important strategy that has been used in investigations of avoidance behavior involves the independent measurement of fear and instrumental avoidance responding. This approach is based on the assumption that if fear motivates and reinforces avoidance responding, then the conditioning of fear and the conditioning of instrumental avoidance behavior should go hand in hand. Contrary to this prediction, however, conditioned fear and avoidance responding are not always highly correlated (Mineka, 1979).

Fairly early in the investigation of avoidance learning, it was noted that animals become less fearful as they become more proficient in performing the avoidance

Figure 9.5 Mean latencies to cross from one side to the other in the shuttle box for control and experimental groups. The shuttle crossing resulted in termination of the CS on that trial. For the experimental group, the CS was previously conditioned with shock. Such conditioning was not conducted with the control group. (From "The Role of Fear in the Motivation and Acquisition of Responses" by J. S. Brown & A. Jacobs, *Journal of Experimental Psychology*, 1949, *39*, pp. 747–759)

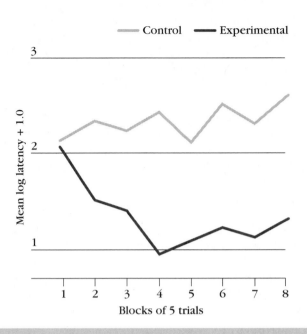

response (Solomon, Kamin, & Wynne, 1953; Solomon & Wynne, 1953). Since then, more systematic measurements of fear have been used. One popular behavioral technique for measuring fear involves the conditioned suppression procedure described in Chapter 3. In this technique, animals are first conditioned to press a response lever for food reinforcement. A shock-conditioned CS is then presented while the animals are responding to obtain food. Generally, the CS produces a suppression in the lever-press behavior, and the extent of this response suppression is assumed to reflect the amount of fear elicited by the CS.

If the warning signal in an avoidance procedure comes to elicit fear, then presentation of that warning stimulus in a conditioned suppression procedure should result in suppression of food-reinforced behavior. This prediction was tested for the first time in a famous experiment by Kamin, Brimer, and Black (1963). The rats in the experiment were initially trained to press a response lever for food reinforcement on a variable interval schedule. The animals were then trained to avoid shock in response to an auditory CS in a shuttle box. Training was continued for independent groups of animals until they successfully avoided shock on 1, 3, 9, or 27 consecutive trials. The animals were then returned to the Skinner box for lever pressing. The auditory CS that had been used in the shuttle box was periodically presented to see how much suppression of lever pressing it would produce.

The results are summarized in Figure 9.6. Lower values of the suppression index indicate greater disruptions of lever pressing by the shock-avoidance CS. Increasing degrees of response suppression were observed among groups of rats that had received avoidance training until they successfully avoided shock on 1 to 9 successive trials. With more extensive avoidance training, however, response suppression declined. Animals trained until they avoided shock on 27 consecutive trials showed less conditioned suppression to the avoidance CS than those trained to a criterion of 9 consecutive avoidances. This outcome indicates that fear, as measured by conditioned suppression, decreases during extended avoidance training and is at a minimal level

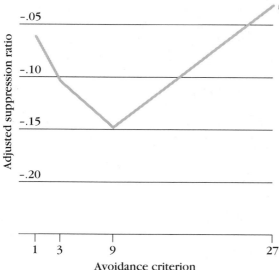

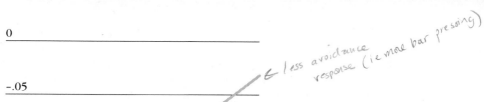

← less avoidance response (ie more bar pressing)

Figure 9.6 Suppression of lever pressing for food during a CS that was previously conditioned in a shock-avoidance procedure. Independent groups received avoidance training until they met a criterion of 1, 3, 9, or 27 consecutive avoidance responses. The suppression scores were adjusted for the degree of suppression produced by the CS before avoidance conditioning. Lower values of the adjusted ratio indicate greater suppression of lever pressing. (From "Conditioned Suppression as a Monitor of Fear of the CS in the Course of Avoidance Training" by L. J. Kamin, C. J. Brimer, & A. H. Black, *Journal of Comparative and Physiological Psychology*, 1963, *56*, pp. 497–501.)

after extensive training (see also Cook, Mineka, & Trumble, 1987; Neuenschwander, Fabrigoule, & Mackintosh, 1987; Starr & Mineka, 1977). Interestingly, however, the decrease in fear is not accompanied by a decrease in the strength of the avoidance response (Mineka & Gino, 1980).

The decline in fear to the CS with extended avoidance training presents a puzzle for two-process theory. However, recent evidence and theoretical argument suggest that the scope of two-process theory can accommodate this finding. Although it is well accepted that fear declines as avoidance conditioning proceeds, declining levels of fear do not preclude continued reinforcement of the avoidance response. McAllister and McAllister (1991) pointed out that as long as the CS elicits some degree of fear, CS termination can result in fear reduction and hence reinforcement of the avoidance behavior (see also Levis, 1989). Furthermore, as the avoidance response becomes well learned, a small degree of fear reduction may be sufficient to maintain the response.

S. Mineka

Asymptotic Avoidance Performance. Two-process theory not only specifies mechanisms responsible for the acquisition of avoidance behavior but also makes predictions about the nature of performance once the response has been well learned. More specifically, it predicts that the strength of the avoidance response will fluctuate in cycles.

Whenever a successful avoidance response occurs, the shock is omitted on that trial, which becomes an extinction trial for the conditioned fear response. Repetition of the avoidance response (and thus the CS-alone extinction trials) should lead to the extinction of fear. As the CS becomes extinguished, there will be less reinforcement resulting from the reduction of fear, and the avoidance response should also become extinguished. However, when shock is not avoided, the CS is paired with the US. This pairing should reinstate fear to the CS and reestablish the potential for reinforcement through fear reduction. Hence, the avoidance response should become reconditioned. Thus, the theory predicts that after initial acquisition, the avoidance response will go through cycles of extinction and reacquisition.

Although evidence of cyclic avoidance responding at asymptote has been obtained (for example, Sheffield, 1948), such findings are not always observed. In fact, some have argued that one of the hallmarks of avoidance behavior is its persistence. Avoidance responding may continue for many trials after shocks are discontinued, as long as the response continues to be effective in terminating the CS. In one experiment (Solomon et al., 1953), for example, a dog was reported to have performed the avoidance response on 650 successive trials after only a few shocks.

In terms of two-process theory, there are several approaches to explaining instances in which avoidance behavior persists after the unconditioned aversive stimulus is no longer delivered. One approach is based on the observation that once an avoidance response has been well learned, it occurs with a short latency. Because the animal responds quickly to turn off the CS, later segments of the CS are never experienced and therefore do not have the opportunity to undergo extinction. The short latency of well-learned avoidance responses serves to protect later segments of the CS from becoming extinguished and thereby contributes to the persistence of avoidance behavior. This mechanism, first proposed by Solomon and Wynne (1953), is called **conservation of fear.** (For elaborations on this idea, see Levis, 1981, 1989, 1991. For additional factors involved in the persistence of avoidance behavior, see Soltysik, Wolfe, Nicholas, Wilson, & Garcia-Sanchez, 1983).

Extinction of Avoidance Behavior Through Response-Blocking and CS-Alone Exposure. As I have noted, if the avoidance response is effective in terminating the CS and no shocks are presented, avoidance responding may persist for a long time. How might avoidance behavior be extinguished? The answer to this question is very important not only for theoretical analyses of avoidance behavior but also for forms of behavior therapy whose purpose is to extinguish maladaptive or pathological avoidance responses.

An effective and extensively investigated extinction procedure for avoidance behavior is called **flooding,** or **response prevention** (Baum, 1970). It involves presenting the CS in the avoidance situation, but with the apparatus altered in such a way that the participant is prevented from making the avoidance response. Thus, the organism is exposed to the CS without being permitted to terminate it. In a sense, it is "flooded" with the CS.

One of the most important variables determining the effects of a flooding procedure is the duration of the forced exposure to the CS. This was convincingly illustrated in an experiment by Schiff, Smith, and Prochaska (1972). Rats were trained to avoid shock in response to an auditory CS by going to a safe compartment. After acquisition, the safe compartment was blocked off by a barrier, and the rats received various amounts of exposure to the CS without shock. Different groups received 1, 5, or 12 blocked trials, and on each of these trials the CS was presented for 1, 5, 10, 50, or 120 seconds. The barrier blocking the avoidance response was then removed, and the animals were tested for extinction. At the start of each extinction trial the animal was placed in the apparatus, and the CS was presented until it crossed into the safe compartment. Shocks never occurred during the extinction trials and each animal was tested until it took at least 120 seconds to cross into the safe compartment on three consecutive trials. The strength of the avoidance response was measured by the number of trials required to reach this extinction criterion.

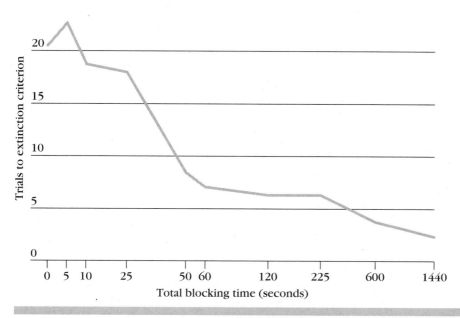

Figure 9.7 Trials to extinction criterion for independent groups of animals that previously received various durations of blocked exposure to the CS. (From "Extinction of Avoidance in Rats as a Function of Duration and Number of Blocked Trials" by R. Schiff, N. Smith, & J. Prochaska, *Journal of Comparative and Physiological Psychology,* 1972, *81,* pp. 356–359. Copyright © 1972 by the American Psychological Association. Reprinted by permission.)

The results of the experiment are summarized in Figure 9.7. As expected, blocked exposure to the CS facilitated extinction of the avoidance response. Furthermore, this effect was determined mainly by the total duration of exposure to the CS. The number of flooding trials administered (1, 5, or 12) facilitated extinction only because each trial added to the total amount of inescapable exposure to the CS. Increases in the total duration of blocked exposure to the CS resulted in more rapid extinction (see also Baum, 1969; Weinberger, 1965).

Two-process theory predicts that flooding will extinguish avoidance behavior because forced exposure to the CS is expected to produce extinction of fear. The fact that more extensive exposure to the CS results in more rapid extinction is consistent with this view. However, detailed investigations of the role of fear in flooding procedures have also provided evidence contrary to two-process theory. Independent measurements of fear (with the conditioned suppression technique, for example) have shown that in some situations flooding extinguishes avoidance behavior more rapidly than it extinguishes fear, whereas in other situations the reverse holds (see, for example, Coulter, Riccio, & Page, 1969; Mineka & Gino, 1979; Mineka, Miller, Gino, & Giencke, 1981). These results suggest that extinction of fear is only one factor responsible for the effects of flooding procedures. Other variables may be related to the fact that during flooding, organisms not only receive forced exposure to the CS but are prevented from making the avoidance response. (For further discussion, see Baum, 1970; Katzev & Berman, 1974; Mineka, 1979.)

Nondiscriminated (Free-Operant) Avoidance.   As we have seen, two-process theory places great emphasis on the role of the warning signal, or CS, in avoidance learning. Can animals also learn to avoid shock if there is no external warning stimulus in the situation? Within the context of two-factor theory, this is a heretical question. However, progress in science requires posing bold questions, and Sidman (1953a, 1953b)

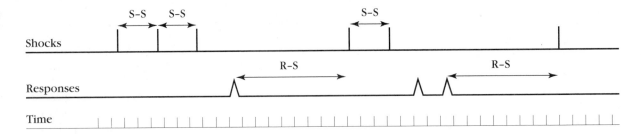

Figure 9.8 Diagram of the nondiscriminated, or free-operant, avoidance procedure. Each occurrence of the response initiates a period without shock, as set by the R-S interval. In the absence of a response, the next shock occurs a fixed period after the last shock, as set by the S-S interval. Shocks are not signaled by an exteroceptive stimulus and are usually brief and inescapable.

did just that. He devised an avoidance conditioning procedure that did not involve a warning stimulus. The procedure has come to be called **nondiscriminated, or free-operant, avoidance.**

In a free-operant avoidance procedure, a brief shock is scheduled to occur periodically without warning—let's say every 10 seconds. Each time the participant makes the avoidance response, it obtains a period of safety—let's say 30 seconds long—during which shocks do not occur. Repetition of the avoidance response before the end of the shock-free period serves to start the safe period over again.

A free-operant avoidance procedure is constructed from two time intervals (see Figure 9.8). One of these is the interval between shocks in the absence of a response. This is called the **S-S (shock-shock) interval.** The other critical time period is the interval between the avoidance response and the next scheduled shock. This is called the **R-S (response-shock) interval.** The R-S interval is the period of safety created by each response. In the example, the S-S interval was 10 seconds, and the R-S interval was 30 seconds.

In addition to lacking a warning stimulus, the free-operant avoidance procedure differs from discriminated avoidance in allowing for avoidance responses to occur at any time. In discriminated avoidance procedures, the avoidance response is effective in preventing the delivery of shock only if it is made during the CS. Responses in the absence of the CS (the intertrial interval) have no effect. In fact, in some experiments (particularly those involving one-way avoidance), the animals are removed from the apparatus between trials. By contrast, in the free-operant procedure, an avoidance response occurring at any time will reset the R-S interval. If the R-S interval is 30 seconds, shock is scheduled 30 seconds after each response. By always responding just before this R-S interval is over, the organism can always reset the R-S interval and thereby prolong its period of safety indefinitely.

Characteristics of Free-Operant Avoidance Learning. There are several striking characteristics of free-operant avoidance experiments. First, these studies generally involve much longer periods of training than discriminated avoidance experiments. Sometimes it takes a lot of experience with shock before participants learn to make a free-operant avoidance response regularly. Extensive training is also often used because the investigators are specifically interested in what kind of steady-state adjustment participants make to free-operant schedules of aversive stimulation. Thus, in many cases the initial learning of the avoidance behavior is not the primary focus of the experiment. Another general characteristic of these experiments is that animals often never get good enough to avoid all shocks, even after extensive training. Finally, participants often differ greatly in how they respond to the identical free-operant avoidance procedure.

Figures 9.9 and 9.10 illustrate the kinds of results that can be obtained with free-operant avoidance training. Each figure shows the cumulative record of lever pressing

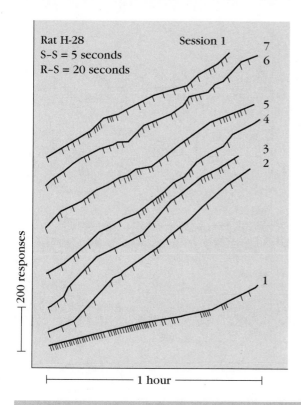

Figure 9.9 Cumulative record of lever pressing for a rat the first time it was exposed to a nondiscriminated avoidance procedure. Numerals at the right label successive hours of exposure to the procedure. Oblique slashes indicate delivery of shock. (From "Avoidance Behavior" by M. Sidman. In W. K. Honig (Ed.), *Operant Behavior.* Copyright © 1966 by Prentice-Hall. Reprinted by permission.)

by a rat during successive 1-hour periods of the rat's first exposure to the avoidance procedure. In the absence of lever presses, the animals received shock every 5 seconds (the S-S interval). Each lever-press response initiated a 20-second period without shocks (the R-S interval). Shocks are indicated by downward deflections of the cumulative recorder pen.

Rat H-28 (Figure 9.9) received a lot of shocks at first but started to press the lever even during the first hour of training. It responded a great deal during the second hour of the session and then settled down to a steady rate of lever pressing for the next 5 hours that the procedure was in effect. This was its stable response pattern under these conditions. Rat H-28 was a particularly fast learner. However, even at the end of the 7 hours of training it received more than 25 shocks per hour.

Rat O-10 (Figure 9.10) did not perform as well as rat H-28. It received many more shocks and never achieved a high rate of responding. Its stable pattern of behavior after several hours of training involved responding just after shock delivery and then not responding again until the next shock occurred at the end of the R-S interval. Therefore, it ended up receiving a shock about every 20 seconds, as set by the R-S interval.

Numerous experiments have been conducted on free-operant avoidance behavior (see Hineline, 1977; Sidman, 1966). The rate of responding is controlled by the values of the S-S and R-S intervals. The more frequently shocks are scheduled in the absence of responding (the S-S interval), the more likely the animal is to learn the avoidance response. Increasing the periods of safety produced by the response (the R-S interval) also promotes the avoidance behavior. In addition, the relative value of the S-S and R-S intervals is important. For example, the animal is not likely to make the instrumental response if the R-S interval is shorter than the S-S interval.

263

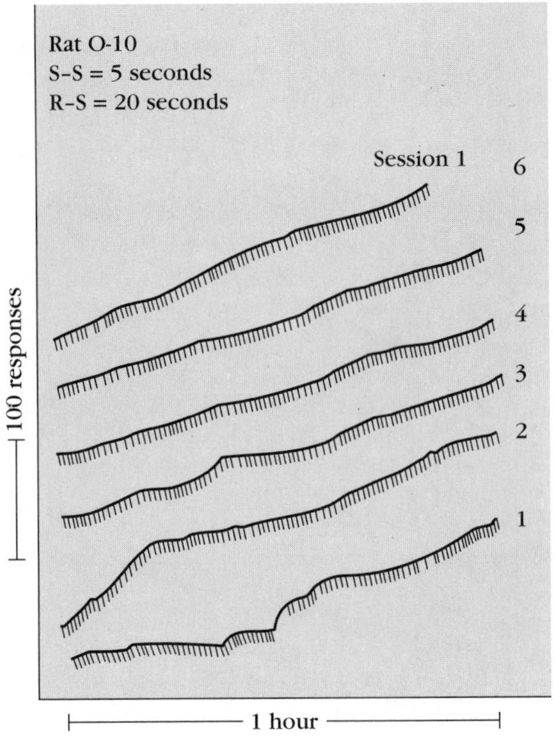

Figure 9.10 Cumulative record of lever pressing for a rat the first time it was exposed to a nondiscriminated avoidance procedure. Numerals at the right label successive hours of exposure to the procedure. Oblique slashes indicate delivery of shock. (From "Avoidance Behavior" by M. Sidman. In W. K. Honig (Ed.), *Operant Behavior.* Copyright © 1966 by Prentice-Hall. Reprinted by permission.)

Free-Operant Avoidance and Two-Process Theory. Free-operant avoidance behavior presents a challenge for two-process theory because there is no explicit CS to elicit conditioned fear, and it is not clear how the avoidance response reduces fear. However, two-process theory has not been entirely abandoned in attempts to explain free-operant avoidance (see Anger, 1963). The S-S and R-S intervals used in effective procedures are usually rather short (less than 1 minute). Furthermore, they remain fixed during an experiment so that the intervals are highly predictable. Therefore, it is reasonable to suggest that the animals might learn to respond to the passage of time as a signal for shock. This assumption of temporal conditioning permits application of the mechanisms of two-process theory to free-operant avoidance procedures.

According to the two-process explanation of free-operant avoidance, the passage of time after the last shock (in the case of the S-S interval) or after the last response (in the case of the R-S interval) becomes conditioned to elicit fear. Since the timing starts over again with each avoidance response, the response effectively removes the fear-eliciting temporal cues. Termination of these time signals can then reinforce the avoidance response through fear reduction. Thus, the temporal cues that predict shock are assumed to have the same role in free-operant avoidance procedures as the explicit CS has in signaled avoidance.

The preceding analysis predicts that organisms will not distribute their responses randomly in a nondiscriminated avoidance procedure. Rather, they will concentrate their responses at the end of the R-S interval because it is here that the temporal cues presumably elicit the greatest amount of fear. Results consistent with this prediction have been obtained. However, many animals successfully avoid a great many shocks without distributing their responses in the manner predicted by two-process theory.

Furthermore, the predicted distribution of responses often develops only after extensive training—after the participants are avoiding a great many of the scheduled shocks (see Sidman, 1966). In addition, avoidance behavior has been successfully conditioned with the use of free-operant procedures in which the S-S and R-S intervals are varied throughout the experiment (for example, Herrnstein & Hineline, 1966). Making the S-S and R-S intervals unpredictable makes it more difficult to use the passage of time as a signal for shock. These types of results have discouraged some investigators from accepting two-process theory as an explanation of free-operant avoidance learning. (For further discussion, see Herrnstein, 1969; Hineline, 1977, 1981.)

Alternative Theoretical Accounts of Avoidance Behavior

In the preceding discussion of experimental investigations of avoidance behavior, I used two-process theory to provide the conceptual framework. This was reasonable because many of the research questions were stimulated in one way or another by two-process theory. However, alternative approaches to the analysis of avoidance learning also have been proposed, as investigators have gradually moved away from using traditional discrete-trial discriminated avoidance procedures. I will now discuss some of the more important of these alternative theories.

P. N. Hineline

In two-process theory, reinforcement for the avoidance response is assumed to be provided by the reduction of fear. This is a case of negative reinforcement—reinforcement due to removal of an aversive state. Several subsequent theoretical treatments have proposed that avoidance procedures also provide for positive reinforcement of the avoidance response, whereas others have suggested that neither negative reinforcement nor positive reinforcement is important in avoidance learning.

Positive Reinforcement Through Conditioned Inhibition of Fear.   Performance of an avoidance response always results in distinctive feedback stimuli, such as the spatial cues involved in going from one side to the other in a shuttle box or tactile and other external stimuli involved in pressing a response lever. Because the avoidance response produces a period of safety in all avoidance conditioning procedures, response feedback stimuli may acquire conditioned inhibitory properties and become signals for the absence of aversive stimulation. Such stimuli are called **safety signals.** Since a shock-free period is desirable, a conditioned inhibitory stimulus for shock may serve as a positive reinforcer. Thus, according to the *safety-signal hypothesis*, the stimuli that accompany avoidance responses may provide positive reinforcement for avoidance behavior.

In most avoidance experiments, no special steps are taken to ensure that the avoidance response is accompanied by vivid feedback stimuli that could acquire conditioned inhibitory properties. Spatial, tactile, and proprioceptive stimuli that are not specifically programmed but inevitably accompany the avoidance response serve this function. However, any avoidance procedure can easily be modified to provide a distinctive stimulus such as a brief light or tone after each occurrence of the avoidance response. The safety-signal hypothesis predicts that introducing an explicit feedback stimulus will facilitate the learning of an avoidance response. Numerous experiments have found this to be true (for example, Bolles & Grossen, 1969; Cándido, Maldonado, & Vila, 1991; D'Amato, Fazzaro, & Etkin, 1968; Keehn & Nakkash, 1959; see also McAllister & McAllister, 1992).

Other studies have shown that during the course of avoidance training, a response feedback stimulus becomes a conditioned inhibitor of fear (for example,

OBSERVATIONAL LEARNING OF FEARS AND PHOBIAS

Excessive fears and phobias can be debilitating and may require therapeutic intervention. Some of the most successful treatment procedures, such as flooding and systematic desensitization, were designed on the basis of conditioning principles. A persistent problem for theoretical analyses of such fears is that people with clinically significant fear and anxiety often have no known history of conditioning with traumatic events. Many people, for example, have an intense fear of snakes even though they have never been bitten by a snake.

If an individual has no known experience with traumatic events, how might that person have acquired a fear or phobia? Research with rhesus monkeys (*Macaca mulatta*) suggests that significant fears may be acquired through observational learning (Mineka & Cook, 1988.) Rhesus monkeys reared in the wild have an intense fear of snakes. In response to the sight of a snake, they exhibit a variety of fear responses, including fear grimacing, ear flapping, clutching the cage, averting their eyes, and piloerection (erection of the hair follicles). Fear is also evident in their reluctance to reach over the snake to obtain a food treat. By contrast, monkeys reared in the laboratory do not show these behaviors. Mineka and Cook investigated whether laboratory-reared monkeys could acquire a fear of snakes by observing the fear reactions of wild-reared monkeys in response to a snake.

A discriminative observational conditioning procedure was used. During preliminary training, the demonstrator monkeys were taught to reach over a clear plastic container to obtain a food treat. Observer monkeys were then given the opportunity to watch the reactions of the demonstrator monkeys. On some trials, a live or toy snake was placed in the plastic container. During other trials, the plastic container held a neutral object (a block of wood, for example). The demonstrators showed intense fear of the snake stimuli but not of the neutral objects. After as few as two fear-observation trials, most of the observer monkeys showed similar fear reactions to the snake stimuli. The level of fear they acquired was closely related to the level of fear shown by the demonstrator monkeys. Furthermore, once the observers became fearful of the snakes, they could serve effectively as demonstrators in the observational conditioning of other rhesus monkeys. These results indicate that observational learning could be the basis for wide social transmission of fear among members of a monkey troupe or other social group (see also Cook & Mineka, 1990).

Morris, 1974; Rescorla, 1968a). Furthermore, there is also direct evidence that a feedback stimulus that has been conditioned to inhibit fear during avoidance training is an effective positive reinforcer for new responses (Morris, 1975; Weisman & Litner, 1972; see also Dinsmoor & Sears, 1973). Thus, there is considerable evidence for safety signals as sources of positive reinforcement in avoidance learning.

There are important similarities and differences between positive reinforcement of avoidance behavior through conditioned inhibition and the negative reinforcement process assumed by two-process theory. Both mechanisms involve a reduction of fear. However, the manner in which this occurs is different in the two cases. Whereas a conditioned inhibitor actively inhibits fear, CS termination is assumed to lead to the passive dissipation of fear. Because both mechanisms involve fear reduction, the operation of both processes depends on the existence of fear. However, the conditioned inhibition reinforcement process is less restrictive about the source of the fear. The fear may be elicited by an explicit warning stimulus or by contextual cues or cues of the environment in which the avoidance procedure is conducted.

The fact that fear elicited by situational cues can provide the basis for conditioned inhibition reinforcement makes the safety-signal hypothesis particularly well suited to explaining free-operant avoidance behavior. Participants often experience numerous shocks during acquisition of free-operant avoidance behavior. This and the absence of an exteroceptive warning stimulus make it highly likely that the entire experimental situation becomes conditioned to elicit fear. Because shocks never occur for the duration of the R-S interval after a response is made, the proprioceptive and tactile stimuli that accompany the response can become conditioned inhibitors of fear. Thus, response-associated feedback cues can come to provide positive reinforcement for the free-operant avoidance response (Dinsmoor, 1977; Rescorla, 1968a).

It is important to realize that the conditioned inhibition reinforcement mechanism is not incompatible with, or necessarily a substitute for, the negative reinforcement process assumed by two-process theory. That is, negative reinforcement through CS termination and positive reinforcement through conditioned inhibitory feedback cues could well be operative simultaneously, both processes contributing to the strength of the avoidance behavior (see Cicala & Owen, 1976; Owen, Cicala, & Herdegen, 1978).

Reinforcement of Avoidance Through Reduction of Shock Frequency. As we have seen, positive reinforcement through conditioned inhibition can occur alongside the negative reinforcement mechanism of two-process theory. In contrast, another reinforcement mechanism, **shock-frequency reduction,** has been proposed as an alternative to two-process theory (deVilliers, 1974; Herrnstein, 1969; Herrnstein & Hineline, 1966; Hineline, 1981). By definition, avoidance responses prevent the delivery of shock and thereby reduce the frequency of shocks an organism receives. The theories of avoidance I have discussed so far have viewed the reduction of shocks almost as an incidental by-product of avoidance responses rather than as an immediate primary cause of avoidance behavior. By contrast, the shock-frequency reduction hypothesis views the avoidance of shock as critical to the reinforcement of avoidance behavior.

Shock-frequency reduction as the cause of avoidance behavior was first entertained by Sidman (1962) to explain results he obtained in a concurrent free-operant avoidance experiment. Rats were exposed to two free-operant avoidance schedules at the same time. Responses on one response lever prevented shocks on one of the schedules, and responses on the other lever prevented shocks on the second schedule. Sidman concluded that the animals distributed their responses between the two levers so as to reduce the overall frequency of shocks they received. The idea that shock frequency reduction can serve to reinforce avoidance behavior was later encouraged by evidence of learning in a free-operant avoidance procedure specifically designed to minimize the role of fear-conditioned temporal cues (Herrnstein & Hineline, 1966). Studies of the relative importance of various components of the discriminated avoidance procedure have also shown that the avoidance component significantly contributes to the learning (for example, Bolles, Stokes, & Younger, 1966; see also Bolles, 1972a; Kamin, 1956).

Although the evidence just cited clearly indicates that avoidance of shock is important, the mechanisms responsible for these results are debatable. Several experiments have shown that animals can learn to make an avoidance response, even if the response does not reduce the frequency of shocks delivered (Gardner & Lewis, 1976; Hineline, 1976; see also Hineline, 1981). Responding in these studies delayed the onset of the next scheduled shock but did not prevent its delivery. Thus, overall shock frequency was unchanged by the instrumental response. Such results can be explained in terms of the shock-frequency reduction hypothesis by assuming that organisms calculate shock frequencies over only a limited period following an avoidance response.

However, the hypothesis does not specify the duration of these intervals, leaving them to be determined experimentally (see, for example, Logue, 1982).

In evaluating the shock-frequency reduction hypothesis, the extent to which evidence consistent with the hypothesis can be explained in other ways must also be considered. Conditioned inhibition reinforcement often presents a serious alternative. If a response reduces the frequency of shocks, external and proprioceptive stimuli involved in making the response will come to signal the absence of shock and become conditioned inhibitors of fear. The conditioned inhibitory properties of these stimuli can then reinforce the avoidance behavior.

SSDR Theory. In the theories discussed so far, the main emphasis was on how the events that precede and follow the avoidance response control avoidance behavior. The exact nature or form of the response itself was not a primary concern of these theories. In addition, the reinforcement mechanisms assumed by the theories all required some time to develop. Before fear reduction can be an effective reinforcer, fear first must be conditioned to the CS; before feedback cues can come to serve as reinforcers, they must become signals for the absence of shock; and before shock-frequency reduction can work, organisms must experience enough shocks to be able to assess shock frequencies. Therefore, these theories tell us little about what determines the organism's behavior during the first few trials of avoidance training.

R. C. Bolles

Lack of concern with what an organism does during the first few trials of avoidance conditioning is a serious weakness of previous theories. For an avoidance mechanism to be useful to an animal in its natural habitat, the mechanism has to generate successful avoidance responses quickly. Consider, for example, an animal trying to avoid a predator. An avoidance mechanism that requires numerous training trials is of no use in this case. If the animal fails to avoid being eaten by the predator during its initial encounter, it will not be around for future training trials. Bolles (1970, 1971) recognized this problem and focused on what controls an organism's behavior during the early stages of avoidance training.

Bolles assumed that aversive stimuli and situations elicit strong unconditioned, or innate, responses. These innate responses are assumed to have evolved because they are successful in defense against pain and injury. Therefore, Bolles called these **species-specific defense reactions** (SSDRs). In rats, for example, prominent species-specific defense reactions include flight (running), freezing (remaining vigilant but motionless, except for breathing), and defensive fighting. Other reactions to danger include thigmotaxis (approaching walls), defensive burying (covering up the source of aversive stimulation), and seeking out dark areas.

Originally, Bolles proposed that the configuration of the environment determined the particular SSDR that occurred. For example, flight may predominate when an obvious escape route is available, and freezing may predominate if there is no way out of the situation. This must be true to some extent. Defensive fighting, for example, is not possible without an opponent, and defensive burying is not possible if something like sand is not available for burying the source of danger. However, other factors such as the imminence and intensity of the danger also determine which SSDR occurs (Fanselow, 1989; Fanselow & Lester, 1988).

The SSDR theory of avoidance behavior states that species-specific defense reactions predominate during the initial stages of avoidance training. If the most likely SSDR is successful in preventing shocks, this behavior will persist as long as the avoidance procedure is in effect. If the first SSDR is not effective, it will be followed by shock, which will suppress the behavior through punishment. The animal will then make the next most likely SSDR. If shocks persist, this second SSDR will also become suppressed by punishment, and the organism will make the third most likely SSDR.

The response-selection process is assumed to end when a response is found that is effective in avoiding shocks, so that the behavior will not be suppressed by punishment. Thus, according to the SSDR account, *punishment is responsible for the selection of the instrumental avoidance response* from other activities of the organism. Reinforcement, be it positive or negative, is assumed to have a minor role, if any, in avoidance learning. According to SSDR theory, the correct avoidance response is not strengthened by reinforcement. Rather, it occurs because other SSDRs are suppressed by punishment.

One obvious prediction of the SSDR theory is that some types of responses will be more easily learned in avoidance experiments than others. Consistent with this prediction, Bolles (1969) found that rats can rapidly learn to run in a running wheel to avoid shock. By contrast, their performance of a rearing response (standing on the hind legs) did not improve much during the course of avoidance training. Presumably, running was learned faster because it was closer to the rat's species-specific defense reactions in the running wheel (see also Grossen & Kelley, 1972).

SSDR theory made significant contributions to the understanding of avoidance learning by calling attention to the importance of species-typical behavior in aversive situations. However, it has not been entirely successful in explaining experimental findings. For example, contrary to SSDR theory, defensive responses that are ineffective in avoiding aversive stimulation are not necessarily suppressed by punishment. In fact, punishment sometimes actually facilitates the occurrence of species-specific defense reactions (for example, Bolles & Riley, 1973; Melvin & Ervey, 1973; Walters & Glazer, 1971).

Predatory Imminence and the Distinction Between Defensive and Recuperative Behavior. Shortcomings of SSDR theory have stimulated alternative formulations that have introduced the concept of predatory imminence (Fanselow & Lester, 1988; Fanselow, 1989). These formulations also make a distinction between defensive responses that presumably reflect the anticipation of a painful event or injury and recuperative responses that are assumed to be performed after the aversive or injurious stimulus (Bolles & Fanselow, 1980).

The concept of **predatory imminence** can be illustrated by considering the circumstances faced by a small rodent (a rat, for example) that is a potential source of food for cats, coyotes, snakes, and other predators. The rat is presumably safest in its nest in a burrow, but it has to go out periodically to forage for food. When it is out foraging, it is not in much danger as long as no cats or snakes are around. When a snake appears, the rat's level of danger increases, but not by much if the snake is far away. However, as the snake gets closer, the level of danger rises. The situation is very dangerous when the snake is about to strike, and maximally dangerous when the strike occurs. This progression of increasing levels of danger is called predatory imminence and is illustrated in Figure 9.11.

Different species-typical defense responses are assumed to occur at different levels of predatory imminence. If a rat is forced to forage for food in a location where it periodically encounters snakes, it is likely to leave its burrow to get food less often but eat a larger meal each time (Fanselow, Lester, & Helmstetter, 1988). Thus, the response to a low level of predatory imminence is an adjustment of meal patterns. When a snake appears but is not yet about to strike, the rat's defensive behavior is likely to change to freezing. Freezing will reduce the chance that a predator will see or hear the rat. Many

M. S. Fanselow

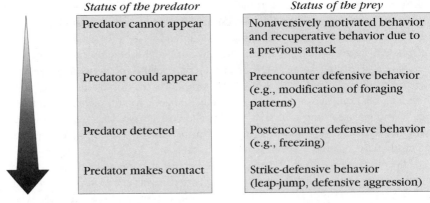

Status of the predator	*Status of the prey*
Predator cannot appear	Nonaversively motivated behavior and recuperative behavior due to a previous attack
Predator could appear	Preencounter defensive behavior (e.g., modification of foraging patterns)
Predator detected	Postencounter defensive behavior (e.g., freezing)
Predator makes contact	Strike-defensive behavior (leap-jump, defensive aggression)

Figure 9.11 The predatory-imminence continuum. (From "A Functional Behavioristic Approach to Aversively Motivated Behavior: Predatory Imminence as a Determinant of the Topography of Defensive Behavior" by M. S. Fanselow & L. S. Lester. In R. C. Bolles and M. D. Beecher (Eds.), *Evolution and Learning,* pp. 185–212. Copyright © 1988 by Lawrence Erlbaum and Associates. Reprinted by permission.)

predators will strike only at moving prey. Freezing by the prey also may result in the predator shifting its attention to something else (Suarez & Gallup, 1981).

When the snake actually touches the rat, the rat is likely to leap into the air. It is as if the rat's prior freezing behavior prepares it to explode into the air when it is touched. If the rat does not successfully escape the predator at this point, it is likely to engage in defensive aggressive activities. If the defensive behavior is successful and the rat manages to get away from the snake, the rat is likely to engage in grooming and other recuperative responses that should promote healing of its injuries.

The predatory-imminence hypothesis differs from the SSDR theory in two important respects. First, as our scenario illustrates, species-specific defense responses such as freezing, fleeing, and aggression are most likely to occur in anticipation of injury rather than in response to the injury itself. The injury actually stimulates recuperative responses. Thus, unlike the SSDR theory, the predatory-imminence hypothesis makes a distinction between defensive and recuperative responses to aversive stimulation. Secondly, in the predatory-imminence hypothesis, the primary determinant of the particular defense response that is observed is assumed to be the level of predatory imminence rather than the configuration of the environment. Thus, selection among possible SSDRs is not through suppression of ineffective SSDRs by punishment, as the SSDR theory proposes, but by different levels of perceived danger.

Despite these differences, both the SSDR theory and the predatory-imminence hypothesis assume that defensive behavior initially occurs as unconditioned responding. Stimuli that become associated with an aversive event can come to elicit a defensive response as well. The available evidence suggests that in rats the defensive response that comes to be elicited by a conditioned stimulus is usually one level lower on the predatory-imminence scale than the response elicited by the unconditioned stimulus (Fanselow, 1989). Thus, if the unconditioned stimulus elicits the leap and jump characteristic of peak predatory imminence, the conditioned stimulus is likely to elicit the freezing behavior of the level just below.

Another important similarity between the predatory-imminence hypothesis and the SSDR theory is that neither of them assumes that positive reinforcement is involved in the development of avoidance behavior. In fact, the predatory-imminence hypothesis takes a more radical position than the SSDR theory in rejecting the importance of instrumental conditioning, since it does not even include a punishment mechanism. However, the predatory-imminence hypothesis was developed as an explanation of defensive behavior—not as an explanation of the diverse findings that have been obtained in avoidance learning experiments. Therefore, it was not intended to serve as a complete account of what happens in avoidance conditioning experiments.

The Avoidance Puzzle: Concluding Comments

We have learned a great deal about avoidance behavior since Mowrer and Lamoreaux (1942) puzzled about how "not getting something" can motivate avoidance responses; numerous ingenious answers to this puzzle have been provided. Two-process theory, conditioned inhibition reinforcement, and shock-frequency reduction reinforcement all provide different views of what happens after an avoidance response to reinforce it. By contrast, the SSDR account focuses on unconditioned aspects of defensive behavior, a theme that is further elaborated through the concept of predatory imminence.

None of the major theories can explain everything that occurs in aversive conditioning situations. However, each provides ideas that are useful for understanding various aspects of avoidance behavior. For example, two-process theory is uniquely suited to explaining the results of the acquired drive experiments. The safety-signal theory is particularly useful in explaining free-operant avoidance learning, the role of response feedback stimuli in avoidance conditioning, and the maintenance of avoidance behavior in the absence of an explicit warning stimulus. Finally, the concept of predatory imminence provides the most useful account of what happens during the early stages of avoidance training. Given the complexities of the various avoidance learning paradigms, we should not be surprised that several conceptual frameworks are needed to explain all of the available data.

PUNISHMENT

Although most of us engage in avoidance behavior of one sort or another every day, there is little public awareness of it. As a society, we are not particularly concerned about what is involved in making avoidance responses. This may be because avoidance conditioning is rarely used to control others' behavior. By contrast, **punishment** has always been of great concern to people. Sometimes punishment is used as a form of retribution or as a price for undesirable behavior. Punishment is also frequently used to encourage adherence to religious and civil codes of conduct. Many institutions and rules have evolved to ensure that punishment will be administered in ways that are deemed ethical and acceptable to society. However, what constitutes justified punishment in the criminal justice system, in childrearing, in schools, and elsewhere is a matter of continual debate.

Despite longstanding societal concerns about punishment, for many years experimental psychologists did not devote much attention to the topic. On the basis of a few experiments, Thorndike (1932) and Skinner (1938, 1953) concluded that punishment was not a very effective method for controlling behavior and that it had only temporary effects at best (see also Estes, 1944). This claim was not seriously challenged until the 1960s, when punishment processes began to be more extensively investigated (Azrin & Holz, 1966; Campbell & Church, 1969; Church, 1963; Solomon, 1964). We now know that punishment can be an effective technique for modifying behavior. Given the appropriate procedural parameters, responding can be suppressed nearly totally in just one or two trials. With less severe parameters, the suppression of behavior may be incomplete, and responding may recover.

Experimental Analysis of Punishment

The basic punishment procedure involves presenting an aversive stimulus after a specified response. The usual outcome is that the specified response becomes suppressed. By not making the punished response, the organism avoids the aversive stimulation. Because punishment involves the suppression of behavior, it can be observed only with responses that are likely to occur in the absence of punishment. To ensure occurrence of the behavior, experimental studies of punishment usually also involve reinforcement of the punished response with something like food or water. This sets up a conflict between responding to obtain positive reinforcement and withholding responding to avoid punishment. The degree of response suppression that occurs is determined both by variables related to presentation of the aversive stimulus and by variables related to the availability of positive reinforcement.

Characteristics of the Aversive Stimulus and Its Method of Introduction. A great variety of aversive stimuli have been used in punishment experiments, including electric shock, a sudden burst of air, loud noise, verbal reprimands, a physical slap, a squirt of lemon juice in the mouth, and a cue previously conditioned with shock (Azrin, 1958; Hake & Azrin, 1965; Hall, Axelrod, Foundopoulos, Shellman, Campbell, & Cranston, 1971; Masserman, 1946; Sajwaj, Libet, & Agras, 1974; Skinner, 1938). Other response suppression procedures have involved the loss of positive reinforcement, time out from positive reinforcement, and overcorrection (Foxx & Azrin, 1973; Thomas, 1968; Trenholme & Baron, 1975).

N. H. Azrin

Time out refers to removal of the opportunity to obtain positive reinforcement. Time out is often used to punish children, as when a child is told "Go to your room" after doing something bad. **Overcorrection** involves requiring a person not only to rectify what was done badly but to overcorrect for the mistake. For example, a child who has placed an object in his mouth may be asked to remove the object and also to wash his mouth out with an antiseptic solution.

The response suppression produced by punishment depends in part on certain features of the aversive stimulus. The effects of various characteristics of the aversive event have been most extensively investigated with shock. The general finding has been that more intense and longer shocks are more effective in suppressing responding. (See reviews by Azrin & Holz, 1966; Church, 1969; Walters & Grusec, 1977.) Low-intensity aversive stimulation produces only moderate suppression of responding, and responding may recover with continued exposure to the mild punishment procedure (for example, Azrin, 1960). By contrast, if the aversive stimulus is sufficiently intense, responding will be completely suppressed for a long time. In one experiment, for example, high-intensity punishment completely suppressed the instrumental response for 6 days (Azrin, 1960).

Another very important factor in punishment is how the aversive stimulus is introduced. If high-intensity shock is used from the beginning when the punishment procedure is introduced, the instrumental response will be severely suppressed. Much less suppression of behavior will occur if the shock intensity is gradually increased during the course of continued punishment training (Azrin, Holz, & Hake, 1963; Miller, 1960; see also Banks, 1976). This is a very important finding because it shows that an organism becomes resistant to the effects of intense punishment if it is first exposed to lower levels of shock that do not produce much response suppression. Spending two weeks in jail is not a disturbing experience for someone who has become accustomed to shorter periods of incarceration.

The preceding findings suggest that how organisms respond during their *initial exposure* to punishment determines how they will respond to punishment subsequently (Church, 1969). This idea has an interesting implication. Suppose that individuals are first exposed to intense shock that results in a very low level of responding. If the shock intensity is subsequently reduced, the severe suppression of behavior should persist. Thus, after exposure to intense shock, mild shock should be more effective in suppressing behavior than if the mild shock had been used from the beginning. Results such as this have been obtained by Raymond (reported in Church, 1969). Taken together, the evidence indicates that initial exposure to mild aversive stimulation that does not disrupt behavior reduces the effects of later intense punishment. By contrast, initial exposure to intense aversive stimulation increases the suppressive effects of later mild punishment.

Response-Contingent Versus Response-Independent Aversive Stimulation. Another important variable that determines the extent to which aversive stimulation suppresses behavior is whether the aversive stimulus is presented contingent on a specified response or independently of behavior. Response-independent aversive stimulation can result in some suppression of instrumental behavior. However, the general finding is that significantly more suppression of behavior occurs if the aversive stimulus is produced by the instrumental response (for example, Azrin, 1956; Bolles, Holtz, Dunn, & Hill, 1980; Camp, Raymond, & Church, 1967; Frankel, 1975).

In one study demonstrating the importance of the response contingency in punishment, Goodall (1984) compared a CER, or conditioned suppression, procedure (in which footshock during a CS was delivered independent of behavior) and a discriminative punishment procedure (in which shock during the CS was delivered contingent on lever pressing). A group of rats was trained initially to press a lever for food reinforcement on a VI 60-sec schedule. After responding had stabilized, two conditioned stimuli were introduced, a tone and a light. One of the stimuli (let's say the tone) was designated as the punishment cue, and the other stimulus (the light) was designated as the cue for response-independent aversive stimulation. Two trials with each of the CSs were presented each day in alternation, starting with the punishment cue. During the punishment stimulus, the rats received a brief shock after every third lever-press response. Thus, punishment was delivered on an FR 3 schedule. Each CER trial was yoked to the preceding punishment trial, so that the rats received the same number and distribution of shocks during the CER cue as they had received during the immediately preceding punishment trial. However, shocks during the CER cue were always delivered independent of the lever-press behavior.

The results of the experiment are presented in Figure 9.12 in terms of suppression of lever pressing during the CER and punishment cues. Given the brief and mild shocks that were used (0.5 mA, 0.5 sec), not much suppression of behavior was

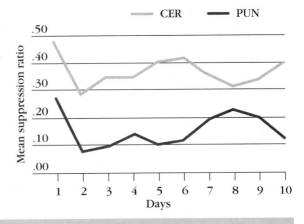

Figure 9.12 Suppression of lever pressing during punishment and CER stimuli during 10 successive sessions. During the punishment cue, lever pressing was punished on an FR 3 schedule. During the CER cue, the same number and distribution of shocks were delivered independent of behavior. (From "Learning Due to the Response-Shock Contingency in Signalled Punishment" by G. Goodall, *The Quarterly Journal of Experimental Psychology*, 1984, *36B*, pp. 259–279. Copyright © 1984 by Lawrence Erlbaum and Associates. Reprinted by permission.)

evident during the CER stimulus. By contrast, the same number and distribution of shocks substantially suppressed responding during the punishment stimulus. This difference illustrates that delivering shocks contingent on an instrumental response is more effective in suppressing that response than delivering aversive stimulation independent of behavior.

Effects of Delay of Punishment. Another important factor in punishment is the interval between the instrumental behavior and the aversive stimulation. The general finding is that increasing the delay of punishment results in less suppression of behavior (for example, Baron, 1965; Camp et al., 1967). This relation is particularly important in attempts to use punishment to modify behavior outside the laboratory. Inadvertent delays may occur if the undesired response is not detected right away, if it takes time to investigate who is actually at fault for an error, or if preparing the aversive stimulus requires time. Such delays can make punishment totally ineffective in modifying the undesired behavior.

Effects of Schedules of Punishment. Just as positive reinforcement does not have to be provided for each occurrence of the instrumental response, as we saw in the experiment by Goodall, punishment may also be delivered only intermittently. In the Goodall study, punishment was delivered on an FR 3 schedule. More systematic studies have shown that the degree of response suppression produced by punishment depends on the proportion of responses that are punished.

In a study of fixed ratio punishment by Azrin and his colleagues (1963), pigeons were first reinforced with food on a variable interval schedule for pecking a response key. Punishment was then introduced. Various fixed ratio punishment procedures were tested while food reinforcement continued to be provided for the pecking behavior. The results are summarized in Figure 9.13. When every response was shocked (FR 1 punishment), key pecking ceased entirely. With the other punishment schedules, the rate of responding depended on the frequency of punishment. Higher fixed ratio schedules allowed more responses to go unpunished. Not surprisingly, therefore, higher rates of responding occurred when higher fixed ratio punishment schedules were used. However, some suppression of behavior was observed, even when only every thousandth response was followed by shock.

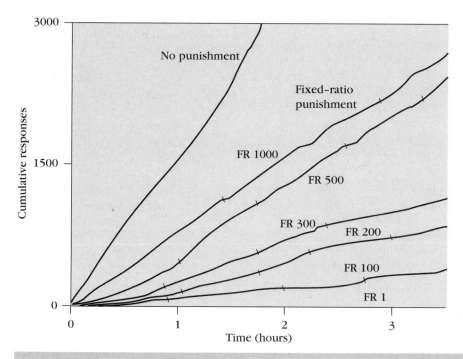

Figure 9.13 Cumulative record of pecking when the response was not punished and when the response was punished according to various fixed ratio schedules of punishment. The oblique slashes indicate the delivery of punishment. Responding was reinforced on a variable interval 3-min schedule. (From "Fixed-Ratio Punishment" by N. H. Azrin, W. C. Holz, & D. R. Hake, *Journal of the Experimental Analysis of Behavior,* 1963, 6, pp. 141–148.)

Effects of Schedules of Positive Reinforcement. As I noted earlier, in most studies of punishment the instrumental response is simultaneously maintained by a positive reinforcement schedule so that there is some level of responding available to be punished. As it turns out, the effects of a punishment procedure are in part determined by this positive reinforcement. When behavior is maintained by either a fixed or a variable interval schedule of positive reinforcement, punishment produces a decrease in the overall rate of responding. However, the temporal distribution of the behavior is not disturbed. That is, during the punishment procedure, variable interval positive reinforcement produces a suppressed but stable rate of responding (see Figure 9.13), whereas fixed interval positive reinforcement produces the typical scalloped pattern of responding (for example, Azrin & Holz, 1961).

The outcome is different if the behavior is maintained by a fixed ratio schedule of positive reinforcement. As I noted in Chapter 6, fixed ratio schedules produce a pause in responding just after reinforcement (the postreinforcement pause), followed by a high and steady rate of responding to complete the number of responses necessary for the next reinforcer (the ratio run). Punishment usually increases the length of the postreinforcement pause but has little effect on the ratio run (Azrin, 1959; see also Church, 1969; Dardano & Sauerbrunn, 1964).

Availability of Alternative Sources of Positive Reinforcement. In many experiments, the punished response is also the only response the individual can perform to obtain positive reinforcement such as food. By reducing its rate of responding, the individual may decrease the number of food pellets it receives. This predicament does not exist if alternative sources of positive reinforcement are available. If they are, the individual can entirely cease making the punished response without having to forgo reinforcement altogether.

Figure 9.14 Cumulative record of responding when responses are not punished, when responses are punished and there is no alternative source of reinforcement, and when responses are punished but an alternative reinforced response is available. (From "Punishment" by N. H. Azrin & W. C. Holz. In W. K. Honig (Ed.), *Operant Behavior.* Copyright © 1966 by Prentice-Hall.)

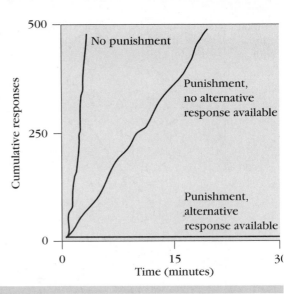

As might be expected, the availability of an alternative source of reinforcement greatly increases the suppression of responding produced by punishment. In a study by Herman and Azrin (1964), for example, adult males were seated in front of two response levers. Pressing either lever was reinforced with a cigarette on a variable interval schedule. After the behavior was occurring at a stable rate, responses on one of the levers resulted in a brief obnoxious noise. In one experimental condition, only one response lever was available during the punishment phase. In another condition, both response levers were accessible, and responding on one of them was punished with the loud noise. Figure 9.14 shows the results. When the punished response was the only way to obtain cigarettes, punishment produced a moderate suppression of behavior. By contrast, when the alternative response lever was available, responding on the punished lever ceased altogether. Thus, the availability of an alternative response for obtaining positive reinforcement greatly increased the suppressive effects of punishment. Similar results have been obtained in other situations. For example, children punished for playing with certain toys are much less likely to play with these if they are allowed to play with other toys instead (Perry & Parke, 1975).

Effects of a Discriminative Stimulus for Punishment. As we saw in Chapter 8, if positive reinforcement is available for responding in the presence of a distinctive stimulus but is not available in its absence, the organism will learn to respond only when the stimulus is present. The suppressive effects of punishment can also be brought under stimulus control. This occurs if responding is punished in the presence of a discriminative stimulus but is not punished when the stimulus is absent. Such a procedure is called **discriminative punishment.** With continued exposure to discriminative punishment, the suppressive effects of punishment will come to be limited to the presence of the discriminative stimulus (for example, Dinsmoor, 1952).

The fact that the suppressive effects of punishment can be limited to the presence of a discriminative stimulus is often problematic in applications of punishment. In many situations, the person who administers the punishment also serves as a discriminative stimulus for punishment, with the result that the undesired behavior is suppressed only as long as the monitor is present. For example, children learn which teachers are strict about discipline and learn to suppress their rambunctious behavior in those classes more than in other classes. As another example, a highway patrol car is a discriminative stimulus for punishment for speeding. Drivers are more likely to obey speed laws in areas where they see patrol cars than in unpatrolled stretches of highway.

Punishment as a Signal for the Availability of Positive Reinforcement.   Punishment does not always suppress behavior. In fact, in certain situations people seem to seek out punishment. Does this represent a breakdown of the normal mechanisms of behavior, or can such behavior be explained by the principles discussed so far? Experimental evidence suggests that conventional behavioral mechanisms may lead to such seemingly abnormal behavior. Punishment seeking can result from a situation in which positive reinforcement is available only when the instrumental response is also punished. In such circumstances, punishment may become a signal, or discriminative stimulus, for the availability of positive reinforcement. If this occurs, punishment will increase rather than suppress responding.

In one demonstration of the discriminative stimulus properties of punishment, pigeons were first trained to peck a response key for food reinforcement on a variable interval schedule (Holz & Azrin, 1961). Each response was then punished by a mild shock sufficient to reduce the response rate by about 50%. In the next phase of the experiment, periods in which the punishment procedure was in effect were alternated with periods in which punishment was not scheduled. In addition, the pecking response was intermittently reinforced with food only during the punishment periods. The punishment and safe periods were not signaled by an exteroceptive stimulus such as a light or a tone. Therefore, the only way for the pigeons to tell whether reinforcement would occur was to see whether they were punished for pecking. Under these circumstances higher rates of pecking occurred during punishment periods than during safe periods. Punishment became a discriminative stimulus for food reinforcement. (For other examples of self-punitive behavior, see Brown, 1969; Brown & Cunningham, 1981; Dean & Pittman, 1991; Melvin, 1971).

Theories of Punishment

In contrast to the study of avoidance behavior, investigations of punishment, by and large, have not been motivated by theoretical considerations. Most of the evidence available about the effects of punishment has been the product of empirical curiosity. The investigators were interested in finding out how punishment is influenced by various manipulations rather than in testing certain theoretical formulations. In fact, there are few systematic theories of punishment, and most of these were formulated about 50 years ago. I will describe three of the most prominent theories.

The Conditioned Emotional Response Theory of Punishment.   One of the first theories of punishment was proposed by Estes (1944) and is based on the observation by Estes and Skinner (1941) that a conditioned stimulus that has been paired with shock will suppress the performance of food-reinforced instrumental behavior. I discussed this conditioned suppression, or conditioned emotional response, procedure earlier in this chapter as well as in Chapter 3. The standard conditioned suppression experiment involves first conditioning animals to make an instrumental response, such as lever pressing, for food reinforcement. Classical conditioning is then conducted in which a CS (a tone or light, for example) is paired with a brief shock. The conditioned aversive stimulus is then presented while the animal is allowed to lever press for the food reinforcement. The usual result is that responding is disrupted during presentations of the CS. This response suppression was originally interpreted as resulting from competing responses elicited by the CS. The basic idea was that the conditioned stimulus came to elicit certain emotional responses (such as freezing) by virtue of being paired with shock. These conditioned emotional responses were presumably incompatible with making the lever-press response (the rat could not freeze and press the lever at the same time). Therefore, the rate of lever pressing was suppressed during presentations of the CS.

Estes (1944) proposed that punishment suppresses behavior through the same mechanism that produces conditioned suppression to a shock-paired CS. In contrast to the conditioned suppression experiment, however, punishment procedures usually do not involve an explicit CS that signals the impending delivery of shock. Estes suggested that the various stimuli an individual experiences just before making the punished response serve this function. For example, just before a rat presses a response lever, it experiences the visual and other spatial cues that exist near the lever, the tactile cues of the lever, and perhaps proprioceptive stimuli that result from its posture just as it is about to make the lever press. When the response is punished, all these stimuli become paired with shock. With repetition of the punishment episode, the various pre-response stimuli become strongly conditioned by the shock. As these cues acquire conditioned aversive properties, they will come to elicit conditioned emotional responses that are incompatible with the punished behavior. Thus, the punished response will become suppressed.

The conditioned emotional response theory can explain many punishment effects. For example, the fact that more intense and longer duration shocks produce more response suppression can be explained by assuming that the stimuli conditioned by these aversive events elicit more vigorous conditioned emotional responses. The theory can also explain why response-contingent aversive stimulation produces more response suppression than response-independent delivery of shock. If shock is produced by the instrumental response, the stimuli that become conditioned by the shock are more likely to be closely related to performance of this behavior. Therefore, the conditioned emotional responses are more likely to interfere with the punished response.

In a reformulation of the conditioned emotional response theory, Estes (1969) proposed an alternative account of the mechanisms of conditioned suppression. The new formulation may be paraphrased in motivational terms. The basic idea is that a shock-conditioned stimulus disrupts food-reinforced responding because it evokes an emotional or motivational state (let us say fear) that is incompatible with the motivation maintaining the food-reinforced behavior. The shock-conditioned stimulus is assumed to inhibit the motivation to respond based on positive reinforcement. This revision is compatible with modern two-process theory, which I will describe in Chapter 10.

The Avoidance Theory of Punishment. Another alternative to the conditioned emotional response theory regards punishment as a form of avoidance behavior. This theory is most closely associated with Dinsmoor (1954, 1977) and follows the tradition of a two-process theory of avoidance. Dinsmoor accepted the idea that the stimuli that accompany the instrumental response acquire aversive properties when the response is punished. Dinsmoor proposed that organisms learn to escape from the conditioned aversive stimuli related to the punished response by engaging in some other behavior that is incompatible with the punished activity. Since this other behavior is incompatible with the punished response, performance of the alternative activity results in suppression of the punished behavior. Thus, the avoidance theory explains punishment in terms of the acquisition of incompatible avoidance responses.

The avoidance theory of punishment is an ingenious proposal. It suggests that all changes produced by aversive instrumental conditioning, be they increases or decreases in the likelihood of a response, can be explained by the same avoidance learning mechanisms. Suppression of behavior is not viewed as reflecting the weakening of the punished response. Rather, it is explained in terms of the strengthening of competing avoidance responses.

Despite its cleverness and parsimony, the avoidance theory of punishment has been controversial. Because it explains punishment in terms of avoidance mechanisms, all the theoretical problems that have been troublesome in the analysis of avoidance behavior become problems in the analysis of punishment as well. Another challenge for the theory is that its critical elements are not stated in a way that makes them easily accessible to experimental proof (Rachlin & Herrnstein, 1969; Schuster

& Rachlin, 1968). The stimuli that are assumed to acquire conditioned aversive properties are not under the direct control of the experimenter. Rather, they are events that an organism is assumed to experience when it is about to make the punished response. The avoidance responses that are presumably acquired are also ill specified. The theory does not say what these responses will be in a given situation or how they might be identified and measured.

Punishment and the Negative Law of Effect. The third and last explanation of punishment I will describe is also the oldest. Thorndike (1911) originally proposed that positive reinforcement and punishment involve symmetrically opposite processes. Just as positive reinforcement strengthens behavior, so punishment weakens it. In later years Thorndike abandoned the idea that punishment weakens behavior because he failed to find supporting evidence in some of his experiments (Thorndike, 1932). However, the belief that there is a negative law of effect that is comparable but opposite to a positive law of effect has retained favor with some investigators (for example, Azrin & Holz, 1966; Rachlin & Herrnstein, 1969).

One approach to the analysis of the negative law of effect was initiated by Premack and his colleagues. As I said in Chapter 7, Premack proposed that positive reinforcement occurs when the opportunity to engage in a highly valued activity is made to depend on the prior performance of an activity of lower value. According to Premack, the punishment contingency reverses this relation. In punishment, a low-valued activity is made to occur contingent on the performance of a higher-valued behavior. Undergoing shock, for example, has a much lower probability than pressing a lever for food. Hence, shock can punish lever pressing. (For further discussion, see Premack, 1971a; Weisman & Premack, 1966).

With a reinforcement procedure, the instrumental response is increased, and the reinforcing response is decreased relative to a baseline free-responding situation. With a punishment procedure, the instrumental response is decreased, and the reinforcing or punishing response is increased relative to a baseline condition. Moreover, in both cases the response that increases is the low-valued behavior, and the one that decreases is the higher-valued behavior (see Table 9.1). Viewed in this way, the procedures of reinforcement and punishment produce the same effects. Operationally, there is only one significant difference. In punishment, the individual has to be forced to engage in the lower-valued activity. Rats do not ordinarily apply electrical shocks to themselves or run more than they want. In reinforcement, the individual is "induced" to engage in the lower-valued activity by the contingency itself.

The similarity between punishment and reinforcement I have just described was tested in an interesting experiment involving toy-playing behavior in children (Burkhard, Rachlin, & Schrader, 1978). In a baseline phase, the children were observed playing with three toys. The toys were ranked high, medium, and low on the basis of how much time the children spent with each one. The children were assigned to reinforcement and punishment groups. For the reinforcement group, 1 minute of playing with the high-ranked toy was allowed after 1 minute of play with the low-ranked toy. For the punishment group, 1 minute of play with the low-ranked toy was required after 1 minute of play with the high-ranked toy. In both cases, the toy ranked as medium provided background activity and could be used freely. If Premack's punishment hypothesis is correct, the reinforcement and punishment procedures should have produced the same new distribution of time among the three toys. This in fact was the result. The reinforcement and punishment groups were indistinguishable in how much time they ended up playing with each toy. Playing

TABLE 9.1	RESPONSE REALLOCATION IN POSITIVE REINFORCEMENT AND PUNISHMENT	
PROCEDURE	RESPONSE-REINFORCER CONTINGENCY	RESULTANT BEHAVIOR CHANGE
Positive reinforcement	L→H	L increases H decreases
Punishment	H→L	L increases H decreases

L = low-valued activity; H = high-valued activity

with the low-ranked toy increased, and playing with the high-ranked toy decreased to comparable levels for the two groups.

Premack's perspective suggests that punishment is similar to positive reinforcement in that it imposes a restriction against which behavior has to be adjusted. The negative law of effect is a statement of the way behavior changes under these restrictions: a low-valued activity produces a decrease in a higher-valued activity. Economically minded theorists propose, as in the case of positive reinforcement (see Chapter 7), that organisms respond so as to maximize overall value. The maximization process, with both reinforcement and punishment procedures, involves an increase in a low-valued activity balanced against a decrease in a high-valued activity.

Punishment Outside the Laboratory

As we have seen, punishment can be a highly effective procedure for rapidly suppressing behavior. However, the effectiveness of punishment in laboratory studies is not sufficient to justify the use of punishment outside the laboratory. Punishment procedures are easily misused, and even if the procedures are administered effectively there are serious ethical constraints on their application.

Punishment is typically not applied in an effective manner. Often punishment is first introduced at low intensities (a reprimand for the first offense, for example). The aversive stimulus may not be administered rapidly after the target response but delayed until it is convenient to administer it ("Wait until I tell your parents about this"). Punishment is usually administered on an intermittent schedule, and the chances of getting "caught" may not be high. Appropriate alternative behavior may not be recognized and positively reinforced at the same time that transgressions are punished. Often there are clear discriminative stimuli for punishment. The undesired behavior may be monitored only at particular times or by a particular person, making it likely that the punished response will be suppressed only at those times. Finally, punishment may be the only source of attention, making punishment a discriminative stimulus for positive reinforcement.

The preceding problems with the uses of punishment outside the laboratory can be overcome. However, it is difficult to guard against these pitfalls in common interpersonal interactions. People who punish others often do so because they are frustrated and angry. A frustrative act of punishment is likely to violate many of the guidelines for effective use of punishment. Punishing someone in an act of anger and frustration is a form of abuse—not a form of systematic behavior modification.

Abuse is not as likely in the hands of professionals if punishment is used as part of a systematic training or therapeutic program for the treatment of severe behavior problems. In such cases, punishment is usually attempted only after other treatment efforts have failed. In one study, for example, punishment was used to suppress recurrent vomiting by a 9-month-old infant (Linscheid & Cunningham, 1977). The recurrent vomiting had resulted in excessive weight loss and malnutrition. Without treatment, the infant risked potentially fatal medical complications. Brief (0.5-second) shocks sufficient to elicit a startle response, but not sufficient to elicit crying, were used as the aversive stimulus. Within three days, vomiting was nearly totally suppressed by the punishment procedure. The suppression of vomiting persisted after discharge from the hospital. The infant started gaining weight again and was soon within normal range.

Cases like the preceding illustrate that punishment can be beneficial. However, even in such instances there are serious ethical dilemmas that must be resolved. There is an ongoing debate about when, if ever, punishment is justified as a treatment procedure, and therapists are continuing their search for alternative ways to deal with potentially life-threatening behavior problems (see Repp & Singh, 1990.) Many states have adopted stringent procedures to review and monitor the use of aversive control procedures in therapeutic settings and have banned certain forms of aversive control altogether. Professional and patient rights organizations also have adopted detailed and restrictive guidelines for the therapeutic uses of aversive control.

SAMPLE QUESTIONS

1. What is the fundamental problem in the analysis of avoidance behavior, and how is this problem resolved by two-process theory?

2. Compare and contrast discriminated and free-operant avoidance procedures.

3. How can the concept of a safety signal be used to explain free-operant avoidance learning?

4. Describe factors that enhance the effectiveness of punishment in suppressing behavior.

5. In what ways is punishment similar to positive reinforcement? In what ways is it different?

KEY TERMS

acquired drive A source of motivation for instrumental behavior caused by the presentation of a stimulus that was previously conditioned with a primary, or unconditioned, reinforcer.

avoidance procedure An instrumental conditioning procedure in which the participant's behavior prevents the delivery of an aversive stimulus.

avoidance trial A trial in a discriminated avoidance procedure in which the occurrence of the avoidance response prevents the delivery of the aversive stimulus.

conservation of fear The assumption that conditioned fear is maintained in a signaled avoidance procedure if participants respond rapidly to turn off the CS because later segments of the CS are not experienced.

discriminated avoidance An avoidance conditioning procedure in which occurrences of the aversive stimulus are signaled by a conditioned stimulus. Responding during presentation of the conditioned stimulus terminates the CS and prevents the delivery of the aversive unconditioned stimulus. Also called *signaled avoidance.*

discriminative punishment A procedure in which responding is punished in the presence of a particular stimulus and not punished in the absence of that stimulus.

escape trial A type of trial during avoidance training in which the required avoidance response is not made, and the aversive unconditioned stimulus is presented. Performance of the instrumental response during the aversive stimulus results in termination of the aversive stimulus. Thus, the organism is able to escape from the aversive stimulus.

flooding A procedure for extinguishing avoidance behavior in which the conditioned stimulus is presented while the participant is prevented from making the avoidance response. Also called *response prevention.*

free-operant avoidance Same as *nondiscriminated avoidance.*

nondiscriminated avoidance An avoidance conditioning procedure in which occurrences of the aversive stimulus are not signaled by an external stimulus. In the absence of avoidance behavior, the aversive stimulus is presented periodically, as set by the S-S interval. Each occurrence of the avoidance response prevents delivery of aversive stimulation for a fixed period (the R-S interval). Also called *free operant avoidance*; originally called *Sidman avoidance.*

overcorrection A procedure for discouraging behavior in which the participant is not only required to correct or rectify a mistake but is also required to go beyond that by, for example, extensively practicing the correct response alternative.

predatory imminence The perceived likelihood of being attacked by a predator. Different species-typical defense responses are assumed to be performed in the face of different degrees of predatory imminence.

punishment An instrumental conditioning procedure in which there is a positive contingency between the instrumental response and an aversive stimulus. If the participant performs the instrumental response, it receives the aversive stimulus; if the participant does not perform the instrumental response, it does not receive the aversive stimulus.

R-S interval The interval between the occurrence of an avoidance response and the next scheduled presentation of the aversive stimulus in a nondiscriminated avoidance procedure.

response prevention Same as *flooding.*

safety signal A stimulus that signals the absence of an aversive event.

shock-frequency reduction A hypothesis according to which reduction in the frequency of shock serves to reinforce avoidance behavior.

shuttle avoidance A type of avoidance conditioning procedure in which the required instrumental response consists in going back and forth (shuttling) between two sides of an experimental apparatus.

signaled avoidance Same as *discriminated avoidance*

species-specific defense reactions Species-typical responses that animals perform in an aversive situation. The responses may involve freezing, fleeing, or fighting.

S-S interval The interval between successive presentations of the aversive stimulus in a nondiscriminated avoidance procedure when the avoidance response is not performed.

time out A period during which the opportunity to obtain reinforcement is removed. This may involve removal of the participant from the situation where reinforcers may be obtained.

two-process theory of avoidance A theory originally developed to explain discriminated avoidance learning that presumes the operation of two mechanisms: (1) classical conditioning of fear to the warning signal and (2) instrumental reinforcement of the avoidance response through termination of the warning signal and consequent fear reduction.

CLASSICAL-INSTRUMENTAL INTERACTIONS AND THE ASSOCIATIVE STRUCTURE OF INSTRUMENTAL CONDITIONING

The Role of Instrumental Reinforcement in Classical Conditioning Procedures

    The Omission Control Procedure

    Conditioned Response Modifications of the US

The Associative Structure of Instrumental Conditioning

    S-R and S-O Associations and the r_g-s_g Mechanism

    S-O Associations and Modern Two-Process Theory

    R-O and S-(R-O) Associations

Concluding Comments

I N Chapter 10 I will discuss in greater detail the possible interactions between classical and instrumental conditioning, as well as issues related to the associative structure of instrumental conditioning. I will begin with a description of experiments concerning the possible role of instrumental reinforcement in classical conditioning procedures. I will then describe some of the extensive theoretical and empirical work on the associative structure of instrumental conditioning. Instrumental conditioning involves a response R and the reinforcer outcome O, as well as the stimuli S, in the presence of which the response is reinforced. I will describe the role of S-R and S-O associations in instrumental conditioning within the context of the r_g-s_g mechanism and S-O associations within the context of modern two-process theory. I will then present evidence for the learning of R-O and S-(R-O) relations in instrumental conditioning.

Classical and instrumental conditioning are clearly distinguishable conceptually and procedurally. As we saw in Chapters 3 and 4, classical conditioning is assumed to involve the learning of relations, or associations, between stimuli (usually the CS and the US), and classical conditioning procedures focus on when the stimuli occur in relation to each other, independent of the actions of the organism. By contrast, as I noted in Chapters 5-7, instrumental conditioning is assumed to involve the learning or redistribution of the organism's responses, and instrumental conditioning procedures focus on the relation between occurrences of a specified (instrumental) response and delivery of the reinforcer or response outcome.

Despite these conceptual and procedural distinctions between classical and instrumental conditioning, in practice most conditioning procedures involve instrumental as well as classical components. Conditioning procedures typically involve both stimulus-stimulus and response-outcome relations. Furthermore, isolating the effects of these components can be difficult and is sometimes impossible.

We already have seen examples of the interaction of classical and instrumental conditioning processes in analyses of discrimination learning (Chapter 8) and avoidance behavior and punishment (Chapter 9). In the present chapter we will consider the interaction of classical and instrumental conditioning more generally. I will first describe the potential role of instrumental conditioning processes in classical conditioning experiments and ways in which investigators have tried to rule out these instrumental factors. I will then describe the potential role of classical conditioning processes in instrumental learning. That research has provided information about the associative structure of instrumental conditioning, which is our second major topic.

THE ROLE OF INSTRUMENTAL REINFORCEMENT IN CLASSICAL CONDITIONING PROCEDURES

In classical conditioning procedures, a conditioned stimulus is periodically presented, followed by an unconditioned stimulus. With repeated pairings of the CS with the US, the organism comes to make a conditioned response, but the occurrence of the CR does not determine whether the US is presented. The US is presented irrespective of the CR. In fact, this is one of the primary bases for distinguishing classical from instrumental training procedures. Nevertheless, investigators have been concerned for a long time with the fact that opportunities for instrumental reinforcement exist in many classical conditioning procedures, and instrumental reinforcement may be partly responsible for the ensuing learning. (See Coleman & Gormezano, 1979, for a historical discussion of this issue.)

The potential for instrumental reinforcement in classical conditioning is most obvious in situations where the conditioned response occurs before presentation of the unconditioned stimulus on a given trial. If the CR occurs before the US, instrumental reinforcement may occur in two different ways. First, if the US is a positive reinforcer such as food, its presentation shortly after the CR may reinforce the CR directly. Second, the occurrence of the CR may somehow alter the US so as to make it either more rewarding or more effective in conditioning (Hebb, 1956; Perkins, 1955, 1968).

The possibility that conditioned responses may make the US more effective or rewarding was first recognized by Schlosberg (1937). He proposed, for example, that dogs may learn to salivate when food is used as the US because anticipatory salivation makes it easier to dissolve and swallow dry food. When a drop of acid serves as the US, salivation may become conditioned because anticipatory salivation helps to dilute the aversive taste of the acid. Analogous instrumental modifications of the US can be postulated to occur in all classical conditioning experiments.

Two experimental strategies have been devised to evaluate the role of instrumental reinforcement in classical conditioning situations. One of these effectively eliminates the possibility of reinforcement of the CR by presentation of the US. The other technique evaluates possible modifications of the US caused by the CR by specifically arranging for such changes in the US. Experiments using both strategies have indicated that instrumental reinforcement is not necessary for learning to take place in classical conditioning procedures.

The Omission Control Procedure

As I noted, if the US is a positive reinforcer such as food, presentation of the US following the CR may result in unintended instrumental reinforcement of the CR. Investigators have attempted to rule out this source of reinforcement by modifying the standard classical conditioning procedure. The modified technique, called the **omission control procedure,** is diagrammed in Figure 10.1. In the omission control procedure, presentation of the US on a given trial depends on whether or not the CR of interest has occurred. In the absence of the CR, the CS is followed by the US in the usual manner. By contrast, if the CR occurs, the US is omitted on that trial. Thus, the CR results in omission of the US. The omission contingency makes it impossible for the CR to be instrumentally reinforced by the US.

The omission control procedure was introduced by Sheffield (1965) in the study of salivary conditioning in dogs. He tested dogs in conditioning with food and acid in the mouth as unconditioned stimuli. With both types of USs, omitting the US when a CR occurred did not prevent development of conditioned salivation. Acquisition of conditioned salivation was generally slower with the omission control procedure than with presentations of the US on every trial. Nevertheless, the omission procedure was remarkably effective. One dog, for example, continued to salivate on about 50% of trials after 800 trials on the omission control procedure.

Since its introduction, the omission control procedure has been tested in a variety of classical conditioning situations (for example, Gormezano & Hiller, 1972; Patten & Rudy, 1967; Crawford & Domjan, 1993). It has been perhaps most frequently used in studies of sign tracking (for reviews, see Locurto, 1981; Tomie et al., 1989). As I have noted, in sign tracking, animals come to approach and touch (peck, in the case of pigeons) stimuli that signal the delivery of a positive reinforcer such as food.

In one notable demonstration of sign tracking in an omission control procedure (Peden, Browne, & Hearst, 1977), pigeons were tested in an experimental chamber that had a food hopper built into one wall and a response key built into an adjacent wall 35 cm away. The key light was periodically illuminated for 8 seconds, followed by access to grain for 5 seconds. Approaching the key light was considered the conditioned response. In the first phase of the experiment (omission control), food delivery at the end of a trial was canceled if the pigeon approached within 20–25 cm of the key-light CS. In Phase 2, food always followed illumination of the key light regardless of what the pigeons were doing. The investigators measured the percentage of trials on which the animals approached the light CS during each phase of the experiment.

E. Hearst

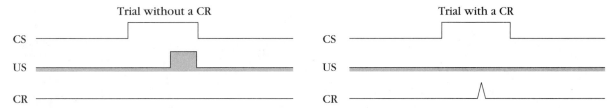

Figure 10.1 Diagram of the omission control procedure. On trials without a conditioned response (left), the CS is followed by the US in the usual manner. On trials with a conditioned response (right), the US is omitted.

The results are shown in Figure 10.2. The remarkable finding was that the pigeons persisted in approaching the key-light CS during the first phase of the experiment, even though their approach responses canceled the delivery of food. Fifty trials were conducted each day, and even after about 2000 trials, the pigeons were observed to approach the CS approximately 40% of the time. This occurred even when subjects were not in the vicinity of the response key at the start of the trial. Thus, as was true in Sheffield's (1965) experiment, instrumental reinforcement was not necessary for the acquisition of the conditioned response. Other research has shown that substantially fewer CS-approach responses occur if the CS and food are presented randomly so that the CS does not signal food (Peden et al., 1977, Experiment 2).

As mentioned previously, in Sheffield's experiment with dogs, acquisition of conditioned salivation was slower with the omission control procedure than with a standard classical conditioning procedure. Peden et al. obtained similar results in sign tracking. In the second phase of their experiment, when every trial ended in food delivery, approach responses increased (see Figure 10.2). A higher performance level with standard classical conditioning than with the omission control procedure is a common finding in studies of this kind (for example, Schwartz & Williams, 1972). The difference between the omission control and standard classical conditioning procedures in sign tracking experiments has been the subject of considerable debate (Jenkins, 1977; Locurto, 1981).

Why does the omission control procedure lead to lower levels of responding than standard classical conditioning? One explanation emphasizes Pavlovian processes and attributes the results to the fact that the US is not presented on every trial when occurrences of the CR prevent delivery of the US in the omission control procedure. Classical conditioning generally leads to lower levels of performance if only some presentations of the CS end in delivery of the US. Other explanations emphasize instrumental processes. The omission control procedure may produce lower levels of responding because the CR is punished by withholding the expected reward. Alternatively, the omission control procedure may decrease conditioned responding by providing reinforcement for activities incompatible with the target CR (since only non-CR responses can be followed by the US). Regardless of which explanation turns out to be correct, the results of omission control studies demonstrate that substantial levels of classical conditioning can occur in the absence of instrumental reinforcement.

Conditioned Response Modifications of the US

A second experimental technique that has been used to evaluate the contribution of instrumental reinforcement to the learning that occurs in classical conditioning procedures has focused on possible modifications of the US caused by the conditioned response. Consider, for example, a classical conditioning situation in which the US is an aversive stimulus. In such cases participants might learn to make the conditioned

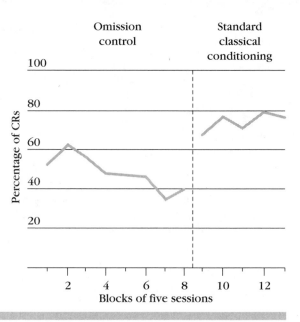

Figure 10.2 Percentage of trials on which a conditioned response (approach to the CS) was observed during blocks of five sessions. Each session consisted of 50 trials. During the first eight blocks of sessions (2000 trials) an omission control procedure was in effect. During the remainder of the experiment a standard classical conditioning procedure was in effect. (From "Persistent Approaches to a Signal for Food Despite Food Omission for Approaching" by B. F. Peden, M. P. Browne, and E. Hearst, *Journal of Experimental Psychology: Animal Behavior Processes*, 1977, *3*, pp. 377–399. Copyright © 1977 by American Psychological Association. Reprinted by permission.)

response because this somehow reduces the aversiveness of the US. (By making the CR, the participant may "brace" itself against the US.) If this is true, then explicitly arranging for the intensity of the US to be reduced when the CR occurs should facilitate acquisition of the CR.

The importance of CR modifications of the US was investigated in an experiment on the conditioning of the nictitating membrane response in rabbits (Coleman, 1975; see also Gormezano & Coleman, 1973). The CS was a tone, and the US was a brief shock to the skin near one eye. Retraction of the nictitating membrane (the secondary eyelid) over the eyes was measured as the conditioned response. Four groups of rabbits were tested. All received a brief shock of 5.0 milliamperes (mA) after the CS when a conditioned response did not occur. For Group 5-5, the shock was also 5.0 mA when the rabbits made a CR. For the other groups, the shock intensity was decreased when a conditioned response occurred. For Group 5-3, the shock was decreased to 3.3 mA; for Group 5-1, the CR decreased the shock intensity to 1.7 mA, and for Group 5-0, the CR prevented delivery of the shock altogether. (Essentially, Group 5-0 received an omission control procedure). If shock reduction provides important instrumental reinforcement for the conditioned response in this type of classical conditioning, better learning should have occurred in Groups 5-3, 5-1, and 5-0 than in Group 5-5.

The results are shown in Figure 10.3. Contrary to the instrumental reinforcement prediction, the speed and level of conditioning were not increased by reducing the shock intensity whenever the conditioned response occurred. Groups 5-3, 5-1, and 5-0 did not learn the nictitating membrane response faster than group 5-5. In fact, the only difference evident between the groups was that eliminating the shock altogether whenever the CR occurred (Group 5-0) resulted in less responding in that group than in the other groups. This outcome probably reflects the fact that Group 5-0 did not receive shock on every trial, whereas the other groups did.

These results provide strong evidence that modifications of the US caused by the CR were not necessary for classical conditioning of the nictitating membrane

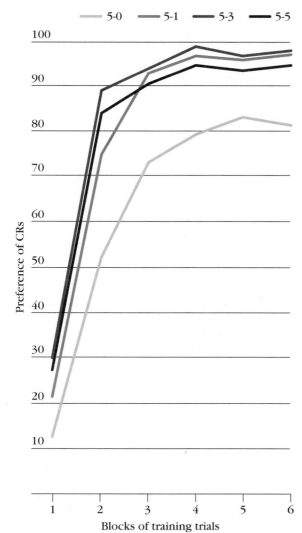

Figure 10.3 Percentage of conditioned responses in an experiment on nictitating membrane conditioning with rabbits. The conditioned response resulted in reduction of the intensity of the shock US for Groups 5-3 and 5-1 and omission of the US for Group 5-0. By contrast, the conditioned response had no effect on the delivery of the US in Group 5-5. (From "Consequences of Response-Contingent Change in Unconditioned Stimulus Intensity Upon the Rabbit (*Oryctolagus cuniculus*) Nictitating Membrane Response" by S. R. Coleman, *Journal of Comparative and Physiological Psychology*, 1975, *88,* pp. 591–595. Copyright © 1975 by the American Psychological Association. Reprinted by permission.)

response and did not even facilitate learning. Thus, classical conditioning can occur in the absence of instrumental reinforcement. However, this does not mean that instrumental reinforcement is not involved in any classical conditioning situation. The contribution of instrumental reinforcement has to be evaluated separately in each case with the techniques I have described.

THE ASSOCIATIVE STRUCTURE OF INSTRUMENTAL CONDITIONING

As I noted in Chapters 5 and 8, in an instrumental conditioning procedure the instrumental response occurs in the presence of certain distinctive stimuli and is followed by a response outcome or reinforcer. This sequence of events is reviewed in Fig-

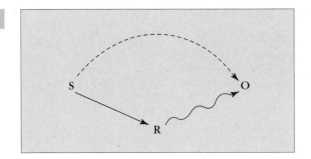

Figure 10.4 Diagram of instrumental conditioning. The instrumental response (R) occurs in the presence of distinctive stimuli (S) and results in delivery of the reinforcer outcome (O). This allows for the establishment of several different types of associations. Historically, investigators emphasized the S-R and S-O associations.

ure 10.4, where S represents the stimuli that are present when the instrumental response is made, R represents the instrumental response, and O represents the reinforcer or response outcome. The wavy line between the response and the reinforcing stimulus signifies that the response causes the delivery of the reinforcer. This causal relation ensures that the reinforcer will be paired with the participant's exposure to stimuli S. The S-O pairing is indicated by the dashed line.

The basic structure of an instrumental conditioning procedure permits the development of several different types of associations. The first association that was identified in instrumental conditioning is the S-R association. The S-R association was postulated by Thorndike to be the key to instrumental learning in his law of effect (see Chapter 5). Another association that attracted the attention of early investigators was the S-O association. The S-O association may develop because the response outcome O is delivered in the presence of stimuli S. This association is presumably established by Pavlovian processes. S acts in the role of a conditioned stimulus, and O acts in the role of an unconditioned stimulus.

In the preceding section I discussed ways in which instrumental reinforcement can be ruled out as a contributing factor in classical conditioning experiments. Unfortunately, analogous strategies do not exist for ruling out classical conditioning in instrumental procedures. The establishment of an S-O association cannot be prevented using anything analogous to the omission control procedure. The reinforcer cannot be omitted after the participant's exposure to stimuli S, because this would also result in nonreinforcement of the instrumental response and would eliminate the instrumental aspects of the procedure.

Specification of an instrumental response ensures that the participant will always experience certain distinctive stimuli (S) in connection with making the response. These stimuli may involve the place where the response is to be performed, the texture of the object the participant is to manipulate, or distinctive olfactory or visual cues. Whatever the stimuli may be, reinforcement of the instrumental response will inevitably result in a pairing between stimuli S and the reinforcer. Such pairings provide the potential for classical conditioning and the establishment of an association between S and O.

Rather than try to construct "pure" instrumental procedures that do not permit the occurrence of classical conditioning, investigators have tried to understand how instrumental and classical conditioning processes interact in producing learning. A highly influential proposal was the r_g-s_g mechanism.

S-R and S-O Associations and the r_g-s_g Mechanism

One of the earliest and most influential accounts of the role of classical conditioning in instrumental behavior was originally proposed by Clark Hull (1930, 1931) and was elaborated by Kenneth Spence (1956). Essentially, Hull and Spence added a classical conditioning component to Thorndike's law of effect. According to Thorndike, reinforcement of an instrumental response increases the future likelihood of the behavior by establishing an association between the response and the stimuli present at the time the response is made. Thus, Thorndike focused on the S-R association.

Hull and Spence suggested that there is also a classical conditioning process that comes to motivate the instrumental behavior. More specifically, they assumed that during the course of instrumental conditioning, animals not only learn to make response R in the presence of stimuli S but also come to expect the reinforcer. Furthermore, they assumed that the expectancy of reward serves to motivate the instrumental response. The expectancy of reward is mediated by the S-O association. Because of the S-O association, the presence of stimuli S elicits an expectation that the reinforcer outcome O will occur.

K. W. Spence

Fractional Anticipatory Goal Responses. Hull and Spence recognized that whenever the instrumental response R was followed by the reinforcer outcome O, the stimulus S present at the time of the response became paired with the reinforcer O. It was their belief that classical conditioning occurred by stimulus substitution. As I noted in Chapter 4, according to the concept of stimulus-substitution, the conditioned stimulus comes to acquire properties of the unconditioned stimulus. Therefore, Hull and Spence assumed that S will come to elicit some of the same responses that are elicited by the reinforcer. If the reinforcer is food, during the course of instrumental training, the animal will presumably come to salivate and perhaps make chewing movements when it experiences stimuli S. These classically conditioned responses are rarely as vigorous as the salivation and chewing elicited by the food itself, and they occur in anticipation of the food delivery. Therefore, they are called **fractional anticipatory goal responses.** The conventional symbol for a fractional anticipatory goal response is r_g.

The fractional anticipatory goal response is assumed to be similar to other types of responses. As noted in Chapter 2, responses typically produce some sensory feedback. That is, the act of making a response usually creates distinctive bodily sensations. The sensory feedback produced by the fractional anticipatory goal response is represented by the symbol s_g.

The fractional anticipatory goal response, with its feedback stimulus, s_g, is assumed to constitute the expectancy of reward, r_g-s_g. Figure 10.5 illustrates the full sequence of events in the r_g-s_g mechanism. The fractional anticipatory goal response, r_g, is elicited by S before the instrumental response occurs. Thus, the instrumental response is made in the presence of the sensory feedback s_g from r_g. Because the instrumental response is reinforced when it is made after exposure to s_g, a connection becomes established between s_g and the response R.

The outcome of these events is that as instrumental conditioning proceeds, the instrumental response comes to be stimulated by two factors (arrows *a* and *b* in Figure 10.5). First, the presence of S comes to evoke the instrumental response directly

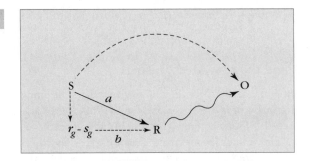

Figure 10.5 The r_g-s_g mechanism. During instrumental conditioning, the instrumental response R is followed by the reinforcer outcome O. Because this happens in the presence of distinctive situational cues S, an association is formed between S and R (arrow *a*). Delivery of the reinforcer following exposure to S results in the classical conditioning of S by the reinforcer. Therefore, S comes to elicit a classically conditioned fractional anticipatory goal response r_g with its feedback cues s_g. Because the instrumental response R is reinforced in the presence of s_g, an association also becomes established between s_g and R (arrow *b*).

by association with R. Second, the instrumental activity also comes to be made in response to the expectancy of reward (r_g-s_g) because of an association between s_g and R.

Concurrent Measurement of Instrumental Behavior and Classically Conditioned Responses. A major implication of the r_g-s_g mechanism is that classically conditioned responses develop during instrumental conditioning. In addition, the r_g-s_g mechanism predicts that the classically conditioned responses occur before the instrumental behavior (see Figure 10.5). These predictions can be tested by measuring classically conditioned responses during the course of instrumental learning. This is the approach taken by **concurrent-measurement experiments.**

Numerous concurrent measurement experiments have been carried out in positive and negative reinforcement situations. (For reviews, see Black, 1971; Rescorla & Solomon, 1967.) These experiments have shown over and over again that classically conditioned responses are learned during instrumental conditioning. Dogs, for example, come to show conditioned salivary responses when they are reinforced with food for making a lever-press response (for example, Williams, 1965). However, contrary to the r_g-s_g mechanism, classically conditioned responses do not invariably begin before the instrumental response.

Figure 10.6 shows a case in point. The dog, whose data are shown in Figure 10.6, was reinforced with food for pressing a response lever on a fixed ratio 33 schedule of reinforcement. As you may recall from Chapter 6, on a fixed ratio schedule there is a postreinforcement pause after the delivery of the reinforcer. This pause is then followed by a high and steady rate of responding (the ratio run). Consistent with that pattern, the dog showed a low rate of lever pressing during the first 3 seconds of the fixed ratio cycle, followed by much higher rates during seconds 4–13. However, salivation did not appear until the 10th second of the cycle. Thus, classically conditioned salivary responding started only after instrumental responding was well under way, contrary to predictions of the r_g-s_g mechanism. (For other dramatic examples of

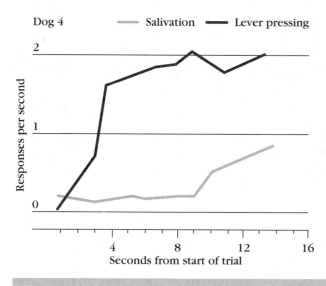

Figure 10.6 Rate of lever pressing and salivation observed with a dog during successive 1-second periods leading up to the next delivery of food reinforcement on a fixed ratio 33 schedule of reinforcement. (From "Classical Conditioning and Incentive Motivation" by D. R. Williams. In W. F. Prokasy (Ed.), *Classical Conditioning.* Copyright © 1965 Prentice-Hall. Reprinted by permission.)

the dissociation of instrumental and classically conditioned behavior, see Ellison & Konorski, 1964.)

Failure of concurrent measurement experiments to confirm predictions of the r_g-s_g mechanism have encouraged investigators to pursue other characterizations of how S-O associations may be involved in the behavior that results from instrumental conditioning procedures. One of the most influential of these alternative approaches has been modern two-process theory.

S-O Associations and Modern Two-Process Theory

Modern two-process theory was brought into focus in 1967 by Rescorla and Solomon. However, it was developed from ideas entertained as early as the 1940s, especially in connection with theorizing about the mechanisms of avoidance learning (see Mowrer, 1960; Rescorla & Solomon, 1967). I term the model "modern two-process theory" to distinguish it from the two-process theory of avoidance learning discussed in Chapter 9.

Modern two-process theory is similar to the fractional anticipatory goal response mechanism in that it assumes that classical conditioning is important in motivating instrumental behavior. However, it adopts a different view of classical conditioning and a different view of how S-O associations influence instrumental behavior.

In contrast to the r_g-s_g mechanism, modern two-process theory does not regard classical conditioning as involving the learning of particular responses. Rather, it assumes that the primary outcome of classical conditioning is that a previously "neutral" stimulus comes to elicit a particular type of motivation called a **central emotional state.** The emotional state that comes to be elicited by a conditioned stimulus corresponds to the particular type of unconditioned stimulus that is used and is considered to be a characteristic of the central nervous system. It is a mood, if you will.

Emotional states do not invariably lead to particular responses. On the contrary, they may be manifest in any one of a variety of actions. Anger, for example, may result in fighting, shouting, a frown, or refusal to acknowledge someone's presence, depending on the circumstances.

Because instrumental conditioning procedures allow for the acquisition of an S-O association, modern two-process theory assumes that central emotional states are conditioned during ordinary instrumental training. These states become conditioned either to situational cues or to discriminative stimuli present during reinforcement of the instrumental response. The emotional states are assumed to motivate the instrumental behavior.

A Basic Implication. The fact that classically conditioned emotional states can be manifest in a variety of different responses makes modern two-process theory much less precise than the r_g-s_g mechanism. It also makes the concurrent measurement of instrumental behavior and classically conditioned responses irrelevant to evaluation of the theory. However, the theory makes one important and unambiguous prediction about behavior—namely, that *the rate of an instrumental response will be modified by the presentation of a classically conditioned stimulus.* This prediction is based on the following considerations. During instrumental conditioning, a conditioned central emotional state is assumed to develop to motivate the instrumental response. Classically conditioned stimuli also are assumed to elicit central emotional states. Therefore, presentation of a classically conditioned stimulus during performance of an instrumental response will alter the emotional state that was maintaining the instrumental response. This will be evident in a change in the rate of the instrumental behavior.

We have already seen an example of how a classically conditioned stimulus can alter instrumental behavior in the conditioned emotional response (CER) procedure, described in earlier chapters. You may recall that in the CER procedure, animals are first trained to press a response lever for food reinforcement. A discrete stimulus such as a light or a tone is then repeatedly paired with shock. This classically conditioned fear stimulus is then presented while the animals are lever pressing for food. Consistent with the prediction of modern two-process theory, presentation of the shock-conditioned CS produces a change in the rate of the lever-press response. The rate of lever pressing for food decreases.

Classically conditioned stimuli do not always suppress instrumental behavior, as in the CER procedure. According to two-process theory, the kinds of changes that various classically conditioned stimuli will produce will depend on the emotional state created by these CSs and the emotional state created by the instrumental reinforcement schedule. If the classically conditioned stimulus produces emotions that are opposite to those that motivate the instrumental behavior, the rate of the instrumental response will decrease. This is presumably what happens in the CER procedure. The food-reinforcement schedule motivates lever pressing by way of a positive emotional state conditioned by food. This emotion is disrupted when the shock conditioned CS is presented because the CS elicits an aversive emotional state.

In other situations, the classically conditioned stimulus may evoke an emotion that is similar to the emotional state created by the instrumental reinforcement schedule. When this occurs, the two emotions will summate, and the rate of the instrumental behavior will increase.

Specific Predictions of Modern Two-Process Theory. Specific predictions about how classically conditioned stimuli will influence instrumental behavior can be made by considering the types of emotions elicited by various types of CSs and by instrumental reinforcement schedules. Borrowing language introduced by Mowrer (1960), Table 10.1 provides metaphorical labels for the emotional states presumably elicited by some common types of classically conditioned stimuli.

295

*Classical-Instrumental
Interactions and the
Associative Structure
of Instrumental
Conditioning*

TABLE 10.1	EMOTIONAL STATES ELICITED BY THE CS AFTER VARIOUS TYPES OF CLASSICAL CONDITIONING	
	UNCONDITIONED STIMULUS	
CONDITIONED STIMULUS	**APPETITIVE (SUCH AS FOOD)**	**AVERSIVE (SUCH AS SHOCK)**
CS+	Hope	Fear
CS–	Disappointment	Relief

Let us first consider classical conditioning with a positive (appetitive) unconditioned stimulus such as food or water. If the stimulus is a CS+, meaning that it becomes associated with the impending presentation of the US, we may refer to the emotional state created by the CS as **hope.** By contrast, if the stimulus is a CS–, meaning that it has become associated with the removal or the absence of the appetitive US, we may refer to the emotional state created as **disappointment.** In the case of a CS+ for the impending presentation of an aversive US such as shock, the conditioned emotional state is called **fear.** Finally, if the conditioned stimulus is a CS associated with the removal or absence of an aversive US, we may presume that **relief** is elicited by presentations of the CS.

Using this same terminology, we may assume that instrumental behavior reinforced by the presentation of food (or other appetitive reinforcers) is motivated by "hope" and that instrumental behavior reinforced by the avoidance or removal of shock (or other aversive events) is motivated by "fear." It is important to note that these labels are used for convenience only and do not imply that the Pavlovian CSs involved necessarily elicit the same emotions that people experience when they describe their feelings using the terms hope, disappointment, fear, and relief.

If presentation of a classically conditioned stimulus alters instrumental behavior solely by changing the emotions that motivate the instrumental response, what should we expect in various situations? Table 10.2 lists the predicted outcomes when classically conditioned stimuli that elicit hope, disappointment, fear, or relief are presented to animals responding either to obtain food (positive reinforcement) or to avoid shock (negative reinforcement). These predictions are based on the assumption that hope and relief are compatible (both being positive emotions) and that fear and disappointment are compatible (both being negative emotions) (Goodman & Fowler, 1983). By contrast, hope and fear (and relief and disappointment) are assumed to be incompatible (Dickinson & Pearce, 1977).

Let us first consider predictions in the case of positive reinforcement (cells 1–4). The underlying emotional state created by positive reinforcement is hope. Hope is assumed to be incompatible with fear, and hence the rate of the instrumental response is expected to decline when a CS+ for an aversive US is presented (cell 1). Hope and relief are assumed to be compatible emotions. Therefore, we predict an increase in the positively reinforced instrumental behavior when a CS– for an aversive US is presented (cell 2). The classically conditioned stimulus is also predicted to facilitate the instrumental behavior in cell 3 because here the CS elicits hope, which is the same type of emotion as the motivational state created by the instrumental procedure.

TABLE 10.2 PREDICTED EFFECTS OF CLASSICALLY CONDITIONED STIMULI ON THE RATE OF INSTRUMENTAL BEHAVIOR

INSTRUMENTAL SCHEDULE	AVERSIVE US		APPETITIVE US	
	CS+ (FEAR)	CS− (RELIEF)	CS+ (HOPE)	CS− (DISAPPOINTMENT)
Positive reinforcement (procurement of food) *(hope)*	1 Decrease	2 Increase	3 Increase	4 Decrease
Negative reinforcement (avoidance of shock) *(fear)*	5 Increase	6 Decrease	7 Decrease	8 Increase

By contrast, the instrumental behavior is predicted to decrease when a CS− for food is presented (cell 4) because the disappointment it elicits is incompatible with the hope that motivates the instrumental behavior.

Cells 5–8 state the predictions when the instrumental procedure involves negative reinforcement such as shock avoidance. The underlying emotion that motivates the instrumental behavior in this case is fear. This fear is enhanced when a CS is presented that also elicits fear (cell 5). Hence, an increase in the rate of the instrumental response is predicted. The fear is reduced by presentation of a CS that has been associated with the removal or absence of an aversive US (cell 6). Instrumental responding therefore declines. Fear is presumably also reduced when the classically conditioned stimulus elicits hope (cell 7) because fear and hope are incompatible emotions. Finally, performance of the instrumental response is expected to increase when a CS− for an appetitive US is presented (cell 8) because disappointment and fear are both aversive emotional states.

Results Consistent with Modern Two-Process Theory. I have already noted that the concurrent measurement of instrumental behavior and classically conditioned responses cannot be used to evaluate modern two-process theory. How, then, can the predictions in Table 10.2 be experimentally tested? The experiments that have been performed to evaluate modern two-process theory were modeled after the CER procedure and are called **transfer-of-control experiments.** Such experiments consist of three phases, as outlined in Table 10.3. Phase 1 involves instrumental conditioning of an operant response using some schedule of positive or negative reinforcement. In Phase 2 the participants are given classical conditioning in which an explicit CS is associated with either the presence or absence of an unconditioned stimulus. Phase 3 is the critical *transfer phase.* Here the participants are allowed to engage in the instrumental response, and the CS from Phase 2 is periodically presented to observe its effect on the rate of the instrumental behavior.

In some applications of the transfer-of-control design, the classical conditioning phase is conducted before instrumental conditioning. In some other experiments, Phases 1 and 2 are conducted concurrently—that is, classical conditioning trials with the CS and US are periodically presented while the participant is being trained on the

297

*Classical-Instrumental
Interactions and the
Associative Structure
of Instrumental
Conditioning*

TABLE 10.3	OUTLINE OF TRANSFER-OF-CONTROL EXPERIMENTS	

PHASE 1	PHASE 2	PHASE 3
Instrumental conditioning of the baseline response	Classical conditioning of the CS	Transfer test: the CS is presented during performance of the baseline response

instrumental reinforcement schedule. These variations in the basic design usually lead to similar results in Phase 3, the critical transfer phase.

Modern two-process theory has stimulated a great deal of research using the transfer-of-control design. Many of the results of these experiments have been consistent with the predictions outlined in Table 10.2. I cannot review all the evidence here, but I will cite some illustrative examples.

Let us first consider the effects of classically conditioned stimuli on the performance of instrumental behavior maintained by positive reinforcement (cells 1–4 in Table 10.2). As I have already noted, cell 1 represents the conditioned emotional response procedure. The common finding is that a CS+ conditioned with an aversive US suppresses the rate of positively reinforced instrumental behavior. (For reviews, see Blackman, 1977; Davis, 1968; Lyon, 1968.) The effects of a signal for the absence of an aversive US (a CS–) on positively reinforced responding (cell 2) have not been as extensively investigated. However, the available data are again consistent with the prediction. Hammond (1966), for example, found that lever pressing in rats reinforced by food increased when a CS– for shock was presented (see also Davis & Shattuck, 1980).

In certain situations, food-reinforced instrumental behavior is also increased by the presentation of a CS+ for food, consistent with the prediction in cell 3 (for example, Estes, 1943, 1948; LoLordo, 1971; Lovibond, 1983). Research on the effects of a signal for the absence of an appetitive reinforcer (CS–) on positively reinforced responding (cell 4) has not been extensive. However, evidence consistent with two-process theory (a suppression of the instrumental response) has been observed in the available studies (for example, Gutman & Maier, 1978; Hearst & Peterson, 1973).

Many experiments have been performed to determine how stimuli that signal an aversive US (CS+) or its absence (CS–) influence the rate of negatively reinforced instrumental behavior (cells 5 and 6). These studies generally support predictions of modern two-process theory. The rate of avoidance behavior is increased by the presentation of a CS+ for shock and decreased by the presentation of a CS– for shock (for example, Bull & Overmier, 1968; Desiderato, 1969; Rescorla & LoLordo, 1965; Weisman & Litner, 1969). Presentation of a signal for the presence of food (CS+) has also been noted to decrease the rate of instrumental avoidance behavior, as cell 7 predicts (for example, Bull, 1970; Davis & Kreuter, 1972; Grossen, Kostansek, & Bolles, 1969). The effects of a signal for the absence of food (CS–) on avoidance behavior (cell 8) have not been extensively investigated. One experiment that included a test of the prediction in cell 8 failed to find any effect on avoidance responding (Bull, 1970). However, in another study (Grossen et al., 1969), a classically conditioned CS– for food facilitated instrumental avoidance behavior, as predicted in cell 8.

J. B. Overmier

Response Interactions in Transfer-of-Control Experiments. Classically conditioned stimuli elicit not only emotional states but also overt responses. Consequently, a classically conditioned stimulus may influence instrumental behavior through the overt responses it elicits. Consider, for example, a hypothetical situation in which the classically conditioned stimulus makes the animal remain still, and the instrumental response is shuttling back and forth in a shuttle box. In this case, presentation of the CS will decrease the instrumental response simply because the tendency to stop moving elicited by the CS will interfere with the shuttle behavior. An appeal to central emotional states is not necessary to understand such an outcome. An appeal to central emotional states is also unnecessary if a classically conditioned stimulus elicited overt responses that were similar to the instrumental behavior. In this case, presentation of the CS would probably increase responding because responses elicited by the CS would be added to the responses the animal was performing to receive instrumental reinforcement.

Investigators have been very concerned with the possibility that the results of transfer-of-control experiments are due to the fact that Pavlovian CSs elicit overt responses that either interfere with or facilitate the behavior required for instrumental reinforcement. This concern has given rise to a number of strategies to rule out this possibility. (For a review, see Overmier & Lawry, 1979.) These strategies generally have been successful in showing that many transfer-of-control effects are not produced by interactions between overt responses (see, for example, Grossen et al., 1969; Lovibond, 1983; Overmier, Bull, & Pack, 1971; Scobie, 1972). However, overt classically conditioned responses have been important in some transfer-of-control experiments.

Response interactions are especially important to consider in transfer-of-control experiments in which classical conditioning is conducted with an appetitive stimulus such as food or water that the participants have to obtain in a particular location—from a cup placed in a corner of the experimental chamber, for example. If the participants have to go to a particular location to obtain the US, a CS+ may suppress instrumental responding because it elicits approach to the site of US delivery (for example, Karpicke, 1978).

Response interactions are also important to consider when the classically conditioned stimulus is a discrete localized stimulus such as a spot of light, because such CSs elicit sign tracking. As I noted in Chapter 3, when a localized stimulus becomes a CS+ for food, animals tend to approach it. By contrast, if the stimulus becomes a CS+ for shock, it comes to elicit withdrawal, or negative sign tracking (for example, Leclerc & Reberg, 1980). Positive and negative sign tracking elicited by classically conditioned stimuli may increase or decrease an instrumental response, depending on whether the sign tracking is compatible or incompatible with the instrumental behavior (for example, LoLordo, McMillan, & Riley, 1974; Schwartz, 1976).

Conditioned Central Emotional States or Reward-Specific Expectancies? Modern two-process theory assumes that classical conditioning mediates instrumental behavior through the conditioning of central emotional states such as hope, disappointment, fear, and relief. However, the result of several experiments indicate that in certain situations animals acquire specific reward expectancies instead of more general central emotional states during instrumental and classical conditioning (Peterson & Trapold, 1980).

Baxter and Zamble (1982), for example, compared electrical stimulation of the brain (ESB) and food as rewards in transfer-of-control experiments with rats. Since both of these USs are positive reinforcers, they would be expected to condition the emotional state of hope. Baxter and Zamble found that a CS+ for brain stimulation increased instrumental lever pressing reinforced with ESB and a CS+ for food increased lever pressing reinforced with food. However, a CS+ for ESB did not increase lever pressing for food reinforcement. Thus, a positive classically conditioned stimulus increased instrumental responding only if it signaled the same US that had been used to condition the instrumental response.

In another study, solid food pellets and a sugar solution were used as USs in the classical and instrumental conditioning of rats (Kruse, Overmier, Konz, & Rokke, 1983). A CS+ for food facilitated instrumental responding reinforced with food much more than instrumental behavior reinforced with the sugar solution. Correspondingly, a CS+ for sugar increased instrumental behavior reinforced with sugar more than instrumental behavior reinforced with food pellets. Thus, as in the study by Baxter and Zamble (1982), expectancies for specific rewards rather than a more general central emotional state of hope determined the results (see also Hendersen, Patterson, & Jackson, 1980).

The studies I have just described clearly indicate that under some circumstances animals acquire reinforcer-specific expectancies rather than more general emotional states during instrumental and classical conditioning. (For another line of evidence indicating the learning of reinforcer-specific expectancies, see, for example, DeMarse & Urcuioli, 1993; Urcuioli & DeMarse, 1996). Reinforcer-specific expectancy learning is a challenging alternative to modern two-process theory in explaining certain types of results. However, expectancy theory cannot replace modern two-process theory entirely.

Reinforcer-specific expectancies cannot explain why a CS– for food facilitates shock avoidance instrumental behavior (cell 8 of Table 10.2). The specific reinforcer expectancy elicited by a CS– for food is certainly not the same as the specific reinforcer expectancy presumably responsible for instrumental shock-avoidance behavior. However, the emotion elicited by a CS– for food (disappointment) is similar to the emotion presumably acquired during avoidance training (fear). Therefore, two-process theory is more successful in explaining such transfer results. For similar reasons, two-process theory is also more successful than expectancy theory in explaining why a CS– for shock facilitates food-reinforced instrumental behavior (cell 2 of Table 10.2).

R-O and S-(R-O) Associations

So far I have described different two-factor theories of instrumental behavior. The response outcome (O), or reinforcer, is assumed to have two different roles in these theories. The first of these is described by Thorndike's law of effect, which is the traditional instrumental reinforcement process. According to the law of effect, the reinforcer acts to establish an S-R association—an association between the instrumental response and the stimuli present when the response occurs. The reinforcer is not assumed to participate directly in this association but is assumed to "stamp in" or provide the "glue" for the S-R association. The second way in which the reinforcer is assumed to be involved in instrumental conditioning is by participating in the S-O association, or classical conditioning of the external cues (S) present in the instrumental conditioning situation.

As we have seen, two-process models assume that the three basic elements of an instrumental conditioning procedure (S, R, and O) are organized into two associations,

S-R and S-O. Upon further reflection, however, this account may seem a bit odd for a couple of reasons (see Colwill & Rescorla, 1986). First, notice that neither of the presumed associations in two-process models involves a direct link between the response R and the reinforcer, or response outcome, O. The response outcome O is not directly represented in the S-R association, or otherwise associated with the response. This is counterintuitive. If you asked someone why they were performing an instrumental response, the reply would be that they expected the response (R) to result in the reinforcer (O). In other words, intuitive explanations of instrumental behavior are based on R-O associations. You comb your hair because you expect that doing so will improve your appearance; you go to see a movie because you expect that watching the movie will be entertaining; and you open the refrigerator because you anticipate that doing so will enable you to get something to eat. Although our informal explanations of instrumental behavior emphasize R-O associations, such associations do not exist in two-process models.

Another peculiarity of the associative structure of instrumental conditioning assumed by two-process theories is that S is assumed to become associated directly with O on the assumption that the pairing of S with O is sufficient for the occurrence of classical conditioning. However, as we saw in Chapter 4, CS-US pairings are not sufficient for the development of Pavlovian associations. The CS must also provide information about the US, or in some way be related to the US. In an instrumental conditioning situation, the reinforcer O cannot be predicted from S alone. Rather O occurs if the participant makes response R in the presence of S. Thus, instrumental conditioning involves a conditional relation in which S is followed by O only if R occurs. This conditionality in the relation of S to O is ignored in two-process theories.

I previously discussed the conditionality of the outcome in Chapter 8 in the context of discrimination training. There, I noted that in a discrimination procedure, reinforcement of the instrumental response is conditional upon the presence of the S+. These considerations suggest that the associative structure of instrumental conditioning is not adequately described by S-R and S-O associations. Rather, the associative structure might also include a conditional, or hierarchical, relation: S-(R-O).

Contemporary efforts to explore the associative structure of instrumental conditioning have concentrated on demonstrating R-O and conditional S-(R-O) relations.

Evidence of R-O Associations. A number of investigators have suggested that instrumental conditioning leads to the learning of response-outcome associations (for example, Bolles, 1972b; Mackintosh & Dickinson, 1979), and several different types of evidence have been obtained in support of this possibility. A common technique involves devaluing the reinforcer after conditioning to see if this decreases the instrumental response. (For reviews, see Colwill, 1994; Colwill & Rescorla, 1986; Rescorla, 1991.) The strategy is analogous to the strategy of US devaluation in studies of Pavlovian conditioning (see Chapter 4). In Pavlovian conditioning, US devaluation is used to determine whether the conditioned response is mediated by a CS-US association. If US devaluation after conditioning disrupts the CR, it is clear that the CR was mediated by the CS-US association. In a corresponding fashion, reinforcer devaluation has been used to determine if an instrumental response is mediated by an association between the response and its reinforcer outcome.

In an interesting demonstration, Colwill and Rescorla (1986) first reinforced rats for pushing a vertical rod either to the right or the left. Responding in either direction was reinforced on a variable interval 1-minute schedule of reinforcement. Both response alternatives were always available during training sessions. The only differ-

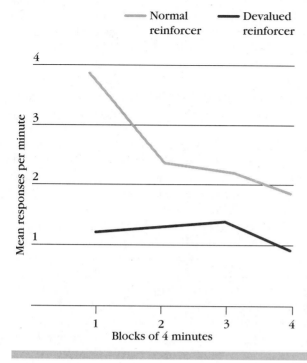

Figure 10.7 Effects of reinforcer devaluation on instrumental behavior. Devaluation of a reinforcer selectively reduces the response that was previously reinforced with that reinforcer. (From "Associative Structures in Instrumental Learning" by R. M. Colwill and R. A. Rescorla. In G. H. Bower (Ed.), *The Psychology of Learning and Motivation*, Vol. 20, pp. 55–104. Copyright © 1986 Academic Press. Reprinted by permission.)

ence was that responses in one direction were reinforced with food pellets, and responses in the opposite direction were always reinforced with a bit of sugar solution (sucrose).

After both responses had become well established, the rod was removed and the reinforcer devaluation procedure was introduced. One of the reinforcers (either food pellets or sugar solution) was periodically presented in the experimental chamber, followed by an injection of lithium chloride to condition an aversion to that reinforcer. After an aversion to the selected reinforcer had been conditioned, the vertical rod was returned, and the rats received an extinction test during which they were free to push the rod either to the left or to the right.

The results of the extinction test are presented in Figure 10.7. The important finding was that during the extinction test the rats were less likely to make the response whose reinforcer had been made aversive by pairings with lithium chloride. For example, if sucrose was used to reinforce responses to the left, and an aversion was then conditioned to sucrose, the rats were less likely to push the rod to the left than to the right.

The selective response suppression that was obtained is difficult to explain in terms of the S-O or S-R associations that are assumed to be learned according to two-process theory. S-R associations cannot produce the results because the reinforcer is not included in an S-R association. Therefore, changes in the value of the reinforcer cannot alter behavior mediated by an S-R association. The results cannot be explained in terms of S-O associations because the two responses, pushing the vertical rod left or right, were made in the same place, with the same manipulandum, and therefore in the presence of the same external stimuli S. If devaluation of one of the reinforcers had altered the properties of S, that should have changed the two responses equally. Instead, devaluation of a reinforcer selectively depressed the particular response that

301

had been trained with that reinforcer. This outcome suggests that each response was associated separately with its own reinforcer. The participants evidently learned separate R-O associations. (For additional evidence of R-O learning, see Colwill, 1994; Rescorla, 1992; Rescorla & Colwill, 1989.)

Evidence of the Learning of a Hierarchical S-(R-O) Relation. The evidence cited above clearly shows that organisms learn to associate an instrumental response with its outcome. However, R-O associations cannot act alone to produce instrumental behavior. As Mackintosh and Dickinson (1979) have pointed out, the fact that the instrumental response activates an expectancy of the reinforcer does not explain what causes the response in the first place. An additional factor is required to activate the R-O association. One possibility is that the R-O association is activated by the stimuli S that are present when the response is reinforced.

Skinner (1938) suggested many years ago that S, R, and O in instrumental conditioning are connected through a conditional S-(R-O) relation. This suggestion has been vigorously pursued in recent years. A variety of direct and indirect lines of evidence have been developed that point to the learning of S-(R-O) relations in instrumental conditioning (Colwill & Rescorla, 1990; Davidson et al., 1988; Holman & Mackintosh, 1981; Goodall & Mackintosh, 1987; Rescorla, 1990a, 1990b). Most of these studies have involved rather complicated discrimination training procedures. The design of one of the experiments (Colwill & Delameter, 1995, Experiment 2) is outlined in Table 10.4.

The experiment required training rats on two special kinds of discrimination problems called *biconditional discriminations.* In one problem, the discriminative stimuli were two different auditory cues, a noise and a tone (A1 and A2). In the other problem, the discriminative stimuli were two different visual cues, a steady light and a flashing light (L1 and L2). Only one problem was in effect during a particular session, with the discriminative stimuli being presented one at a time. Training on the two problems took place on alternate days. The rats were reinforced for making one of two responses during each session. During some sessions they could press a response lever or pull a chain. During alternate sessions they could perform a nose-poke response or pull a handle that was positioned below the grid floor. Each discrimination problem was set up so that one response was reinforced during one cue (A1-R1-O), and the other response was reinforced during the alternate cue (A2-R2-O). If the rat made the wrong response (for example, R2 in the presence of A1), it was not reinforced. One other detail is important—a different reinforcer (food pellets or liquid sucrose) was used with each biconditional discrimination problem. All of the stimulus, response, and reinforcer combinations are outlined in Table 10.4.

How could rats solve the discrimination problems outlined in Table 10.4? Let us consider the auditory discrimination. How could rats learn to make R1 when A1 was presented and R2 when A2 was presented? The structure of the task rules out solutions involving S-O and R-O associations. The task cannot be solved by learning reward expectancies or S-O associations, because each stimulus is associated with the same reinforcer outcome. Thus, S-O learning would result in learning the associations A1-O1 and A2-O1. Since both A1 and A2 are associated with the same outcome O1, these associations do not help in deciding which response to make during A1 and A2.

The structure of a biconditional discrimination also prevents a solution based on R-O associations. R1 and R2 are both reinforced with the same outcome, O1. Therefore, R-O associations cannot help in deciding whether to make R1 or R2.

303

*Classical-Instrumental
Interactions and the
Associative Structure
of Instrumental
Conditioning*

TABLE 10.4	OUTLINE OF PROCEDURES USED TO DEMONSTRATE THE LEARNING OF S-(R-O) RELATIONS IN INSTRUMENTAL CONDITIONING (Colwill & Delameter, 1995).

Training	A1: R1→O1, R2→nothing
	A2: R2→O1, R1→nothing
	L1: R3→O2, R4→nothing
	L2: R4→O2, R3→nothing
Devaluation	Aversion conditioned to O1 or O2
Test	A1: R1 vs. R2
	A2: R1 vs. R2
	L1: R3 vs. R4
	L2: R3 vs. R4

Note: A1 and A2 were different auditory cues (noise or tone); L1 and L2 were different visual cues (steady or pulsating light); O1 and O2 were different reinforcers (solid food or liquid sucrose); and R1, R2, R3, and R4 were different responses (lever-press, chain-pull, nose-poke, and handle-pull).

The traditional explanation of how organisms learn a biconditional discrimination focuses on S-R associations. The assumption is that A1 comes to be associated with R1 and A2 comes to be associated with R2. These S-R associations then enable the rats to make R1 when A1 is presented and R2 when A2 is presented.

An alternative interpretation is that each discriminative stimulus comes to activate a corresponding R-O associative unit. Thus, A1 comes to activate the R1-O1 association, and A2 comes to activate the R2-O1 association. Such an account assumes that animals learn a hierarchical S-(R-O) association.

How can we decide between the S-R and S-(R-O) explanations of biconditional discrimination learning? Notice that a representation of the response outcome or reinforcer is not included in the S-R learning mechanism. Therefore, the S-R learning explanation predicts that changes in the value of the reinforcer will not alter biconditional discrimination performance. In contrast, the response outcome is a part of the S-(R-O) mechanism. Therefore, decreasing the value of the response outcome after the discrimination has been learned should affect performance according to the S-(R-O) mechanism. This prediction was tested by Colwill and Delameter (1995).

Following acquisition of the biconditional discrimination, for some of the rats an aversion was conditioned to O1 using a food-aversion conditioning procedure. For other rats, an aversion was conditioned to O2. All of the animals were then tested during extinction on each biconditional discrimination (see Table 10.4).

The results of the test sessions are summarized in Figure 10.8. The figure shows the rates of correct and incorrect responses on the discrimination problem whose reinforcer had been devalued, as well as the discrimination problem whose reinforcer had not been devalued. (Incorrect responses were R1 during A2, R2 during A1, R3 during L2, and R4 during L1.) The rates of incorrect responding were low and similar on the devalued and valued discrimination tasks. In contrast, large differences were obtained in the rates of correct responding. Devaluation of the reinforcer produce a large decrement in the rate of correct responding.

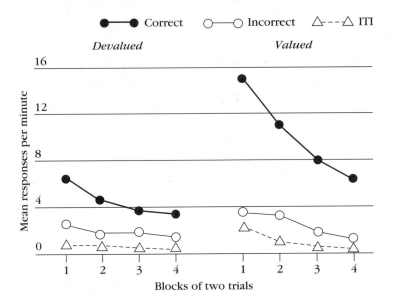

Figure 10.8 Rates of correct responses, incorrect responses, and responding during the intertrial interval (ITI) during the test phase of the biconditional discrimination experiment outlined in Table 10.4. (From "An Associative Analysis of Instrumental Biconditional Discrimination Learning" by R. M. Colwill and B. A. Delamater, *Animal Learning & Behavior*, 1995, *23*, pp. 218–233. Copyright © 1995 by the Psychonomic Society. Reprinted by permission.)

These findings cannot be explained in terms of S-R mechanisms because reinforcer devaluation is not predicted to change responding according to S-R mechanisms. However, the results are consistent with the assumption that the animals learned a hierarchical S-(R-O) association. As predicted by S-(R-O) learning, devaluation of the reinforcer produced a decrement in responding. Furthermore, the effect was specific to the discrimination task whose reinforcer was devalued.

CONCLUDING COMMENTS

Classical and instrumental conditioning procedures are clearly different from each other. However, instrumental reinforcement can be involved in classical conditioning procedures, and Pavlovian processes can be involved in instrumental conditioning procedures. Experimental investigations have shown that classical conditioning can take place in the absence of the opportunity for instrumental reinforcement. However, comparable investigations cannot be conducted to show that instrumental conditioning is possible without the occurrence of classical conditioning.

All instrumental conditioning procedures allow for the occurrence of classical conditioning. Concurrent-measurement experiments have confirmed that classically conditioned responses in fact develop during instrumental conditioning procedures. However, the concurrent measurement of classically and instrumentally conditioned responses has not been very helpful in elucidating the interaction of these two processes. Another experimental technique, the transfer-of-control design, has provided more enlightening information. Transfer-of-control experiments have confirmed the basic tenet of two-process theory—that classically conditioned stimuli can influence the performance of an independently established instrumental response. Research has shown that the transfer of control from Pavlovian conditioned stimuli to instrumental behavior is governed by several factors. One important factor is the nature of the central emotional state elicited by the Pavlovian CS in comparison with the central emotional state established by the baseline instrumental reinforcement schedule. (This factor has been emphasized by modern two-process theory.) A second important variable is the overt responses elicited by the Pavlovian CS and the extent to which these are compatible or incompatible with the instrumental behavior. Finally, transfer-of-control experiments can also involve reinforcer-specific expectancies. Generally, particular transfer-of-control experiments have been designed to highlight the importance of a particular variable. Therefore, results of individual experiments often provide evidence consistent with just one perspective on the interrelation of classical and instrumental conditioning. However, the totality of the evidence suggests that the interaction of classical and instrumental conditioning procedures is multiply determined.

In addition to elucidating the relation between classical and instrumental conditioning, two-process theories provide an account of the associative structure of instrumental conditioning. That account emphasizes stimulus-reinforcer (S-O) and stimulus-response (S-R) associations. External cues (S) in the instrumental conditioning situation are assumed to become classically conditioned by the reinforcer (O), producing the S-O association. In addition, the instrumental response is assumed to become associated both with external discriminative stimuli and with internal cues that are by-products of the S-O associations.

In addition to these S-R and S-O associations, contemporary views of the associative structure of instrumental conditioning assume the existence of associations between the instrumental response and the reinforcer (R-O associations). Furthermore, contemporary views assume that the three basic terms of instrumental conditioning (S, R, and O) are related not only in binary associations (S-R, S-O, and R-O) but also in a hierarchical fashion—S-(R-O)—that enables S to activate the R-O association.

SAMPLE QUESTIONS

1. How might instrumental reinforcement contribute to the acquisition of classically conditioned responses?

2. How can a classical conditioning procedure be modified so as to prevent the possible instrumental reinforcement of the conditioned response?

3. Compare and contrast the r_g-s_g mechanism and modern two-process theory.

4. What major factors determine the outcome of transfer-of-control experiments?

5. What investigative strategy can be used to distinguish between S-R and R-O associations?

KEY TERMS

central emotional state The general state of the nervous system assumed to be produced by the presentation of a classically conditioned stimulus.

concurrent-measurement experiment An experiment in which classically and instrumentally conditioned responses are measured at the same time.

disappointment A hypothetical emotional state presumably elicited by classically conditioned stimuli that signal the absence or removal of a positive reinforcer such as food.

fear A hypothetical emotional state presumably elicited when either an unconditioned aversive stimulus or a stimulus that was previously conditioned with an aversive event is presented.

fractional anticipatory goal response A theoretical entity or response that, according to the r_g-s_g mechanism, becomes classically conditioned to stimuli that are present when an instrumental response is reinforced. Abbreviated r_g.

hope A hypothetical emotional state presumably elicited by classically conditioned stimuli that signal the presentation of a positive reinforcer such as food.

omission control procedure A procedure in which the unconditioned stimulus is presented after the conditioned stimulus (CS) only if the conditioned response does not occur. If the conditioned response occurs during the CS, the unconditioned stimulus is not presented on that trial.

relief A hypothetical emotional state presumably elicited by classically conditioned stimuli that signal the absence or removal of an aversive stimulus such as shock.

r_g The conventional symbol for a fractional anticipatory goal response.

s_g The conventional symbol for the sensory feedback produced by the fractional anticipatory goal response.

transfer-of-control experiment An experiment that assesses the effects of a classically conditioned stimulus (CS) on the performance of instrumental behavior. The CS and the instrumental behavior are first conditioned in independent phases of the experiment. The effects of the CS on instrumental behavior are then determined in a transfer phase.

ANIMAL COGNITION: MEMORY MECHANISMS

What Is Animal Cognition?

Animal Memory Paradigms

Working and Reference Memory

Delayed Matching to Sample

Spatial Memory in a Radial Maze

Spatial Memory in Food-Storing Birds

Memory Mechanisms

Acquisition and the Problem of Stimulus Coding

Retention and the Problem of Rehearsal

Retrieval

Forgetting

Proactive and Retroactive Interference

Retrograde Amnesia

Concluding Comments

I N Chapter 11 we turn to a consideration of animal cognition. Although interest in animal cognition dates back to Darwin's writings about the evolution of intelligence, much of the systematic experimental work in this area has been done in the last 25 years. Chapter 11 begins with a definition of animal cognition and a brief discussion of some cognitive effects I have already described. The rest of the chapter is devoted to one of the most important cognitive processes—memory. I will start by describing the relationship between learning and memory and the distinction between working memory and reference memory. I will then discuss several prominent working memory paradigms. In the next section, I will describe research relevant to three different stages of memory—acquisition, retention, and retrieval—and will then end the chapter with a discussion of different sources of forgetting.

As I noted in Chapter 1, interest in animal cognition dates back to the founding of the field of animal learning more than a century ago. Early experimental efforts to study animal cognition employed animal learning paradigms. However, studies of animal learning soon came to have a life of their own. Through much of the 20th century, learning processes have been investigated in animals for what they told us about behavior in general rather than for what they told us about animal cognition or animal intelligence in particular. However, the past 25 years have witnessed a resurgence of interest in animal cognition and animal intelligence (for example, Griffin, 1976; Hulse, Fowler, & Honig, 1978; Ristau, 1991; Roitblat, Bever, & Terrace, 1984; Spear & Riccio, 1994; Zentall, 1993).

The renewed focus on issues relevant to animal cognition is a part of the "cognitive revolution" that has swept over many areas of psychology. These developments have stimulated considerable theoretical debate (for example, Amsel, 1989; Hintzman, 1991). Regardless of that debate, an important consequence of contemporary interest in animal cognition has been the extension of the study of animal learning to numerous new paradigms. These extensions have raised many new and interesting questions about behavior—questions that were not explored in conventional studies of classical and instrumental conditioning. I will describe some of these developments in this chapter and the next.

In addition to providing important new information about learning and memory processes, studies of animal cognition help address the kind of theoretical questions about the evolution of intelligence that captivated Darwin. Exploring the cognitive skills of animals will tell us about the uniqueness of various human cognitive skills, just as exploring other planets tells us about the uniqueness of our terrestrial habitat. Studies of animal cognition are also important because they provide model systems for the investigation of the neurophysiological bases of cognitive functions. Memory-enhancing drugs, for example, cannot be developed without first developing animal model systems for the study of memory mechanisms. Studies of the mechanisms of cognition in animals may also help researchers design intelligent machines and robots.

WHAT IS ANIMAL COGNITION?

The word *cognition* comes from the Latin meaning "knowledge or thinking" and is commonly used in reference to thought processes. In casual discourse, we regard thinking as involving voluntary, deliberate, and conscious reflection on some topic, usually with the use of language. Thinking is informally considered to involve a form of "talking to oneself."

The second prominent characteristic of thinking is that it can lead to actions that cannot be explained on the basis of the external stimuli a person experiences at the time. For example, on your way to work, you may start thinking that you did not lock the door to your apartment when you left home. This thought may stimulate you to return home to check whether the door is locked. Your returning cannot be explained by the external stimuli to which you are exposed on your way to work. You encounter these same stimuli every day, but usually they do not make you return home. Rather, your behavior is attributed to the thought of the unlocked door.

In the scientific study of animal behavior, cognition is used in a more restricted sense than in casual discourse. Animal cognition shares the second feature of cognition just noted, but not the first. Animal cognition does not refer to voluntary or conscious reflection on a topic. Thus, animal cognition does not imply anything about awareness, consciousness, or verbal reasoning. As Terrace (1984) has commented, "The rationale for the study of cognitive processes in animals requires no reference to animal consciousness" (p. 8). Rather **animal cognition** refers to *the use of a neural representation, or model, of some past experience as a basis for action.*

A neural representation is an internal or "mental" record, if you will. Internal representations may encode various types of information, such as particular features of stimuli or relations between stimuli. Internal representations cannot be investigated directly by looking into the nervous system. Rather, they have to be inferred from behavior. Thus, an internal representation is a theoretical construct, in the same sense that gravity is a theoretical construct inferred from the behavior of falling objects. (For a more detailed discussion, see Roitblat, 1982.)

Research on animal cognition is concerned with questions such as how representations are formed, what aspects of experience they encode, how the information is stored, and how it is used later to guide behavior. I have already discussed research relevant to such questions in analyses of classical and instrumental conditioning. For example, I noted in Chapter 4 that classical conditioning involves the learning of an association between a CS and a US. As a result of this association, presentation of the CS activates a representation ("mental image" if you will) of the US, and the conditioned response is performed because of this representation. In Chapter 10 I noted that instrumental conditioning results in the establishment of S-O and R-O associations. Because of these associations, an internal representation of the reinforcer O is activated by the stimuli of the conditioning situation (S) as well as by the instrumental response (R). Additional evidence suggests that S can also activate a representation of the R-O association. Another area that clearly involves cognitive processes is the study of memory (Spear & Riccio, 1994), to which we turn next.

H. L. Roitblat

ANIMAL MEMORY PARADIGMS

The term **memory** is commonly used in reference to the ability to respond to or recount information that was experienced at an earlier time. Thus, we are said to remember what happened in our childhood if we talk about our childhood experiences, and we are said to remember someone's name if we call that person by the correct name. Unfortunately, similar tests of memory with most animals are impractical. We cannot ask a pigeon to tell us what it did last week. Instead, we have to use the bird's nonverbal responses as a clue to its memory.

If your cat goes down the street but finds its way back to your house, you might conclude that it remembered where you live. If your dog greets you with unusual exuberance after a long vacation, you might conclude that it remembered you. These and similar cases illustrate that the existence of memory in animals is identified by the fact that *their current behavior can be predicted from some aspect of their earlier experiences.* Any time an animal's behavior is determined by past events, we can conclude that some type of memory mechanism is involved.

You may notice that the definition of memory is very similar to the definition of learning stated in Chapter 1, where learning was characterized as an enduring change in responding to a particular situation as a result of prior experience with that type of situation. Thus, evidence of learning is also identified on the basis of changes in behavior that are due to earlier experiences. Indeed, learning is not possible without memory.

TABLE 11.1	COMPARISON OF LEARNING AND MEMORY EXPERIMENTS	
PHASE	STUDIES OF LEARNING	STUDIES OF MEMORY
Acquisition	Varied	Constant
Retention	Constant (long)	Varied (short and long)
Retrieval	Constant	Varied

How, then, are studies of memory to be distinguished from studies of learning? The differences may be clarified by considering the components that are common to both learning and memory experiments (see Table 11.1). The first thing that happens in both types of experiments is that the participants are exposed to certain kinds of stimuli or information. This phase is termed **acquisition.** The information that was acquired is then retained for some time—a period called the **retention interval.** At the end of the retention interval, the participants are tested for their memory of the original experience, which requires **retrieval** or reactivation of the information encountered during acquisition. Thus, studies of learning and studies of memory both involve basically three phases: acquisition, retention, and retrieval.

Consider, for example, riding a bicycle. Skilled bicyclists initially had to be trained to balance, pedal, and steer the bike (acquisition). They have to remember those training experiences (retention). And, when they get on a bicycle again, they have to reactivate their knowledge of bike riding (retrieval).

In studies of learning, the focus is on the acquisition phase. Learning experiments deal with the kind of information we acquire and the ways in which we acquire it. Thus, *learning experiments involve manipulations of the conditions of acquisition.* The retention interval is always fairly long (a day or longer) because short-term changes in behavior are not considered to be instances of learning. Furthermore, the retention interval typically is not varied within the experiment. Because the emphasis is on the conditions of acquisition, the conditions of retrieval are also kept constant. All participants in a given experiment are tested for their knowledge using the same test procedures.

In contrast to studies of learning, *studies of memory focus on retention and retrieval.* Issues concerning acquisition are of interest only to the extent that they are relevant to retention and retrieval. The retention interval is often varied to determine how the availability of the acquired information changes with time. Unlike studies of learning, which employ only long retention intervals, studies of memory can employ retention intervals of any duration. In fact, many studies of animal memory involve short retention intervals.

Studies of memory also focus on the circumstances of retrieval. Consider, for example, taking a vocabulary test on a set of technical terms in a college course. You may miss many items if the test consists of a series of fill-in-the-blank questions for which you have to provide the technical terms. In contrast, you are likely to do much better if you are provided with a list of the technical terms and are merely required to match up each term with its definition. These different forms of the test involve different conditions of retrieval.

Working and Reference Memory

Memory mechanisms have been classified in various ways depending on what is remembered (the contents of memory) and how long it is remembered (the retention interval). A particularly useful classification has employed the distinction between working and reference memory.

One of the earliest experimental investigations of animal memory was conducted by the American psychologist Walter S. Hunter (1913). Hunter tested rats, dogs, and raccoons in a simple memory task. The apparatus consisted of a start area from which the animals could enter any one of three goal compartments. Only one of the goal compartments was baited with a piece of food on each trial, and the baited compartment was marked by turning on a light above that compartment at the start of the trial. Which compartment was baited (and marked by the light) was varied from trial to trial.

After the animals learned to always choose the compartment in which the light was turned on, Hunter made the task a bit more difficult. Now the light marking the baited goal compartment remained on for only a short time. After the signal was turned off, the animal was detained in the start area for a while before being allowed to choose among the three compartments. Therefore, the animal had to somehow remember which light had been lit in order to find the food. The longer the animals were delayed before being allowed to make a choice, the less likely they were to go to the correct compartment. The maximum delay that rats could handle was about 10 seconds. The performance of dogs did not deteriorate until the delay interval was extended past 5 minutes, and raccoons performed well as long as the delay was no more than 25 seconds.

The species also differed in what they did during the delay interval. Rats and dogs were observed to maintain a postural orientation toward the correct compartment during the delay interval. No such postural orientations were observed in the raccoons. Since the raccoons did not maintain a postural orientation during the delay interval, their behavior required some type of internal memory mechanism.

With the delay procedure, the animals had to remember which compartment had been illuminated at the start of that trial. However, once the trial was finished, this information was no longer useful because the food could be in any of the three goal compartments on the next trial. Thus, memory for which compartment had been recently illuminated was required only to complete the work during a given trial. This type of memory is called **working memory.**

Working memory is operative when information has to be retained only long enough to complete a particular task, after which the information is best discarded because it is not needed, or (as in Hunter's experiment) it may interfere with successful completion of the next trial. If you have to go to several stores in a shopping mall, for example, it is useful to remember which stores you have already visited as you decide where to go next. However, this information is useful only during that particular shopping trip. A mechanic changing the oil and lubricating a car has to remember which steps of the job he already finished, but only as long as that particular car is being serviced. In cooking a good stew, you have to remember which spices you have already put in before adding others, but once the stew is finished, you can forget this information. All these illustrate instances of working memory.

Working memory is often shortlasting. In Hunter's experiment, the memory lasted for only 10 seconds in rats and for 25 seconds in raccoons. However, as we will see, in other situations working memory may last for several hours or days.

Examples of working memory illustrate the retention, for a limited duration, of recently acquired information. However, such information is useful only in the context of more enduring knowledge. In Hunter's experiment, for example, remembering which compartment had been illuminated at the start of a trial was not enough to obtain food. This information was useful only in the context of the knowledge that the light marked the baited compartment. In contrast to information in working memory that was disposed of after each trial, information about the relation between the light and food had to be remembered on all trials. Such memory is called **reference memory** (Honig, 1978).

Reference memory is *long-term retention of information necessary for successful use of incoming and recently acquired information.* To shop efficiently in a mall, you have to remember not only what stores you have already been to but also general information about shopping malls. Similarly, information about what a mechanic has done recently is useless without more general information about cars and lubrication procedures. Knowing which spices you have already added to a stew is useful only if you have some background information about cooking and flavoring food. All successful uses of working memory require appropriate reference memories.

Since Hunter's research, increasingly sophisticated techniques have been developed for the study of working memory. I will describe three of these. The first procedure—delayed matching to sample—is a laboratory procedure that was developed without much regard for the behavioral predispositions of animals and can be adapted to the study of how animals remember a variety of different events. The other techniques are related to species-specific foraging strategies and illustrate some remarkable adaptive specializations in working memory for spatial stimuli.

Delayed Matching to Sample

The delayed-matching-to-sample procedure is one of the most versatile techniques for the study of working memory. It is a substantial refinement of the technique that Hunter originally used. As in Hunter's procedure, the participant is exposed to a cue that identifies the correct response on a particular trial. This stimulus is then removed before the animal is permitted to perform the designated behavior. In the typical experiment with pigeons, for example, the experimental chamber contains three response keys arranged in a row, as in Figure 11.1. The cue that designates the correct response is called the *sample* and is presented on the center key. After a delay, the pigeons are given a choice between the sample and an alternative stimulus, and pecks on the test stimulus that matches the sample are reinforced.

The test stimuli might consist of an array of horizontal or vertical lines projected on the response keys from the rear. The start of a trial is signaled by illumination of the center key with a white light, the start cue (see row A in Figure 11.1). The pigeon is first required to peck the start cue, to make sure it is facing the pecking keys. Then, the sample for that trial—the horizontal array, for example—is projected on the center key (row B in Figure 11.1). Usually several pecks at the sample stimulus are required, after which the sample is turned off and the two side keys are lit up. One of the side keys is illuminated with the sample for that trial (horizontal), and the other key is illuminated with the alternative pattern (vertical) (row C in Figure 11.1). If the pigeon pecks the test stimulus that matches the sample (in this case horizontal), it is reinforced with access to grain. If it pecks the other stimulus, no reinforcement is provided. Thus, the reinforced response "matches" the sample.

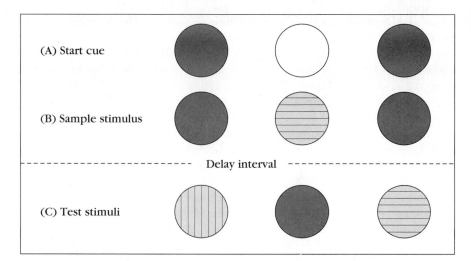

Figure 11.1 Diagram of the delayed-matching-to-sample procedure for pigeons. The experimental chamber has three response keys arranged in a row. At the start of a trial, the center key is illuminated with a white light, the start cue (row A). After the pigeon pecks the start cue, the sample stimulus (horizontal) is projected on the center key (row B). This stimulus is then removed, and after a delay, two choice stimuli (horizontal and vertical) are presented on the side keys (row C). Pecks at the choice stimulus that matches the sample are reinforced.

Which of the test stimuli serves as the sample is randomly varied from one trial to the next. In addition, the matching stimulus is equally likely to be presented on the right or left key during the choice test. Therefore, the pigeon can never predict which stimulus will be the sample on a given trial or where the matching stimulus will appear during the choice.

During the initial stages of matching-to-sample training, the sample stimulus remains visible until the pigeon has made the correct choice. Thus, in the example, the horizontal pattern on the center key would remain illuminated until the bird correctly pecks the horizontal side key. Such a procedure is called **simultaneous matching to sample**. Simultaneous matching to sample does not require working memory because the cue for the correct response is visible when the choice response is made. Once a bird has mastered the simultaneous matching procedure, the sample stimulus can be presented only briefly and removed before the choice stimuli are provided. Introduction of a delay between exposure to the sample stimulus and availability of the choice cues changes the procedure to **delayed matching to sample,** which requires working memory.

As I mentioned, the matching stimulus is equally likely to appear on the left or the right choice key at the end of a trial. Because of this, the participants cannot make the correct choice by orienting to the right or left when the sample appears on the center key and holding this body posture until the choice stimuli are presented. Thus, in contrast to Hunter's procedure, simple postural orientations cannot be used to increase the likelihood of making the correct choice. The participants are forced to use more sophisticated memory processes. (For an especially effective matching-to-sample procedure, see Wright & Delius, 1994.)

D. S. Grant

Procedural Determinants of Delayed Matching to Sample. The delayed-matching-to-sample procedure has been used extensively with a variety of species, including monkeys, pigeons, dolphins, sea lions, goldfish, rats, and people (Baron & Menich, 1985; Blough, 1959; D'Amato, 1973; D'Amato & Colombo, 1985; Forestell & Herman, 1988; Jarrad & Moise, 1971; Iversen, 1993a; Kastak & Schusterman, 1994; Roberts & Grant, 1976; Steinert, Fallon, & Wallace, 1976). In addition, the procedure has been adapted to investigate how animals remember a variety of stimuli, including visual shapes, numbers of responses performed, presence or absence of reward, the spatial location of stimuli, and the order of two successively presented events (for example, D'Amato, 1973; Maki, Moe, & Bierley, 1977; MacDonald, 1993; Wilkie & Summers, 1982).

Three aspects of the matching-to-sample procedure are critical in determining the accuracy of performance. One of these is the nature of the stimulus that has to be remembered. Some stimuli are remembered better than others. Wilkie and Summers (1982), for example, tested the ability of pigeons to remember the spatial position of illuminated lights. Nine lights were arranged in three rows of three lights each. Three of the lights were illuminated on each trial. Memory for the position of the illuminated lights was much better when the three lights were in a straight line than when they formed a discontinuous pattern. (I will discuss the importance of patterns of stimulation further in Chapter 12.)

The two other factors that are important in determining the accuracy of delayed matching to sample are the delay interval and the duration of exposure to the sample stimulus at the start of the trial. In one experiment, for example, Grant (1976) tested pigeons in a standard three-key apparatus after they had received extensive training on delayed matching to sample with visual stimuli. Two pairs of colors—red/green and blue/yellow—served as sample and comparison stimuli on alternate trials. At the start of each trial, the center key was illuminated with a white light. After the pigeon pecked the start cue, the sample color for that trial was presented on the center key for 1, 4, 8, or 14 seconds. This was followed by delay intervals of 0, 20, 40, or 60 seconds, after which the two side keys were illuminated, one with the sample-matching color and the other with the paired alternate color. After the bird made its choice, all the keys were turned off for a 2-minute intertrial interval.

The results of the experiment are summarized in Figure 11.2. If pigeons had pecked the choice keys randomly, they would have been correct 50% of the time. Better than chance performance indicates the use of working memory. For all the sample durations evaluated, the accuracy of matching decreased as longer delays were introduced between exposure to the sample and opportunity to make the choice response. In fact, if the sample was presented for only 1 second, and the opportunity to make a choice was delayed 40 seconds or more, the pigeons responded at chance level. Performance improved if the birds were exposed to the sample for longer periods. When the sample was presented for 4, 8, or 14 seconds, the birds performed above chance levels, even when the delay interval was as long as 60 seconds. Thus, accuracy in the delayed-matching-to-sample procedure decreased as a function of the delay interval and increased as a function of the duration of exposure to the sample stimulus (see also Guttenberger & Wasserman, 1985).

Response Strategies in Matching to Sample. The matching-to-sample procedure is analogous to a discrimination problem in that the participant has to respond to a correct stimulus and refrain from responding to an incorrect one to get reinforced. As I noted in discussions of what is learned in discrimination training in Chapter 8, such

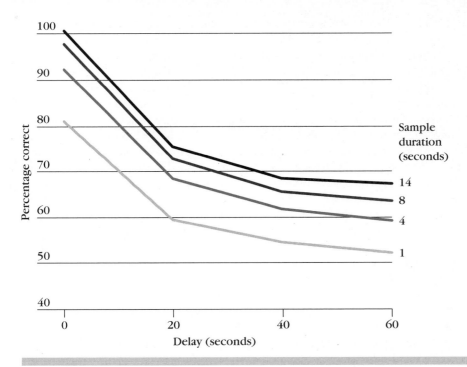

Figure 11.2 Percentage of correct responses in a delayed-matching-to-sample task as a function of the duration of the sample stimulus (1–14 seconds) and the delay between the sample and the choice stimuli (0–60 seconds). (From "Effect of Sample Presentation Time on Long Delay Matching in the Pigeon" by D. S. Grant, *Learning and Motivation,* 1976, *7,* pp. 580–590. Copyright © 1976 by Academic Press. Reprinted by permission.)

a two-alternative task can be solved in several ways. The participant can make the correct choice by just focusing on the correct stimulus, by inhibiting behavior to the incorrect stimulus, or by using both these response strategies. In discrimination learning (which involves the establishment of a reference memory) participants appear to use the combined response strategy. By contrast, participants in matching to sample appear to focus primarily on the correct choice.

In one interesting experiment supporting this conclusion, the investigators used a three-key apparatus for pigeons that was specially constructed so that the stimulus projected on a response key was visible only if the pigeon was standing directly in front of that key (Wright & Sands, 1981). This apparatus enabled the experimenters to determine which response keys the pigeons looked at before making their choice. The results showed that the birds focused on the correct alternative. If they saw the matching stimulus, they pecked it without bothering to check what stimulus was presented on the other side (see also Roitblat, Penner, & Nachtigall, 1990; Wright, 1990, 1992; Zentall, Edwards, Moore, & Hogan, 1981).

General versus Specific Rule Learning. The evidence I have just reviewed indicates that animals focus on the correct choice in matching to sample. What leads them to identify a stimulus as correct? One possibility is that they learn a general rule involving the sample and choice stimuli. The rule may be, for example, "Choose the choice stimulus that is the same as the sample." Another possibility is that the animals learn a series of specific rules or stimulus-response relations. In the experiment by Grant (1976), for example, pairs of colors were used—red/green and blue/yellow. The pigeons may have learned a series of specific stimulus-response relations: "Select red after exposure to red," "Select green after exposure to green," and so on. Most matching-to-sample procedures can be solved either by learning a general "same as" rule or by learning a series of specific stimulus-response relations.

The two alternative strategies can be evaluated by testing transfer of training to new stimuli. After matching-to-sample training with one set of stimuli, another matching problem may be presented with a new set of stimuli. The hypothesis of specific stimulus-response learning predicts little positive (or negative) transfer of matching behavior to new stimuli because the new task requires learning a new set of stimulus-response relations. By contrast, the hypothesis of general-rule learning predicts considerable positive carryover because the general "same as" rule can be used to solve any matching-to-sample problem. Thus, in transfer of training from one matching-to-sample problem to another, the general-rule-learning hypothesis predicts better transfer performance than the specific-rule-learning hypothesis.

In a study with infant chimpanzees, Oden, Thompson, and Premack (1988) first provided training on a matching-to-sample task with just one pair of stimulus objects—a stainless steel measuring cup and a brass bolt lock. One of the objects was presented at the start of the trial, followed by a choice of both objects. If the chimp selected the matching object, it was reinforced with effusive praise, tickling, cuddling, or an edible treat, depending on its preference. After the animals learned the task with the two training stimuli, they were tested with a variety of other stimulus objects. Remarkably, with most of the test objects, the transfer performance was better than 80% accurate. Thus, the chimps seemed to have learned a general "same as" rule with just two training stimuli.

Chimpanzees are more likely to show evidence of generalized matching than pigeons and other species. However, the preponderance of evidence suggests that both general-rule learning and specific stimulus-response learning can occur as a result of matching-to-sample training in a variety of species. Which type of learning predominates appears to be related to the size of the stimulus set used in the matching-to-sample procedure. A study such as Grant's (1976), in which sample and comparison stimuli were selected from two pairs of colors, is likely to favor the learning of specific stimulus-response relations. By contrast, procedures that employ a wide range of stimuli are more likely to favor the learning of a general rule. The extreme of a procedure of this type is the **trials-unique procedure.**

In a trials-unique procedure, a different stimulus serves as the sample on each trial and is paired with another stimulus during the choice phase. Because a given sample stimulus is not presented on more than one trial, accurate performance with a trials-unique procedure is possible only if the participant learns to respond on the basis of a general "same as" rule. Successful learning of the "same as" concept has been obtained with the trials-unique procedure with visual stimuli in pigeons and auditory stimuli in monkeys (Wright, Cook, Rivera, Sands, & Delius, 1988; Wright, Shyan, & Jitsumori, 1990).

A. A. Wright

Passive versus Active Memory Processes. Another important issue in the analysis of delayed-matching-to-sample behavior concerns the type of memory involved. Results such as those shown in Figure 11.2 have encouraged an interpretation of short-term memory known as the **trace decay hypothesis** (Roberts & Grant, 1976). This hypothesis assumes that presentation of a stimulus produces changes in the nervous system that gradually dissipate, or decay, after the stimulus has been removed. The initial strength of the stimulus trace is assumed to reflect the physical energy of the stimulus. Thus, longer or more intense stimuli are presumed to result in stronger stimulus traces. However, no matter what the initial strength of the trace, it is assumed to decay at the same rate after the stimulus ends.

The extent to which the memory of an event exerts control over the organism's actions is assumed to depend on the strength of the stimulus trace at that moment. The stronger the trace, the stronger is the effect of the past stimulus on the organism's behavior. The trace decay model predicts results exactly like those summarized in Figure 11.2. Increasing the delay interval in the matching-to-sample procedure reduces the accuracy of performance presumably because the trace of the sample stimulus is weaker after longer delays. By contrast, increasing the duration of exposure to the sample improves performance presumably because longer exposures to the sample establish stronger stimulus traces.

The trace decay hypothesis emphasizes the physical characteristics of the sample stimulus and is a passive memory mechanism. After the stimulus has been terminated, the decay of its trace is assumed to proceed automatically. As the trace decays, information about the stimulus is assumed to become irretrievably lost.

Contrary to the trace decay hypothesis, various types of results suggest that working memory does not depend entirely on the physical features of the event to be remembered; rather, it involves active processes (Roitblat, 1993). For example, delayed-matching-to-sample performance improves with practice. The learning history of a monkey named Roscoe provides a dramatic illustration. After 4500 training trials, Roscoe could not perform at an above-chance level if a 20-second interval was introduced between the sample and choice stimuli. However, after 17,500 trials he correctly matched the sample stimulus nearly 80% of the time with a 2-minute sample-to-choice delay interval, and after approximately 30,000 trials his performance was better than chance with a 9-minute delay interval (D'Amato, 1973).

Another important determinant of working memory is the extent to which the stimulus is surprising. Several lines of evidence indicate that surprising events are remembered better than expected events (Maki, 1979; Terry & Wagner, 1975). Finally, numerous studies have shown that memory processes can be brought under external stimulus control. (See the discussion of "directed forgetting" later in this chapter.) These various results all support the conclusion that working memory involves active rather than passive processes.

Spatial Memory in a Radial Maze

The matching-to-sample procedure can be adapted to investigate how animals remember a variety of stimuli. The next technique I will describe has more limited applicability but focuses on a very important type of memory—memory for places.

To be able to move about their habitat efficiently, animals have to remember how their environment is laid out—where open spaces, sheltered areas, and potential food sources are located. In many environments, once food has been eaten at one location, it is not available there again for some time until it is replenished. Therefore, animals have to remember where they last found food and avoid that location for awhile. For example, the amakihi (*Loxops virens*), a species of Hawaiian honeycreeper, feeds on the nectar of mamane flowers (Kamil, 1978). After feeding on a cluster of flowers, these birds have to avoid returning to the same flowers for about an hour. By delaying their return to clusters they have recently visited, the birds increase the chance that they will find nectar in the flowers they search. They appear to remember the spatial location of recently visited flower clusters (see also Healy & Hurly, 1995).

Memory for locations in space—spatial memory—has been studied in the laboratory with the use of complex mazes (for example, Olton, 1979). An especially

D. S. Olton

BOX **11.1**

MATCHING TO SAMPLE
IN ELDERLY PEOPLE

A matching-to-sample task can be solved either by learning a matching rule ("same as") or by learning a set of stimulus-response associations. Which of these strategies is learned depends on the characteristics of the participants. This is illustrated by a comparison of matching-to-sample learning in elderly people diagnosed to have Alzheimer-type dementia and normal elderly people (Morris, 1987).

Both groups of participants were about 79 years old. The matching-to-sample task required selecting a color chip that was the same as the sample stimulus on each trial. Training was conducted with red, white, and orange chips. Each trial started with one of these chips presented in the middle of a response panel. The sample chip was then removed, and the participants were presented with two color chips on either side of the sample position. One of the comparisons was the same as the sample; the other was one of the other colors. The participants had to select the matching comparison stimulus. Correct responses were reinforced with a token hidden under the correct chip.

Each participant was trained with red, white, and orange chips until he or she responded correctly on 20 of the 24 trials of a session. At this point the original color chips were replaced with three new ones (yellow, green, and blue) and matching-to-sample training continued. If a participant had learned to respond on the basis of a general "same as" rule, this learning should have transferred to the new color chips, and there should have been no disruption in performance when the new colors were introduced. By contrast, transfer was not expected to occur if a participant had learned a series of stimulus-response rules during the first phase of training.

The results obtained with some of the people are presented in Figure 11.3 by way of illustration. Notice that the Alzheimer's patients were as slow to learn the matching task in Phase 2 of the experiment as in Phase 1. Thus, having learned the matching problem with the first three colors did not facilitate their performance when a new set of colors was introduced in Phase 2.

The results obtained with normal elderly people were very different. They learned the matching task much faster originally, responding with 100% accuracy by the third session. In addition, during Phase 2 when three new stimuli were introduced, their performance remained perfectly accurate. These findings suggest that the Alzheimer's patients learned specific stimulus-response associations in the matching task, whereas the normal elderly participants learned to respond on the basis of a "same as" rule.

---

popular technique involves the use of a radial arm maze (see Figure 11.4). Olton and Samuelson (1976), for example, tested rats in a maze that had eight arms radiating from a central choice area, with a food cup at the end of each arm (see Figure 11.5). Before the start of each trial, a pellet of food was placed in each food cup. The rat was then placed in the center of the maze and allowed to go from one arm to another and pick up all the food. Once a food pellet had been consumed, that arm of the maze remained without food for the rest of the trial.

How could the rat have gone about finding food in this situation? It could have randomly selected which alley to enter each time. Thus, the rat might have entered an alley, eaten the food there, returned to the center area and then randomly selected another arm of the maze to enter next. With such a strategy, however, the rat would have ended up going down alleys from which it had already removed the food. A more efficient strategy would have been to enter only those arms of the maze that had not yet been visited and therefore still had food. This is in fact what the animals did.

The results of the experiment are summarized in Figure 11.6. Entering an arm that had not been visited previously was considered to be a correct choice. Figure 11.6

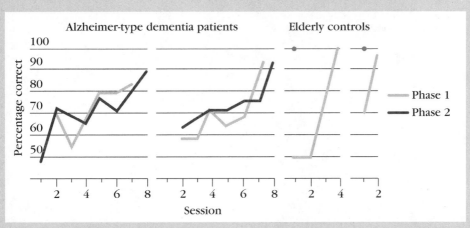

Figure 11.3 Accuracy in responding on a matching-to-sample task by two elderly Alzheimer's patients and two normal elderly people during original training with three stimuli (Phase 1) and a transfer training phase with three new stimuli (Phase 2). (From "Identity Matching and Oddity Learning in Patients with Moderate to Severe Alzheimer-Type Dementia" by R. G. Morris, *Quarterly Journal of Experimental Psychology,* 1987, *39B*, pp. 215–227. Copyright © 1987 The Experimental Psychology Society. Reprinted by permission.)

summarizes the number of correct choices the rats made during the first eight choices of successive tests. During the first five test runs after familiarization with the maze, the rats made a mean of nearly seven correct choices during each test. With continued practice, the mean number of correct choices was consistently above seven, indicating that the animals rarely entered an arm they had previously chosen on that trial.

Rats do not require much training to perform efficiently in the radial maze. The radial maze task appears to take advantage of a preexisting tendency of rats to move about without returning to recently visited places. This tendency is, in fact, so strong that the failure of rats to return to a place where they recently have obtained food may not be related to having obtained food there (Gaffan & Davies, 1981). Several investigators have found that performance on a radial maze is equally accurate (in the sense of the rats not returning to recently visited arms of the maze) whether or not the maze arms are baited with food (FitzGerald, Isler, Rosenberg, Oettinger, & Battig, 1985; Timberlake & White, 1990; see also Maki, 1987).

There are several mechanisms by which rats could choose to enter only previously unchosen arms of a maze without necessarily remembering which arms they had already visited. For example, they may mark each arm they visit with a drop of urine

Figure 11.4 Rat foraging on a radial maze.

and then avoid maze arms with this odor marker, or they may always select arms in a fixed sequence, for example, by entering successive arms in a clockwise order.

Various procedures have convincingly ruled out the use of odor cues in the selection of maze arms (for example, Olton, Collison, & Werz, 1977; Olton & Samuelson, 1976; Zoladek & Roberts, 1978). The available evidence also indicates that rats in a radial maze experiment can perform efficiently without using response chains or entering maze arms in a fixed order from one trial to the next. As long as the central choice area is fairly small so that the rats can easily reach all the arms from anywhere in the central area, they do not choose arms in a fixed order (Olton & Samuelson, 1976; see also Olton et al., 1977). Furthermore, rats select previously unvisited arms, even if procedures are introduced that should disrupt response chains (for example, Beatty & Shavalia, 1980a, 1980b).

The studies I have cited have been important in ruling out various potential cues for radial maze performance and suggest that spatial stimuli are critical. What are spatial cues, and how are they identified? Spatial cues are stimuli that identify the location of an object in the environment. Rats appear to use such things as a window, door, corner of the room, or poster on the wall as landmarks of the experimental environment and to locate maze arms relative to these landmarks. Movement of these landmarks relative to the maze causes the rats to treat the maze arms as being in new locations (Suzuki, Augerinos, & Black, 1980). Thus, spatial location is identified relative to distal room cues, not to local stimuli inside the maze (see also Morris, 1981). Furthermore, the distal environmental cues seem to be perceived visually (Mazmanian & Roberts, 1983).

Because radial maze performance usually depends on memory for recently visited locations, the radial maze procedure has become a popular technique for the study of memory processes, both at the behavioral and physiological level. The memory capacity revealed by the technique is rather remarkable. For example, rats and gerbils have been observed to perform well in radial mazes with as many as 17 arms

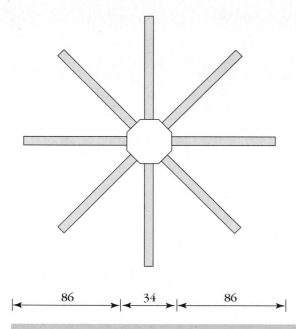

Figure 11.5 Top view of an eight-arm radial maze used in the study of spatial memory. Numbers indicate dimensions in centimeters. (From "Remembrance of Places Passed: Spatial Memory in Rats" by D. S. Olton and R. J. Samuelson, *Journal of Experimental Psychology: Animal Behavior Processes,* 1976, *2,* 97–116. Copyright © 1976 the American Psychological Association. Reprinted by permission.)

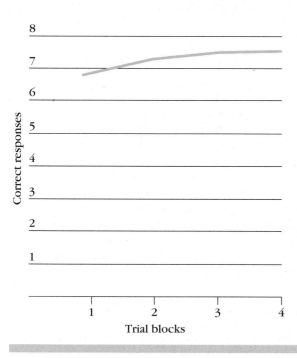

Figure 11.6 Mean number of correct responses rats made in the first eight choices during blocks of five test trials in the eight-arm radial maze. (Adapted from Olton, 1978.)

(Olton et al., 1977; Wilkie & Slobin, 1983), and this probably does not represent the limit of their spatial memory (Roberts, 1979). The duration of spatial working memory is also remarkable.

In a notable test of the limits of spatial memory, Beatty and Shavalia (1980b) allowed rats to make four choices in the eight-arm radial maze in the usual manner. The animals were then detained in their home cages for various periods of up to 24

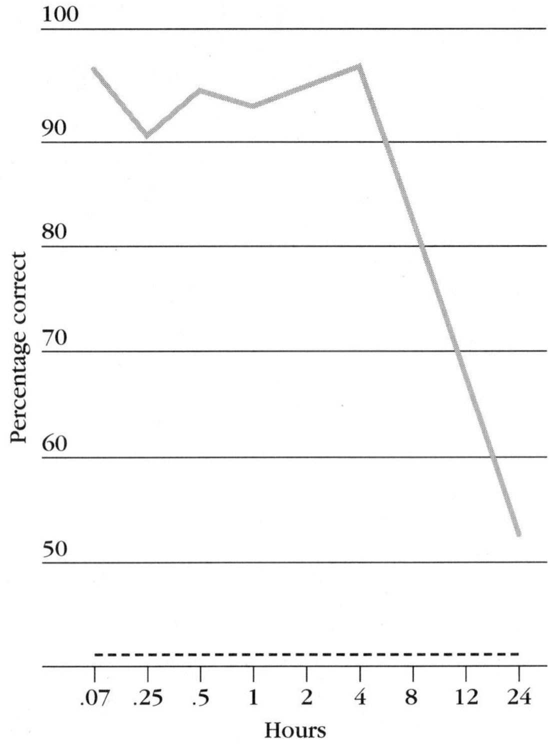

Figure 11.7 Percentage correct responses on choices 5–8 in an eight-arm radial maze. Between choices 4 and 5 the animals were returned to their home cages for varying intervals ranging from .07 to 24 hours. The dashed line indicates chance performance (41%). (From "Rat Spatial Memory: Resistance to Retroactive Interference at Long Retention Intervals" by W. W. Beatty and D. A. Shavalia, *Animal Learning & Behavior*, 1980, *8*, pp. 550–552. Copyright © 1980 by Academic Press. Reprinted by permission.)

hours. After the delay interval, they were returned to the maze and allowed to make choices 5–8. An entry into an alley they had not previously chosen was considered a correct choice, and an entry into a previously visited alley was considered an error.

Figure 11.7 shows the percentage of correct choices as a function of the delay interval. Delays of up to 4 hours after the first four choices did not disrupt performance. Longer periods of confinement in the home cage produced progressively more errors. In fact, only one rat out of five showed significant retention of the first four choices after a 24-hour period. These data show that spatial memory is not permanent. However, remarkably spatial memory can last for several hours (see also Maki, Beatty, Hoffman, Bierley, & Clouse, 1984; Spetch, 1990; Strijkstra & Bolhuis, 1987; Willson & Wilkie, 1991).

Spatial Memory in Food-Storing Birds

Animals tested on a radial maze have to recover food items that were previously stored in various locations by the experimenter. This is similar to natural situations in which animals have no control over the location of food items. Another interesting spatial memory problem involves the recovery of food items that were stored in various places by the animal itself. Under these circumstances, the location of the food items is under the animal's own control. A number of bird and mammalian species (including chipmunks and squirrels) hoard food in various places during times of plenty and visit these caches later to recover the stored food items. (For a review, see Sherry, 1985.)

One remarkable example of cache recovery is provided by the Clark's nutcracker (*Nucifraga columbiana*) (Balda & Turek, 1984; Kamil & Balda, 1990). These birds live in alpine areas of the western United States and harvest seeds from pine cones in late summer and early autumn. They hide the seeds in underground caches and recover them many months later in the winter and spring when other food sources are scarce. A Clark's nutcracker may store as many as 33,000 seeds in caches of four or five seeds each and recover several thousand of these during the next winter. Cache recovery also has been extensively investigated in the marsh tit (*Parus palustris*), a small, lively bird found in England, and in its North American relative, the chickadee (Shettleworth, 1983b; Sherry, 1988). Marsh tits and chickadees store several hundred food items and recover them within a few days. Thus, these smaller birds do not use food storing to mitigate seasonal changes in the food supply.

What mechanisms might food-storing birds use to recover food they previously placed in caches? One possibility is that they remember where they stored each food item and subsequently return to the remembered cache locations. However, before such a memory interpretation can be accepted, other possibilities have to be ruled out. The possible alternatives to a memory interpretation are similar to those I discussed in the analysis of spatial memory in a radial maze. One possibility is that birds find caches by searching randomly among possible cache sites. Another possibility is that they store food only in particular types of locations and then go around to these favored places to recover the food items. They also may mark food-storage sites somehow and then look for these marks when it comes time to recover the food. Yet another possibility is that they are able to smell or see the stored food and identify caches in that way.

Ruling out nonmemory interpretations has required laboratory studies of the food-storing and retrieval behavior of the birds (for example, Kamil & Balda, 1985, 1990a, 1990b; Sherry, 1984; Sherry, Krebs, & Cowie, 1981; Shettleworth & Krebs, 1986). In one such laboratory study, Kamil and Balda (1985) tested nutcrackers in a room that had a special floor with 180 recessed cups of sand (see left panel of Figure 11.8). After habituation to the experimental situation and while they were hungry, the birds were given three sessions during which they could store pinyon pine seeds in the sand cups. During each caching session, only 18 cups were available; the rest of the cups were covered with lids. This procedure forced the birds to store food in cups selected by the experimenter rather than in cups or locations the birds might have found especially attractive.

Starting 10 days after the seeds had been stored by the nutcrackers, four recovery sessions were conducted on successive days. During recovery sessions none of the 180 sand cups was covered with a lid, but seeds were buried only in the cups where the birds had previously stored seeds. The results are summarized on the right side of Figure 11.8. Notice that on average the birds performed much better than chance in going to the sand cups where they had previously stored food. The correct locations could not be identified by disturbed sand because the experimenters raked the sand smooth at the start of each recovery session. Other tests showed that the correct locations were not identified by the smell of the seeds buried in the sand because the birds visited places where they had previously stored food, even if the food was removed before the test session. These control studies indicate that cache recovery is guided by a fairly longlasting spatial memory.

Given the remarkable performance of food-storing birds in controlled memory experiments, it is tempting to conclude that they have evolved unusual and specialized spatial memory skills (Sherry & Schacter, 1987). To determine the extent of this

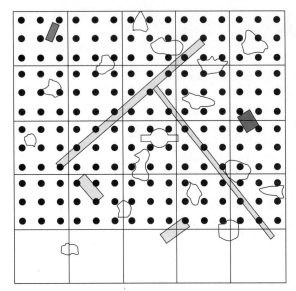
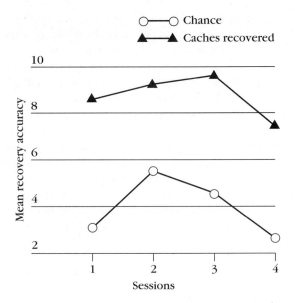

Figure 11.8 Left panel: Floor plan of the apparatus used by Kamil and Balda (1985) to test the spatial memory of Clark's nutcrackers. Filled circles represent sand cups. Other symbols represent rocks, logs, and a feeder in the middle. Right panel: Recovery accuracy, compared to chance, during four successive recovery sessions started 10 days after the birds stored pine seeds. (From "Cache Recovery and Spatial Memory in Clark's Nutcrackers (*Nucifraga columbiana*)," by A. C. Kamil and R. P. Balda, *Journal of Experimental Psychology: Animal Behavior Processes,* 1985, *11,* 95–111. Copyright © 1985 by American Psychological Association. Reprinted by permission.)

specialization, investigators have compared directly the memory performance of bird species that store food and those that do not engage in such behavior. These comparisons had to be made with tasks that both types of species can perform—tasks that do not involve storing food. In some experiments, birds were required to return to a place where they previously ate food placed there by the experimenter; other experiments employed a matching-to-sample procedure. The results were somewhat unexpected. Food-storing and nonstoring species of birds do not seem to differ much in how long they remember stimuli encountered in nonstoring tasks (Healy & Krebs, 1992a, 1992b; Healy, 1995; Hilton & Krebs, 1990; but see Olson, 1991). However, food-storing species seem to have a bias toward paying attention to spatial cues rather than color and pattern stimuli (Brodbeck, 1994; Brodbeck & Shettleworth, 1995; see also Clayton & Krebs, 1994).

MEMORY MECHANISMS

In the preceding section, I described several prominent techniques for the study of memory processes in animals. Next, I turn to a discussion of factors that determine what we remember and how well we remember it. As I noted earlier, memory processes involve three phases: acquisition, retention, and retrieval (see Table 11.1). What we remember and how well we remember it depend on all three of these phases, often in combination with each other. In this part of the chapter, I will discuss animal research relevant to each of the three phases of memory processes.

Acquisition and the Problem of Stimulus Coding

Obviously, we cannot remember something (the winning play in a championship game, for example) if we were never exposed to the event in the first place. Memory depends on our having experienced an event and having made some kind of a record of that experience. However, even when our memory is excellent, it is not because we have retained a perfect or literal record of the earlier experience.

Experiences cannot be recorded in a literal sense, even by machines. A movie camera can do a remarkably good job in recording the sights and sounds of the winning play in a championship game. The visual aspects of the event are recorded in terms of a series of stationary images; the auditory aspects are recorded in terms of a pattern of magnetized particles on the film. Thus, the winning play is coded in terms of still photographs and magnetic patterns for the purposes of retention. However, the coded record (a strip of film with a soundtrack) bears little resemblance to the actual event.

In a similar fashion, we do not have a literal record of a past experience in memory. Rather, the past experience is coded in the nervous system in some way for the purposes of retention. Our memory is based on how a past experience was coded and how that code is retrieved at a later time. Thus, **stimulus coding** is a critical feature of the acquisition phase of memory.

Investigators have been interested in several aspects of the problem of coding (Zentall, 1993). Consider, for example, rats foraging for food in a radial maze (see Figure 11.5). The animals have to enter the various arms of the maze to obtain the food located at the end of each arm. So as not to waste effort, they have to select only the arms they have not yet tried that day. As we have seen, rats rely on their memory to do this. But, what do they keep in mind? How is memory coded?

Cognitive Maps. One possibility is that the animals make a serial list of the maze arms they visit, adding an item to the list with each new arm visited. Given the excellent performance of rats on mazes with 17 arms or more (Olton et al., 1977; Roberts, 1979; Wilkie & Slobin, 1983), this would involve a rather long list. Such extensive list learning seems unlikely, since even humans have difficulty maintaining 17 items or more in working memory at one time. Another possibility is that the animals form a mental map or mental representation of how the maze and the food cups are arranged. They then use this mental map to decide which arm of the maze to enter next (Roberts, 1984).

D. Wilkie

Investigators have been able to answer rather sophisticated questions about the kinds of information that are included in a mental map. One may inquire, for example, whether the distance between two points in a mental map corresponds to the physical distance between those points in the real world. Using multidimensional scaling and correlational analyses of errors in a spatial learning task, Wilkie (1989) was able to demonstrate that mental distances in a spatial representation do in fact correspond to physical distances. Another interesting question is whether a mental representation of space highlights places where the animal has found food or also includes information about the paths the animal has used to get to those places (Brown & Mellgren, 1994).

Retrospective and Prospective Coding. In addition to understanding the kinds of spatial information that are included in a mental map, we also have to figure out what aspects of the map animals keep in mind as they go about foraging in the radial maze. Perhaps the most obvious possibility is that the animals keep in mind where they have already been. This is called **retrospective memory**, or **retrospection**. An equally effective memory strategy is for the animals to keep in mind which maze arms they have yet to visit. This strategy is called **prospective memory**, or **prospection**. Investigators of animal memory processes have become very much interested in the distinction between retrospective and prospective memory (Honig & Thompson, 1982; Wasserman, 1986; Grant, 1993). Because all animal memory paradigms have a limited range of outcomes, they can all be solved successfully either by remembering a past event (retrospection) or by remembering a plan for future action (prospection).

Consider going shopping at a mall. Let's assume that to complete your shopping, you have to visit six stores: a shoe store, a record store, a book shop, a bakery, a clothing store, and a pharmacy. What memory strategy could you use to avoid going to the same place twice? One possibility would be to form a memory code for each store after visiting that store. This would be a retrospective code. You could then decide whether to enter the next store on the list based on whether or not you remembered already having gone there. With such a retrospective strategy, the contents of your working memory would increase by one item with each store you visit. Thus, how much you have to remember (the memory load) would increase as you progress through the task (see Figure 11.9).

The alternative would be to memorize a list of all the stores you intend to visit before you start your trip. Such memory would involve prospection, because it would be memory for what you intend to do. After visiting a particular store, you could delete that store from your list. Thus, in this scheme, a visit to a store would be "recorded" by having that store removed from the prospective memory list. Because you would be keeping in mind only the stores you still have to visit, the memory load would decrease as you progress through your shopping, as shown in Figure 11.9.

Numerous ingenious experiments have been conducted to determine whether animals use retrospective or prospective memory. Many of these have involved variations of the matching-to-sample procedure with pigeons as participants. The experiments have demonstrated that animals use both retrospective and prospective memory, but under different circumstances (Santi, Musgrave, & Bradford, 1988; Zentall, Jagielo, Jackson-Smith, & Urcuioli, 1987; Zentall, Urcuioli, Jagielo, & Jackson-Smith, 1989). Such experiments illustrate that coding strategies are flexible, with different strategies adopted in response to different task demands. (For other evidence of coding flexibility, see Ducharme & Santi, 1993; Grant, 1991; Grant & Spetch, 1993.)

Coding Strategies and Task Demands. To illustrate how coding strategies might change as a function of task demands, let us return to the example of having to shop in six different stores in a mall. As I have noted, with a retrospective coding strategy the demands on working memory increase as you progress through the shopping trip, from having to remember the first store you visited to having to remember all six stores. Conversely, with a prospective coding strategy the demands on working memory decrease as you progress through the six stores, starting with having to remember all six stores to visit and ending with having to remember none (see Figure 11.9). The question arises, How might you minimize the demands on your memory? Is there a way to keep the demands on working memory to three items or fewer throughout the shopping trip? As it turns out there is, if you change your memory strategy halfway through the task.

Since the memory load is least for a retrospective strategy at the beginning of the trip, you should use a retrospective strategy to start with. Remembering where you have been works well for the first three stores you visit. After that, the memory load for retrospection begins to exceed the memory load for prospection (see Figure 11.9). Therefore, after having visited three stores, you should switch to a prospective code and keep in mind only which stores remain to be visited. By switching coding strate-

P. Urcuioli

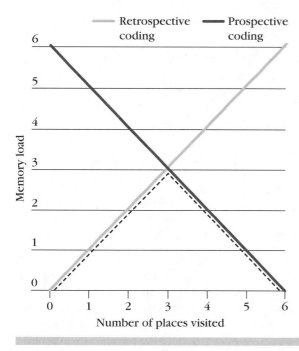

Figure 11.9 Memory load following different numbers of places visited, out of a possible total of six, given retrospective and prospective coding strategies. The dashed line represents memory load when the coding strategy is changed from retrospection to prospection halfway through the task.

gies halfway through, you minimize how much you have to remember at any one time. If you use retrospection followed by prospection, memory load will at first increase and then decrease as you complete the task, as illustrated by the dashed line in Figure 11.9.

Do animals (and people) actually have such flexibility in coding strategies, and if so how could that be proved? Several experiments have been performed indicating that coding strategies change from retrospection to prospection as an individual goes through a list of places or items. Individuals remember what has happened early in the list and what remains to be done later in the list (Cook, Brown, & Riley, 1985; Zentall, Steirn, & Jackson-Smith, 1990; see also Brown, Wheeler, & Riley, 1989).

In one study (Kesner & DeSpain, 1988), both rats and college students were tested for their coding strategies. If individuals switch from retrospection to prospection in the course of remembering a series of places, memory load should first increase and then decrease. Memory load was estimated from the rate of errors the participants made on a test that was conducted after the participants had visited different numbers of places.

The rats in Kesner and DeSpain's study were first trained to forage for food on a 12-arm radial maze in the standard manner. Once they had become proficient at obtaining food by going to each maze arm, a series of test trials was conducted. On each test trial, the rats were allowed to make a certain number of arm entries. They were then removed from the maze for 15 minutes. At the end of the delay, they were returned to the maze and allowed to enter one of two alleys selected by the experimenter. One was an alley they had entered earlier; the other one was new. Selecting the new alley was judged to be the correct response. The rate of errors the rats made during the test phase is presented in the left graph of Figure 11.10. As the number of visited locations before the test increased from 2 to 8 arms of the maze, the error rate increased. This finding is consistent with the hypothesis that the rats were using a retrospective coding strategy during the first eight arm entries. Interestingly, however,

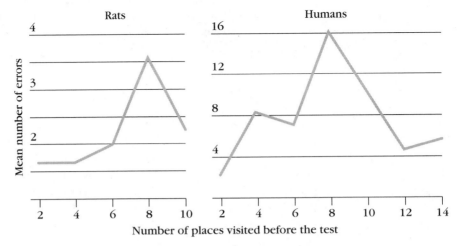

Figure 11.10 Error rate of rats (left) and college students (right) on spatial memory tasks requiring identification of a new place after a delay. The delay was imposed after the participants had "visited" various numbers of locations. (From "Correspondence Between Rats and Humans in the Utilization of Retrospective and Prospective Codes" by R. P. Kesner and M. J. DeSpain, *Animal Learning and Behavior*, 1988, *16*, pp. 299–302. Copyright © by the Psychonomic Society. Reprinted by permission.)

when the rats were tested after having entered 10 arms, they made fewer errors. This improvement in memory performance after more alleys suggests that the animals switched to a prospective coding strategy.

The college students in the study were presented with a grid having 16 squares (corresponding to 16 places in a maze). During the course of a trial, the symbol X traveled from one square to another in an irregular order, simulating movement from one place to another in a maze. After the X had been presented at various locations, a delay of 5 seconds was introduced, followed by a test of two test locations. One test location was a place where the X had been; the other was a new square. The participants had to identify which was the new square.

The rate of errors the students made is presented in the right graph of Figure 11.10 as a function of the number of places where the X had been before the test. The results were remarkably similar to the pattern of errors obtained with the rats. The error rate initially increased, consistent with a retrospective coding strategy. After the X had been at eight places, however, the error rate decreased, consistent with a prospective coding strategy.

Results such as these illustrate that memory performance is a function of coding strategies and that coding strategies may vary as a function of task demands. Given alternative possible coding strategies, participants switch strategies so as to reduce memory load and thereby improve response accuracy.

Retention and the Problem of Rehearsal

The second phase of memory processes is retention. With working-memory tasks, a prominent issue in the context of retention is rehearsal. Rehearsal refers to keeping information in an active state—a state in which the information is readily available for use. If someone tells you a phone number, you may rehearse the number by repeating it to yourself over and over again until you get to a phone. If someone is giving you directions for getting to the post office, you may try to create a mental image of the route and imagine yourself following the route a number of times. Such rehearsal strategies facilitate keeping newly acquired information readily at hand so that it is available to guide behavior.

Rehearsal processes were first investigated in animal memory as they relate to the learning or establishment of new associations. Models of learning and memory typically assume that associations are formed between two events (occurrence of a conditioned and an unconditioned stimulus, for example), provided that the two events are rehearsed at the same time (for example, Wagner, 1976, 1981). Given this assumption, learning is expected to be disrupted by manipulations that disrupt rehearsal. Early studies of rehearsal processes in animal memory focused on how manipulations that disrupt rehearsal influence the learning of new associations (for example, Wagner, Rudy, & Whitlow, 1973). More recently, the focus of research has been on the role of rehearsal in working memory paradigms. An important line of evidence for rehearsal processes in working memory comes from studies of **directed forgetting.**

It is now well established that human memory performance can be modified by cues or instructions indicating that something will or will not be important to remember (for example, Bjork, 1972; Johnson, 1994). In this research, participants are first exposed to a list of items. Some of the items are accompanied by a remember cue (R-cue), indicating that the item will appear later in a test of memory. Other items are accompanied by a forget cue (F-cue), indicating that the item will not be included in the memory test. Occasionally probe trials are included in which participants are tested for their memory of a item that was accompanied by the F-cue. The results of these probe trials indicate that memory is disrupted by the forget cue.

Demonstrations of directed forgetting are important because they provide evidence that memory is an active process that can be brought under stimulus control. Research on directed forgetting in people has sparked interest in finding analogous effects with nonhuman animals. (See review by Rilling, Kendrick, & Stonebraker, 1984.) How might a procedure be devised to study directed forgetting in animals?

One possibility is to use a variation of the delayed-matching-to-sample procedure. In a matching task, each trial begins with exposure to a sample stimulus (a horizontal grid, for example). The animal is then presented with both the sample (horizontal grid) and a distractor stimulus (vertical grid). Responses to the sample are reinforced; responses to the distractor stimulus do not produce reinforcement. Cues to remember or forget can be introduced into the matching task after the sample stimulus, as is shown in Figure 11.11 (left panel). On R-cue trials, the animals are tested for their memory of the sample; on F-cue trials such a memory test is not conducted; the F-cue is followed directly by the intertrial interval.

Early research on directed forgetting in animals used procedures similar to the one outlined in the left panel of Figure 11.11. After extensive training on such a procedure, probe trials were introduced that tested for memory of the sample after an F-cue. As in the human research, these probe trials indicated that memory is disrupted by the F-cue. Why might such a disruption occur? One possibility is that the F-cue disrupts rehearsal and thereby leads to poorer memory performance. Unfortunately, however, the procedure outlined in Figure 11.11 (left panel) allows for other possibilities as well (see Roper & Zentall, 1993). Notice, for example, that during the training trials the animals cannot earn reinforcement on F-cue trials.

T. Zentall

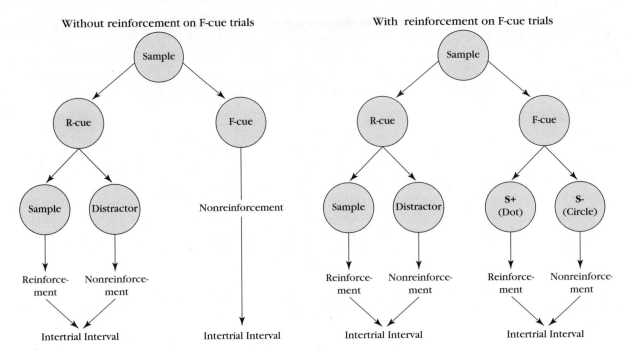

Without reinforcement on F-cue trials

With reinforcement on F-cue trials

Figure 11.11 Two versions of the delayed-matching-to-sample procedure used for the study of directed forgetting in animals. In both procedures, a sample stimulus is presented at the beginning of each trial. This is then followed by either a remember cue (R-cue) or a forget cue (F-cue). In the procedure on the left, reinforcement cannot be obtained on F-cue trials. In the procedure on the right, reinforcement can be obtained on both R-cue and F-cue trials.

Research has indicated that the absence of reinforcement on F-cue trials can produce disruptions of memory performance independent of any effects on rehearsal (Zentall, Roper, & Sherburne, 1995). Therefore, directed forgetting experiments have to be designed in a way that allows animals to earn reinforcement on both R-cue and F-cue trials. Such a procedure is outlined in the right panel of Figure 11.11. Again a delayed-matching-to-sample procedure is used. During the training phase, R-cue trials end in presentation of either the sample or a distractor stimulus, and responses to the sample stimulus are reinforced. On F-cue trials, in place of the sample and distractor stimuli, the birds receive a simple discrimination that does not require working memory. They are reinforced for pecking in the presence of S+ (a dot, for example) and are not reinforced for pecking in the presence of S− (a circle) (see Figure 11.11, right panel). After extensive training, probe trials are introduced in which both the R-cue and the F-cue are followed by tests of the sample and a distractor stimulus.

Grant and Soldat (1995) conducted an experiment using the procedures outlined in Figure 11.11 (right panel). The results are summarized in Figure 11.12. Performance was highly accurate on the R-cue probe trials; the birds responded much more to the sample than to the distractor test stimulus. In contrast, they did not respond accurately on the F-cue probe trials. On these trials they pecked both the sample and the distractor at high rates. Thus, on F-cue trials they failed to distinguish between the sample and the distractor. These results illustrate that directed forgetting effects can occur in animals and that such effects are evident in the absence of suppressed responding to the distractor stimulus.

Results such as those presented in Figure 11.12 indicate that rehearsal and memory processes in animals can be brought under stimulus control (see also Roper, Kaiser, & Zentall, 1995). These findings indicate that even in animals, memory does not involve the passive storage of information. Rather, memory involves active processes.

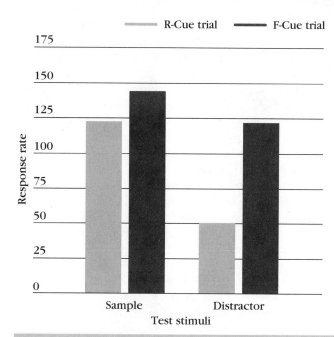

Figure 11.12   Directed forgetting in pigeons trained on a matching-to-sample task. On remember-cue trials (R-cue), the birds responded much more to the sample than to the distractor stimulus. On forget-cue probe trials (F-cue), the birds responded indiscriminantly to the two stimuli. (Based on Grant & Soldat, 1995.)

Retrieval

In the third phase of memory processes—retrieval—stored information is recovered so that it can be used to guide behavior. Whereas problems of coding and rehearsal are primarily being investigated in working-memory paradigms, research on retrieval has focused on reference memory and, more specifically, on memory for learned associations. Retrieval processes are of special interest because instances of memory failure are often due to a deficit in recovering information from memory—**retrieval failure**—rather than the loss of that information from memory.

During the course of our daily lives, we learn many things, all of which are somehow stored in the brain. Which aspect of our extensive knowledge we think of at a particular time depends on which pieces of information are retrieved from our long-term memory store. At any moment, we recall only a minute proportion of what we know. Retrieval processes are triggered by reminders, or **retrieval cues.** If you are discussing summer camp experiences with your friends, the things they say will serve as retrieval cues to remind you of things you did at summer camp.

Retrieval cues are effective in reminding you of a past experience because they are associated with the memory for that experience. A song may remind you of the concert you attended on your first date. Balancing on a bicycle will remind you of what you have to do to ride a bicycle. The sensations of sinking in a swimming pool will remind you of what you learned about swimming, and the voice of a friend you have not seen for a long time will stimulate retrieval of memories for the things you used to do together.

Retrieval Cues and Memory for Instrumental Behavior in Human Infants. Various stimuli that are present during acquisition of a memory can come to serve as retrieval cues for that memory. Borovsky and Rovee-Collier (1990), for example, investigated retrieval of the memory for instrumental conditioning in 6-month-old infants. The

C. Rovee-Collier

infants were trained in their own homes in playpens whose sides were covered with a cloth liner. Some of these liners were striped, and others had a square pattern. The investigators were interested in the role of the cloth liner as a retrieval cue for the instrumental response.

A mobile was mounted above the playpen. Each infant was seated in the playpen in a reclining baby seat so that it could see the mobile. One end of a satin ribbon was looped around the infant's ankle, and the other end was attached to the stand that supported the mobile. With this arrangement, each time the infant kicked, it moved the mobile. The instrumental response was kicking the leg, and the reinforcer was movement of the mobile. The kicking response first was conditioned in two short training sessions. The infants then received a test session 24 hours later.

The cues present during the test session were varied for different groups of infants. Some of the babies were tested in a crib with the same cloth liner that had been present during the training sessions (Group Same). Others were tested with the alternate cloth liner that was new to them (Group Diff). For a third group, the alternate cloth liner was familiar, but it had not been present during the training trials (Group Diff-Fam). Finally, a fourth group of babies was tested without a liner and could look around their familiar playroom (None-Fam).

The results of the experiment are summarized in Figure 11.13. The best retention performance was evident in the group that was tested with the same playpen liner that had been present during conditioning. Each of the other groups showed significantly poorer memory performance. Infants tested with a novel liner (Group Diff) may have shown poor performance because novelty somehow disrupted their behavior (Thomas & Empedocles, 1992). However, the poor performance of Group Diff-Fam indicates that novelty was not entirely responsible for the disruptions of memory that occurred. A change in the crib liner from conditioning to testing resulted in poor performance, even if the liner used during testing was familiar. The inferior performance of Group Diff-Fam as compared to Group Same provides strong evidence that the cloth liner served as a retrieval cue for the instrumental kicking behavior (see also Bhatt, Rovee-Collier, & Shyi, 1994; Rovee-Collier & Bhatt, 1993).

Contextual Cues and the Retrieval of Conflicting Memories. Changing the cloth pattern on the playpen liner changed the contextual cues of the playpen. Thus, the study by Borovsky and Rovee-Collier was a study of the role of contextual cues in memory retrieval. We previously encountered another example of contextual cues in memory retrieval in the discussion of contextual stimulus control in Chapter 8. There I described an experiment by Thomas, McKelvie, and Mah (1985) in which discrimination training was conducted with pigeons. In the first phase, the pigeons were reinforced for pecking when a vertical line (S+ = 90°) was projected on the response key and were not reinforced when a horizontal (S– = 0°) line appeared. This initial discrimination training was provided in the presence of certain contextual cues. The contextual cues were then changed (by altering the sounds and lighting in the chamber), and the pigeons were trained on the reversal of the original discrimination. Now, the horizontal line was the cue for reinforcement of pecking (S+ = 0°), and the vertical line was the cue for nonreinforcement (S– = 90°).

Subsequent generalization tests in each context indicate that responding to the vertical and horizontal lines depended on the context in which the lines were tested. In the original context, the pigeons responded in accord with the original discrimina-

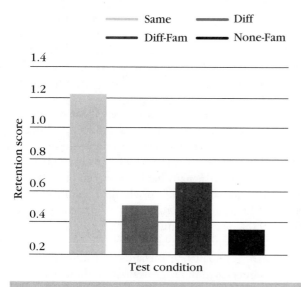

Figure 11.13 Retention scores of 6-month-old infants in a test of instrumental conditioning. Group Same was tested in a playpen with the same cloth liner that had been present during conditioning. Group Diff was tested with a new cloth liner. Group Diff-Fam was tested with a familiar cloth liner that was different from the one that had been in the playpen during conditioning. Group None-Fam was tested without a cloth liner but in a familiar playpen in a familiar room. (From "Contextual Constraints on Memory Retrieval at Six Months" by D. Borovsky and C. Rovee-Collier, *Child Development, 61,* pp. 1569–1583. Copyright © 1990 by University of Chicago Press. Reprinted by permission.)

tion contingencies; in the altered context, they responded in accord with the reversal discrimination contingencies (see Figure 8.12). These results indicate that the contextual cues served as retrieval cues for the two discriminations. Which discrimination was retrieved (and which controlled the behavior of the birds) depended on which set of contextual cues the pigeons experienced during the test. The study illustrates that organisms can retain memories of diametrically opposing response tendencies. Which of the conflicting memories controls behavior depends on which memory is retrieved at the time.

Training participants on diametrically opposed tasks, as Thomas, McKelvie, and Mah did, may seem a bit unusual. However, the principle illustrated by their study may have considerable generality. (For other examples of involving the retrieval of conflicting memories, see Dekeyne & Deweer, 1990; Fiori, Barnet, & Miller, 1994; Haggbloom & Morris, 1994.) Contingencies of reinforcement rarely remain the same during an organism's lifetime. Although it may be rare for contingencies to become reversed, alterations in contingencies are fairly common. One such change in contingencies is extinction. Reinforced responses may undergo extinction as food supplies change, or the animal is forced into a new habitat by changes in the weather or by predators. The study by Thomas, McKelvie, and Mah suggests that organisms may not forget or unlearn things when extinction is introduced; rather, they may simply learn a new relationship. Whether the memory of original reinforcement or of extinction is reactivated will depend on the retrieval cues present in a test situation.

The role of retrieval processes in extinction has been investigated extensively by Bouton and his colleagues (Bouton, 1991, 1993, 1994; Bouton & Bolles, 1985; Bouton & Peck, 1989; Brooks & Bouton, 1993; Peck & Bouton, 1990). One important finding in this research has been that the effects of extinction are context-specific. If reinforced training is conducted in one context, and extinction is conducted in another, returning the animals to the context of reinforcement results in renewal of the conditioned responding. Thus, whether performance appropriate to reinforcement or performance appropriate to extinction is observed depends on whether contextual cues retrieve the memory of reinforcement or the memory of extinction.

N. E. Spear

The Generality of Reminder Treatments. Much has been learned about the facilitation of memory retrieval by reminder treatments (see Gordon, 1981; Spear, 1978, 1981; Spear & Riccio, 1994). As we have seen, contextual cues are especially effective in stimulating memory retrieval (Gordon & Klein, 1994). In addition, various other reminder procedures have been found to facilitate recall, including exposure to the *unconditioned stimulus* (MacArdy & Riccio, 1995; Miller, Jagielo, & Spear, 1991; Quartermain, McEwen, & Azmitia, 1970), exposure to the *reinforced conditioned stimulus* (CS+) (Gisquet-Verrier & Alexinsky, 1990; Gordon & Mowrer, 1980), and exposure to a *nonreinforced conditioned stimulus* (CS–) that was present during training (Campbell & Randall, 1976; Miller, Jagielo, & Spear, 1990a, 1991, 1992).

Reminder treatments can be used to reverse many instances of memory loss. (For a review, see Miller, Kasprow, & Schachtman, 1986.) For example, reminder treatments have been used to facilitate memory retrieval from short-term memory (Feldman & Gordon, 1979; Kasprow, 1987). They can remind older animals (and babies) of forgotten early-life experiences (for example, Campbell & Randall, 1976; Fagen & Rovee-Collier, 1983; Haroutunian & Riccio, 1979; Richardson, Riccio, & Jonke, 1983). Reminder treatments can counteract stimulus-generalization decrements that occur when learned behavior is tested in a new situation (Gordon, McCracken, Dess-Beech, & Mowrer, 1981; Mowrer & Gordon, 1983). Reminder treatments also have been observed to increase the low levels of conditioned responding that typically occur in latent inhibition, overshadowing, and blocking procedures (Kasprow, Cacheiro, Balaz, & Miller, 1982; Kasprow, Catterson, Schachtman, & Miller, 1984; Miller, Jagielo, & Spear, 1990b; Schachtman, Gee, Kasprow, & Miller, 1983; see also Gordon, McGinnis, & Weaver, 1985).

FORGETTING

As we have seen, memory mechanisms involve many different factors. Some of these concern coding and the acquisition of information. Others involve rehearsal and the retention of information. Still others involve processes of retrieval. Things can go wrong at any point along the way. Therefore, failures of memory, or forgetting, can occur for a variety of reasons.

When we fail to remember something, it could be because the information was never put into a memory store properly. This may have occurred for lack of a viable coding scheme or for lack of rehearsal necessary for moving information into a long-term store. Failures of memory also may be attributable to lack of necessary retrieval mechanisms. Retrieval failures can also occur if the retrieval processes do not fit the way in which the information was originally coded and stored. Consider, for example, trying to retrieve a book from the library. Libraries in the United States use either the Dewey decimal system or the Library of Congress system for coding and organizing their collections. If you had the Dewey decimal code for the book, but the library was organized according to the Library of Congress code, you would have a great deal of difficulty retrieving the book. For successful remembering, retrieval mechanisms have to be consistent with how the information was originally coded.

In studies of animal memory, forgetting has been extensively investigated in the context of two types of phenomena—interference effects and retrograde amnesia. In the concluding sections of this chapter, we will consider these phenomena in turn.

Proactive and Retroactive Interference

The most common sources of memory disruption arise from exposure to prominent stimuli either before or after the event a person is trying to remember. Consider meeting people at a party, for example. If the only new people you meet at the party are a young couple new to town, chances are you will not have much trouble remembering who they are. However, if you are introduced to a number of new people before and/or after meeting this couple, you may find it much harder to remember their names.

There are numerous well-documented and analyzed situations in which memory for something is disrupted by earlier exposure to other information. In these cases the interfering information acts forward to disrupt the memory of a future target event. Therefore, the disruption of memory is called **proactive interference.** In other cases memory for something is disrupted by subsequent exposure to other information. In these situations the interfering stimulus acts backward to disrupt the memory of a preceding target event. Therefore, the disruption of memory is called **retroactive interference.**

The mechanisms of proactive and retroactive interference have been extensively investigated in human memory (Postman, 1971; Slamecka & Ceraso, 1960; Underwood, 1957). Proactive and retroactive interference also have been investigated in various animal memory paradigms including delayed matching to sample (for example, Grant, 1975; Grant & Roberts, 1973, 1976), spatial memory (for example, Cohen, Reid, & Chew, 1994; Gordon & Feldman, 1978; Hoffman & Maki, 1986; Maki et al., 1979; Roitblat & Harley, 1988), and serial list learning (Jitsumori, Wright, & Cook, 1988).

W. S. Maki

Proactive Interference. Proactive interference can be investigated in the delayed-matching-to-sample procedure by exposing participants to an interfering stimulus just before presentation of the sample stimulus on each trial (see Grant, 1982; Medin, 1980; Reynolds & Medin, 1981). Recall that in the standard matching-to-sample procedure, animals are given a sample (let us say S1), followed by two choice stimuli (S1 and S2), one of which (S1) matches the sample. The participants are reinforced only for responding to the matching stimulus.

In one study of proactive interference with monkeys, illumination of stimulus panels with a red or a green light served as the S1 and S2 stimuli (Jarvik, Goldfarb, & Carley, 1969). The experimental chamber had three stimulus panels arranged in a row. The sample was always presented on the center panel. One second after the sample stimulus, the two side panels were illuminated with the choice stimuli. To investigate the effects of proactive interference, the monkeys were exposed to an interfering stimulus for 3 seconds at various intervals ranging from 1 to 18 seconds before presentation of the sample. The interfering cue was always the incorrect choice for that trial. If the sample on a given trial was the green color, the preceding interfering stimulus was exposure to the red color on the center key, and vice versa. The monkeys also received control trials not preceded by an interfering stimulus.

The results are summarized in Figure 11.14. On control trials—that is, when an interfering cue was not presented before the sample—the monkeys made the correct choice nearly 100% of the time. They responded less accurately when the sample was preceded by an interfering cue. Furthermore, greater disruptions of performance occurred when the interfering stimulus more closely preceded the sample stimulus.

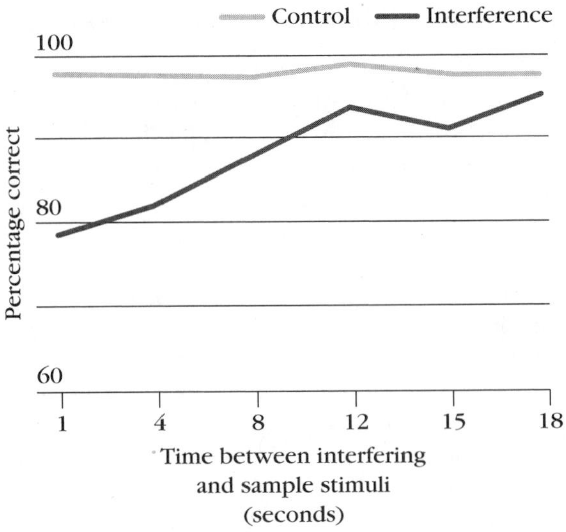

Figure 11.14 Percentage correct responses in a delayed-matching-to-sample task. On some trials a 3-second interfering stimulus was presented 1–18 seconds before the sample stimulus. (From "Influence of Interference on Delayed Matching in Monkeys" by M. E. Jarvik, T. L. Goldfarb, and J. L. Carley, *Journal of Experimental Psychology*, 1969, *81*, pp. 1–6. Copyright © 1969 by the American Psychological Association. Reprinted by permission.)

There was no significant proactive interference if the interfering stimulus was presented more than 8 seconds before the sample.

In the study just described, proactive interference was produced by introducing an explicit interfering stimulus before a regular matching-to-sample trial. Proactive interference in working-memory tasks can also arise from events experienced during the preceding regular trial, without there being an explicit interfering stimulus (for example, Edhouse & White, 1988a, 1988b; Jitsumori, Wright, & Shyan, 1989; Roitblat & Scopatz, 1983). In these cases, participants remember the stimuli and/or responses they made on the preceding trial, and this disrupts their performance on the next trial. In one study (with monkeys), stimuli presented on one day were observed to cause proactive interference with responding during the next day's session (Jitsumori, Wright, & Cook, 1988).

Most cases of proactive interference are not the result of memory failure. Interference does not occur because the participants do not remember the right thing. Rather, the problem is that they remember too much and end up basing their responses on irrelevant information. The participants may remember not only the correct response for the current trial but also the correct response for the preceding trial. Errors occur because of confusion between trials. Information about the current trial is mixed up with information from preceding trials.

Retroactive Interference. In contrast to commonly observed proactive interference effects, retroactive interference is usually caused by memory loss rather than confusion (Cook, 1980; Roberts & Grant, 1978; Thompson, Van Hemel, Winston, & Pappas, 1983; Wright, Urcuioli, Sands, & Santiago, 1981). The memory loss is due to disruption of rehearsal caused by introduction of interfering sources of stimulation.

Retroactive interference can be studied in the delayed-matching-to-sample procedure by introducing an interfering stimulus between exposure to the sample and presentation of the test stimuli. If the delayed-matching-to-sample task involves visual cues, memory is readily disrupted by visual cues presented during the delay interval (for example, Worsham & D'Amato, 1973; see also Thompson, et al., 1983).

By contrast, if the sample is an auditory stimulus, memory is readily disrupted by auditory stimuli presented in the delay interval (Colombo & D'Amato, 1986).

Perhaps the simplest way to present interfering visual stimuli is to turn on a light so that the animals can see various features of the experimental chamber. Several experiments have demonstrated that illumination of the experimental chamber during the delay interval impairs memory in a visual matching-to-sample task (for example, Grant & Roberts, 1976; Worsham & D'Amato, 1973). In one experiment, pigeons first received extensive matching-to-sample training with stimuli that consisted of vertical or horizontal lines (Roberts & Grant, 1978). During a test of retroactive interference, the choice stimuli were presented 0–12 seconds after exposure to the sample, and the experimental chamber was either illuminated or dark during the delay period.

Figure 11.15 shows the results. The birds correctly chose the matching stimulus over 90% of the time when there was no delay after the sample stimulus. Accuracy decreased as the interval between the sample and choice cues increased. However, this decrement in performance was much greater when the house lights were on during the delay interval. Thus, exposure to various features of the experimental chamber during the delay interval disrupted memory in the matching task (see also Grant, 1988).

Retrograde Amnesia

Severe head injury often causes loss of memory, which is technically called **amnesia.** For example, people in a car accident involving a blow to the head are likely to suffer memory loss. However, the memory loss is selective. They may forget how the injury occurred, where the accident took place, or who else was in the car at the time. But, they will continue to remember their name and address, where they grew up, and what they prefer for dessert.

The first extensive study of memory loss following brain injury in humans was conducted by Russell and Nathan (1946). They found that there is a temporal gradient of memory loss going back in time from the point of injury. The closer an episode

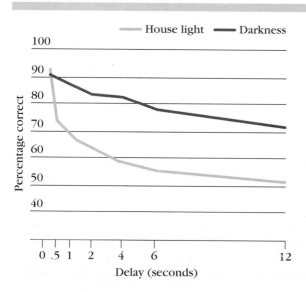

Figure 11.15 Percentage of correct responses in a delayed-matching-to-sample task as a function of increasing delays (0–12 seconds) between the sample and the choice stimuli. On some trials the delay interval was spent in darkness. On other trials the house lights were on during the delay interval. (From "An Analysis of Light-Induced Retroactive Inhibition in Pigeon Short-Term Memory" by W. A. Roberts and D. S. Grant, *Journal of Experimental Psychology: Animal Behavior Processes,* 1978, *4,* pp. 219–236. Copyright © 1978 by the American Psychological Association. Reprinted by permission.)

is to the time of injury, the more likely the person is to forget that information. This phenomenon is called **retrograde amnesia.**

Retrograde amnesia has been extensively studied in animal laboratory experiments. The first studies of this sort used electroconvulsive shock (ECS) to induce amnesia. Electroconvulsive shock, introduced as a treatment for mental illness many years ago (Cerletti & Bini, 1938), involves a brief electrical current passed through the brain between electrodes placed on each side of the head. We do not know exactly how ECS helps alleviate some forms of mental illness. Investigators interested in memory started to study the effects of ECS because patients often reported amnesia after ECS treatment (for example, Mayer-Gross, 1943).

In the first laboratory investigation of the amnesic effects of ECS, Duncan (1949) trained rats to perform an instrumental avoidance response. One conditioning trial was conducted a day for 18 days. The rats received an electroconvulsive shock after each training trial. The ECS was delivered at different times ranging from 20 seconds to 4 hours after each training trial for different groups of animals. The question of interest was whether, and to what extent, ECS would disrupt avoidance learning.

The results are summarized in Figure 11.16. ECS given 1 hour or more after each training trial did not disrupt avoidance learning. By contrast, the performance of the animals given ECS within 15 minutes of each trial was severely disrupted. In fact, there was a gradient of interference: administration of ECS closer to the training trials resulted in poorer avoidance performance. This pattern of results is consistent with a retrograde-amnesia interpretation. Presumably, events closer to the ECS were forgotten more readily than earlier events. Therefore, delivery of ECS shortly after a conditioning trial disrupted retention of that conditioning experience more than ECS that was delayed 1 hour or more after the trial.

Numerous studies have provided convincing evidence of experimentally induced retrograde amnesia in a wide variety of learning tasks. (For reviews, see McGaugh & Herz, 1972; Spear, 1978; Spear & Riccio, 1994.) In addition, experiments have shown that retrograde amnesia can be produced by many treatments that affect the nervous system, including anesthesia (McGaugh & Petrinovich, 1965); temporary cooling of the body, or hypothermia (Riccio, Hodges, & Randall, 1968); and injection of drugs that inhibit protein synthesis (for example, Flexner, Flexner, & Stellar, 1963).

Why do various neural insults produce a graded loss of memory? One explanation of retrograde amnesia is based on the concept of **memory consolidation** (see McGaugh & Herz, 1972). According to the memory-consolidation hypothesis, when an event is first experienced, it enters a short-term, or temporary, memory store. While in short-term memory, the information is vulnerable and can be lost because of interfering stimuli or other disruptive manipulations. However, if the proper conditions are met, the information gradually becomes consolidated into a relatively permanent form.

Memory consolidation is assumed to be a physiological process by which information is gradually transformed into a long-term or permanent state. Neurophysiological disturbances such as electroconvulsive shock, anesthesia, and body cooling are assumed to interfere with the consolidation process and thereby disrupt the transfer of information to long-term memory. Disruption of consolidation produces amnesia only for information stored in short-term memory. Once information has been transferred to long-term memory, it cannot be lost because of disruptions of consolidation. Amnesic agents presumably lead to loss of memory for only recently experienced

D. C. Riccio

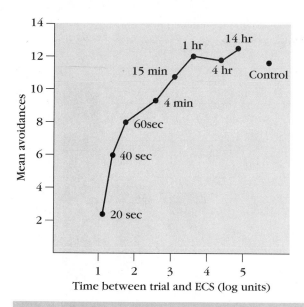

Figure 11.16 Mean number of avoidance responses for independent groups of rats given electroconvulsive shock (ECS) at various intervals after each avoidance trial. The control group was not given ECS. (From "The Retroactive Effect of Electroshock on Learning" by C. P. Duncan, *Journal of Comparative and Physiological Psychology,* 1949, *42,* pp. 32–44.)

events because only the recent events are in short-term memory and are thus susceptible to disruptions of consolidation.

Disruptions of performance caused by amnesic agents can also be explained in a very different way. According to this alternative account, amnesia results not from loss of the memory but from inability to retrieve or reactivate the memory (Lewis, 1979; Miller & Springer, 1973; Riccio & Richardson, 1984; Spear, 1973). This explanation is called the *retrieval-failure hypothesis* and assumes that the amnesic agent alters the coding of new memories so as to make subsequent recovery of the information difficult. Thus, unlike the memory-consolidation view, the retrieval-failure hypothesis assumes that the information surrounding an amnesic episode is acquired and retained in memory. However, the information is retained in a form that makes it inaccessible.

What kinds of evidence would help theorists decide between the memory-consolidation and retrieval-failure interpretations? If information is lost because of a failure of consolidation, it cannot ever be recovered. By contrast, the retrieval-failure view assumes that amnesia can be reversed if the proper procedure is found to reactivate the memory. Thus, to decide between the alternatives, techniques that can reverse the effects of amnesic agents must be found. Several such procedures have, in fact, been discovered.

Numerous experiments have shown that the memory deficits that characterize retrograde amnesia can be overcome by various reminder treatments. (For reviews, see Gordon, 1981; Spear, 1978; Spear & Riccio, 1994.) In one study, for example, four groups of rats were conditioned to make a one-way avoidance response (Gordon & Mowrer, 1980). The apparatus consisted of two compartments, one white and the other black. At the beginning of each trial, a rat was placed in the white compartment. Several seconds later, a flashing light was presented, and the door to the black compartment was opened. If the rat crossed over to the black side within 5 seconds, it avoided shock. If it did not cross in time, the shock was presented until the rat entered the black compartment. Conditioning trials continued until successful

W. C. Gordon

339

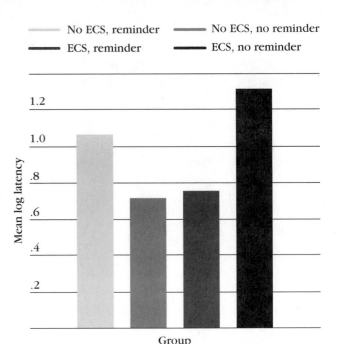

Figure 11.17 Latency of the avoidance response during a retention test for four groups of rats. Two of the groups were not given electroconvulsive shock (ECS) after training and were tested either after a reminder extinction trial or without the reminder trial. The other two groups were treated with ECS after training and were also tested either after a reminder extinction trial or without the reminder trial. (Adapted from Gordon & Mowrer, 1980.)

avoidance responses occurred on three consecutive trials. Immediately after this training, two groups of rats were given electroconvulsive shock to induce amnesia.

Memory for the avoidance response was tested three days after the end of training. During the retention test the shock was never turned on, no matter how long the rats took to cross to the black side. The most important aspect of the experiment involved giving a reminder treatment to some of the animals 15 minutes before the beginning of the retention test. This reminder treatment consisted of placing the rats in the white compartment of the apparatus for 60 seconds with the flashing light turned on. No shock was delivered at the end of this stimulus exposure. Thus, the reminder treatment was an extinction trial. Ordinarily an extinction trial would be expected to decrease avoidance performance. However, if the CS-alone trial acts as a reminder treatment, it might facilitate retrieval of the memory of avoidance conditioning in the ECS treated rats.

The results of the study are summarized in Figure 11.17. The data are presented in terms of the latency of avoidance responses during the retention test. Lower scores indicate faster performance of the avoidance response. Higher scores indicate amnesia for the avoidance training. Let us first consider the two groups of rats that had not been given electroconvulsive shock. For these animals, administration of the reminder extinction trial 15 minutes before the retention test resulted in slower avoidance behavior. This is the usual outcome of extinction. Let us next consider the results for the rats that were treated with ECS. Electroconvulsive shock in the absence of a reminder treatment (ECS, no reminder) resulted in the slowest avoidance responses. This outcome indicates that ECS produced amnesia for the prior avoidance training. However, if the ECS-treated rats got the extinction reminder trial before the retention test, their performance was much improved. In fact, the ECS rats given the reminder treatment responded as fast as the animals that had not received either ECS or extinction.

These results suggest that the reminder treatment fully restored the memory of the prior avoidance training. Thus, the amnesic effects of ECS were entirely reversed by exposing the animals to the extinction trial. Since the extinction trial produced a decrement in performance in the absence of ECS, these results cannot be explained in terms of any new learning produced by the reminder treatment. (For a review of similar findings, see Riccio & Richardson, 1984.)

CONCLUDING COMMENTS

The study of memory processes is central to the understanding of animal cognition. Memory processes involve acquisition and coding of information, rehearsal and retention, and retrieval. Difficulties in any of these phases or problems involving interactions among the phases can result in failures of memory, or forgetting. Several ingenious techniques for the study of memory processes in animals have been developed in the past 30 years. These techniques have revealed much about the coding of information, rehearsal processes, and retrieval processes. This information has, in turn, permitted a better understanding of failures of memory that occur in interference paradigms and in retrograde amnesia.

SAMPLE QUESTIONS

1. Compare and contrast working and reference memory.
2. Describe the delayed-matching-to-sample procedure and alternative strategies that can be used to respond accurately in such a procedure. How can these response strategies be distinguished experimentally?
3. Describe control procedures that have to be tested to prove that food-storing birds are using memory mechanisms to find previously stored food.
4. How can retrospective and prospective coding be differentiated experimentally?
5. What is retrograde amnesia, and how can it be reversed?

KEY TERMS

acquisition The initial stage of learning.

amnesia Loss of memory. (See also *retrograde amnesia*.)

animal cognition The use of a neural representation, or code, as a basis for action.

delayed matching to sample A procedure in which participants are reinforced for responding to a test stimulus that is the same as a sample stimulus that was presented some time earlier.

directed forgetting Forgetting that occurs because of a stimulus (a forget cue) that indicates that working memory will not be tested on that trial. Directed forget-

ting is an example of the stimulus control of memory.

memory A term used to characterize instances in which an organism's current behavior is determined by some aspect of its previous experience.

memory consolidation The establishment of a memory in relatively permanent form, or the transfer of information from short-term to long-term memory.

proactive interference Disruption of memory caused by exposure to stimuli before the event to be remembered.

prospection Same as *prospective memory*.

prospective memory Memory for an expected future event or response.

reference memory Long-term retention of background information necessary for successful use of incoming and recently acquired information. (Compare with *working memory*.)

rehearsal A theoretical process whereby information is maintained in an active state, available to influence behavior and/or the processing of other information.

retention interval The time between acquisition of information and a test of memory for that information.

retrieval The recovery of information from a memory store.

retrieval cue A stimulus related to an experience that facilitates the recall of other information related to that experience.

retrieval failure A deficit in recovering information from a memory store.

retroactive interference Disruption of memory caused by exposure to stimuli following the event to be remembered.

retrograde amnesia A gradient of memory loss going back in time from the occurrence of a major injury or physiological disturbance. Amnesia is greatest for events that took place closest to the time of injury.

retrospection Same as *retrospective memory*.

retrospective memory Memory for a previously experienced event. Also called *retrospection*.

simultaneous matching to sample A procedure in which participants are reinforced for responding to a test stimulus that is the same as a sample stimulus. The sample and the test stimuli are presented at the same time. (Compare with *delayed matching to sample*.)

stimulus coding How a stimulus is represented in memory.

trace decay hypothesis The idea that exposure to a stimulus produces changes in the nervous system that gradually and automatically decrease after the stimulus has been terminated.

trials-unique procedure A matching-to-sample procedure in which different sample and comparison stimuli are used on each trial.

working memory Short-term retention of information that is needed for successful responding on the task at hand but not on subsequent (or previous) similar tasks. (Compare with *reference memory*.)

Timing

Techniques for the Measurement of Timing Behavior

The Concept of an Internal Clock

Characteristics of the Internal Clock

Models of Timing

Serial Pattern Learning

Possible Bases of Serial Pattern Behavior

Tests of Serial Pattern Learning with Simultaneous
Stimulus Arrays

Effects of the Structure of Serial Patterns: Evidence of
Chunking

Perceptual Concept Learning

Generalization to Novel Exemplars

Concept Training and Pseudoconcept Training Compared

Discrimination Between Perceptual Categories

Development of Conceptual Errors

Mechanisms of Perceptual Concept Learning

Language Learning in Nonhuman Animals

Approaches to Language Training

Documenting Language Skills

Language Training Procedures

Components of Linguistic Competence

C HAPTER 12 explores a diversity of contemporary research areas in animal cognition that involve the processing of various types of information. I will start by discussing research on timing and will then turn to serial pattern learning and perceptual concept formation. In the concluding section, I will describe research on some of the most complex forms of cognition in animals. These involve efforts to teach language skills to chimpanzee and bonobo great apes. Recent results provide compelling evidence of complex linguistic skill in a bonobo ape.

The various aspects of behavior I will discuss in this chapter—timing, serial pattern learning, perceptual concept formation, and language learning—have more apparent differences among them than similarities. They are not all reflections of a common underlying mechanism, nor are they all involved in the solution of a common behavioral problem or challenge to survival. However, they all involve contemporary areas of research in animal cognition that have stimulated a great deal of interest. This interest has come in part because until recently the cognitive processes involved were considered to be associated primarily with human behavior. In addition, each of these areas of research has stimulated considerable controversy.

The controversies have centered on whether complex cognitive processes had to be postulated to explain the various behaviors that were observed. Opponents of cognitive interpretations have argued that the phenomena of timing, serial pattern learning, perceptual concept formation, and language learning could be explained by traditional learning principles. By contrast, proponents of cognitive interpretations have argued that cognitive mechanisms provide simpler explanations for the phenomena and are more productive in stimulating new research. Work in animal cognition has amply borne out this latter justification. Without a cognitive perspective, much of the research I will describe in this chapter would never have been done, and many of the phenomena would never have been discovered.

TIMING

Many aspects of animal behavior reflect sensitivity to time (Richelle & Lejeune, 1980). The study of timing is of particular interest because all of animal and human experience is embedded in a temporal context. Some things occur closely together in time; others are separated by longer intervals. In either case, the effects of stimuli are determined by their temporal distribution.

Interest in how behavior is controlled by the passage of time has a long history. However, only in the past 30 years has substantial progress been made toward understanding the psychological processes that are responsible for timing in animals. (For reviews, see Killeen & Fetterman, 1988; Gibbon & Allan, 1984; Gibbon & Church, 1992; Maier & Church, 1991.) Timing is investigated in situations where an animal's behavior is related to the duration of a stimulus, or the passage of time. A critical methodological requirement is to make sure that the passage of time is not correlated with an external stimulus such the noise of a clock ticking or the gradual increase in light that occurs as the sun comes up in the morning. Experimental situations have to be set up carefully to eliminate time-related external stimuli that might inadvertently "tip off" the organism and permit accurate responding without the use of an internal timing process.

Techniques for the Measurement of Timing Behavior

We have already seen time-dependent behavioral phenomena in many of the previous chapters. Habituation, sensitization, and spontaneous recovery (Chapter 2) are all time-dependent effects. Pavlovian conditioning critically depends on the temporal relation between conditioned and unconditioned stimuli (Chapter 3); instrumental conditioning depends on the temporal relation between response and reinforcer (Chapter 5); and some schedules of reinforcement involve important temporal factors

(Chapter 6). We have also encountered important time-dependent effects in our discussions of avoidance learning (Chapter 9) and memory (Chapter 11).

Various powerful techniques have been developed to investigate animal timing. Some tasks involve **duration estimation.** A duration estimation task is basically a discrimination procedure in which the discriminative stimulus is the duration of an event. One study (Fetterman, 1995), for example, employed a modified matching-to-sample procedure. Pigeons were trained in an experimental chamber that had three pecking keys arranged in a row. The sample stimulus at the start of the trial was an amber light presented on the center key for either 2 seconds or 10 seconds. The sample was followed by illumination of one side key with a red light and the other side key with a green light. If the sample on that trial had been short (the 2-second stimulus), pecks on the red key were reinforced. If the sample had been long (the 10-second stimulus), pecks on the green key were reinforced. Pigeons and rats can learn to perform accurately in such tasks without too much difficulty (see also Church, Getty, & Lerner, 1976; Wasserman, DeLong, & Larew, 1984).

Other useful techniques for the study of timing have involved duration production instead of duration estimation. One popular technique, called the **peak procedure,** involves a discrete-trial variation of a fixed interval schedule. Each trial begins with the presentation of a discriminative stimulus—a noise or a light. A specified duration after the start of the trial stimulus, a food pellet is set up, or made ready for delivery. Once the food pellet has been set up, the organism can obtain it by performing a specified instrumental response.

A study by Roberts (1981) nicely illustrates use of the peak procedure to investigate timing in laboratory rats. The animals were tested in a standard lever-press chamber housed in a sound-attenuating enclosure to minimize extraneous stimuli. Some trials began with a light; other trials began with a noise. In the presence of the light, food was set up after 20 seconds; in the presence of the noise, food was set up after 40 seconds. Most of the trials ended when the rats responded and obtained the food pellet. However, a small proportion of the trials were test trials and continued for 80 seconds or more and ended without food reward. These extra-long trials were included to see how the animals would respond after the usual time of reinforcement had passed.

Figure 12.1 summarizes the results of the experiment in terms of rates of responding at various points during a trial. The figure shows that during the 20-second signal, the highest rate of responding occurred around 20 seconds into the trial. By contrast, during the 40-second signal, the highest rate of responding occurred around 40 seconds into the trial. The results were remarkably orderly. In addition, the peak response rates occurred near the times that food became available during training. These features make the peak procedure especially useful in animal studies of timing. However, it should be noted that the results required extensive training. The data in Figure 12.1 were obtained after 10 daily training sessions of 6 hours each. (For additional information about the peak procedure, see Cheng & Westwood, 1993; Cheng, Westwood, & Crystal, 1993; Church, Miller, Meck, & Gibbon, 1991; Church, Meck, & Gibbon, 1994.)

The Concept of an Internal Clock

Results such as those presented in Figure 12.1 also have been obtained with human participants (Wearden & McShane, 1988) and clearly indicate that behavior can be exquisitely tuned to the passage of time. How might such findings be interpreted?

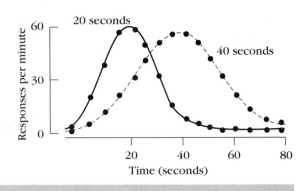

Figure 12.1 Rate of responding at various times during nonreinforced test trials. During training, food became available for delivery after 20 seconds in the presence of one stimulus (solid line) and after 40 seconds in the presence of another stimulus (dashed line). (From "Isolation of an Internal Clock" by S. Roberts, *Journal of Experimental Psychology: Animal Behavior Processes,* 1981, *7,* pp. 242–268. Copyright © 1981 by the American Psychological Association. Reprinted by permission.)

R. M. Church

One highly productive theoretical approach has been to assume that animals (including people) use some kind of an internal clock and respond differentially based on the readings of this internal clock. Although the assumption of an internal clock may seem a bit fanciful at first glance, the suggestion is not that animals have something like a pocket watch that they can pull out and read now and then. Rather, the suggestion is that organisms have a timing mechanism localized somewhere in the nervous system that has clock-like properties.

Why should we entertain the possibility that organisms have an internal clock? The advantage of such a hypothesis is that it helps organize research. As Church (1978) has pointed out, the concept of an internal clock may simplify the explanation and discussion of instances of behavior controlled by time cues. The concept of a clock can also stimulate questions about animal timing that we would not be likely to ask otherwise. I will explain this shortly. Finally, an internal clock may be a physiological reality. We are more likely to find a biological clock if we first postulate its existence and investigate its properties at the behavioral level (for example, Meck, 1988; Meck, Church, & Olton, 1984; Meck, Church, Wenk, & Olton, 1987).

Characteristics of the Internal Clock

If the concept of an internal clock is useful in explaining results of the peak procedure and other timing situations, we should be able to use the concept to generate interesting research questions. We may ask, for example, whether the clock can be stopped and restarted without loss of information about how much time has already elapsed. Roberts (1981) designed an experiment to answer this question (see also Roberts & Church, 1978). The experimental chamber used was ordinarily dark. Each trial started with the presentation of a light, and food was set up 40 seconds after the start of the trial. On special test trials without food reinforcement, the light was turned off for 10 seconds, starting 10 seconds after the start of the trial. Roberts was interested in how the interruption influenced when the rats showed their peak responding.

Figure 12.2 shows the resulting distributions of response rates at various times during trials with and without the 10-second break. Introducing the 10-second break shifted the peak response rate to the right by a bit more than 10 seconds (13.3 seconds, to be exact). These results suggest that the internal clock of the rats stopped timing when the break was introduced. Some information about elapsed time was distorted by the break, but when the stimulus resumed, the clock resumed timing without being reset (see also de Vaca, Brown, & Hemmes, 1994).

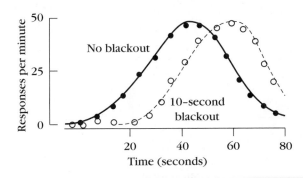

Figure 12.2 Rate of responding as a function of time during a signal in the presence of which food was set up after 40 seconds. On some trials, the signal was interrupted for a 10-second blackout period (dashed line). On other trials, no blackout occurred (solid line). (From "Isolation of an Internal Clock" by S. Roberts, *Journal of Experimental Psychology: Animal Behavior Processes,* 1981, 7, pp. 242–268. Copyright © 1981 by the American Psychological Association. Reprinted by permission.)

Other research on animal timing has shown that the internal clock of rats has many of the same properties as a stopwatch. For example, like a stopwatch, the internal clock measures how much time has elapsed from the start of a stimulus (rather than how much time remains until the stimulus usually ends). Rats seem to use the same internal clock to measure the duration of stimuli from different sensory modalities (visual and auditory); they also use the same clock and clock speed to measure intervals of different durations (Meck & Church, 1982; Roberts, 1981, 1982; Roberts & Church, 1978). (For a somewhat different pattern of results, see Brown, Hemmes, & de Vaca, 1992; Roberts, Cheng, & Cohen, 1989.)

Investigators have also started studying what determines the speed and accuracy of the internal clock. Increasing the rate of food reinforcement appears to increase the speed of the internal clock (Bizo & White, 1994, 1995a, 1995b; MacEwen & Killeen, 1991). The speed of the clock is also altered by diet (Meck & Church, 1987b), body temperature (Wearden & Penton-Voak, 1995), and psychoactive drugs. For example, methamphetamine has been observed to increase the speed of the internal clock, whereas other drugs, such as haliperidol, have been noted to decrease clock speed (see Maricq, Roberts, & Church, 1981; Meck, 1983; Meck & Church, 1987a).

Models of Timing

So far we have considered the notion of an internal clock somewhat loosely. What might be the details of a mechanism that permits animals (and people) to respond on the basis of temporal information?

Information Processing Model of Timing. A prominent model of time estimation, summarized in Figure 12.3, was proposed by Gibbon and Church (1984) (see also Gibbon, Church, & Meck, 1984; Church, Meck, & Gibbon, 1994). The model shows the relationship of three independent processes: a clock process, a memory process, and a decision process.

The clock process is activated by the start of the interval to be timed. Timing is assumed to be accomplished by a pacemaker that generates pulses at a certain rate (something like a cardiac pacemaker). The pacemaker pulses are fed to a switch, which is turned on by the start of the interval to be timed. This allows the pacemaker pulses to go to an accumulator that counts the number that come through. When the interval to be timed ends, the switch closes, thereby blocking any further accumulations

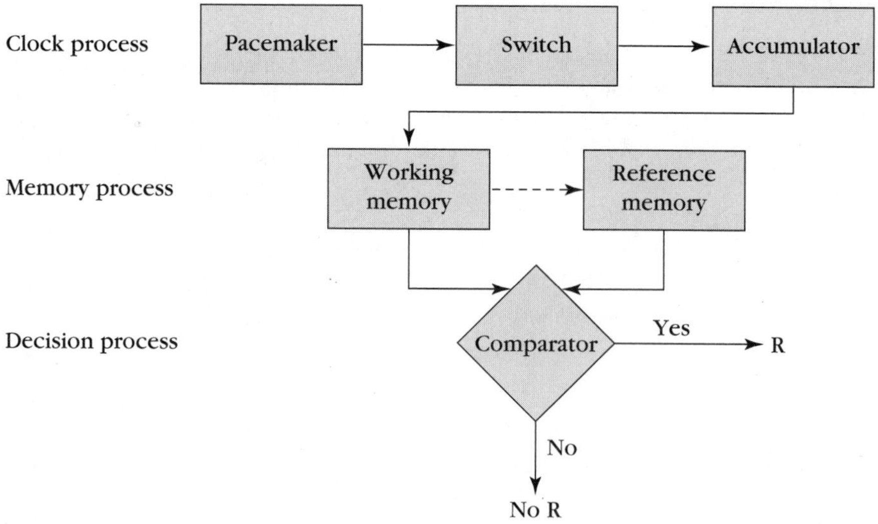

Figure 12.3 Diagram of an information processing model of timing. (From "Sources of Variance in an Information Processing Theory of Timing" by J. Gibbon and R. M. Church. In H. L. Roitblat, T. G. Bever, & H. S. Terrace (Eds.), *Animal Cognition.* Copyright © 1984 Lawrence Erlbaum & Associates.)

of pacemaker pulses. Thus, the accumulator accumulates information about elapsed time.

Information about the contents of the accumulator is relayed to working memory, providing input about the current trial. The nervous system is also assumed to have information about the duration of similar stimuli in reference memory from past training. The contents of working and reference memory are compared in the decision process, and this comparison provides the basis for the animal's response. For example, in the peak procedure, if the time information in working memory matches the information in reference memory concerning availability of reinforcement, the decision is to respond. If information in working and reference memory does not match closely enough, the decision is to not respond. This mechanism produces a peak response rate close to the time when reinforcement is set up.

A detailed hypothetical model of timing is necessary to guide analyses of fine-grained details of timing behavior (see Church, Meck, & Gibbon, 1994; Gibbon & Church, 1984). The model also helps explain different ways in which timing behavior can be altered. Evidence, for example, suggests that certain drugs alter timing behavior by changing the speed of the internal clock (altering the frequency of pulses generated by the pacemaker). By contrast, other drugs change timing behavior by altering the memory process, that is, by changing the remembered duration of past time intervals (Meck, 1983). These contrasting influences on timing behavior would be difficult to interpret without a model that distinguishes a clock process from a memory process.

Behavioral Theory of Timing. All models of timing assume that there is a clock process consisting of a pacemaker and an accumulator. However, some models do not assume that animals form mental representations of time and do not include the kind of memory and decision processes outlined in Figure 12.3. A prominent alternative to the Gibbon-Church information processing model was offered by Killeen and Fetterman (1988, 1993; see also Killeen, 1991), who characterized the timing process in more behavioral terms.

The behavioral theory of timing is based on the observation that situations in which the primary basis for the delivery of a reinforcer is the passage of time produce systematic time-related activities, called **adjunctive behaviors.** These activities are akin to the pacing or finger tapping that people engage in during periods of forced waiting. Those adjunctive behaviors that predominate early in the timed interval are known as **interim responses;** others (**terminal responses**) predominate later in the interval. (You may recall that I previously described interim and terminal responses in Chapter 5 in the section, "Reinterpretation of the superstition experiment.")

In the behavioral theory of timing, a clock process is assumed to produce the adjunctive behaviors. Because different responses emerge at different intervals in a forced waiting period, these various responses can be used to tell time. Killeen and Fetterman proposed that in timing experiments, animals come to use their adjunctive responses as discriminative stimuli for the experimentally required timing responses. Thus, instead of reading an internal clock, animals are assumed to "read" their adjunctive behavior to tell time. The behavioral theory of timing makes no assumptions about memory and decision processes.

The behavioral theory of timing is a provocative proposal that has met with considerable success (for example, Bizo & White, 1994; Fetterman & Killeen, 1995; MacEwen & Killeen, 1991). However, in many situations the behavioral theory makes predictions that are similar to the predictions of the Gibbon-Church information processing model, and therefore the two models are difficult to distinguish. In situations where predictions from the two theories diverge, sometimes the Gibbon-Church model appears more consistent with the data (for example, Leak & Gibbon, 1995), and other times the behavioral theory makes better predictions (for example, Fetterman & Killeen, 1995). Presently, then, neither model provides a complete account of data on animal timing.

P. R. Killeen

SERIAL PATTERN LEARNING

Time is one ubiquitous characteristic of events in the environment. Another ubiquitous feature is serial order. Stimuli rarely occur randomly and independently of each other. Rather, many aspects of the environment involve orderly sequences of events. One thing leads to the next in a predictable fashion. Stimuli are arranged in orderly sequences as you walk from one end of a street to the other, as you work to open a package, or as you eat your dinner from start to finish. Stimulus order is also very important in language. "The hunters ate the bear" is very different from "The bear ate the hunters." Investigators of animal cognition have been interested in whether animals recognize order in a series of stimuli, whether they can form a representation of the serial order of stimuli, and what mechanisms they use to respond correctly to a series of stimuli.

Possible Bases of Serial Pattern Behavior

There are several possible ways in which to respond to a series of stimuli. By way of illustration, consider playing through a six-hole miniature golf course, a schematic of which is shown to the left in Figure 12.4. Each hole involves a unique set of stimuli and may be represented by letters of the alphabet: A, B, C, D, E, and F. Each hole also requires a unique response—a unique way in which the ball must be hit to get it into the hole. Let's label the responses R1, R2, . . . , R6. In playing the course, you have to

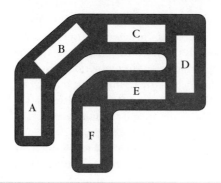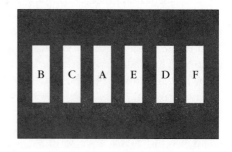

Figure 12.4 Two possible layouts of a six-hole miniature golf course. A sequential arrangement is shown on the left, and a simultaneous arrangement is shown on the right.

go in order from the first to the last hole, A→F. In addition, you have to make the correct response on each hole: R1 on hole A, R2 on B, and so on.

How might you learn to play the course successfully? The simplest way would be to learn which response goes with which stimulus. This would involve learning a set of S-R associations: A-R1, B-R2, . . . , F-R6. In the presence of A, you would automatically make R1, which would get you to stimulus B; in the presence of B, you would automatically make R2, which would get you to C; in the presence of C, you would automatically make R3, which would get you to D, and so on. Such a mechanism is called a **response chain.** In a response chain, each response produces the stimulus for the next response in the sequence, and correct responses occur because the organism has learned a series of S-R associations.

Although a response chain can result in responding appropriately to a series of stimuli, it does not require actually learning the stimulus sequence or forming a mental representation of the order in which the stimuli or responses occur. Response chains do not require cognitive mechanisms any more complex than S-R associations. A response-chain strategy works perfectly well on the usual miniature golf course, because the successive holes are laid out so that the player is forced to go through them in the correct sequence, A→F.

Now, let us consider a course with a different layout. The rules are the same in that you have to play in order from A to F, but this course is laid out in such a way that you are not forced to go in that order. Imagine having the holes lined up next to each other in a random order on a playing field, as shown to the right in Figure 12.4. After having played hole A, for example, your movement would not be restricted to hole B. You could go to any other hole next. To earn points, however, you would still have to play B after having finished with A, and then go to C, then D, and so forth. Learning a series of stimulus-response associations (A-R1, B-R2, and so on) would not be enough to succeed on such a course. Even if someone got you started in the right place, after playing hole A, you would not know where to go next.

What would you have to learn in order to respond in the correct sequence with a simultaneous stimulus array? This time, you would be forced to learn something about the order of the stimuli. You could get by with just knowing the order of successive pairs of stimuli. You could learn that A is followed by B, B is followed by C, and so forth. These would constitute a set of independent stimulus-stimulus associations (A-B, B-C, C-D, and so on). This type of mechanism is called **paired-associate learning.** Once you know the correct independent paired associates, having played hole A, you would know to go to B; having played B, you would know to go to C; and so on until you had completed the course.

Obviously, learning more than just the order of successive pairs of stimuli would also enable you to perform the task accurately. At the extreme, you might form a mental representation of the entire sequence: A-B-C-D-E-F. This alternative is called **serial representation learning.** A serial representation can be formed in different ways. One possibility is to string together a series of paired associates, such that A activates the representation of B, which in turn activates the representation of C, and so forth. Thus, a serial representation could consist of a chain of associations. Alternatively, you could learn that stimulus A is in position 1, B is in position 2, and so forth.

How might we decide among possible mechanisms of serial pattern behavior? An especially powerful technique involves presenting carefully constructed test trials after training. Returning to our simultaneous layout of the miniature golf course (Figure 12.4, to the right), consider being given a choice between holes C and E after having learned to respond to the entire sequence, A→F, in the correct order. In a choice between C and E, which hole would you play first? If you had learned a representation of the entire stimulus sequence, you could respond without difficulty because you would know that C occurs before E in the sequence. Other possible mechanisms would create problems for various reasons. For example, if you had learned a response chain in which one response leads to the next stimulus, you would be in trouble because the response preceding C is not available in a choice of only C and E. You would also be in trouble if you had learned just the order of successive pairs of stimuli because C and E do not form a successive pair.

Tests of Serial Pattern Learning with Simultaneous Stimulus Arrays

Several different techniques have been developed to study the learning of serial representations in animals (for example, Hulse, 1978; Roitblat, Bever, Helweg, & Harley, 1991; Roitblat, Scopatz, Bever, 1987; Terrace, 1986a, 1986b). Straub and Terrace (1981) introduced the technique of training animals with a set of stimuli presented in a simultaneous array and then testing them with subsets of those stimuli (see also Terrace, 1987). This technique was then adopted by D'Amato and Colombo (1988) in a study with cebus monkeys (*Cebus apella*). The monkeys were trained on a five-stimulus sequence, A→B→C→D→E. The stimuli were various visual patterns (dots, circles, and the like), which could be projected on any of five square panels. Which pattern appeared on which panel varied from one trial to the next, but all five stimuli were presented at the same time on each training trial. The task was to press the panels in the prescribed order, A→B→C→D→E.

H. S. Terrace

Training started with presentation of stimulus A. After the monkeys had learned to press A, B was added; after they had learned the A→F sequence, C was added, and so forth. After having learned the entire five-item sequence, the monkeys were tested with subsets of two and three stimuli. They performed with above-chance accuracy on all these subsets—even on subsets that included only stimuli in the middle of the series (BC, CD, BD, and BCD). These results indicate that the monkeys learned the prescribed order of the five stimuli.

D'Amato and Colombo also measured the latencies of the correct responses during the tests with subsets of the five-element series. These results were particularly interesting and are shown in Figure 12.5. The left-hand graph shows the latency of responding to the first item of subsets of stimuli. Some of these subsets started with A

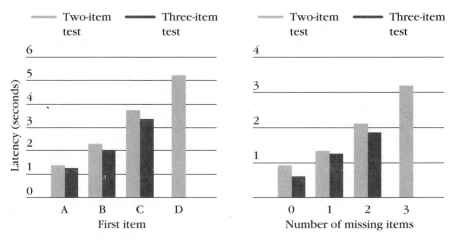

Figure 12.5   Latency of correct responses during tests of two- and three-item subsets of a five-item list with cebus monkeys. Left: Latency of responding to the first item of the subset as a function of the position of that item in the original sequence. Right: Latency of responding to the second item of the subset as a function of the number of items missing between the first and second item. (From "Representation of Serial Order in Monkeys (*Cebus apella*)," by M. R. D'Amato and M. Colombo, *Journal of Experimental Psychology: Animal Behavior Processes,* 1988, *14,* pp. 131–139. Copyright © 1988 by the American Psychological Association. Reprinted by permission.)

(as in the subset AC, for example); some started with B (as in the subset BC or BD); some started with C (as in CD), and one started with D (DE).

When the first item of the subset was A, the monkeys responded rapidly. When the first item was B, responding was slower. Responding was slower still when the first item was C or D. Loosely speaking, these latencies suggest that at the start of a trial the monkeys started to walk through the sequence mentally. When they came to one of the stimuli presented on that trial, they responded to that stimulus. Since they encountered A first in this mental scan of the series, they responded to A quickest. Longer latencies occurred with items that came up later in their mental scan of the series. Such mental scanning would have been possible only if the monkeys had formed a mental representation of the entire stimulus sequence. Thus, the latency data provide evidence of this mental representation.

Additional evidence for mental scanning of the stimulus sequence was provided by the latency of responding to the second item in the subset tests. Some of the subsets involved adjacent items in the list, such as subset BC. Others involved one missing item, such as subset BD or CE. Still others involved two missing items (BE) or three missing items (AD). If the monkeys were walking through the list mentally as they performed the subset tests, how long they took to respond between the first and second item would depend on the number of missing items. With more missing items between stimuli in a subset, the monkeys should take longer to respond to the second item. This is exactly what occurred (see Figure 12.5, right). These results provide additional evidence that the monkeys had formed a mental representation of the stimulus sequence. (For additional studies of the nature of that mental representation, see D'Amato and Colombo, 1989, 1990.)

Effects of the Structure of Serial Patterns: Evidence of Chunking

In the study by D'Amato and Colombo (1988), evidence of serial pattern learning was obtained by looking at the accuracy of performance on subsets of stimuli and measuring the latency of responses. The structure or pattern of the list of items was not altered. All of the monkeys were trained on the same type of A→B→C→D→E stimulus sequence. Another powerful approach to the study of whether animals form representations of a series of stimuli has involved seeing whether they recognize the pattern of the stimuli. Recognition of a pattern requires knowledge of the sequence and structure of a set of stimuli and hence is not likely to result from mechanisms that do not involve some form of representation of the serial order of the stimuli.

Behavior in response to serial patterns of stimuli has been extensively investigated in humans (for example, Jones, 1974; Restle & Brown, 1970; Simon & Kotovsky, 1963). Consider, for example, what you would do if you were asked to memorize the following list of numbers: 1234234534564567. You could learn the numbers by memorizing which number is in each of the 16 positions of the list. If you knew that 1 is in the first position, 2 in the second and fifth positions, 3 in the third, sixth, and ninth positions, and so on, you could recall the numbers in the correct order. However, this would be the hard way of doing it. A simpler way to memorize the list would be to identify regularities in the list and break the list into smaller units based on those regularities. Dividing the list into small organized units makes the list easier to memorize.

The list 1234234534564567 has a pattern that is more obvious if the numbers are rewritten as 1234—2345—3456—4567. In this form, it is clear that the list consists of several four-digit segments. Each segment is made up of four consecutive numbers, and successive segments start with successive integers, starting with the number 1. Recognizing this structure makes it much easier to memorize the 16-item list. Subdividing a series of items into subsets, each with its own internal structure, is called **chunking**.

There is considerable evidence that human beings respond on the basis of the patterns inherent in the stimuli they experience. Starting with the work of Hulse (1978), a great deal of evidence has been accumulated indicating that nonhuman animals, too, can respond on the basis of patterns in serially presented stimuli. Chunking in animal learning has been observed using a variety of procedures with both laboratory rats and pigeons (for example, Capaldi, 1992; Capaldi, Miller, Alptekin, & Barry, 1990; Dallal & Meck, 1990; Fountain, 1990; Fountain & Rowan, 1995a 1995b; Macuda & Roberts, 1995; Wathen & Roberts, 1994). In an extensive series of experiments, Terrace (1991a, 1991b, 1991c) investigated chunking in serial pattern learning in pigeons using a simultaneous stimulus array. I will now describe a part of one of these experiments (Terrace, 1991a, Experiment 1).

Terrace's pigeons faced a stimulus panel on which five stimuli were projected at the beginning of each trial. The stimuli could occur in any of eight different positions, and positions were varied between trials. Three of the stimuli were colors (for example, red, green, and blue), and two were shapes (a horizontal line and a diamond). The pigeons had to peck the stimuli in a particular order for food reinforcement, which was delivered when they completed the series. In these respects, the experiment was similar to the study I previously described with cebus monkeys (D'Amato & Colombo, 1988). Unlike D'Amato and Colombo, however, Terrace varied the nature of the series the participants had to learn.

For one group of pigeons, the three color stimuli and the two shapes were segregated in the series. The birds had to learn to go through the series of stimuli by first pecking the three colors and then the two shapes. The segregated series may be symbolized as A→B→C→D′→E′, where the primed letters designate the shapes, and the nonprimed letters designate the color stimuli. A second group of pigeons had to learn to go through the series in a different way. For them, the shape stimuli were mixed in with the color stimuli in the sequence. They had to learn the sequence A→B′→C→D′→E. This group of birds had to select a shape as the second and fourth items rather than as the fourth and fifth items.

The segregated sequence A→B→C→D′→E′ can be easily subdivided into two subsets or chunks. One chunk consists of the three color stimuli, A→B→C; the other chunk consists of the two shapes D′→E′. By contrast, the mixed sequence A→B′→C→D′→E does not have such internal structure and cannot be so obviously divided into subsets. As I noted earlier, chunking a series makes it easier to learn. Therefore, if the pigeons had chunked the lists, we would expect that the segregated list would have been learned faster than the mixed list. This was indeed what happened. The birds took an average of 59 sessions to learn to respond correctly on the segregated list. They took more than twice as long (an average of 140 sessions) to learn the mixed list. They also differed in how they went through a list once they had mastered it.

As I mentioned in connection with the experiment by D'Amato and Colombo, the time it takes to respond can provide interesting insights into cognitive processes. Terrace also found this to be true. "Thinking" in the monkeys was evident in their latency to respond (see Figure 12.5). For the pigeons, "thinking" seemed to be reflected in repeated responding to a particular stimulus. D'Amato and Colombo's monkeys hardly ever made repeat responses. By contrast, the pigeons sometimes perseverated (or dwelled) on a stimulus before moving on to the next one in the sequence. (As with taking extra time in playing a hole of golf, there was no penalty for this, provided the bird selected the next stimulus correctly.) How long the pigeon stayed with a particular stimulus is called the *dwell time*.

Figure 12.6 shows the dwell times of the pigeons on each stimulus as a function of the position of that stimulus in the five-element sequence. (The first response to the fifth stimulus ended the trial; therefore, there are no data for dwelling on the fifth stimulus.) Pigeons that received the mixed order of stimuli A→B′→C→D′→E dwelled longest on stimulus A and picked up the pace as they went through the sequence. Importantly, they did not dwell on any of the interior elements of the series any longer than they took with stimulus A.

For pigeons trained on the segregated pattern A→B→C→D′→E′, the results were dramatically different. These pigeons got off to a fast start, not dwelling very much on stimuli A and B, perhaps because the segregated series was easier to learn than the mixed series. However, they seemed to get stuck on stimulus C. The birds dwelled on stimulus C much longer than on the preceding or following stimuli. Stimulus C was the last of the color stimuli before the two shape cues. It was as if the pigeons had to take a bit of extra time thinking about what to do next as they moved from the color stimuli to the shape cues. This kind of increased dwell time at stimulus C is exactly what is expected if the pigeons chunked the series into two subsets. Increased processing time is expected to occur at boundaries of chunks. Therefore, the dwell time data provide additional evidence that the pigeons were sensitive to the internal structure of the series of stimuli.

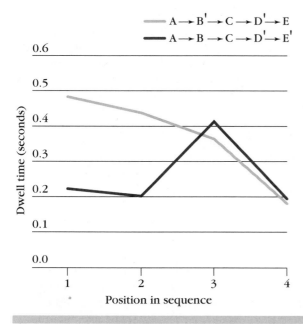

Figure 12.6 The dwell time of pigeons on each of the first four stimuli of a five-element series. One group was trained on a segregated series of stimuli (A→B→C→D′→E′). Another group was trained on a mixed series of stimuli (A→B′→C→D′→E). (From "Chunking During Serial Learning by a Pigeon: I. Basic Evidence" by H. S. Terrace, *Journal of Experimental Psychology: Animal Behavior Processes,* 1991, *17,* pp. 81–93. Copyright © 1991 by the American Psychological Association. Reprinted by permission.)

PERCEPTUAL CONCEPT LEARNING

Organisms experience a great variety of stimuli during their lifetime. However, as we have seen, they do not have to respond to stimuli as independent and isolated events. I discussed one type of cognitive organization in the preceding section—responding to a series of stimuli on the basis of the structural pattern of the series. An even more basic form of cognitive organization of responses to stimuli involves perceptual concept learning. Consider, for example, seeing a chair. You may note some of its specific features: its color, shape, height, and firmness. You would also immediately identify it as a "chair." We can all agree on which things are chairs and which things are not chairs, even though chairs come in a variety of shapes, sizes, and colors. "Chair" is an example of a perceptual concept.

We rely on perceptual concepts in much of our interaction with the world. We have perceptual concepts of physical objects such as chairs, houses, trees, water, cats, and cars. We also have perceptual concepts of events such as rain and wind or day and night. Perceptual concepts are important because they help us organize the wide variety of stimuli that we encounter during the course of normal experience into a manageable number of groupings or categories. Perceptual concepts are also important in language. Many words in our vocabulary are labels for perceptual concepts.

In the rough and tumble of life, nothing occurs exactly the same way twice. Even the same tree viewed from the same vantage point appears slightly different each time you look at it. The sun may be shining on it from a different angle, clouds may be casting a different pattern of shadows, and a breeze may be moving the branches and leaves. Perceptual concepts help organisms navigate through the maze of ever-changing stimuli in the world.

Through perceptual concepts, certain variations among stimuli are ignored. For example, you recognize your cat as the same animal, even though strictly speaking, the visual image the cat presents is different every time you see it. You also recognize various objects such as chairs, even though they may differ in color, size, and firmness. By contrast, other differences are emphasized. You distinguish your cat from your neighbor's cat, and you distinguish your cat from your parakeet. You also distinguish between things that are called chairs and things that are called tables. Thus, perceptual concepts involve *generalization within a category* or set of stimuli and *discrimination between categories* or sets of stimuli.

A great deal of research has been done on the learning of perceptual concepts since the early work of Herrnstein and Loveland (1964) more than 30 years ago (for example, Cerella, 1982; Commons, Herrnstein, Kosslyn, & Mumford, 1990; Herrnstein, 1984, 1990; Lea, 1984; Macintosh, 1995; Pearce, 1994a; Wasserman & Astley, 1994). In the tradition of Herrnstein and Loveland, much of the research has been done with pigeons responding to complex visual stimuli. A variety of visual concepts has been conditioned. Pigeons have learned to respond to the presence or absence of water in various forms (lakes, oceans, puddles, and so on) and to the presence or absence of a particular person (in various types of clothing, in various situations, and engaged in various activities) (Herrnstein, Loveland, & Cable, 1976). In other studies, pigeons have been conditioned to respond to the presence or absence of fish in underwater photographs (Herrnstein & deVilliers, 1980), to the presence of the letter A as opposed to other letters of the alphabet in various fonts (Morgan, Fitch, Holman, & Lea, 1976), and to various views of a particular location on campus (Honig & Stewart, 1988; Wilkie, Willson, & Kardal, 1989). As I noted in Chapter 8, pigeons have also been conditioned to distinguish the music of Bach from that of Stravinsky (Porter & Neuringer, 1984) and to discriminate pictures of Monet from those of Picasso (Watanabe et al., 1995).

Studies have also demonstrated perceptual concept learning in other species, including monkeys, quail, and dolphins (for example, D'Amato & Van Sant, 1988; Helweg, Roitblat, Nachtigall, & Hautus, 1996; Jitsumori, 1994; Kluender, Diehl, & Killeen, 1987; Roberts & Mazmanian, 1988; Schrier & Brady, 1987). In all of these cases, the participants learned to respond similarly to stimuli belonging to the category in question, even though members of the category differed in numerous respects. As I noted in Chapter 8, perceptual concept learning is a form of stimulus equivalence learning. Through equivalence training, physically different stimuli come to be treated in the same manner by the organism. Stimulus equivalence training produces generalization within a set of stimuli.

In one study with pigeons (Herrnstein et al., 1976), for example, color slides of various scenes were projected on one wall of the experimental chamber near a response key. If the scene included a tree or some part of a tree, the pigeons were reinforced with food for pecking the response key. If the picture did not include a tree or any part of one, pecking was not reinforced. Each experimental session consisted of 80 slide presentations, about 40 of which included a tree. During training, the stimuli for any given day were randomly selected from 500–700 pictures depicting various scenes from all four seasons of the year in New England. The same photographs were used more than once only occasionally. The reinforced stimuli included trees (or parts of trees) of all descriptions. However, the trees were not necessarily the main point of interest in the pictures. Some slides showed a tree far in the distance; others showed trees that were partly obstructed so that only some of the branches were visible.

Generalization to Novel Exemplars

The pigeons tested by Herrnstein and his associates (1976) learned the requirements of the task without much difficulty. Soon they were pecking at a much higher rate in the presence of pictures that included a tree than in the presence of pictures without trees. What might have been responsible for the accuracy of their performance? One possibility is that the pigeons memorized what the reinforced and nonreinforced pictures looked like without paying particular attention to the presence or absence of trees. This is a distinct possibility. Pigeons have been found to be able to memorize several hundred pictures (Vaughan & Greene, 1984).

Herrnstein and his associates (1976) attempted to rule out picture memorization by testing the pigeons with a new set of pictures at the end of training. The pigeons performed nearly as accurately on the new pictures as on those used during training. Much higher rates of pecking occurred in the presence of new slides that included a tree (or part of one) than in the presence of new slides without trees. Such evidence of generalization to novel exemplars is often used to support a concept-learning interpretation. However, several other interesting approaches also have been used.

Concept Training and Pseudoconcept Training Compared

All perceptual concept experiments involve presenting a series of stimuli, some of which exemplify the concept under investigation and some of which do not. Edwards and Honig (1987), for example, investigated the learning of the concept "person" with a series of photographic slides. Half the slides depicted one or more people in various places. The remaining slides depicted the same scenes, but without the people (see Figure 12.7). One group of pigeons (the concept group) was reinforced for pecking whenever a slide that included a person appeared and was not reinforced on trials that did not include a person. The pigeons quickly learned to respond more on trials depicting people than on trials without people.

Edwards and Honig were concerned with the possibility of picture memorization, just as Herrnstein, Loveland, and Cable (1976) had been in their experiment on concept learning. Edwards and Honig's birds might have simply memorized which slides were reinforced and which were not without categorizing the slides in terms of the presence or absence of a person. Here, too, this was a distinct possibility because the experiment included only 40 slides with people and 40 without. If the pigeons had treated the slides as a series of arbitrary pictures, it should not have mattered which were in the reinforced set and which were in the nonreinforced set. To see if this was the case, Edwards and Honig trained another group of pigeons with the same 80 slides, but this time the slides were assigned to the reinforced and nonreinforced sets at random. This second group of pigeons was designated the *pseudoconcept* group.

How the two groups of pigeons learned to discriminate between the reinforced and nonreinforced sets of pictures is summarized in Figure 12.8. The response measure presented is the percentage of all responses made that occurred on reinforced trials. During the first block of trials, the birds responded about equally to the reinforced and nonreinforced stimuli, making about 50% of their responses to the reinforced stimuli. As training progressed the concept group learned the discrimination, so that by the fourth block of trials, 75% of its responses were made to the reinforced stimuli. By contrast, the pseudoconcept group continued to respond about equally to the reinforced and nonreinforced slides.

Figure 12.7 Photos illustrating the concept "person." A positive exemplar is shown on the right; a negative exemplar is shown on the left.

The results indicate that it was much easier for the birds to learn to distinguish the two sets of slides if one set included all the pictures with people, and the other set included all the slides of only the backgrounds. If the people and background-only slides were intermixed as reinforced and nonreinforced slides, the birds did not learn the discrimination. This finding indicates that the birds in the concept group were not treating the pictures as an arbitrary collection of reinforced and nonreinforced stimuli. Rather, they seemed to recognize that pictures with people had something in common. (For other comparisons of concept and pseudoconcept training, see Herrnstein & de Villiers, 1980; Wasserman, Kiedinger, & Bhatt, 1988.)

Discrimination between Perceptual Categories

In the studies of perceptual concept learning described so far, the participants had to discriminate between stimuli that contained an exemplar of the concept from stimuli that did not—pictures of a person versus pictures of just the background, for example. However, there was no unifying concept to the nonreinforced stimuli. The experiments demonstrated generalization within a category but not discrimination between categories, which is a companion criterion for a perceptual concept.

How a concept discrimination is learned depends not only on the reinforced category but also on the nonreinforced stimuli. Roberts and Mazmanian (1988), for example, found that both pigeons and monkeys had difficulty learning to discriminate pictures of birds from pictures of other types of animals. However, the participants could discriminate pictures of birds from pictures not containing animals. Other aspects of their study demonstrated that the failure to discriminate birds from other animals was not due to a general inability to distinguish between two cate-

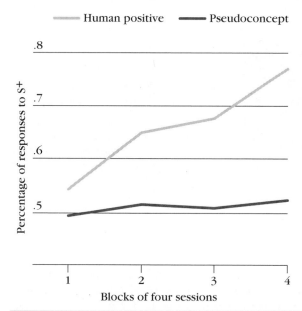

Figure 12.8 Percentage of total responses that were made to reinforced stimuli consisting of slide pictures. For the concept group, all reinforced stimuli included a person, and nonreinforced stimuli showed only the backgrounds. For the pseudoconcept group, reinforced and nonreinforced stimuli consisted of mixtures of person and background-only slides. (From "Memorization and 'Feature Selection' in the Acquisition of Natural Concepts in Pigeons," by C. A. Edwards and W. K. Honig, *Learning and Motivation*, 1987, *18*, pp. 235–260. Copyright © 1987 by Academic Press. Reprinted by permission.)

gories. Rather, the difficulty was related to the level of abstractness of the concepts. The pigeons and monkeys easily learned to discriminate various views of a particular bird, the common kingfisher, from pictures of other types of birds. In other studies pigeons have been shown to be able to discriminate among four concrete perceptual categories simultaneously: cat, person, flower, and car or chair (Bhatt, Wasserman, Reynolds, & Knauss, 1988).

Development of Conceptual Errors

Training several concept discriminations at the same time provides an opportunity for direct observation of the development of generalization within categories and discrimination between categories. As the participants learn to group items together in a perceptual category, they become more likely to generalize among those items and confuse them. This leads to the counterintuitive outcome that perceptual concept learning can lead to an increase in confusion errors between members of the category. This effect can be observed with a task that requires discriminating subsets of items within a category. I will now describe a study of this type.

Wasserman, Kiedinger, and Bhatt (1988) taught pigeons a discrimination involving two perceptual categories—cats and flowers, for example. Slides depicting cats and flowers of various sorts were projected onto a square viewing screen in the experimental chamber. Each corner of the viewing screen had a pecking key, as shown in Figure 12.9. There were 20 different slides of cats and 20 different slides of flowers. Each of these sets of 20 slides was arbitrarily divided into two subsets of 10 each, and for each subset of 10 slides, a different pecking key was reinforced. One pattern of these assignments is shown in Figure 12.9. Here, responses on key 1 were reinforced whenever cat slides 1–10 appeared; responses on key 4 were reinforced with cat slides 11–20; responses on key 2 were reinforced with flower slides 1–10; and responses on key 3 were reinforced with flower slides 11–20. (Different pigeons were trained with the other possible response assignments.)

E. A. Wasserman

359

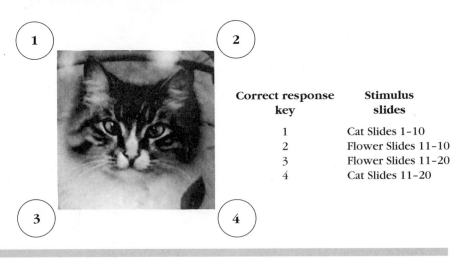

Figure 12.9 Outline of the experimental situation employed by Wasserman, Kiedinger, and Bhatt (1988). Slides were projected on a square screen that had a response key near each corner. Each response key was associated with a different set of 10 slides. One set of assignments is indicated to the right.

Correct response key	Stimulus slides
1	Cat Slides 1–10
2	Flower Slides 11–10
3	Flower Slides 11–20
4	Cat Slides 11–20

The pigeons in this task had to learn which of the four responses to make with each slide. Consider a trial in which cat slide 3 was presented. On this trial, response key 1 was correct, and keys 2, 3, and 4 were incorrect. Keys 2 and 3 were incorrect because they were associated with flower stimuli, and key 4 was incorrect because it was associated with a different set of cat slides. If the pigeons were unsure of the correct response to cat slide 3, what kinds of errors would they have made? If they had treated the slides as an arbitrary and independent collection of pictures, they would have distributed their errors equally among the three incorrect choices. They would have confused cat slide 3 as much with flower slides as with other cat slides. By contrast, if the pigeons had been learning to group cat slides together as different from flower slides, they would have confused cat slide 3 with other cat slides, more so than with flower slides. In that case, they would have pecked the wrong cat response key (key 4) more often than the incorrect flower response keys (keys 2 and 3). Such errors are called **conceptual errors** because they reflect confusion within a perceptual concept category.

The results of the experiment are presented in Figure 12.10. The left-hand graph shows that as training progressed, the pigeons made progressively more correct responses. A correct response in this task can be made by chance 25% of the time. By the end of training, the pigeons were selecting the correct response key over 70% of the time. Another way to think about the increase in accuracy with training is that the overall rate of errors declined. That is expected to happen in learning experiments. Interestingly, however, when the errors were analyzed more closely, it was found that the rate of conceptual errors actually increased with increased training. These remarkable findings are presented in the right-hand graph.

Although the number of mistakes decreased overall, the mistakes that remained tended to be conceptual errors. Of the three possible incorrect responses on each trial, one was a conceptual error, and the other two were not (see the preceding description). Therefore, the rate of a conceptual error by chance was 33%. Figure 12.10 shows that the rate of conceptual errors started under 40% (near chance) and increased to about 55%. Furthermore, once the error rate had reached about 55%, it remained there for the remainder of the experiment (72 sessions). In this experiment, further training was ineffective in reducing the rate of conceptual errors. (For a different analysis of this type of error, see Aitken, Bennett, McLaren, & Mackintosh, 1996; Mackintosh, 1995.)

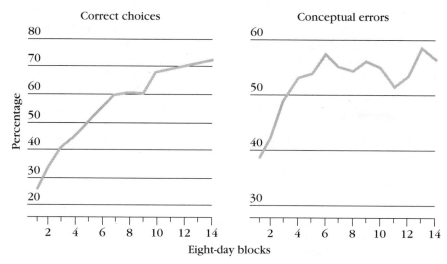

Figure 12.10 Rate of correct responses (left) and rate of conceptual errors (right) in the concept-discrimination experiment by Wasserman, Kiedinger, and Bhatt (1988). (From "Conceptual Behavior in Pigeons: Categories, Subcategories, and Pseudocategories," by E. A. Wasserman, R. E. Kiedinger, and R. S. Bhatt, *Journal of Experimental Psychology: Animal Behavior Processes*, 1988, *14*, pp. 235–246. Copyright © 1988 by the American Psychological Association. Reprinted by permission.)

Mechanisms of Perceptual Concept Learning

Evidence of generalization to novel exemplars, better learning of concept discriminations than pseudoconcept discriminations, and the development of conceptual errors with training provide diverse but converging evidence of perceptual concept learning in animals. Such evidence demonstrates that animals group stimuli into perceptual categories and generalize within those categories; however, it does not reveal how such perceptual categorization is accomplished. Three major alternative explanations are provided by *prototype theory, feature theory,* and *exemplar theory.*

Prototype Theory. Among the various explanations of concept learning that we will consider, prototype theory relies most heavily on higher-order cognitive mechanisms. According to prototype theory, exposure to a number of exemplars of a perceptual category results in the abstraction of a **prototype** or "standard" representative of the concept. For the category "chair," for example, the prototype would be of an average or typical chair, one that has four legs and a back. Once the organism has abstracted or formed the prototype, it will respond to new instances of the category based on how similar these new instances are to the prototype.

Although prototype theory provides a plausible explanation for perceptual concept learning, it has not been easy to differentiate predictions of this theory from predictions of other accounts of perceptual concept learning (but see Aydin & Pearce, 1994). Because prototype theory is no more successful than the simpler behavioral theories I will turn to next, people have questioned the value and necessity of assuming that animals engage in the kind of complex cognitive processes that are required to abstract a prototype from a set of stimuli that represent a perceptual concept.

Feature Theory. Feature theory assumes that members of a perceptual category have certain stimulus features in common—features to which the instrumental response becomes conditioned when the organism is reinforced. Investigators of perceptual concept learning have argued against a simple feature-analysis explanation because a single feature common to all positive instances of natural perceptual concepts is difficult (and sometimes impossible) to identify. In Herrnstein, Loveland, and Cable's (1976) tree-concept experiment, for example, many of the trees had green coloration and were leafy, vertical, woody, and branching. However, the pigeons also responded to pictures of trees that did not have these characteristics. In addition, they failed to respond to pictures that did not include a tree but had some green, leafy, vertical, woody, and branching components. Thus, it is difficult to identify a critical feature or combination of features that might have controlled the behavior of the pigeons.

Because of the difficulties posed by the richness and complexity of photographs of natural scenes, investigators interested in feature theory have turned to studying perceptual concept learning with specially constructed artificial stimuli (for example, Lea & Ryan, 1983; Jitsumori, 1993, 1994). Huber and Lenz (1993), for example, used simple line drawings of faces like those shown in Figure 12.11. Four features of the drawings were varied: the distance between the eyes, the height of the forehead, the length of the nose, and the size of the chin. Each of these features could take on one of three values, designated as −1, 0, and +1. Two categories were created from the resultant drawings by adding the values of the four features. One category (called "positive") was composed of drawings that had feature sums greater than zero; another category (called "negative") was made of drawings that had feature sums less than zero.

The drawing on the left of Figure 12.11 represents the face with the highest negative sum of the features, and the drawing on the right represents the face with the highest positive sum of the features. The pigeons were reinforced for pecking in the presence of faces with a positive feature sum and were not reinforced for pecking in the presence of faces with a negative feature sum. The birds learned the concept discrimination in about 20 sessions, and detailed analyses of their performance indicated that their behavior was controlled by the four features that were manipulated. Responding of each pigeon was highly correlated with the sum of the features that appeared in a test stimulus. Greater feature sums produced proportionately greater rates of responding.

Although feature theory has met with some success, pigeons do not always take advantage of the features that are available in a perceptual category (Lea, Lohmann, & Ryan, 1993). Furthermore, pigeons and monkeys do not invariably treat independent features as separate and additive predictors of reinforcement. Rather, they tend to respond to combinations or configurations of features (Jitsumori, 1993, 1994). These factors can disrupt performance when the animals are tested with new stimuli that contain the relevant features.

Exemplar Theory. The simplest, and in some ways the most successful, explanation of perceptual concept learning is the exemplar theory (Wasserman & Astley, 1994). This theory is based on conventional concepts of discrimination learning and stimulus generalization such as those discussed in Chapter 8. Reinforcement for responding in the presence of a stimulus is assumed to result in the conditioning of excitation to that stimulus. In contrast, nonreinforcement is assumed to result in the absence of excitation and perhaps the conditioning of inhibition to the stimulus. Both conditioned excitation and inhibition are assumed to generalize to other stimuli, with the

Figure 12.11   Examples of drawings of faces used by Huber and Lenz (1993). The face on the left represents the highest negative sum of facial features. The face in the middle has a feature sum of zero, and the face on the right has the highest positive feature sum. (From "A Test of the Linear Feature Model of Polymorphous Concept Discrimination with Pigeons," by L. Huber and R. Lenz, *The Quarterly Journal of Experimental Psychology,* 1993, *46B,* 1–18. Copyright © 1993 the Experimental Psychology Society. Reprinted by permission.)

degree of generalization determined by the degree of similarity between the new and old stimuli.

These basic ideas can explain many aspects of perceptual concept learning. For example, generalization of a learned concept to new exemplars presumably occurs because the new test stimuli are in some ways similar to the stimuli used in original training of the perceptual concept. Better performance on a concept discrimination task than on a pseudoconcept discrimination is explained on the assumption that the reinforced and nonreinforced stimuli are more perceptually distinct in a concept discrimination than in a pseudoconcept discrimination. Finally, the increase in conceptual errors with concept discrimination learning is explained on the assumption that subsets of stimuli within one perceptual category are more similar than stimuli between perceptual categories.

Although exemplar theory is highly successful in explaining many aspects of perceptual concept learning, it should be pointed out that this theory may well operate in combination with the mechanisms of feature theory. In fact, exemplar theory is difficult to distinguish from feature theory in situations where organisms respond to examples of a perceptual concept in terms of the salient features that those examples have in common. The advantage of exemplar theory, however, is that it can predict various aspects of categorization behavior without first identifying which stimulus features are important to a perceptual category (for further details, see Wasserman & Astley, 1994).

LANGUAGE LEARNING IN NONHUMAN ANIMALS

Perhaps the most complex cognitive skill is linguistic competence. In fact, many have assumed that linguistic skill is so complex and specialized that it is uniquely human. According to this view, the ability to use language depends on certain innate processes that have evolved only in our own species (for example, Chomsky, 1972; Lennenberg, 1967). By contrast, others have proposed that people are able to use language because our species is especially intelligent and because we have had the necessary training. This second view suggests that nonhuman organisms may also acquire language skills if they are sufficiently intelligent and if they receive the proper training. Encouraged by this possibility, investigators have tried to teach language skills to various species.

The language training of animals raises the intriguing possibility that someday we might be able to communicate with nonhuman organisms and thereby gain unique insights into their lives. Whether or not people will ever have heart-to-heart talks with animals, research on language learning in nonhuman species can tell us a great deal about the cognitive prerequisites and components of language competence. Such research can also provide information about how best to teach linguistic skills. This information can then be put to good use in language instruction for persons with cognitive disabilities (Sevcik, Romski, & Wilkenson, 1991).

Approaches to Language Training

Most efforts to teach animals language have involved chimpanzees because chimpanzees have many characteristics in common with human beings. Despite these similarities, however, chimpanzees do not learn to speak when they are given the same types of experiences that children have as they learn to speak. Nadezhda Kohts, of the Darwinian museum in Moscow, raised a chimpanzee in her home from 1913 to 1916 without once having it imitate the human voice or utter a word of Russian (see A. J. Premack, 1976). More detailed accounts of life with a chimpanzee are available from the experiences of Winthrop and Louise Kellogg, who raised a baby chimpanzee along with their baby boy (Kellogg, 1933). Their adopted charge also did not learn to speak like a person. Undaunted by this evidence, Cathy and Keith Hayes raised a chimpanzee named Viki with the explicit intent of teaching her to talk (Hayes & Hayes, 1951). Despite several years of training, Viki learned to say only three words: mama, papa, and cup.

The failure of the Hayeses to teach language to Viki despite their great efforts discouraged others from trying to teach chimpanzees to talk. However, people remained intrigued with the possibility that animals might acquire some language skills. The search for linguistic competence in chimpanzees got a big boost from the innovative work of Allen and Beatrice Gardner and their students (Gardner & Gardner, 1969, 1975, 1978). Instead of trying to teach their chimpanzee Washoe to talk using vocal speech, the Gardners taught Washoe American Sign Language.

American Sign Language consists of manual gestures in place of words. Chimpanzees are much more adept at making hand movements and gestures than they are at making the vocal-laryngeal contractions required for the production of speech sounds. Washoe was a good student. She learned to sign well over 100 words. Washoe's success suggested that earlier efforts to teach speech to chimpanzees may have failed not because of the inability of the chimpanzee to learn linguistic skills but because an inappropriate response medium (vocalization) was used. Washoe held out the promise that animals would acquire linguistic competence with the appropriate response medium.

The success of the Gardners with Washoe encouraged other language training efforts with chimpanzees, as well as with other species. These included a gorilla (Patterson, 1978); dolphins (Herman, 1987); sea lions (Gisiner & Schusterman, 1992; Schusterman & Gisiner, 1988); and an African grey parrot (Pepperberg, 1990). Some investigators followed the approach of the Gardners in using American Sign Lan-

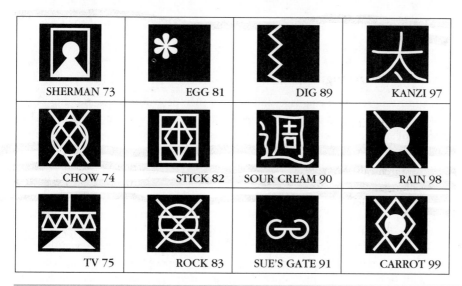

Figure 12.12 Examples of lexigrams used at the Language Research Center of Georgia State University. (Courtesy of Language Research Center, Georgia State University.)

guage to train chimpanzees (see Gardner, Gardner, & Van Cantfort, 1989) and gorillas (Patterson, 1978). Another approach has also avoided trying to teach chimpanzees vocalization. However, instead of adopting a human language in active use, such as sign language, this approach has employed artificial languages.

One artificial language, developed and used by David Premack and his associates, consists of various shapes made of plastic in place of words (Premack, 1971b, 1976). Another artificial language was developed by Duane Rumbaugh and his colleagues at the Language Research Center associated with Georgia State University (Rumbaugh, 1977; see also Savage-Rumbaugh, 1986). In this artificial language, simple designs of various shapes and colors represent words (see Figure 12.12). These symbols, called lexigrams, are presented on a board. The chimpanzee can select a word by pointing to or pressing the corresponding lexigram on the board. Computer records of these lexigram responses provide detailed information about the linguistic performance of the research participant.

Early language training efforts attempted to determine whether nonhuman animals are capable of language. However, it has become evident that this is not an answerable question (Roitblat, Harley, & Helweg, 1993). Such a question is as difficult to answer as it is to determine at what point human infants have language. Language is not a unitary entity that an individual either does or does not have. Rather, it consists of component skills. A human infant's language abilities improve gradually as the infant acquires and integrates increasingly sophisticated language skills. In this developmental sequence, there is no one point at which the young child graduates from not having language to having it.

Based on such considerations, investigators have come to recognize that instead of trying to prove (or disprove) that nonhuman animals can learn language, a more productive approach is to investigate the acquisition of various components of language competence. There are two major issues in contemporary work on animal language training. One issue concerns documenting the nature of the language skills that animals acquire through training. The second issue involves trying to identify the kinds of training procedures that are necessary for acquisition of the skills that are found.

Documenting Language Skills

Documenting acquired language skill is easier than determining the training procedures responsible for those skills. When an animal has presumably acquired a language skill, tests can be conducted that conclusively demonstrate the skill in question. Special test procedures are necessary because language training typically involves extensive interactions with the participant under conditions in which hints or prompts might be provided, or conditions in which a trainer might give the animal the benefit of the doubt and credit the animal with more intelligent behavior than is warranted. Terrace and his colleagues (Terrace, 1979; Terrace, Petitto, Sanders, & Bever, 1979), for example, studied videotaped records of the sign language behavior of their chimpanzee, Nim, and found that Nim often imitated signs previously made by the trainer. They considered imitative signing to be poor evidence of language skill.

Not only must test procedures be set up in a way that precludes inadvertent prompts, they must also be constructed to allow for objective measurement of behavior. In a test of sign language vocabulary, for example, Gardner and Gardner (1984), presented pictures to Washoe for her to identify by signing. Two observers recorded the signs Washoe made. To minimize the possibility of prompting, neither observer could see the picture Washoe was trying to name. To ensure objective independent observations, the observers also could not see each other. With these elaborate procedures, Washoe could not be tipped off as to the correct sign. Since the observers did not know what the correct sign was on each trial, they could not give her credit for incorrect responses. Despite these precautions, Washoe responded correctly about 80% of the time.

Washoe's vocabulary test was a test of word production. Subsequently, Savage-Rumbaugh and her colleagues reported on a bonobo chimpanzee, Kanzi, who learned to recognize spoken English words. Kanzi, like other chimpanzees, could not produce the sounds of English words, but he could identify the meaning of spoken words. In one test of this comprehension skill (Savage-Rumbaugh, McDonald, Sevcik, Hopkins, & Rubert, 1986), English words were "spoken" by a speech synthesizer to make sure Kanzi was not responding to the intonation of human speech. After each word, Kanzi was asked to select the lexical symbol for that word from a selection of three lexigrams (see Figure 12.13). The experimenter did not see the possible choices, and thus could not inadvertently indicate which was correct. The choice alternatives were presented by a second experimenter, who then did not observe Kanzi's choices so she could not prompt the correct response either. Each of 66 words was presented three times. Kanzi responded correctly each time 51 of the words was presented. In a similar test with spoken human speech, Kanzi erred on only one of the 66 words. Thus, synthesized speech was more difficult for Kanzi to comprehend, as it is for human listeners sometimes.

Interestingly, two other language-trained chimpanzees, Austin and Sherman, showed no evidence of comprehension of human spoken speech in similar tests after similar extensive experience with spoken English. Austin and Sherman are common chimpanzees of the same species as Washoe (*Pan troglodytes*), whereas Kanzi is a bonobo chimpanzee (*Pan paniscus*). Their differences in comprehension of spoken English may reflect species differences in this skill. However, given the small numbers of chimpanzees tested so far, we cannot be sure.

Figure 12.13 The bonobo chimpanzee, Kanzi, participating in a test of English comprehension. Words were presented to him through the earphones, and he had to respond by pressing lexigrams on the panel in the background.

Language Training Procedures

Comparisons between Species. A variety of procedures have been employed to train language skills. For example, Pepperberg (for example, 1990, 1993), working with the African Grey parrot, Alex, has employed an observational learning procedure known as the **model-rival technique.** This technique involves two people interacting with Alex. One person acts as a trainer, and the other acts as a rival student who competes with Alex for the attention of the trainer. The trainer may present an object of interest to Alex and ask what color it is. The person acting as the student then responds, sometimes correctly and sometimes incorrectly. An incorrect response results in a reprimand from the trainer and temporary removal of the object. A correct response results in praise and a chance to manipulate the object. Alex observes these interactions and attempts to gain the attention of the trainer (and obtain the object) by responding correctly before the rival human "student" does so.

I. M. Pepperberg, with Alex

In the dolphin and sea lion language training projects, more conventional stimulus discrimination procedures have been used (for example, Herman, Pack, & Morrel-Samuels, 1993; Schusterman & Krieger, 1986). The instructional stimuli were provided by a person making a particular gesture (arms crossed against the chest, for example) at the edge of the pool. The correct response on the part of the marine mammal to the gesture was reinforced with food; incorrect responses were not reinforced. Thus, the training procedures used with the African grey parrot and the marine mammals differ in numerous respects, including opportunities for observational learning and the reinforcers employed. Observed differences between the language skills of the avian and marine animals may reflect species differences or any of the numerous differences in the training procedures used.

Comparisons within the Same Species. Specific aspects of language training procedures that are responsible for acquired language competence are potentially easier to identify if the comparisons are made within a single species. Starting with the pioneering work of training sign language to Washoe, language training has been conducted with more than a dozen chimpanzees. It is possible that different training procedures produce differences in language competence among chimpanzees. However, even these comparisons have to be made with caution.

One methodological problem arises from the complexity of the language training procedures employed with chimpanzees. For example, sign language training conducted by the Gardners and their associates was usually within the context of an established social relationship between the trainers and the chimpanzees. The chimpanzees lived in a rich home-like environment and were cared for by a small number of people throughout the day, each of whom was adept in sign language. Every effort was made to engage the chimpanzees in active conversation (through signing) during their waking hours. New signs were learned during games, in the course of getting dressed, or in going from place to place. The intent was to teach language to the chimpanzees in the way that children presumably learn to talk during the normal course of interacting with parents and other children.

In contrast to the efforts to create a naturalistic context for the training of sign language, early investigators using artificial languages conducted language training in more confined laboratory settings with the use of explicit reinforcers (D. Premack, 1976; Rumbaugh, 1977). For example, in the initial efforts of Rumbaugh and his associates (Rumbaugh, 1977), the chimpanzee Lana was taught an artificial language consisting of lexigrams, each of which represented a different word. The lexigrams appeared on a modified keyboard hooked up to a computer. Lana could "talk" to the computer and make various requests. The computer, in turn, was programmed to reply with lexigrams presented on a display console. This procedure obviously was very different from that employed by the Gardners and their associates. Such differences in training procedures make it difficult to identify the specific component of a training procedure that is primarily responsible for differences in observed results.

A second difficulty is that although language training has been conducted with more than a dozen chimpanzees altogether, each procedure has been employed with just a few experimental participants (and only one in some cases). Individuals of a single species (rats or pigeons, for example) can vary considerably in how they respond to the same complex learning task. There is no reason to assume that chimpanzees do not show similar individual differences. Therefore, differences observed across training procedures may reflect nonspecific individual differences between the participants rather than differences in the efficacy of those procedures.

Finally, different training procedures have been used by different investigators in different laboratories. Therefore, unknown and unintended differences in laboratory procedures and personnel may lead to differences in the performance of the animals. Terrace and his associates (Terrace et al., 1979), for example, attempted to teach sign language to their chimpanzee, Nim, at Columbia University, using the same procedures that had been used by the Gardners to train Washoe at the University of Nevada. However, the Gardners have disputed that the Columbia University project successfully replicated the procedures of the Nevada project (for example, Gardner & Gardner, 1989).

Comparisons at the Georgia State University Language Research Center. Although problematic, it is tempting to try to relate language competence to training method, especially in cases where striking differences in results are observed in the same laboratory. Several such opportunities have arisen at the Language Research Center at

Georgia State University, the site of the longest continuing investigation of language learning in chimpanzees. Investigators at the Center have varied their training regimes as new participants entered the language training program.

The training procedure employed with the first chimpanzee at the Center, Lana, was described briefly earlier. Lana's training emphasized the naming of objects and the learning of short sequences of symbols. Two other chimpanzees, Austin and Sherman, entered the program after Lana (see Savage-Rumbaugh, 1986). In contrast to Lana, Austin and Sherman were reared with more extensive human contact, and, perhaps more importantly, they learned language within the context of interacting not only with humans but also with each other. However, they were trained with the same lexigram language system that had been used in training Lana rather than American Sign Language. Austin and Sherman interacted with caretakers and with each other by pointing to or pressing lexigrams on a stimulus board. Portable versions of the lexigram board were available to extend training to a variety of settings.

Austin and Sherman showed more sophisticated language competence than Lana. For example, as I will describe shortly, Austin and Sherman learned to use words more abstractly than Lana. Unlike Lana, Austin and Sherman were able to use words to label categories of other words.

The most sophisticated demonstrations of language competence to date have been obtained with Kanzi, a bonobo great ape (*Pan paniscus*) (Savage-Rumbaugh, Murphy, Sevcik, Brakke, Williams, & Rumbaugh, 1993; Savage-Rumbaugh, Sevcik, Brakke, & Rumbaugh, 1990). (See Figure 12.14.) Bonobos are more similar to human beings than chimpanzees but they are rare both in the wild and in captivity. Kanzi's language acquisition was unusual in comparison to previous language training efforts with chimpanzees in that Kanzi did not receive formal language training. During the first 2.5 years of his life he lived with his mother, Matata, who was born in the wild and started language training at the Language Research Center of Georgia State University when Kanzi was 6 months old.

Matata was trained with standard procedures in which she had to indicate the lexigram names of food objects to obtain those foods. However, she progressed slowly and never attained the language competence of Austin and Sherman. For several years, Kanzi observed these training sessions but did not participate in them. Matata was then removed for a period for breeding purposes. During this separation Kanzi began to interact with the lexigram board spontaneously. The investigators took advantage of this spontaneous use of the lexigram board and allowed Kanzi to continue to use it in addition to communicating with manual gestures. They also allowed Kanzi to continue to learn language skills by listening to spoken English and observing humans communicating with gestures and lexigrams.

D. M. Rumbaugh and
E. S. Savage-Rumbaugh

Every effort was made to provide Kanzi with as rich and as natural an environment as possible. He was allowed to go on excursions in a 50-acre wooded area adjacent to the laboratory. The woods were provisioned with food stations at fixed locations. Excursions in the woods provided numerous opportunities for conversation concerning which food site to visit, what to take along, and so on. Kanzi was also allowed to visit various areas of the laboratory, including areas in which other apes were housed, and periodically he was taken on car rides.

Spoken and lexical language were incorporated into Kanzi's daily activities such as diaper changes, food preparation, and various games. The hope was that Kanzi would acquire language incidentally during his normal daily activities, as children do. No explicit language training sessions were conducted, and Kanzi's use of language was not explicitly reinforced with food. However, the reinforcement contingencies

Figure 12.14 Kanzi working with a lexigram board.

inherent in social interactions were probably important in Kanzi's language learning (Sundberg, 1996).

Components of Linguistic Competence

As I noted earlier, research on language learning in nonhuman species has come to focus on various components of linguistic competence rather than on whether or not animals are capable of language. I will now describe the components of linguistic competence in greater detail.

Learning a Vocabulary. One of the undisputed results of language training programs is that animals can learn to associate arbitrary symbols (be they manual signs or lexigrams) with objects. They can learn to correctly name a large number of different objects. To what extent does this skill represent having learned what we call words in human language?

A word in human language is an abstract representation that can be used in a variety of ways. A word can be used as a label for its referent object (as in saying "tomato" when presented with an example of the vegetable). A word can also be used to identify the referent object in response to the word (as in picking out a tomato when asked, "Which is the tomato?"). Or a word can be used in relation to other words (as in saying "tomato" when asked to name examples of "vegetables").

In various types of tests of the use of lexigrams, Lana was found to be just as skillful as Austin and Sherman in labeling various objects and in sorting a set of objects into two categories—"food" and "tool"—by putting the objects into separate piles (Savage-Rumbaugh, Rumbaugh, Smith, & Lawson, 1980). However, in contrast to Austin and Sherman, Lana was unable to generalize the labels "food" and "tool" to novel examples of foods and tools, even though she could sort these new objects accurately when required to put them into separate piles. Thus, Lana's knowledge of the words "food" and "tool" was much more restricted than Austin's and Sherman's.

In further training (see Savage-Rumbaugh et al., 1980), Austin and Sherman readily learned to label pictures of foods and tools and generalized this skill to novel photographs of exemplars of each category. In a final phase of the experiment, Austin and Sherman were trained to label lexigrams of various foods (beancake, orange, and bread) and tools (key, money, and stick) as "food" and "tool." They were then tested with a variety of symbols of new tools (magnet, sponge, lever, string, for example) and foods (M & M, banana, corn, for example). They had previously learned the lexigrams for each of these new tools and foods. However, they had not been explicitly trained to categorize or label these items in terms of their uses (tool and food). Nevertheless, Austin and Sherman performed with nearly perfect accuracy in categorizing these new lexigrams. Thus, they were able to use words to label and categorize other words.

This linguistic skill shows a level of abstractness similar to that used in human language. Other studies of animal language have failed to demonstrate such sophisticated usage of words. It is tempting to attribute the superior performance of Austin and Sherman, as compared to Lana, to the differences in how language training was conducted with the former chimpanzees. However, any such conclusion has to be tempered by the fact that the training procedures differed in numerous features. Therefore, the critical difference cannot be identified with much confidence.

Evidence of "Grammar" in Great Apes. Although it is agreed that great apes (and Alex the Grey parrot, and dolphins, and sea lions) can learn a vocabulary, language is more than just a collection of words. Language also involves the arrangement of words into sequences according to certain rules set forth by the grammar and syntax of the language. Hence, a critical issue in chimpanzee language research is whether chimpanzees can learn word sequences on the basis of grammatical rules. There has been considerable debate about this.

The smallest word sequence contains two words. However, the utterance of a pair of words does not prove that the participant is using grammar to create the sequence. An often-recounted incident involving a two-word sequence occurred when the chimp Washoe saw a swan in the water. She had never been exposed to a swan before. When asked, "What is that?" she signed "Water bird." In this sequence was Washoe using "water" as an adjective to specify the kind of bird she saw? Perhaps. However, an equally plausible interpretation is that she signed "water" because she saw the water and "bird" because she saw a bird. That is, she may have signed "water bird" as two independent words rather than as an utterance of two words related to each other as adjective and noun (Terrace et al., 1979).

Early detailed studies of language production in the chimpanzee failed to provide convincing evidence of responding on the basis of some kind of grammar or set of rules for word combinations (Terrace, 1979; Terrace et al., 1979). The chimpanzee Nim, who was taught sign language by Terrace and his associates, performed sequences of signs, but these appeared to be imitations of the trainer and included meaningless repetitions. For example, Nim's most common four-sign combination was "eat-drink-eat-drink."

Convincing evidence of the development of grammatical word sequences has been obtained in studies of the language behavior of the bonobo ape Kanzi (Greenfield & Savage-Rumbaugh, 1990; see also Savage-Rumbaugh et al., 1990). Data for the analysis of the possible existence of grammatical structure in Kanzi's language production were first obtained when Kanzi was 5.5 years old (Greenfield & Savage-Rumbaugh, 1990). Over a 5-month period of observations, Kanzi communicated

13,691 "words." Of these, about 10% contained more than one element, or "word." The analysis of word sequences was limited to spontaneous communications. Thus, responses to directed questions were excluded from the analyses, as were responses that Kanzi performed to obtain something that was otherwise withheld, or responses that involved some degree of imitation. Unlike Nim, Kanzi rarely repeated himself or combined words that did not make sense together. Analyses of the multiple-word communications revealed a structure indicative of rules for word order.

Kanzi's word combinations could be categorized according to the types of words that were involved. By way of example, Table 12.1 summarizes data from three different types of two-word combinations. The first type involves a word for an action and a word for an agent. A total of 132 such action/agent combinations were observed. Of these, in 119 instances the word identifying the action preceded the word identifying the agent. In only 13 of the 132 cases did the word for the agent precede the word for the action. A similar bias in favor of a particular word order is evident with the other types of two-word combinations—action/object and goal/action. Notice that the "grammatical" rule is not a simple one. One of the words in all three of these types of two-word combinations involved an action. However, the action word did not come first predominantly in all three types of two-word combinations. When talking about an action and a goal, Kanzi tended to state the goal first.

Some of the rules for word order that were manifest in Kanzi's word combinations were probably learned by observing his human caretakers. However, other grammatical rules appeared to be Kanzi's original inventions. Perhaps the most prominent of these concerned word combinations that Kanzi made involving a lexigram and a hand gesture. In such cases, Kanzi nearly always performed the lexigram response first, followed by the gesture. For example, in requesting to be carried, Kanzi would press the lexigram for CARRY, followed by a gesture pointing to the caretaker. Kanzi faithfully followed the rule of making the lexigram response before any manual gestures, but the caretakers usually performed such word sequences in the opposite order.

Language Comprehension versus Production. Historically, studies of ape language have focused on whether apes can learn to produce orderly linguistic responses, be those words or word sequences. Starting with the findings obtained with the bonobo Kanzi, the focus has shifted toward investigations of language comprehension. The initial observations of Kanzi's language competence were incidental and serendipitous. Recall that Kanzi was not in an organized language training program but was present while his mother received explicit language training. Savage-Rumbaugh and her colleagues noticed that Kanzi seemed to understand the words that were being used with his mother. This incidental observation led them to investigate language comprehension rather than production in a systematic fashion. The shift in emphasis has provided dramatic results (for example, Brakke & Savage-Rumbaugh, 1995; Savage-Rumbaugh et al., 1993).

Comprehension precedes the ability to speak a language in human language learning. Individuals learning a second language, for example, can often understand more of that language than they are able to speak. This raises the possibility that studies of language comprehension may reveal sophisticated aspects of linguistic competence that are not evident in language production.

A prominent feature of human language is its variety and flexibility. A limited set of words can be combined to form a great variety of different sentences, and you can understand a new sentence even if you have never seen that particular sequence of words before. It has been difficult to prove that animals can use language in as flexible

| TABLE 12.1 | FREQUENCY OF VARIOUS TWO-ELEMENT COMMUNICATIONS BY KANZI (lexigram responses are indicated by small capital letters) | |

WORD ORDER	FREQUENCY	EXAMPLE OF DOMINANT ORDER
Action → Agent	119	CARRY → gesture to Phil, who agrees
Agent → Action	13	to carry Kanzi
Action → Object	39	KEEP AWAY BALLOON → wanting to tease
Object → Action	15	Bill with a balloon and start a fight
Goal → Action	46	COKE CHASE → researcher chases Kanzi
Action → Goal	10	to place in woods where Coke is kept

Source: Adapted from Greenfield and Savage-Rumbaugh, 1990.

a fashion as human beings (see, for example, Thompson & Church, 1980). Recent tests of comprehension conducted with Kanzi provide promising results.

Savage-Rumbaugh et al. (1993) conducted detailed evaluations of the language comprehension of Kanzi when he was 8 years old and compared his performance to that of a 2-year-old child, Alia. Alia's mother, Jeannine Murphy, was one of Kanzi's caretakers. She worked with Kanzi in the mornings and spent the afternoons with Alia in a double-wide mobile home at the Language Research Center that was set up like Kanzi's laboratory. Alia participated in games and other activities similar to those that were used with Kanzi and received similar exposure to lexigrams and spoken English.

The test sentences involved instructions to manipulate various objects that were familiar and available to Kanzi and Alia. Kanzi faced up to 12 objects, and Alia was given up to 8. In the critical test phase, the sentences were spoken by an experimenter hidden by a one-way mirror so that the experimenter could not make gestures that might prompt the correct response. All trials were recorded on videotape. Usually two or three other people were present in the room so that sentences involving inter- actions with these people could be included in the test. However, the additional in- dividuals wore headphones that played loud music so that they could not hear the instructions given Kanzi or Alia. To further preclude inadvertent influences on the data, the results of tests with Kanzi were not known to the person conducting the tests with Alia, and vice versa.

Kanzi was tested with 415 sentences, and Alia was tested with 407. The sen- tences were distributed among seven different types. Some were fairly simple, such as "Put object X in object Y," "Give object X to person A," "Do action A on object X," and "Take object X to location Y." Others were more complicated, such as "Make pretend animate A do action X on recipient Y." (For example, "Make the [toy] doggie bite the [toy] snake.") Both Kanzi and Alia did remarkably well. Each responded cor- rectly more than 50% of the time on all but one sentence type. Overall, Kanzi did a bit better than Alia. Kanzi responded correctly on 74% of the trials, and Alia responded correctly on 65% of the trials.

Both Kanzi and Alia responded correctly when tested with sentences involving the same words but in different orders. For example, they responded correctly to the sentences, "Take the umbrella outdoors" and "Go outdoors and get the umbrella"; "Take the potato to the bedroom" and "Go to the bedroom and get the potato"; "Put some water on the carrot" and "Put the carrot in the water"; and "Kanzi/Alia is going to chase Liz/Nathaniel" and "Liz/Nathaniel is going to chase Kanzi/Alia." Kanzi was more accurate on sentence pairs involving the same words in different orders. Kanzi made the correct response on 66% of such pairs of sentences, whereas Alia was correct on 38% of them.

Kanzi and Alia also responded correctly to sentences involving unusual instructions that they had not previously encountered. For example, on one occasion the objects available to Kanzi included a tomato and a sponge ball. The ball was shaped in the form of a head, with eyes, nose and a mouth. One of Kanzi's test sentences was, "Feed your ball some tomato." Before this test item, the word "feed" had never been used with "ball." Nevertheless, in response to "Feed your ball some tomato," Kanzi took the tomato and put it into the mouth on the sponge ball. (See Figure 12.15.)

Both Kanzi and Alia also came up with some unusual solutions to the instructions they were given. Both had seen food washed in the kitchen sink. Therefore, in response to, "Wash the hot dogs," the experimenters expected that they would take the hot dogs to the sink. But, neither did so. Rather, they responded in a way that did not require going to the sink. Kanzi washed the hot dogs with a hose that was in the room to clean the floor. Alia, in contrast, rubbed the hot dogs with a sponge that was close at hand.

Kanzi's performance provides the best evidence available so far that a nonhuman mammal can acquire sophisticated linguistic skills. Kanzi acquired a substantial vocabulary and also showed evidence of syntax in language production. In addition,

Figure 12.15 Video sequence showing Kanzi's response to the instruction, "Feed your ball some tomato." (Courtesy of Duane Rumbaugh, Language Research Center, Georgia State University.)

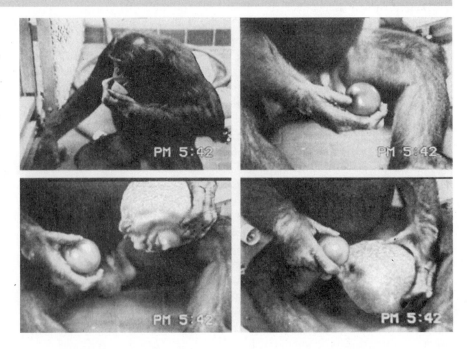

he mastered some of the flexibility of language. He could understand differences in meaning created by different word orders and new messages created by combining familiar words in unfamiliar sentences. The language sophistication of Kanzi proves that many important linguistic skills are not uniquely human attributes. Thus, these findings vindicate Darwin's belief that seemingly unique human abilities and skills do not reflect a discontinuity in the animal kingdom.

SAMPLE QUESTIONS

1. Describe the peak procedure and how results obtained with the peak procedure may be explained by an information processing model.

2. Compare and contrast the information processing model of timing and the behavioral theory of timing.

3. Explain why tests with subsets of items from a simultaneous array are useful in assessing the mechanisms of serial pattern learning.

4. Compare and contrast three different theories of perceptual concept learning.

5. Describe how responsiveness to word order may be evaluated in the language comprehension of chimpanzees and children.

KEY TERMS

adjunctive behaviors Systematic activities or responses that occur when reinforcers are delivered at fixed intervals.

chunking The subdivision of a series of items into subsets, each of which has its own internal structure.

conceptual error An error that results from failure to differentiate the subset of a category to which a stimulus belongs.

duration estimation A discrimination procedure in which the discriminative stimulus is the duration of an event.

interim response A response that increases in frequency after the delivery of a periodic reinforcer and then declines as time for the next reinforcer approaches.

model-rival technique An observational learning procedure in which the participant observes a trainer teaching a student and tries to compete with that student for the trainer's attention.

paired-associate learning Learning of associations between successive pairs of an ordered list of stimuli.

peak procedure A discrete-trial variation of a fixed interval schedule used to study timing in animals.

prototype An exemplar of a category that is the average, typical, or "standard" representation of that category.

response chain A consecutively ordered series of responses in which each response produces the cue for the next response in the sequence.

serial representation learning The learning of a mental representation of the order of an entire list or series of stimuli.

terminal response A response that is most likely to occur at the end of the interval between successive reinforcements that are presented at fixed intervals.

REFERENCES

Abramson, L. Y., Metalsky, G. I., & Alloy, L. B. (1989). Hopelessness depression: A theory-based subtype of depression. *Psychological Review, 96,* 358–372.

Adams, G. P. (1903). On the negative and positive phototropism of the earthworm *Allolobophora foetida* as determined by light of different intensities. *American Journal of Physiology, 9,* 26–34.

Ader, R. (1985). Conditioned taste aversions and immunopharmacology. *Annals of the New York Academy of Sciences, 443,* 293–307.

Aguado, L., Symonds, M., & Hall, G. (1994). Interval between preexposure and test determines the magnitude of latent inhibition: Implications for an interference account. *Animal Learning & Behavior, 22,* 188–194.

Aitken, M. R. F., Bennett, C. H., McLaren, I. P. L., & Mackintosh, N. J. (1996). Perceptual differentiation during categorization learning by pigeons. *Journal of Experimental Psychology: Animal Behavior Processes, 22,* 43–50.

Akins, C. K., Domjan, M., & Gutiérrez, G. (1994). Topography of sexually conditioned behavior in male Japanese quail (*Coturnix japonica*) depends on the CS-US interval. *Journal of Experimental Psychology: Animal Behavior Processes, 20,* 199–209.

Allan, R. W., & Zeigler, H. P. (1994). Autoshaping the pigeon's gape response: Acquisition and topography as a function of reinforcer type and magnitude. *Journal of the Experimental Analysis of Behavior, 62,* 201–223.

Allen, A. A. (1934). Sex rhythm in the ruffed grouse (*Bonasa umbellus*) and other birds. *Auk, 51,* 180–199.

Allison, J. (1983). Behavioral economics. New York: Praeger.

Allison, J. (1989). The nature of reinforcement. In S. B. Klein & R. R. Mowrer (Eds.), *Contemporary learning theories: Instrumental conditioning and the impact of biological constraints on learning* (pp. 13–39). Hillsdale, NJ: Erlbaum.

Allison, J. (1993). Response deprivation, reinforcement, and economics. *Journal of the Experimental Analysis of Behavior, 60,* 129–140.

Allison, J., Buxton, A., & Moore, K. E. (1987). Bliss points, stop lines, and performance under schedule constraint. *Journal of Experimental Psychology: Animal Behavior Processes, 13,* 331–340.

Allison, J., Moore, K. E., Gawley, D. J., Mondloch, C. J., & Mondloch, M. V. (1986). The temporal patterns of unconstrained drinking: Rats' responses to inversion and identity constraints. *Journal of the Experimental Analysis of Behavior, 45,* 5–13.

Amsel, A. (1958). The role of frustrative nonreward in noncontinuous reward situations. *Psychological Bulletin, 55,* 102–119.

Amsel, A. (1962). Frustrative nonreward in partial reinforcement and discrimination learning. *Psychological Review, 69,* 306–328.

Amsel, A. (1967). Partial reinforcement effects on vigor and persistence. In K. W. Spence & J. T. Spence (Eds.), *The psychology of learning and motivation*

(Vol. 1, pp. 1–65). New York: Academic Press.

Amsel, A. (1989). *Behaviorism, neobehaviorism, and cognitivism in learning theory.* Hillsdale, NJ: Erlbaum.

Amsel, A. (1992). *Frustration theory.* Cambridge, England: Cambridge University Press.

Amsel, A., & Rashotte, M. E. (1984). *Mechanisms of adaptive behavior: Clark L. Hull's theoretical papers, with commentary.* New York: Columbia University Press.

Anderson, D. C., Crowell, C. R., Cunningham, C. L., & Lupo, J. V. (1979). Behavior during shock exposure as a determinant of subsequent interference with shuttle box escape-avoidance learning in the rat. *Journal of Experimental Psychology: Animal Behavior Processes, 5,* 243–257.

Anderson, M. C., & Shettleworth, S. J. (1977). Behavioral adaptation to fixed-interval and fixed-time food delivery in golden hamsters. *Journal of the Experimental Analysis of Behavior, 25,* 33–49.

Anger, D. (1963). The role of temporal discrimination in the reinforcement of Sidman avoidance behavior. *Journal of the Experimental Analysis of Behavior, 6,* 477–506.

Anisman, H., de Catanzaro, D., & Remington, G. (1978). Escape performance following exposure to inescapable shock: Deficits in motor response maintenance. *Journal of Experimental Psychology: Animal Behavior Processes, 4,* 197–218.

Anisman, H., Hamilton, M., & Zacharko, R. M. (1984). Cue and response-choice acquisition and reversal after exposure to uncontrollable shock: Induction of response perseveration. *Journal of Experimental Psychology: Animal Behavior Processes, 10,* 229–243.

Aydin, A., & Pearce, J. M. (1994). Prototype effects in categorization by pigeons. *Journal of Experimental Psychology: Animal Behavior Processes, 20,* 264–277.

Ayres, J. J. B., Haddad, C., & Albert, M. (1987). One-trial excitatory backward conditioning as assessed by suppression of licking in rats: Concurrent observations of lick suppression and defensive behaviors. *Animal Learning & Behavior, 15,* 212–217.

Azorlosa, J. L., & Cicala, G. A. (1986). Blocking of conditioned suppression with 1 or 10 compound trials. *Animal Learning & Behavior, 14,* 163–167.

Azrin, N. H. (1956). Some effects of two intermittent schedules of immediate and non-immediate punishment. *Journal of Psychology, 42,* 3–21.

Azrin, N. H. (1958). Some effects of noise on human behavior. *Journal of the Experimental Analysis of Behavior, 1,* 183–200.

Azrin, N. H. (1959). Punishment and recovery during fixed ratio performance. *Journal of the Experimental Analysis of Behavior, 2,* 301–305.

Azrin, N. H. (1960). Effects of punishment intensity during variable-interval reinforcement. *Journal of the Experimental Analysis of Behavior, 3,* 123–142.

Azrin, N. H., & Holz, W. C. (1961). Punishment during fixed-interval reinforcement. *Journal of the Experimental Analysis of Behavior, 4,* 343–347.

Azrin, N. H., & Holz, W. C. (1966). Punishment. In W. K. Honig (Ed.), *Operant behavior: Areas of research and application* (pp. 380–447). New York: Appleton-Century-Crofts.

Azrin, N. H., Holz, W. C., & Hake, D. F. (1963). Fixed-ratio punishment. *Journal of the Experimental Analysis of Behavior, 6,* 141–148.

Azrin, N. H., Hutchinson, R. R., & Hake, D. F. (1966). Extinction-

induced aggression. *Journal of the Experimental Analysis of Behavior, 9,* 191–204.

Babkin, B. P. (1949). *Pavlov: A biography.* Chicago: University of Chicago Press.

Baer, D. M., & Wolf, M. M. (1970). The entry into natural communities of reinforcement. In R. Ulrich, T. Stachnik, & J. Mabry (Eds.), *Control of human behavior* (Vol. 2, pp. 319–324). Glenview, IL: Scott Foresman.

Baerends, G. P. (1957). The ethological analysis of fish behavior. In M. E. Brown (Ed.), *The physiology of fishes.* New York: Academic Press.

Baerends, G. P. (1985). Do the dummy experiments with sticklebacks support the IRM-concept? *Behaviour, 93,* 258–277.

Baerends, G. P. (1988). Ethology. In R. C. Atkinson, R. J. Herrnstein, G. Lindzey, & R. D. Luce (Eds.), *Stevens' handbook of experimental psychology: Vol. 1.* (pp. 765–830). New York: Wiley.

Baerends, G. P., & Drent, R. H. (Eds.). (1982). The herring gull and its egg. Part II. The responsiveness to egg features. *Behaviour, 82,* 1–417.

Baker, A. G., & Baker, P. A. (1985). Does inhibition differ from excitation? Proactive interference, contextual conditioning, and extinction. In R. R. Miller & N. E. Spear (Eds.), *Information processing in animals: Conditioned inhibition* (pp. 151–183). Hillsdale, NJ: Erlbaum.

Baker, T. B., & Tiffany, S. T. (1985). Morphine tolerance as habituation. *Psychological Review, 92,* 78–108.

Balaz, M. A., Kasprow, W. J., & Miller, R. R. (1982). Blocking with a single compound trial. *Animal Learning & Behavior, 10,* 271–276.

Balda, R. P., & Turek, R. J. (1984). The cache-recovery system as an example of memory capabilities in Clark's nutcracker. In H. L. Roitblat, T. G. Bever, & H. S. Terrace (Eds.), *Animal cognition* (pp. 513–532). Hillsdale, NJ: Erlbaum.

Balsam, P. D. (1985). The functions of context in learning and performance. In P. D. Balsam & A. Tomie (Eds.),

Context and learning (pp. 1–21). Hillsdale, NJ: Erlbaum.

Balsam, P. D. (1988). Selection, representation, and equivalence of controlling stimuli. In R. C. Atkinson, R. J. Herrnstein, G. Lindzey, & R. D. Luce (Eds.), *Stevens' handbook of experimental psychology: Vol. 2. Learning and cognition* (pp. 111–166). New York: Wiley.

Balsam, P. D., & Tomie, A. (Eds.). (1985). *Context and learning.* Hillsdale, NJ: Erlbaum.

Banks, R. K. (1976). Resistance to punishment as a function of intensity and frequency of prior punishment experience. *Learning and Motivation, 7,* 551–558.

Barker, L. M., Best, M. R., & Domjan, M. (Eds.). (1977). *Learning mechanisms in food selection.* Waco, TX: Baylor University Press.

Barnet, R. C., Arnold, H. M., & Miller, R. R. (1991). Simultaneous conditioning demonstrated in second-order conditioning: Evidence for similar associative structure in forward and simultaneous conditioning. *Learning and Motivation, 22,* 253–268.

Baron, A. (1965). Delayed punishment of a runway response. *Journal of Comparative and Physiological Psychology, 60,* 131–134.

Baron, A., & Leinenweber, A. (1994). Molecular and molar analyses of fixed-interval performance. *Journal of the Experimental Analysis of Behavior, 61,* 11–18.

Baron, A., & Menich, S. R. (1985). Reaction times of younger and older men: Effects of compound samples and a prechoice signal on delayed matching-to-sample performances. *Journal of the Experimental Analysis of Behavior, 44,* 1–14.

Barrett, J. E., & Hoffmann, S. M. (1991). Neurochemical changes correlated with behavior maintained under fixed-interval and fixed-ratio schedules of reinforcement. *Journal of the Experimental Analysis of Behavior, 56,* 395–405.

Barton, L. E., Brulle, A. R., & Repp, A. C. (1986). Maintenance of therapeutic change by momentary DRO.

Journal of Applied Behavior Analysis, 19, 277–282.

Bashinski, H., Werner, J., & Rudy, J. (1985). Determinants of infant visual attention: Evidence for a two-process theory. *Journal of Experimental Child Psychology, 39*, 580–598.

Bateson, M., & Kacelnik, A. (1995). Preference for fixed and variable food sources: Variability in amount and delay. *Journal of the Experimental Analysis of Behavior, 63*, 313–329.

Baum, M. (1969). Extinction of avoidance response following response prevention: Some parametric investigations. *Canadian Journal of Psychology, 23*, 1–10.

Baum, M. (1970). Extinction of avoidance responding through response prevention (flooding). *Psychological Bulletin, 74*, 276–284.

Baum, W. M. (1974). On two types of deviation from the matching law: Bias and undermatching. *Journal of the Experimental Analysis of Behavior, 22*, 231–242.

Baum, W. M. (1975). Time allocation in human vigilance. *Journal of the Experimental Analysis of Behavior, 23*, 45–53.

Baum, W. M. (1979). Matching, undermatching, and overmatching in studies of choice. *Journal of the Experimental Analysis of Behavior, 32*, 269–281.

Baum, W. M. (1981). Optimization and the matching law as accounts of instrumental behavior. *Journal of the Experimental Analysis of Behavior, 36*, 387–403.

Baum, W. M. (1993). Performances on ratio and interval schedules of reinforcement: Data and theory. *Journal of the Experimental Analysis of Behavior, 59*, 245–264.

Baxter, D. J., & Zamble, E. (1982). Reinforcer and response specificity in appetitive transfer of control. *Animal Learning & Behavior, 10*, 201–210.

Beardsley, S. D., & McDowell, J. J. (1992). Application of Herrnstein's hyperbola to time allocation of naturalistic human behavior maintained by naturalistic social reinforcement.

Journal of the Experimental Analysis of Behavior, 57, 177–185.

Beatty, W. W., & Shavalia, D. A. (1980a). Rat spatial memory: Resistance to retroactive interference at long retention intervals. *Animal Learning & Behavior, 8*, 550–552.

Beatty, W. W., & Shavalia, D. A. (1980b). Spatial memory in rats: Time course of working memory and effects of anesthetics. *Behavioral and Neural Biology, 28*, 454–462.

Bechterev, V. M. (1913). *La psychologie objective.* Paris: Alcan.

Belke, T. W. (1992). Stimulus preference and the transitivity of preference. *Animal Learning & Behavior, 20*, 401–406.

Belke, T. W., & Heyman, G. M. (1994a). A matching law analysis of the reinforcing efficacy of wheel running in rats. *Animal Learning & Behavior, 22*, 267–274.

Belke, T. W., & Heyman, G. M. (1994b). Increasing and signaling background reinforcement: Effect on the foreground response-reinforcer relation. *Journal of the Experimental Analysis of Behavior, 61*, 65–81.

Belke, T. W., & Spetch, M. (1994). Choice between reliable and unreliable reinforcement alternatives revisited: Preference for unreliable reinforcement. *Journal of the Experimental Analysis of Behavior, 62*, 353–366.

Berlyne, D. E. (1969). The reward value of indifferent stimulation. In J. Tapp (Ed.), *Reinforcement and behavior* (pp. 178–214). New York: Academic Press.

Bernstein, D. J., & Ebbesen, E. B. (1978). Reinforcement and substitution in humans: A multiple response analysis. *Journal of the Experimental Analysis of Behavior, 30*, 243–253.

Bernstein, I. L. (1978). Learned taste aversions in children receiving chemotherapy. *Science, 200*, 1302–1303.

Bernstein, I. L. (1991). Aversion conditioning in response to cancer and cancer treatment. *Clinical Psychology Review, 11*, 185–191.

Bernstein, I. L., & Borson, S. (1986). Learned food aversion: A component

of anorexia syndromes. *Psychological Review, 93*, 462–472.

Bernstein, I. L., & Webster, M. M. (1980). Learned taste aversions in humans. *Physiology and Behavior, 25*, 363–366.

Berridge, K. C., & Schulkin, J. (1989). Palatability shift of a salt-associated incentive during sodium depletion. *Quarterly Journal of Experimental Psychology, 41B*, 121–138.

Best, M. R., Dunn, D. P., Batson, J. D., Meachum, C. L., & Nash, S. M. (1985). Extinguishing conditioned inhibition in flavour-aversion learning: Effects of repeated testing and extinction of the excitatory element. *Quarterly Journal of Experimental Psychology, 37B*, 359–378.

Bevins, R. A., & Ayres, J. J. B. (1994). Factors affecting rats' location during conditioned suppression training. *Animal Learning and Behavior, 22*, 302–308.

Bhatt, R. S., & Wasserman, E. A. (1987). Choice behavior of pigeons on progressive and multiple schedules: A test of optimal foraging theory. *Journal of Experimental Psychology: Animal Behavior Processes, 13*, 40–51.

Bhatt, R. S., Rovee-Collier, C., & Shyi, G. C.-W. (1994). Global and local processing of incidental information and memory retrieval at 6 months. *Journal of Experimental Child Psychology, 52*, 141–162.

Bhatt, R. S., Wasserman, E. A., Reynolds, W. F., Jr., & Knauss, K. S. (1988). Conceptual behavior in pigeons: Categorization of both familiar and novel examples from four classes of natural and artificial stimuli. *Journal of Experimental Psychology: Animal Behavior Processes, 14*, 219–234.

Bickel, W. K., DeGrandpre, R. J., Hughes, J. R., & Higgins, S. T. (1991). Behavioral economics of drug self administration. II. A unit-price analysis of cigarette smoking. *Journal of the Experimental Analysis of Behavior, 55*, 145–154.

Bickel, W. K., Green, L., & Vuchinich, R. E. (1995). Behavioral economics.

Journal of the Experimental Analysis of Behavior, 64, 257–262.

Bitterman, M. E. (1964). Classical conditioning in the goldfish as a function of the CS-US interval. *Journal of Comparative and Physiological Psychology, 58,* 359–366.

Bitterman, M. E. (1975). The comparative analysis of learning. *Science, 188,* 699–709.

Bitterman, M. E. (1988). Vertebrate-invertebrate comparisons. In H. J. Jerison & I. Jerison (Eds.), *Intelligence and evolutionary biology* (NATO ASI Series, Vol. G17, pp. 251–276). Berlin: Springer.

Bitterman, M. E. (1996). Comparative analysis of learning in honeybees. *Animal Learning & Behavior, 24,* 123–141.

Bizo, L. A., & White, K. G. (1994). Pacemaker rate in the behavioral theory of timing. *Journal of Experimental Psychology: Animal Behavior Processes, 20,* 308–321.

Bizo, L. A., & White, K. G. (1995a). Biasing the pacemaker in the behavioral theory of timing. *Journal of the Experimental Analysis of Behavior, 64,* 225–235.

Bizo, L. A., & White, K. G. (1995b). Reinforcement context and pacemaker rate in the behavioral theory of timing. *Animal Learning & Behavior, 23,* 376–382.

Bjork, R. A. (1972). The updating of human memory. In G. H. Bower (Ed.), *The psychology of learning and motivation* (Vol. 12, pp. 235–259). New York: Academic Press.

Black, A. H. (1971). Autonomic aversive conditioning in infrahuman subjects. In F. R. Brush (Ed.), *Aversive conditioning and learning* (pp. 3–104). New York: Academic Press.

Black, A. H. (1977). Comments on "Learned helplessness: Theory and evidence" by Maier and Seligman. *Journal of Experimental Psychology: General, 106,* 41–43.

Blackman, D. (1977). Conditioned suppression and the effects of classical conditioning on operant behavior. In W. K. Honig & J. E. R. Staddon (Eds.), *Handbook of operant behavior* (pp. 340–363). Englewood Cliffs, NJ: Prentice-Hall.

Blakely, E., & Schlinger, H. (1988). Determinants of pausing under variable-ratio schedules: Reinforcer magnitude, ratio size, and schedule configuration. *Journal of the Experimental Analysis of Behavior, 50,* 65–73.

Blakemore, C., & Cooper, G. F. (1970). Development of the brain depends on visual environment. *Science, 228,* 477–478.

Blass, E. M., Ganchrow, J. R., & Steiner, J. E. (1984). Classical conditioning in newborn humans 2–48 hours of age. *Infant Behavior and Development, 7,* 223–235.

Blough, D. S. (1959). Delayed matching in the pigeon. *Journal of the Experimental Analysis of Behavior, 2,* 151–160.

Boakes, R. A. (1984). *From Darwin to behaviourism.* Cambridge: Cambridge University Press.

Boakes, R. A., & Halliday, M. S. (Eds.). (1972). *Inhibition and learning.* London: Academic Press.

Boice, R. (1973). Domestication. *Psychological Bulletin, 80,* 215–230.

Boice, R. (1977). Burrows of wild and albino rats: Effects of domestication, outdoor raising, age, experience, and maternal state. *Journal of Comparative and Physiological Psychology, 91,* 649–661.

Boice, R. (1981). Behavioral comparability of wild and domesticated rats. *Behavior Genetics, 11,* 545–553.

Bolles, R. C. (1969). Avoidance and escape learning: Simultaneous acquisition of different responses. *Journal of Comparative and Physiological Psychology, 68,* 355–358.

Bolles, R. C. (1970). Species-specific defense reactions and avoidance learning. *Psychological Review, 71,* 32–48.

Bolles, R. C. (1971). Species-specific defense reactions. In F. R. Brush (Ed.), *Aversive conditioning and learning* (pp. 183–233). New York: Academic Press.

Bolles, R. C. (1972a). The avoidance learning problem. In G. H. Bower (Ed.), *The psychology of learning and motivation* (Vol. 6, pp. 97–145). New York: Academic Press.

Bolles, R. C. (1972b). Reinforcement, expectancy, and learning. *Psychological Review, 79,* 394–409.

Bolles, R. C. (1975). *Theory of motivation* (2nd ed.). New York: Harper & Row.

Bolles, R. C., & Fanselow, M. S. (1980). A perceptual defensive-recuperative model of fear and pain. *Behavioral and Brain Sciences, 3,* 291–323.

Bolles, R. C., & Grossen, N. E. (1969). Effects of an informational stimulus on the acquisition of avoidance behavior in rats. *Journal of Comparative and Physiological Psychology, 68,* 90–99.

Bolles, R. C., & Riley, A. L. (1973). Freezing as an avoidance response: Another look at the operant-respondent distinction. *Learning and Motivation, 4,* 268–275.

Bolles, R. C., Holtz, R., Dunn, T., & Hill, W. (1980). Comparisons of stimulus learning and response learning in a punishment situation. *Learning and Motivation, 11,* 78–96.

Bolles, R. C., Stokes, L. W., & Younger, M. S. (1966). Does CS termination reinforce avoidance behavior? *Journal of Comparative and Physiological Psychology, 62,* 201–207.

Bonardi, C., Rey, V., Richmond, M., & Hall, G. (1993). Acquired equivalence of cues in pigeon autoshaping: Effects of training with common consequences and with common antecedents. *Animal Learning & Behavior, 21,* 369–376.

Borovsky, D., & Rovee-Collier, C. (1990). Contextual constraints on memory retrieval at six months. *Child Development, 61,* 1569–1583.

Borszcz, G. S., Cranney, J., & Leaton, R. N. (1989). Influence of long-term sensitization on long-term habituation of the acoustic startle response in rats: Central gray lesions, preexposure, and extinction. *Journal of Experimental Psychology: Animal Behavior Processes, 15,* 54–64.

Bouton, M. E. (1991). Context and retrieval in extinction and in other examples of interference in simple associative learning. In L. Dachowski & C. F. Flaherty (Eds.), *Current topics in animal learning* (pp. 25–53). Hillsdale, NJ: Erlbaum.

Bouton, M. E. (1993). Context, time, and memory retrieval in the interference paradigms of Pavlovian learning. *Psychological Bulletin, 114,* 80–99.

Bouton, M. E. (1994). Conditioning, remembering, and forgetting. *Journal of Experimental Psychology: Animal Behavior Processes, 20,* 219–231.

Bouton, M. E., & Bolles, R. C. (1980). Conditioned fear assessed by freezing and by the suppression of three different baselines. *Animal Learning & Behavior, 8,* 429–434.

Bouton, M. E., & Bolles, R. C. (1985). Contexts, event memories, and extinction. In P. Balsam & A. Tomie (Eds.), *Context and conditioning* (pp. 133–166). Hillsdale, NJ: Erlbaum.

Bouton, M. E., & Peck, C. A. (1989). Context effects on conditioning, extinction, and reinstatement in an appetitive conditioning preparation. *Animal Learning & Behavior, 17,* 188–198.

Bouton, M. E., & Swartzentruber, D. (1986). Analysis of the associative and occasion-setting properties of contexts participating in a Pavlovian discrimination. *Journal of Experimental Psychology: Animal Behavior Processes, 12,* 333–350.

Bowe, C. A., Miller, J. D., & Green, L. (1987). Qualities and locations of stimuli and responses affecting discrimination learning of chinchillas (*Chinchilla laniger*) and pigeons (*Columbia livia*). *Journal of Comparative Psychology, 101,* 132–138.

Brakke, K. E., & Savage-Rumbaugh, E. S. (1995). The development of language skills in bonobo and chimpanzee. I. Comprehension. *Language & Communication, 15,* 121–148.

Braveman, N. S., & Bronstein, P. (Eds.). (1985). *Annals of the New York Academy of Sciences: Vol. 443. Experimental assessments and clinical applications of conditioned food aversions.* New York: New York Academy of Sciences.

Breland, K., & Breland, M. (1961). The misbehavior of organisms. *American Psychologist, 16,* 681–684.

Brener, J., & Mitchell, S. (1989). Changes in energy expenditure and work during response acquisition in rats. *Journal of Experimental Psychology: Animal Behavior Processes, 15,* 166–175.

Brodbeck, D. R. (1994). Memory for spatial and local cues: A comparison of a storing and a nonstoring species. *Animal Learning & Behavior, 22,* 119–133.

Brodbeck, D. R., & Shettleworth, S. J. (1995). Matching location and color of a compound stimulus: Comparison of a food-storing and a nonstoring bird species. *Journal of Experimental Psychology: Animal Behavior Processes, 21,* 64–77.

Brogden, W. J., Lipman, E. A., & Culler, E. (1938). The role of incentive in conditioning and extinction. *American Journal of Psychology, 51,* 109–117.

Brooks, D. C., & Bouton, M. E. (1993). A retrieval cue for extinction attenuates spontaneous recovery. *Journal of Experimental Psychology: Animal Behavior Processes, 19,* 77–89.

Brown, B. L., Hemmes, N. S., & de Vaca, S. C. (1992). Effects of intra-trial stimulus change on fixed-interval performance: The roles of clock and memory processes. *Animal Learning & Behavior, 20,* 83–93.

Brown, J. S. (1969). Factors affecting self-punitive behavior. In B. Campbell & R. M. Church (Eds.), *Punishment and aversive behavior* (pp. 467–514). New York: Appleton-Century-Crofts.

Brown, J. S., & Cunningham, C. L. (1981). The paradox of persisting self-punitive behavior. *Neuroscience & Biobehavioral Reviews, 5,* 343–354.

Brown, J. S., & Jacobs, A. (1949). The role of fear in the motivation and acquisition of responses. *Journal of Experimental Psychology, 39,* 747–759.

Brown, M. F., Wheeler, E. A., & Riley, D. A. (1989). Evidence for a shift in the choice criterion of rats in a 12-arm radial maze. *Animal Learning & Behavior, 17,* 12–20.

Brown, P. L., & Jenkins, H. M. (1968). Auto-shaping the pigeon's key peck. *Journal of the Experimental Analysis of Behavior, 11,* 1–8.

Brown, S. W., & Mellgren, R. L. (1994). Distinction between places and paths in rats' spatial representations. *Journal of Experimental Psychology: Animal Behavior Processes, 20,* 20–31.

Bruner, D., Gibbon, J., & Fairhurst, S. (1994). Choice between fixed and variable delays with different reward amounts. *Journal of Experimental Psychology: Animal Behavior Processes, 20,* 331–346.

Bull, J. A., III, & Overmier, J. B. (1968). Additive and subtractive properties of excitation and inhibition. *Journal of Comparative and Physiological Psychology, 66,* 511–514.

Bull, J. A., III. (1970). An interaction between appetitive Pavlovian CS's and instrumental avoidance responding. *Learning and Motivation, 1,* 18–26.

Burkhard, B., Rachlin, H., & Schrader, S. (1978). Reinforcement and punishment in a closed system. *Learning and Motivation, 9,* 392–410.

Burkhardt, P. E., & Ayres, J. J. B. (1978). CS and US duration effects in one-trial simultaneous conditioning as assessed by conditioned suppression of licking in rats. *Animal Learning and Behavior, 6,* 225–230.

Burns, M., & Domjan, M. (1996). Sign tracking versus goal tracking in the sexual conditioning of male Japanese quail (*Coturnix japonica*). *Journal of Experimental Psychology: Animal Behavior Processes, 22,* 297–306.

Cameron, J., & Pierce, W. D. (1994). Reinforcement, reward, and intrinsic motivation: A meta-analysis. *Review of Educational Research, 64,* 363–423.

Camhi, J. M. (1984). *Neuroethology.* Sunderland, MA: Sinauer.

Camp, D. S., Raymond, G. A., & Church, R. M. (1967). Temporal relationship between response and punishment. *Journal of Experimental Psychology, 74,* 114–123.

Campbell, B. A., & Church, R. M. (Eds.). (1969). *Punishment and aversive behavior.* New York: Appleton-Century-Crofts.

Campbell, B. A., & Randall, P. K. (1976). The effect of reinstatement stimulus conditions on the maintenance of long-term memory. *Developmental Psychobiology, 9,* 325–333.

Cándido, A., Maldonado, A., & Vila, J. (1991). Effects of duration of feedback on signaled avoidance. *Animal Learning & Behavior, 19,* 81–87.

Capaldi, E. J. (1967). A sequential hypothesis of instrumental learning. In K. W. Spence & J. T. Spence (Eds.), *The psychology of learning and motivation* (Vol. 1, pp. 67–156). New York: Academic Press.

Capaldi, E. J. (1971). Memory and learning: A sequential viewpoint. In W. K. Honig & P. H. R. James (Eds.), *Animal memory* (pp. 115–154). New York: Academic Press.

Capaldi, E. J. (1992). Levels of organized behavior in rats. In W. K. Honig & J. G. Fetterman (Eds.), *Cognitive aspects of stimulus control* (pp. 385–404). Hillsdale, NJ: Erlbaum.

Capaldi, E. J., Alptekin, S., & Birmingham, K. M. (1996). Instrumental performance and time between reinforcements: Intimate relation to learning or memory retrieval? *Animal Learning & Behavior, 24,* 211–220.

Capaldi, E. J., Alptekin, S., Miller, D. J., & Barry, K. (1992). The role of instrumental responses in memory retrieval in a T-maze. *Quarterly Journal of Experimental Psychology, 45B,* 65–76.

Capaldi, E. J., Miller, D. J., & Alptekin, S. (1989). Multiple food-unit-incentive effect: Nonconservation of weight of food reward by rats. *Journal of Experimental Psychology: Animal Behavior Processes, 15,* 75–80.

Capaldi, E. J., Miller, D. J., Alptekin, S., & Barry, K. (1990). Organized responding in instrumental learning: Chunks and superchunks. *Learning and Motivation, 21,* 415–433.

Carew, T. J., Hawkins, R. D., & Kandel, E. R. (1983). Differential classical conditioning of a defensive withdrawal reflex in *Aplysia californica. Science, 219,* 397–400.

Carr, W. J., Loeb, L. S., & Dissinger, M. E. (1965). Responses of rats to sex odors. *Journal of Comparative and Physiological Psychology, 59,* 370–377.

Carrell, L. E., Cannon, D. S., Best, M. R., & Stone, M. J. (1986). Nausea and radiation-induced taste aversions in cancer patients. *Appetite, 7,* 203–208.

Carroll, M. E., Carmona, G. G., & May, S. A. (1991). Modifying drug-reinforced behavior by altering the economic conditions of the drug and nondrug reinforcer. *Journal of the Experimental Analysis of Behavior, 56,* 361–376.

Carter, M. M., Hollon, S. D., Carson, R., & Shelton, R. C. (1995). Effects of a safe person on induced distress following a biological challenge in panic disorder with agoraphobics. *Journal of Abnormal Psychology, 104,* 156–163.

Case, D. A., Nichols, P., & Fantino, E. (1995). Pigeons' preference for variable-interval water reinforcement under widely varied water budgets. *Journal of the Experimental Analysis of Behavior, 64,* 299–311.

Caspy, T., & Lubow, R. E. (1981). Generality of US preexposure effects: Transfer from food to shock or shock to food with and without the same response requirements. *Animal Learning & Behavior, 9,* 524–532.

Cerella, J. (1982). Mechanisms of concept formation in the pigeon. In D. J. Ingle, M. A. Goodale, & R. J. W. Mansfield (Eds.), *Analysis of visual behavior.* Cambridge, MA: M.I.T. Press.

Cerletti, U., & Bini, L. (1938). Electric shock treatment. *Bollettino ed atti della Accademia medica di Roma, 64,* 36.

Charlop, M. H., Kurtz, P. F., & Casey, F. G. (1990). Using aberrant behaviors as reinforcers for autistic children. *Journal of Applied Behavior Analysis, 23,* 163–181.

Cheng, K., & Spetch, M. L. (1995). Stimulus control in the use of landmarks by pigeons in a touch-screen task. *Journal of the Experimental Analysis of Behavior, 63,* 187–201.

Cheng, K., & Westwood, R. (1993). Analysis of single trials in pigeons' timing performance. *Journal of Experimental Psychology: Animal Behavior Processes, 19,* 56–67.

Cheng, K., Westwood, R., & Crystal, J. D. (1993). Memory variance in the peak procedure of timing in pigeons. *Journal of Experimental Psychology: Animal Behavior Processes, 19,* 68–76.

Chomsky, N. (1972). *Language and mind.* New York: Harcourt Brace Jovanovich.

Chung, S.-H., & Herrnstein, R. J. (1967). Choice and delay of reinforcement. *Journal of the Experimental Analysis of Behavior, 10,* 67–74.

Church, R. M. (1963). The varied effects of punishment on behavior. *Psychological Review, 70,* 369–402.

Church, R. M. (1969). Response suppression. In B. A. Campbell & R. M. Church (Eds.), *Punishment and aversive behavior* (pp. 111–156). New York: Appleton-Century-Crofts.

Church, R. M. (1978). The internal clock. In S. H. Hulse, H. Fowler, & W. K. Honig (Eds.), *Cognitive processes in animal behavior* (pp. 277–310). Hillsdale, NJ: Erlbaum.

Church, R. M. (1989). Theories of timing. In S. B. Klein & R. R. Mowrer (Eds.), *Contemporary learning theories: Instrumental conditioning and the impact of biological constraints on learning* (pp. 41–71). Hillsdale, NJ: Erlbaum.

Church, R. M., Getty, D. J., & Lerner, N. D. (1976). Duration discrimination by rats. *Journal of Experimental Psychology: Animal Behavior Processes, 2,* 303–312.

Church, R. M., Meck, W. H., & Gibbon, J. (1994). Application of scalar timing theory to individual trials. *Journal of Experimental Psychology: Animal Behavior Processes, 20,* 135–155.

Church, R. M., Miller, K. D., Meck, W. H., & Gibbon, J. (1991). Symmetrical and asymmetrical sources of variance in temporal generalization. *Animal Learning & Behavior, 19,* 207–214.

Cicala, G. A., & Owen, J. W. (1976). Warning signal termination and a feedback signal may not serve the same function. *Learning and Motivation, 7,* 356–367.

Clayton, N. S., & Krebs, J. R. (1994). One-trial associative memory: Comparison of food-storing and nonstoring species of birds. *Animal Learning & Behavior, 22,* 366–372.

Cleland, G. G., & Davey, G. C. L. (1982). The effects of satiation and reinforcer devaluation on signal-centered behavior in the rat. *Learning and Motivation, 13,* 343–360.

Cleland, G. G., & Davey, G. C. L. (1983). Autoshaping in the rat: The effects of localizable visual and auditory signals for food. *Journal of the Experimental Analysis of Behavior, 40,* 47–56.

Cohen, J. S., Reid, S., & Chew, K. (1994). Effects of varying trial distribution, intra- and extramaze cues, and amount of reward on proactive interference in the radial maze. *Animal Learning & Behavior, 22,* 134–142.

Cohen, L. B. (1988). An information processing view of infant cognitive development. In L. Weiskrantz (Ed.), *Thought without language* (pp. 211–228). Oxford: Oxford University Press.

Cole, M. R. (1994). Response-rate differences in variable-interval and variable-ratio schedules: An old problem revisited. *Journal of the Experimental Analysis of Behavior, 61,* 441–451.

Cole, R. P., Barnet, R. C., & Miller, R. R. (1995). Effect of relative stimulus validity: Learning or performance deficit? *Journal of Experimental Psychology: Animal Behavior Processes, 21,* 293–303.

Coleman, S. R. (1975). Consequences of response contingent change in unconditioned stimulus intensity upon the rabbit (*Oryctolagus cuniculus*) nictitating membrane response. *Journal of Comparative and Physiological Psychology, 88,* 591–595.

Coleman, S. R., & Gormezano, I. (1979). Classical conditioning and the "Law of Effect": Historical and empirical assessment. *Behaviorism, 7,* 1–33.

Collias, N. E. (1990). Statistical evidence for aggressive response to red by male three-spined sticklebacks. *Animal Behaviour, 39,* 401–403.

Collier, G., Johnson, D. F., & Morgan, C. (1992). The magnitude-of-reinforcement function in closed and open economies. *Journal of the Experimental Analysis of Behavior, 57,* 81–89.

Colombo, M., & D'Amato, M. R. (1986). A comparison of visual and auditory short-term memory in monkeys (*Cebus apella*). *Quarterly Journal of Experimental Psychology, 38B,* 425–448.

Colwill, R. M. (1994). Associative representations of instrumental contingencies. *The psychology of learning and motivation* (Vol. 31, pp. 1–72). San Diego: Academic Press.

Colwill, R. M., & Delamater, B. A. (1995). An associative analysis of instrumental biconditional discrimination learning. *Animal Learning & Behavior, 23,* 218–233.

Colwill, R. M., & Motzkin, D. K. (1994). Encoding of the unconditioned stimulus in Pavlovian conditioning. *Animal Learning & Behavior, 22,* 384–394.

Colwill, R. M., & Rescorla, R. A. (1986). Associative structures in instrumental learning. In G. H. Bower (Ed.), *The psychology of learning and motivation* (Vol. 20, pp. 55–104). Orlando, FL: Academic Press.

Colwill, R. M., & Rescorla, R. A. (1990). Evidence for the hierarchical structure of instrumental learning. *Animal Learning & Behavior, 18,* 71–82.

Commons, M. L., Herrnstein, R. J., & Rachlin, H. (Eds.). (1982). *Quantitative analyses of behavior: Vol. 2. Matching and maximizing accounts.* Cambridge, MA: Ballinger.

Commons, M. L., Herrnstein, R. J., Kosslyn, S. M., & Mumford, D. B. (Eds.). (1990). *Quantitative analyses of behavior: Vol. 8. Behavioral approaches to pattern recognition and concept formation.* Hillsdale, NJ: Erlbaum.

Commons, M. L., Kacelnik, A., & Shettleworth, S. J. (Eds.). (1987). *Quantitative analyses of behavior: Vol. 6. Foraging.* Hillsdale, NJ: Erlbaum.

Conger, R., & Killeen, P. (1974). Use of concurrent operants in small group research. *Pacific Sociological Review, 17,* 399–416.

Cook, M., & Mineka, S. (1990). Selective associations in the observational conditioning of fear in rhesus monkeys. *Journal of Experimental Psychology: Animal Behavior Processes, 16,* 372–389.

Cook, M., Mineka, S., & Trumble, D. (1987). The role of response-produced and exteroceptive feedback in the attenuation of fear over the course of avoidance learning. *Journal of Experimental Psychology: Animal Behavior Processes, 13,* 239–249.

Cook, R. G. (1980). Retroactive interference in pigeon short-term memory by a reduction in ambient illumination. *Journal of Experimental Psychology: Animal Behavior Processes, 6,* 326–338.

Cook, R. G., Brown, M. F., & Riley, D. A. (1985). Flexible memory processing by rats: Use of prospective and retrospective information in the radial maze. *Journal of Experimental Psychology: Animal Behavior Processes, 11,* 453–469.

Cooper, L. D. (1991). Temporal factors in classical conditioning. *Learning and Motivation, 22,* 129–152.

Cooper, L. D., Aronson, L., Balsam, P. D., & Gibbon, J. (1990). Duration of signals for intertrial reinforcement and nonreinforcement in random control procedures. *Journal of Experimental Psychology: Animal Behavior Processes, 16,* 14–26.

Coulter, X., Riccio, D. C., & Page, H. A. (1969). Effects of blocking an instrumental avoidance response: Facilitated extinction but persistence of "fear." *Journal of Comparative and Physiological Psychology, 68,* 377–381.

Craske, M. G., Glover, D., & DeCola, J. (1995). Predicted vs. unpredicted panic attacks: Acute versus general distress. *Journal of Abnormal Psychology, 104,* 214–223.

Crawford, L. L., & Domjan, M. (1993). Sexual approach conditioning: Omission contingency tests. *Animal Learning & Behavior, 21,* 42–50.

Crespi, L. P. (1942). Quantitative variation in incentive and performance in the white rat. *American Journal of Psychology, 55,* 467–517.

Critchfield, T. S., & Lattal, K. A. (1993). Acquisition of a spatially defined operant with delayed reinforcement. *Journal of the Experimental Analysis of Behavior, 59,* 373–387.

Cronin, P. B. (1980). Reinstatement of post response stimuli prior to reward in delayed-reward discrimination learning by pigeons. *Animal Learning & Behavior, 8,* 352–358.

Crossman, E. K., Bonem, E. J., & Phelps, B. J. (1987). A comparison of response patterns on fixed-, variable-, and random-ratio schedules. *Journal of the Experimental Analysis of Behavior, 48,* 395–406.

Crozier, W. J., & Navez, A. E. (1930). The geotropic orientation of gastropods. *Journal of General Physiology, 3,* 3–37.

Culler, E. A. (1938). Recent advances in some concepts of conditioning. *Psychological Review, 45,* 134–153.

Cunningham, C. L. (1993). Pavlovian drug conditioning. In F. van Haaren (Ed.), *Methods in behavioral pharmacology* (pp. 349–381). Amsterdam: Elsevier.

Cunningham, C. L. (1997). Drug conditioning and drug-seeking behavior. In W. O'Donohue (Ed.), *Learning and behavior therapy,* 156.

D'Amato, M. R. (1973). Delayed matching and short-term memory in monkeys. In G. H. Bower (Ed.), *The psychology of learning and motivation* (Vol. 7, pp. 227–269). New York: Academic Press.

D'Amato, M. R., & Colombo, M. (1985). Auditory matching-to-sample in monkeys (*Cebus apella*). *Animal Learning & Behavior, 13,* 375–382.

D'Amato, M. R., & Colombo, M. (1988). Representation of serial order in monkeys (*Cebus apella*). *Journal of Experimental Psychology: Animal Behavior Processes, 14,* 131–139.

D'Amato, M. R., & Colombo, M. (1989). Serial learning with wild card items by monkeys (*Cebus apella*): Implications for knowledge of ordinal position. *Journal of Comparative Psychology, 103,* 252–261.

D'Amato, M. R., & Colombo, M. (1990). The symbolic distance effect in monkeys (*Cebus apella*). *Animal Learning & Behavior, 18,* 133–140.

D'Amato, M. R., & Salmon, D. P. (1982). Tune discrimination in monkeys (*Cebus apella*) and in rats. *Animal Learning & Behavior, 10,* 126–134.

D'Amato, M. R., & Van Sant, P. (1988). The person concept in monkeys (*Cebus apella*). *Journal of Experimental Psychology: Animal Behavior Processes, 14,* 43–55.

D'Amato, M. R., Fazzaro, J., & Etkin, M. (1968). Anticipatory responding and avoidance discrimination as factors in avoidance conditioning. *Journal of Comparative and Physiological Psychology, 77,* 41–47.

Dallal, N. L., & Meck, W. H. (1990). Hierarchical structures: Chunking by food type facilitates spatial memory. *Journal of Experimental Psychology: Animal Behavior Processes, 16,* 69–84.

Dardano, J. F., & Sauerbrunn, D. (1964). An aversive stimulus as a correlated block counter in FR performance. *Journal of the Experimental Analysis of Behavior, 7,* 37–43.

Darwin, C. (1897). *The descent of man and selection in relation to sex.* New York: Appleton-Century-Crofts.

Davey, G. C. L. (1995). Preparedness and phobias: Specific evolved associations or a generalized expectancy bias? *Behavioral and Brain Sciences, 18,* 289–325.

Davey, G. C. L., & Cleland, G. G. (1982). Topography of signal-centered behavior in the rat: Effects of deprivation state and reinforcer type. *Journal of the Experimental Analysis of Behavior, 38,* 291–304.

Davey, G. C. L., Phillips, S., & Cleland, G. G. (1981). The topography of signal-centered behaviour in the rat: The effects of solid and liquid food reinforcers. *Behaviour Analysis Letters, 1,* 331–337.

Davidson, T. L., Aparicio, J., & Rescorla, R. A. (1988). Transfer between Pavlovian facilitators and instrumental discriminative stimuli. *Animal Learning & Behavior, 16,* 285–291.

Davidson, T. L., Flynn, F. W., & Jarrard, L. E. (1992). Potency of food deprivation intensity cues as discriminative stimuli. *Journal of Experimental Psychology: Animal Behavior Processes, 18,* 174–181.

Davis, E. R., & Platt, J. R. (1983). Contiguity and contingency in the acquisition and maintenance of an operant. *Learning and Motivation, 14,* 487–512.

Davis, H. (1968). Conditioned suppression: A survey of the literature. *Psychonomic Monograph Supplements, 2* (14, Whole No. 30), 283–291.

Davis, H., & Kreuter, C. (1972). Conditioned suppression of an avoidance response by a stimulus paired with food. *Journal of the Experimental Analysis of Behavior, 17,* 277–285.

Davis, H., & Shattuck, D. (1980). Transfer of conditioned suppression and conditioned acceleration from instrumental to consummatory baselines. *Animal Learning & Behavior, 8,* 253–257.

Davis, M. (1974). Sensitization of the rat startle response by noise. *Journal of Comparative and Physiological Psychology, 87,* 571–581.

Davis, M., & File, S. E. (1984). Intrinsic and extrinsic mechanisms of habituation and sensitization: Implications for the design and analysis of experiments. In H. V. S. Peeke & L. Petrinovich (Eds.), *Habituation, sensitization, and behavior.* New York: Academic Press.

Davis, M., Hitchcock, J. M., & Rosen, J. B. (1987). Anxiety and the amygdala: Pharmacological and anatomical analysis of the fear-potentiated startle paradigm. In G. H. Bower (Ed.), *The psychology of learning and motivation* (Vol. 21, pp. 263–304). Orlando, FL: Academic Press.

Davis, D. G., Staddon, J. E. R., Machado, A., & Palmer, R. G. (1993). The process of recurrent choice. *Psychological Review, 100,* 320–341.

Davison, M. (1991a). Choice, changeover, and travel: A quantitative model. *Journal of the Experimental Analysis of Behavior, 55,* 47–61.

Davison, M. (1991b). Concurrent schedules: Effects of time and response-allocation constraints. *Journal of the Experimental Analysis of Behavior, 55,* 189–200.

Davison, M. (1992). Choice between repleting/depleting patches: A concurrent-schedule procedure. *Journal of the Experimental Analysis of Behavior, 58,* 445–469.

Davison, M., & Jones, B. M. (1995). A quantitative analysis of extreme choice. *Journal of the Experimental Analysis of Behavior, 64,* 147–162.

Davison, M., & McCarthy, D. (1988). *The matching law: A research review.* Hillsdale, NJ: Erlbaum.

Davison, M., & McCarthy, D. (1994). Leaving patches: An investigation of a laboratory analogue. *Journal of the Experimental Analysis of Behavior, 62,* 89–108.

Dawson, G. R., & Dickinson, A. (1990). Performance on ratio and interval schedules with matched reinforcement rates. *Quarterly Journal of Experimental Psychology, 42B,* 225–239.

Dean, S. J., & Pittman, C. M. (1991). Self-punitive behavior: A revised analysis. In M. R. Denny (Ed.), *Fear, avoidance and phobias* (pp. 259–284). Hillsdale, NJ: Erlbaum.

DeCarlo, L. T. (1985). Matching and maximizing with variable-time schedules. *Journal of the Experimental Analysis of Behavior, 43,* 75–81.

DeCola, J. P., & Rosellini, R. A. (1990). Unpredictable/ uncontrollable stress proactively interferes with appetitive Pavlovian conditioning. *Learning and Motivation, 21,* 137–152.

DeCola, J. P., Rosellini, R. A., & Warren, D. A. (1988). A dissociation of the effects of control and prediction. *Learning and Motivation, 19,* 269–282.

DeGrandpre, R. J., Bickel, W. K., Rizvi, S. A. T., & Hughes, J. R. (1993). Effect of income on drug choice in humans. *Journal of the Experimental Analysis of Behavior, 59,* 483–500.

Deich, J. D., Allan, R. W., & Zeigler, H. P. (1988). Conjunctive differentiation of gape during food-reinforced keypecking in the pigeon. *Animal Learning & Behavior, 16,* 268–276.

DeKeyne, A., & Deweer, B. (1990). Interaction between conflicting memories in the rat: Contextual pretest cuing reverses control of behavior by testing context. *Animal Learning & Behavior, 18,* 1–12.

Delprato, D. J. (1969). Extinction of one-way avoidance and delayed warning signal termination. *Journal of Experimental Psychology, 80,* 192–193.

DeMarse, T. B., & Urcuioli, P. J. (1993). Enhancement of matching acquisition by differential comparison–outcome associations. *Journal of Experimental Psychology: Animal Behavior Processes, 19,* 317–326.

Desiderato, O. (1969). Generalization of excitation and inhibition in control of avoidance responding by Pavlovian CS's in dogs. *Journal of Comparative and Physiological Psychology, 68,* 611–616.

deVaca, S. C., Brown, B. L., Hemmes, N. S. (1994). Internal clock and memory processes in animal timing. *Journal of Experimental Psychology: Animal Behavior Processes, 20,* 184–198.

deVilliers, P. A. (1974). The law of effect and avoidance: A quantitative relationship between response rate and shock-frequency reduction. *Journal of the Experimental Analysis of Behavior, 21,* 223–235.

DeVito, P. L., & Fowler, H. (1986). Effects of contingency violations on the extinction of a conditioned fear inhibitor and conditioned fear excitor. *Journal of Experimental Psychology: Animal Behavior Processes, 12,* 99–115.

DeVito, P. L., & Fowler, H. (1987). Enhancement of conditioned inhibition via an extinction treatment. *Animal Learning & Behavior, 15,* 448–454.

Dickinson, A., & Dearing, M. F. (1979). Appetitive aversive interactions and inhibitory processes. In A. Dickinson & R. A. Boakes (Eds.), *Mechanisms of learning and motivation* (pp. 203–231). Hillsdale, NJ: Erlbaum.

Dickinson, A., & Pearce, J. M. (1977). Inhibitory interactions between appetitive and aversive stimuli. *Psychological Bulletin, 84,* 690–711.

Dickinson, A., Nicholas, D. J., & Macintosh, N. J. (1983). A re-examination of one-trial blocking in conditioned suppression. *Quarterly Journal of Experimental Psychology, 35,* 67–79.

Dickinson, A., Watt, A., & Griffiths, W. J. H. (1992). Free-operant acquisition with delayed reinforcement. *Quarterly Journal of Experimental Psychology, 45B,* 241–258.

Dinsmoor, J. A. (1952). A discrimination based on punishment. *Quarterly Journal of Experimental Psychology, 4,* 27–45.

Dinsmoor, J. A. (1954). Punishment: I. The avoidance hypothesis. *Psychological Review, 61,* 34–46.

Dinsmoor, J. A. (1962). Variable-interval escape from stimuli accompanied by shocks. *Journal of the Experimental Analysis of Behavior, 5,* 41–48.

Dinsmoor, J. A. (1977). Escape, avoidance, punishment: Where do we stand? *Journal of the Experimental Analysis of Behavior, 28,* 83–95.

Dinsmoor, J. A., & Sears, G. W. (1973). Control of avoidance by a response-produced stimulus. *Learning and Motivation, 4,* 284–293.

Dobrzecka, C., Szwejkowska, G., & Konorski, J. (1966). Qualitative versus directional cues in two forms of differentiation. *Science, 153,* 87–89.

Dolan, J. C., Shishimi, A., & Wagner, A. R. (1985). The effects of signaling the US in backward conditioning: A shift from excitatory to inhibitory learning. *Animal Learning & Behavior, 13,* 209–214.

Dollard, J., & Miller, N. E. (1950). *Personality and psychotherapy.* New York: McGraw-Hill.

Dollard, J., Miller, N. E., Doob, L. W., Mowrer, O. H., & Sears, R. R. (1939). *Frustration and aggression.* New Haven, CT: Yale University Press.

Domjan, M. (1976). Determinants of the enhancement of flavored-water intake by prior exposure. *Journal of Experimental Psychology: Animal Behavior Processes, 2,* 17–27.

Domjan, M. (1980). Ingestional aversion learning: Unique and general processes. In J. S. Rosenblatt, R. A. Hinde, C. Beer, & M. Busnel (Eds.), *Advances in the study of behavior* (Vol. 11, pp. 275–336). New York: Academic Press.

Domjan, M. (1983). Biological constraints on instrumental and classical conditioning: Implications for general process theory. In G. H. Bower (Ed.), *The psychology of learning and motivation* (Vol. 17, pp. 215–277). New York: Academic Press.

Domjan, M. (1987). Animal learning comes of age. *American Psychologist, 42,* 556–564.

Domjan, M., & Holloway, K. S. (1997). Sexual learning. In G. Greenberg and M. M. Harraway (Eds.), *The encyclopedia of comparative psychology.* New York: Garland.

Domjan, M., & Ravert, R. D. (1991). Discriminating the sex of conspecifics by male Japanese quail (*Coturnix coturnix japonica*). *Journal of Comparative Psychology, 105,* 157–164.

Domjan, M., Lyons, R., North, N. C., & Bruell, J. (1986). Sexual Pavlovian conditioned approach behavior in male Japanese quail (*Coturnix coturnix japonica*). *Journal of Comparative Psychology, 100,* 413–421.

Dougherty, D. M., & Lewis, P. (1991). Stimulus generalization, discrimination learning, and peak shift in horses. *Journal of the Experimental Analysis of Behavior, 56,* 97–104.

Dreyfus, L. R., DePorto-Callan, D., & Pesillo, S. A. (1993). Changeover contingencies and choice on concurrent schedules. *Animal Learning & Behavior, 21,* 203–213.

Ducharme, M. J., & Santi, A. (1993). Alterations in the memory code for temporal events induced by differential outcome expectancies in pigeons. *Animal Learning & Behavior, 21,* 73–81.

Duncan, C. P. (1949). The retroactive effect of electroshock on learning. *Journal of Comparative and Physiological Psychology, 42,* 32–44.

Durkin, M., Prescott, L., Furchtgott, E., Cantor, J., & Powell, D. A. (1993). Concomitant eyeblink and heart rate classical conditioning in young, mid-

dle-aged, and elderly human subjects. *Psychology and Aging, 8,* 571–581.

Durlach, P. J. (1983). Effect of signaling intertrial unconditioned stimuli in autoshaping. *Journal of Experimental Psychology: Animal Behavior Processes, 9,* 374–389.

Dweck, C. S., & Wagner, A. R. (1970). Situational cues and correlation between conditioned stimulus and unconditioned stimulus as determinants of the conditioned emotional response. *Psychonomic Science, 18,* 145–147.

Dworkin, B. R. (1993). *Learning and physiological regulation.* Chicago and London: University of Chicago Press.

Edhouse, W. V., & White, K. G. (1988a). Cumulative proactive interference in animal memory. *Animal Learning & Behavior, 16,* 461–467.

Edhouse, W. V., & White, K. G. (1988b). Sources of proactive interference in animal memory. *Journal of Experimental Psychology: Animal Behavior Processes, 14,* 56–70.

Edwards, C. A., & Honig, W. K. (1987). Memorization and "feature selection" in the acquisition of natural concepts in pigeons. *Learning and Motivation, 18,* 235–260.

Ehrman, R. N., Robbins, S. J., Childress, A. R., & O'Brien, C. P. (1992). Conditioned responses to cocaine-related stimuli in cocaine abuse patients. *Psychopharmacology, 107,* 523–529.

Eibl-Eibesfeldt, I. (1970). *Ethology: The biology of behavior.* New York: Holt, Rinehart and Winston.

Eisenberger, R., & Adornetto, M. (1986). Generalized self-control of delay and effort. *Journal of Personality and Social Psychology, 51,* 1020–1031.

Eisenberger, R., & Cameron, J. (1996). Detrimental effects of reward: Reality or myth? *American Psychologist, 51,* 1153–1166.

Eisenberger, R., Karpman, M., & Trattner, J. (1967). What is the necessary and sufficient condition for reinforcement in the contingency situation? *Journal of Experimental Psychology, 74,* 342–350.

Elliffe, D., & Alslop, B. (1996). Concurrent choice: Effects of overall reinforcer rate and the temporal distribution of reinforcers. *Journal of the Experimental Analysis of Behavior, 65,* 445–463.

Ellins, S. R., Cramer, R. E., & Martin, G. C. (1982). Discrimination reversal learning in newts. *Animal Learning & Behavior, 10,* 301–304.

Ellison, G. D. (1964). Differential salivary conditioning to traces. *Journal of Comparative and Physiological Psychology, 57,* 373–380.

Ellison, G. D., & Konorski, J. (1964). Separation of the salivary and motor responses in instrumental conditioning. *Science, 146,* 1071–1072.

English, J. A., Rowlett, J. K., & Woolverton, W. L. (1995). Unit-price analysis of opioid consumption by monkeys responding under a progressive-ratio schedule of drug injection. *Journal of the Experimental Analysis of Behavior, 64,* 361–371.

Estes, W. K. (1943). Discriminative conditioning: I. A discriminative property of conditioned anticipation. *Journal of Experimental Psychology, 32,* 150–155.

Estes, W. K. (1944). An experimental study of punishment. *Psychological Monographs, 57* (3, Whole No. 263).

Estes, W. K. (1948). Discriminative conditioning: II. Effects of a Pavlovian conditioned stimulus upon a subsequently established operant response. *Journal of Experimental Psychology, 38,* 173–177.

Estes, W. K. (1969). Outline of a theory of punishment. In B. A. Campbell & R. M. Church (Eds.), *Punishment and aversive behavior* (pp. 57–82). New York: Appleton-Century-Crofts.

Estes, W. K., & Skinner, B. F. (1941). Some quantitative properties of anxiety. *Journal of Experimental Psychology, 29,* 390–400.

Fagen, J. W., & Rovee-Collier, C. (1983). Memory retrieval: A time-locked process in infancy. *Science, 222,* 1349–1351.

Falls, W. A., & Kelsey, J. E. (1989). Procedures that produce context-specific tolerance to morphine in rats also produce context-specific withdrawal. *Behavioral Neuroscience, 103,* 842–849.

Fanselow, M. S. (1989). The adaptive function of conditioned defensive behavior: An ecological approach to Pavlovian stimulus-substitution theory. In R. J. Blanchard, P. F. Brain, D. C. Blanchard, & S. Parmigiani (Eds.), *Ethoexperimental approaches to the study of behavior* (NATO ASI Series D, Vol. 48, pp. 151–166). Boston: Kluver Academic Publishers.

Fanselow, M. S., & Lester, L. S. (1988). A functional behavioristic approach to aversively motivated behavior: Predatory imminence as a determinant of the topography of defensive behavior. In R. C. Bolles & M. D. Beecher (Eds.), *Evolution and learning* (pp. 185–212). Hillsdale, NJ: Erlbaum.

Fanselow, M. S., Lester, L. S., & Helmstetter, F. J. (1988). Changes in feeding and foraging patterns as an antipredator defensive strategy: A laboratory simulation using aversive stimulation in a closed economy. *Journal of the Experimental Analysis of Behavior, 50,* 361–374.

Fantino, E., & Abarca, N. (1985). Choice, optimal foraging, and the delay-reduction hypothesis. *Behavioral & Brain Sciences, 8,* 315–330.

Fantino, E., & Preston, R. A. (1988). Choice and foraging: Effects of accessibility on acceptability. *Journal of the Experimental Analysis of Behavior, 50,* 395–403.

Farley, J., & Alkon, D. L. (1980). Neural organization predicts stimulus specificity for a retained associative behavioral change. *Science, 210,* 1373–1375.

Feldman, D. T., & Gordon, W. C. (1979). The alleviation of short-term retention decrements with reactivation. *Learning and Motivation, 10,* 198–210.

Felton, M., & Lyon, D. O. (1966). The post-reinforcement pause. *Journal of the Experimental Analysis of Behavior, 9,* 131–134.

Ferster, C. B., & Skinner, B. F. (1957). *Schedules of reinforcement.* New York: Appleton-Century-Crofts.

Fetterman, J. G. (1995). The psychophysics of remembered duration. *Animal Learning & Behavior, 23,* 49–62.

Fetterman, J. G. (1996). Dimensions of stimulus complexity. *Journal of Experimental Psychology: Animal Behavior Processes, 22,* 3–18.

Fetterman, J. G., & Killeen, P. R. (1995). Categorical scaling of time: Implications for clock-counter models. *Journal of Experimental Psychology: Animal Behavior Processes, 21,* 43–63.

Fiori, L. M., Barnet, R. C., & Miller, R. R. (1994). Renewal of Pavlovian conditioned inhibition. *Animal Learning & Behavior, 22,* 47–52.

FitzGerald, R. E., Isler, R., Rosenberg, E., Oettinger, R., & Battig, K. (1985). Maze patrolling by rats with and without food reward. *Animal Learning & Behavior, 13,* 451–462.

Flaherty, C. F. (1982). Incentive contrast: A review of behavioral changes following shifts in reward. *Animal Learning & Behavior, 10,* 409–440.

Flaherty, C. F. (1991). Incentive contrast and selected animal models of anxiety. In L. Dachowski & C. F. Flaherty (Eds.), *Current topics in animal learning* (pp. 207–243). Hillsdale, NJ: Erlbaum.

Flaherty, C. F., & Rowan, G. A. (1986). Successive, simultaneous, and anticipatory contrast in the consumption of saccharin solutions. *Journal of Experimental Psychology: Animal Behavior Processes, 12,* 381–393.

Flexner, J. B., Flexner, L. B., & Stellar, E. (1963). Memory in mice as affected by intracerebral puromycin. *Science, 141,* 57–59.

Foa, E. B., Zinbarg, R., & Rothbaum, B. O. (1992). Uncontrollability and unpredictability in post-traumatic stress disorder: An animal model. *Psychological Review, 112,* 218–238.

Foltin, R. W. (1991). An economic analysis of "demand" for food in baboons. *Journal of the Experimental Analysis of Behavior, 56,* 445–454.

Foltin, R. W. (1994). Does package size matter? A unit-price analysis of "demand" for food in baboons. *Journal of the Experimental Analysis of Behavior, 62,* 293–306.

Foree, D. D., & LoLordo, V. M. (1973). Attention in the pigeon: The differential effects of food-getting vs. shock avoidance procedures. *Journal of Comparative and Physiological Psychology, 85,* 551–558.

Forestell, P. H., & Herman, L. M. (1988). Delayed matching of visual materials by a bottlenosed dolphin aided by auditory symbols. *Animal Learning & Behavior, 16,* 137–146.

Forzano, L. B., & Logue, A. W. (1994). Self-control in adult humans: Comparison of qualitatively different reinforcers. *Learning and Motivation, 25,* 65–82.

Foster, T. M., Temple, W., Robertson, B., Nair, V., & Poling, A. (1996). Concurrent-schedule performance in dairy cows: Persistent undermatching. *Journal of the Experimental Analysis of Behavior, 65,* 57–80.

Fountain, S. B. (1990). Rule abstraction, item memory, and chunking in rat serial-pattern tracking. *Journal of Experimental Psychology: Animal Behavior Processes, 16,* 96–105.

Fountain, S. B., & Rowan, J. D. (1995a). Coding of hierarchical versus linear pattern structure in rats and humans. *Journal of Experimental Psychology: Animal Behavior Processes, 21,* 187–202.

Fountain, S. B., & Rowan, J. D. (1995b). Sensitivity to violations of "run" and "trill" structures in rat serial-pattern learning. *Journal of Experimental Psychology: Animal Behavior Processes, 21,* 78–81.

Fowler, H., Kleiman, M. C., & Lysle, D. T. (1985). Factors controlling the acquisition and extinction of conditioned inhibition suggest a "slave" process. In R. R. Miller & N. E. Spear (Eds.), *Information processing in animals: Conditioned inhibition* (pp. 113–150). Hillsdale, NJ: Erlbaum.

Fowler, H., Lysle, D. T., & DeVito, P. L. (1991). Conditioned excitation and conditioned inhibition of fear: Asymmetrical processes as evident in extinction. In M. R. Denny (Ed.), *Fear, avoidance and phobias* (pp. 317–362). Hillsdale, NJ: Erlbaum.

Foxx, R. M., & Azrin, N. H. (1973). The elimination of autistic self-stimulatory behavior by overcorrection. *Journal of Applied Behavioral Analysis, 6,* 1–14.

Fraenkel, G. S., & Gunn, D. L. (1961). *The orientation of animals* (2nd ed.). New York: Dover.

France, K. G., & Hudson, S. M. (1990). Behavior management of infant sleep disturbance. *Journal of Applied Behavior Analysis, 23,* 91–98.

Frankel, F. D. (1975). The role of response-punishment contingency in the suppression of a positively reinforced operant. *Learning and Motivation, 6,* 385–403.

Gaffan, E. A., & Davies, J. (1981). The role of exploration in win-shift and win-stay performance on a radial maze. *Learning and Motivation, 12,* 282–299.

Galbicka, G. (1988). Differentiating the behavior of organisms. *Journal of the Experimental Analysis of Behavior, 50,* 343–354.

Gallup, G. G., Jr., & Suarez, S. D. (1985). Alternatives to the use of animals in psychological research. *American Psychologist, 40,* 1104–1111.

Gamzu, E. R., & Williams, D. R. (1971). Classical conditioning of a complex skeletal act. *Science, 171,* 923–925.

Gamzu, E. R., & Williams, D. R. (1973). Associative factors underlying the pigeon's key pecking in autoshaping procedures. *Journal of the Experimental Analysis of Behavior, 19,* 225–232.

Gantt, W. H. (1966). Conditional or conditioned, reflex or response? *Conditioned Reflex, 1,* 69–74.

Garb, J. J., & Stunkard, A. J. (1974). Taste aversions in man. *American Journal of Psychiatry, 131,* 1204–1207.

Garber, J., & Seligman, M. E. P. (Eds.). (1980). *Human helplessness: Theory and application.* New York: Academic Press.

Garcia, J., & Koelling, R. A. (1966). Relation of cue to consequence in avoidance learning. *Psychonomic Science, 4,* 123–124.

Garcia, J., Ervin, F. R., & Koelling, R. A. (1966). Learning with prolonged delay of reinforcement. *Psychonomic Science, 5,* 121–122.

Gardner, E. T., & Lewis, P. (1976). Negative reinforcement with shock-frequency increase. *Journal of the Experimental Analysis of Behavior, 25,* 3–14.

Gardner, R. A., & Gardner, B. T. (1969). Teaching sign language to a chimpanzee. *Science, 165,* 664–672.

Gardner, R. A., & Gardner, B. T. (1975). Early signs of language in child and chimpanzee. *Science, 187,* 752–753.

Gardner, R. A., & Gardner, B. T. (1978). Comparative psychology and language acquisition. *Annals of the New York Academy of Science, 309,* 37–76.

Gardner, R. A., & Gardner, B. T. (1984). A vocabulary test for chimpanzees (*Pan troglodytes*). *Journal of Comparative Psychology, 98,* 381–404.

Gardner, R. A., & Gardner, B. T. (1989). A cross-fostering laboratory. In R. A. Gardner, B. T. Gardner, & T. E. Van Cantfort (Eds.), *Teaching sign language to chimpanzees* (pp. 1–28). Albany: State University of New York Press.

Gardner, R. A., Gardner, B. T., & Van Cantfort, T. E. (Eds.). (1989). *Teaching sign language to chimpanzees.* Albany: State University of New York Press.

Gawley, D. J., Timberlake, W., & Lucas, G. A. (1987). System-specific differences in behavior regulation: Overrunning and underdrinking in molar nondepriving schedules. *Journal of Experimental Psychology: Animal Behavior Processes, 13,* 354–365.

Gemberling, G. A., & Domjan, M. (1982). Selective association in one-day-old rats: Taste-toxicosis and texture-shock aversion learning. *Journal of Comparative and Physiological Psychology, 96,* 105–113.

George, J. T., & Hopkins, B. L. (1989). Multiple effects of performance-contingent pay for waitpersons. *Journal of Applied Behavior Analysis, 22,* 131–141.

Gibbon, J., & Allan, L. (Eds.). (1984). *Annals of the New York Academy of Sciences: Vol. 423. Time and time perception.* New York: New York Academy of Sciences.

Gibbon, J., & Balsam, P. (1981). Spreading association in time. In C. M. Locurto, H. S. Terrace, & J. Gibbon (Eds.), *Autoshaping and conditioning theory* (pp. 219–253). New York: Academic Press.

Gibbon, J., & Church, R. M. (1984). Sources of variance in an information processing theory of timing. In H. L. Roitblat, T. G. Bever, & H. S. Terrace (Eds.), *Animal cognition* (pp. 465–488). Hillsdale, NJ: Erlbaum.

Gibbon, J., & Church, R. M. (1992). Comparison of variance and covariance patterns in parallel and serial theories of timing. *Journal of the Experimental Analysis of Behavior, 57,* 393–406.

Gibbon, J., & Fairhurst, S. (1994). Ratio versus difference comparators in choice. *Journal of the Experimental Analysis of Behavior, 62,* 409–434.

Gibbon, J., Church, R. M., & Meck, W. H. (1984). Scalar timing in memory. *Annals of the New York Academy of Sciences, 423,* 52–77.

Gibbon, J., Church, R. M., Fairhurst, S., & Kacelnik, A. (1988). Scalar expectancy theory and choice between delayed rewards. *Psychological Review, 95,* 102–114.

Gillan, D. J., & Domjan, M. (1977). Taste-aversion conditioning with expected versus unexpected drug treatment. *Journal of Experimental Psychology: Animal Behavior Processes, 3,* 297–309.

Gillette, K., Martin, G. M., & Bellingham, W. P. (1980). Differential use of food and water cues in the formation of conditioned aversions by domestic chicks (*Gallus gallus*). *Journal of Experimental Psychology: Animal Behavior Processes, 6,* 99–111.

Gisiner, R., & Schusterman, R. J. (1992). Sequence, syntax, and semantics: Responses of a language-trained sea lion (*Zalophus californianus*) to novel sign combinations. *Journal of Comparative Psychology, 106,* 78–91.

Gisquet-Verrier, P., & Alexinsky, T. (1990). Facilitative effect of a pretest exposure to the CS: Analysis and implications for the memory trace. *Animal Learning & Behavior, 18,* 323–331.

Goodall, G. (1984). Learning due to the response-shock contingency in signalled punishment. *Quarterly Journal of Experimental Psychology, 36B,* 259–279.

Goodall, G., & Mackintosh, N. J. (1987). Analysis of the Pavlovian properties of signals for punishment. *Quarterly Journal of Experimental Psychology, 39B,* 1–21.

Goodman, J. H., & Fowler, H. (1983). Blocking and enhancement of fear conditioning by appetitive CSs. *Animal Learning & Behavior, 11,* 75–82.

Gordon, W. C. (1981). Mechanisms for cue-induced retention enhancement. In N. E. Spear & R. R. Miller (Eds.), *Information processing in animals: Memory mechanisms* (pp. 319–339). Hillsdale, NJ: Erlbaum.

Gordon, W. C., & Feldman, D. T. (1978). Reactivation induced interference in a short-term retention paradigm. *Learning and Motivation, 9,* 164–178.

Gordon, W. C., & Klein, R. L. (1994). Animal memory: The effects of context change on retention performance. In N. J. Mackintosh (Ed.), *Animal learning and cognition* (pp. 255–279). San Diego: Academic Press.

Gordon, W. C., & Mowrer, R. R. (1980). An extinction trial as a reminder treatment following electroconvulsive shock. *Animal Learning & Behavior, 8,* 363–367.

Gordon, W. C., McCracken, K. M., Dess-Beech, N., & Mowrer, R. R. (1981). Mechanisms for the cueing phenomenon: The addition of the cueing context to the training memory. *Learning and Motivation, 12,* 196–211.

Gordon, W. C., McGinnis, C. M., & Weaver, M. S. (1985). The effect of cuing after backward conditioning trials. *Learning and Motivation, 16,* 444–463.

Gormezano, I. (1966). Classical conditioning. In J. B. Sidowski (Ed.), *Experimental methods and instrumentation in psychology.* New York: McGraw-Hill.

Gormezano, I., & Coleman, S. R. (1973). The law of effect and CR contingent modification of the UCS. *Conditioned Reflex, 8,* 41–56.

Gormezano, I., & Hiller, G. W. (1972). Omission training of the jaw-movement response of the rabbit to a water US. *Psychonomic Science, 29,* 276–278.

Gormezano, I., Kehoe, E. J., & Marshall, B. S. (1983). Twenty years of classical conditioning research with the rabbit. In J. M. Prague & A. N. Epstein (Eds.), *Progress in psychobiology and physiological psychology* (Vol. 10). New York: Academic Press.

Grace, R. C. (1995). Independence of reinforcement delay and magnitude in concurrent chains. *Journal of the Experimental Analysis of Behavior, 63,* 255–276.

Graham, J. M., & Desjardins, C. (1980). Classical conditioning: Induction of luteinizing hormone and testosterone secretion in anticipation of sexual activity. *Science, 210,* 1039–1041.

Grant, D. S. (1975). Proactive interference in pigeon short-term memory. *Journal of Experimental Psychology: Animal Behavior Processes, 1,* 207–220.

Grant, D. S. (1976). Effect of sample presentation time on long-delay matching in the pigeon. *Learning and Motivation, 7,* 580–590.

Grant, D. S. (1982). Intratrial proactive interference in pigeon short-term memory: Manipulation of stimulus dimension and dimensional similarity. *Learning and Motivation, 13,* 417–433.

Grant, D. S. (1988). Sources of visual interference in delayed matching-to-sample with pigeons. *Journal of Experimental Psychology: Animal Behavior Processes, 14,* 368–375.

Grant, D. S. (1991). Symmetrical and asymmetrical coding of food and no-food samples in delayed matching in pigeons. *Journal of Experimental Psychology: Animal Behavior Processes, 17,* 186–193.

Grant, D. S. (1993). Coding processes in pigeons. In T. R. Zentall (Ed.), *Animal cognition* (pp. 193–216). Hillsdale, NJ: Erlbaum.

Grant, D. S., & Roberts, W. A. (1973). Trace interaction in pigeon short-term memory. *Journal of Experimental Psychology, 101,* 21–29.

Grant, D. S., & Roberts, W. A. (1976). Sources of retroactive inhibition in pigeon short-term memory. *Journal of Experimental Psychology: Animal Behavior Processes, 2,* 1–16.

Grant, D. S., & Soldat, A. S. (1995). A postsample cue to forget does initiate an active forgetting process in pigeons. *Journal of Experimental Psychology: Animal Behavior Processes, 21,* 218–228.

Grant, D. S., & Spetch, M. L. (1993). Analogical and nonanalogical coding of samples differing in duration in a choice-matching task in pigeons. *Journal of Experimental Psychology: Animal Behavior Processes, 19,* 15–25.

Green, L., & Freed, D. E. (1993). The substitutability of reinforcers. *Journal of the Experimental Analysis of Behavior, 60,* 141–158.

Green, L., & Rachlin, H. (1991). Economic substitutability of electrical brain stimulation, food, and water. *Journal of the Experimental Analysis of Behavior, 55,* 133–143.

Greenfield, P. M., & Savage-Rumbaugh, E. S. (1990). Grammatical combination in *Pan paniscus*: Processes of learning and invention in the evolution and development of language. In S. T. Parker & K. R. Gibson (Eds.), *Language and intelligence in monkeys and apes* (pp. 540–578). Cambridge: Cambridge University Press.

Greenfield, P. M., & Savage-Rumbaugh, E. S. (1993). Comparing communicative competence in child and chimp: The pragmatics of repetition. *Journal of Child Language, 20,* 1–26.

Grice, G. R. (1948). The relation of secondary reinforcement to delayed reward in visual discrimination learning. *Journal of Experimental Psychology, 38,* 1–16.

Griffin, D. R. (1976). *The question of animal awareness.* New York: Rockefeller University Press.

Griffiths, R. R., & Thompson, T. (1973). The postreinforcement pause: A misnomer. *Psychological Record, 23,* 229–235.

Grossen, N. E., & Kelley, M. J. (1972). Species-specific behavior and acquisition of avoidance behavior in rats. *Journal of Comparative and Physiological Psychology, 81,* 307–310.

Grossen, N. E., Kostansek, D. J., & Bolles, R. C. (1969). Effects of appetitive discriminative stimuli on avoidance behavior. *Journal of Experimental Psychology, 81,* 340–343.

Groves, P. M., & Thompson, R. F. (1970). Habituation: A dual-process theory. *Psychological Review, 77,* 419–450.

Groves, P. M., Lee, D., & Thompson, R. F. (1969). Effects of stimulus frequency and intensity on habituation and sensitization in acute spinal cat. *Physiology and Behavior, 4,* 383–388.

Guha, D., Dutta, S. N., & Pradhan, S. N. (1974). Conditioning of gastric secretion by epinephrine in rats. *Proceedings of the Society for Experimental Biology and Medicine, 147,* 817–819.

Gunther, M. (1961). Infant behavior at the breast. In B. Foss (Ed.), *Determinants of infant behavior.* London: Wiley.

Gutiérrez, G., & Domjan, M. (1996). Learning and male-male sexual competition in Japanese quail (*Coturnix japonica*). *Journal of Comparative Psychology, 110,* 170–175.

Gutman, A., & Maier, S. F. (1978). Operant and Pavlovian factors in cross-response transfer of inhibitory stimulus control. *Learning and Motivation, 9,* 231–254.

Guttenberger, V. T., & Wasserman, E. A. (1985). Effects of sample duration, retention interval, and passage of time in the test on pigeons' matching-to-sample performance. *Animal Learning & Behavior, 13,* 121–128.

Guttman, N., & Kalish, H. I. (1956). Discriminability and stimulus generalization. *Journal of Experimental Psychology, 51,* 79–88.

Haggbloom, S. J., & Morris, K. M. (1994). Contextual cues and the retrieval of competing memories of goal events. *Animal Learning & Behavior, 22,* 165–172.

Haggbloom, S. J., Lovelace, L., Brewer, V. R., Levins, S. M., & Owens, J. D. (1990). Replacement of event-generated memories of nonreinforcement with signal-generated memories of reinforcement during partial reinforcement training: Effects on resistance to extinction. *Animal Learning & Behavior, 18,* 315–322.

Hailman, J. P. (1967). The ontogeny of an instinct. *Behaviour Supplements, 15,* 1–159.

Hake, D. F., & Azrin, N. H. (1965). Conditioned punishment. *Journal of the Experimental Analysis of Behavior, 8,* 279–293.

Hall, G. (1991). *Perceptual and associative learning.* Oxford, England: Clarendon Press.

Hall, G. (1994). Pavlovian conditioning. In N. J. Mackintosh (Ed.), *Animal learning and cognition* (pp. 15–43). San Diego: Academic Press.

Hall, G., & Honey, R. C. (1989). Contextual effects in conditioning, latent inhibition, and habituation: Associative and retrieval functions of contextual cues. *Journal of Experimental Psychology: Animal Behavior Processes, 15,* 232–241.

Hall, G., Kaye, H., & Pearce, J. M. (1985). Attention and conditioned inhibition. In R. R. Miller & N. E. Spear (Eds.), *Information processing in animals: Conditioned inhibition* (pp. 185–207). Hillsdale, NJ: Erlbaum.

Hall, G., Ray, E., & Bonardi, C. (1993). Acquired equivalence between cues trained with a common antecedent. *Journal of Experimental Psychology: Animal Behavior Processes, 19,* 391–399.

Hall, R. V., Axelrod, S., Foundopoulos, M., Shellman, J., Campbell, R. A., & Cranston, S. S. (1971). The effective use of punishment to modify behav-ior in the classroom. *Educational Technology, 11*(4), 24–26.

Hall, S. M., Hall, R. G., & Ginsberg, D. (1990). Pharmacological and behavioral treatment for cigarette smoking. In M. Hersen, R. M. Eisler, & P. M. Miller (Eds.), *Progress in behavior modification* (Vol. 25, pp. 86–118). Newbury Park, CA: Sage.

Hallam, S. C., Grahame, N. J., Harris, K., & Miller, R. R. (1992). Associative structures underlying enhanced negative summation following operational extinction of a Pavlovian inhibitor. *Learning and Motivation, 23,* 43–62.

Hallam, S. C., Matzel, L. D., Sloat, J. S., & Miller, R. R. (1990). Excitation and inhibition as a function of post-training extinction of the excitatory cue used in Pavlovian inhibition training. *Learning and Motivation, 21,* 59–84.

Hammond, L. J. (1966). Increased responding to CS in differential CER. *Psychonomic Science, 5,* 337–338.

Hammond, L. J. (1968). Retardation of fear acquisition by a previously inhibitory CS. *Journal of Comparative and Physiological Psychology, 66,* 756–759.

Hankins, W. G., Rusiniak, K. W., & Garcia, J. (1976). Dissociation of odor and taste in shock-avoidance learning. *Behavioral Biology, 18,* 345–358.

Hanson, H. M. (1959). Effects of discrimination training on stimulus generalization. *Journal of Experimental Psychology, 58,* 321–333.

Hanson, J., & Green, L. (1986). Time and response matching with topographically different responses. *Animal Learning & Behavior, 14,* 435–442.

Hanson, S. J., & Timberlake, W. (1983). Regulation during challenge: A general model of learned performance under schedule constraint. *Psychological Review, 90,* 261–282.

Harlow, H. F. (1969). Age-mate or peer affectional system. In D. S. Lehrman, R. H. Hinde, & E. Shaw (Eds.), *Advances in the study of behavior* (Vol. 2). New York: Academic Press.

Haroutunian, V., & Riccio, D. C. (1979). Drug-induced "arousal" and the effectiveness of CS exposure in the reinstatement of memory. *Behavioral and Neural Biology, 26,* 115–120.

Hart, B. L. (1973). Reflexive behavior. In G. Bermant (Ed.), *Perspectives in animal behavior.* Glenview, IL: Scott, Foresman.

Hastjarjo, T., & Silberberg, A. (1992). Effects of reinforcer delays on choice as a function of income level. *Journal of the Experimental Analysis of Behavior, 57,* 119–125.

Hastjarjo, T., Silberberg, A., & Hursh, S. R. (1990a). Quinine pellets as an inferior good and a Giffen good in rats. *Journal of the Experimental Analysis of Behavior, 53,* 263–271.

Hastjarjo, T., Silberberg, A., & Hursh, S. R. (1990b). Risky choice as a function of amount and variance in food supply. *Journal of the Experimental Analysis of Behavior, 53,* 155–161.

Hayes, K. J., & Hayes, C. (1951). The intellectual development of a home-raised chimpanzee. *Proceedings of the American Philosophical Society, 95,* 105–109.

Healy, S. D. (1995). Memory for objects and positions: Delayed non-matching-to-sample in storing and non-storing tits. *Quarterly Journal of Experimental Psychology, 48B,* 179–191.

Healy, S. D., & Hurly, R. A. (1995). Spatial memory in rufous hummingbirds (*Selasphorus rufus*): A field test. *Animal Learning & Behavior, 23,* 63–68.

Healy, S. D., & Krebs, J. R. (1992a). Comparing spatial memory in two species of tit: Recalling a single positive location. *Animal Learning & Behavior, 20,* 121–126.

Healy, S. D., & Krebs, J. R. (1992b). Delayed-matching-to-sample by marsh tits and great tits. *Quarterly Journal of Experimental Psychology, 45B,* 33–47.

Hearst, E. (1968). Discrimination learning as the summation of excitation and inhibition. *Science, 162,* 1303–1306.

Hearst, E. (1969). Excitation, inhibition, and discrimination learning. In N. J. Mackintosh & W. K. Honig (Eds.), *Fundamental issues in associative learning.* Halifax: Dalhousie University Press.

Hearst, E. (1975). Pavlovian conditioning and directed movements. In G. Bower (Ed.), *The psychology of learning and motivation* (Vol. 9, pp. 215–262). New York: Academic Press.

Hearst, E. (1989). Backward associations: Differential learning about stimuli that follow the presence versus the absence of food in pigeons. *Animal Learning and Behavior, 17,* 280–290.

Hearst, E., & Franklin, S. R. (1977). Positive and negative relations between a signal and food: Approach withdrawal behavior to the signal. *Journal of Experimental Psychology: Animal Behavior Processes, 3,* 37–52.

Hearst, E., & Jenkins, H. M. (1974). *Sign-tracking: The stimulus-reinforcer relation and directed action.* Austin, TX: Psychonomic Society.

Hearst, E., & Peterson, G. B. (1973). Transfer of conditioned excitation and inhibition from one operant response to another. *Journal of Experimental Psychology, 99,* 360–368.

Hebb, D. O. (1956). The distinction between "classical" and "instrumental." *Canadian Journal of Psychology, 10,* 165–166.

Heiligenberg, W. (1974). Processes governing behavioral states of readiness. In D. S. Lehrman, J. S. Rosenblatt, R. Hinde, & E. Shaw (Eds.), *Advances in the study of behavior* (Vol. 5, pp. 173–200). New York: Academic Press.

Helweg, D. A., Roitblat, H. L., Nachtigall, P. E., & Hautus, M. J. (1996). Recognition of aspect-dependent three-dimensional objects by an echolocating Atlantic bottlenose dolphin. *Journal of Experimental Psychology: Animal Behavior Processes, 22,* 19–31.

Hendersen, R. W., Patterson, J. M., & Jackson, R. L. (1980). Acquisition and retention of control of instrumental behavior by a cue signaling airblast: How specific are conditioned anticipations? *Learning and Motivation, 11,* 407–426.

Hepper, P. G., & Shahidullah, S. (1992). Habituation in normal and Down's syndrome fetuses. *Quarterly Journal of Experimental Psychology, 44B,* 305–317.

Herman, L. M. (1987). Receptive competencies of language-trained animals. In J. S. Rosenblatt, C. Beer, M.-C. Busnel, & P. J. B. Slater (Eds.), *Advances in the study of behavior* (Vol. 17, pp. 1–60). Orlando, FL: Academic Press.

Herman, L. M., Pack, A. A., & Morrel-Samuels, P. (1993). Representational and conceptual skills of dolphins. In H. L. Roitblat, L. M. Herman, & P. E. Nachtigall (Eds.), *Language and communication: Comparative perspectives* (pp. 403–442). Hillsdale, NJ: Erlbaum.

Herman, R. L., & Azrin, N. H. (1964). Punishment by noise in an alternative response situation. *Journal of the Experimental Analysis of Behavior, 7,* 185–188.

Herrnstein, R. J. (1961). Relative and absolute strength of response as a function of frequency of reinforcement. *Journal of the Experimental Analysis of Behavior, 4,* 267–272.

Herrnstein, R. J. (1969). Method and theory in the study of avoidance. *Psychological Review, 76,* 49–69.

Herrnstein, R. J. (1970). On the law of effect. *Journal of the Experimental Analysis of Behavior, 13,* 243–266.

Herrnstein, R. J. (1984). Objects, categories, and discriminative stimuli. In H. L. Roitblat, T. G Bever, & H. S. Terrace (Eds.), *Animal cognition* (pp. 233–261). Hillsdale, NJ: Erlbaum.

Herrnstein, R. J. (1990). Levels of stimulus control: A functional approach. *Cognition, 37,* 133–166.

Herrnstein, R. J., & deVilliers, P. A. (1980). Fish as a natural category for people and pigeons. In G. H. Bower (Ed.), *The psychology of learning and motivation* (Vol. 14, pp. 60–97). New York: Academic Press.

Herrnstein, R. J., & Heyman, G. M. (1979). Is matching compatible with reinforcement maximization on concurrent variable interval, variable ratio? *Journal of the Experimental Analysis of Behavior, 31*, 209–223.

Herrnstein, R. J., & Hineline, P. N. (1966). Negative reinforcement as shock-frequency reduction. *Journal of the Experimental Analysis of Behavior, 9*, 421–430.

Herrnstein, R. J., & Loveland, D. H. (1964). Complex visual concept in the pigeon. *Science, 146*, 549–551.

Herrnstein, R. J., & Vaughan, W., Jr. (1980). Melioration and behavioral allocation. In J. E. R. Staddon (Ed.), *Limits to action.* New York: Academic Press.

Herrnstein, R. J., Loveland, D. H., & Cable, C. (1976). Natural concepts in pigeons. *Journal of Experimental Psychology: Animal Behavior Processes, 2*, 285–301.

Herzog, H. A., Jr. (1988). The moral status of mice. *American Psychologist, 43*, 473–474.

Heth, C. D. (1976). Simultaneous and backward fear conditioning as a function of number of CS-UCS pairings. *Journal of Experimental Psychology: Animal Behavior Processes, 2*, 117–129.

Heth, C. D., & Rescorla, R. A. (1973). Simultaneous and backward fear conditioning in the rat. *Journal of Comparative and Physiological Psychology, 82*, 434–443.

Heyman, G. M. (1983). Optimization theory: Close but no cigar. *Behaviour Analysis Letters, 3*, 17–26.

Heyman, G. M., & Herrnstein, R. J. (1986). More on concurrent interval-ratio schedules: A replication and review. *Journal of the Experimental Analysis of Behavior, 46*, 331–351.

Heyman, G. M., & Monaghan, M. M. (1994). Reinforcer magnitude (sucrose concentration) and the matching law theory of response strength. *Journal of the Experimental Analysis of Behavior, 61*, 505–516.

Hilgard, E. R. (1936). The nature of the conditioned response: I. The case for and against stimulus substitution. *Psychological Review, 43*, 366–385.

Hilton, S. C., & Krebs, J. K. (1990). Spatial memory of four species of

Parus: Performance in an open-held analogue of a radial maze. *Quarterly Journal of Experimental Psychology, 42B*, 345–368.

Hineline, P. N. (1976). Negative reinforcement without shock reduction. *Journal of the Experimental Analysis of Behavior, 14*, 259–268.

Hineline, P. N. (1977). Negative reinforcement and avoidance. In W. K. Honig & J. E. R. Staddon (Eds.), *Handbook of operant behavior* (pp. 364–414). Englewood Cliffs, NJ: Prentice-Hall.

Hineline, P. N. (1981). The several roles of stimuli in negative reinforcement. In P. Harzem & M. D. Zeiler (Eds.), *Predictability, correlation, and contiguity.* Chichester, England: Wiley.

Hinson, J. M., & Staddon, J. E. R. (1983a). Hill-climbing by pigeons. *Journal of the Experimental Analysis of Behavior, 39*, 25–47.

Hinson, J. M., & Staddon, J. E. R. (1983b). Matching, maximizing, and hill-climbing. *Journal of the Experimental Analysis of Behavior, 40*, 321–331.

Hinson, R. E., & Siegel, S. (1980). Trace conditioning as an inhibitory procedure. *Animal Learning & Behavior, 8*, 60–66.

Hinson, R. E., Poulos, C. X., & Cappell, H. (1982). Effects of pentobarbital and cocaine in rats expecting pentobarbital. *Pharmacology, Biochemistry and Behavior, 16*, 661–666.

Hintzman, D. L. (1991). Twenty-five years of learning and memory: Was the cognitive revolution a mistake? In D. E. Meyer & S. Kornblum (Eds.), *Attention and performance XIVP.* Hillsdale, NJ: Erlbaum.

Hoffman, H. S., & Fleshler, M. (1964). An apparatus for the measurement of the startle-response in the rat. *American Journal of Psychology, 77*, 307–308.

Hoffman, H. S., & Solomon, R. L. (1974). An opponent-process theory of motivation: III. Some affective dynamics in imprinting. *Learning and Motivation, 5*, 149–164.

Hoffman, N., & Maki, W. S. (1986). Two sources of proactive interference

in spatial working memory: Multiple effects of repeated trials on radial maze performance by rats. *Animal Learning & Behavior, 14*, 65–72.

Hogan, J. A. (1974). Responses in Pavlovian conditioning studies. *Science, 186*, 156–157.

Holland, P. C. (1977). Conditioned stimulus as a determinant of the form of the Pavlovian conditioned response. *Journal of Experimental Psychology: Animal Behavior Processes, 3*, 77–104.

Holland, P. C. (1980). Influence of visual conditioned stimulus characteristics on the form of Pavlovian appetitive conditioned responding in rats. *Journal of Experimental Psychology: Animal Behavior Processes, 6*, 81–97.

Holland, P. C. (1984). Origins of behavior in Pavlovian conditioning. In G. H. Bower (Ed.), *The psychology of learning and motivation* (Vol. 18, pp. 129–174). Orlando, FL: Academic Press.

Holland, P. C. (1985). The nature of conditioned inhibition in serial and simultaneous feature negative discriminations. In R. R. Miller & N. E. Spear (Eds.), *Information processing in animals: Conditioned inhibition* (pp. 267–297). Hillsdale, NJ: Erlbaum.

Holland, P. C. (1986). Temporal determinants of occasion setting in feature-positive discriminations. *Animal Learning and Behavior, 14*, 111–120.

Holland, P. C. (1989a). Feature extinction enhances transfer of occasion setting. *Animal Learning & Behavior, 17*, 269–279.

Holland, P. C. (1989b). Occasion setting with simultaneous compounds in rats. *Journal of Experimental Psychology: Animal Behavior Processes, 15*, 183–193.

Holland, P. C. (1989c). Transfer of negative occasion setting and conditioned inhibition across conditioned and unconditioned stimuli. *Journal of Experimental Psychology: Animal Behavior Processes, 15*, 311–328.

Holland, P. C. (1991). Acquisition and transfer of occasion setting in operant feature positive and feature negative discriminations. *Learning and Motivation, 22,* 366–387.

Holland, P. C. (1992). Occasion setting in Pavlovian conditioning. In D. L. Medin (Ed.), *The psychology of learning and motivation,* (Vol. 28, pp. 69–125). San Diego, CA: Academic Press.

Holland, P. C., & Rescorla, R. A. (1975a). The effect of two ways of devaluing the unconditioned stimulus after first- and second-order appetitive conditioning. *Journal of Experimental Psychology: Animal Behavior Processes, 1,* 355–363.

Holland, P. C., & Rescorla, R. A. (1975b). Second-order conditioning with food unconditioned stimulus. *Journal of Comparative and Physiological Psychology, 88,* 459–467.

Holland, P. C., & Straub, J. J. (1979). Differential effect of two ways of devaluing the unconditioned stimulus after Pavlovian appetitive conditioning. *Journal of Experimental Psychology: Animal Behavior Processes, 5,* 65–78.

Holliday, M., & Hirsch, J. (1986). Excitatory conditioning of individual *Drosophila melanogaster. Journal of Experimental Psychology: Animal Behavior Processes, 12,* 131–142.

Hollis, K. L. (1982). Pavlovian conditioning of signal-centered action patterns and autonomic behavior: A biological analysis of function. *Advances in the Study of Behavior, 12,* 1–64.

Hollis, K. L., Cadieux, E. L., & Colbert, M. M. (1989). The biological function of Pavlovian conditioning: A mechanism for mating success in the blue gourami (*Trichogaster trichopterus*). *Journal of Comparative Psychology, 103,* 115–121.

Hollis, K. L., Pharr, V. L., Dumas, M. J., Britton, G. B., & Field, J. (1997). Classical conditioning provides paternity advantage for territorial male blue gouramis (*Trichogaster trichopterus*). *Journal of Comparative Psychology,* in press.

Holloway, K. S., & Domjan, M. (1993). Sexual approach conditioning: Tests of unconditioned stimulus devaluation using hormone manipulations.

Journal of Experimental Psychology: Animal Behavior Processes, 19, 47–55.

Holman, J. G., & Mackintosh, N. J. (1981). The control of appetitive instrumental responding does not depend on classical conditioning to the discriminative stimulus. *Quarterly Journal of Experimental Psychology, 33B,* 21–31.

Holz, W. C., & Azrin, N. H. (1961). Discriminative properties of punishment. *Journal of the Experimental Analysis of Behavior, 4,* 225–232.

Honey, R. C., & Hall, G. (1989). Acquired equivalence and distinctiveness of cues. *Journal of Experimental Psychology: Animal Behavior Processes, 15,* 338–346.

Honey, R. C., & Hall, G. (1991). Acquired equivalence and distinctiveness of cues using a sensory-preconditioning procedure. *Quarterly Journal of Experimental Psychology, 43B,* 121–135.

Honey, R. C., Pye, C., Lightbown, Y., Rey, V., & Hall, G. (1992). Contextual factors in neophobia and its habituation: The role of absolute and relative novelty. *Quarterly Journal of Experimental Psychology, 45B,* 327–347.

Honey, R. C., Willis, A., & Hall, G. (1990). Context specificity in pigeon autoshaping. *Learning and Motivation, 21,* 125–136.

Honig, W. K. (1978). Studies of working memory in the pigeon. In S. H. Hulse, H. Fowler, & W. K. Honig (Eds.), *Cognitive processes in animal behavior* (pp. 211–248). Hillsdale, NJ: Erlbaum.

Honig, W. K., & Stewart, K. E. (1988). Pigeons can discriminate locations presented in pictures. *Journal of the Experimental Analysis of Behavior, 50,* 541–551.

Honig, W. K., & Thompson, R. K. R. (1982). Retrospective and prospective processing in animal working memory. In G. H. Bower (Ed.), *The psychology of learning and motivation* (Vol. 16, pp. 239–283). Orlando, FL: Academic Press.

Honig, W. K., & Urcuioli, P. J. (1981). The legacy of Guttman and Kalish

(1956): 25 years of research on stimulus generalization. *Journal of the Experimental Analysis of Behavior, 36,* 405–445.

Honig, W. K., Boneau, C. A., Burstein, K. R., & Pennypacker, H. S. (1963). Positive and negative generalization gradients obtained under equivalent training conditions. *Journal of Comparative and Physiological Psychology, 56,* 111–116.

Hoyert, M. S. (1992). Order and chaos in fixed-interval schedules of reinforcement. *Journal of the Experimental Analysis of Behavior, 57,* 339–363.

Huber, L., & Lenz, R. (1993). A test of the linear feature model of polymorphous concept discrimination with pigeons. *Quarterly Journal of Experimental Psychology, 46B,* 1–18.

Hull, C. L. (1930). Knowledge and purpose as habit mechanisms. *Psychological Review, 30,* 511–525.

Hull, C. L. (1931). Goal attraction and directing ideas conceived as habit phenomena. *Psychological Review, 38,* 487–506.

Hulse, S. H. (1978). Cognitive structure and serial pattern learning by animals. In S. H. Hulse, H. Fowler, & W. K. Honig (Eds.), *Cognitive processes in animal behavior* (pp. 311–340). Hillsdale, NJ: Erlbaum.

Hulse, S. H., Fowler, H., & Honig, W. K. (Eds.). (1978). *Cognitive processes in animal behavior.* Hillsdale, NJ: Erlbaum.

Hulse, S. H., Page, S. C., & Braaten, R. F. (1990). Frequency range size and the frequency range constraint in auditory perception by European starlings (*sturnus vulgaris*). *Animal Learning & Behavior, 18,* 238–245.

Hunter, W. S. (1913). The delayed reaction in animals and children. *Behavior Monographs, 2,* serial #6.

Hursh, S. R. (1980). Economic concepts for the analysis of behavior. *Journal of the Experimental Analysis of Behavior, 34,* 219–238.

Hursh, S. R. (1984). Behavioral economics. *Journal of the Experimental Analysis of Behavior, 42,* 435–452.

Hursh, S. R. (1991). Behavioral economics of drug self-administration and drug abuse policy. *Journal of the Experimental Analysis of Behavior, 56,* 377–393.

Hursh, S. R., Raslear, T. G., Shurtleff, D., Bauman, R., & Simmons, L. (1988). A cost-benefit analysis of demand for food. *Journal of the Experimental Analysis of Behavior, 50,* 419–440.

Hutt, P. J. (1954). Rate of bar pressing as a function of quality and quantity of food reward. *Journal of Comparative and Physiological Psychology, 47,* 235–239.

Imada, H., & Imada, S. (1983). Thorndike's (1898) puzzle box experiments revisited. *Kwansei Gakuin University Annual Studies, 32,* 167–184.

Innis, N. K., Reberg, D., Mann, B., Jacobson, J., & Turton, D. (1983). Schedule-induced behavior for food and water: Effects of interval duration. *Behaviour Analysis Letters, 3,* 191–200.

Innis, N. K., Simmelhag-Grant, V. L., & Staddon, J. E. R. (1983). Behavior induced by periodic food delivery: The effects of interfood interval. *Journal of the Experimental Analysis of Behavior, 39,* 309–322.

Irwin, J., Suissa, A., & Anisman, H. (1980). Differential effects of inescapable shock on escape performance and discrimination learning in a water escape task. *Journal of Experimental Psychology: Animal Behavior Processes, 6,* 21–40.

Israel, A. C., Devine, V. T., O'Dea, M. A., & Hamdi, M. E. (1974). Effect of delayed conditioned stimulus termination on extinction of an avoidance response following differential termination conditions during acquisition. *Journal of Experimental Psychology, 103,* 360–362.

Ito, M., & Fantino, E. (1986). Choice, foraging, and reinforcer duration. *Journal of the Experimental Analysis of Behavior, 46,* 93–103.

Iversen, I. H. (1993a). Acquisition of matching-to-sample performance in rats using visual stimuli on nose keys. *Journal of the Experimental Analysis of Behavior, 59,* 471–482.

Iversen, I. H. (1993b). Techniques for establishing schedules with wheel running as reinforcement in rats. *Journal of the Experimental Analysis of Behavior, 60,* 219–238.

Jackson, R. L., & Minor, T. R. (1988). Effects of signaling inescapable shock on subsequent escape learning: Implications for theories of coping and "learned helplessness." *Journal of Experimental Psychology: Animal Behavior Processes, 14,* 390–400.

Jackson, R. L., Alexander, J. H., & Maier, S. F. (1980). Learned helplessness, inactivity, and associative deficits: Effects of inescapable shock on response choice escape learning. *Journal of Experimental Psychology: Animal Behavior Processes, 6,* 1–20.

Jacobs, E. A., & Hackenberg, T. D. (1996). Humans' choices in situations of time-based diminishing returns: Effects of fixed-interval duration and progressive-interval step size. *Journal of the Experimental Analysis of Behavior, 65,* 5–19.

Janssen, M., Farley, J., & Hearst, E. (1995). Temporal location of unsignaled food deliveries: Effects on conditioned withdrawal (inhibition) in pigeon signtracking. *Journal of Experimental Psychology: Animal Behavior Processes, 21,* 116–128.

Jarrard, L. E., & Moise, S. L. (1971). Short-term memory in the monkey. In L. E. Jarrard (Ed.), *Cognitive processes of nonhuman primates.* New York: Academic Press.

Jarvik, M. E., Goldfarb, T. L., & Carley, J. L. (1969). Influence of interference on delayed matching in monkeys. *Journal of Experimental Psychology, 81,* 1–6.

Jenkins, H. M. (1962). Resistance to extinction when partial reinforcement is followed by regular reinforcement. *Journal of Experimental Psychology, 64,* 441–450.

Jenkins, H. M. (1977). Sensitivity of different response systems to stimulus-reinforcer and response-reinforcer relations. In H. Davis & H. M. B. Hurwitz (Eds.), *Operant-Pavlovian interactions* (pp. 47–62). Hillsdale, NJ: Erlbaum.

Jenkins, H. M., & Harrison, R. H. (1960). Effects of discrimination training on auditory generalization. *Journal of Experimental Psychology, 59,* 246–253.

Jenkins, H. M., & Harrison, R. H. (1962). Generalization gradients of inhibition following auditory discrimination learning. *Journal of the Experimental Analysis of Behavior, 5,* 435–441.

Jenkins, H. M., & Moore, B. R. (1973). The form of the autoshaped response with food or water reinforcers. *Journal of the Experimental Analysis of Behavior, 20,* 163–181.

Jenkins, H. M., Barnes, R. A., & Barrera, F. J. (1981). Why autoshaping depends on trial spacing. In C. M. Locurto, H. S. Terrace, & J. Gibbon (Eds.), *Autoshaping and conditioning theory* (pp. 255–284). New York: Academic Press.

Jenkins, H. M., Barrera, F. J., Ireland, C., & Woodside, B. (1978). Signal-centered action patterns of dogs in appetitive classical conditioning. *Learning and Motivation, 9,* 272–296.

Jitsumori, M. (1993). Category discrimination of artificial polymorphous stimuli based on feature learning. *Journal of Experimental Psychology: Animal Behavior Processes, 19,* 244–254.

Jitsumori, M. (1994). Discrimination of artificial polymorphous categories by rhesus monkeys (*Macaca mulatta*). *Quarterly Journal of Experimental Psychology, 47B,* 371–386.

Jitsumori, M., Wright, A. A., & Cook, R. G. (1988). Long-term proactive interference and novelty enhancement effects in monkey list memory. *Journal of Experimental Psychology: Animal Behavior Processes, 14,* 146–154.

Jitsumori, M., Wright, A. A., & Shyan, M. R. (1989). Buildup and release from proactive interference in a rhesus monkey. *Journal of Experimental Psychology: Animal Behavior Processes, 15,* 329–337.

Job, R. F. S. (1987). Learned helplessness in an appetitive discrete-trial T-maze discrimination test. *Animal Learning & Behavior, 15,* 342–346.

Job, R. F. S. (1989). A test of proposed mechanisms underlying the interference effect produced by noncontingent food presentations. *Learning and Motivation, 20,* 153–177.

Johnson, H. M. (1994). Processes of successful intentional forgetting. *Psychological Bulletin, 116,* 274–292.

Jones, F. R. H. (1955). Photo-kinesis in the ammocoete larva of the brook lamprey. *Journal of Experimental Biology, 32,* 492–503.

Jones, M. R. (1974). Cognitive representations of serial patterns. In B. Kantowitz (Ed.), *Human information processing: Tutorials in performance and cognition.* Hillsdale, NJ: Erlbaum.

Kagel, J. H., Rachlin, H., Green, L., Battalio, R. C., Basmann, R. L., & Klemm, W. R. (1975). Experimental studies of consumer demand behavior using laboratory animals. *Economic Inquiry, 13,* 22–38.

Kalat, J. W. (1974). Taste salience depends on novelty, not concentration, in taste-aversion learning in the rat. *Journal of Comparative and Physiological Psychology, 86,* 47–50.

Kamil, A. C. (1978). Systematic foraging by a nectarfeeding bird, the amakihi (*Loxops virens*). *Journal of Comparative and Physiological Psychology, 92,* 388–396.

Kamil, A. C., & Balda, R. P. (1985). Cache recovery and spatial memory in Clark's nutcrackers (*Nucifraga columbiana*). *Journal of Experimental Psychology: Animal Behavior Processes, 11,* 95–111.

Kamil, A. C., & Balda, R. P. (1990a). Differential memory for different cache sites by Clark's nutcrackers (*Nueifraga columbiana*). *Journal of Experimental Psychology: Animal Behavior Processes, 16,* 162–168.

Kamil, A. C., & Balda, R. P. (1990b). Spatial memory in seed-caching corvids. In G. H. Bower (Ed.), *The psychology of learning and motivation,* (Vol. 26, pp. 1–25). San Diego: Academic Press.

Kamil, A. C., & Clements, K. C. (1990). Learning, memory, and foraging behavior. In D. A. Dewsbury (Ed.), *Contemporary issues in comparative psychology* (pp. 7–30). Sunderland, MA: Sinauer.

Kamil, A. C., & Sargent, T. D. (Eds.). (1981). Foraging behavior. New York: Garland STPM.

Kamil, A. C., Krebs, J. R., & Pulliam, H. R. (Eds.). (1987). *Foraging behavior.* New York: Plenum.

Kamil, A. C., Yoerg, S. I., & Clements, K. C. (1988). Rules to leave by: Patch departure in foraging blue jays. *Animal Behaviour, 36,* 843–853.

Kamin, L. J, Brimer, C. J., & Black, A. H. (1963). Conditioned suppression as a monitor of fear of the CS in the course of avoidance training. *Journal of Comparative and Physiological Psychology, 56,* 497–501.

Kamin, L. J. (1956). The effects of termination of the CS and avoidance of the US on avoidance learning. *Journal of Comparative and Physiological Psychology, 49,* 420–424.

Kamin, L. J. (1965). Temporal and intensity characteristics of the conditioned stimulus. In W. F. Prokasy (Ed.), *Classical conditioning* (pp. 118–147). New York: Appleton-Century-Crofts.

Kamin, L. J. (1968). "Attention-like" processes in classical conditioning. In M. R. Jones (Ed.), *Miami symposium on the prediction of behavior: Aversive stimulation* (pp. 9–31). Miami: University of Miami Press.

Kamin, L. J. (1969). Predictability, surprise, attention, and conditioning. In B. A. Campbell & R. M. Church (Eds.), *Punishment and aversive behavior* (pp. 279–296). New York: Appleton-Century-Crofts.

Kamin, L. J., & Brimer, C. J. (1963). The effects of intensity of conditioned and unconditioned stimuli on a conditioned emotional response. *Canadian Journal of Psychology, 17,* 194–198.

Kamin, L. J., & Schaub, R. E. (1963). Effects of conditioned stimulus intensity on the conditioned emotional response. *Journal of Comparative and Physiological Psychology, 56,* 502–507.

Kandel, E. R., Schwartz, J. H., & Jessell, T. M. (Eds.). (1991). *Principles of neural science.* New York: Elsevier.

Kaplan, P. S. (1984). The importance of relative temporal parameters in trace autoshaping: From excitation to inhibition. *Journal of Experimental Psychology: Animal Behavior Processes, 10,* 113–126.

Kaplan, P. S., & Hearst, E. (1982). Bridging temporal gaps between CS and US in autoshaping: Insertion of other stimuli before, during, and after the CS. *Journal of Experimental Psychology: Animal Behavior Processes, 8,* 187–203.

Kaplan, P. S., Goldstein, M. H., Huckeby, E. R., Cooper, R. P. (1995). Habituation, sensitization, and infants' responses to motherese speech. *Developmental Psychobiology, 28,* 45–57.

Kaplan, P. S., Werner, J. S., & Rudy, J. W. (1990). Habituation, sensitization, and infant visual attention. In C. Rovee-Collier & L. P. Lipsitt (Eds.), *Advances in infancy research* (Vol. 6, pp. 61–109). Norwood, NJ: Ablex.

Karpicke, J. (1978). Directed approach responses and positive conditioned suppression in the rat. *Animal Learning & Behavior, 6,* 216–224.

Kasprow, W. J. (1987). Enhancement of short-term retention by appetitive-reinforcer reminder treatment. *Animal Learning & Behavior, 15,* 412–416.

Kasprow, W. J., Cacheiro, H., Balaz, M. A., & Miller, R. R. (1982). Reminder-induced recovery of associations to an overshadowed stimulus. *Learning and Motivation, 13,* 155–166.

Kasprow, W. J., Catterson, D., Schachtman, T. R., & Miller, R. R. (1984). Attenuation of latent inhibition by post-acquisition reminder. *Quarterly Journal of Experimental Psychology, 36B,* 53–63.

Kasprow, W. J., Schachtman, T. R., & Miller, R. R. (1987). The comparator hypothesis of conditioned response generation: Manifest conditioned excitation and inhibition as a function of relative excitatory strengths of CS and conditioning context at the time of testing. *Journal of Experimental Psychology: Animal Behavior Processes, 13,* 395–406.

Kastak, D., & Schusterman, R. J. (1994). Transfer of visual identity matching-to-sample in two California sea lions (*Zatophus californianus*). *Animal Learning & Behavior, 22,* 427–435.

Katzev, R. D. (1967). Extinguishing avoidance responses as a function of delayed warning signal termination. *Journal of Experimental Psychology, 75,* 339–344.

Katzev, R. D. (1972). What is both necessary and sufficient to maintain avoidance responding in the shuttle box? *Quarterly Journal of Experimental Psychology, 24,* 310–317.

Katzev, R. D., & Berman, J. S. (1974). Effect of exposure to conditioned stimulus and control of its termination in the extinction of avoidance behavior. *Journal of Comparative and Physiological Psychology, 87,* 347–353.

Kaufman, L. W., & Collier, G. (1983). Cost and meal pattern in wild-caught rats. *Physiology and Behavior, 30,* 445–449.

Keehn, J. D., & Nakkash, S. (1959). Effect of a signal contingent upon an avoidance response. *Nature, 184,* 566–568.

Kehoe, E. J. (1986). Summation and configuration in conditioning of the rabbit's nictitating membrane response to compound stimuli. *Journal of Experimental Psychology: Animal Behavior Processes, 12,* 186–195.

Kehoe, E. J., & Graham, P. (1988). Summation and configuration: Stimulus compounding and negative patterning in the rabbit. *Journal of Experimental Psychology: Animal Behavior Processes, 14,* 320–333.

Kehoe, E. J., Cool, V., & Gormezano, I. (1991). Trace conditioning of the rabbit's nictitating membrane response as a function of CS-US interstimulus interval and trials per session. *Learning and Motivation, 22,* 269–290.

Kelley, M. J. (1986). Selective attention and stimulus reinforcer interactions in the pigeon. *Quarterly Journal of Experimental Psychology, 38B,* 97–110.

Kellogg, W. N. (1933). *The ape and the child.* New York: McGraw-Hill.

Kesner, R. P., & DeSpain, M. J. (1988). Correspondence between rats and humans in the utilization of retrospective and prospective codes. *Animal Learning & Behavior, 16,* 299–302.

Khallad, Y., & Moore, J. (1996). Blocking, unblocking, and overexpectation in autoshaping with pigeons. *Journal of the Experimental Analysis of Behavior, 65,* 575–591.

Killeen, P. R. (1991). Behavior's time. In G. H. Bower (Ed.), *The psychology of learning and motivation.* (Vol. 27, pp. 295–334). San Diego: Academic Press.

Killeen, P. R., & Fetterman, J. G. (1988). A behavioral theory of timing. *Psychological Review, 95,* 274–295.

Killeen, P. R., & Fetterman, J. G. (1993). The behavioral theory of timing: Transition analyses. *Journal of the Experimental Analysis of Behavior, 59,* 411–422.

Kim, S. D., Rivers, S., Bevins, R. A., & Ayres, J. J. B. (1996). Conditioned stimulus determinants of conditioned response form in Pavlovian fear conditioning. *Journal of Experimental Psychology: Animal Behavior Processes, 22,* 87–104.

King, G. R., & Logue, A. W. (1987). Choice in a self-control paradigm with human subjects: Effects of changeover delay duration. *Learning and Motivation, 18,* 421–438.

Klein, M., & Rilling, M. (1974). Generalization of free operant avoidance behavior in pigeons. *Journal of the Experimental Analysis of Behavior, 21,* 75–88.

Kluender, K. R., Diehl, R. L., & Killeen, P. R. (1987). Japanese quail can learn phonetic categories. *Science, 237,* 1195–1197.

Köhler, W. (1939). Simple structural functions in the chimpanzee and in the chicken. In W. D. Ellis (Ed.), *A source book of Gestalt psychology* (pp. 217–227). New York: Harcourt Brace Jovanovich.

Konorski, J., & Miller, S. (1930). Méthode d'examen de l'analysateur moteur par les réactions salivomatrices.

Compte et Mémoires de la Société de Biologie, 104, 907–910.

Konorski, J., & Szwejkowska, G. (1950). Chronic extinction and restoration of conditioned reflexes: I. Extinction against the excitatory background. *Acta Biologiae Experimentalis, 15,* 155–170.

Konorski, J., & Szwejkowska, G. (1952). Chronic extinction and restoration of conditioned reflexes: IV. The dependence of the course of extinction and restoration of conditioned reflexes on the "history" of the conditioned stimulus (The principle of the primacy of first training). *Acta Biologiae Experimentalis, 16,* 95–113.

Koshland, D. E., Jr. (1989). Animal rights and animal wrongs. *Science, 243,* 1253.

Kraemer, P. J., & Roberts, W. A. (1985). Short-term memory for simultaneously presented visual and auditory signals in the pigeon. *Journal of Experimental Psychology: Animal Behavior Processes, 11,* 13–39.

Kraemer, P. J., Hoffmann, H., Randall, C. K., & Spear, N. E. (1992). Devaluation of Pavlovian conditioning in the 10-day-old rat. *Animal Learning & Behavior, 20,* 219–222.

Kraemer, P. J., Randall, C. K., & Carbary, T. J. (1991). Release from latent inhibition with delayed testing. *Animal Learning & Behavior, 19,* 139–145.

Krank, M. D. (1987). Conditioned hyperalgesia depends on the pain sensitivity measure. *Behavioral Neuroscience, 101,* 854–857.

Krebs, J. R., & McCleery, R. H. (1984). Optimization in behavioural ecology. In J. R. Krebs & N. B. Davies (Eds.), *Behavioural ecology* (2nd ed.). Sunderland, MA: Sinauer.

Kremer, E. F. (1978). The Rescorla-Wagner model: Losses in associative strength in compound conditioned stimuli. *Journal of Experimental Psychology: Animal Behavior Processes, 4,* 22–36.

Kruse, J. M., Overmier, J. B., Konz, W. A., & Rokke, E. (1983). Pavlovian conditioned stimulus effects upon instrumental choice behavior are reinforcer specific. *Learning and Motivation, 14,* 165–181.

Lachnit, H., & Kimmel, H. D. (1993). Positive and negative patterning in human classical skin conductance response conditioning. *Animal Learning & Behavior, 21,* 314–326.

Lamarre, J., & Holland, P. C. (1987). Transfer of inhibition after serial feature negative discrimination training. *Learning and Motivation, 18,* 319–342.

Lamb, R. J., & Henningfield, J. E. (1994). Human d-amphetamine drug discrimination: Methamphetamine and hydromorphone. *Journal of the Experimental Analysis of Behavior, 61,* 169–180.

Lansdell, H. (1988). Laboratory animals need only humane treatment: Animal "rights" may debase human rights. *International Journal of Neuroscience, 42,* 169–178.

Lashley, K. S., & Wade, M. (1946). The Pavlovian theory of generalization. *Psychological Review, 53,* 72–87.

Lattal, K. A., & Gleeson, S. (1990). Response acquisition with delayed reinforcement. *Journal of Experimental Psychology: Animal Behavior Processes, 16,* 27–39.

Lattal, K. A., & Metzger, B. (1994). Response acquisition by Siamese fighting fish (*Betta spendens*) with delayed visual reinforcement. *Journal of the Experimental Analysis of Behavior, 61,* 35–44.

Lavin, M. J. (1976). The establishment of flavor-flavor associations using a sensory preconditioning training procedure. *Learning and Motivation, 7,* 173–183.

Lawler, C. P., & Cohen, P. S. (1992). Temporal patterns of schedule-induced drinking and pawgrooming in rats exposed to periodic food. *Animal Learning & Behavior, 20,* 266–280.

Lea, S. E. G. (1978). The psychology and economics of demand. *Psychological Bulletin, 85,* 441–466.

Lea, S. E. G. (1984). In what sense do pigeons learn concepts? In H. L. Roitblat, T. G. Bever, & H. S. Terrace (Eds.), *Animal cognition* (pp. 263–276). Hillsdale, NJ: Erlbaum.

Lea, S. E. G., & Ryan, C. M. E. (1983). Feature analysis of pigeon's acquisition of concept discrimination. In M. L. Commons, R. J. Herrnstein, & A. R. Wagner (Eds.), *Quantitative analyses of behavior: Vol. 4. Discrimination processes* (pp. 239–253). Cambridge, MA: Ballinger.

Lea, S. E. G., Lohmann, A., & Ryan, C. M. E. (1993). Discrimination of five-dimensional stimuli by pigeons: Limitations of feature analysis. *Quarterly Journal of Experimental Psychology, 46B,* 19–42.

Leak, T. M., & Gibbon, J. (1995). Simultaneous timing of multiple intervals: Implications of the scalar property. *Journal of Experimental Psychology: Animal Behavior Processes, 21,* 3–19.

Leaton, R. N. (1976). Long-term retention of the habituation of lick suppression and startle response produced by a single auditory stimulus. *Journal of Experimental Psychology: Animal Behavior Processes, 2,* 248–259.

Leclerc, R., & Reberg, D. (1980). Sign-tracking in aversive conditioning. *Learning and Motivation, 11,* 302 317.

Lee, R. K. K., & Maier, S. F. (1988). Inescapable shock and attention to internal versus external cues in a water discrimination escape task. *Journal of Experimental Psychology: Animal Behavior Processes, 14,* 302–310.

Leinbach, M. D., & Fagot, B. I. (1993). Categorical habituation to male and female faces: Gender schematic processing in infancy. *Infant Behavior and Development, 16,* 317–332.

Lejeune, H., & Wearden, J. H. (1991). The comparative psychology of fixed-interval responding: Some quantitative analyses. *Learning and Motivation, 22,* 84–111.

Lennenberg, E. H. (1967). *Biological foundations of language.* New York: Wiley.

Lepper, M. R., Greene, D., & Nisbett, R. E. (1973). Undermining children's intrinsic interest with extrinsic reward: A test of the "overjustification"

hypothesis. *Journal of Personality and Social Psychology, 28,* 129–137.

Levine, F. M., & Sandeen, E. (1985). *Conceptualization in psychotherapy: The models approach.* Hillsdale, NJ: Erlbaum.

Levis, D. J. (1976). Learned helplessness: A reply and alternative S-R interpretation. *Journal of Experimental Psychology: General, 105,* 47–65.

Levis, D. J. (1981). Extrapolation of two-factor learning theory of infrahuman avoidance behavior to psychopathology. *Neuroscience & Biobehavioral Reviews, 5,* 355–370.

Levis, D. J. (1989). The case for a return to a two-factor theory of avoidance: The failure of non-fear interpretations. In S. B. Klein & R. R. Mowrer (Eds.), *Contemporary learning theories: Pavlovian conditioning and the status of learning theory* (pp. 227–277). Hillsdale, NJ: Erlbaum.

Levis, D. J. (1991). A clinician's plea for a return to the development of nonhuman models of psychopathology: New clinical observations in need of laboratory study. In M. R. Denny (Ed.), *Fear, avoidance and phobias* (pp. 395–427). Hillsdale, NJ: Erlbaum.

Lewis, D. J. (1979). Psychobiology of active and inactive memory. *Psychological Bulletin, 86,* 1054–1083.

Lieberman, D. A., & Thomas, G. V. (1986). Marking, memory and superstition in the pigeon. *Quarterly Journal of Experimental Psychology, 38B,* 449–459.

Lieberman, D. A., Davidson, F. H., & Thomas, G. V. (1985). Marking in pigeons: The role of memory in delayed reinforcement. *Journal of Experimental Psychology: Animal Behavior Processes, 11,* 611–624.

Lieberman, D. A., McIntosh, D. C., & Thomas, G. V. (1979). Learning when reward is delayed: A marking hypothesis. *Journal of Experimental Psychology: Animal Behavior Processes, 5,* 224–242.

Liebman, J. M., & Cooper, S. J. (Eds.) (1989). *The neuropharmacological basis of reward.* Oxford: Clarendon Press.

Linscheid, T. R., & Cunningham, C. E. (1977). A controlled demonstration of the effectiveness of electric shock in the elimination of chronic infant rumination. *Journal of Applied Behavior Analysis, 10,* 500.

Little, A. H., Lipsitt, L. P., & Rovee-Collier, C. (1984). Classical conditioning and retention of the infant's eyelid response: Effects of age and interstimulus interval. *Journal of Experimental Child Psychology, 37,* 512–524.

Lockard, R. B. (1968). The albino rat: A defensible choice or a bad habit? *American Psychologist, 23,* 734–742.

Locurto, C. M. (1981). Contributions of autoshaping to the partitioning of conditioned behavior. In C. M. Locurto, H. S. Terrace, & J. Gibbon (Eds.), *Autoshaping and conditioning theory* (pp. 101–135). New York: Academic Press.

Locurto, C. M., Terrace, H. S., & Gibbon, J. (Eds.). (1981). *Autoshaping and conditioning theory.* New York: Academic Press.

Loeb, J. (1900). *Comparative physiology of the brain and comparative psychology.* New York: G. P. Putman.

Logue, A. W. (1982). Expecting shock. *Behavioral and Brain Sciences, 5,* 680–681.

Logue, A. W. (1985). Conditioned food aversion learning in humans. *Annals of the New York Academy of Sciences, 443,* 316–329.

Logue, A. W. (1988a). A comparison of taste aversion learning in humans and other vertebrates: Evolutionary pressures in common. In R. C. Bolles & M. D. Beecher (Eds.), *Evolution and learning* (pp. 97–116). Hillsdale, NJ: Erlbaum.

Logue, A. W. (1988b). Research on self-control: An integrating framework. *Behavioral and Brain Sciences, 11,* 665–709.

Logue, A. W., & Chavarro, A. (1987). Effect on choice of absolute and relative values of reinforcer delay, amount, and frequency. *Journal of Experimental Psychology: Animal Behavior Processes, 13,* 280–291.

Logue, A. W., Forzano, L. B., & Tobin, H. (1992). Independence of reinforcer amount and delay: The generalized matching law and self-control

in humans. *Learning and Motivation, 23,* 326–342.

Logue, A. W., King, G. R., Chavarro, A., & Volpe, J. S. (1990). Matching and maximizing in a self-control paradigm using human subjects. *Learning and Motivation, 21,* 340–368.

Logue, A. W., Ophir, I., & Strauss, K. E. (1981). The acquisition of taste aversions in humans. *Behaviour Research and Therapy, 19,* 319–333.

Logue, A. W., Peña-Correal, T. E., Rodriguez, M. L., & Kabela, E. (1986). Self-control in adult humans: Variation in positive reinforcer amount and delay. *Journal of the Experimental Analysis of Behavior, 46,* 159–173.

LoLordo, V. M. (1971). Facilitation of food-reinforced responding by a signal for response-independent food. *Journal of the Experimental Analysis of Behavior, 15,* 49–55.

LoLordo, V. M. (1979). Selective associations. In A. Dickinson & R. A. Boakes (Eds.), *Mechanisms of learning and motivation* (pp. 367–398). Hillsdale, NJ: Erlbaum.

LoLordo, V. M., & Fairless, J. L. (1985). Pavlovian conditioned inhibition: The literature since 1969. In R. R. Miller & N. E. Spear (Eds.), *Information processing in animals: Conditioned inhibition* (pp. 1–49). Hillsdale, NJ: Erlbaum.

LoLordo, V. M., Jacobs, W. J., & Foree, D. D. (1982). Failure to block control by a relevant stimulus. *Animal Learning & Behavior, 10,* 183–193.

LoLordo, V. M., McMillan, J. C., & Riley, A. L. (1974). The effects upon food-reinforced pecking and treadle-pressing of auditory and visual signals for response-independent food. *Learning and Motivation, 5,* 24–41.

Losey, G. S., & Sevenster, P. (1995). Can three-spined sticklebacks learn when to display? Rewarded displays. *Animal Behaviour, 49,* 137–150.

Lovibond, P. F. (1983). Facilitation of instrumental behavior by a Pavlovian appetitive conditioned stimulus. *Journal of Experimental Psychology: Animal Behavior Processes, 9,* 225–247.

Lubow, R. E. (1989). *Latent inhibition and conditioned attention theory.* Cam-

bridge, England: Cambridge University Press.

Lubow, R. E., & Gewirtz, J. C. (1995). Latent inhibition in humans: Data, theory, and implications for schizophrenia. *Psychological Bulletin, 117,* 87–103.

Lubow, R. E., Weiner, I., & Schnur, P. (1981). Conditioned attention theory. In G. H. Bower (Ed.), *The psychology of learning and motivation* (Vol. 15, pp. 1–49). Orlando, FL: Academic Press.

Lucas, G. A., Timberlake, W., & Gawley, D. J. (1988). Adjunctive behavior of the rat under periodic food delivery in a 24-hour environment. *Animal Learning & Behavior, 16,* 19–30.

Lyon, D. O. (1968). Conditioned suppression: Operant variables and aversive control. *Psychological Record, 18,* 317–338.

Lysle, D. T., & Fowler, H. (1985). Inhibition as a "slave" process: Deactivation of conditioned inhibition through extinction of conditioned excitation. *Journal of Experimental Psychology: Animal Behavior Processes, 11,* 71–94.

MacArdy, E. A., & Riccio, D. C. (1995). Time-dependent changes in the effectiveness of a noncontingent footshock reminder. *Learning and Motivation, 26,* 29–42.

MacDonald, S. E. (1993). Delayed matching-to-successive-samples in pigeons: Short-term memory for item and order information. *Animal Learning & Behavior, 21,* 59–67.

MacEwen, D., & Killeen, P. (1991). The effects of rate and amount of reinforcement on the speed of the pacemaker in pigeons' timing behavior. *Animal Learning & Behavior, 19,* 164–170.

Machado, A. (1989). Operant conditioning of behavioral variability using a percentile reinforcement schedule. *Journal of the Experimental Analysis of Behavior, 52,* 155–166.

Machado, A. (1992). Behavioral variability and frequency-dependent selection. *Journal of the Experimental Analysis of Behavior, 58,* 241–263.

Machado, A. (1994). Polymorphic response patterns under frequency-dependent selection. *Animal Learning & Behavior, 22,* 53–71.

Mackintosh, N. J. (1974). *The psychology of animal learning.* London: Academic Press.

Mackintosh, N. J. (1975). A theory of attention: Variations in the associability of stimuli with reinforcement. *Psychological Review, 82,* 276–298.

Mackintosh, N. J. (1995). Categorization by people and pigeons: The twenty-second Bartlett memorial lecture. *Quarterly Journal of Experimental Psychology, 48B,* 193–214.

Mackintosh, N. J., Bygrave, D. J., & Picton, B. M. B. (1977). Locus of the effect of a surprising reinforcer in the attenuation of blocking. *Quarterly Journal of Experimental Psychology, 29,* 327–336.

Mackintosh, N. J., & Dickinson, A. (1979). Instrumental (Type II) conditioning. In A. Dickinson & R. A. Boakes (Eds.), *Mechanisms of learning and motivation* (pp. 143–169). Hillsdale, NJ: Erlbaum.

Macuda, T., & Roberts, W. A. (1995). Further evidence for hierarchical chunking in rat spatial memory. *Journal of Experimental Psychology: Animal Behavior Processes, 21,* 20–32.

Maier, S. F. (1990). Role of fear in mediating shuttle escape learning deficit produced by inescapable shock. *Journal of Experimental Psychology: Animal Behavior Processes, 16,* 137–149.

Maier, S. F., & Church, R. M. (Eds.) (1991). Special issue on animal timing. *Learning and Motivation, 22,* 1–252.

Maier, S. F., & Jackson, R. L. (1979). Learned helplessness: All of us were right (and wrong): Inescapable shock has multiple effects. In G. H. Bower (Ed.), *The psychology of learning and motivation* (Vol. 13, pp. 155–218). New York: Academic Press.

Maier, S. F., & Seligman, M. E. P. (1976). Learned helplessness: Theory and evidence. *Journal of Experimental Psychology: General, 105,* 3–46.

Maier, S. F., & Warren, D. A. (1988). Controllability and safety signals exert dissimilar proactive effects on nociception and escape performance. *Journal of Experimental Psychology: Animal Behavior Processes, 14,* 18–25.

Maier, S. F., Jackson, R. L., & Tomie, A. (1987). Potentiation, overshadowing, and prior exposure to inescapable shock. *Journal of Experimental Psychology: Animal Behavior Processes, 13,* 260–270.

Maier, S. F., Rapaport, P., & Wheatley, K. L. (1976). Conditioned inhibition and the UCS-CS interval. *Animal Learning & Behavior, 4,* 217–220.

Maier, S. F., Seligman, M. E. P., & Solomon, R. L. (1969). Pavlovian fear conditioning and learned helplessness. In B. A. Campbell & R. M. Church (Eds.), *Punishment and aversive behavior* (pp. 299–342). New York: Appleton-Century-Crofts.

Maki, W. S. (1979). Pigeon's short-term memories for surprising vs. expected reinforcement and nonreinforcement. *Animal Learning & Behavior, 7,* 31–37.

Maki, W. S. (1987). On the nonassociative nature of working memory. *Learning and Motivation, 18,* 99–117.

Maki, W. S., Beatty, W. W., Hoffman, N., Bierley, R. A., & Clouse, B. A. (1984). Spatial memory over long retention intervals: Nonmemorial factors are not necessary for accurate performance on the radial arm maze by rats. *Behavioral and Neural Biology, 41,* 1–6.

Maki, W. S., Moe, J. C., & Bierley, C. M. (1977). Short-term memory for stimuli, responses, and reinforcers. *Journal of Experimental Psychology: Animal Behavior Processes, 3,* 156–177.

March, J., Chamizo, V. D., & Mackintosh, N. J. (1992). Reciprocal overshadowing between intra-maze and extra-maze cues. *Quarterly Journal of Experimental Psychology, 45,* 49–63.

Marchant, H. G., III, Mis, F. W., & Moore, J. W. (1972). Conditioned inhibition of the rabbit's nictitating membrane response. *Journal of Experimental Psychology, 95,* 408–411.

Maricq, A. V., Roberts, S., & Church, R. M. (1981). Methamphetamine and time estimation. *Journal of Experimental Psychology: Animal Behavior Processes, 7,* 18–30.

Marlin, N. A. (1981). Contextual associations in trace conditioning. *Animal Learning & Behavior, 9,* 519–523.

Marlin, N.A., & Miller, R. R. (1981). Associations to contextual stimuli as a determinant of long-term habituation. *Journal of Experimental Psychology: Animal Behavior Processes, 7,* 313–333.

Marsh, G. (1972). Prediction of the peak shift in pigeons from gradients of excitation and inhibition. *Journal of Comparative and Physiological Psychology, 81,* 262–266.

Martens, B. K., Lochner, D. G., & Kelly, S. Q. (1992). The effects of variable-interval reinforcement on academic engagement: A demonstration of matching theory. *Journal of Applied Behavior Analysis, 25,* 143–151.

Masserman, J. H. (1946). *Principles of dynamic psychiatry.* Philadelphia: Saunders.

Mast, M., Blanchard, R. J., & Blanchard, D. C. (1982). The relationship of freezing and response suppression in a CER situation. *Psychological Record, 32,* 151–167.

Matthews, T. J., Bordi, F., & Depollo, D. (1990). Schedule induced kinesic and taxic behavioral stereotypy in the pigeon. *Journal of Experimental Psychology: Animal Behavior Processes, 16,* 335–344.

Matzel, L. D., Brown, A. M., & Miller, R. R. (1987). Associative effects of US preexposure: Modulation of conditioned responding by an excitatory training context. *Journal of Experimental Psychology: Animal Behavior Processes, 13,* 65–72.

Matzel, L. D., Gladstein, L., & Miller, R. R. (1988). Conditioned excitation and conditioned inhibition are not mutually exclusive. *Learning and Motivation, 19,* 99–121.

Matzel, L. D., Held, F. P., & Miller, R. R. (1988). Information and expression of simultaneous and backward associations: Implications for contiguity theory. *Learning and Motivation, 19,* 317–344.

Mayer-Gross, W. (1943). Retrograde amnesia. *Lancet, 2,* 603–605.

Mazmanian, D. S., & Roberts, W. A. (1983). Spatial memory in rats under restricted viewing conditions. *Learning and Motivation, 14,* 123–139.

Mazur, J. E. (1991). Choice with probabilistic reinforcement: Effects of delay and conditioned reinforcers. *Journal of the Experimental Analysis of Behavior, 55,* 63–77.

Mazur, J. E., & Romano, A. (1992). Choice with delayed and probabilistic reinforcers: Effects of variability, time between trials, and conditioned reinforcers. *Journal of the Experimental Analysis of Behavior, 58,* 513–525.

McAllister, D. E., & McAllister, W. R. (1991). Fear theory and aversively motivated behavior: Some controversial issues. In M. R. Denny (Ed.), *Fear, avoidance and phobias* (pp. 135–163). Hillsdale, NJ: Erlbaum.

McAllister, W. R., & McAllister, D. E. (1971). Behavioral measurement of fear. In F. R. Brush (Ed.), *Aversive conditioning and learning* (pp. 105–179). New York: Academic Press.

McAllister, W. R., & McAllister, D. E. (1992). Fear determines the effectiveness of a feedback stimulus in aversively motivated instrumental learning. *Learning and Motivation, 23,* 99–115.

McCarthy, D., Voss, P., & Davison, M. (1994). Leaving patches: Effects of travel requirements. *Journal of the Experimental Analysis of Behavior, 62,* 185–200.

McDowell, J. J. (1981). On the validity and utility of Herrnstein's hyperbola in applied behavioral analysis. In C. M. Bradshaw, E. Szabadi, & C. F. Lowe (Eds.), *Quantification of steady-state operant behaviour.* Amsterdam: Elsevier/North-Holland.

McDowell, J. J. (1982). The importance of Herrnstein's mathematical statement of the law of effect for behavior therapy. *American Psychologist, 37,* 771–779.

McDowell, J. J., & Wixted, J. T. (1988). The linear system theory's account of behavior maintained by variable ratio schedules. *Journal of the Experimental Analysis of Behavior, 49,* 143–169.

McDowell, J. J., & Wood, H. M. (1985). Confirmation of linear system theory prediction: Rate of change of Herrnstein's k as a function of response-force requirement. *Journal of the Experimental Analysis of Behavior, 43,* 61–73.

McGaugh, J. L., & Herz, M. J. (1972). *Memory consolidation.* San Francisco: Albion.

McGaugh, J. L., & Petrinovich, L. F. (1965). Effects of drugs on learning and memory. *International Review of Neurobiology, 8,* 139–196.

McGee, G. G., Krantz, P. J., & McClannahan, L. E. (1986). An extension of incidental teaching procedures to reading instruction for autistic children. *Journal of Applied Behavior Analysis, 19,* 147–157.

McSweeney, F. K., & Melville, C. L. (1993). Behavioral contrast for key pecking as a function of component duration when only one component varies. *Journal of the Experimental Analysis of Behavior, 60,* 311–343.

McSweeney, F. K., Melville, C. L., Buck, M. A., & Whipple, J. E. (1983). Local rates of responding and reinforcement during concurrent schedules. *Journal of the Experimental Analysis of Behavior, 40,* 79–98.

Meachum, C. L., & Bernstein, I. L. (1990). Conditioned responses to a taste conditioned stimulus paired with lithium-chloride administration. *Behavioral Neuroscience, 104,* 711–715.

Meck, W. H. (1983). Selective adjustment of the speed of internal clock and memory processes. *Journal of Experimental Psychology: Animal Behavior Processes, 9,* 171–201.

Meck, W. H. (1988). Hippocampal function is required for feedback control of an internal clock's criterion. *Behavioral Neuroscience, 102,* 54–60.

Meck, W. H., & Church, R. M. (1982). Abstraction of temporal attributes. *Journal of Experimental Psychology: Animal Behavior Processes, 8,* 226–243.

Meck, W. H., & Church, R. M. (1987a). Cholinergic modulation of the content of temporal memory. *Behavioral Neuroscience, 101,* 457–464.

Meck, W. H., & Church, R. M. (1987b). Nutrients that modify the speed of internal clock and memory storage processes. *Behavioral Neuroscience, 101,* 465–475.

Meck, W. H., Church, R. M., & Olton, D. S. (1984). Hippocampus, time, and memory. *Behavioral Neuroscience, 98,* 3–22.

Meck, W. H., Church, R. M., Wenk, G. L., & Olton, D. S. (1987). Nucleus basalis magnocellularis and medial septal area lesions differentially impair temporal memory. *Journal of Neuroscience, 7,* 3505–3511.

Medin, D. L. (1980). Proactive interference in monkeys: Delay and intersample interval effects are noncomparable. *Animal Learning & Behavior, 8,* 553–560.

Meehl, P. E. (1950). On the circularity of the law of effect. *Psychological Bulletin, 47,* 52–75.

Mehrabian, A. (1970). A semantic space for nonverbal behavior. *Journal of Consulting and Clinical Psychology, 35,* 248–257.

Mehrabian, A., & Weiner, M. (1966). Decoding of inconsistent communications. *Journal of Personality and Social Psychology, 6,* 109–114.

Mellgren, R. L. (1972). Positive and negative contrast effects using delayed reinforcement. *Learning and Motivation, 3,* 185–193.

Mellgren, R. L. (1982). Foraging in simulated natural environments: There's a rat loose in the lab. *Journal of the Experimental Analysis of Behavior, 38,* 93–100.

Melvin, K. B. (1971). Vicious circle behavior. In H. D. Kimmel (Ed.), *Experimental psychopathology.* New York: Academic Press.

Melvin, K. B., & Ervey, D. H. (1973). Facilitative and suppressive effects of punishment of species-typical aggressive display in *Betta splendens. Journal of Comparative and Physiological Psychology, 83,* 451–457.

Midgley, M., Lea, S. E. G., & Kirby, R. M. (1989). Algorithmic shaping and misbehavior in the acquisition of token deposit by rats. *Journal of the Experimental Analysis of Behavior, 52,* 27–40.

Miller, H. L. (1976). Matching-based hedonic scaling in the pigeon. *Journal of the Experimental Analysis of Behavior, 26,* 335–347.

Miller, J. S., Jagielo, J. A., & Spear, N. E. (1990a). Alleviation of short-term forgetting: Effects of the CS– and other conditioning elements in prior cueing or as context during test. *Learning and Motivation, 21,* 96–109.

Miller, J. S., Jagielo, J. A., & Spear, N. E. (1990b). Changes in the retrievability of associations to elements of the compound CS determine the expression of overshadowing. *Animal Learning & Behavior, 18,* 157–161.

Miller, J. S., Jagielo, J. A., & Spear, N. E. (1991). Differential effectiveness of various prior-cuing treatments in the reactivation and maintenance of memory. *Journal of Experimental Psychology: Animal Behavior Processes, 17,* 249–258.

Miller, J. S., Jagielo, J. A., & Spear, N. E. (1992). The influence of the information value provided by prior-cuing treatment on the reactivation of memory in preweanling rats. *Animal Learning & Behavior, 20,* 233–239.

Miller, J. S., Jagielo, J. A., & Spear, N. E. (1993). The influence of retention interval on the US preexposure effect: Changes in contextual blocking over time. *Learning and Motivation, 24,* 376–394.

Miller, N. E. (1948). Studies of fear as an acquirable drive: I. Fear as motivation and fear-reduction as reinforcement in the learning of new responses. *Journal of Experimental Psychology, 38,* 89–101.

Miller, N. E. (1951). Learnable drives and rewards. In S. S. Stevens (Ed.), *Handbook of experimental psychology.* New York: Wiley.

Miller, N. E. (1960). Learning resistance to pain and fear: Effects of overlearning, exposure, and rewarded exposure

in context. *Journal of Experimental Psychology, 60,* 137–145.

Miller, N. E. (1985). The value of behavioral research on animals. *American Psychologist, 40,* 423–440.

Miller, N. E., & Dollard, J. (1941). *Social learning and imitation.* New Haven, CT: Yale University Press.

Miller, N. E., & Kessen, M. L. (1952). Reward effect of food via stomach fistula compared with those of food via mouth. *Journal of Comparative and Physiological Psychology, 45,* 555–564.

Miller, R. R., & Matzel, L. D. (1988). The comparator hypothesis: A response rule for the expression of associations. In G. H. Bower (Ed.), *The psychology of learning and motivation* (pp. 51–92). Orlando, FL: Academic Press.

Miller, R. R., & Matzel, L. D. (1989). Contingency and relative associative strength. In S. B. Klein and R. R. Mowrer (Eds.), *Contemporary learning theories: Pavlovian conditioning and the status of learning theory* (pp. 61–84). Hillsdale, NJ: Erlbaum.

Miller, R. R., & Spear, N. E. (Eds.). (1985). *Information processing in animals: Conditioned inhibition.* Hillsdale, NJ: Erlbaum.

Miller, R. R., & Springer, A. D. (1973). Amnesia, consolidation, and retrieval. *Psychological Review, 80,* 69–79.

Miller, R. R., Barnet, R. C., & Grahame, N. J. (1992). Responding to a conditioned stimulus depends on the current associative status of other cues present during training of that specific stimuuls. *Journal of Experimental Psychology: Animal Behavior Processes, 18,* 251–264.

Miller, R. R., Barnet, R. C., & Grahame, N. J. (1995). Assessment of the Rescorla-Wagner model. *Psychological Bulletin, 117,* 363–386.

Miller, R. R., Hallam, S. C., & Grahame, N. J. (1990). Inflation of comparator stimuli following CS training. *Animal Learning & Behavior, 18,* 434–443.

Miller, R. R., Hallam, S. C., Hong, J. Y., & Dufore, D. S. (1991). Associative structure of differential inhibition: Implications for models of conditioned inhibition. *Journal of Experi-*

mental Psychology: Animal Behavior Processes, 17, 141–150.

Miller, R. R., Kasprow, W. J., & Schachtman, T. R. (1986). Retrieval variability: Sources and consequences. *American Journal of Psychology, 99,* 145–218.

Miller, V., & Domjan, M. (1981). Selective sensitization induced by lithium malaise and footshock in rats. *Behavioral and Neural Biology, 31,* 42–55.

Mineka, S. (1979). The role of fear in theories of avoidance learning, flooding, and extinction. *Psychological Bulletin, 86,* 985–1010.

Mineka, S., & Cook, M. (1988). Social learning and the acquisition of snake fear in monkeys. In T. Zentall & B. G. Galef, Jr. (Eds.), *Social learning* (pp. 51–73). Hillsdale, NJ: Erlbaum.

Mineka, S., & Gino, A. (1979). Dissociative effects of different types and amounts of nonreinforced CS exposure on avoidance extinction and the CER. *Learning and Motivation, 10,* 141–160.

Mineka, S., & Gino, A. (1980). Dissociation between conditioned emotional response and extended avoidance performance. *Learning and Motivation, 11,* 476–502.

Mineka, S., Miller, S., Gino, A., & Giencke, L. (1981). Dissociative effects of flooding on a multivariate assessment of fear reduction and on jump-up avoidance extinction. *Learning and Motivation, 12,* 435–461.

Mineka, S., Suomi, S. J., & DeLizio, R. (1981). Multiple separations in adolescent monkeys: An opponent process interpretation. *Journal of Experimental Psychology: General, 110,* 56–85.

Minor, T. R., Dess, N. K., & Overmier, J. B. (1991). Inverting the traditional view of "learned helplessness." In M. R. Denny (Ed.), *Fear, avoidance and phobias* (pp. 87–133). Hillsdale, NJ: Erlbaum.

Minor, T. R., Trauner, M. A., Lee, C.-Y., & Dess, N. K. (1990). Modeling signal features of escape response: Effects of cessation conditioning in "learned helplessness" paradigm. *Journal of*

Experimental Psychology: Animal Behavior Processes, 16, 123–136.

Mitchell, S. H., & Brener, J. (1991). Energetic and motor responses to increasing food requirements. Journal of Experimental Psychology: Animal Behavior Processes, 17, 174–185.

Morgan, C. L. (1903). Introduction to comparative psychology (Rev. ed.). New York: Scribner.

Morgan, L., & Neuringer, A. (1990). Behavioral variability as a function of response topography and reinforcement contingency. Animal Learning & Behavior, 18, 257–263.

Morgan, M. J., Fitch, M. D., Holman, J. G., & Lea, S. E. G. (1976). Pigeons learn the concept of an "A." Perception, 5, 57–66.

Morris, C. J. (1987). The operant conditioning of response variability: Free-operant versus discrete-response procedures. Journal of the Experimental Analysis of Behavior, 47, 273–277.

Morris, R. G. (1987). Identity matching and oddity learning in patients with moderate to severe Alzheimer-type dementia. Quarterly Journal of Experimental Psychology, 39B, 215–227.

Morris, R. G. M. (1974). Pavlovian conditioned inhibition of fear during shuttlebox avoidance behavior. Learning and Motivation, 5, 424–447.

Morris, R. G. M. (1975). Preconditioning of reinforcing properties to an exteroceptive feedback stimulus. Learning and Motivation, 6, 289–298.

Morris, R. G. M. (1981). Spatial localization does not require the presence of local cues. Learning and Motivation, 12, 239–260.

Mowrer, O. H. (1947). On the dual nature of learning: A reinterpretation of "conditioning" and "problem-solving." Harvard Educational Review, 17, 102–150.

Mowrer, O. H. (1960). Learning theory and behavior. New York: Wiley.

Mowrer, O. H., & Lamoreaux, R. R. (1942). Avoidance conditioning and signal duration: A study of secondary motivation and reward. Psychological Monographs, 54 (Whole No. 247).

Mowrer, R. R., & Gordon, W. C. (1983). Effects of cuing in an "irrelevant" context. Animal Learning & Behavior, 11, 401–406.

Moye, T. B., & Thomas, D. R. (1982). Effects of memory reactivation treatments on postdiscrimination generalization performance in pigeons. Animal Learning & Behavior, 10, 159–166.

Myerson, J., & Hale, S. (1988). Choice in transition: A comparison of melioration and the kinetic model. Journal of the Experimental Analysis of Behavior, 49, 291–302.

Napier, R. M., Macrae, M., & Kehoe, E. J. (1992). Rapid reacquisition in conditioning of the rabbit's nictitating membrane response. Journal of Experimental Psychology: Animal Behavior Processes, 18, 182–192.

Nash, S., & Domjan, M. (1991). Learning to discriminate the sex of conspecifics in male Japanese quail (Coturnix coturnix japonica): Tests of "biological constraints." Journal of Experimental Psychology: Animal Behavior Processes, 17, 342–353.

Nash, S., Domjan, M., & Askins, M. (1989). Sexual discrimination learning in male Japanese quail (Coturnix coturnix japonica). Journal of Comparative Psychology, 103, 347–358.

Nation, J. R., & Cooney, J. B. (1982). The time course of extinction-induced aggressive behavior in humans: Evidence for a stage model of extinction. Learning and Motivation, 13, 95–112.

Neill, J. C., & Harrison, J. M. (1987). Auditory discrimination: The Konorski quality-location effect. Journal of the Experimental Analysis of Behavior, 48, 81–95.

Neuenschwander, N., Fabrigoule, C., & Mackintosh, N. J. (1987). Fear of the warning signal during overtraining of avoidance. Quarterly Journal of Experimental Psychology, 39B, 23–33.

Neuringer, A. (1991). Operant variability and repetition as functions of interresponse time. Journal of Experimental Psychology: Animal Behavior Processes, 17, 3–12.

Neuringer, A. (1992). Choosing to vary and repeat. Psychological Science, 3, 246–250.

Neuringer, A. (1993). Reinforced variation and selection. Animal Learning & Behavior, 21, 83–91.

Nevin, J. A. (1969). Interval reinforcement of choice behavior in discrete trials. Journal of the Experimental Analysis of Behavior, 12, 875–885.

Nevin, J. A. (1979). Overall matching versus momentary maximizing: Nevin (1969) revisited. Journal of Experimental Psychology: Animal Behavior Processes, 5, 300–306.

Nicoll, C. S., & Russell, S. M. (1990). Analysis of animal rights literature reveals the underlying motives of the movement: Ammunition for counter offensive by scientists. Endocrinology, 127, 985–989.

Noble, G. K., & Vogt, W. (1935). An experimental study of sex recognition in birds. Auk, 52, 278–286.

Obal, F. (1966). The fundamentals of the central nervous system of vegetative homeostasis. Acta Physiologica Academiae Scientiarum Hungaricae, 30, 15–29.

Oden, D. L., Thompson, R. K. R., & Premack, D. (1988). Spontaneous transfer of matching by infant chimpanzees (Pan troglodytes). Journal of Experimental Psychology: Animal Behavior Processes, 14, 140–145.

Öhman, A., Dimberg, U., & Öst, L. G. (1985). Animal and social phobias: Biological constraints on learned fear responses. In S. Reiss & R. R. Bootzin (Eds.), Theoretical issues in behavior therapy. Orlando, FL: Academic Press.

Olds, J., & Milner, P. (1954). Positive reinforcement produced by electrical stimulation of septal area and other regions of the rat brain. Journal of Comparative and Physiological Psychology, 47, 419–427.

Olds, M. E., & Olds, J. (1963). Approach-avoidance analysis of rat diencephalon. Journal of Comparative Neurology, 120, 259–295.

Olson, D. J. (1991). Species differences in spatial memory among Clark's nutcrackers, scrub jays, and pigeons.

Journal of Experimental Psychology: Animal Behavior Processes, 17, 363–376.

Olson, D. J., & Maki, W. S. (1983). Characteristics of spatial memory in pigeons. *Journal of Experimental Psychology: Animal Behavior Processes, 9,* 266–280.

Olton, D. S. (1978). Characteristics of spatial memory. In S. H. Hulse, H. Fowler, & W. K. Honig (Eds.), *Cognitive processes in animal behavior* (pp. 341–374). Hillsdale, NJ: Erlbaum.

Olton, D. S. (1979). Mazes, maps, and memory. *American Psychologist, 34,* 583–596.

Olton, D. S., & Samuelson, R. J. (1976). Remembrance of places passed: Spatial memory in rats. *Journal of Experimental Psychology: Animal Behavior Processes, 2,* 97–116.

Olton, D. S., Collison, C., & Werz, M. A. (1977). Spatial memory and radial arm maze performance of rats. *Learning and Motivation, 8,* 289–314.

Ost, J. W. P., & Lauer, D. W. (1965). Some investigations of salivary conditioning in the dog. In W. F. Prokasy (Ed.), *Classical conditioning* (pp. 192–207). New York: Appleton-Century-Crofts.

Overmier, J. B., & Burke, P. D. (Eds.) (1992). *Animal models of human pathology: A bibliography of a quarter century of behavioral research, 1967–1992.* Washington, D.C.: American Psychological Association.

Overmier, J. B., & Lawry, J. A. (1979). Pavlovian conditioning and the mediation of behavior. In G. H. Bower (Ed.), *The psychology of learning and motivation* (Vol. 13, pp. 1–55). New York: Academic Press.

Overmier, J. B., & Seligman, M. E. P. (1967). Effects of inescapable shock upon subsequent escape and avoidance learning. *Journal of Comparative and Physiological Psychology, 63,* 23–33.

Overmier, J. B., Bull, J. A., & Pack, K. (1971). On instrumental response interaction as explaining the influences of Pavlovian CSs upon avoidance behavior. *Learning and Motivation, 2,* 103–112.

Owen, J. W., Cicala, G. A., & Herdegen, R. T. (1978). Fear inhibition and species specific defense reaction termination may contribute independently to avoidance learning. *Learning and Motivation, 9,* 297–313.

Page, S., & Neuringer, A. (1985). Variability as an operant. *Journal of Experimental Psychology: Animal Behavior Processes, 11,* 429–452.

Palya, W. L. (1993). Bipolar control in fixed interfood intervals. *Journal of the Experimental Analysis of Behavior, 60,* 345–359.

Papadouka, V., & Matthews, T. J. (1995). Motivational mechanisms and schedule-induced behavioral stereotypy. *Animal Learning & Behavior, 23,* 461–469.

Papini, M. R., & Bitterman, M. E. (1993). The two-test strategy in the study of inhibitory conditioning. *Journal of Experimental Psychology: Animal Behavior Processes, 19,* 342–352.

Papini, M. R., & Bitterman, M. E. (1990). The role of contingency in classical conditioning. *Psychological Review, 97,* 396–403.

Parker, B. K., Serdikoff, S. L., Kaminski, B. J., & Critchfield, T. S. (1991). Stimulus control of Pavlovian facilitation. *Journal of the Experimental Analysis of Behavior, 55,* 275–286.

Parker, L. A. (1988). Positively reinforcing drugs may produce a different kind of CTA than drugs which are not positively reinforcing. *Learning and Motivation, 19,* 207–220.

Patten, R. L., & Rudy, J. W. (1967). The Sheffield omission of training procedure applied to the conditioning of the licking response in rats. *Psychonomic Science, 8,* 463–464.

Patterson, F. G. (1978). The gestures of a gorilla: Language acquisition in another pongid. *Brain and Language, 5,* 56–71.

Pavlov, I. P. (1927). *Conditioned reflexes* (G. V. Anrep, trans.). London: Oxford University Press.

Pear, J. J., & Legris, J. A. (1987). Shaping by automated tracking of an arbitrary operant response. *Journal of the Experimental Analysis of Behavior, 47,* 241–247.

Pearce, J. M. (1987). A model for stimulus generalization in Pavlovian conditioning. *Psychological Review, 94,* 61–73.

Pearce, J. M. (1994a). Discrimination and categorization. In N. J. Mackintosh (Ed.), *Animal learning and cognition* (pp. 109–134). San Diego: Academic Press.

Pearce, J. M. (1994b). Similarity and discrimination: A selective review and a connectionist model. *Psychological Review, 101,* 587–607.

Pearce, J. M., & Dickinson, A. (1975). Pavlovian counterconditioning: Changing the suppressive properties of shock by association with food. *Journal of Experimental Psychology: Animal Behavior Processes, 1,* 170–177.

Pearce, J. M., & Hall, G. (1980). A model for Pavlovian learning: Variations in the effectiveness of conditioned but not of unconditioned stimuli. *Psychological Review, 87,* 532–552.

Pearce, J. M., & Redhead, E. S. (1993). The influence of an irrelevant stimulus on two discriminations. *Journal of Experimental Psychology: Animal Behavior Processes, 19,* 180–190.

Pearce, J. M., & Wilson, P. N. (1990a). Configural associations in discrimination learning. *Journal of Experimental Psychology: Animal Behavior Processes, 16,* 250–261.

Pearce, J. M., & Wilson, P. N. (1990b). Feature-positive discrimination learning. *Journal of Experimental Psychology: Animal Behavior Processes, 16,* 315–325.

Peck, C. A., & Bouton, M. E. (1990). Context and performance in aversive-to-appetitive and appetitive-to-aversive transfer. *Learning and Motivation, 21,* 1–31.

Peden, B. F., Browne, M. P., & Hearst, E. (1977). Persistent approaches to a signal for food despite food omission for approaching. *Journal of Experimental Psychology: Animal Behavior Processes, 3,* 377–399.

Peeke, H. V. S., & Petrinovich, L. (Eds.). (1984). *Habituation, sensitization, and behavior.* New York: Academic Press.

Pelchat, M. L., & Rozin, P. (1982). The special role of nausea in the acquisition of food dislikes by humans. *Appetite, 3,* 341–351.

Pelchat, M. L., Grill, H. J., Rozin, P., & Jacobs, J. (1983). Quality of acquired responses to tastes by *Rattus norvegicus* depends on type of associated discomfort. *Journal of Comparative Psychology, 97,* 140–153.

Pepperberg, I. M. (1990). Some cognitive capacities of an African Grey parrot (*Psittacus erithacus*). In P. J. B. Slater, J. S. Rosenblatt, & C. Beer (Eds.), *Advances in the study of behavior* (Vol. 19, pp. 357–409). San Diego: Academic Press.

Pepperberg, I. M. (1993). Cognition and communication in an African Grey parrot (*Psittacus erithacus*): Studies on a nonhuman, nonprimate, nonmammalian subject. In Roitblat, H. L., Herman, L. M., & Nachtigall, P. E. (Eds.), *Language and communication: Comparative perspectives* (pp. 221–248). Hillsdale, NJ: Erlbaum.

Perkins, C. C., Jr. (1955). The stimulus conditions which follow learned responses. *Psychological Review, 62,* 341–348.

Perkins, C. C., Jr. (1968). An analysis of the concept of reinforcement. *Psychological Review, 75,* 155–172.

Perry, D. G., & Parke, R. D. (1975). Punishment and alternative response training as determinants of response inhibition in children. *Genetic Psychology Monographs, 91,* 257–279.

Peterson, C., & Seligman, M. E. P. (1984). Causal explanations as a risk factor for depression: Theory and evidence. *Psychological Review, 91,* 347–374.

Peterson, C., Maier, S. F., & Seligman, M. E. P. (1993). *Learned helplessness: A theory for the age of personal control.* New York: Oxford University Press.

Peterson, G. B., & Trapold, M. A. (1980). Effects of altering outcome expectancies on pigeons' delayed conditional discrimination performance. *Learning and Motivation, 11,* 267–288.

Peterson, G. B., Ackil, J. E., Frommer, G. P., & Hearst, E. S. (1972). Conditioned approach and contact behavior toward signals for food and brain-stimulation reinforcement. *Science, 177,* 1009–1011.

Petry, N. M., & Heyman, G. M. (1994). Effects of qualitatively different reinforcers on the parameters of the response-strength equation. *Journal of the Experimental Analysis of Behavior, 61,* 97–106.

Petry, N. M., & Heyman, G. M. (1995). Behavioral economics of concurrent ethanol-sucrose and sucrose reinforcement in the rat: Effects of altering variable-ratio requirements. *Journal of the Experimental Analysis of Behavior, 64,* 331–359.

Phillips, A. G., & Fibiger, H. C. (1989). Neuroanatomical bases of intracranial self-stimulation: Untangling the Gordian knot. In J. M. Liebman & S. J. Cooper (Eds.), *The neuropharmacological basis of reward* (pp. 66–105). Oxford: Clarendon Press.

Pisacreta, R. (1982). Some factors that influence the acquisition of complex, stereotyped, response sequences in pigeons. *Journal of the Experimental Analysis of Behavior, 37,* 359–369.

Platt, J. R. (1973). Percentile reinforcement: Paradigms for experimental analysis of response shaping. In G. H. Bower (Ed.), *The psychology of learning and motivation* (Vol. 7, pp. 271–296). Orlando, FL: Academic Press.

Platt, S. A., Holliday, M., & Drudge, O. W. (1980). Discrimination learning of an instrumental response in individual *Drosophila melanogaster*. *Journal of Experimental Psychology: Animal Behavior Processes, 6,* 301–311.

Ploog, B. O., & Zeigler, H. P. (1996). Effects of food-pellet size on rate, latency, and topography of autoshaped key pecks and gapes in pigeons. *Journal of the Experimental Analysis of Behavior, 65,* 21–35.

Plotkin, H. C., & Odling-Smee, F. J. (1979). Learning, change, and evolution: An enquiry into the teleonomy of learning. In J. S. Rosenblatt, R. A. Hinde, C. Beer, & M.-C. Busnel (Eds.), *Advances in the study of behavior* (Vol. 10). New York: Academic Press.

Plous, S. (1991). An attitude survey of animal rights activists. *Psychological Science, 2,* 194–196.

Plowright, C. M. S., & Shettleworth, S. J. (1991). Time horizon and choice by pigeons in a prey-selection task. *Animal Learning & Behavior, 19,* 103–112.

Poling, A., Nickel, M., & Alling, K. (1990). Free birds aren't fat: Weight gain in captured wild pigeons maintained under laboratory conditions. *Journal of the Experimental Analysis of Behavior, 53,* 423–424.

Porter, D., & Neuringer, A. (1984). Music discrimination by pigeons. *Journal of Experimental Psychology: Animal Behavior Processes, 10,* 138–148.

Postman, L. (1971). Transfer, interference, and forgetting. In J. W. Kling & L. A. Riggs (Eds.), *Woodworth and Schlosberg's experimental psychology* (3rd ed.). New York: Holt, Rinehart and Winston.

Poulos, C. X., Hinson, R. E., & Siegel, S. (1981). The role of Pavlovian processes in drug tolerance and dependence: Implications for treatment. *Addictive Behaviors, 6,* 205–211.

Premack, A. J. (1976). *Why chimps can read.* New York: Harper & Row.

Premack, D. (1962). Reversibility of the reinforcement relation. *Science, 136,* 255–257.

Premack, D. (1965). Reinforcement theory. In D. Levine (Ed.), *Nebraska Symposium on Motivation* (Vol. 13, pp. 123–180). Lincoln: University of Nebraska Press.

Premack, D. (1971a). Catching up with common sense, or two sides of a generalization: Reinforcement and punishment. In R. Glaser (Ed.), *The nature of reinforcement.* New York: Academic Press.

Premack, D. (1971b). Language in chimpanzee? *Science, 172,* 808–822.

Premack, D. (1976). *Intelligence in ape and man.* Hillsdale, NJ: Erlbaum.

Preston, R. A., & Fantino, E. (1991). Conditioned reinforcement value and choice. *Journal of the Experimental Analysis of Behavior, 55*, 155–175.

Puente, G. P., Cannon, D. S., Best, M. R., & Carrell, L. E. (1988). Occasion setting of fluid ingestion by contextual cues. *Learning and Motivation, 19*, 239–253.

Quartermain, D., McEwen, B. S., & Azmitia, E. C., Jr. (1970). Amnesia produced by electroconvulsive shock or cycloheximide: Conditions for recovery. *Science, 169*, 683–686.

Rachilin, H. (1995). Behavioral economics without anomalies. *Journal of the Experimental Analysis of Behavior, 64*, 397–404.

Rachlin, H. (1989). *Judgement, decision, and choice.* New York: Freeman.

Rachlin, H. C. (1978). A molar theory of reinforcement schedules. *Journal of the Experimental Analysis of Behavior, 30*, 345–360.

Rachlin, H. C., & Burkhard, B. (1978). The temporal triangle: Response substitution in instrumental conditioning. *Psychological Review, 85*, 22–47.

Rachlin, H. C., & Green, L. (1972). Commitment, choice, and self-control. *Journal of the Experimental Analysis of Behavior, 17*, 15–22.

Rachlin, H. C., & Herrnstein, R. L. (1969). Hedonism revisited: On the negative law of effect. In B. A. Campbell & R. M. Church (Eds.), *Punishment and aversive behavior* (pp. 83–109). New York: Appleton-Century-Crofts.

Rachlin, H. C., Battalio, R., Kagel, J., & Green, L. (1981). Maximization theory in behavioral psychology. *Behavioral and Brain Sciences, 4*, 371–417.

Rachlin, H. C., Green, L., Kagel, J. H., & Battalio, R. C. (1976). Economic demand theory and studies of choice. In G. H. Bower (Ed.), *The psychology of learning and motivation* (Vol. 10, pp. 129–154). New York: Academic Press.

Randich, A. (1981). The US preexposure phenomenon in the conditioned suppression paradigm: A role for conditioned situational stimuli. *Learning and Motivation, 12*, 321–341.

Randich, A., & LoLordo, V. M. (1979). Associative and non-associative theories of the UCS preexposure phenomenon: Implications for Pavlovian conditioning. *Psychological Bulletin, 86*, 523–548.

Rashotte, M. E., Griffin, R. W., & Sisk, C. L. (1977). Second-order conditioning of the pigeon's keypeck. *Animal Learning & Behavior, 5*, 25–38.

Reberg, D. (1972). Compound tests for excitation in early acquisition and after prolonged extinction of conditioned suppression. *Learning and Motivation, 3*, 246–258.

Reberg, D., & Black, A. H. (1969). Compound testing of individually conditioned stimuli as an index of excitatory and inhibitory properties. *Psychonomic Science, 17*, 30–31.

Reberg, D., Innis, N. K., Mann, B., & Eizenga, C. (1978). "Superstitious" behavior resulting from periodic response-independent presentations of food or water. *Animal Behaviour, 26*, 506–519.

Redhead, E. S., & Pearce, J. M. (1995a). Similarity and discrimination learning. *Quarterly Journal of Experimental Psychology, 48B*, 46–66.

Redhead, E. S., & Pearce, J. M. (1995b). Stimulus salience and negative patterning. *Quarterly Journal of Experimental Psychology, 48B*, 67–83.

Redhead, E., & Tyler, P. A. (1988). An experimental analysis of optimal foraging behaviour in patchy environments. *Quarterly Journal of Experimental Psychology, 40B*, 83–102.

Reed, P. (1991). Multiple determinants of the effects of reinforcement magnitude on free-operant response rates. *Journal of the Experimental Analysis of Behavior, 55*, 109–123.

Reed, P., & Wright, J. E. (1989). Effects of magnitude of food reinforcement on free-operant response rates. *Journal of the Experimental Analysis of Behavior, 49*, 75–85.

Reed, P., Mitchell, C., & Nokes, T. (1996). Intrinsic reinforcing properties of putatively neutral stimuli in an instrumental two-lever discrimination task. *Animal Learning & Behavior, 24*, 38–45.

Repp, A. C., & Singh, N. N. (Eds.). (1990). *Perspectives on the use of non-aversive and aversive interventions for persons with developmental disabilities.* Sycamore, IL: Sycamore.

Rescorla, R. A. (1967a). Inhibition of delay in Pavlovian fear conditioning. *Journal of Comparative and Physiological Psychology, 64*, 114–120.

Rescorla, R. A. (1967b). Pavlovian conditioning and its proper control procedures. *Psychological Review, 74*, 71–80.

Rescorla, R. A. (1968a). Pavlovian conditioned fear in Sidman avoidance learning. *Journal of Comparative and Physiological Psychology, 65*, 55–60.

Rescorla, R. A. (1968b). Probability of shock in the presence and absence of CS in fear conditioning. *Journal of Comparative and Physiological Psychology, 66*, 1–5.

Rescorla, R. A. (1969a). Conditioned inhibition of fear resulting from negative CS-US contingencies. *Journal of Comparative and Physiological Psychology, 67*, 504–509.

Rescorla, R. A. (1969b). Pavlovian conditioned inhibition. *Psychological Bulletin, 72*, 77–94.

Rescorla, R. A. (1973). Effect of US habituation following conditioning. *Journal of Comparative and Physiological Psychology, 82*, 137–143.

Rescorla, R. A. (1980a). *Pavlovian second-order conditioning.* Hillsdale, NJ: Erlbaum.

Rescorla, R. A. (1980b). Simultaneous and successive associations in sensory preconditioning. *Journal of Experimental Psychology: Animal Behavior Processes, 6*, 207–216.

Rescorla, R. A. (1982a). Effect of a stimulus intervening between CS and US in autoshaping. *Journal of Experimental Psychology: Animal Behavior Processes, 8*, 131–141.

Rescorla, R. A. (1982b). Some consequences of associations between the excitor and the inhibitor in a conditioned inhibition paradigm. *Journal of Experimental Psychology: Animal Behavior Processes, 8*, 288–298.

Rescorla, R. A. (1985). Conditioned inhibition and facilitation. In R. R.

Miller & N. E. Spear (Eds.), *Information processing in animals: Conditioned inhibition* (pp. 299–326). Hillsdale, NJ: Erlbaum.

Rescorla, R. A. (1986). Extinction of facilitation. *Journal of Experimental Psychology: Animal Behavior Processes, 12,* 16–24.

Rescorla, R. A. (1987). Facilitation and inhibition. *Journal of Experimental Psychology: Animal Behavior Processes, 13,* 250–259.

Rescorla, R. A. (1988a). Facilitation based on inhibition. *Animal Learning & Behavior, 16,* 169–176.

Rescorla, R. A. (1988b). Pavlovian conditioning: It's not what you think it is. *American Psychologist, 43,* 151–160.

Rescorla, R. A. (1990a). Evidence for an association between the discriminative stimulus and the response–outcome association in instrumental learning. *Journal of Experimental Psychology: Animal Behavior Processes, 16,* 326–334.

Rescorla, R. A. (1990b). The role of information about the response-outcome relation in instrumental discrimination learning. *Journal of Experimental Psychology: Animal Behavior Processes, 16,* 262–270.

Rescorla, R. A. (1991). Associative relations in instrumental learning: The eighteenth Bartlett memorial lecture. *Quarterly Journal of Experimental Psychology, 43B,* 1–23.

Rescorla, R. A. (1992). Response-outcome versus outcome-response associations in instrumental learning. *Animal Learning & Behavior, 20,* 223–232.

Rescorla, R. A., & Colwill, R. M. (1989). Associations with anticipated and obtained outcomes in instrumental learning. *Animal Learning & Behavior, 17,* 291–303.

Rescorla, R. A., & Durlach, P. J. (1981). Within-event learning in Pavlovian conditioning. In N. E. Spear & R. R. Miller (Eds.), *Information processing in animals: Memory mechanisms* (pp. 81–112). Hillsdale, NJ: Erlbaum.

Rescorla, R. A., & LoLordo, V. M. (1965). Inhibition of avoidance behavior. *Journal of Comparative and Physiological Psychology, 59,* 406–412.

Rescorla, R. A., & Solomon, R. L. (1967). Two-process learning theory: Relationships between Pavlovian conditioning and instrumental learning. *Psychological Review, 74,* 151–182.

Rescorla, R. A., & Wagner, A. R. (1972). A theory of Pavlovian conditioning: Variations in the effectiveness of reinforcement and nonreinforcement. In A. H. Black & W. F. Prokasy (Eds.), *Classical conditioning II: Current research and theory* (pp. 64–99). New York: Appleton-Century-Crofts.

Rescorla, R. A., Durlach, P. J., & Grau, J. W. (1985). Contextual learning in Pavlovian conditioning. In P. Balsam & A. Tomie (Eds.), *Context and learning* (pp. 23–56). Hillsdale, NJ: Erlbaum.

Rescorla, R. A., Grau, J. W., & Durlach, P. J. (1985). Analysis of the unique cue in configural discriminations. *Journal of Experimental Psychology: Animal Behavior Processes, 11,* 356–366.

Restle, F., & Brown, E. (1970). Organization of serial pattern learning. In G. H. Bower & J. T. Spence (Eds.), *The psychology of learning and motivation* (Vol. 4, pp. 249–331). New York: Academic Press.

Revusky, S. H., & Garcia, J. (1970). Learned associations over long delays. In G. H. Bower & J. T. Spence (Eds.), *The psychology of learning and motivation* (Vol. 4, pp. 1–84). New York: Academic Press.

Reynolds, G. S. (1961). Attention in the pigeon. *Journal of the Experimental Analysis of Behavior, 4,* 203–208.

Reynolds, G. S. (1975). *A primer of operant conditioning.* Glenview, IL: Scott, Foresman.

Reynolds, T. J., & Medin, D. L. (1981). Stimulus interaction and between-trials proactive interference in monkeys. *Journal of Experimental Psychology: Animal Behavior Processes, 7,* 334–347.

Riccio, D. C., & Richardson, R. (1984). The status of memory following experimentally induced amnesias: Gone, but not forgotten. *Physiological Psychology, 12,* 59–72.

Riccio, D. C., Hodges, L. A., & Randall, P. R. (1968). Retrograde amnesia produced by hypothermia in rats. *Journal of Comparative and Physiological Psychology, 3,* 618–622.

Richardson, R., Riccio, D. C., & Jonke, T. (1983). Alleviation of infantile amnesia in rats by means of a pharmacological contextual state. *Developmental Psychobiology, 16,* 511–518.

Richardson, R., Riccio, D. C., & Smoller, D. (1987). Counterconditioning of memory in rats. *Animal Learning & Behavior, 15,* 321–326.

Richelle, M., & Lejeune, H. (1980). *Time in animal behavior.* New York: Pergamon.

Riegert, P. W. (1959). Humidity reactions of *Melanoplus birittatus* (Say) and *Camnula pellucida* (Scudd.) (Orthoptera, Acrididae): Reactions of normal grasshoppers. *Canadian Entomologist, 91,* 35–40.

Riley, A. L., & Tuck, D. L. (1985). Conditioned food aversions: A bibliography. *Annals of the New York Academy of Sciences, 443,* 381–437.

Rilling, M., Kendrick, D. F., & Stonebraker, T. B. (1984). Directed forgetting in context. In G. H. Bower (Ed.), *The psychology of learning and motivation* (Vol. 18). New York: Academic Press.

Ristau, C. A. (Ed.). (1991). *Cognitive ethology.* Hillsdale, NJ: Erlbaum.

Robbins, S. J. (1988). Role of context in performance on a random schedule of autoshaping. *Journal of Experimental Psychology: Animal Behavior Processes, 14,* 413–424.

Robbins, S. J. (1990). Mechanisms underlying spontaneous recovery in autoshaping. *Journal of Experimental Psychology: Animal Behavior Processes, 16,* 235–249.

Roberts, S. (1981). Isolation of an internal clock. *Journal of Experimental Psychology: Animal Behavior Processes, 7,* 242–268.

Roberts, S. (1982). Cross-modal use of an internal clock. *Journal of Experi-*

mental *Psychology: Animal Behavior Processes, 8,* 2–22.

Roberts, S., & Church, R. M. (1978). Control of an internal clock. *Journal of Experimental Psychology: Animal Behavior Processes, 4,* 318–337.

Roberts, W. A. (1979). Spatial memory in the rat on a hierarchical maze. *Learning and Motivation, 10,* 117–140.

Roberts, W. A. (1984). Some issues in animal spatial memory. In H. L. Roitblat, T. G. Bever, & H. S. Terrace (Eds.), *Animal cognition* (pp. 425–443). Hillsdale, NJ: Erlbaum.

Roberts, W. A., & Grant, D. S. (1976). Studies of short-term memory in the pigeon using the delayed matching to sample procedure. In D. L. Medin, W. A. Roberts, & R. T. Davis (Eds.), *Processes of animal memory.* Hillsdale, NJ: Erlbaum.

Roberts, W. A., & Grant, D. S. (1978). An analysis of light-induced retroactive inhibition in pigeon short term memory. *Journal of Experimental Psychology: Animal Behavior Processes, 4,* 219–236.

Roberts, W. A., & Mazmanian, D. S. (1988). Concept learning at different levels of abstraction by pigeons, monkeys, and people. *Journal of Experimental Psychology: Animal Behavior Processes, 14,* 247–260.

Roberts, W. A., Cheng, K., & Cohen, J. S. (1989). Timing light and tone signals in pigeons. *Journal of Experimental Psychology: Animal Behavior Processes, 15,* 23–35.

Rogers, R. F., Schiller, K. M., & Matzel, L. D. (1996). Chemosensory-based contextual conditioning in *Hermissendra crassicornis. Animal Learning & Behavior, 24,* 28–37.

Roitblat, H. L. (1980). Codes and coding processes in pigeon short-term memory. *Animal Learning & Behavior, 8,* 341–351.

Roitblat, H. L. (1982). The meaning of representation in animal memory. *Behavioral and Brain Sciences, 5,* 353–406.

Roitblat, H. L. (1993). Representations and processes in working memory. In T. R. Zentall (Ed.). *Animal cogni-*

tion (pp. 175–192). Hillsdale, NJ: Erlbaum.

Roitblat, H. L., & Harley, H. E. (1988). Spatial delayed matching-to-sample performance by rats: Learning, memory, and proactive interference. *Journal of Experimental Psychology: Animal Behavior Processes, 14,* 71–82.

Roitblat, H. L., Harley, H. E., & Helweg, D. A. (1993). Cognitive processing in artificial language research. In H. L. Roitblat, L. M. Herman, & P. E. Nachtigall (Eds.). *Language and communication: Comparative perspectives* (pp. 1–23). Hillsdale, NJ: Erlbaum.

Roitblat, H. L., & Scopatz, R. A. (1983). Sequential effects in pigeon delayed matching-to-sample performance. *Journal of Experimental Psychology: Animal Behavior Processes, 9,* 202–221.

Roitblat, H. L., Bever, T. G., & Terrace, H. S. (Eds.). (1984). *Animal cognition.* Hillsdale, NJ: Erlbaum.

Roitblat, H. L., Bever, T. G., Helweg, D. A., & Harley, H. E. (1991). On-line choice and the representation of serially structured stimuli. *Journal of Experimental Psychology: Animal Behavior Processes, 17,* 55–67.

Roitblat, H. L., Penner, R. H., & Nachtigall, P. E. (1990). Matching-to-sample by an echo locating dolphin (*Tursiops truncatus*). *Journal of Experimental Psychology: Animal Behavior Processes, 16,* 85–95.

Roitblat, H. L., Scopatz, R. A., & Bever, T. G. (1987). The hierarchical representation of three-item sequences. *Animal Learning & Behavior, 15,* 179–192.

Romanes, G. J. (1884). *Animal intelligence.* New York: Appleton.

Roper, K. L., & Zentall, T. R. (1993). Directed forgetting in animals. *Psychological Bulletin, 113,* 513–532.

Roper, K. L., Kaiser, D. H., & Zentall, T. R. (1995). True directed forgetting in pigeons may occur only when alternative working memory is required on forget-cue trials. *Animal Learning & Behavior, 23,* 280–285.

Rosellini, R. A., & DeCola, J. P. (1981). Inescapable shock interferes with the

acquisition of a low-activity response in an appetitive context. *Animal Learning & Behavior, 9,* 487–490.

Rosellini, R. A., DeCola, J. P., & Shapiro, N. R. (1982). Cross-motivational effects of inescapable shock are associative in nature. *Journal of Experimental Psychology: Animal Behavior Processes, 8,* 376–388.

Rosellini, R. A., DeCola, J. P., Plonsky, M., Warren, D. A., & Stilman, A. J. (1984). Uncontrollable shock proactively increases sensitivity to response-reinforcer independence in rats. *Journal of Experimental Psychology: Animal Behavior Processes, 10,* 346–359.

Rosellini, R. A., Warren, D. A., & DeCola, J. P. (1987). Predictability and controllability: Differential effects upon contextual fear. *Learning and Motivation, 18,* 392–420.

Ross, R. T. (1983). Relationships between the determinants of performance in serial feature-positive discriminations. *Journal of Experimental Psychology: Animal Behavior Processes, 9,* 349–373.

Ross, R. T., & Holland, P. C. (1981). Conditioning of simultaneous and serial feature-positive discriminations. *Animal Learning & Behavior, 9,* 293–303.

Rovee-Collier, C. K., Sullivan, M. W., Enright, M., Lucas, D., & Fagen, J. W. (1980). Reactivation of infant memory. *Science, 208,* 1159–1161.

Rovee, C. K., & Rovee, D. T. (1969). Conjugate reinforcement of infant exploratory behavior. *Journal of Experimental Child Psychology, 8,* 33–39.

Rovee-Collier, C., & Bhatt, R. S. (1993). Evidence of long-term memory in infancy. In R. Vasta (Ed.), *Annals of Child Development,* Vol. 9 (p. 1–45). London: Jessica Kingsley.

Rozin, P., & Schull, J. (1988). The adaptive-evolutionary point of view in experimental psychology. In R. C. Atkinson, R. J. Herrnstein, G. Lindzey, & R. D. Luce (Eds.), *Stevens' handbook of experimental psychology* (2nd ed., Vol. 1, pp. 503–546). New York: Wiley.

Rozin, P., & Zellner, D. (1985). The role of Pavlovian conditioning in the acquisition of food likes and dislikes. *Annals of the New York Academy of Sciences, 443,* 189–202.

Rumbaugh, D. M. (Ed.). (1977). *Language learning by a chimpanzee: The Lana project.* New York: Academic Press.

Russell, W. R., & Nathan, P. W. (1946). Traumatic amnesia. *Brain, 69,* 280–300.

Sahley, C., Rudy, J. W., & Gelperin, A. (1981). An analysis of associative learning in a terrestrial mollusc: I. Higher-order conditioning, blocking, and a transient US-pre-exposure effect. *Journal of Comparative Physiology-A, 144,* 1–8.

Sajwaj, T., Libet, J., & Agras, S. (1974). Lemon-juice therapy: The control of life-threatening rumination in a six-month-old infant. *Journal of Applied Behavior Analysis, 7,* 557–563.

Saladin, M. E., ten Have, W. N., Saper, Z. L., Labinsky, J. S., & Tait, R. W. (1989). Retardation of rabbit nictitating membrane conditioning following US preexposures depends on the distribution and numbers of US presentations. *Animal Learning & Behavior, 17,* 179–187.

Santi, A., Musgrave, S., & Bradford, S. A. (1988). Utilization of cues signaling different test stimulus dimensions in delayed matching to sample by pigeons. *Learning and Motivation, 19,* 87–98.

Savage-Rumbaugh, E. S. (1986). *Ape language.* New York: Columbia University Press.

Savage-Rumbaugh, E. S., McDonald, K., Sevcik, R. A., Hopkins, W. D., & Rubert, E. (1986). Spontaneous symbol acquisition and communicative use by pigmy chimpanzees (*Pan paniscus*). *Journal of Experimental Psychology: General, 115,* 211–235.

Savage-Rumbaugh, E. S., Rumbaugh, D. M., Smith, S. T., & Lawson, J. (1980). Reference: The linguistic essential. *Science, 210,* 922–925.

Savage-Rumbaugh, E. S., Sevcik, R. A., Brakke, K. E., & Rumbaugh, D. M. (1990). Symbols: Their communicative use, comprehension, and combination by bonobos (*Pan paniscus*). In C. Rovee-Collier & L. P. Lipsitt (Eds.), *Advances in infancy research* (Vol. 6, pp. 221–278). Norwood, NJ: Ablex.

Savage-Rumbaugh, E. S., Murphy, J., Sevcik, R. A., Brakke, K. E., Williams, S. L., & Rumbaugh, D. M. (1993). Language comprehension in ape and child. *Monographs of the Society for Research in Child Development,* Vol. 58 (Nos. 3–4), Serial No. 233.

Savastano, H., & Fantino, E. (1994). Human choice in concurrent ratio-interval schedules of reinforcement. *Journal of the Experimental Analysis of Behavior, 61,* 453–463.

Scavio, M. J., Jr., & Gormezano, I. (1974). CS intensity effects on rabbit nictitating membrane conditioning, extinction and generalization. *Pavlovian Journal of Biological Science, 9,* 25–34.

Schachtman, T. R., Brown, A. M., Gordon, E. L., Catterson, D. A., & Miller, R. R. (1987). Mechanisms underlying retarded emergence of conditioned responding following inhibitory training: Evidence for the comparator hypothesis. *Journal of Experimental Psychology: Animal Behavior Processes, 13,* 310–322.

Schachtman, T. R., Gee, J.-L., Kasprow, W. J., & Miller, R. R. (1983). Reminder-induced recovery from blocking as a function of the number of compound trials. *Learning and Motivation, 14,* 154–164.

Schachtman, T. R., Kasprow, W. J., Meyer, R. C., Bourne, M. J., & Hart, J. A. (1992). Extinction of the overshadowing CS after overshadowing in conditioned taste aversion. *Animal Learning & Behavior, 20,* 207–218.

Schafe, G. E., Sollars, S. I., & Bernstein, I. L. (1995). The CS-US interval and taste aversion learning: A brief look. *Behavioral Neuroscience, 109,* 799–802.

Schiff, R., Smith, N., & Prochaska, J. (1972). Extinction of avoidance in rats as a function of duration and number of blocked trials. *Journal of Comparative and Physiological Psychology, 81,* 356–359.

Schindler, C. W., & Weiss, S. J. (1982). The influence of positive and negative reinforcement on selective attention in the rat. *Learning and Motivation, 13,* 304–323.

Schlinger, H., Blakely, E., & Kaczor, T. (1990). Pausing under variable-ratio schedules: Interaction of reinforcer magnitude, variable-ratio size, and lowest ratio. *Journal of the Experimental Analysis of Behavior, 53,* 133–139.

Schlosberg, H. (1934). Conditioned responses in the white rat. *Journal of Genetic Psychology, 45,* 303–335.

Schlosberg, H. (1936). Conditioned responses in the white rat: II. Conditioned responses based upon shock to the foreleg. *Journal of Genetic Psychology, 49,* 107–138.

Schlosberg, H. (1937). The relationship between success and the laws of conditioning. *Psychological Review, 44,* 379–394.

Schneiderman, N., & Gormezano, I. (1964). Conditioning of the nictitating membrane of the rabbit as a function of CS-US interval. *Journal of Comparative and Physiological Psychology, 57,* 188–195.

Schneiderman, N., Fuentes, I., & Gormezano, I. (1962). Acquisition and extinction of the classically conditioned eyelid response in the albino rabbit. *Science, 136,* 650–652.

Schreibman, L., Koegel, R. L., Charlop, M. H., & Egel, A. L. (1990). Infantile autism. In A. S. Bellack, M. Hersen, & A. E. Kazdin (Eds.), *International handbook of behavior modification and therapy* (pp. 763–789). New York: Plenum.

Schrier, A. M., & Brady, P. M. (1987). Categorization of natural stimuli by monkeys (*Macaca mulatta*): Effects of stimulus set size and modification of exemplars. *Journal of Experimental Psychology: Animal Behavior Processes, 13,* 136–143.

Schuster, R. H., & Rachlin, H. (1968). Indifference between punishment and free shock: Evidence for the negative law of effect. *Journal of the Experimental Analysis of Behavior, 11,* 777–786.

Schusterman, R. J., & Gisiner, R. (1988). Artificial language comprehension in dolphins and sea lions: The essential cognitive skills. *Psychological Record, 38,* 311–348.

Schusterman, R. J., & Krieger, K. (1986). Artificial language comprehension and size transposition by a California sea lion (*Zalophus californianus*). *Journal of Comparative Psychology, 100,* 348–355.

Schwartz, B. (1976). Positive and negative conditioned suppression in the pigeon: Effects of the locus and modality of the CS. *Learning and Motivation, 7,* 86–100.

Schwartz, B. (1980). Development of complex, stereotyped behavior in pigeons. *Journal of the Experimental Analysis of Behavior, 33,* 153–166.

Schwartz, B. (1981). Reinforcement creates behavioral units. *Behavioural Analysis Letters, 1,* 33–41.

Schwartz, B. (1982). Interval and ratio reinforcement of a complex sequential operant in pigeons. *Journal of the Experimental Analysis of Behavior, 37,* 349–357.

Schwartz, B. (1985). On the organization of stereotyped response sequences. *Animal Learning & Behavior, 13,* 261–268.

Schwartz, B. (1986). Allocation of complex, sequential operants on multiple and concurrent schedules of reinforcement. *Journal of the Experimental Analysis of Behavior, 45,* 283–295.

Schwartz, B. (1988). The experimental synthesis of behavior: Reinforcement, behavioral stereotypy, and problem solving. In G. H. Bower (Ed.), *The psychology of learning and motivation* (Vol. 22, pp. 93–138). Orlando, FL: Academic Press.

Schwartz, B., & Williams, D. R. (1972). The role of the response-reinforcer contingency in negative automaintenance. *Journal of the Experimental Analysis of Behavior, 17,* 351–357.

Schweitzer, J. B., & Sulzer-Azaroff, B. (1988). Self-control: Teaching tolerance for delay in impulsive children. *Journal of the Experimental Analysis of Behavior, 50,* 173–186.

Scobie, S. R. (1972). Interaction of an aversive Pavlovian conditioned stimulus with aversively and appetitively motivated operants in rats. *Journal of Comparative and Physiological Psychology, 79,* 171–188.

Seligman, M. E. P. (1971). Phobias and preparedness. *Behavior Therapy, 2,* 307–320.

Seligman, M. E. P. (1975). *Helplessness: On depression, development and death.* San Francisco: W. H. Freeman.

Seligman, M. E. P., & Maier, S. F. (1967). Failure to escape traumatic shock. *Journal of Experimental Psychology, 74,* 1–9.

Seligman, M. E. P., & Weiss, J. (1980). Coping behavior: Learned helplessness, physiological activity, and learned inactivity. *Behaviour Research and Therapy, 18,* 459–512.

Sevcik, R. A., Romski, M. A., & Wilkenson, K. (1991). Roles of graphic symbols in the language acquisition process for persons with severe cognitive disabilities. *Journal of Augmentative and Alternative Communication, 7,* 161–170.

Sevenster, P. (1973). Incompatibility of response and reward. In R. A. Hinde & J. Stevenson-Hinde (Eds.), *Constraints on learning.* London: Academic Press.

Shah, K., Bradshaw, C. M., & Szabadi, E. (1991). Relative and absolute reinforcement frequency as determinants of choice in concurrent variable interval schedules. *Quarterly Journal of Experimental Psychology, 43,* 25–38.

Shapiro, K. L., & LoLordo, V. M. (1982). Constraints on Pavlovian conditioning of the pigeon: Relative conditioned reinforcing effects of redlight and tone CSs paired with food. *Learning and Motivation, 13,* 68–80.

Shapiro, K. L., Jacobs, W. J., & LoLordo, V. M. (1980). Stimulus-reinforcer interactions in Pavlovian conditioning of pigeons: Implications for selective associations. *Animal Learning & Behavior, 8,* 586–594.

Sheffield, F. D. (1948). Avoidance training and the contiguity principle. *Journal of Comparative and Physiological Psychology, 41,* 165–177.

Sheffield, F. D. (1965). Relation between classical conditioning and instrumental learning. In W. F. Prokasy (Ed.), *Classical conditioning* (pp. 302–322). New York: Appleton-Century-Crofts.

Sheffield, F. D., Roby, T. B., & Campbell, B. A. (1954). Drive reduction versus consummatory behavior as determinants of reinforcement. *Journal of Comparative and Physiological Psychology, 47,* 349–354.

Sheffield, F. D., Wulff, J. J., & Backer, R. (1951). Reward value of copulation without sex drive reduction. *Journal of Comparative and Physiological Psychology, 44,* 3–8.

Sherry, D. F. (1984). Food storage by black-capped chickadees: Memory for the location and contents of caches. *Animal Behaviour, 32,* 451–464.

Sherry, D. F. (1985). Food storage by birds and mammals. *Advances in the Study of Behavior, 15,* 153–188.

Sherry, D. F. (1988). Learning and adaptation in foodstoring birds. In R. C. Bolles & M. D. Beecher (Eds.), *Evolution and learning* (pp. 79–95). Hillsdale, NJ: Erlbaum.

Sherry, D. F., & Schachter, D. L. (1987). The evolution of multiple memory systems. *Psychological Review, 94,* 439–454.

Sherry, D. F., Krebs, J. R., & Cowie, R. J. (1981). Memory for the location of stored food in marsh tits. *Animal Behaviour, 29,* 1260–1266.

Shettleworth, S. J. (1975). Reinforcement and the organization of behavior in golden hamsters: Hunger, environment, and food reinforcement. *Journal of Experimental Psychology: Animal Behavior Processes, 1,* 56–87.

Shettleworth, S. J. (1983). Memory in food-hoarding birds. *Scientific American, 248,* 102–110.

Shettleworth, S. J. (1988). Foraging as operant behavior and operant behavior as foraging: What have we learned? In G. H. Bower (Ed.), *The psychology of learning and motivation* (Vol. 22, pp. 1–49). Orlando, FL: Academic Press.

Shettleworth, S. J. (1989). Animals foraging in the lab: Problems and promises.

Journal of Experimental Psychology: Animal Behavior Processes, 15, 81–87.

Shettleworth, S. J., & Krebs, J. R. (1986). Stored and encountered seeds: A comparison of two spatial memory tasks in marsh tits and chickadees. *Journal of Experimental Psychology: Animal Behavior Processes, 12,* 248–257.

Shimp, C. P. (1966). Probabilistically reinforced choice behavior in pigeons. *Journal of the Experimental Analysis of Behavior, 9,* 443–455.

Shimp, C. P. (1969). Optimum behavior in free-operant experiments. *Psychological Review, 76,* 97–112.

Shizgal, P., & Murray, B. (1989). Neuronal basis of intracranial self-stimulation. In J. M. Liebman & S. J. Cooper (Eds.), *The neuropharmacological basis of reward* (pp. 106–163). New York: Oxford University Press.

Shurtleff, D., & Ayres, J. J. B. (1981). One-trial backward excitatory fear conditioning in rats: Acquisition, retention, extinction, and spontaneous recovery. *Animal Learning & Behavior, 9,* 65–74.

Sidman, M. (1953a). Avoidance conditioning with brief shock and no exteroceptive warning signal. *Science, 118,* 157–158.

Sidman, M. (1953b). Two temporal parameters of the maintenance of avoidance behavior by the white rat. *Journal of Comparative and Physiological Psychology, 46,* 253–261.

Sidman, M. (1960). *Tactics of scientific research.* New York: Basic Books.

Sidman, M. (1962). Reduction of shock frequency as reinforcement for avoidance behavior. *Journal of the Experimental Analysis of Behavior, 5,* 247–257.

Sidman, M. (1966). Avoidance behavior. In W. K. Honig (Ed.), *Operant behavior* (pp. 448–498). New York: Appleton-Century-Crofts.

Sidman, M. (1990). Equivalence relations: Where do they come from? In D. E. Blackman & H. Lejeune (Eds.), *Behavioral analysis in theory and practice: Contributions and controversies* (pp. 93–114). Hillsdale, NJ: Erlbaum.

Sidman, M. (1994). Equivalence relations and behavior: A research story. Boston: Author's Cooperative.

Sidman, M. & Tailby, W. (1982). Conditional discrimination vs. matching to sample: An expansion of the testing paradigm. *Journal of the Experimental Analysis of Behavior, 37,* 5–22.

Siegel, S., & Allen, L. G. (1996). The widespread influence of the Rescorla-Wagner model. *Psychonomic Bulletin & Review, 3,* 314–321.

Siegel, S. (1977). A Pavlovian conditioning analysis of morphine tolerance (and opiate dependence). In N. A. Krasnegor (Ed.), *Behavioral tolerance: Research and treatment implications.* National Institute for Drug Abuse, Monograph No. 18. Government Printing Office Stock No. 017–024-00699–8. Washington, DC: Government Printing Office.

Siegel, S. (1983). Classical conditioning, drug tolerance, and drug dependence. In Y. Israel, F. B. Glaser, H. Kalant, R. E. Popham, W. Schmidt, & R. G. Smart (Eds.), *Research advances in alcohol and drug problems* (Vol. 7). New York: Plenum.

Siegel, S. (1989). Pharmacological conditioning and drug effects. In A. J. Goudie & M. W. Emmett-Oglesby (Eds.), *Psychoactive drugs: Tolerance and sensitization* (pp. 115–180). Clifton, NJ: Humana Press.

Siegel, S., & Domjan, M. (1971). Backward conditioning as an inhibitory procedure. *Learning and Motivation, 2,* 1–11.

Sigmundi, R. A., & Bolles, R. C. (1983). CS modality, context conditioning, and conditioned freezing. *Animal Learning & Behavior, 11,* 205–212.

Silberberg, A., Warren-Boulton, F. R., & Asano, T. (1987). Inferior-good and Giffen-good effects in monkey choice behavior. *Journal of Experimental Psychology: Animal Behavior Processes, 13,* 292–301.

Silverman, K., Mumford, G. K., & Griffiths, R. R. (1994). A procedure for studying within-session onset of human drug discrimination. *Journal of the Experimental Analysis of Behavior, 61,* 181–189.

Simon, H. A., & Kotovsky, K. (1963). Human acquisition of concepts for sequential patterns. *Psychological Review, 70,* 534–546.

Simons, R. C. (1996). *Boo! Culture, experience, and the startle reflex.* New York: Oxford University Press.

Singh, N. N., & Solman, R. T. (1990). A stimulus control analysis of the picture-word problem in children who are mentally retarded: The blocking effect. *Journal of Applied Behavior Analysis, 23,* 525–532.

Skinner, B. F. (1938). *The behavior of organisms.* New York: Appleton-Century-Crofts.

Skinner, B. F. (1948). "Superstition" in the pigeon. *Journal of Experimental Psychology, 38,* 168–172.

Skinner, B. F. (1953). *Science and human behavior.* New York: Macmillan.

Slamecka, N. J., & Ceraso, J. (1960). Retroactive and proactive inhibition of verbal learning. *Psychological Bulletin, 57,* 449–475.

Small, W. S. (1899). An experimental study of the mental processes of the rat: 1. *American Journal of Psychology, 11,* 133–164.

Small, W. S. (1900). An experimental study of the mental processes of the rat: 11. *American Journal of Psychology, 12,* 206–239.

Smith, J. C., & Roll, D. L. (1967). Trace conditioning with X-rays as an aversive stimulus. *Psychonomic Science, 9,* 11–12.

Smith, M. C., Coleman, S. R., & Gormezano, I. (1969). Classical conditioning of the rabbit's nictitating membrane response at backward, simultaneous, and forward CS-US intervals. *Journal of Comparative and Physiological Psychology, 69,* 226–231.

Smotherman, W. P., & Robinson, S. R. (1992). Habituation in the rat fetus. *Quarterly Journal of Experimental Psychology, 44B,* 215–230.

Snodgrass, S. H., & McMillan, D. E. (1996). Drug discrimination under a concurrent schedule. *Journal of the Experimental Analysis of Behavior, 65,* 495–512.

Solomon, R. L. (1964). Punishment. *American Psychologist, 19,* 239–253.

Solomon, R. L. (1977). An opponent-process theory of acquired motivation: The affective dynamics of addiction. In J. D. Maser & M. E. P. Seligman (Eds.), *Psychopathology: Experimental models* (pp. 66–103). San Francisco: W. H. Freeman.

Solomon, R. L., & Corbit, J. D. (1973). An opponent-process theory of motivation: II. Cigarette addiction. *Journal of Abnormal Psychology, 81,* 158–171.

Solomon, R. L., & Corbit, J. D. (1974). An opponent-process theory of motivation: I. The temporal dynamics of affect. *Psychological Review, 81,* 119–145.

Solomon, R. L., & Wynne, L. C. (1953). Traumatic avoidance learning: Acquisition in normal dogs. *Psychological Monographs, 67* (Whole No. 354).

Solomon, R. L., Kamin, L. J., & Wynne, L. C. (1953). Traumatic avoidance learning: The outcomes of several extinction procedures with dogs. *Journal of Abnormal and Social Psychology, 48,* 291–302.

Soltysik, S. S., Wolfe, G. E., Nicholas, T., Wilson, W. J., & Garcia-Sanchez, L. (1983). Blocking of inhibitory conditioning within a serial conditioned stimulus conditioned inhibitor compound: Maintenance of acquired behavior without an unconditioned stimulus. *Learning and Motivation, 14,* 1–29.

Sonuga-Barke, E. J. S., Lea, S. E. G., & Webley, P. (1989a). An account of human "impulsivity" on self-control tasks. *Quarterly Journal of Experimental Psychology, 41B,* 161–179.

Sonuga-Barke, E. J. S., Lea, S. E. G., & Webley, P. (1989b). The development of adaptive choice in a self-control paradigm. *Journal of the Experimental Analysis of Behavior, 51,* 77–85.

Spear, N. E. (1973). Retrieval of memory in animals. *Psychological Review, 80,* 163–194.

Spear, N. E. (1978). *The processing of memories: Forgetting and retention.* Hillsdale, NJ: Erlbaum.

Spear, N. E. (1981). Extending the domain of memory retrieval. In N. E. Spear & R. R. Miller (Eds.), *Information processing in animals: Memory mechanisms* (pp. 341–378). Hillsdale, NJ: Erlbaum.

Spear, N. E., & Riccio, D. C. (1994). *Memory: Phenomena and principles.* Boston: Allyn and Bacon.

Spence, K. W. (1936). The nature of discrimination learning in animals. *Psychological Review, 43,* 427–449.

Spence, K. W. (1937). The differential response in animals to stimuli varying within a single dimension. *Psychological Review, 44,* 430–444.

Spence, K. W. (1956). *Behavior theory and conditioning.* New Haven, CT: Yale University Press.

Spetch, M. L. (1990). Further studies of pigeons' spatial working memory in the open-field task. *Animal Learning & Behavior, 18,* 332–340.

Spetch, M. L. (1995). Overshadowing in landmark learning: Touch-screen studies with pigeons and humans. *Journal of Experimental Psychology: Animal Behavior Processes, 21,* 166–181.

Spetch, M. L., Mondloch, M. V., Belke, T. W., & Dunn, R. (1994). Determinants of pigeons' choice between certain and probabilistic outcomes. *Animal Learning & Behavior, 22,* 239–251.

Spetch, M. L., Wilkie, D. M., & Pinel, J. P. J. (1981). Backward conditioning: A reevaluation of the empirical evidence. *Psychological Bulletin, 89,* 163–175.

Spetch, M. L., Wilkie, D. M., & Skelton, R. W. (1981). Control of pigeons' keypecking topography by a schedule of alternating food and water reward. *Animal Learning & Behavior, 9,* 223–229.

Staddon, J. E. R. (1979). Operant behavior as adaptation to constraint. *Journal of Experimental Psychology: General, 108,* 48–67.

Staddon, J. E. R. (1980). Optimality analyses of operant behavior and their relation to optimal foraging. In J. E. R. Staddon (Ed.), *Limits to action.* New York: Academic Press.

Staddon, J. E. R. (1983). *Adaptive behavior and learning.* Cambridge: Cambridge University Press.

Staddon, J. E. R. (1988). Quasi-dynamic choice models: Melioration and ratio invariance. *Journal of the Experimental Analysis of Behavior, 49,* 303–320.

Staddon, J. E. R., & Simmelhag, V. L. (1971). The "superstition" experiment: A reexamination of its implications for the principles of adaptive behavior. *Psychological Review, 78,* 3–43.

Staddon, J. E. R., & Wynne, C. D. L., & Higa, J. J. (1991). The role of timing in reinforcement schedule performance. *Learning and Motivation, 22,* 200–225.

Stanhope, K. J. (1992). The representation of the reinforcer and the force of the pigeon's keypeck in first- and second-order conditioning. *Quarterly Journal of Experimental Psychology, 44B,* 137–158.

Starr, M. D. (1978). An opponent-process theory of motivation: VI. Time and intensity variables in the development of separation-induced distress calling in ducklings. *Journal of Experimental Psychology: Animal Behavior Processes, 4,* 338–355.

Starr, M. D., & Mineka, S. (1977). Determinants of fear over the course of avoidance learning. *Learning and Motivation, 8,* 332–350.

Steinert, P., Fallon, D., & Wallace, J. (1976). Matching to sample in goldfish (*Carassuis auratus*). *Bulletin of the Psychonomic Society, 8,* 265.

Stellar, J. R., & Rice, M. B. (1989). Pharmacological basis of intracranial self-stimulation reward. In J. M. Liebman and S. J. Cooper (Eds.), *The neuropharmacological basis of reward* (pp. 14–65). Oxford: Clarendon Press.

Stephens, D. W., & Krebs, J. R. (1986). *Foraging theory.* Princeton, NJ: Princeton University Press.

Stephenson, D., & Siddle, D. (1983). Theories of habituation. In D. Siddle (Ed.), *Orienting and habituation: - Perspectives in human research* (pp. 183–236). Chichester, England: Wiley.

Stevens, S. S. (1951). Mathematics, measurement and psychophysics. In S. S.

Stevens (Ed.), *Handbook of experimental psychology* (pp. 1–49). New York: Wiley.

Stewart, J., & Eikelboom, R. (1987). Conditioned drug effects. In L. L. Iversen, S. D. Iversen, & S. H. Snyder (Eds.), *Handbook of psychopharmacology* (Vol. 19, pp. 1–57). New York: Plenum.

Stokes, P., & Balsam, P. D. (1991). Effects of reinforcing preselected approximations on the topography of the rat's bar press. *Journal of the Experimental Analysis of Behavior, 55,* 213–231.

Stokes, T. F., & Baer, D. M. (1977). An implicit technology of generalization. *Journal of Applied Behavior Analysis, 10,* 349–367.

Straub, R. O., & Terrace, H. S. (1981). Generalization of serial learning in the pigeon. *Animal Learning & Behavior, 9,* 454–468.

Strijkstra, A. M., & Bolhuis, J. J. (1987). Memory persistence of rats in a radial maze vanes with training procedure. *Behavioral and Neural Biology, 47,* 158–166.

Suarez, S. D., & Gallup, G. G. (1981). An ethological analysis of open-field behavior in rats and mice. *Learning and Motivation, 12,* 342–363.

Sundberg, M. L. (1996). Toward granting linguistic competence to apes: A review of Savage-Rumbaugh et al.'s *Language comprehension in ape and child. Journal of the Experimental Analysis of Behavior, 65,* 477–492.

Suomi, S. J., Mineka, S., & Harlow, H. F. (1983). Social separation in monkeys as viewed from several motivational perspectives. In E. Satinoff & P. Teitelbaum (Eds.), *Handbook of neurobiology: Vol. 6. Motivation.* New York: Plenum.

Susswein, A. J., & Schwarz, M. (1983). A learned change of response to inedible food in Aplysia. *Behavioral and Neural Biology, 39,* 1–6.

Suzuki, S., Augerinos, G., & Black, A. H. (1980). Stimulus control of spatial behavior on the eight-arm maze in rats. *Learning and Motivation, 11,* 1–18.

Swartzentruber, D. (1993). Transfer of contextual control across similarly trained conditioned stimuli. *Animal Learning & Behavior, 21,* 14–22.

Swartzentruber, D. (1995). Modulatory mechanisms in Pavlovian conditioning. *Animal Learning & Behavior, 23,* 123–143.

Tait, R. W., & Saladin, M. E. (1986). Concurrent development of excitatory and inhibitory associations during backward conditioning. *Animal Learning & Behavior, 14,* 133–137.

Terrace, H. S. (1979). *Nim.* New York: Knopf.

Terrace, H. S. (1984). Animal cognition. In H. L. Roitblat, T. G. Bever, & H. S. Terrace (Eds.), *Animal cognition* (pp. 7–28). Hillsdale, NJ: Erlbaum.

Terrace, H. S. (1986a). A nonverbal organism's knowledge of ordinal position in a serial learning task. *Journal of Experimental Psychology: Animal Behavior Processes, 12,* 203–214.

Terrace, H. S. (1986b). Positive transfer from sequence production to sequence discrimination in a nonverbal organism. *Journal of Experimental Psychology: Animal Behavior Processes, 12,* 215–234.

Terrace, H. S. (1987). Chunking by a pigeon in a serial learning task. *Nature, 325,* 149–151.

Terrace, H. S. (1991a). Chunking during serial learning by a pigeon: I. Basic evidence. *Journal of Experimental Psychology: Animal Behavior Processes, 17,* 81–93.

Terrace, H. S. (1991b). Chunking during serial learning by a pigeon: 11. Integrity of a chunk on a new list. *Journal of Experimental Psychology: Animal Behavior Processes, 17,* 94–106.

Terrace, H. S. (1991c). Chunking during serial learning by a pigeon: III. What are the necessary conditions for establishing a chunk? *Journal of Experimental Psychology: Animal Behavior Processes, 17,* 107–118.

Terrace, H. S., Petitto, L. A., Sanders, R. J., & Bever, T. G. (1979). Can an ape create a sentence? *Science, 206,* 891–1201.

Terry, W. S., & Wagner, A. R. (1975). Short-term memory for "surprising" versus "expected" unconditioned stimuli in Pavlovian conditioning. *Journal of Experimental Psychology: Animal Behavior Processes, 1,* 122–133.

Theios, J. (1962). The partial reinforcement effect sustained through blocks of continuous reinforcement. *Journal of Experimental Psychology, 64,* 1–6.

Thomas, D. R. (1993). A model for adaptation-level effects on stimulus generalization. *Psychological Review, 100,* 658–673.

Thomas, D. R., & Empedocles, S. (1992). Novelty vs. retrieval cue value in the study of long-term memory in pigeons. *Journal of Experimental Psychology: Animal Behavior Processes, 18,* 22–23.

Thomas, D. R., Cook, S. C., & Terrones, J. P. (1990). Conditional discrimination learning by pigeons: The role of simultaneous versus successive stimulus presentations. *Journal of Experimental Psychology: Animal Behavior Processes, 16,* 390–401.

Thomas, D. R., Curran, P. J., & Russell, R. J. (1988). Factors affecting conditional discrimination learning by pigeons: II. Physical and temporal characteristics of stimuli. *Animal Learning & Behavior, 16,* 468–476.

Thomas, D. R., McKelvie, A. R., & Mah, W. L. (1985). Context as a conditional cue in operant discrimination reversal learning. *Journal of Experimental Psychology: Animal Behavior Processes, 11,* 317–330.

Thomas, G. V., & Lieberman, D. A. (1990). Commentary: Determinants of success and failure in experiments on marking. *Learning and Motivation, 21,* 110–124.

Thomas, G. V., Robertson, D., & Lieberman, D. A. (1990). The effects of relative intensity of cue and marker on marked trace conditioning in pigeons. *Quarterly Journal of Experimental Psychology, 42B,* 267–287.

Thomas, J. R. (1968). Fixed ratio punishment by timeout of concurrent variable-interval behavior. *Journal of the Experimental Analysis of Behavior, 11,* 609–616.

Thompson, C. R., & Church, R. M. (1980). An explanation of the language of a chimpanzee. *Science, 208,* 313–314.

Thompson, R. F., & Spencer, W. A. (1966). Habituation: A model phenomenon for the study of neuronal substrates of behavior. *Psychological Review, 73,* 16–43.

Thompson, R. F., Groves, P. M., Teyler, T. J., & Roemer, R. A. (1973). A dual-process theory of habituation: Theory and behavior. In H. V. S. Peeke & M. J. Herz (Eds.), *Habituation.* New York: Academic Press.

Thompson, R. K. R., Van Hemel, P. E., Winston, K. M., & Pappas, N. (1983). Modality-specific interference with overt mediation by pigeons in a delayed discrimination task. *Learning and Motivation, 14,* 271–303.

Thorndike, E. L. (1898). Animal intelligence: An experimental study of the association processes in animals. *Psychological Review Monograph, 2* (Whole No. 8).

Thorndike, E. L. (1911). *Animal intelligence: Experimental studies.* New York: Macmillan.

Thorndike, E. L. (1932). *The fundamentals of learning.* New York: Teachers College, Columbia University.

Tierney, K. J., Smith, H. V., & Gannon, K. N. (1987). Some tests of molar models of instrumental performance. *Journal of Experimental Psychology: Animal Behavior Processes, 13,* 341–353.

Timberlake, W. (1980). A molar equilibrium theory of learned performance. In G. H. Bower (Ed.), *The psychology of learning and motivation* (Vol. 14, pp. 1–58). New York: Academic Press.

Timberlake, W. (1983a). The functional organization of appetitive behavior: Behavior systems and learning. In M. D. Zeiler & P. Harzem (Eds.), *Advances in analysis of behavior: Vol. 3. Biological factors in learning* (pp. 177–221). Chichester, England: Wiley.

Timberlake, W. (1983b). Rats' responses to a moving object related to food or water: A behavior-systems analysis. *Animal Learning & Behavior, 11,* 309–320.

Timberlake, W. (1984). Behavior regulation and learned performance: Some misapprehensions and disagreements. *Journal of the Experimental Analysis of Behavior, 41,* 355–375.

Timberlake, W. (1990). Natural learning in laboratory paradigms. In D. A. Dewsbury (Ed.) *Contemporary issues in comparative psychology* (pp. 31–54). Sunderland, MA: Sinauer.

Timberlake, W. (1993). Behavior systems and reinforcement: An integrative approach. *Journal of the Experimental Analysis of Behavior, 60,* 105–128.

Timberlake, W., & Allison, J. (1974). Response deprivation: An empirical approach to instrumental performance. *Psychological Review, 81,* 146–164.

Timberlake, W., & Farmer-Dougan, V. A. (1991). Reinforcement in applied settings: Figuring out ahead of time what will work. *Psychological Bulletin, 110,* 379–391.

Timberlake, W., & Grant, D. S. (1975). Auto-shaping in rats to the presentation of another rat predicting food. *Science, 190,* 690–692.

Timberlake, W., & Lucas, G. A. (1985). The basis of superstitious behavior: Chance contingency, stimulus substitution, or appetitive behavior? *Journal of the Experimental Analysis of Behavior, 44,* 279–299.

Timberlake, W., & Lucas, G. A. (1989). Behavior systems and learning: From misbehavior to general principles. In S. B. Klein & R. R. Mowrer (Eds.), *Contemporary learning theories: Instrumental conditioning and the impact of biological constraints on learning* (pp. 237–275). Hillsdale, NJ: Erlbaum.

Timberlake, W., & Lucas, G. A. (1991). Period water, interwater interval, and adjunctive behavior in a 24-hour multiresponse environment. *Animal Learning & Behavior, 19,* 369–380.

Timberlake, W., & Washburne, D. L. (1989). Feeding ecology and laboratory predatory behavior toward live and artificial moving prey in seven rodent species. *Animal Learning & Behavior, 17,* 2–11.

Timberlake, W., & White, W. (1990). Winning isn't everything: Rats need

only food deprivation and not food reward to efficiently traverse a radial arm maze. *Learning and Motivation, 21,* 153–163.

Timberlake, W., Gawley, D. J., & Lucas, G. A. (1987). Time horizons in rats foraging for food in temporally separated patches. *Journal of Experimental Psychology: Animal Behavior Processes, 13,* 302–309.

Timberlake, W., Gawley, D. J., & Lucas, G. A. (1988). Time horizons in rats: The effects of operant control of access to future food. *Journal of the Experimental Analysis of Behavior, 50,* 405–417.

Timberlake, W., Wahl, G., & King, D. (1982). Stimulus and response contingencies in the misbehavior of rats. *Journal of Experimental Psychology: Animal Behavior Processes, 8,* 62–85.

Tinbergen, N. (1951). *The study of instinct.* Oxford: Clarendon Press.

Tinbergen, N., & Perdeck, A. C. (1950). On the stimulus situation releasing the begging response in the newly hatched herring gull chick (*Larus argentatus argentatus Pont.*). *Behaviour, 3,* 1–39.

Tobin, H., Logue, A. W., Chelonis, J. J., Ackerman, K. T., & May, J. G., III (1996). Self-control in the monkey *Macaca fascicularis. Animal Learning and Behavior, 24,* 168–174.

Tolman, E. C. (1938). The determiners of behavior at a choice point. *Psychological Review, 45,* 1–41.

Tomie, A., Brooks, W., & Zito, B. (1989). Sign-tracking: The search for reward. In S. B. Klein & R. R. Mowrer (Eds.), *Contemporary learning theories: Pavlovian conditioning and the status of learning theory* (pp. 191–223). Hillsdale, NJ: Erlbaum.

Tomie, A., Carelli, R., & Wagner, G. C. (1993). Negative correlation between tone (S-) and water increases target biting during S- in rats. *Animal Learning & Behavior, 21,* 355–359.

Trenholme, I. A., & Baron, A. (1975). Immediate and delayed punishment of human behavior by loss of reinforcement. *Learning and Motivation, 6,* 62–79.

Turkkan, J. S. (1989). Classical conditioning: The new hegemony. *The Behavioral and Brain Sciences, 12,* 121–179.

Twitmyer, E. B. (1974). A study of the knee jerk. *Journal of Experimental Psychology, 103,* 1047–1066.

Underwood, B. J. (1957). Interference and forgetting. *Psychological Review, 64,* 49–60.

Urcuioli, P. J., & DeMarse, T. (1996). Associative processes in differential outcome discriminations. *Journal of Experimental Psychology: Animal Behavior Processes, 22,* 192–204.

Urcuioli, P. J., & Kasprow, W. J. (1988). Long-delay learning in the T-maze: Effects of marking and delay-interval location. *Learning and Motivation, 19,* 66–86.

Vaccarino, F. J., Schiff, B. B., & Glickman, S. E. (1989). Biological view of reinforcement. In S. B. Klein & R. R. Mowrer (Eds.), *Contemporary learning theories: Instrumental conditioning and the impact of biological constraints on learning* (pp. 111–142). Hillsdale, NJ: Erlbaum.

Vaughan, W., Jr. (1981). Melioration, matching, and maximizing. *Journal of the Experimental Analysis of Behavior, 36,* 141–149.

Vaughan, W., Jr. (1985). Choice: A local analysis. *Journal of the Experimental Analysis of Behavior, 43,* 383–405.

Vaughan, W., Jr., & Greene, S. L. (1984). Pigeon visual memory capacity. *Journal of Experimental Psychology: Animal Behavior Processes, 10,* 256–271.

Viken, R. J., & McFall, R. M. (1994). Paradox lost: Implications of contemporary reinforcement theory for behavior therapy. *Current Directions in Psychological Science, 3,* 121–125.

Vyse, S. A., & Belke, T. W. (1992). Maximizing versus matching on concurrent variable-interval schedules. *Journal of the Experimental Analysis of Behavior, 58,* 325–334.

Wagner, A. R. (1976). Priming in STM: An information processing mechanism for self-generated or retrieval generated depression in performance. In T. J. Tighe & R. N. Leaton (Eds.),

Habituation: Perspectives from child development, animal behavior, and neurophysiology (pp. 95–128). Hillsdale, NJ: Erlbaum.

Wagner, A. R. (1981). SOP: A model of automatic memory processing in animal behavior. In N. E. Spear & R. R. Miller (Eds.), *Information processing in animals: Memory mechanisms* (pp. 5–47). Hillsdale, NJ: Erlbaum.

Wagner, A. R., & Brandon, S. E. (1989). Evolution of a structured connectionist model of Pavlovian conditioning (AESOP). In S. B. Klein & R. R. Mowrer (Eds.), *Contemporary learning theories: Pavlovian conditioning and the status of learning theory* (pp. 149–189). Hillsdale, NJ: Erlbaum.

Wagner, A. R., & Larew, M. B. (1985). Opponent processes and Pavlovian inhibition. In R. R. Miller & N. E. Spear (Eds.), *Information processing in animals: Conditioned inhibition* (pp. 233–265). Hillsdale, NJ: Erlbaum.

Wagner, A. R., & Rescorla, R. A. (1972). Inhibition in Pavlovian conditioning: Application of a theory. In R. A Boakes & M. S. Halliday (Eds.), *Inhibition and learning.* London: Academic Press.

Wagner, A. R., Logan, F. A., Haberlandt, K., & Price, T. (1968). Stimulus selection in animal discrimination learning. *Journal of Experimental Psychology, 76,* 171–180.

Wagner, A. R., Rudy, J. W., & Whitlow, J. W. (1973). Rehearsal in animal conditioning. *Journal of Experimental Psychology, 97,* 407–426.

Walter, H. E. (1907). The reaction of planarians to light. *Journal of Experimental Zoology, 5,* 35–162.

Walters, G. C., & Glazer, R. D. (1971). Punishment of instinctive behavior in the Mongolian gerbil. *Journal of Comparative and Physiological Psychology, 75,* 331–340.

Walters, G. C., & Grusec, J. F. (1977). *Punishment.* San Francisco: W. H. Freeman.

Wanchisen, B. A., Tatham, T. A., & Hineline, P. N. (1988). Pigeons' choices in situations of diminishing returns: Fixed versus progressive-ratio

schedules. *Journal of the Experimental Analysis of Behavior, 50,* 375–394.

Wasserman, E. A. (1973). Pavlovian conditioning with heat reinforcement produces stimulus-directed pecking in chicks. *Science, 181,* 875–877.

Wasserman, E. A. (1974). Responses in Pavlovian conditioning studies (reply to Hogan). *Science, 186,* 157.

Wasserman, E. A. (1981). Response evocation in autoshaping: Contributions of cognitive and comparative evolutionary analyses to an understanding of directed action. In C. M. Locurto, H. S. Terrace, & J. Gibbon (Eds.), *Autoshaping and conditioning theory* (pp. 21–54). New York: Academic Press.

Wasserman, E. A. (1986). Prospection and retrospection as processes of animal short-term memory. In D. F. Kendrick, M. E. Rilling, & M. R. Denny (Eds.), *Theories of animal memory* (pp. 53–75). Hillsdale, NJ: Erlbaum.

Wasserman, E. A. (1993). Comparative cognition: Beginning the second century of the study of animal intelligence. *Psychological Bulletin, 113,* 211–228.

Wasserman, E. A., & Astley, S. L. (1994). A behavioral analysis of concepts: Its application to pigeons and children. In D. L. Medin (Ed.), *The psychology of learning and motivation,* Vol. 31 (pp. 73–132). San Diego: Academic Press.

Wasserman, E. A., & Miller, R. R. (1977). What's elementary about associative learning? *Annual Review of Psychology, 48,* 573–607.

Wasserman, E. A., DeLong, R. E., & Larew, M. B. (1984). Temporal order and duration: Their discrimination and retention by pigeons. *Annals of the New York Academy of Sciences, 423,* 103–115.

Wasserman, E. A., Franklin, S. R., & Hearst, E. (1974). Pavlovian appetitive contingencies and approach versus withdrawal to conditioned stimuli in pigeons. *Journal of Comparative and Physiological Psychology, 86,* 616–627.

Wasserman, E. A., Kiedinger, R. E., & Bhatt, R. S. (1988). Conceptual behavior in pigeons: Categories, subcategories, and pseudocategories. *Journal of Experimental Psychology: Animal Behavior Processes, 14,* 235–246.

Watanabe, S., Sakamoto, J., & Wakita, M. (1995). Pigeons' discrimination of paintings by Monet and Picasso. *Journal of the Experimental Analysis of Behavior, 63,* 165–174.

Wathen, C. N., & Roberts, W. A. (1994). Multiple-pattern learning by rats on an eight-arm radial maze. *Animal Learning & Behavior, 22,* 155–164.

Wearden, J. H., & Burgess, I. S. (1982). Matching since Baum (1979). *Journal of the Experimental Analysis of Behavior, 38,* 339–348.

Wearden, J. H., & Clark, R. B. (1988). Interresponse-time reinforcement and behavior under aperiodic reinforcement schedules: A case study using computer modeling. *Journal of Experimental Psychology: Animal Behavior Processes, 14,* 200–211.

Wearden, J. H., & McShane, B. (1988). Interval production as an analogue of the peak procedure: Evidence for similarity of human and animal timing processes. *Quarterly Journal of Experimental Psychology, 40B,* 363–375.

Wearden, J. H., & Penton-Voak, I. S. (1995). Feeling the heat: Body temperature and the rate of subjective time, revisited. *Quarterly Journal of Experimental Psychology, 48B,* 129–141.

Weinberger, N. (1965). Effect of detainment on extinction of avoidance responses. *Journal of Comparative and Physiological Psychology, 60,* 135–138.

Weisman, R. G., & Litner, J. S. (1969). The course of Pavlovian excitation and inhibition of fear in rats. *Journal of Comparative and Physiological Psychology, 69,* 667–672.

Weisman, R. G., & Litner, J. S. (1972). The role of Pavlovian events in avoidance training. In R. A. Boakes & M. S. Halliday (Eds.), *Inhibition and learning.* London: Academic Press.

Weisman, R. G., & Premack, D. (1966). *Reinforcement and punishment produced by the same response depending upon the probability relation between the instrumental and contingent responses.* Paper presented at the meeting of the Psychonomic Society, St. Louis.

Weiss, S. J., & Schindler, C. W. (1981). Generalization peak shift in rats under conditions of positive reinforcement and avoidance. *Journal of the Experimental Analysis of Behavior, 35,* 175–185.

Weiss, S. J., & Weissman, R. D. (1992). Generalization peak shift for autoshaped and operant key pecks. *Journal of the Experimental Analysis of Behavior, 57,* 27–143.

Weiss, S. J., Panlilio, L. V., & Schindler, C. W. (1993a). Selective associations produced solely with appetitive contingencies: The stimulus-reinforcer interaction revisited. *Journal of the Experimental Analysis of Behavior, 59,* 309–322.

Weiss, S. J., Panlilio, L. V., & Schindler, C. W. (1993b). Single-incentive selective associations produced solely as a function of compound-stimulus conditioning context. *Journal of Experimental Psychology: Animal Behavior Processes, 19,* 284–294.

Welsh, J. H. (1933). Light intensity and the extent of activity of locomotor muscles as opposed to cilia. *Biological Bulletin, 65,* 168–174.

Wesierska, M., & Zielinski, K. (1980). Enhancement of bar-pressing rate in rats by the conditioned inhibitor of the CER. *Acta Neurobiological Experimentalis, 40,* 945–963.

Westbrook, R. F., Smith, F. J., & Charnock, D. J. (1985). The extinction of an aversion: Role of the interval between nonreinforced presentations of the averted stimulus. *Quarterly Journal of Experimental Psychology, 37B,* 255–273.

Whitlow, J. W., Jr., & Wagner, A. R. (1984). Memory and habituation. In H. V. S. Peeke & L. Petrinovich (Eds.), *Habituation, sensitization, and behavior.* New York: Academic Press.

Wigglesworth, V. B., & Gillett, J. D. (1934). The function of the antennae of *Rhodnius prolixus* (Hemiptera) and the mechanisms of orientation to the host. *Journal of Experimental Biology, 11,* 120–139.

Wilkenfield, J., Nickel, M., Brakely, E., & Poling, A. (1992). Acquisition of lever-press responding in rats with delayed reinforcement: A comparison of three procedures. *Journal of the Experimental Analysis of Behavior, 58,* 431–443.

Wilkie, D. M. (1989). Evidence that pigeons represent Euclidian properties of space. *Journal of Experimental Psychology: Animal Behavior Processes, 15,* 114–123.

Wilkie, D. M., & Slobin, P. (1983). Gerbils in space: Performance on the 17-arm radial maze. *Journal of the Experimental Analysis of Behavior, 40,* 301–312.

Wilkie, D. M., & Summers, R. J. (1982). Pigeons' spatial memory: Factors affecting delayed matching of key location. *Journal of the Experimental Analysis of Behavior, 37,* 45–56.

Wilkie, D. M., Willson, R. J., & Kardal, S. (1989). Pigeons discriminate pictures of a geographic location. *Animal Learning & Behavior, 17,* 163–171.

Williams, B. A. (1991). Choice as a function of local versus molar contingencies of reinforcement. *Journal of the Experimental Analysis of Behavior, 56,* 455–473.

Williams, B. A. (1994). Reinforcement and choice. In N. J. Mackintosh (Ed.) *Animal learning and cognition* (pp. 81–108). San Diego: Academic Press.

Williams, B. A. (1983). Another look at contrast in multiple schedules. *Journal of the Experimental Analysis of Behavior, 39,* 345–384.

Williams, B. A. (1988). Reinforcement, choice, and response strength. In R. C. Atkinson, R. J. Herrnstein, G. Lindzey, & R. D. Luce (Eds.), *Stevens' handbook of experimental psychology: Vol. 2. Learning and cognition* (pp. 167–244) New York: Wiley.

Williams, B. A. (1990). Pavlovian contingencies and anticipatory contrast. *Animal Learning & Behavior, 18,* 44–50.

Williams, B. A. (1991). Marking and bridging versus conditioned reinforcement. *Animal Learning & Behavior, 19,* 264–269.

Williams, B. A. (1992a). Dissociation of theories of choice via temporal spacing of choice opportunities. *Journal of Experimental Psychology: Animal Behavior Processes, 18,* 287–297.

Williams, B. A. (1992b). Inverse relations between preference and contrast. *Journal of the Experimental Analysis of Behavior, 58,* 303–312.

Williams, B. A. (1993). Molar versus local reinforcement probability as determinants of stimulus value. *Journal of the Experimental Analysis of Behavior, 59,* 163–172.

Williams, B. A. (1994). Conditioned reinforcement: Neglected or outmoded explanatory construct? *Psychonomic Bulletin & Review, 1,* 457–475.

Williams, B. A., & Dunn, R. (1991). Preference for conditioned reinforcement. *Journal of the Experimental Analysis of Behavior, 55,* 37–46.

Williams, D. A. (1986). On extinction of inhibition: Do explicitly unpaired conditioned inhibitors extinguish? *American Journal of Psychology, 99,* 515–525.

Williams, D. A., & Overmier, J. B. (1988a). Backward inhibitory conditioning with signaled and unsignaled unconditioned stimuli: Distribution of trials across days and intertrial interval. *Journal of Experimental Psychology: Animal Behavior Processes, 14,* 26–35.

Williams, D. A., & Overmier, J. B. (1988b). Some types of conditioned inhibitors carry collateral excitatory associations. *Learning and Motivation, 19,* 345–368.

Williams, D. A., Butler, M. M., & Overmier, J. B. (1990). Expectancies of reinforcer location and quality as cues for a conditional discrimination in pigeons. *Journal of Experimental Psychology: Animal Behavior Processes, 16,* 3–13.

Williams, D. A., Overmier, J. B., & LoLordo, V. M. (1992). A reevaluation of Rescorla's early dictums about Pavlovian conditioned inhibition. *Psychological Bulletin, 111,* 275–290.

Williams, D. R. (1965). Classical conditioning and incentive motivation. In W. F. Prokasy (Ed.), *Classical conditioning* (pp. 340–357). New York: Appleton-Century-Crofts.

Willson, R. J., & Wilkie, D. M. (1991). Discrimination training facilitates pigeons' performance on one-trial-per-day delayed matching of key location. *Journal of the Experimental Analysis of Behavior, 55,* 201–212.

Wilson, M. I., & Bermant, G. (1972). An analysis of social interaction in Japanese quail (*Coturnix coturnix japonica*). *Animal Behaviour, 20,* 252–258.

Wilson, P. N., & Pearce, J. M. (1990). Selective transfer of responding in conditional discriminations. *Quarterly Journal of Experimental Psychology, 42B,* 41–58.

Winter, J., & Perkins, C. C. (1982). Immediate reinforcement in delayed reward learning in pigeons. *Journal of the Experimental Analysis of Behavior, 38,* 169–179.

Witcher, E. S., & Ayres, J. J. B. (1984). A test of two methods for extinguishing Pavlovian conditioned inhibition. *Animal Learning & Behavior, 12,* 149–156.

Wolpe, J. (1990). *The practice of behavior therapy.* (4th ed.). New York: Pergamon.

Woodworth, R. S., & Schlosberg, H. (1954). *Experimental psychology.* New York: Holt, Rinehart and Winston.

Worsham, R. W., & D'Amato, M. R. (1973). Ambient light, white noise, and monkey vocalization as sources of interference in visual short-term memory of monkeys. *Journal of Experimental Psychology, 99,* 99–105.

Wright, A. A. (1990). Markov choice processes in simultaneous matching-to-sample at different levels of discriminability. *Animal Learning & Behavior, 18,* 277–286.

Wright, A. A. (1992). Learning mechanisms in matching to sample. *Journal of Experimental Psychology: Animal Behavior Processes, 18,* 67–79.

Wright, A. A., & Delius, J. D. (1994). Scratch and match: Pigeons learn matching and oddity with gravel stimuli. *Journal of Experimental Psychology: Animal Behavior Processes, 20,* 108–112.

Wright, A. A., & Sands, S. F. (1981). A model of detection and decision processes during matching to sample by pigeons: Performance with 88 different wavelengths in delayed and simultaneous matching tasks. *Journal of Experimental Psychology: Animal Behavior Processes, 7,* 191–216.

Wright, A. A., Cook, R. G., Rivera, J. J., Sands, S. F., & Delius, J. D. (1988). Concept learning by pigeons: Matching-to-sample with trial-unique video picture stimuli. *Animal Learning & Behavior, 16,* 436–444.

Wright, A. A., Shyan, M. R., & Jitsumori, M. (1990). Auditory same/different concept learning by monkeys. *Animal Learning & Behavior, 18,* 287–294.

Wright, A. A., Urcuioli, P. J., Sands, S. F., & Santiago, H. C. (1981). Interference of delayed matching to sample in pigeons: Effects of interpolation at different periods within a trial and stimulus similarity. *Animal Learning & Behavior, 9,* 595–603.

Yeomans, J. S. (1990). *Principles of brain stimulation.* New York: Oxford University Press.

Yerkes, R. M., & Morgulis, S. (1909). The method of Pavlov in animal psychology. *Psychological Bulletin, 6,* 257–273.

Yin, H., Barnet, R. C., & Miller, R. R. (1994). Second-order conditioning and Pavlovian conditioned inhibition: Operational similarities and differences. *Journal of Experimental Psychology: Animal Behavior Processes, 20,* 419–428.

Zalaquett, C. P., & Parker, L. A. (1989). Further evidence that CTAs produced by lithium and amphetamine are qualitatively different. *Learning and Motivation, 20,* 413–427.

Zamble, E., Hadad, G. M., Mitchell, J. B., & Cutmore, T. R. H. (1985). Pavlovian conditioning of sexual arousal: First- and second-order effects. *Journal of Experimental Psychology: Animal Behavior Processes, 11,* 598–610.

Zeiler, M. D. (1987). On optimal choice strategies. *Journal of Experimental Psychology: Animal Behavior Processes, 13,* 31–39.

Zeiler, M. D. (1992). On immediate function. *Journal of the Experimental Analysis of Behavior, 57,* 417–427.

Zener, K. (1937). The significance of behavior accompanying conditioned salivary secretion for theories of the conditioned response. *American Journal of Psychology, 50,* 384–403.

Zentall, T. R. (Ed.). (1993). *Animal cognition.* Hillsdale, NJ: Erlbaum.

Zentall, T. R., Edwards, C. A., Moore, B. S., & Hogan, D. E. (1981). Identity: The basis for both matching and oddity learning in pigeons. *Journal of Experimental Psychology: Animal Behavior Processes, 7,* 70–86.

Zentall, T. R., Jagielo, J. A., Jackson-Smith, P. & Urcuioli, P. J. (1987). Memory codes in pigeon short-term memory: Effects of varying the number of sample and comparison stimuli. *Learning and Motivation, 18,* 21–33.

Zentall, T. R., Roper, K. L., & Sherburne, L. M. (1995). Most directed forgetting in pigeons can be attributed to the absence of reinforcement on forget trials during training or to other procedural artifacts. *Journal of the Experimental Analysis of Behavior, 63,* 127–137.

Zentall, T. R., Sherburne, L. M., & Urcuioli, P. J. (1993). Common coding by pigeons in a many-to-one delayed matching task as evidenced by facilitation and interference effects. *Animal Learning & Behavior, 21,* 233–237.

Zentall, T. R., Sherburne, L. M., Steirn, J. N. (1993). Common coding and stimulus class formation in pigeons. In T. R. Zentall (Ed.). *Animal cognition* (pp. 217–236). Hillsdale, NJ: Erlbaum.

Zentall, T. R., Sherburne, L. M., Steirn, J. N., Randall, C. K., Roper, K. L., & Urcuioli, P. J. (1992). Common coding in pigeons: Partial versus total reversals of one-to-many conditional discriminations. *Animal Learning & Behavior, 20,* 373–381.

Zentall, T. R., Steirn, J. N., & Jackson-Smith, P. (1990). Memory strategies in pigeons' performance of a radial-arm-maze analog task. *Journal of Experimental Psychology: Animal Behavior Processes, 16,* 358–371.

Zentall, T. R., Steirn, J. N., Sherburne, L. M., & Urcuioli, P. J. (1991). Common coding in pigeons assessed through partial versus total reversals of many-to-one conditional and simple discriminations. *Journal of Experimental Psychology: Animal Behavior Processes, 17,* 194–201.

Zentall, T. R., Urcuioli, P. J., Jagielo, J. A., & Jackson-Smith, P. (1989). Interaction of sample dimension and sample comparison mapping on pigeons' performance of delayed conditional discriminations. *Animal Learning & Behavior, 17,* 172–178.

Zhuikov, A. Y., Couvillon, P. A., & Bitterman, M. E. (1994). Quantitative two-process analysis of avoidance conditioning in goldfish. *Journal of Experimental Psychology: Animal Behavior Processes, 20,* 32–43.

Zimmer-Hart, C. L., & Rescorla, R. A. (1974). Extinction of Pavlovian conditioned inhibition. *Journal of Comparative and Physiological Psychology, 86,* 837–845.

Zoladek, L., & Roberts, W. A. (1978). The sensory basis of spatial memory in the rat. *Animal Learning & Behavior, 6,* 77–81.

NAME INDEX

Abarca, N., 213
Abramson, L. Y., 153
Ackerman, K. T., 185
Ackil, J. E., 98
Adams, G. P., 35
Adornetto, M., 186
Agras, S., 272
Aguado, L., 89
Aitken, M. R. F., 360
Akins, C. K., 106, 107
Albert, M., 73
Alexander, J. H., 153
Alexinsky, T., 334
Alkon, D. L., 19
Allan, L., 344
Allan, R. W., 97, 129, 130
Allen, A. A., 234
Allen, L. G., 109
Alling, K., 22
Allison, J., 197, 200, 201, 206, 207
Alloy, L. B., 153
Alptekin, S., 172, 191, 353
Alslop, B., 176
Amsel, A., 171, 191, 308
Anderson, D. C., 153
Anderson, M. C., 150
Anger, D., 264
Anisman, H., 153
Aparicio, J., 245
Aristotle, 6
Arnold, H. M., 73, 94
Aronson, L., 115
Asano, T., 209
Askins, M., 234
Astley, S. L., 356, 362, 363
Augerinos, G., 320
Axelrod, S., 272
Aydin, A., 361
Ayres, J. J. B., 64, 73, 79, 103, 113
Azmitia, E. C., Jr., 334
Azorlosa, J. L., 114
Azrin, N. H., 169, 272, 273, 274, 275, 276, 277, 280

Babkin, B. P., 11
Backer, R., 192
Baer, D. M., 222
Baerends, G. P., 31, 32, 33, 34, 36
Baker, A. G., 74
Baker, P. A., 74
Baker, T. B., 103
Balaz, M. A., 114, 334
Balda, R. P., 323, 324
Balsam, P. D., 114, 115, 129, 233, 243, 246
Banks, R. K., 273
Barker, L. M., 66
Barnes, R. A., 114
Barnet, R. C., 73, 79, 93, 94, 113, 117, 333
Baron, A., 164, 272, 274, 314
Barrera, F. J., 105, 114
Barrett, J. E., 165
Barry, K., 172, 353
Barton, L. E., 135
Bashinksi, H., 36, 37
Bateson, M., 211
Batson, J. D., 77
Battalio, R., 179
Battig, K., 319
Baum, M., 260, 261
Baum, W. M., 166, 167, 176, 177, 180
Bauman, R., 209
Baxter, D. J., 298, 299
Beardsley, S. D., 178
Beatty, W. W., 320, 321, 322
Bechterev, V., 252
Beecher, M. D., 270
Belke, T. W., 178, 180, 181, 182
Bell, C., 7
Bellingham, W. P., 224
Bennett, C. H., 360
Berlyne, D. E., 192
Berman, J. S., 261
Bermant, G., 29, 234
Bernstein, I. L., 73, 83, 98
Berridge, K. C., 95

Best, M. R., 66, 77, 78, 83, 113, 117, 247
Bever, T. G., 308, 348, 351, 366
Bevins, R. A., 64, 103
Bhatt, R. S., 212, 332, 358, 359, 360, 361
Bickel, W. K., 207, 208, 209, 210
Bierley, C. M., 314
Bierley, R. A., 322
Bini, L., 338
Birmingham, K. M., 172
Bitterman, M. E., 16, 19, 71, 73, 74, 78, 255
Bizo, L. A., 347, 349
Bjork, R. A., 329
Black, A. H., 78, 79, 153, 258, 259, 292, 320
Blackman, D., 297
Blakely, E., 146, 162
Blakemore, C., 15
Blanchard, D. C., 64
Blanchard, R. J., 64
Blass, E. M., 83
Blough, D. S., 314
Boakes, R. A., 59, 74
Boice, R., 21
Bolhuis, J. J., 322
Bolles, R. C., 64, 103, 192, 265, 267, 268, 269, 270, 273, 297, 300, 333
Bonardi, C., 242
Boneau, C. A., 236
Bonem, E. J., 162
Bordi, F., 150
Borovsky, D., 331, 333
Borson, S., 83
Borszcz, G. S., 44
Bourne, M. J., 225
Bouton, M. E., 64, 81, 82, 103, 247, 333
Bowe, C. A., 228
Bower, G. H., 301
Braaten, R. F., 241
Bradford, S. A., 326
Bradshaw, C. M., 177

Brady, P. M., 356
Brakke, K. E., 369, 372
Brandon, S. E., 117, 119
Braveman, N. S., 66
Breland, K., 140
Breland, M., 140
Brener, J., 129
Brewer, V. R., 172
Brimer, C. J., 64, 89, 258, 259
Brodbeck, D. R., 324
Brogden, W. J., 253, 254
Bronstein, P., 66
Brooks, D. C., 81, 333
Brooks, W., 62
Brown, A. M., 117
Brown, B. L., 346
Brown, E., 353
Brown, J. S., 257, 258, 277
Brown, M. F., 327
Brown, P. L., 62
Brown, S. W., 325
Brown, T., 6
Browne, M. P., 286, 288
Bruell, J., 84
Brulle, A. R., 135
Bruner, D., 182
Buck, M. A., 181
Bull, J. A., III, 297, 298
Burgess, I. S., 176
Burke, P. D., 13
Burkhard, B., 280
Burns, M., 62, 72, 84
Burstein, K. R., 236
Butler, M. M., 228
Buxton, A., 206
Bygrave, D. J., 114

Cable, C., 241, 356, 357, 362
Cacheiro, H., 334
Cadieux, E. L., 84
Cameron, J., 139
Camhi, J. M., 31
Camp, D. S., 273, 274
Campbell, B. A., 194, 272, 334
Campbell, R. A., 272
Cándido, A., 265
Cannon, D. S., 83, 247
Cantor, J., 65
Capaldi, E. J., 172, 191, 353
Cappell, H., 103
Carbary, T. J., 89
Carelli, R., 170
Carew, T. J., 19
Carley, J. L., 335, 336
Carmona, G. G., 210
Carrell, L. E., 83, 247
Carroll, M. E., 210
Carson, R., 80

Carter, M. M., 80
Case, D. A., 211
Casey, F. G., 198, 199
Caspy, T., 151
Catterson, D. A., 117, 334
Ceraso, J., 335
Cerella, J., 356
Cerletti, U., 338
Chamizo, V. D., 225
Charlop, M. H., 198, 199, 222
Charnock, D. J., 80
Chavarro, A., 185
Chelonis, J. J., 185
Cheng, K., 218, 345, 347
Chew, K., 335
Childress, A. R., 101, 102
Chomsky, N., 363
Church, R. M., 213, 272, 273, 275, 344,
    345, 346, 347, 348, 373
Cicala, G. A., 114, 267
Clark, R. B., 167
Clayton, N. S., 324
Cleland, G. G., 63, 98, 99
Clements, K. C., 212
Clouse, B. A., 322
Cohen, J. S., 335, 347
Cohen, L. B., 44
Cohen, P. S., 150
Colbert, M. M., 84
Cole, M. R., 166, 167
Coleman, S. R., 73, 285, 288, 289
Collier, G., 21, 142
Collison, C., 320
Colombo, M., 314, 337, 351, 352, 353
Colwill, R. M., 99, 300, 301, 302, 303,
    304
Commons, M. L., 178, 210, 356
Conger, R., 177
Cook, M., 92, 259, 266
Cook, R. G., 316, 327, 335, 336
Cook, S. C., 248
Cool, V., 72
Cooney, J. B., 170
Cooper, G. F., 15
Cooper, L. D., 115
Cooper, R. P., 44
Cooper, S. J., 193
Corbit, J. D., 48, 49, 50, 51, 52
Coulter, X., 261
Couvillon, P. A., 255
Cowie, R. J., 323
Cramer, R. E., 19
Cranney, J., 44
Cranston, S. S., 272
Craske, M. G., 80
Crawford, L. L., 286
Crespi, L. P., 143
Critchfield, T. S., 146, 246

Cronin, P. B., 147
Crossman, E. K., 162
Crowell, C. R., 153
Crozier, W. J., 35
Crystal, J. D., 345
Culler, E., 253, 254
Cunningham, C. E., 282
Cunningham, C. L., 102, 153, 277
Curran, P. J., 248
Cutmore, T. R. H., 84

Dallal, N. L., 353
D'Amato, M. R., 233, 265, 314, 317,
    336, 337, 351, 352, 353, 356
Dardano, J. F., 275
Darwin, C., 9, 18
Davey, G. C. L., 63, 92, 98, 99
Davidson, F. H., 147
Davidson, T. L., 233, 245, 302
Davies, J., 319
Davis, D. G., 181
Davis, E. R., 156
Davis, H., 297
Davis, M., 37, 39, 44, 45
Davison, M., 176, 178, 197, 212
Dawson, G. R., 167
Dean, S. J., 277
Dearing, M. F., 94
de Cantanzaro, D., 153
DeCarlo, L. T., 180
DeCola, J. P., 80, 152, 153, 156
DeGrandpre, R. J., 208, 209
Deich, J. D., 129, 130
Dekeyne, A., 333
Delamater, B. A., 302, 303, 304
Delius, J. D., 313, 316
DeLizio, R., 54
DeLong, R. E., 345
Delprato, D. J., 257
DeMarse, T. B., 299
Depollo, D., 150
DePorto-Callan, D., 176
Descartes, R., 3–4, 7
Desiderato, O., 297
Desjardins, C., 84
DeSpain, M. J., 327, 328
Dess, N. K., 151, 156
Dess-Beech, N., 334
de Vaca, S. C., 346, 347
deVilliers, P. A., 267, 356, 358
Devine, V. T., 257
DeVito, P. L., 74, 79, 113
Deweer, B., 333
Dickinson, A., 94, 114, 146, 167, 295,
    300, 302
Diehl, R. L., 356
Dimberg, U., 92
Dinsmoor, J. A., 257, 266, 267, 276, 279

Dobrzecka, C., 226, 227
Dolan, J. C., 73
Dollard, J., 11, 13
Domjan, M., 9, 47, 62, 66, 72, 73, 77,
    84, 91, 99, 106, 107, 114, 234, 235,
    286
Doob, L. W., 11
Dougherty, D. M., 239
Drent, R. H., 32, 33
Dreyfus, L. R., 176
Drudge, O., 19
Ducharme, M. J., 326
Dufore, D. S., 76
Duncan, C. P., 338, 339
Dunn, D. P., 77
Dunn, R., 182
Dunn, T., 273
Durkin, M., 65
Durlach, P. J., 63, 95, 115, 245, 246
Dutta, S. N., 100
Dweck, C. S., 76
Dworkin, B. R., 103

Ebbinghaus, H., 6
Edhouse, W. V., 336
Edwards, C. A., 315, 357, 359
Egel, A. L., 222
Ehrman, R. N., 101, 102
Eibl-Eibesfeldt, I., 34
Eikelboom, R., 101, 103
Eisenberger, R., 139, 186, 200
Eizenga, C., 151
Elliffe, D., 176
Ellins, S. R., 19
Ellison, G. D., 72, 293
Empedocles, S., 332
English, J. A., 210
Ervey, D. H., 269
Ervin, F. R., 67
Estes, W. K., 63, 272, 277, 278, 279, 297
Etkin, M., 265

Fabrigoule, C., 259
Fagen, J. W., 334
Fagot, B. I., 44
Fairhurst, S., 177, 182, 213
Fairless, J. L., 74, 76
Fallon, D., 314
Falls, W. A., 103
Fanselow, M. S., 268, 269, 270
Fantino, E., 180, 211, 213
Farley, J., 19, 77
Farmer-Dougan, V. A., 204
Fazzaro, J., 265
Feldman, D. T., 334, 335
Felton, M., 161
Ferster, C. B., 160, 162
Fetterman, J. G., 219, 344, 345, 349

Fibiger, H. C., 193, 194
File, S. E., 44
Fiori, L. M., 79, 333
Fitch, M. D., 356
FitzGerald, R. E., 319
Flaherty, C. F., 143, 145
Fleshler, M., 38
Flexner, J. B., 338
Flexner, L. B., 338
Flynn, F. W., 233
Foa, E. B., 153
Foltin, R. W., 209
Foree, D. D., 91, 225, 226
Forestell, P. H., 314
Forzano, L. B., 185
Foster, T. M., 176
Foundopolous, M., 272
Fountain, S. B., 353
Fowler, H., 74, 79, 113, 117, 295, 308
Foxx, R. M., 272
Fraenkel, G. S., 35
France, K. G., 232
Frankel, F. D., 273
Franklin, S. R., 77
Freed, D. E., 209
Frommer, G. P., 98
Fuentes, I., 66
Furchtgott, E., 65

Gaffan, E. A., 319
Galbicka, G., 131
Gallup, G. G., 24, 270
Gamzu, E. R., 62
Ganchrow, J. R., 83
Gannon, K. N., 205
Gantt, W. H., 61
Garb, J. J., 82, 91
Garber, J., 153
Garcia, J., 67, 90, 91
Garcia-Sanchez, L., 260
Gardner, B. T., 364, 365, 366, 368
Gardner, E. T., 267
Gardner, R. A., 364, 365, 366, 368
Gawley, D. J., 150, 197, 205, 206, 213
Gee, J.-L., 334
Gelperin, A., 19
Gemberling, G. A., 91
George, J. T., 168
Getty, D. J., 345
Gewirtz, J. C., 89
Gibbon, J., 61, 114, 115, 177, 182, 213,
    344, 345, 347, 348, 349
Giencke, L., 261
Gillan, D. J., 114
Gillett, J. D., 35
Gillette, K., 224
Gino, A., 259, 261
Ginsberg, D., 92

Gisiner, R., 364
Gisquet-Verrier, P., 334
Gladstein, L., 113
Glazer, R. D., 269
Gleeson, S., 146
Glickman, S. E., 193
Glisson, F., 7
Glover, D., 80
Goldfarb, T. L., 335, 336
Goldstein, M. H., 44
Goodall, G., 245, 273, 274, 302
Goodman, J. H., 295
Gordon, E. L., 117
Gordon, W. C., 334, 335, 339
Gormezano, I., 65, 66, 71, 72, 73, 89,
    285, 286, 288
Grace, R. C., 177
Graham, J. M., 84
Graham, P., 228
Grahame, N. J., 113, 117
Grant, D. S., 103, 104, 314, 315, 316,
    326, 330, 331, 335, 336, 337
Grau, J. W., 63, 245, 246
Green, L., 177, 179, 183, 184, 207, 209,
    228
Greene, D., 139
Greene, S. L., 357
Greenfield, P. M., 371, 374
Grice, G. R., 146
Griffin, D. R., 308
Griffin, R. W., 99
Griffiths, R. R., 234
Griffiths, W. J. H., 146
Grossen, N. E., 265, 269, 297, 298
Groves, P. M., 41, 42, 45
Grusec, J. F., 272
Guha, D., 100
Gunn, D. L., 35
Gunther, M., 30
Gutiérrez, G., 84, 106, 107
Gutman, A., 297
Guttenberger, V. T., 314
Guttman, N., 220, 221

Haberlandt, K., 107
Hackenberg, T. D., 212
Hadad, G. M., 84
Haddad, C., 73
Haggbloom, S. J., 172, 333
Hailman, J. P., 34
Hake, D. F., 169, 272, 273, 275
Hale, S., 181
Hall, G., 46, 89, 107, 114, 242, 244
Hall, R. G., 92
Hall, R. V., 272
Hall, S. M., 92
Hallam, S. C., 76, 113, 117
Halliday, M. S., 74

Hamdi, M. E., 257
Hamilton, M., 153
Hammond, L. J., 77, 79, 297
Hanson, H. M., 237, 238
Hanson, J., 177
Hanson, S. J., 201
Harley, H. E., 335, 351, 365
Harlow, H. F., 15, 54
Haroutunian, V., 334
Harris, K., 113
Harrison, J. M., 228
Harrison, R. H., 232, 234, 241
Hart, B. L., 29
Hart, J. A., 225
Hastjarjo, T., 209
Hautus, M. J., 356
Hawkins, R. D., 19
Hayes, C., 364
Hayes, K. J., 364
Healy, S. D., 317, 324
Hearst, E. S., 61, 62, 72, 73, 77, 98, 241,
    286, 288, 297
Hebb, D. O., 285
Heiligenberg, W., 45
Held, F. P., 73
Helmstetter, F. J., 269
Helweg, D. A., 351, 356, 365
Hemmes, N. S., 346, 347
Henderson, R. W., 299
Henningfield, J. E., 234
Hepper, P. G., 44
Herdegen, R. T., 267
Herman, L. M., 314, 364, 367
Herman, R. L., 276
Herrnstein, R. J., 174, 175, 178, 180,
    241, 265, 267, 279, 280, 356, 357,
    358, 362
Herz, M. J., 338
Herzog, H. A., Jr., 23
Heth, C. D., 73
Heyman, G. M., 178, 180, 210
Higa, J. J., 165
Higgins, S. T., 208
Hilgard, E. R., 98
Hill, W., 273
Hiller, G. W., 286
Hilton, S. C., 324
Hineline, P. N., 212, 263, 264, 265, 267
Hinson, J. M., 103, 179
Hinson, R. E., 72
Hintzman, D. L., 308
Hirsch, J., 19
Hitchcock, J. M., 44
Hobbes, T., 5
Hodges, L. A., 338
Hoffman, H. S., 38, 48, 54, 99
Hoffman, N., 322, 335
Hoffman, S. M., 165

Hogan, D. E., 315
Hogan, J. A., 105
Holland, P. C., 98, 99, 103, 104, 244,
    246, 247, 248
Holliday, M., 19
Hollis, K. L., 73, 84
Hollon, S. D., 80
Holloway, K. S., 84, 99
Holman, J. G., 245, 302, 356
Holtz, R., 273
Holz, W. C., 272, 273, 275, 276, 277,
    280
Honey, R. C., 46, 242, 244
Hong, J. Y., 76
Honig, W. K., 220, 236, 237, 239, 263,
    264, 308, 312, 326, 356, 357, 359
Hopkins, B. L., 168
Hopkins, W. D., 366
Hoyert, M. S., 164
Huber, L., 362, 363
Huckeby, E. R., 44
Hudson, S. M., 232
Hughes, J. R., 208, 209
Hull, C., 191, 291
Hulse, S. H., 241, 308, 351
Hunter, W. S., 311
Hurly, R. A., 317
Hursh, S. R., 207, 209
Hutchinson, R. R., 169
Hutt, P. J., 142, 143

Imada, H., 124
Imada, S., 124
Innis, N. K., 150, 151
Ireland, C., 105
Irwin, J., 153
Isler, R., 319
Israel, A. C., 257
Ito, M., 211
Iversen, I. H., 202, 314

Jackson, R. L., 151, 153, 154, 156, 299
Jackson-Smith, P., 326, 327
Jacobs, A., 257, 258
Jacobs, E. A., 212
Jacobs, W. J., 91
Jacobson, J., 150
Jagielo, J. A., 89, 326, 334
Janssen, M., 77
Jarrard, L. E., 233, 314
Jarvik, M. E., 335, 336
Jenkins, H. M., 61, 62, 63, 97, 105, 114,
    115, 171, 232, 234, 241, 245, 287
Jessell, T. M., 11
Jitsumori, M., 316, 335, 336, 356, 362
Job, R. F. S., 151
Johnson, D. F., 142
Johnson, H. M., 329

Jones, B. M., 176
Jones, M. R., 353
Jonke, T., 334

Kabela, E., 185
Kacelnik, A., 210, 211, 213
Kaczor, T., 162
Kagel, J., 179, 208
Kaiser, D. H., 330
Kalat, J. W., 90
Kalish, H. I., 220, 221
Kamil, A. C., 210, 212, 213, 317, 323,
    324
Kamin, L. J., 63, 64, 72, 89, 108, 258,
    259, 267
Kaminski, B. J., 246
Kandel, E. R., 11, 19
Kaplan, P. S., 36, 44, 47, 48, 72
Kardal, S., 356
Karpicke, J., 298
Karpman, M., 200
Kasprow, W. J., 114, 117, 147, 225, 334
Kastak, D., 314
Katzev, R. D., 257, 261
Kaufman, L. W., 21
Kaye, H., 114
Keehn, J. D., 265
Kehoe, E. J., 65, 72, 81, 228
Kelley, M. J., 91, 225, 269
Kellogg, W. N., 364
Kelly, S. Q., 177
Kelsey, J. E., 103
Kendrick, D. F., 329
Kesner, R. P., 327, 328
Kessen, M. L., 192
Khallad, Y., 111
Kiedinger, R. E., 358, 359, 360, 361
Killeen, P. R., 177, 344, 347, 348, 349,
    356
Kim, S. D., 103
Kimmel, H. D., 228
King, D., 141
King, G. R., 185
Kirby, R. M., 131
Kleiman, M. C., 74
Klein, M., 241
Klein, R. L., 334
Kluender, K. R., 356
Knauss, K. S., 359
Koegel, R. L., 222
Köhler, W., 241
Kohts, N., 364
Konorski, J., 81, 226, 227, 293
Konz, W. A., 299
Koshland, D. E., 22
Kosslyn, S. M., 356
Kostansek, D. J., 297

Kotovsky, K., 353
Kraemer, P. J., 89, 99, 225
Krank, M. D., 103
Krantz, P. J., 222
Krebs, J. R., 210, 323, 324
Kremer, E. F., 111
Kreuter, C., 297
Krieger, K., 367
Kruse, J. M., 299
Kurtz, P. F., 198, 199

Labinsky, J. S., 89
Lachnit, H., 228
Lamb, R. J., 234
Lamoreaux, R. R., 255, 271
Lansdell, H., 23
Larew, M. B., 117, 345
Lashley, K. S., 230
Lattal, K. A., 146
Lauer, D. W., 71
Lavin, M. J., 95
Lawler, C. P., 150
Lawry, J. A., 298
Lawson, J., 370
Lea, S. E. G., 131, 185, 207, 356, 362
Leak, T. M., 349
Leaton, R. N., 44, 45, 46
Leclerc, R., 298
Lee, C.-Y., 156
Lee, R. K. K., 155
Legris, J. A., 131
Leinbach, M. D., 44
Leinenweber, A., 164
Lejeune, H., 164, 344
Lennenberg, E. H., 363
Lenz, R., 362, 363
Lepper, M. R., 139
Lerner, N. D., 345
Lester, L. S., 268, 269, 270
Levins, S. M., 172
Levis, D. J., 153, 255, 259, 260
Lewis, D. J., 339
Lewis, P., 239, 267
Libe, J., 272
Lieberman, D. A., 72, 147, 148
Liebman, J. M., 193
Lightbown, Y., 46
Linscheid, T. R., 282
Lipman, E. A., 253, 254
Lipsitt, L. P., 48, 65
Litner, J. S., 266, 297
Little, A. H., 65
Lochner, D. G., 177
Lockard, R. B., 21
Locke, J., 5
Locurto, C. M., 61, 286, 287
Loeb, J., 18
Logan, F. A., 107

Logue, A. W., 82, 91, 183, 184, 185, 268
Lohmann, A., 362
LoLordo, V. M., 74, 75, 76, 89, 91, 225, 226, 297, 298
Losey, G. S., 123
Lovelace, L., 172
Loveland, D. H., 241, 356, 357, 362
Lovibond, P. F., 297, 298
Lubow, R. E., 89, 151
Lucas, G. A., 105, 140, 150, 151, 205, 213
Lupo, J. V., 153
Lyon, D. O., 161, 297
Lyons, R., 84
Lysle, D. T., 74, 113, 117

MacArdy, E. A., 334
MacDonald, S. E., 314
MacEwen, D., 347, 349
Machado, A., 137, 179, 181
Mackintosh, N. J., 114, 142, 225, 245, 259, 300, 302, 356, 360
Macrae, M., 81
Macuda, T., 353
Magendie, F., 7
Mah, W. L., 243, 244, 332
Maier, S. F., 73, 151, 152, 153, 154, 155, 156, 297, 344
Maki, W. S., 314, 317, 319, 322, 335
Maldonado, A., 265
Mann, B., 150, 151
March, J., 225
Marchant, H. G., III, 75
Maricq, A. V., 347
Marlin, N. A., 46
Marsh, G., 241
Marshall, B. S., 65
Martens, B. K., 177
Martin, G. C., 19
Martin, G. M., 224
Masserman, J. H., 272
Mast, M., 64
Matthews, T. J., 150, 151
Matzel, L. D., 19, 73, 74, 113, 115, 117
May, J. G., 185
May, S. A., 210
Mayer-Gross, W., 338
Mazmanian, D. S., 320, 356, 358
Mazur, J. E., 182
McAllister, D. E., 255, 257, 259, 265
McAllister, W. R., 255, 257, 259, 265
McCarthy, D., 176, 178, 212
McClannahan, L. E., 222
McCleery, R. H., 210
McCracken, K. M., 334
McDonald, K., 366
McDowell, J. J., 167, 177, 178, 181
McEwen, B. S., 334 ·

McFall, R. M., 204
McGaugh, J. L., 338
McGee, G. G., 222
McGinnis, C. M., 334
McIntosh, D. C., 147, 148
McKelvie, A. R., 243, 244, 332
McLaren, I. P. L., 360
McMillan, D. E., 234
McMillan, J. C., 298
McShane, B., 345
McSweeney, F. K., 145, 181
Meachum, C. L., 77, 98
Meck, W. H., 345, 346, 347, 348, 353
Medin, D. L., 335
Meehl, P. E., 190
Mellgren, R. L., 143, 144, 145, 211, 325
Melville, C. L., 145, 181
Melvin, K. B., 269, 277
Menich, S. R., 314
Metalsky, G. I., 153
Metzger, B., 146
Meyer, R. C., 225
Midgley, M., 131, 137
Miller, D. J., 172, 191, 353
Miller, H. L., 177
Miller, J. D., 228
Miller, J. S., 89, 334
Miller, K. D., 345
Miller, N. E., 11, 13, 192, 255, 273
Miller, R. R., 46, 73, 74, 76, 78, 79, 93, 94, 107, 113, 114, 115, 117, 333, 334, 339
Miller, S., 261
Miller, V., 47
Milner, P., 193
Mineka, S., 54, 92, 257, 259, 261, 266
Minor, T. R., 151, 155, 156
Mis, F. W., 75
Mitchell, C., 192
Mitchell, J. B., 84
Mitchell, S., 129
Moe, J. C., 314
Moise, S. L., 314
Monaghan, M. M., 178
Mondloch, M. V., 182, 197
Moore, B. R., 97
Moore, B. S., 315
Moore, J., 111
Moore, J. W., 75
Moore, K. E., 197, 206
Morgan, C., 142
Morgan, C. L., 18
Morgan, L., 137
Morgan, M. J., 356
Morgulis, S., 59
Morrel-Samuels, P., 367
Morris, C. J., 137
Morris, K. M., 333

Morris, R. G., 266, 318, 319, 320
Motzkin, D. K., 99
Mowrer, O. H., 11, 255, 271, 293, 294, 334
Mowrer, R. R., 334, 339, 340
Moye, T. B., 239
Mumford, D. B., 356
Mumford, G. K., 234
Murphy, J., 369, 373
Murray, B., 193
Musgrave, S., 326
Myerson, J., 181

Nachtigall, P. E., 315, 356
Nair, V., 176
Nakkash, S., 265
Napier, R. M., 81
Nash, S., 234, 235
Nash, S. M., 77
Nathan, P. W., 337
Nation, J. R., 170
Navez, A. E., 35
Neill, J. C., 228
Neuenschwander, N., 259
Neuringer, A., 137, 138, 233, 356
Nevin, J. A., 179
Nicholas, D. J., 114
Nicholas, T., 260
Nichols, P., 211
Nickel, M., 22, 146
Nicoll, C. S., 23, 24
Nisbett, R. E., 139
Noble, G. K., 234
Nokes, T., 192
North, N. C., 84

Obal, F., 100
O'Brien, C. P., 101, 102
O'Dea, M. A., 257
Oden, D. L., 316
Odling-Smee, F. J., 16
Oettinger, R., 319
Öhman, A., 92
Olds, J., 193
Olds, M. E., 193
Olson, D. J., 324
Olton, D. S., 317, 318, 320, 321, 325, 346
Ophir, I., 82
Ost, J. W. P., 71
Öst, L. G., 92
Overmier, J. B., 13, 73, 74, 113, 151, 228, 297, 298, 299
Owen, J. W., 267
Owens, J. D., 172

Pack, A. A., 367
Pack, K., 298

Page, H. A., 261
Page, S., 137, 138
Page, S. C., 241
Palmer, R. G., 181
Palya, W. L., 77
Panlilio, L. V., 225
Papadouka, V., 151
Papini, M. R., 71, 74, 78
Pappas, N., 336
Parke, R. D., 276
Parker, B. K., 246
Parker, L. A., 98
Patten, R. L., 286
Patterson, F. G., 364, 365
Patterson, J. M., 299
Pavlov, I. P., 7, 8, 10–11, 58–59, 60, 72, 75, 78, 81, 92, 225
Pear, J. J., 131
Pearce, J. M., 94, 114, 228, 229, 295, 356, 361
Peck, C. A., 333
Peden, B. F., 286, 287, 288
Peeke, H. V. S., 39
Pelchat, M. L., 91, 98
Peña-Correal, T. E., 185
Penner, R. H., 315
Pennypacker, H. S., 236
Penton-Voak, I. S., 347
Pepperberg, I. M., 364, 367
Perdeck, A. C., 32
Perkins, C. C., 147, 285
Perry, D. G., 276
Pesillo, S. A., 176
Peterson, C., 151, 153
Peterson, G. B., 98, 297, 298
Petitto, L. A., 366
Petrinovich, L. F., 39, 338
Petry, N. M., 178, 210
Phelps, B. J., 162
Phillips, A. G., 193, 194
Phillips, S., 98
Picton, B. M. B., 114
Pierce, W. D., 139
Pinel, J. P. J., 73
Pisacreta, R., 137
Pittman, C. M., 277
Platt, J. R., 131, 156
Platt, S. A., 19
Plonsky, M., 153
Ploog, B. O., 97
Plotkin, H. C., 16
Plous, S., 24
Plowright, C. M. S., 211
Poling, A., 22, 146, 176
Porter, D., 233, 356
Postman, L., 335
Poulos, C. X., 103
Pradhan, S. N., 100

Premack, A. J., 364, 365
Premack, D., 195, 196, 200, 280, 316, 368
Prescott, L., 65
Preston, R. A., 211
Price, T., 107
Prochaska, J., 260, 261
Prokasy, W. F., 293
Puente, G. P., 247
Pulliam, H. R., 210
Pye, C., 46

Quartermain, D., 334

Rachlin, H. C., 178, 179, 183, 184, 207, 208, 209, 279, 280
Randall, C. K., 89, 99, 334
Randall, P. R., 338
Randich, A., 89
Rapaport, P., 73
Rashotte, M. E., 99, 191
Raslear, T. G., 209
Ravert, R. D., 234
Ray, E., 242
Raymond, G. A., 273
Reberg, D., 78, 79, 81, 150, 151, 298
Redhead, E. S., 212, 228
Reed, P., 142, 192
Reid, S., 335
Remington, G., 153
Repp, A. C., 135, 282
Rescorla, R. A., 61, 63, 71, 72, 73, 74, 75, 76, 79, 81, 93, 95, 98, 99, 107, 109, 113, 245, 246, 247, 266, 267, 292, 293, 297, 300, 301, 302
Restle, F., 353
Revusky, S. H., 67
Rey, V., 46, 242
Reynolds, G. S., 165, 166, 218, 219, 222
Reynolds, T. J., 335
Reynolds, W. F., Jr., 359
Riccio, D. C., 261, 308, 309, 334, 338, 339, 341
Rice, M. B., 193
Richardson, R., 334, 339, 341
Richelle, M., 344
Richmond, M., 242
Riegert, P. W., 35
Riley, A. L., 82, 269, 298
Riley, D. A., 327
Rilling, M., 241, 329
Ristau, C. A., 308
Rivera, J. J., 316
Rivers, S., 103
Rizvi, S. A. T., 209
Robbins, S. J., 81, 101, 102, 113, 117
Roberts, S., 345, 346, 347

Roberts, W. A., 225, 314, 316, 320, 321, 325, 335, 336, 337, 347, 353, 356, 358
Robertson, B., 176
Robertson, D., 72
Robinson, S. R., 44
Roby, T. B., 194
Rodriguez, M. L., 185
Roemer, R. A., 42
Rogers, R. F., 19
Roitblat, H. L., 308, 309, 315, 317, 335, 336, 348, 351, 356, 365
Rokke, E., 299
Roll, D. L., 67, 68
Romanes, G. J., 9
Romano, A., 182
Romski, M. A., 364
Roper, K. L., 329, 330
Rosellini, R. A., 152, 153, 156
Rosen, J. B., 44
Rosenberg, E., 319
Ross, R. T., 246, 247, 248
Rothbaum, B. O., 153
Rovee-Collier, C., 48, 65, 331, 332, 333, 334
Rowan, G. A., 145
Rowan, J. B., 353
Rowlett, J. K., 210
Rozin, P., 16, 82, 91
Rubert, E., 366
Rudy, J. W., 19, 36, 37, 47, 48, 286, 329
Rumbaugh, D. M., 365, 368, 369, 370, 374
Russell, R. J., 248
Russell, S. M., 23, 24
Russell, W. R., 337
Ryan, C. M. E., 362

Sahley, C., 19
Sajwaj, T., 272
Sakamoto, J., 233
Saladin, M. E., 73, 89, 113, 119
Salmon, D. P., 233
Samuelson, R. J., 318, 320, 321
Sanders, R. J., 366
Sands, S. F., 315, 316, 336
Santi, A., 326
Santiago, H. C., 336
Saper, Z. L., 89
Sargent, T. D., 210
Sauerbrunn, D., 275
Savage-Rumbaugh, E. S., 365, 366, 369, 370, 371, 372, 373, 374
Savastano, H., 180
Scavio, M. J., Jr., 89
Schachter, D. L., 16, 323
Schachtman, T. R., 117, 225, 334
Schafe, G. E., 73

Schaub, R. E., 89
Schiff, B. B., 193
Schiff, R., 260, 261
Schiller, K. M., 19
Schindler, C. W., 225, 239
Schlinger, H., 162
Schlosberg, H., 173, 253, 285
Schneiderman, N., 66, 71
Schnur, P., 89
Schrader, S., 280
Schreibman, L., 222
Schrier, A. M., 356
Schulkin, J., 95
Schull, J., 16
Schuster, R. H., 279
Schusterman, R. J., 314, 364, 367
Schwartz, B., 137, 287, 298
Schwartz, J. H., 11
Schwarz, M., 19
Schweitzer, J. B., 186
Scobie, S. R., 298
Scopatz, R. A., 336, 351
Sears, G. W., 266
Sears, R. R., 11
Sechenov, I. M., 7–8
Seligman, M. E. P., 92, 151, 152, 153
Serdikoff, S. L., 246
Sevcik, R. A., 364, 366, 369
Sevenster, P., 123, 139
Shah, K., 177
Shahidullah, S., 44
Shapiro, K. L., 91, 225
Shapiro, N. R., 152
Shattuck, D., 297
Shavalia, D. A., 320, 321, 322
Sheffield, F. D., 192, 194, 260, 286, 287
Shellman, J., 272
Shelton, R. C., 80
Sherburne, L. M., 330
Sherry, D. F., 16, 322, 323
Shettleworth, S. J., 141, 150, 210, 211, 212, 323, 324
Shimp, C. P., 179
Shishimi, A., 73
Shizgal, P., 193
Shurtleff, D., 73, 209
Shyan, M. R., 316, 336
Shyi, G. C.-W., 332
Siddle, D., 44
Sidman, M., 242, 261, 263, 264, 265, 267
Siegel, S., 72, 73, 100, 101, 103, 109
Sigmundi, R. A., 103
Silberberg, A., 209
Silverman, K., 234
Simmelhag, V. L., 149, 150
Simmelhag-Grant, V. L., 150

Simmons, L., 209
Simon, H. A., 353
Simons, R. C., 39
Singh, N. N., 109, 282
Sisk, C. L., 99
Skelton, R. W., 97
Skinner, B. F., 11, 63, 127, 148, 160, 162, 245, 272, 277, 302
Slamecka, N. J., 335
Sloat, J. S., 117
Slobin, P., 321, 325
Small, W. S., 126
Smith, F. J., 80
Smith, H. V., 205
Smith, J. C., 67, 68
Smith, M. C., 73
Smith, N., 260, 261
Smith, S. T., 370
Smotherman, W. P., 44
Snarsky, A., 59
Snodgrass, S. H., 234
Soldat, A. S., 330, 331
Sollars, S. I., 73
Solman, R. T., 109
Solomon, R. L., 48, 49, 50, 51, 52, 54, 152, 258, 260, 272, 292, 293
Soltysik, S. S., 260
Sonuga-Barke, E. J. S., 185
Spear, N. E., 74, 78, 89, 99, 308, 309, 334, 338, 339
Spence, K. W., 235, 239, 291
Spencer, W. A., 46, 47
Spetch, M. L., 73, 97, 182, 218, 225, 322, 326
Springer, A. D., 339
Staddon, J. E. R., 149, 150, 165, 179, 181, 203, 207
Stanhope, K. J., 97
Starr, M. D., 54, 259
Steiner, J. E., 83
Steinert, P., 314
Steirn, J. N., 327
Stellar, E., 338
Stellar, J. R., 193
Stephens, D. W., 210
Stephenson, D., 44
Stevens, S. S., 219
Stewart, J., 101, 103
Stewart, K. E., 356
Stilman, A. J., 153
Stokes, L. W., 267
Stokes, P., 129
Stokes, T. F., 222
Stone, M. J., 83
Stonebraker, T. B., 329
Straub, J. J., 99
Straub, R. O., 351
Strauss, K. E., 82

Strijkstra, A. M., 322
Stunkard, A. J., 82, 91
Suarez, S. D., 24, 270
Suissa, A., 153
Sulzer-Azaroff, B., 186
Summers, R. J., 314
Sundberg, M. L., 370
Suomi, S. J., 54
Susswein, A. J., 19
Suzuki, S., 320
Swammerdam, J., 7
Swartzentruber, D., 244, 247, 248
Symonds, M., 89
Szabadi, E., 177
Szwejkowska, G., 81, 226, 227

Tailby, W., 242
Tait, R. W., 73, 89, 113, 119
Tatham, T. A., 212
Temple, W., 176
ten Have, W. N., 89
Terrace, H. S., 61, 308, 309, 348, 351,
    353, 355, 366, 368, 371
Terrones, J. P., 248
Terry, W. S., 317
Teyler, T. J., 42
Theios, J., 171
Thomas, D. R., 239, 241, 243, 244, 248,
    332
Thomas, G. V., 72, 147, 148
Thomas, J. R., 272
Thompson, C. R., 373
Thompson, R. F., 41, 42, 45, 46, 47
Thompson, R. K. R., 316, 326, 336
Thorndike, E. L., 18–19, 124–125, 272,
    280
Tierney, K. J., 205, 206
Tiffany, S. T., 103
Timberlake, W., 20, 103, 104, 105, 140,
    141, 142, 150, 151, 190, 200, 201,
    204, 205, 213, 319
Tinbergen, N., 32, 34
Tobin, H., 185
Tomie, A., 62, 153, 154, 170, 243, 246,
    286
Trapold, M. A., 298
Trattner, J., 200
Trauner, M. A., 156
Trenholme, I. A., 272
Trumble, D., 259
Tuck, D. L., 82
Turek, R. J., 323
Turkkan, J. S., 61, 82
Turton, D., 150
Twitmyer, E. B., 58
Tyler, P. A., 212

Underwood, B. J., 335
Urcuioli, P. J., 147, 220, 299, 326, 336

Vaccarino, F. J., 193
Van Cantfort, T. E., 365
Van Hemel, P. E., 336
Van Sant, P., 356
Vaughan, W., Jr., 180, 357
Viken, R. J., 204
Vila, J., 265
Vogt, W., 234
Volpe, J. S., 185
Voss, P., 212
Vuchinich, R. E., 207
Vyse, S. A., 180

Wade, M., 230
Wagner, A. R., 46, 73, 76, 107, 109, 117,
    119, 317, 329
Wagner, G. C., 170
Wahl, G., 141
Wakita, M., 233
Wallace, J., 314
Walter, H. E., 35
Walters, G. C., 269, 272
Wanchisen, B. A., 212
Warren, D. A., 153, 156
Warren-Boulton, F. R., 209
Washburne, D. L., 142
Wasserman, E. A., 10, 77, 105, 107, 212,
    314, 326, 345, 356, 358, 359, 360,
    361, 362, 363
Watanabe, S., 233, 356
Wathen, C. N., 353
Watt, A., 146
Wearden, J. H., 164, 167, 176, 345, 347
Weaver, M. S., 334
Webley, P., 185
Webster, M. M., 83
Weinberger, N., 261
Weiner, I., 89
Weisman, R. G., 266, 280, 297
Weiss, J., 151
Weiss, S. J., 225, 239
Weissman, R. D., 239
Welsh, J. H., 35
Wenk, G. L., 346
Werner, J. S., 36, 37, 47, 48
Werz, M. A., 320
Wesierska, M., 77
Westbrook, R. F., 80
Westwood, R., 345
Wheatley, K. L., 73
Wheeler, E. A., 327
Whipple, J. E., 181
White, K. G., 336, 347, 349

White, W., 319
Whitlow, J. W., 46, 329
Wigglesworth, V. B., 35
Wilkenfield, J., 146
Wilkenson, K., 364
Wilkie, D. M., 73, 97, 314, 321, 322,
    325, 356
Williams, B. A., 145, 147, 176, 178, 179,
    181
Williams, D. A., 73, 74, 79, 113, 228
Williams, D. R., 62, 72, 287, 292, 293
Willis, A., 244
Willson, R. J., 322, 356
Wilson, M. I., 234
Wilson, P. N., 228
Wilson, W. J., 260
Winston, K. M., 336
Winter, J., 147
Witcher, E. S., 79, 113
Wixted, J. T., 167
Wolf, M. M., 222
Wolfe, G. E., 260
Wolfson, S., 59
Wolpe, J., 94
Wood, H. M., 181
Woodside, B., 105
Woodworth, R. S., 173
Woolverton, W. L., 210
Worsham, R. W., 336, 337
Wright, A. A., 313, 315, 316, 335, 336
Wright, J. E., 142
Wulff, J. J., 192
Wynne, C. D. L., 165
Wynne, L. C., 258, 260

Yeomans, J. S., 193
Yerkes, R. M., 59
Yin, H., 93
Yoerg, S. I., 212
Younger, M. S., 267

Zacharko, R. M., 153
Zalaquett, C. P., 98
Zamble, E., 84, 298, 299
Zeigler, H. P., 97, 129, 130
Zeiler, M. D., 16
Zellner, D., 82
Zener, K., 98
Zentall, T. R., 308, 315, 325, 326, 327,
    329, 330
Zhuikov, A. Y., 255
Zielinski, K., 77
Zimmer-Hart, C. L., 113
Zinbarg, R., 153
Zito, B., 62
Zoladek, L., 320

SUBJECT INDEX

Abusive punishment, 282
Accidental reinforcement, 149, 157
Acquired drive experiments, 256–257, 282
Acquisition
  defined, 341
  in learning vs. memory processes, 310
  stimulus coding and, 324–328
Active avoidance, 252
Active memory processes, 316–317
Activity deficits, 153
Adaptation phase, 49
Addiction, 53
Adjunctive behaviors, 349, 375
Adventitious reinforcement, 149, 157
AESOP model, 117, 119
Affective after-reaction, 49, 53–54
Afferent neurons, 28, 55
Aggression
  defensive, 270
  extinction-induced, 169–170
Alcoholism, 52–53
Alex (African Grey parrot), 367
Alzheimer's disease, 318–319
American Sign Language, 364–365, 369
Amnesia
  defined, 337, 341
  memory loss as, 337–341
Animal cognition
  defined, 308–309, 341
  forgetting and, 334–341
  language learning and, 363–375
  memory mechanisms and, 324–334
  memory paradigms and, 309–324
  perceptual concept learning and, 355–363
  serial pattern learning and, 349–355
  timing and, 344–349
Animal Intelligence (Romanes), 9
Animal research
  models of human behavior derived from, 11–13
  normal behavior of animals and, 21

  public debate about, 22–25
  rationale for, 20–21
Animal spirits, 7
Annoying event, 125
Anorexia nervosa, 83
Anxiety, 80
Appetitive stimulus, 131, 157
a process, 50, 51, 55, 74
Artificial languages, 365
Association
  concept of, 5–6
  of CS and US, 106–119
  defined, 25
  rules of, 6
Associative interference, 89
Asymptotic avoidance performance, 259–260
Attachment, 53–54
Attentional deficits, 153–155
Autistic children, 198, 199, 222
Autoshaping, 61–63, 85
Aversion conditioning
  avoidance behavior and, 252–271
  cigarette smoking and, 92
  punishment and, 271–282
  taste aversion learning and, 66–67, 68, 82–83
Aversive stimulus
  characteristics of, 272
  defined, 131, 157
  introduction of, 273
  response-contingent vs. response-independent, 273–274
Avoidance behavior. *See also* Punishment
  alternative theories of, 265–271
  defined, 157
  discriminated avoidance procedure and, 253–254
  experimental analysis of, 256–265
  explained, 133–134
  origins of the study of, 252–253
  punishment and, 279–280
  two-process theory of, 255–256

Avoidance procedure, 252, 282
Avoidance theory of punishment, 279–280
Avoidance trial, 254, 282

Backward conditioning
  defined, 69, 85
  effectiveness of, 73
Baseline phase, 196
Behavior. *See also* Human behavior
  changing, 14–16
  choice, 172–181
  elicited, 28–38
  regulating, 201–214
  shaping of, 129–131
  superstitious, 149
Behavioral bliss point approach
  behavior therapy and, 204–205
  contingency constraints and, 202–203
  contributions of, 206
  defined, 215
  explained, 201–202
  problems with, 204–206
  reinforcement effects and, 203–204
Behavioral regulation
  bliss point approach and, 201–206
  economic concepts and, 206–209
  explained, 201
  optimal foraging theory and, 209–214
Behavioral theory of timing, 348–349
Behavioral variability, 137–138
Behavior systems theory, 104–106, 1
  40–142, 150–151
Behavior therapy
  bliss point approach and, 204–205
  omission training and, 135
  punishment and, 282
  stimulus generalization and, 222
Belongingness
  in classical conditioning, 90–92
  defined, 157
  in instrumental conditioning, 138–140
Bias, response, 177

Biconditional discrimination, 302–303
Bidirectional response systems, 77–78
Binary relations, 244
Biological strength, 92–95
Bliss point approach. *See* Behavioral bliss point approach
Blocking effect, 107–109, 110, 120
b process, 50, 51, 52, 55, 74
Brain injury, 337–338
Brain-mind connection, 4, 5
Brain-stimulation reinforcement, 193–194
British empiricists, 5–6

Cartesian dualism, 3, 4
Causation, 145–146
Central emotional states, 293–294, 306
CER procedure. *See* Conditioned emotional response (CER) procedure
Children. *See also* Infants
   autistic, 198, 199, 222
   stimulus control of sleeping in, 232
Chimpanzee language training, 364–366, 367, 368
Choice behavior
   concurrent-chain schedules and, 181–183
   explained, 172–173
   matching law and, 174–178
   measures of, 173–174
   mechanisms of, 178–181
   self-control and, 183–185
Choice link, 181–182
Choice with commitment, 182
Chunking, 253–255, 375
Classical conditioning. *See also* Instrumental conditioning
   avoidance behavior and, 255–256
   conditional control in, 245–247
   CS-US associations in, 106–119
   determinants of the CR in, 96–106
   early studies in, 58–61
   effective stimuli in, 88–95
   excitatory, 67–73
   experiments in, 61–67
   extinction and, 79–82
   inhibitory, 73–79
   instrumental reinforcement in, 285–304
   paradigm of, 60–61
   prevalence of, 82–84
   stimulus discrimination procedure in, 250
Clock mechanism. *See* Internal clocks
Coding strategies. *See also* Stimulus coding
   task demands and, 326–328
   types of, 325–326

Cognition, 308. *See also* Animal cognition
Cognitive maps, 325
Cognitive revolution, 308
Comparator hypothesis, 115–117, 120
Compensatory-response model, 100–103, 120
Compound stimulus, 228–229
Compound-stimulus test, 78, 79, 80, 85
Computer simulations, 24–25
Concept training, 357–358
Conceptual errors, 359–361, 375
Concurrent-chain schedules of reinforcement
   defined, 187
   explained, 181–183
   self-control and, 183–185
Concurrent-measurement experiments, 292–293, 306
Concurrent schedules of reinforcement
   defined, 187
   explained, 172–173
   matching law and, 174–181
   measures of choice behavior and, 173–174
Conditional relations
   defined, 244, 249
   stimulus control and, 244–248
Conditioned compensatory-response model, 100–103, 120
Conditioned emotional response (CER) procedure, 63–65, 85, 294
Conditioned emotional response theory of punishment, 277–279
Conditioned excitation, 74
Conditioned inhibition, 74, 111–112
Conditioned reinforcer, 147, 157
Conditioned response (CR)
   behavior systems theory and, 104–106
   compensatory-response model of, 100–103
   CS as a determinant of, 103, 104
   defined, 61, 85
   measurement of, 69–70
   modifications of the US by, 287–289
   stimulus-substitution model of, 96–99
Conditioned stimulus (CS)
   association of US with, 106–119
   biological strength of, 92–95
   defined, 60–61, 85
   intensity of, 89–90
   novelty of, 88–89
   relevance or belongingness of, 90–92
Conditioned suppression procedure, 63–65, 85
Conditioning trial, 68, 85
Configural conditioning, 248
Configural-cue approach, 228–229, 249
Conflicting memories, 332–333

Conservation of fear, 260, 282–283
Consumer demand concept
   drug abuse and, 210
   elasticity of demand and, 208–209
   explained, 207–208
Consummatory response theory, 194, 215
Contextual cues
   memory retrieval and, 332–333
   stimulus control and, 242–244
Contiguity, 6, 145, 146–147, 157
Contingencies
   behavioral bliss point and, 202–203
   positive vs. negative, 134, 136
   response-reinforcer, 146, 148
Continuous reinforcement (CRF), 161, 187
Contrast effects, 145
Contrast principle, 6
Controllability of reinforcers, 151–156
Control procedures, 70–71
Counterconditioning, 94, 121
CR. *See* Conditioned response
CRF. *See* Continuous reinforcement
CS. *See* Conditioned stimulus
CS-modification models, 113–114
CS-preexposure effect, 89, 121
CS-US interval, 68, 85, 106, 107
Cumulative recorder, 131, 132, 157
Cyclic avoidance performance, 259–260

Defensive behavior, 269–271
Delayed echolalia, 198
Delayed-matching-to-sample procedure
   defined, 341
   described, 312–313
   directed forgetting and, 329–331
   elderly people and, 318
   general vs. specific rule learning and, 315–316
   memory interference and, 335–337
   passive vs. active memory processes and, 316–317
   procedural determinants of, 314
   response strategies and, 314–315
Delayed punishment, 274
Delayed reinforcement
   instrumental conditioning and, 146–147
   self-control and, 183–185, 186
Delayed unconditional response, 100
Demand curve, 207, 215
Descent of Man and *Selection in Relation to Sex, The* (Darwin), 9
Devaluation of reinforcers, 301, 303–304
Differential inhibition, 75–76, 85
Differential probability principle, 195, 215

Differential reinforcement of high rates (DRH), 167, 187
Differential reinforcement of low rates (DRL), 167, 187
Differential reinforcement of other behavior (DRO), 134, 135, 157
Differential responding, 218–219
Directed forgetting, 329–331, 341
Disappointment, 295, 306
Discrete-trial procedures, 125–126, 157
Discriminated avoidance procedure, 253–254, 255, 283
Discrimination between categories, 356
Discrimination hypothesis, 171, 187
Discrimination learning theory, 235–241
Discrimination training. *See also* Equivalence training
   biconditional discrimination and, 302–303
   explained, 230–232
   intradimensional discrimination and, 237–239
   learning acquired through, 235–241
   perceptual concept learning and, 358–359
   stimulus control and, 232–235
Discriminative punishment, 276–277, 283
Discriminative stimulus, 230, 249
Dishabituation, 47–48, 55, 81
Disinhibition, 81
DRH. *See* Differential reinforcement of high rates
Drive reduction theory, 191, 215
Drive state, 191
DRL. *See* Differential reinforcement of low rates
DRO. *See* Differential reinforcement of other behavior
Drug abuse
   consumer demand and, 210
   evidence of conditioning in, 101–102
   opponent-process theory of, 52–53
Drug anticipatory conditioned response, 100
Drug tolerance, 53, 55, 100–101, 121
Dualism, 3, 4, 25
Dual-process theory of habituation and sensitization
   applications of, 43
   explained, 41–43
   implications of, 43–44
Duration estimation, 345, 375
Dwell time, 354–355

Economic concepts, 206–209
ECS. *See* Electroconvulsive shock
Effect

law of, 125, 157, 280–281, 299
   negative law of, 280–281
Efferent neurons, 28–29, 55
Elasticity of demand
   defined, 208, 215
   determinants of, 208–209
Elderly people, 318–319
Electrical stimulation of the brain (ESB), 298–299
Electric shock
   animal research debate and, 22
   avoidance behavior studies and, 253, 254, 255, 257, 258, 262–263
   fear conditioning and, 63–64
   shock-frequency reduction theory and, 267–268
Electroconvulsive shock (ECS), 338, 339, 340–341
Elicited behavior
   emotional responses and, 48–54
   examples of, 36–38
   habituation and sensitization and, 38–48
   modal action patterns and, 30–32, 33
   reflexes and, 28–30
   response feedback and, 32–36
Emotional responses
   modern two-process theory and, 293–299
   opponent-process theory and, 50–54
   standard pattern of affective dynamics and, 48–50
Empiricism, 5, 25
Equivalence training. *See also* Discrimination training
   stimulus control and, 241–242
ESB. *See* Electrical stimulation of the brain
Escape behavior, 133, 155–156, 157
Escape trial, 254, 283
Ethics of animal research, 23
Ethologists, 31
Excitatory conditioning. *See also* Inhibitory conditioning
   common procedures for, 67–69
   control procedures for, 70–71
   effectiveness of procedures for, 71–73
   extinction of, 112
   measurement of conditioned responses and, 69–70
   modulation vs., 247–248
Excitatory stimulus generalization gradient
   defined, 249
   discrimination learning and, 235–236
Exemplar theory, 362–363
Experimental techniques, 16–17
Experiments

avoidance behavior, 256–265
   classical conditioning, 61–67
   punishment, 272–277
   triadic design, 151–156
Explicitly unpaired control procedure, 71, 85
Extinction
   of avoidance behavior, 260–261
   defined, 85, 187
   effects of, 169–172
   explained, 79–80
   habituation and, 80–81
   learning involved in, 81–82
   Rescorla-Wagner model of, 112–113
   retrieval processes and, 333
   schedules of reinforcement and, 168–172
Extinction burst, 169
Eyeblink conditioning, 65–66

Facilitation, 246–247, 249
Fatigue
   behavioral change and, 15
   defined, 25, 55
   habituation vs., 40–41
F-cue (forget cue), 329–331
Fear
   classical conditioning of, 63–65, 255–256, 295
   conditioned inhibition of, 265–267
   conservation of, 260
   defined, 306
   higher order conditioning of, 94
   independent measurement of, 257–259
   instrumental conditioning of, 255–256
   observational learning of, 266
Feature theory, 362, 363
Feedback function, 166, 187
Feedback stimulus, 32, 55
First-order conditioning, 93
Fixed interval scallop, 164, 187
Fixed interval schedules, 163–164, 187
Fixed ratio schedules, 161–162, 187, 274–275
Flooding, 260–261, 283
Food aversion learning. *See* Taste aversion learning
Food magazine, 128
Food-storing birds, 322–324
Foraging behavior
   decisions involved in, 211–212
   optimal foraging theory and, 209–214
Forget cue (F-cue), 329–331
Forgetting. *See also* Memory
   defined, 85
   directed, 329–331
   explained, 334
   extinction procedure and, 80

Forgetting *(continued)*
    proactive interference and, 335–336
    retroactive interference and, 335,
        336–337
    retrograde amnesia and, 337–341
Fractional anticipatory goal responses,
    291–293, 306
Free-operant avoidance procedure
    characteristics of, 262–263, 264
    defined, 283
    described, 261–262
    two-process theory of avoidance and,
        264–265
Free-operant procedures, 127–131, 157
Freezing behavior, 269–270
Frustration, 169, 187
Frustration theory, 171, 187
Functional neurology, 10–11

Gape response, 129–130
Generality of learning phenomena, 19, 20
Generalization
    behavior therapy and, 222
    stimulus, 47, 219–220
Generalization to novel exemplars, 357
Generalization within a category, 356
General laws, 18
General-process approach
    elements of, 17–19
    methodological implications of, 19–20
General-rule learning hypothesis,
    315–316
Georgia State University Language
    Research Center, 365, 368–370, 373
Grammar learning by animals, 371–372

Habituation. *See also* Sensitization
    adaptiveness and pervasiveness of,
        39–40
    drug tolerance as, 53
    dual-process theory of, 41–44
    effects of strong extraneous stimuli on,
        47–48
    emotional responses and, 48–54
    extinction and, 80–81
    sensory adaptation and response fatigue
        vs., 40–41
    stimulus specificity of, 46–47
    time course of, 45–46
Habituation effects, 38, 55
Habituation process, 41, 55
Hedonism, 5, 25
Helplessness
    human behavior and, 153
    learned, 151–156
Higher-order conditioning, 93–94, 121
Homeostatic theory, 50
Hope, 295, 306

Human behavior. *See also* Behavior
    animal models of, 11–13, 153
    controllability of reinforcers and, 153

Incentive motivation, 191, 215
Independent measurement of fear, 257–
    259
Infants
    elicited behavior in, 36–37
    habituation and sensitization in, 44,
        47–48
    linguistic development in, 365
    memory for instrumental behavior in,
        331–332, 333
    reflexive behavior in, 29–30
    sucking response in, 83–84
Information processing model of timing,
    347–348
Inhibition of delay, 72, 85
Inhibitory conditioning. *See also*
        Excitatory conditioning
    defined, 85
    explained, 73–74
    extinction of, 112–113
    measuring, 77–79
    procedures for, 74–76
    Rescorla-Wagner model and, 111–112,
        113
    stress management and, 80
Inhibitory stimulus generalization
        gradient
    defined, 249–250
    discrimination learning and, 235–236
Instinctive drift, 140, 141–142, 157
Instrumental behavior, 123, 157
Instrumental conditioning. *See also*
        Classical conditioning
    associative structure of, 289–304
    avoidance behavior and, 255–256
    behavioral regulation theories and,
        201–214
    classical conditioning procedures and,
        285–304
    concurrent-chain schedules of
        reinforcement and, 181–185
    concurrent schedules of reinforcement
        and, 172–181
    early investigations of, 124–125
    extinction procedures and, 168–172
    fundamental elements of, 136–156
    modern approaches to study of,
        125–131
    procedures used in, 131–136
    reinforcers as special responses in,
        194–199
    reinforcers as special stimuli in,
        190–194

response deprivation hypothesis and,
    200–201
simple schedules of reinforcement and,
    160–168
stimulus control of behavior and,
    216–250
stimulus discrimination procedure in,
    250
Instrumental reinforcer, 142–145
Instrumental response
    instrumental conditioning and,
        136–142
    stimulus control and, 226–228
Intelligence. *See also* Animal cognition
    early definition of, 9
Intensity, 89–90
Interference
    associative, 89
    memory, 89
    proactive, 335–336
    retroactive, 335, 336–337
Interim responses, 149, 150, 157, 349,
    375
Intermittent reinforcement, 161, 187
Internal clocks
    characteristics of, 346–347
    concept of, 345–346
    models of timing and, 347–349
Internal representation, 309
Interneurons, 29, 55
Interstimulus interval, 68, 85–86, 106,
    107
Intertrial interval, 68, 85, 304
Interval schedules
    compared to ratio schedules, 165–167
    defined, 187
    fixed interval schedules, 163–164
    limited hold restrictions and, 165
    variable interval schedules, 164–165
Intracranial self-stimulation, 193, 215
Intradimensional discrimination,
    237–239, 250
Involuntary behavior, 3

Kanzi (bonobo ape), 366, 367, 369, 370,
    371–375
Kinesis, 35, 55

Laboratory animals
    public debate on, 22–25
    wild animals compared to, 21
Lana (chimpanzee), 368, 369, 370
Language comprehension, 372–375
Language learning by animals
    approaches to training for, 364–366
    components of linguistic competence
        and, 370–375

documentation of language skills and, 366

overview of, 363–364

training procedures for, 367–370

Language production, 371–372

Language Research Center (Georgia State University), 365, 368–370, 373

Latency, 70, 86, 126, 157

Latent-inhibition effect, 89, 121

Laws

general, 18

law of effect, 125, 157, 280–281, 299

matching law, 174–181

negative law of effect, 280–281

Learned helplessness effect, 151–156, 157

Learned helplessness hypothesis, 152–153, 157

Learning

animal use in research on, 20–25

contemporary study of, 9–13

definition of, 13–16, 26

experimental approach to the study of, 16–17

extinction procedures and, 81–82

general-process approach to the study of, 17–20

historical antecedents to the study of, 3–8

memory vs., 309–310

observational learning, 266

perceptual concept learning, 355–363

serial pattern learning, 349–355

stimulus control and, 229–242

survival and, 2

Lever-press training, 127–129, 136–137

Lexigram language system, 365, 366, 367, 368, 369–370, 371

Limited hold, 165, 187

Linguistic competence

grammar and, 371–372

language comprehension and, 372–375

vocabulary and, 370–371

Local rate of a response, 180

Long-delayed conditioning, 69, 72

Long-delay learning, 67

Long-term habituation, 45

Love, 53–54

Magazine training, 128, 157–158

Magnitude of the conditioned response, 70, 86

MAPs. See Modal action patterns

Marking procedure, 147, 148, 158

Matching law

defined, 187

explained, 174–178

mechanisms of, 178–181

Matching-to-sample procedures

delayed, 312–317

elderly people and, 318–319

simultaneous, 313

Maturation

defined, 26

learning and, 15–16

Mazes, 126

Mechanisms of behavior, 14

Melioration theory, 180–181, 187

Memory. See also Forgetting

acquisition process and, 310, 324–328

defined, 309, 341

failures of, 334–341

learning vs., 309–310

matching-to-sample procedures and, 312–317

reference, 312

retention interval and, 310, 328–331

retrieval process and, 310, 331–334

spatial, 317–324

working, 311–312

Memory consolidation, 338–339, 341

Memory interference, 89, 335–337

Mentalism, 4

Mind

brain-mind connection and, 4, 5

historical developments in study of, 4–6

Minimum deviation model, 203, 215

Modal action patterns (MAPs)

defined, 55

eliciting stimuli for, 31–32, 33

explained, 30–31

response feedback and, 33–34

Model-rival technique, 367, 375

Modern two-process theory. See also Two-process theory of avoidance

S-O associations and, 293–299

Modulation

configural conditioning vs., 248

excitation vs., 247–248

Modulator, 244, 250

Molar maximizing theories, 178, 179–180

Molecular maximizing theories, 178, 179

Motivation

brain-stimulation reinforcement and, 193–194

opponent-process theory of, 50–54

primary vs. incentive, 191–192

Motor neurons, 28, 55

Multiple schedules of reinforcement, 231–232, 250

Nativism, 5, 26

Negative behavioral contrast, 145, 158

Negative CS-US contingency procedure, 76, 77

Negative geotaxis, 35

Negative law of effect, 280–281

Negative phototaxis, 35

Negative reinforcement. See also Positive reinforcement; Reinforcement

avoidance learning and, 265

defined, 158

explained, 133–134

instrumental behavior and, 296

Nervism, 10–11, 26

Neural representation, 309

Nondiscriminated avoidance procedure

characteristics of, 262–263, 264

defined, 283

described, 261–262

Nonreinforced conditioned stimulus, 334

Nonsense syllables, 6, 26

Novelty, 88–89, 137

Nursing interaction, 83–84

Object learning, 60, 86

Observational learning, 266

Observational techniques, 24

Occasion setting, 246–247, 250

Omission control procedure, 286–287, 306

Omission training, 134, 135, 158

One-way avoidance, 254

Operant response, 128, 158

Opponent processes

defined, 55

examples of, 52–54

explained, 50–52

Opponent-process theory of motivation, 50–54

Optimal foraging theory, 209–214

Orientation, 223–224

Orosensory stimuli, 59–60

Overcorrection, 272, 283

Overmatching, 176, 187

Overshadowing

configural-cue approach and, 228–229

defined, 250

explained, 224–225

Paired-associate learning, 350, 375

Panic attacks, 80

Partial reinforcement, 161, 187

Partial reinforcement extinction effect (PREE), 170–172, 187

Passive avoidance, 252

Passive memory processes, 316–317

Pavlov, Ivan P., biographical sketch, 60

Pavlovian conditioning. See Classical conditioning

Peak procedure, 345, 375

Peak reaction, 49

Peak-shift effect, 239–241, 250

Perceptual concept learning
  concept vs. pseudoconcept training
    and, 357–358
  development of conceptual errors and,
    359–361
  discrimination between perceptual
    categories and, 358–359
  explained, 355–356
  generalization to novel exemplars and,
    357
  mechanisms of, 361–363
Performance
  defined, 26
  learning distinguished from, 13–14
Perseverative behavior, 198
Phobias, 266
Physiological homeostasis, 191, 215
Pineal gland, 4
Plants, 24
Pleasant events, 131
Poison avoidance learning, 66
Positive behavioral contrast, 145, 158
Positive punishment, 133
Positive reinforcement. See also Negative
    reinforcement; Reinforcement
  avoidance learning and, 265–267
  defined, 158
  explained, 132
  instrumental behavior and, 295–296
  punishment and, 275–276, 277,
    280–281
  schedules of, 275
Positive thermotaxis, 35
Postreinforcement pause, 161, 163,
    187–188
Predatory imminence, 269–271, 283
PREE. See Partial reinforcement
    extinction effect
Preexposure effects, 89
Premack's theory of reinforcement,
    194–199
Primary motivation, 191, 215
Primary process, 50–51, 55
Primary response, 50
Proactive interference, 335–336, 341
Probability of responding, 70, 86,
    196–199
Procrastination, 163
Proprioceptive stimuli, 32, 55
Prospection, 325–326, 341
Prospective memory, 325–326, 342
Prototype, 361, 375
Prototype theory, 361
Pseudoconcept training, 357–358
Pseudo-conditioning, 71, 86
Punishment. See also Avoidance behavior
  controversy about, 271–272, 281–282
  defined, 158, 283

delayed, 274
discriminative, 276–277
experimental analysis of, 272–277
explained, 132–133
outside the laboratory, 281–282
positive reinforcement and, 275–276,
    277
schedules of, 274–275
species-specific defense responses and,
    269
theories of, 277–281
Puzzle boxes, 124, 125

Radial maze experiments, 317–322
Random control procedure, 71, 86
Rate of occurrence, 131
Ratio run, 161, 188
Ratio schedules
  compared to interval schedules,
    165–167
  defined, 188
  fixed ratio schedules, 161–162
  variable ratio schedules, 162–163
Ratio strain, 161–162, 188
Rats
  conditioned suppression in, 63–65
  radial maze performance of, 318–322
  startle response in, 37–38, 45–46
R-cue (remember cue), 329–331
Reading instruction, 109
Recuperative behavior, 269–270
Reference memory, 312, 342
Reflex arc, 29, 42, 55
Reflexes
  defined, 3, 26
  elicited behavior and, 28–30
  eyeblink conditioning and, 65–66
  historical developments in study of,
    7–8
  neural organization of, 28–29
Reflexology, 4
Rehearsal processes, 328–331, 342
Reinforced conditioned stimulus, 334
Reinforcement. See also Negative
    reinforcement; Positive
    reinforcement; Schedules of
    reinforcement
  accidental, 149
  avoidance learning and, 265–268
  behavioral regulation theories and,
    201–214
  behavior therapy and, 204–205
  brain-stimulation, 193–194
  delayed, 146–147
  detrimental effects of, 139
  of earlier response forms, 129
  of an existing response, 136
  Premack's theory of, 194–199

punishment and, 275–276, 277,
    280–281
response deprivation hypothesis and,
    200–201
sensory, 192–193
stimulus control and, 225–228
of successive approximations, 129
Reinforcement effects, 203–204
Reinforcers
  conditioned, 147
  devaluation of, 301, 303–304
  effects of controllability of, 151–156
  instrumental, 142–145
  as special responses, 194–199
  as special stimuli, 190–194
Reinforcer-specific expectancies, 298–299
Relative rate of responding, 174
Relative waiting time hypothesis,
    114–115, 121
Releasing stimulus, 32, 55
Relevance
  in classical conditioning, 90–92
  in instrumental conditioning, 138–140
Relevant features, 12
Relief, 295, 306
Remember cue (R-cue), 329–331
Remembering. See Forgetting; Memory
Reminder treatments, 334, 339–341
Rescorla-Wagner model, 109–113
Respiratory occlusion reflex, 29–30
Response bias, 177
Response chain, 350, 375
Response contingency phase, 196
Response-contingent aversive stimulation,
    273–274
Response deprivation hypothesis,
    200–201, 215
Response fatigue, 40–41
Response-independent aversive
    stimulation, 273–274
Response interactions, 298
Response-outcome associations, 299–304
Response prevention, 260–261, 283
Response probability, 196–199
Response rate, 131
Response-rate schedules of reinforcement,
    167, 188
Response-reinforcer contingency, 146,
    148, 158
Response-reinforcer relation, 145–156
Response shaping, 129–131
Response variability, 137
Retardation-of-acquisition test, 79, 86
Retention interval
  defined, 342
  in learning vs. memory processes, 310
  rehearsal and, 328–331
Retrieval

defined, 342
in learning vs. memory processes, 310
memory mechanisms and, 331–334
Retrieval cues, 331–332, 342
Retrieval failure, 331, 339, 342
Retroactive interference, 335, 336–337, 342
Retrograde amnesia, 337–341, 342
Retrospection, 325–326, 342
Retrospective memory, 325–326, 342
Reward-specific expectancies, 298–299
r_g symbol, 291, 306
R-O associations, 299–304
r_g-s_g mechanism, 291–293
R-S interval, 262, 283
Running speed, 126, 144, 158
Run of bad luck, 213
Runway maze, 126, 136

S-(R-O) associations, 299–304
Safety-signal feedback cues, 155
Safety-signal hypothesis, 265
Safety signals, 265, 283
Sample stimulus, 312
Satisfying event, 125
Scalar expectancy hypothesis, 114–115
Schedules of reinforcement. *See also* Reinforcement
    concurrent-chain schedules, 181–185
    concurrent schedules, 172–181
    defined, 160, 188
    extinction and, 168–172
    multiple schedules, 231–232
    punishment and, 274–275
    simple schedules, 160–168
    wage scales as, 168
Science, 22
Scientific American, 126
Secondary reinforcer, 147, 158
Second-order conditioning, 93–94
Self-control
    explanations of, 183–185
    studies of, 183
    training in, 186
Sensitization. *See also* Habituation
    adaptiveness and pervasiveness of, 39–40
    dual-process theory of, 41–44
    stimulus specificity of, 47
    time course of, 45
Sensitization effects, 38, 55
Sensitization process, 41, 55
Sensory adaptation, 40–41, 55
Sensory capacity, 223–224
Sensory neurons, 28, 55
Sensory preconditioning, 94–95, 121
Sensory reinforcement, 192–193
Sequential modification, 222

Sequential theory, 172, 188
Serial compound, 248
Serial pattern learning
    chunking and, 253–255
    possible mechanisms of, 349–351
    tests of, 351–352
Serial representation learning, 351, 375
Sexual behavior, 84
s_g symbol, 291, 306
Shaping
    defined, 129, 158
    of response forms, 129–131
Shock-cessation feedback cues, 155
Shock-frequency reduction, 267–268, 283
Short-delayed conditioning
    defined, 68, 86
    effectiveness of, 71
Short-term habituation, 45
Shuttle avoidance procedures, 254, 283
Signaled avoidance procedure, 253–254, 255, 283
Sign language, 364–365, 368, 369
Sign stimulus, 32, 55
Sign tracking, 61–63, 86
Similarity principle, 6
Simple schedules of reinforcement
    comparison of, 165–167
    interval schedules, 163–165
    matching law and, 178
    ratio schedules, 161–163
    response-rate schedules, 167
Simultaneous behavioral contrast, 145, 158
Simultaneous conditioning
    defined, 69, 86
    effectiveness of, 73
Simultaneous matching to sample, 313, 342
Skinner box, 127–128
Sleep reinforcement procedure, 232
Smoking aversion conditioning, 92
S-O associations
    modern two-process theory and, 293–299
    r_g-s_g mechanism and, 291–293
Social reinforcement, 204–205
SOP model, 117–119
Spatial memory
    in a radial maze, 317–322
    in food-storing birds, 322–324
Species-specific defense reactions (SSDRs), 268–269, 283
Specific-rule learning hypothesis, 315–316
Spence's theory of discrimination learning, 235–236
    peak-shift effect and, 239–241

Spontaneous recovery
    in classical conditioning, 46, 81
    defined, 55–56
    in instrumental conditioning, 169
S-R associations, 291–293
S-R learning, 99, 121, 125
S-R systems, 42–44, 56
SSDRs. *See* Species-specific defense reactions
SSDR theory of avoidance, 268–269
S-S interval, 262, 283
S-S learning, 99, 121
Stabilimeter chamber, 37
"Stamping in" process, 190, 214, 299
Standard conditioned inhibition procedure, 75
Standard pattern of affective dynamics, 48–50, 51–52, 56
Startle response, 37–38, 45–46
State system, 43, 56
Steady state, 49
Stereotyped responses, 137–138
Stimulus coding
    cognitive maps and, 325
    defined, 342
    memory acquisition and, 324–325
    prospection and, 325–326
    retrospection and, 325–326
    task demands and, 326–328
Stimulus control
    conditional relations and, 244–248
    contextual cues and, 242–244
    discrimination training and, 230–241
    equivalence training and, 241–242
    explained, 217
    identification and measurement of, 217–222
    learning factors in, 229–242
    sleeping habits of children and, 232
    stimulus and response factors in, 222–229
Stimulus dimensions, 237
Stimulus discrimination, 218, 250
Stimulus discrimination procedure, 230, 250
Stimulus discrimination training. *See* Discrimination training
Stimulus-element approach, 228–229, 250
Stimulus equivalence, 241, 250
Stimulus equivalence training, 241–242
Stimulus generalization
    behavior therapy and, 222
    defined, 250
    of habituation, 47
    stimulus control and, 219–220
Stimulus generalization gradient, 220–221, 250

Stimulus-response learning, 99, 121
Stimulus specificity, 46–47
Stimulus-stimulus learning, 99, 121
Stimulus-substitution model, 96–99, 121
Straight-alley maze, 126
Stress, 80
Sucking response, 83
Summation test, 78, 86
Supernormal stimulus, 32, 56
Superstition experiment, 148–150
Superstitious behavior, 149, 158
Suppression, conditioned, 63–65
Suppression ratio, 64
Suprisingness, 109–110
Survival basis for learning, 2, 66
Synthesized speech, 366

Tabula rasa, 5
Taste aversion learning, 66–67, 68,
    82–83
Taxis, 35, 56
Temporal contiguity, 145, 146–147, 158
Terminal link, 182
Terminal responses, 149, 150, 158, 349,
    375
Test trial, 70, 86
Therapy. *See* Behavior therapy
Third-order conditioning, 93
Thorndike, Edward L., biographical
    sketch, 125
Time course
    of habituation, 45–46
    of sensitization, 45

Time out, 272, 283
Timing
    behavioral theory of, 348–349
    information processing model of,
        347–348
    internal clocks and, 345–347
    measurement techniques, 344–345
    response-reinforcer relation and,
        145–146
    self-control studies and, 183–185
Tissue cultures, 24
T-maze, 126, 136
Trace conditioning
    defined, 68–69, 86
    effectiveness of, 71–72
Trace decay hypothesis, 316–317, 342
Trace interval, 69, 86
Training sessions, 68
Transfer-of-control experiments
    defined, 306
    described, 296–297
    response interactions in, 298
Triadic design experiments, 151–156
Trials-unique procedure, 316, 342
Two-process theory of avoidance. *See also*
        Modern two-process theory
    defined, 283
    experimental research based on,
        256–265
    explained, 255–256
    free-operant avoidance procedure and,
        264–265
Two-way shuttle avoidance, 254

Unconditioned response (UR), 61, 86
Unconditioned stimulus (US)
    association of CS with, 106–119
    biological strength of, 92–95
    conditioned response modifications of,
        287–289
    defined, 61, 86
    intensity of, 89–90
    novelty of, 88–89
    relevance or belongingness of, 90–92
    reminder procedures and, 334
Undermatching, 176, 188
Unpleasant events, 131
UR. *See* Unconditioned response
US. *See* Unconditioned stimulus
US devaluation, 98, 121
US-modification models, 113–114
US-preexposure effect, 89, 121

Variable interval schedules, 164–165, 188
Variable ratio schedules, 162–163, 188
Visual attention, 36–37
Vocabulary learning, 370–371
Voluntary behavior, 3

Wage systems, 168
Washoe (chimpanzee), 364, 366, 368,
    371
Working memory
    defined, 342
    delayed-matching-to-sample procedure
        and, 312–317
    explained, 311–312

PHOTO CREDITS

Chapter 1: **4**, Bettmann Archive; **8**, Sovfoto; **10**, Bettmann Archive. **Chapter 2: 30**, photo courtesy of Allen Zak; **32 and 48**, Donald A. Dewsbury. **Chapter 3: 60**, Bettmann Archive; **64**, courtesy of the author; **65**, courtesy of I. Gormezano; **67, 76**, **82 and 84**, Donald A. Dewsbury. **Chapter 4: 100**, Donald A. Dewsbury; **108**, courtesy of L. J. Kamin; **114**, top, Donald A. Dewsbury; below, courtesy of J. Gibbon; **115**, top, Donald A. Dewsbury; below, courtesy of R. R. Miller; **117**, Donald A. Dewsbury. **Chapter 5: 127**, Bettmann Archive; **128**, Omikron / Photo Researchers, Inc.; **140**, Donald A. Dewsbury; **141**, top, Animal Behavior Enterprises; below, Donald A. Dewsbury; **143 and 145**, Donald A. Dewsbury; **147**, courtesy of D. A. Lieberman; **149 and 151**, top, Donald A. Dewsbury; **151**, below, courtesy of M. E .P. Seligman. **Chapter 6: 171**, courtesy of A. Amsel; **172**, courtesy of E. J. Capaldi; **175**, Donald A. Dewsbury; **176**, courtesy of W. M. Baum; **178**, courtesy of B. A. Williams; **180**, Donald A. Dewsbury; **183**, top, courtesy of L. Green; below, courtesy of A. W. Logue. **Chapter 7: 193**, © Robert Brenner / PhotoEdit; **200**, courtesy of W. Timberlake; **201**, courtesy of J. Allison; **210**, Donald A. Dewsbury. **Chapter 8: 224**, photo courtesy of the author; **225, 228 and 241**, Donald A. Dewsbury. **Chapter 9: 255, 257, 264, 268 and 269**, Donald A. Dewsbury; **272**, courtesy of N. H. Azrin. **Chapter 10: 286**, courtesy of E. Hearst; **291**, courtesy of the University of Iowa; **297**, Donald A. Dewsbury. **Chapter 11: 309**, Donald A. Dewsbury; **314**, courtesy of D. S. Grant; **316 and 317**, Donald A. Dewsbury; **320**, courtesy of Catherine Green, from Patricia Sharp Lab, Department of Psychology, Yale University; **325**, courtesy of Dr. D. M. Wilkie; **326**, courtesy of P. Urcuioli; **329**, courtesy of T. Zentall; **332**, Donald A. Dewsbury; **334**, courtesy of N. E. Spear; **335**, Donald A. Dewsbury; **338**, courtesy of D. C. Riccio; **339**, courtesy of W. C. Gordon. **Chapter 12: 346**, courtesy of R. M. Church; **349**, Arizona State University photo; **351**, Donald A. Dewsbury; **358**, courtesy of Gail Meese, Meese Photo Research; **359**, courtesy of E. A. Wasserman; **360**, photo courtesy of Merlin; **367**, top, courtesy of Duane Rumbaugh, Language Research Center, Georgia State University; below, courtesy of I. M. Pepperberg; **369**, courtesy of D. M. Rumbaugh; **370 and 374**, courtesy of Duane Rumbaugh, Language Research Center, Georgia State University.

Sniffy™ the Virtual Rat, Version 4.5

by Lester Krames, Jeff Graham, and Tom Alloway, all of the University of Toronto, Erindale

Train Sniffy to perform any of 30 behaviors!

Sniffy is a popular, affordable program for Windows® or Macintosh® that allows you to explore the principles of shaping and partial reinforcement in operant conditioning using a "virtual rat" named *Sniffy*. Each user learns by doing — conditioning his or her own "rat" — and receives many of the benefits of true animal experimentation with none of the drawbacks associated with using live animals.

The *Sniffy* software comes packaged with a brief, hands-on student lab manual that walks you through the steps you'll follow as you condition *Sniffy* to perform up to 30 behaviors. The lab manual offers a comprehensive discussion of the principles of operant conditioning, integrated with guidelines for using *Sniffy* to explore these principles, and is an ideal supplement to Michael Domjan's *Principles of Learning and Behavior, Fourth Edition*.

With *Sniffy*, you can learn about:

- **Magazine training:** by training *Sniffy* to orient to the sound of food being delivered.
- **Shaping:** by conditioning *Sniffy* to press the bar for food.
- **Reinforcement schedules:** by exploring the changes in *Sniffy's* behavior as conditioning occurs.
- **Extinction:** by measuring the elapsed time before extinction, after reinforcement is no longer delivered.

Test drive Sniffy from the Web!
To download a free demonstration copy of Sniffy, go to:
http://www.brookscole.com/technology/products/sniffy/4.5/mtsnf.html.

TO THE OWNER OF THIS BOOK:

I hope that you have found *The Principles of Learning and Behavior*, Fourth Edition, useful. So that this book can be improved in a future edition, would you take the time to complete this sheet and return it? Thank you.

School and address: _____

Department: _____

Instructor s name: _____

1. What I like most about this book is: _____

_____

_____

2. What I like least about this book is: _____

_____

_____

3. My general reaction to this book is: _____

_____

4. The name of the course in which I used this book is: _____

_____

5. Were all of the chapters of the book assigned for you to read? _____

   If not, which ones weren t? _____

6. In the space below, or on a separate sheet of paper, please write specific suggestions for improving this book and anything else you d care to share about your experience in using the book.

_____

_____

_____

_____

_____

Optional:

Your name: _____ Date: _____

May Brooks/Cole quote you, either in promotion for *The Principles of Learning and Behavior,* Fourth Edition, or in future publishing ventures?

Yes: _____ No: _____

Sincerely,

Michael Domjan

FOLD HERE

BUSINESS REPLY MAIL

FIRST CLASS   PERMIT NO. 358   PACIFIC GROVE, CA

POSTAGE WILL BE PAID BY ADDRESSEE

ATT: *Michael Domjan* _____

Brooks/Cole Publishing Company
511 Forest Lodge Road
Pacific Grove, California 93950-9968

NO POSTAGE
NECESSARY
IF MAILED
IN THE
UNITED STATES

FOLD HERE